The CRC Press Terrorism Reader

The CRC Press Terrorism Reader

Marie-Helen Maras

CRC Press is an imprint of the
Taylor & Francis Group, an **informa** business

CRC Press
Taylor & Francis Group
6000 Broken Sound Parkway NW, Suite 300
Boca Raton, FL 33487-2742

Printed on acid-free paper
Version Date: 20130715

International Standard Book Number-13: 978-1-4665-8832-5 (Hardback)

Library of Congress Cataloging-in-Publication Data

Maras, Marie-Helen, 1979-
The CRC Press terrorism reader / Marie-Helen Maras.
pages cm
Includes bibliographical references and index.
ISBN 978-1-4665-8832-5 (hardback)
1. Terrorism. 2. Terrorism--Prevention. I. Title.

HV6431.M362673 2013
363.325--dc23 2013025175

Visit the Taylor & Francis Web site at
http://www.taylorandfrancis.com

and the CRC Press Web site at
http://www.crcpress.com

To my beloved niece, Hera-Demetra Maras

May you always follow your dreams

Contents

Introduction

From the best and brightest of CRC Press' unrivaled pool of author experts comes the ultimate reader on terrorism. This volume serves as a perfect complement to any course in homeland security, terrorism, or criminal justice curricula because it provides not only a history and background of terrorism, but also covers important policy issues; critical infrastructure protection as it relates to terrorism; terrorism funding; global and domestic groups; transnational terrorist activities, surveillance, planning, and tactic and target selection; weapons of mass destruction; intelligence; antiterrorism efforts; terrorism crisis management and responder issues; regional security issues; and current trends in terrorism and counterterrorism. Unlike other books on the market that cover only theory or history, this volume considers the essentials of terrorism as well as real-world threats and solutions as to how to counter, prepare for, mitigate, manage, and respond to terrorist threats and acts. As such, it is far more practical than the average survey book—this is practitioner knowledge from the field straight into the reader's hands.

The primary goal of this book is to give readers an understanding of what terrorism is; the terrorist threat; ways to prevent, mitigate, and deter attacks; and best practices with which to respond to and mitigate the impact of disasters. To accomplish this, it introduces readers to the various definitions of terrorism; key terrorist global and domestic terrorist organizations and a discussion of the varying motivations behind these groups; how terrorist cells operate, surveil, and target others; terrorist funding and money laundering; intelligence, counterterrorism, and antiterrorism methods; responses to terrorism events and planning and preparedness considerations; the terrorist threat in other countries and these countries' responses to various forms of terrorism; emerging trends and influences on the present state; and future threats from terrorism.

This volume is broken up into five sections. Part I includes three chapters (Chapters 1 through 3). Chapter 1 examines the origins and definitions of terrorism. Information for this chapter was retrieved from the following titles:

- Kenneth J. Dudonis, Frank Bolz, and David P. Schulz. (2005). *The Counterterrorism Handbook: Tactics, Procedures, and Techniques*, Third Edition, CRC Press.
- Malcolm W. Nance. (2008). *Terrorist Recognition Handbook: A Practitioner's Manual for Predicting and Identifying Terrorist Activities*, Second Edition, CRC Press.
- Edward Kraft and Michael Marks. (2011). *US Government Counterterrorism: A Guide to Who Does What*. CRC Press.
- Jeffrey A. Larsen and James J. Wirtz. (2008). WMD Terrorism: New Threats, Revised Responses. In Michael A. Opheim, Nicholas Bowen, and Paul R. Viotti (Eds.), *Terrorism and Homeland Security: Thinking Strategically About Policy*. CRC Press.
- David P. Schulz. (2011). *The Counterterrorism Handbook: Tactics, Procedures, and Techniques*, Fourth Edition, CRC Press.
- Herbert K. Tillema. (2009). A Brief Theory of Terrorism and Technology. In Tushar K. Ghosh, Mark A. Prelas, Dabir S. Viswanath, and Sudarshan K. Loyalka (Eds.), *Science and Technology of Terrorism and Counterterrorism*, Second Edition, CRC Press.

- Paul R. Viotti. (2008). Toward a Comprehensive Strategy for Terrorism and Homeland Security. In Michael A. Opheim, Nicholas Bowen, and Paul R. Viotti (Eds.), *Terrorism and Homeland Security: Thinking Strategically About Policy*. CRC Press.

This chapter demonstrates that throughout the years, terrorism has evolved, changing tactics, targets, and objectives. Terrorism is no longer restricted to a particular territory or region of the world. It is in fact global. Governments worldwide have sought to define terrorism, but a common definition cannot (and has not) been agreed upon by all.

Chapter 2 considers the motivations of terrorists and the psychology of terrorism by drawing on the following works:

- Michael E. Diamond. (2009). The Group Psychology of Terrorism. In Tushar K. Ghosh, Mark A. Prelas, Dabir S. Viswanath, and Sudarshan K. Loyalka (Eds.), *Science and Technology of Terrorism and Counterterrorism*, Second Edition, CRC Press.
- Raymond McPartland. (2011). Terrorist Tradecraft I: The Attack Cycle. Fagel, M. J. (Ed.), *Principles of Emergency Management: Hazard Specific Issues and Mitigation Strategies*. CRC Press.
- Malcolm W. Nance. (2008). *Terrorist Recognition Handbook: A Practitioner's Manual for Predicting and Identifying Terrorist Activities*, Second Edition, CRC Press.
- Herbert K. Tillema. (2009). A Brief Theory of Terrorism and Technology. In Tushar K. Ghosh, Mark A. Prelas, Dabir S. Viswanath, and Sudarshan K. Loyalka (Eds.), *Science and Technology of Terrorism and Counterterrorism*, Second Edition, CRC Press.

Terrorists are motivated by various political, religious, and ideological factors. Motivations to engage in terrorism vary according to ethnicity, religion, nationality, region, culture, economic standing, structural conditions of society, and personal factors. Special attention is paid to group psychology and individuals' propensity to engage in terrorism.

Finally, Chapter 3 analyzes international and domestic terrorism by extracting information from the below titles:

- Robert Burke. (2006). *Counter-Terrorism for Emergency Responders*, Second Edition, CRC Press.
- Kenneth J. Dudonis, Frank Bolz, and David P. Schulz. (2005). *The Counterterrorism Handbook: Tactics, Procedures, and Techniques*, Third Edition, CRC Press.
- Malcolm W. Nance. (2008). *Terrorist Recognition Handbook: A Practitioner's Manual for Predicting and Identifying Terrorist Activities*, Second Edition, CRC Press.
- James F. Pastor. (2009). *Terrorism and Public Safety Policing: Implications for the Obama Presidency*. CRC Press.
- Dawn Perlmutter. (2003). *Investigating Religious Terrorism and Ritualistic Crimes*. CRC Press.
- Philip P. Purpura. (2010). *Security: An Introduction*. CRC Press.
- David P. Schulz. (2011). *The Counterterrorism Handbook: Tactics, Procedures, and Techniques*, Fourth Edition, CRC Press.

A geographical typology of terrorism exists; that is, terrorists and terrorist groups have been classified according to their area of operations. International terrorists cross borders and often target and operate within several countries. Conversely, domestic terrorists operate within their target country's borders. This chapter looks at various domestic and international terrorists pursuing different ideologies that exist both in the United States and abroad. Particular emphasis is placed on lone wolves and homegrown terrorist incidents as they pose significant challenges to counterterrorism officials.

Part II includes four chapters (Chapters 4 through 7). Chapter 4 examines terrorist organizations and cells. Information for this chapter was retrieved from the following:

- Kenneth J. Dudonis, Frank Bolz, and David P. Schulz. (2005). *The Counterterrorism Handbook: Tactics, Procedures, and Techniques*, Third Edition, CRC Press.
- Malcolm W. Nance. (2008). *Terrorist Recognition Handbook: A Practitioner's Manual for Predicting and Identifying Terrorist Activities*, Second Edition, CRC Press.

Terrorist organizations are either centralized or decentralized. Modern terrorism has changed from an organized group with a discernible leader to a more ideological approach undertaken by inspired followers. Even though a hierarchical organization still exists for some groups today, these groups or individuals within these groups are using more of a networked approach, connected in an indirect manner. Quite often, current groups are self-organized—leading to single actor or small group "lone wolf" operations—without any direction or connection to a terrorist organization other than the ideology itself.

Chapter 5 investigates terrorist surveillance, planning, targeting, tactics, and operations, utilizing information from the following sources:

- Raymond McPartland. (2011). Terrorist Tradecraft I: The Attack Cycle. Fagel, M. J. (Ed.), *Principles of Emergency Management: Hazard Specific Issues and Mitigation Strategies*. CRC Press.
- Malcolm W. Nance. (2008). *Terrorist Recognition Handbook: A Practitioner's Manual for Predicting and Identifying Terrorist Activities*, Second Edition, CRC Press.

This chapter considers the five phases of a terrorist cycle, including target selection, operational planning and preparation, plan implementation, escape and evasion, and media exploitation. Although all phases are covered, primary emphasis is placed on terrorists' target selection and terrorist surveillance, planning, preparation, and implementation of their plan. Special attention is also given to terrorist tactics, safe houses, supplies, mobility, and communications.

Chapter 6 focuses on a particular tactic of terrorism; namely, the use of weapons of mass destruction (WMD). Information for this chapter was obtained from several works:

- Markus Binder and Michael Moodie. (2009). Jihadists and Chemical Weapons. In Gary Ackerman and Jeremy Tamsett (Eds.), *Jihadists and Weapons of Mass Destruction*. CRC Press.
- Charles P. Blair. (2009). Jihadists and Nuclear Weapons. In Gary Ackerman and Jeremy Tamsett (Eds.), *Jihadists and Weapons of Mass Destruction*. CRC Press.
- Kenneth J. Dudonis, Frank Bolz, and David P. Schulz. (2005). *The Counterterrorism Handbook: Tactics, Procedures, and Techniques*, Third Edition, CRC Press.
- Charles D. Ferguson. (2009). Radiological Weapons and Jihadist Terrorism. In Gary Ackerman and Jeremy Tamsett (Eds.), *Jihadists and Weapons of Mass Destruction*. CRC Press.
- James J. F. Forest and Sammy Salama. (2009). Jihadist Tactics and Targeting. In Gary Ackerman and Jeremy Tamsett (Eds.), *Jihadists and Weapons of Mass Destruction*. CRC Press.
- Jeffrey A. Larsen and James J. Wirtz. (2008). WMD Terrorism: New Threats, Revised Responses. In Michael A. Opheim, Nicholas Bowen, and Paul R. Viotti (Eds.), *Terrorism and Homeland Security: Thinking Strategically About Policy*. CRC Press.
- Cheryl Loeb. (2009). Jihadists and Biological and Toxin Weapons. In Gary Ackerman and Jeremy Tamsett (Eds.), *Jihadists and Weapons of Mass Destruction*, CRC Press.

- Sudarshan K. Loyalka. (2009). Nuclear Terrorism: Nuclear Weapons. In Tushar K. Ghosh, Mark A. Prelas, Dabir S. Viswanath, and Sudarshan K. Loyalka (Eds.), *Science and Technology of Terrorism and Counterterrorism*. Second Edition, CRC Press.
- Sudarshan K. Loyalka and Mark Prelas. (2009). Nuclear Terrorism: Threats and Countermeasures. In Tushar K. Ghosh, Mark A. Prelas, Dabir S. Viswanath, and Sudarshan K. Loyalka (Eds.), *Science and Technology of Terrorism and Counterterrorism*. Second Edition, CRC Press.
- Joseph R. Masci and Elizabeth Bass. (2004). *Bioterrorism: A Guide for Hospital Preparedness*. CRC Press.
- Steven M. Presley, Galen P. Austin, Philip N. Smith, and Ronald J. Kendall. (2008). Threats and Vulnerabilities Associated with Biological and Chemical Terrorism. In Ronald J. Kendall, Steven M. Presley, Galen P. Austin, and Philip N. Smith (Eds.), *Advances in Biological and Chemical Terrorism Countermeasures*. CRC Press.
- David P. Schulz. (2011). *The Counterterrorism Handbook: Tactics, Procedures, and Techniques*, Fourth Edition, CRC Press.

Terrorists have demonstrated interest in the full range of chemical, biological, radiological, and nuclear (CBRN) weapons. CBRN weapons would provide terrorists with different capabilities and pose different operational challenges. This chapter considers the likelihood that future terrorist attacks could involve WMD and the challenges involved in their creation, acquisition, and use by terrorists. Counterterrorism responses to potential WMD attacks are considered as well.

Lastly, Chapter 7 covers the funding of terrorism drawing on the works of Michael Kraft, Edward Marks, and Jennifer L. Hesterman:

- Michael Kraft and Edward Marks. (2010). *US Government Counterterrorism: A Guide to Who Does What*. CRC Press.
- Jennifer L. Hesterman. (2013). *The Terrorist-Criminal Nexus: An Alliance of International Drug Cartels, Organized Crime, and Terror Groups*. CRC Press.

Terrorists and terrorist groups fund their operations from a variety of illegal and legal activities. Several methods terrorists use to earn, move, and store funds are explored in this chapter, including (but not limited to) charities; hawala; Zakat; money laundering; fraudulent activities; and the counterfeiting, smuggling, and theft of commercial goods.

Part III includes four chapters (Chapters 8 through 11). Chapter 8 considers homeland security as it applies to terrorism. Information for this chapter was retrieved from the following:

- Thomas A. Johnson. (2008). *War on Terrorism: A Collision of Values, Strategies and Societies*. CRC Press.
- Dale Jones (2008). Homeland Security: Emerging Discipline, Challenges, and Research. In Jack Pinkowski (Ed.), *Homeland Security Handbook*. CRC Press.
- Dale L. June. (2010). Gemini: Terrorism and Homeland Security. In Dale L. June (Ed.), *Terrorism and Homeland Security: Perspectives, Thoughts, and Opinions*. CRC Press.
- Chuck P. Nemeth. (2012). *Homeland Security: An Introduction to Principles and Practice*. 2nd edition, CRC Press.
- Michael R. Ronczkowski. (2003). *Terrorism and Organized Hate Crime: Intelligence Gathering, Analysis, and Investigations*. CRC Press.
- Paul R. Viotti. (2008). Toward a Comprehensive Strategy for Terrorism and Homeland Security. In Michael A. Opheim, Nicholas Bowen, and Paul R. Viotti (Eds.), *Terrorism and Homeland Security: Thinking Strategically About Policy*. CRC Press.

In developing a strategy for homeland security in relation to terrorist threats, domestic remedies providing better intelligence and early warning of attacks, detecting terrorist threats, and developing and exercising plans for damage limitation are sought. The strategy of homeland security focuses on terrorism prevention and mitigation. A successful strategy for homeland security, thus, incorporates approaches to reducing the threat of terrorism. The next chapters, Chapters 9 and 10, cover such approaches. Specifically, Chapter 9 examines measures that are implemented to mitigate terrorism, looking in particular at antiterrorism measures. This chapter utilized information from the following sources:

- Robert Dzikansky, Mordecai Kleiman, and Gil Slater. (2011). *Terrorist Suicide Bombings: Attack Interdiction, Mitigation, and Response*. CRC Press.
- Ross Johnson. (2013). *Antiterrorism and Threat Response: Planning and Implementation*. CRC Press.
- Malcolm W. Nance. (2008). *Terrorist Recognition Handbook: A Practitioner's Manual for Predicting and Identifying Terrorist Activities*, Second Edition, CRC Press.
- David P. Schulz. (2011). *The Counterterrorism Handbook: Tactics, Procedures, and Techniques*, Fourth Edition. CRC Press.

Moreover, Chapter 10 investigates methods with which to deter terrorists, by drawing on the following works:

- Ross Johnson. (2013). *Antiterrorism and Threat Response: Planning and Implementation*. CRC Press.
- Thomas A. Johnson. (2008). *War on Terrorism: A Collision of Values, Strategies and Societies*. CRC Press.
- James M. Smith and Brent J. Talbot. (2008). Terrorism and Deterrence by Denial. In Michael A. Opheim, Nicholas Bowen, and Paul R. Viotti (Eds.), *Terrorism and Homeland Security: Thinking Strategically About Policy*. CRC Press.

Particularly, this chapter looked at deterrence by denial. Deterrence by denial was applied to the capability (the operational level), opportunity (the tactical level), and objectives (the strategic level) sought by terrorists to advance their cause.

Furthermore, Chapter 11 explores intelligence-driven counterterrorism from the below sources:

- Bartholomew Elias. (2009). *Airport and Aviation Security: US Policy and Strategy in the Age of Global Terrorism*. CRC Press.
- Amos N. Guiora. (2011). *Homeland Security: What Is It and Where Are We Going?* CRC Press.
- Ross Johnson. (2013). *Antiterrorism and Threat Response: Planning and Implementation*. CRC Press.
- Raymond McPartland. (2011). Terrorist Tradecraft I: The Attack Cycle. Fagel, M. J. (Ed.), *Principles of Emergency Management: Hazard Specific Issues and Mitigation Strategies*. CRC Press.
- Malcolm W. Nance. (2008). *Terrorist Recognition Handbook: A Practitioner's Manual for Predicting and Identifying Terrorist Activities*, Second Edition, CRC Press.
- James F. Pastor. (2009). *Terrorism and Public Safety Policing: Implications for the Obama Presidency*. CRC Press.
- Chuck P. Nemeth. (2012). *Homeland Security: An Introduction to Principles and Practice*. 2nd edition, CRC Press.

This chapter specifically looks at the intelligence cycle and its components: direction, collection, processing, and dissemination. It also examines types of intelligence and intelligence-led policing. It further considers domestic and and international cooperation in counterterrorism.

Part IV includes four chapters (Chapters 12 through 15). Chapter 12 examines the terrorist threat from Latin America, using information from the following:

- Juan A. Bacigalupi. (2010). Terrorist Threats South of the Border. In Dale L. June (Ed.), *Terrorism and Homeland Security: Perspectives, Thoughts, and Opinions*. CRC Press.
- Augusto D'Avila. (2010). Mexico Violence That Threatens Our Southern Border: Ripening Conditions for Escalated Terrorism Domestically and Internationally Immediately South of the United States. In Dale L. June (Ed.), *Terrorism and Homeland Security: Perspectives, Thoughts, and Opinions*. CRC Press.
- Jennifer L. Hesterman. (2013). *The Terrorist-Criminal Nexus: An Alliance of International Drug Cartels, Organized Crime, and Terror Groups*. CRC Press.

Chapter 13 covers the terrorist threat in Europe, looking in particular at the domestic and international terrorist threat against Germany and Germany's counterterrorism response to these threats. The work utilized in this analysis is the following:

- Michael Klichling and Azilis Maguer. (2009). Border Security in Germany since 9/11. In Kelly W. Sundberg and John A. Winterdyk (Eds.), *Border Security in the Al-Qaeda Era*. CRC Press.

Additionally, Chapter 14 considers terrorism and border security in the Middle East, drawing on the work of the following:

- Hussei Aghababaei and Hassan Rezaei. (2009). Iran—Borders of an Islamic Republic in the Middle East. In Kelly W. Sundberg and John A. Winterdyk (Eds.), *Border Security in the Al-Qaeda Era*. CRC Press.

The focus of this analysis is on Iran. The final chapter in this part, Chapter 15, explores the threat of terrorism in Asia, looking in particular at the Philippines. Information for this chapter was obtained from the below title:

- Rommel C. Banlaoi. (2009). *Philippine Security in the Age of Terror: National, Regional, and Global Challenges in the Post-9/11 World*. Auerbach Publications.

The last part of this volume, Part V, consists of five chapters (Chapter 16 through 20). Chapter 16 investigates the impact of the Arab Spring based on information retrieved (and updated) from the following source:

- Andrew J. Budka. (2012). The Arab Revolutions of 2011: Promise, Risk, and Uncertainty. Thomas A. Johnson (Ed.), *Power, National Security, and Transformational Global Events: Challenges Confronting America, China, and Iran*. CRC Press.

Chapter 17 explores why suicide bombings are the ultimate terrorist tool by synthesizing the following works:

- Robert Dzikansky, Mordecai Kleiman, and Gil Slater. (2011). *Terrorist Suicide Bombings: Attack Interdiction, Mitigation, and Response*. CRC Press.
- Malcolm W. Nance. (2008). *Terrorist Recognition Handbook: A Practitioner's Manual for Predicting and Identifying Terrorist Activities*, Second Edition, CRC Press.
- Mohammed, A. K. (2010). The Concept of Martyrdom. In Dale L. June (Ed.), *Terrorism and Homeland Security: Perspectives, Thoughts, and Opinions*. CRC Press.

- Mohammed, A. K. (2010). Suicide Bombing as an Ultimate Terrorist Tool. In Dale L. June (Ed.), *Terrorism and Homeland Security: Perspectives, Thoughts, and Opinions*. CRC Press.

Chapter 18 looks at the crime-terror nexus, drawing on the work of Jennifer L. Hesterman:

- Jennifer L. Hesterman. (2013). *The Terrorist-Criminal Nexus: An Alliance of International Drug Cartels, Organized Crime, and Terror Groups*. CRC Press.

Specifically, this chapter examines the operating objectives of drug trafficking organizations, drug cartels, and terrorists; how these individuals are cooperating with each other; and how they are sharing and copying each other's tactics.

Chapter 19 considers critical infrastructure protection as it relates to terrorism. Information for this chapter was obtained from the following source:

- Philip P. Purpura. (2010). *Security: An Introduction*. CRC Press.

To conclude, the last chapter in this volume, Chapter 20, covers technology in terrorism and counterterrorism utilizing the work by George F. Hepner and Richard M. Medina:

- George F. Hepner and Richard M. Medina. (2013). *The Geography of International Terrorism: An Introduction to Spaces and Places of Violent Non-state Groups*. CRC Press.

Particularly, this chapter looks at the use of geospatial intelligence and geospatial technologies by both terrorists and counterterrorists.

Author

Dr. Marie-Helen Maras is an associate professor at the Department of Security, Fire, and Emergency Management at John Jay College of Criminal Justice, City University of New York. She has also served as an adjunct professor at New York University, teaching graduate courses, including *Transnational Terrorism*, *Transnational Security*, and *Cybercrime*. Additionally, she has taught numerous undergraduate and graduate courses on computer forensics, crime scene investigation, transnational organized crime, terrorism and counterterrorism, and crisis management and disaster preparedness (to name a few) at State University of New York–Farmingdale and the King Graduate School of Monroe College. Moreover, she is an international editor for the *Journal of Applied Security Research* and the President of Protect New York, a professional organization that brings together academics and professionals concerned with responding to the threat of terrorism, as well as the creator and co-editor of the *Protect New York Newsletter*.

Dr. Marie-Helen Maras holds several graduate and undergraduate degrees: a DPhil in law and an MPhil in criminology and criminal justice (University of Oxford); an MA in industrial and organizational psychology (University of New Haven); a BS in psychology and a BS in computer and information science (University of Maryland University College). The majority of her research and publications have focused on the legal, economic, social, and political implications of security measures in the United States and the European Union. She has three major works at Jones and Bartlett, books titled *Counterterrorism*; *Computer Forensics: Cybercriminals, Laws and Evidence*; and *Exploring Criminal Justice: The Essentials*. Furthermore, she has provided chapters for edited volumes by Benjamin Goold and Daniel Neyland, titled *New Directions in Privacy and Surveillance* (Willan Publishing, 2009), and Justin Sinclair and Daniel Antonius, titled *The Political Psychology of Terrorism Fears* (Oxford University Press, 2013).

In addition to her teaching and academic work, her background includes approximately seven years of service in the US Navy with significant experience in security and law enforcement from her posts as a Navy law enforcement specialist and command investigator. While in the Navy, she supervised her personnel in conducting more than 130 counter-surveillance operations throughout *Operations Enduring Freedom* and *Iraqi Freedom*.

PART I

Terrorism and Terrorism History

1

Definitions and Origins of Terrorism[1]

The word "terror" derives from the Latin word *terrere*, meaning "to frighten." The word and its derivatives have been applied in a variety of contexts, from a sobriquet for a vicious despot (as in Ivan the Terrible) to eras of violent political turbulence (as in the Reign of Terror during the French Revolution) to the sporadic outbursts of violence the world knows today as terrorism. Violence is not the key characteristic, however, because such violent confrontations as World Wars I and II are not considered terrorism. Rather than being an end in itself, violence is a means to instill fear into (i.e., to terrify) whole populations.

Instilling fear can be purposeful for criminal or political ends that are malevolent in nature. Yet populations can be frightened without terrorism being involved; for example, the cause may be disease, such as the West Nile–type avian virus that plagued sections of the United States, the "mad cow" disease that struck England and parts of Europe and North America, the spread of autoimmune deficiency syndrome (AIDS) through many countries south of the equator, the severe acute respiratory syndrome (SARS) outbreak in China, and the deadly Ebola epidemics in sub-Saharan Africa in the late 1990s and the early 21st century, to name just a few.

The intention of all terrorists is to instill fear in the population at large. With the events surrounding the attacks on the World Trade Center and the Pentagon on September 11, 2001, such fear has been greatly elevated both in the United States and around the world. For terrorists, there is a common motivation to the criminal acts they perpetrate. Because there is a common element to terrorism, counterterrorism is a foundation on which to base defensive strategies and tactics. Anything that can be done to reduce fear and anxiety among the general population is an effective defense against terrorism.

[1] Information for this chapter was drawn from the following titles: (1) H. K. Tillema, A brief theory of terrorism and technology. In T. K. Ghosh, M. A. Prelas, D. S. Viswanath, and S. K. Loyalka (eds.), *Science and Technology of Terrorism and Counterterrorism*, Second Edition, CRC Press, 2009. (2) M. W. Nance, *Terrorist Recognition Handbook: A Practitioner's Manual for Predicting and Identifying Terrorist Activities*, Second Edition, CRC Press, 2008. (3) D. P. Schulz, *The Counterterrorism Handbook: Tactics, Procedures, and Techniques*, Fourth Edition, CRC Press, 2011. (4) K. J. Dudonis, F. Bolz, and D. P. Schulz, *The Counterterrorism Handbook: Tactics, Procedures, and Techniques*, Third Edition, 2005. (5) P. R. Viotti, Toward a comprehensive strategy for terrorism and homeland security. In M. A. Opheim, N. Bowen, and P. R. Viotti (eds.), *Terrorism and Homeland Security: Thinking Strategically About Policy*. CRC Press, 2008. (6) J. A. Larsen and J. J. Wirtz, WMD terrorism: New threats, revised responses. In M. A. Opheim, N. Bowen, and P. R. Viotti (eds.), *Terrorism and Homeland Security: Thinking Strategically About Policy*. CRC Press, 2008. (7) E. Kraft and M. Marks, *US Government Counterterrorism: A Guide to Who Does What*, CRC Press, 2011.

What Is Terrorism?

Terrorists act deliberately. While the desired effect is to make it seem random, each act is deliberate, even if the exact moment of the attack is unknown to the public or to every member of the terrorist cell. Many terrorist attacks may seem arbitrary in their execution, but each event has been deliberately planned to create a specific effect. Terrorism is deliberately selected as a tactic to effect change. The group must make a conscious decision to reject or abandon peaceful political change and further its agenda through the use of terrorist acts and tactics.

Terrorism involves attacks that are ruthless in nature and calculated in their impact on society at large. More specifically, terrorism is the calculated use of criminal violence or the threat of violence by a covert or overt individual, group, entity, special-interest organization, or government agency specifically designed to target people, commerce, and/or infrastructures solely for political or other advantage. The terrorist act must break laws or conspire to break laws that are common to most societies. Though terrorism usually involves violent acts, such as murder, battery, and destruction of property, it could also mean nonviolent disruptive acts that are broad threats to safety and result in the mass spread of fear.

Terrorism is not political activism or "freedom fighting." It is a conscious choice to deliberately select deadly tactics as a criminally symbolic act to spread fear, intimidation, and horror to popularize or gain support for a cause. It includes an intention to extort funds and/or influence an audience beyond the immediate victims. Terrorism is an illegitimate expression of dissent, demand for conflict resolution, or form of psychological warfare that is unjustified at any time.

Terrorism is the targeting of innocent people, including military personnel. At the heart of an act of terrorism are terrorists who specifically focus their acts of violence on killing, injuring, and/or generating fear in innocent victims. The victim may be the immediate target, especially in assassination and physical intimidation attacks, but terrorists care far more about the psychological impact of the attack on society at large. The purpose of carrying out the act is not only to meet tactical objectives but also to terrorize a population.

Terror may be produced by the purposive use of violence, but populations may also be terrorized by other, nonviolent means. Soviet show-trial purges conducted in the 1930s under Stalin, for example, spread fear not only among communist party members, but also within the population as a whole. The "knock on the door" by the police and the arrests that followed (whether in the Soviet Union or Nazi Germany) sent strong messages designed to scare people into compliance with the expectations or mandates of the party or regime—state terror in an oppressive, but not necessarily violent, form. Terrorism needs to be differentiated analytically from other forms of political violence—guerrilla warfare (typically hit-and-run tactics), insurrection or popular uprising (as in the Palestinian Intifada) that usually becomes violent, sectarian or intercommunal (as in tribal, clan, national, or ethnic) strife, civil war between competing parties for control of the state, and combat between regular military units; if it is not, there is a risk that virtually all forms of political violence will be regarded incorrectly as terrorism or the work of terrorists. Unless the meaning of terror is limited by differentiating it from these other forms of violence, terror can be construed to mean virtually anything.

Military personnel may never be targeted legitimately by terrorists. Many terrorist groups have tried to arbitrarily designate military personnel and bases as legitimate targets. Military actions are usually intended to destroy or substantially weaken an enemy's war-making capability. Such actions become terrorist incidents only when the intent is to intimidate, cause fear, or terrorize an adversary. Even in wartime, however, terrorism remains a criminal attack punishable in criminal courts after the conflict.

Terrorism is illegitimate combat, even in war. Indeed, terrorism is not a legitimate form of warfare. The rules of warfare were formalized in Convention (IV): Respecting the Laws and Customs of War on Land and Its Annex: Regulations Concerning the Laws and Customs of War on Land (The Hague, October 18, 1907). These rules, which called for armed forces to specifically avoid targeting civilians, were expanded after World War II. Governments and other groups that target civilians clearly violate these rules. Terrorism is never justified: The use of terrorism is immoral and unjustified. In almost every country, terrorism is a crime. No matter how desperate the situation, choosing to commit an act of terrorism over nonviolent resistance or political activism is not justified.

Terrorists operate in all environments. Many terrorist groups, formerly localized, have begun to operate with increasing ease throughout the world. Most organizations can move easily from urban to rural environments, so the myth that terrorists are mainly urban is no longer applicable. Many terrorists seek the anonymity and privacy rural areas offer. Additionally, most terrorists operate covertly. Terrorist operations are, not surprisingly, usually synonymous with secrecy. A few groups have been known to issue warnings before carrying out an attack, generally with a goal of creating shock value and then benefiting from the media attention the attack generates.

Terrorists often use symbolic acts to attract media and reach a large audience. The publicity surrounding an event is critical for terrorists to gain influence and spread fear. The fear effect must extend beyond the immediate victims and must symbolize the power of the group; therefore, terrorist attacks tend to be spectacular—depending on the tactics and goals of the organization—and spread fear. No matter how large or small the act, its symbolism is of far greater importance to the perpetrators than its immediate impact on the group's victims.

Many attempts have been made to encompass all of the above-mentioned aspects of terms into a single definition. Definitions provided by academics, practitioners, and government agencies will be explored below.

Definitions of Terrorism

On a scholarly level, Brian Jenkins of the Rand Corporation described terrorism as "the calculated use of violence to attain goals that are political, religious or ideological in nature. Terrorism involves a criminal act that is often symbolic in nature and intended to influence an audience beyond the immediate victims."[2] He further noted that terrorism involves "the use or threatened use of force designed to bring about political change."

Although most terrorist acts are politically motivated, in some cases other nonpolitical causes may be served by this intentional use of fear. One can argue, for example, that the 1995 sarin gas attack by Aum Shinrikyo in the subway in Tokyo was politically motivated against the Japanese government, local police, or other government officials, but another nonpolitical motive may be found in the extreme religious beliefs of this cult that defined itself by the term "supreme truth." Bruce Hoffman, a leading scholar on terrorism, describes terrorism as fundamentally and politically about violence. It is "violence—or equally important—the threat of violence—used and directed in pursuit of, or in service of, a political aim."[3] But how that violence is described has been a major difficulty. That difficulty has led to the scores of definitions of terrorism that have been used by various countries, the United Nations (UN), and regional organization resolutions and promoted by scholars.

On the political level, the US Department of State acknowledges that there are a range of definitions for terrorism, influenced particularly by the definer's perspective on any given conflict or group. A middle-of-the-road definition that initially surfaced in the mid-1980s and has retained currency says it best: "Terrorism is a premeditated, politically motivated violence perpetrated against non-combatant targets by substantial groups of clandestine state agents, usu-

[2] As introduced to the US Senate by Senator Abraham Ribicoff of Connecticut on October 25, 1977, and indicated in *On Domestic Terrorism*, a publication of the National Governors Association, Emergency Preparedness Project, Center for Policy Research, Washington, D.C., May 1979.

[3] B. Hoffman. *Inside Terrorism*. New York: Columbia University Press, 2006, 1–41.

ally intended to influence an audience."[4] However, not all terrorists are state agents, but they may be adherents of groups or organizations that often act with the assistance of state agents.

The US Department of Defense holds that terrorism is the "calculated use of violence or threat of violence to inculcate fear, intended to coerce or to intimidate governments or societies in the pursuit of goals that are generally political, religious or ideological." The *Dictionary of Military Terms*[5] further defines terrorism as "the unlawful use of violence or threat of violence to instill fear and coerce governments or societies. Terrorism is often motivated by religious, political, or other ideological beliefs and committed in the pursuit of goals that are usually political." Additionally, according to the US Department of Defense Directive 2000.12H, terrorism involves "the calculated use of violence or threat of violence to attain goals—political, religious or ideological in nature—by instilling fear or using intimidation or coercion. Terrorism involves a criminal act, often symbolic in nature, intended to influence an audience beyond the immediate victims."

The Department of Homeland Security's definition,[6] reflecting its role in protecting the national infrastructure, says the term "terrorism" means any activity that (A) involves an act that (i) is dangerous to human life or potentially destructive of critical infrastructure or key resources and (ii) is a violation of the criminal laws of the United States or of any State or other subdivision of the United States and (B) appears to be intended (i) to intimidate or coerce a civilian population; (ii) to influence the policy of a government by intimidation or coercion; or (iii) to affect the conduct of a government by mass destruction, assassination, or kidnapping.

The most commonly cited definition of terrorism is that of the Federal Bureau of Investigation (FBI). The FBI, the lead agency for investigating terrorism against American targets, defines terrorism as "the unlawful use of force or violence against persons or property to intimidate or coerce a Government, the civilian population, or any segment thereof, in furtherance of political or social objectives."[7] The use of the phrase "social objectives" could be interpreted to include attacks on abortion clinics or medical research facilities by groups such as the Animal Liberation Front or attacks by radical environmentalists on commercial logging operations by ski resorts.[1] This divides the definition into domestic and international terrorism (which will be explored in Chapter 3 of this volume).

Today, laws exist that have defined terrorism and presented penalties for those who engage in terrorism or terrorism-related activity (e.g., the acquisition and/or use of weapons of mass destruction). For example, the US Code defines terrorism as the "premeditated, politically motivated violence perpetrated against noncombatant targets by sub-national groups or clandestine agents." It should be noted that 22 USC 2656f(d) is one of many US statutes and international legal instruments that concern terrorism and acts of violence.

Apart from the United States, other countries have also attempted to define terrorism. A case in point is the British government. They have defined terrorism as "the use of serious violence against persons or property, or the threat to use such violence, to intimidate or coerce a government, the public, or any section of the public for political, religious or ideological ends. The term serious violence would need to be defined so that it included serious disruption, for instance resulting from attacks on computer installations or public utilities." Another country that has defined terrorism in their domestic laws is Russia. Law 130 FZ of the Russian Federation defines terrorism as follows:

---

[4] Patterns of Global Terrorism–194, US Department of State, cover statement, Washington, D.C., 1985.

[5] *Department of Defense Dictionary of Military and Associated Terms*. November 8, 2010 (as amended through January 31, 2011) 1-02, p. 368. Available at http://www.dtic.mil/doctrine/new_pubs/jp1_02.pdf.

[6] Homeland Security Act of 2002, Public Law 107-296, November 25, 2002, 116 Stat. 2135, Sec. 2 (15). Available at http://www.dhs.gov/xlibrary/assets/hr_5005_enr.pdf (accessed July 28, 2011). Also see http://codes.lp.findlaw.com/uscode/8/12/II/II/1182.

[7] FBI Report, "Terrorism 2002–2005." Available at http://www.fbi.gov/stats-services/publications/terrorism-2002-2005 (accessed April 26, 2011).

> Terrorism is violence or the threat of violence against individuals or organizations, and also the destruction (damaging) of or threat to destroy (damage) property and other material objects, such as to threaten to cause loss of life, significant damage to property, or other socially dangerous consequences and are implemented with a view to violating public security, intimidating the population, or influencing the adoption of decisions advantageous to terrorists by organs of power, or satisfying their unlawful material and (or) other interests; attempts on the lives of statesmen or public figures perpetrated with a view to ending their state or other political activity or out of revenge for such activity; attacks on representatives of foreign states or staffers of international organizations enjoying international protection, and also on the official premises or vehicles of persons enjoying international protection if these actions are committed with a view to provoking war or complicating international relations.

International organizations have followed suit in defining terrorism. For instance, the United Nations views terrorism as "a unique form of crime. Terrorist acts often contain elements of warfare, politics and propaganda. For security reasons and due to lack of popular support, terrorist organizations are usually small, making detection and infiltration difficult. Although the goals of terrorists are sometimes shared by wider constituencies, their methods are generally abhorred." By contrast, the Organization of African Unity Convention on the Prevention and Combating of Terrorism of 1999[8] includes acts that should not be considered as terrorism. Specifically, notwithstanding the provisions of Article 1 that contains a lengthy definition of terrorist acts, this Convention holds that "[t]he struggle waged by peoples in accordance with the principles of international law for their liberation or self-determination, including armed struggle against colonialism, occupation, aggression and domination by foreign forces shall not be considered as terrorist acts."

In the past, the lack of a working definition of terrorism presented a serious problem when terrorists were apprehended and brought to trial. Terrorism itself was, for the most part, not prohibited by law, although the planting of explosive devices, kidnapping, arson, robbery, taking hostages, hijacking planes, conspiring to commit illegal acts, and similar activities were prohibited by federal, state, and local laws. The result was that, in court, terrorists argued they were being persecuted for supporting certain political or religious causes and that the proceeding was a political trial rather than a criminal case.

The History of Terrorism

Terrorism is a tactic that has been used in the past; it may be one of the oldest forms of illegitimate political dissent. Political betrayal, treachery, deceit, and violence have been around as long as humans have formed themselves into political groups. The use of violence or the threat of violence to "send a message" to political leaders or society at large has occurred throughout recorded history. Groups such as the Zealots and Sicari in biblical Palestine are often cited as historical terrorists.

Ancient texts, such as the Bible, *The Iliad*, *The Odyssey*, and Egyptian hieroglyphics and letters inscribed in cuneiform on clay tablets, have related specific details about such occurrences in the eastern Mediterranean. The act of murder for political ends, a major component of terrorism, was used by a small group of Ismaili Shiite Muslims late in the 11th century under the direction of Hasam-I Sabbah. His followers, who came to be known as Assassins, were a small fundamentalist religious sect engaged in numerous confrontations with other Shiites and the more dominant Sunni Muslims. The Assassins of 11th-century Persia are, like the Zealots and Sicari, often cited as historical terrorists.

---

[8] UN Documents, Organization of African Unity, Algiers, 2008. Available at http://treaties.un.org/doc/db/Terrorism/OAU-english.pdf.

In the world of Islam, the demarcation between secular and religious authority is blurred so that a religious dispute may equally be viewed as political and vice versa. In addition to their name and legacy of terrorism, the Assassins have also been credited with precipitating the invention of chain-mail body armor as protection against dagger attacks. These loyal followers of Sabbah and his successors were known as *fedai*, or faithful, and as *fadayeen*, men of sacrifice. As religious and domestically political as their motives usually were, the Assassins were not above engaging in terrorism on behalf of others, including, according to some accounts, Richard the Lion-Hearted (King Richard III of England) while he was engaged in one of the crusades to the Holy Land. The Christian religious group, the Order of the Knights Templar, was said to have adopted the Assassins' system of military organization. The Assassins were also trained to participate in suicide missions. They were often paid in advance so they could give the money to their families. The only success was the death of the target whether or not it cost the life of the individual Assassin. The Assassins eventually fell prey to internal squabbles and internecine disputes and were effectively neutralized as a political power by the middle of the 13th century but managed to remain cohesive enough to resurface in the 1830s and again in the 1940s as foes of the Shah of Iran.

Although the Assassins were the most notorious group of historical terrorists, there have been others, including the celebrated Guy Fawkes, bomber of the English Parliament (who nonetheless is viewed by others as a fighter against oppression). The Barbary pirates of North Africa in the 18th and 19th centuries made their living kidnapping citizens of other countries and holding them for ransom. This activity led to the founding of another Christian religious group, the Redemptionist Order, whose members often acted as intermediaries between the states of the Barbary Coast and the foreign governments whose citizens were being held hostage. In the United States, in the early part of the 20th century, anarchists operating under the banner of the Black Hand preyed on newly arrived immigrants, especially on the Lower East Side of New York City's Manhattan. Their tactics of selective assassinations with guns and bombs proved extremely effective for a short period of time.

The 18th and 19th centuries generated forms of terrorism that are still used today. Although various types of violence have permeated societies throughout history, most scholars link the emergence of modern terrorism, and modern warfare for that matter, to the French Revolution. Modern usage of the word "terrorism" owes much to the Jacobins during the French Revolution. The Jacobin movement advocated democracy in the form of universal suffrage and also proclaimed very high standards of probity for personal and public conduct. In September 1793, the radical Committee of Public Safety in France under the leadership of Robespierre and the Jacobins publicly decreed "terror," called by that name, against enemies of the Revolution in order to assure the "reign of virtue." The French Revolution leader, Maximilien Robespierre, publicly advocated the use of terrorism as a political tool and employed public executions by guillotine to seize popular attention and terrify French society.

This type of violence was also used to manipulate elite and public opinion. The Committee of Public Safety, led by Robespierre and his followers, used the guillotine in a Reign of Terror (1793–1794) to gain control of the public bodies of the French Republic. When Robespierre forewarned several of his colleagues that they would soon lose their heads too, members of the Committee became concerned about their own safety and killed him first. But the Reign of Terror allowed 22 people to hold a nation of 27 million hostage, killing at least 40,000 of their countrymen in the process.

Agents of the Committee murdered, maimed, and also seized and destroyed property of alleged enemies for nine months until Robespierre's arrest and execution. Foreign and domestic critics of Jacobin political objectives and methods, including Britain's Edmund Burke and conservative continental European governments, fulminated against the French "Reign of Terror." That period of French history is still commonly identified as "The Reign of Terror." Perhaps this helps to explain the persistently pejorative connotations associated with the word "terrorism."

The Revolution demonstrated that what average people thought and believed mattered and that war was no longer simply the sport of kings, noblemen, or mercenaries. Indeed, this "first generation warfare," a term popularized by Bill Lind and G. I. Wilson, saw many developments that remain the basis of today's armies and contemporary combined arms operations: an increasingly professional officer corps, volunteers for military service, industrial production, and national zeal.[9] At its inception, terrorism emerged as the weapon of the weak, used to instill fear in the hearts of a public audience to achieve a political objective.[10] It was violence directed as a matter of political strategy against innocent persons.[11]

The First Wave

David Rapoport, one of the world's foremost authorities on political violence, divides the evolution of modern terrorism into four waves that roughly correspond to broad generational change and to the major political issues of their day.[12,13] The first wave of terrorism emerged near the end of the 19th century when rebel and revolutionary movements embraced sensational violence to attack local regimes. The fathers of modern terrorism originated largely in Russia, where numerous groups, anarchists, and terror-advocating philosophers emerged, such as Sergi Nachayev and Mikhail Bakunin. The Narodnaya Volya (People's Will) movement in Russia, for instance, deliberately violated social and legal norms by targeting civilians in an effort to prompt a government overreaction, which, in their view, would provoke a revolutionary outburst. Soon various terrorist movements, following in the wake of economic, political, educational, and social advances in Russia and Central Europe, emerged in various countries. Terrorists armed with handguns or dynamite targeted elected officials or royal families to advance the cause of political reform, nationalism, or various ideological movements, such as communism and anarchy. After the Russian Revolution of 1917, Russian terrorism further expanded and was encouraged by the communist leadership. Lenin, also known as the Red Prince, encouraged collective terrorism.

Terrorism spread throughout Europe, where numerous heads of state were assassinated. This first wave ended with the assassination of Austrian Archduke Franz Ferdinand, an act that precipitated the outbreak of the First World War. Gavrilo Princip, the Serbian nationalist who pulled the trigger that day, set off a chain reaction that ultimately led to the deaths of millions of people. The death and destruction that swept Europe set several countries back decades in terms of demographics or economic development, illustrating an important fact about terrorism: its effects often are unforeseen and unintended. Nevertheless, the fact that spectacular acts of terrorism can unleash uncontrollable social, political, and military forces has seemed to encourage those who want to use mayhem to achieve their objectives.

The Second Wave

The second wave of terror, prompted by the forces of decolonization, emerged in the aftermath of World War II. Instead of targeting senior officials and government luminaries, these nationalists targeted the instruments of colonial control, such as local officials, police, and military outposts, to confront colonists with the possibility that by occupying some distant land they would be forced to endure never-ending casualties. Terrorist cells were formed in cities, and attacks

---

[9] W. Lind, K. Nightengale, J. Schmitt, J. Sutton, and G. I. Wilson. The changing face of war: Into the fourth generation. *Marine Corps Gazette*: 22–26, October 1989.

[10] D. Fromkin. The strategy of terrorism. *Foreign Affairs* 53, no. 4: 683–698, July 1975.

[11] P. E. Devine and R. J. Rafalko. International terrorism. On Terror, *Annals of the American Academy of Political and Social Science* 463: 49, September 1982.

[12] D. C. Rapoport. The fourth wave: September 11 in the history of terrorism. *Current History*: 419–424, December 2001.

[13] D. Rapoport. Terrorism. In Lester R. Kurtz and Jennifer E. Turpin (eds.), *Encyclopedia of Violence, Peace, and Conflict*, vol. 3, London: Academic Press, 1999, 497–510

were carried out against prominent urban targets although these attacks were not necessarily directed at civilians. Second-wave terrorists sometimes provided warning of their attacks to minimize casualties, but mistakes occurred. For example, the Irgun bombing of the King David Hotel in Jerusalem in July 1946 knocked out the center of British mandatory rule in Palestine but also killed 91 people, a death toll that undermined Irgun's credibility among friend and foe alike.

The crest of the second wave, however, occurred in Southeast Asia. The "People's War," a strategy whereby terrorism is used to rid the countryside of a government's presence, was put to use by the North Vietnamese and their Viet Cong allies during the Vietnam War to drive the US-supported regime in Saigon from power.[14] The first stage of the people's war involved the use of violence against government officials and supporters to demonstrate to the local population that the colonial power was on the wrong side of history. By reducing the government presence in the countryside, the Viet Cong placed themselves in a position where they were able to communicate their own political program to the peasantry. In theory, the Vietnamese version of the people's war also ended in a burst of revolutionary terrorism, the so-called general offensive general uprising, a spontaneous revolt against the government.[15]

In the United States, the war in Vietnam and opposition to it was a springboard for launching a wave of domestic terrorism unparalleled in this country's history. Such groups as the Weather Underground, the New World Liberation Front, and groups with similar antiwar, antiestablishment, and anarchist sympathies spawned bombing campaigns, armed robberies to finance their activities, and other criminal acts. The attention drawn by these groups to various causes encouraged political radicals of other stripes, spanning the political spectrum, from the Puerto Rican national group FALN to the Black Panthers to the anti-Castro Cuban group Omega-7, to engage in increasingly violent activities. Such domestic terrorism waned following the end of the Vietnam War only to yield to new breeds of terrorists, including antiabortionists, ecoterrorists, animal rights extremists, antiglobalists, and individuals such as Timothy McVeigh, who perpetrated the bombing of a federal office building in Oklahoma City, Oklahoma, in 1995.

The second wave produced its own lesson: Terrorism can be integrated into a complex political-military strategy that, over time, might wear down and defeat even the strongest military power. Terrorism was not just the weapon of the weak, it was an effective weapon of the weak. The Vietnamese success against the United States spurred other organizations to use terrorism as a political instrument although few groups described themselves as terrorists because the term had taken on a pejorative connotation by the 1960s. Many of these organizations, such as the Weather Underground in the United States, the Italian Red Brigades, or the German Red Army Faction, saw themselves as the vanguard for socialist revolution, a view that was welcomed by Soviet officials who looked for every available opportunity to cause trouble for the West.

The Third Wave

The Palestine Liberation Organization (PLO) came to exemplify third-wave terrorism that was inspired by the Viet Cong's struggle against overwhelming odds. Left alone in its fight to regain lost lands following Israel's defeat of the Arabs in the 1967 Six Day War, the PLO's operations had virtually all of the hallmarks of today's Islamic fundamentalists who use terror to advance their cause. Because they lacked access to their own territory, the Palestinians had to create operating and training facilities in countries sympathetic to their plight. They also attacked targets outside the Middle East. Palestinian terrorists struck the Munich Olympics in 1972 and kidnapped OPEC ministers in Vienna in 1975. Because they primarily sought to draw atten-

[14] R. Shultz. The limits of terrorism in insurgency warfare: The case of the Viet Cong. *Polity* 11, no. 1: 67–91, Autumn 1978.

[15] D. Pike, PAVN: *People's Army of Vietnam*. Novato, CA: Presidio Press, 1986.

tion to their cause, the PLO and other third-wave groups adopted hostage taking and airplane hijackings as preferred tactics.

Third-wave terrorists, however, had to strike a delicate balance. Too little violence would fail to draw attention to their cause while too much violence would cause a backlash of international outrage as people turned against the perpetrators of what appeared to be senseless acts of violence. Still, there was a gradual escalation in terms of death and destruction produced by terrorism. Tens of people died in the worst terrorist incidents in the 1970s while hundreds would die in the worst incidents in the 1980s and 1990s.[16] Observers also came to several conclusions about third-wave terrorism. These terrorists appeared to be rational in the sense that they used violence in a calculated way to achieve political objectives. Additionally, terrorists seemed to stick with tried and true operations. Innovation was rare because terrorists often strove to minimize risks in what were inherently demanding operations.[17]

The Fourth Wave

The lessons drawn from the third wave became conventional wisdom as a new generation of fourth-wave terrorists emerged in the aftermath of the Soviet defeat in Afghanistan and the triumph of the Islamic revolution in Iran at the end of the 1970s. After the 1979 Islamic Revolution in Iran and with the encouragement of the Ayatollah Khomeini, religious students seized the American embassy in Tehran. The Iranian government eventually took responsibility for the hostage-taking and held 55 Americans for 444 days in protest of the United States' ongoing support for the exiled Mohammed Reza Pahlavi, the Shah of Iran, who was perceived by many as a corrupt dictator. Iran quickly became a major sponsor of Islamic extremist terrorism worldwide after this event.

Although the Iranian Hostage Crisis demonstrated that Americans were vulnerable to this new type of Islamic terrorism, US policymakers tried to harness the religious forces that motivated Islamic militants in the Cold War by supporting their battle against the Soviets in Afghanistan. Russia's invasion of Afghanistan during the 1980s and its eventual defeat helped catalyze the rise of al-Qaeda. Indeed, al-Qaeda emerged from the remnants of the mujahedin forces, especially foreign volunteers, once allied with the United States. Returning from the brutal struggle in Afghanistan, these individuals found it impossible to reintegrate into what they believed were amoral and corrupt societies. Many began to gravitate toward Osama bin Laden (now deceased), a rich Saudi financier who had built a reputation as a logistics and construction expert during the war in Afghanistan. Bin Laden's motivations and rhetoric evolved over the course of a decade of terrorist activity, but his initial ire seems to have been directed toward what he believed was a hypocritical Wahabi regime in Saudi Arabia and its strongest backer, the United States government.

The US military presence in the Persian Gulf and Saudi Arabia, made necessary by the requirement to maintain sanctions against Baghdad following the first Gulf War, only fueled bin Laden's animosity toward the Saudi royal family and the United States. These former anti-Russian "holy warriors" were drawn from the thousands of Muslim volunteers who had been recruited to fight the Russians with Pakistani, Saudi Arabian, and American support. Known as Afghan-Arabs, postwar terrorists now claim they are fighting to protest US foreign policy in the Middle East and America's military presence in Saudi Arabia and to promote the liberation of Palestine and the establishment of Islamic states throughout the Muslim world.

Al-Qaeda and other jihadists launched a war against the United States in the 1990s. After the first attack on the World Trade Center in 1993, the Central Intelligence Agency collected

---

[16] B. Jenkins. *Countering al Qaeda: An Appreciation of the Situation and Suggestions for Strategy.* Santa Monica, CA: RAND, 2002, 6.

[17] A. K. Cronin. Terrorist motivations for chemical and biological weapons use: Placing the threat in context. *Defense & Security Analysis* 20, no. 4: 317, December 2004.

information on bin Laden. For its part, the US military strengthened security at its facilities in the Persian Gulf region following the attacks on the Khobar Towers in Saudi Arabia. By 1998, bin Laden had held press conferences calling for attacks against American interests and issued a fatwa justifying his actions. In August 1998, al-Qaeda attacked US embassies in Nairobi, Kenya, and Dar Es Salaam, Tanzania. In 2000, after a failed attempt to attack the USS The Sullivans, bin Laden's operatives launched a suicide attack against the USS Cole, inflicting 50 casualties on the crew and nearly sinking the vessel. Bin Laden was quite vocal about his ambitions, which were repeated in an article published by *Foreign Affairs*.[18]

Concluding Thoughts

There are many long definitions of terrorism in the public domain and in the law books of the United States and other countries. If there is any common theme, it is that terrorist acts are calculated acts; they are not carried out randomly. Terrorists use violence. Terrorist operations entail violence or the threat of violence. Some groups that use violent means may also carry out terror operations that do not use violence in the traditional sense but may result in disruption that heightens the sense of fear and terror.

Publicity is essential to terrorism's purposes, even if it is limited to word of mouth, in order to communicate demands and to signal accomplishments. Terrorism normally involves a succession of destructive events. It is difficult to change attitudes and behavior by means of a single isolated act. At the same time, it is customary to distinguish episodic terrorism from continuous military campaigns, including strategic bombings of civilian targets during World War II and other major wars. Terrorist violence aims ultimately to affect public policy and governance and not necessarily other matters. It aims to do so by changing attitudes and behavior among immediate and secondary witnesses, primarily through intimidation.

Since the French Revolution, terrorism has changed its stripes to reflect the outstanding political and social grievances of the day as seen from the viewpoint of the weak. Its targets have been political elites and royalty, government outposts, the international news media, and most recently, the citizens of opposing governments and societies. It seems to be shaped and encouraged by the example of previously triumphant movements, especially campaigns that ultimately proved successful against powerful states. Terrorism also had been distinctly secular and localized until third-wave movements incorporated Islamic fundamentalism into the mix, and the PLO was forced by circumstances to conduct international operations. Over the past several decades, terrorism has become increasingly lethal as transnational organizations use international communication and transportation networks to wreak death and destruction across the globe.

[18] A. Rashid. The Taliban: Exporting extremism. *Foreign Affairs* 78, no. 6: 22–35, November/December 1999. Terrorism has evolved over time, reflecting the ideologies, organizational preferences, and technological sophistication of those who attempt to kill the innocent to achieve their political objectives. This evolution is not necessarily linear, but fourth-generation terrorists do seem unusually interested in generating mass casualty events.

2

Motivations of Terrorists and the Psychology of Terrorism[1]

Terrorism is, by definition, a tactic undertaken for strategic political effect. It helps to think like a terrorist in order to comprehend the political context within which the terrorist operates. Politics generally resembles a strategic game whose outcome rests upon interdependent choices among two or more parties. Politics further involves a bargaining process, not necessarily peaceful, in which parties attempt to influence one another's choices.[2] One may seek to induce another to act in ways he or she did not originally intend. Alternatively, one may seek to deter another from doing what he planned. Various general strategies are available for this purpose, including argumentation (both affirmative and negative), reward, promise, punishment, and threat. Several instruments are available to suit each of these strategies.

Terrorism is an instrument that has been employed in an attempt to change political behavior by the application of punishment and threat. It is an intermediate technique in the spectrum of violence. It is more destructive than most strikes and other demonstrations and less damaging than most conventional military campaigns. The deadly logic of terrorism relies upon the insight that death and damage inflicted upon noncombatants may demoralize observant citizens and government officials, undermine support of established leaders, and eventually lead to change of policies or governments. The person who resorts to terrorism may also employ other instruments at other times, including conventional military force if he or she is able. The terrorist presumably employs terrorism because it suits his or her purpose and is consistent with his or her abilities. The question that follows is: what motivates terrorists? To answer this question, their ideologies and the reasons for engaging in terrorism are examined.

---

[1] Information for this chapter was drawn from the following titles: (1) M. W. Nance, *Terrorist Recognition Handbook: A Practitioner's Manual for Predicting and Identifying Terrorist Activities*, Second Edition, CRC Press, 2008. (2) H. K. Tillema, A brief theory of terrorism and technology. In T. K. Ghosh, M. A. Prelas, D. S. Viswanath, and S. K. Loyalka (eds.), *Science and Technology of Terrorism and Counterterrorism*, Second Edition, CRC Press, 2009. (3) M. E. Diamond, The group psychology of terrorism. In T. K. Ghosh, M. A. Prelas, D. S. Viswanath, and S. K. Loyalka (eds.), *Science and Technology of Terrorism and Counterterrorism*, Second Edition, CRC Press, 2009. (4) R. McPartland, Terrorist tradecraft I: The attack cycle. In M. J. Fagel (ed.), *Principles of Emergency Management: Hazard Specific Issues and Mitigation Strategies*. CRC Press, 2011.

[2] T. C. Schelling. *The Strategy of Conflict*. Cambridge, MA: Harvard University Press, 1960.

Ideologies Terrorists Espouse

When it comes to justifying terrorist violence with a certain ideology, the human imagination knows no boundaries. An ideology is a set of values or principles—a belief system—that may motivate people to act. Most political and religious ideologies are, at their core, based on noble ideas, but, as we see far too often, they can become twisted to serve the ambitions of a few and take on violent tendencies. Other ideologies, such as white supremacy, are based on hate and fear and actually espouse, at their core, the use of violence as the desired means to an end.

People who carry out acts of terrorism invariably claim they are acting in the name of a religious, political, philosophical, or other type of cause. It is important to understand the particular ideology claimed by a terrorist group in order to better predict its targets and methodologies. The following is a partial list of political, religious, and other ideologies that have been used by terrorist organizations to justify their violent actions. First, political and policy-based ideologies are considered; then religious extremist ideologies are examined.

Political and Policy-Based Ideologies

Marxist-Leninist communism: The main objective of this political model is worker ownership of the means of production, resulting from the overthrow (violent, if necessary) of the bourgeois class. Theoretically, such a revolution would produce a classless society. Historical enemies of communists are the property-owning class and the state systems that keep the "owners" in power, including politicians, the military, and the police. Some current terrorist groups with communist roots include the Tupac Amaru Revolutionary Movement (MRTA, or Shining Path) of Peru, which has attempted to replace Peru's government with a revolutionary Marxist regime, and the Red Brigades of Italy, which attacked the Italian government and businesses in an attempt to remove Italy from the Western Alliance and punish Italian participation in NATO. Thought to be defunct after 1991, the New Red Brigades (with new, younger adherents) is believed to have resumed operations in Italy in 2002.

Stalinist communism: The key feature of Stalin's attempts at furthering a socialist revolution was the creation of a one-party state (and the consequent brutal suppression of opposition). The underlying result of Stalinism was the lack of workers' rights, dictatorial rule through a cult of personality, and the distortion of history. Whereas Marx stressed the idea of a proletariat revolution from below, Stalinism emphasized strict implementation of socialism from the top down. In the Soviet Union, this ideology resulted in a classic example of state-run terror campaigns. Some mafia and Old-Guard Russian groups, who have used terrorism as a localized tool, still believe Stalinism is the best system for Russia today.

Maoist communism: Maoism is a Chinese variant on Marxism. It stresses cultural characteristics (such as strong family ties), unceasing class struggle, and constant party oversight. Mao Tse-tung also advocated the use of terrorist campaigns against counterrevolutionaries. Ideologically, Mao adapted Marxism to apply to the peasant masses, rather than the working classes of Europe, and today, many peasant revolutionary terrorist groups throughout Asia and Latin America stem from Maoist-type philosophies rather than those of Marxism because their origins are more rural than urban.

Castro and Guevarist communism: The communism of Fidel Castro (and his deputy, Che Guevara) has been based, since the 1950s, on the Marxist-Leninist model. Its major characteristics include elections to a general assembly, the cult of personality centered on Fidel Castro, and Cuba's explicit efforts to export its brand of communism to other Latin American countries. Groups that have adopted this philosophy include the Colombian Army of National Liberation (ELN), the Revolutionary Armed Forces of Colombia (FARC), and the defunct Farabundo Marti National Movement (FMLN) of El Salvador.

Fascism/neo-fascism: Fascism is a state philosophy based on glorification of that state and its supreme leadership, paired with total individual subordination for the greater good of the state. The state is thus justified in all actions that promote its own survival, such as imperialism, unilateralism in foreign policy, and ethnocentrism. The philosophy since the end of World

War II has been referred to as neo-fascism. Nazi Germany and Italy under Benito Mussolini are classic examples of fascism; modern examples would include Chile under Augusto Pinochet and Francisco Franco's Spain. All used their national intelligence agencies (such as the Nazi Gestapo and Chile's DINA) as terrorist organizations.

European neo-Nazism: A contraction of the German word *Nationalsozialismus*, Nazi ideology in the 1930s and 1940s stressed support for ethnic-based nationalism, anti-Semitism, and anticommunism. Today, neo-Nazi groups in Europe, often youth-based, have mainly nominal and iconographic ties to true Nazism and are generally focused only on racist agendas. They often espouse violence against immigrants and tend to deny Nazi atrocities. European neo-Nazi groups and their cells in Germany have conducted, and been convicted of, fire bombings and murders of Turkish and Arab immigrants.

American neo-Nazism: Characterized by xenophobia and idolization of Adolf Hitler and the Nazi Party, American neo-Nazis are fewer in number and less politically active than their European counterparts. American neo-Nazis, by virtue of the diverse makeup of US society, expanded Hitler's concept of a master race to include non-Aryan ethnicities, including Greeks, Slavs, and Hispanics. They also differ from European neo-Nazis in their use of Christianity to justify racist beliefs and thus gain broader support. Numerous neo-Nazi groups operate quietly within the United States under the umbrella of, and in complete cooperation with, the Christian Identity, a white supremacy movement. Emerging American groups, such as World Church of the Creator and the RAcial HOly WAr movement (RAHOWA), have conducted murder, small-scale arson, and financial robbery in an effort to create a terrorist capability.

Anarchist/nihilist: These two ideologies stress the need for immediate, violent destruction of established order and were popular in Eastern Europe and Russia/the Soviet Union in the late 19th and early 20th centuries. Nihilists see Western values as baseless and maintain no loyalties or fundamental beliefs in an existence they view as purposeless. To nihilists, social justice can be achieved by reason alone. Anarchists, emphasizing individual freedom of action, similarly seek to bring about a stateless world system and to eliminate all hierarchical structure for the good of humanity. Combined, these two concepts make for an extremist, disorganized belief system bent solely on violent overthrow of the current world order. Modern-day anarchists have been connecting in a global movement of civil disobedience and street action and have yet to reach the horrible levels of assassinations seen a century ago.

Ethnic and national independence movements: Perhaps the broadest political category of all—and one encompassing myriad political philosophies—is that of ethnic groups seeking to establish independent nations for their people. In many parts of the world, centuries old "nations" of people were split apart or subsumed by the modern nation-states created in the 19th and 20th centuries; during the past few decades, many have sought to reclaim their historical identities and homelands. Faced with colonial political repression, many nationalist movements have resorted to terrorist acts to achieve their goal of independence, and many have succeeded. Countries such as South Africa, Israel, and Nicaragua have all gained independence using acts of terrorism to pressure existing governments. Active groups, including the Tamil Tigers (LTTE) of Sri Lanka; the Kurdish Workers Party (PKK) in Turkey; and Palestinian groups in Israel, such as the PFLP, PLO, and DFLP, have not yet succeeded in their efforts to gain independent states but have continued using terrorist tactics up through recent years.

Environmentalism: Environmentalists are advocates for the state and quality of the Earth, its inhabitants, and its resources. Some groups choose to act in violent ways that constitute terrorism. For example, the Earth Liberation Front (ELF) operates in decentralized cells acting in the interest of environmental preservation. The ELF seeks to hurt businesses responsible for environmental destruction, drawing attention to its cause through the destruction of property. Its socialist-leaning ideology claims to be based on nonviolence against either humans or animals, but it carries out and advocates performing violent acts that may kill and injure innocent people.

Antiglobalization: These groups seek to slow, halt, or reverse the forces of globalization—the (some believe) uncontrolled and rapid economic, cultural, and technological interaction among diverse parts of the world. Many view globalization—specifically, the increase in international trade and the Westernization of business culture—as a threat to local practices and customs, and they fear the eventual loss of these societal qualities to a new, Western-dominated global order. Others simply oppose negative byproducts of economic globalization, such as accelerated environmental destruction and labor exploitation.

Animal rights: Animal rights advocates preach the ethical and humane treatment of animals. Generally an extremely peaceful movement, it encompasses some smaller groups that have adopted terrorist tactics as a method of protest. For example, the Animal Liberation Front (ALF) resorts to criminal actions—most often the malicious destruction of property—in an ongoing fight to end animal cruelty and the exploitation of the Earth for profit. The ALF is classified as a potential terrorist group due to its advocacy of arson and bombings and the message it sends despite its claims to be opposed to harming human life.

Religious Extremist Ideologies

Islamic extremism. Islamic extremism is the belief that traditional Islamic values must be universally adopted to defeat the encroachment of Western influence and return to the purest form of Islam. Radical Islamists perceive that Western cultural and economic influences, the sponsorship of pro-Western Muslim governments, the creation of the state of Israel, and the dilution of traditional Islamic law (Sharia) are all violations of the Koranic scriptures by illegitimate Muslims who have abdicated their responsibility to maintain the values of the faith and the people.

Christian extremism. Christian extremism is the belief that the teachings of Christianity, with Jesus Christ as the source of spiritual salvation, should be the basis of all political decisions and teachings. Two examples of Christian extremism, Ecumenical Marxism and the Christian Identity movement, are explored below.

- Ecumenical Marxism (liberation theology) is based on the belief that Christianity and its Gospels stipulate preferential treatment of the world's poor; it is therefore every Christian's duty to ensure the fair treatment of all others. Liberation theology, developed in the late 1960s and with its Marxist implications, is often blamed for encouraging violent revolution in defense of social justice and equitable wealth distribution.
- The Christian Identity Movement is a conservative, racist extension of "Anglo-Israelism." It promotes the belief that members of the Anglo Saxon, Celtic, Germanic, and/or Scandinavian cultures are racial descendants of the 10 ancient lost tribes of Israel. Christian Identity, in its various forms, asserts that the people of these cultures are "God's chosen people" while Jews are direct descendants of Satan and Eve. These groups categorize nonwhite races as soulless "mud people" on par with animals. Identity followers emphasize that Christian teachings justify not only racist doctrine, but extremist violence as well. To them, Armageddon will be manifested in an inevitable race war, necessary for the establishment of Christ's kingdom on Earth. The largest representation of this movement has been the Ku Klux Klan, whose adherents often engage in paramilitary survivalist training. The Klan operated in the United States as a domestic terrorist organization with near impunity for a century and remains a threat today.

Anti-abortion/right to life. This political/social movement—predominant in the United States—promotes the belief that human life begins at fertilization; therefore abortion, at any stage of pregnancy, is murder. Extremist proponents of this philosophy believe direct action is necessary to prevent abortions from being performed, including bombing abortion clinics and assassinating abortion providers. The Army of God is one such violence-condoning group;

members believe that they are carrying out God's will as part of a Christian holy war. Hundreds of acts, such as sniper assassinations, bombings, biological agent (anthrax) threats, and acts of physical intimidation, have been perpetrated by anti-abortion terrorists. The 1996 Olympic Park bombing in Atlanta, Georgia, is believed to have been perpetrated by suspected anti-abortion terrorist Eric Robert Rudolph.

Militant Zionism. Militant Zionism stems from the Jewish movement that arose in the late 19th century and was advocated by leading intellectuals, such as Theodore Herzl, in response to growing anti-Semitism in Europe. Zionism called for the reestablishment of the Jewish homeland in Palestine as a solution to the Jewish Diaspora. Modern Zionism is concerned with the support, development, and continuation of the state of Israel. Extremist believers, such as the Kach Group and Kahane Chai, support the perpetuation of a sovereign, all-Jewish homeland in Israel—at almost any cost.

Hindu extremism. Hindu extremism is a henotheistic religion recognizing one God as well as that God's manifestation in other deities. The principal religion of India, Hinduism centers on the principle of the Brahman (one God), positing that all of reality is unified. Hindu scriptures do not support most forms of violence, yet they make allowances for its use in self-defense against the evils of the world. Extremist Hindus support the perpetuation of the Hindu religious majority in India over the minority Muslims and Sikhs. This largely ethnic conflict has led to the formation of many indigenous terrorist groups and corresponding counter-groups (such as Sikh extremists).

Sikh extremism. The Sikh religion is an offshoot of Hinduism, promoting a love of God and humankind. Believing that all people should be treated equally, Sikhs make no distinctions along lines of race, caste, or creed. Sikh men are identifiable by their turbans and uncut hair and beards, and Sikhism's adherents believe in transmigration of the soul as a result of a person's deeds. In modern-day India, a Sikh minority actively seeks to create an independent state of Khalistan in northern India and has carried out numerous attacks, including the assassination of Indian Prime Minister Indira Gandhi in 1984 and the destruction of an Air India 747 airliner over the Atlantic Ocean, which killed 329 passengers.

Messianic salvation/apocalyptic cultism. Messianic salvation/apocalyptic cultism is an extremist belief in Jesus Christ's expected return to Earth for the purpose of delivering salvation to the worthy followers of a particular ideology, such as that of a self-designated prophet who creates a cult around his beliefs. Such cults foresee an inevitable and relatively immediate apocalyptic end of the world and, thus, seek to prepare themselves for the upcoming battle between good and absolute evil. Cultist groups, such as the American Concerned Christians, were expelled from Israel around the millennium celebrations after the discovery of plots to conduct massacres in an effort to bring on the second coming of Christ and the end of the world. In addition, the American Movement for the Establishment of the Temple has threatened to "liberate" the Temple Mount in Jerusalem through force and then blow up the Dome of the Rock Mosque (Islam's third holiest site) and build the Third Temple of Israel on it.

Occultism. The word "occult" derives from a Latin word meaning "concealed." Occultists believe that their secret practices allow them to tap into the paranormal world and thus gain insight into the mysteries of life. Basic beliefs include the ability to contact the dead and work beyond established laws of physics. Occultists are often attracted by promises of power and the appeal of inheriting esoteric knowledge, of which the general public is believed to be ignorant.

Paganism/animism. These belief systems include the ancient view that souls give life to all beings, including apparently inanimate objects, and that these souls are separate beings before birth and after death. Holy men, trances, and idols are common facets of animistic societies, and Earth-centered polytheism is characteristic of pagan societies. In the 1960s, paganism gained popularity as an environmentally friendly ideology emphasizing nature worship and the immanency of multiple deities. The Mau-Mau of Kenya (active in the 1960s) carried out massacres of civilians and acts of terrorism. They combined many pagan and animistic beliefs with political action aimed at expelling Europeans, who were seen as political oppressors.

Terrorist Motivations and Goals

All terrorist groups have both primary and secondary goals motivating them to conduct a terrorist attack. Oftentimes these goals are intertwined and parlay into each other, allowing the consequences of each attack the ability to multiply. It is important to understand the reason for which a terrorist group or individual commits an act of terrorism in order to better prepare for such an event, distinguish possible targets, and easily recognize an event as it occurs. Motivations can originate in a number of ways but often fall into a few central categories. These categories are explained below.

Primary Motivations/Goals

- Instill fear in the targeted population as well as those populations unsympathetic to their cause
- Create mass casualties as well as mass confusion in the targeted population

Secondary Motivation/Goals

- Cause financial distress in a nation, region, or population
- Create political unrest for an organization, regime, or government entity
- Create recognition for their cause through action and exploitation of resulting media
- Coerce a government to make political and even operational changes in matters relating or unrelated to the event at hand

Overall, the principal goal of all terrorists is to undermine the existing structure of society so that it will be forced to accept their demands in order to avoid further destruction. Contrary to popular belief, acts of terrorism, particularly international terrorism, need not involve mass casualties similar to those resulting from wars between nations. Instead, terrorism bases its actions on swift, unpredictable assaults that force a target nation into a state of never-ending vigilance and redirection of its resources into sustained and costly counterterrorism measures that ultimately lead to prolonged economical and political turmoil. Destabilization of the national fabric of life will eventually lead to the introduction of countermeasures that place further burdens on the population, may cause internal strife, and induce racial and ethnic tensions that will continue the process of destabilization. The goal of continual and targeted terrorism is to induce sufficient uncertainty to cause public and political pressure on the governing bodies to "open a dialogue" with the terrorists. Terrorist goals will thus acquire legitimacy by becoming "social grievances" that can be addressed only at the level of a national government or an international organization such as the United Nations (UN).

A terrorist attack constitutes a nonverbal signal intended primarily to convey an intimidating message to particular audiences. Any such act demonstrates an ability and willingness to behave destructively. The magnitude of an attack further signals terrorist strength.[3] Apparent strength implies an ability to conduct more attacks in the future. A terrorist attack may intend to send a signal to any of several audiences for any of several instrumental purposes. It may also be employed in an effort to undermine public support of a government by demonstrating that government's inability to protect its citizens. This is a frequent aim among insurrectionist movements now and has been in the past.

Additionally, it may be employed abroad in order to discourage foreign support for domestic policies and governments, including Palestinian attacks within Europe from the 1960s onward aimed at coercing change in foreign support of Israel. Moreover, it may be employed in order

[3] P. B. Overgaard. The Scale of Terrorist Attacks as a Signal of Resources. *Journal of Conflict Resolution* 38: 452–478, 1994.

to attract new adherents to one's own cause by demonstrating the will and capacity for action. Furthermore, it may be employed in order to reinforce commitment among one's own followers and to forestall decay of an organization due to inaction. One suspects that was one reason why the Provisional Irish Republican Army broke so many truce agreements in Northern Ireland during the 1980s. In practice, the signal represented by a terrorist attack may reach several audiences at once and may serve more than one political objective.

Strictly personal terrorism is uncommon, however. It is difficult to sustain a program without a durable organization. It is difficult to effect important political change if others interpret violence merely as a personal vendetta. Effective terrorist leaders typically portray themselves as representatives of conspicuous groups and movements. Usually they are. Some governments also contribute to terrorism although more sponsor it indirectly than employ it directly. Most refrain from visible involvement in terrorism because either they have no need for it, do not approve of its methods, or fear retaliation. Governments that employ terrorism directly and conspicuously are often comparatively weak and insecure. A few employ terror against their own peoples in an effort to consolidate power as did France's Committee of Public Safety in the 1790s. Others terrorize their own in an effort to forestall collapse as did the government of Mohammed Reza Shah Pahlavi in Iran prior to its downfall in 1979. A few others occasionally employ terrorism for blatantly coercive purposes, including Libya within Chad during the 1970s and 1980s.

Today, fewer acts of terrorism are state sponsored. Increasingly, acts of terrorism are rooted in ethnic, religious, cultural, and nationalistic large-group identities. Given the combined ambiguity and vulnerability of nation-state boundaries and affiliations in a global economy, understanding individual motives behind violent, large-group memberships is crucial. The psychology of large-group defense of borders and boundaries must be understood and appreciated if one wants to increase tolerance and decrease intergroup conflicts and ethnic and religious tensions worldwide.

Terrorism is a group activity in which members share a common ideology, group solidarity, and persecutory group identity. Typically, the group ideology is fundamentalist and homogeneous, a totalistic system of beliefs that governs a way of life, which promotes group cohesion. Members merge via group solidarity behind the idealized godlike image and grandiosity of their charismatic leaders and the perpetuation of absolutist ideas. The terrorist group identity stems from a shared subjective experience of persecution among members of a common ethnic, religious, nationalistic, or cultural group. This shared experience and collective tragic and traumatic memory (what Volkan calls chosen trauma[4]) consists of shame, anger, and a lethal perception of outsiders. These toxic sentiments are then fueled and solidified at historically urgent and opportune moments of intergroup tension and vulnerability.

The essence of this bond of persecution symbolizes a shared experience of unjust treatment by others, specifically those outside of their ethnic, religious, nationalistic, or racial group. This fear of and hostility toward outsiders may simply derive from the others' rejection of the group's ideas and belief system, or it may emerge from the possible threat alleged of outsiders infiltrating and destroying the large-group identity (as is often the case in ethnic tensions). Inevitably, a vulnerable sense of "we-ness," low group self-image, resentment for persecution, and/or opposition (whether real or imagined) fosters a social structure of "us against them." The polarization of group insiders and outsiders is driven by the psychology of the large-group identity and requires further elaboration.

Internal Psychology of Terrorist Acts

Juergensmeyer observes that "acts of terrorism are usually products of an internal logic and not of random crazy thinking: These acts of terrorism are done not to achieve a strategic goal but

[4] V. Volkan. *Blood Lines: From Ethnic Pride to Ethnic Terrorism*. New York: Farrar, Straus and Giroux, 1997.

to make a symbolic statement."[5] For Juergensmeyer, what matters to terrorists is the symbolism, the theatrical nature of an act that draws attention worldwide rather than a well-planned maneuver intended to defeat the evil enemy. Some experts, such as Pape, argue that suicide terrorism, in particular, is strategic and represents a logical choice on the part of otherwise disenfranchised and relatively powerless extremists.[6] And, although there may be a rationale for these acts of desperation, as Pape suggests, it would also seem that the symbolism of particular acts of terror are assumed to reinforce the strategic goals of terrorists.[6] Nevertheless, this does not explain why some individuals become suicide terrorists and what motivates them and not others to engage in mass killings.

Ethnic, religious, cultural, and nationalistic large-group affiliations are vulnerable to provocation of regressive, primitive, and fanatical thinking and extreme emotions, particularly when these groups espouse fundamentalist ideologies and simultaneously feel defenseless and in danger of losing their identity or "we-ness." In the minds of extremists, holding on to that identity and protecting the integrity and preservation of the group are acts worthy of self-sacrifice, and thereby, in the group mind, a threat, real or imagined, justifies violence and mayhem.

In Lifton's study of Aum Shinrikyo, the Japanese cult that released sarin nerve gas in the Tokyo subways, he writes, "[a]ny imagined Armageddon is violent, but the violence tends to be distant and mythic, to be brought about by evil forces that leave God with no other choice, but a total cleansing of this world. With Aum's Armageddon the violence was close at hand and palpable."[7] Lifton writes that Aum was always an actor in its own Armageddon drama, whether as a target of world-destroying enemies or as a fighting force in a great battle soon to begin or already underway. As time went on, however, Aum increasingly saw itself as the initiator, the trigger of the final event.

Similar to rightist American militia groups, these groups perceive themselves as destined to "save the world" and, as Lifton writes, they are driven to do so even if the means necessary to meet their ultimate goal necessitate "destroying the world to save it."[7] Moreover, as is often the case, the vulnerable cult (or large-group identity) comes to believe in the evil of the other by demonizing and dehumanizing the other and thereby rationalizing the destruction of the other as an act of God's will rather than a mass killing. Psychologically, group members perpetrate murderous acts on outsiders when they come to view the other as a nonhuman object of evil (such as vermin, pests, and insects). Staub,[8] among others, has noted that underlying the hostility and violence is a collective self-image of vulnerability. His research indicates that the presence of "difficult life conditions" and "certain cultural and personal characteristics" contribute to violent group activities, such as genocide, terrorism, and ethnic cleansing. Difficult life conditions include economic and political problems, crime, widespread violence, rapid changes in technology, social institutions, values, ways of life, and social disorganization. These conditions promote feelings of powerlessness and confusion. In addition, cultural and personal characteristics provide further context for group violence and encompass low self-concept among group members. The group's low self-image and shared vulnerability foster in-group–out-group differentiation (an "us and them" mentality), exaggerated obedience to authority (as in authoritarianism), monolithic (versus pluralistic) culture, emerging totalitarian or fascistic ideology, and cultural aggressiveness. Staub also suggests that societal and political organizations with authoritarian and totalitarian characteristics are factors contributing to group violence.[8]

---

[5] M. Juergensmeyer. *Terror in the Mind of God: The Global Rise of Religious Violence*. Berkeley: University of California Press, 2000.

[6] R. A. Pape. *Dying to Win: The Strategic Logic of Suicide Terrorism*. New York: Random House, 2005.

[7] R. J. Lifton. *Destroying the World to Save It: Aum Shinrikyo, Apocalyptic Violence and the New Global Terrorism*. New York: Metropolitan Books, 1999.

[8] E. Staub. *The Roots of Evil: The Origins of Genocide and Other Group Violence*. New York: Cambridge University Press, 1992.

Violent group members come to view themselves as potentially innocent victims of the other group's (societal and political institutions) inherently evil nature—what psychoanalysts call "projective identification." Projective identification is a mode of projection in which the subject locates part of himself or herself (psychologically speaking) inside someone else, which permits knowing this person to have the projected attributes.[9] At the same time, the other takes in and identifies with the projected image. Controlling others (into which parts of the self are projected) is central to projective identification. Thus, group members are driven to act out in some fashion as a reaction to their imagined demise. In the case of projective identification, group members externalize and project all bad and evil attributes onto the image of the outsider's group and its leadership. Eventually, the outsiders are depersonalized and dehumanized in the minds of the insiders. In some instances, the outsiders react with aggression and violence, which reinforces one group's image of the other and ties the volatile emotional knot between them—the essence of projective identification. Moreover, as is the case with ethnic tensions, a vicious cycle of conflict is then set in motion with seemingly little hope of finding a peaceful exit. These are the dynamics of large-group identity and what Volkan calls "the need to have enemies and allies"—a proclivity shared by all human beings.[10]

Dynamics of Large-Group Identity

Although some prefer to avoid calling these violent acts (such as projective identification) "mad" or psychotic, these are, in fact, psychotic processes acted out on the social and political stage of international human relations. Thus, exploring the underlying, primitive, motivating psychological dynamics of large-group identities can illuminate our understanding of group violence and terrorism. These large-group characteristics do, in fact, resemble psychotic thinking and acting out. For example, group members' devotion to totalistic ideologies and grand conspiracies are typical of paranoid-schizoid processes of splitting objects (the world of "others") into good and bad camps—viewing the world as black or white. Totalistic, absolutist, and fundamentalist belief systems require compartmentalization and the psychology of splitting. Group vulnerability and the impulse to act out is then triggered by anxieties further provoked by difficult life conditions that often reflect poverty and disenfranchisement, societal-cultural characteristics that foster and reinforce extremist and conspiratorial belief systems, and relatively recent political changes within the larger economic and social systems.

Beck argues for distinguishing between the paranoid perspective of militia groups in the United States and mental illness: "The militants confine their conspiratorial beliefs to a relatively circumscribed domain: their relation with the government and their group. They have normal relations with members of their families and friends, carry on normal business transactions, and appear rational when testifying in court."[11] Nevertheless, Beck submits that "although there are decided differences between people who are members of an extremist group and those who are psychologically disturbed, it is illuminating to examine the similarities in their beliefs and thinking. The comparison between militant group think and paranoid delusions is useful for the light it shines on the nature of the human mind and its tendency to create fantastic explanations for distressing circumstances"[11]—what Freud observed as the human proclivity toward "magical thinking"—a tendency more commonplace in human groups.

---

[9] M. Klein. Notes on Some Schizoid Mechanisms. *International Journal of Psychoanalysis* 27: 99–110, 1946.

[10] V. Volkan. *The Need to Have Enemies & Allies: From Clinical Practice to International Relationships*. New Jersey: Jason Aronson Inc., 1988.

[11] A. T. Beck. *Prisoners of Hate: The Cognitive Basis of Anger, Hostility, and Violence*. New York: HarperCollins Publishers, 1999.

Following this line of logic, Lifton describes the phenomena of "doubling" and "numbing" in his extensive study of the Nazi doctors and their culpability for mass killings and genocide.[12] Lifton reports that despite their horrific and murderous daily chores and the concomitant decision-making responsibilities, sentencing millions to death in gas chambers and many other millions to die in labor camps, he found that these same Nazi physicians were capable of carrying on relatively normal relationships with their families—seemingly evil by day and apparently loving by night—a mental feat he assumed was made possible by a combination of "doubling" and "numbing."[12]

Doubling encompasses processes of (what psychologists call) psychological "splitting." Splitting describes a process in which the self-in-mind cognitively and emotionally splits apart good and bad images of the other based upon one's memories and subjective experiences of the other. It is a form of internal compartmentalization and fragmentation of self and other. When internalized splits cannot be contained, the individual self projects, typically, bad images onto the other. This is what is meant by the psychological concept of projection. Fear, pain, and anguish often provoke these projections, leaving the self, if only momentarily, with the internalized good images. In large groups with common ideologies and emotional cohesion, these projections are commonplace under stressful and vulnerable circumstances. Numbing indicates a psychological distancing and desensitization of one's actions, despite their horrific nature. Hence, it is common for a perpetrator (such as a terrorist) to convey that he felt nothing or has no remorse for his actions. His or her commitment to the grand idea, the ideology, provides a cognitive focal point that takes the self beyond the present experience of destruction and violence.

Under certain circumstances, joining a group may require relinquishing one's true self for the group's required ideological cloak, resulting in the performance of a false self among large-group members, something akin to Lifton's "doubling." For example, in *The Roots of Evil*, Ervin Staub writes that the greater the demands a group makes on its members and the more it guides their lives, the more completely the members can relinquish their burdensome identity and assume a group identity.[13] However, submerging oneself in a group makes it difficult to maintain independent judgment of the group's conduct and more problematic to exert a contrary influence. A loss of individuality or individuation and a lack of inhibition of the usual moral constraint on individual action are likely consequences: Experiments show that aggressiveness is increased by conditions that weaken a sense of identity or increase anonymity, such as wearing masks. Stripping individuals of their distinct individuality and self-identity is correlated with increased aggression and violence. Group membership is acquired at the rather high cost of individual integrity and identity to self and a much greater price to society in the members' ability to commit acts of murder and destruction without guilt or remorse.

The notion of "deindividuation" here has significance in human development. Cognitive and emotional growth and maturity occur along a developmental path from infantile attachment (deindividuation) to childhood (early individuation) toward (eventual separation) relative adult autonomy. Hence, deindividuation signifies a psychologically regressive and backward process taking hold of the individual in his or her experience of group membership. Members of a group, when they regress in the face of stressful conditions, come close to experiencing their enemy as the original container of unintegrated bad parts (punishers) of their childhood selves. Adults, when regressed, reactivate a sense of experiencing the enemy as nonhuman.

Surrendering individuation and the capacity for critical judgment may promote group solidarity and identity while, at the same time, fostering a deeper underlying sense of powerlessness and dissociation. While the group identity offers the illusion of compensatory power for its members, it is an illusion that does not solve the problem of members' deeper feelings of

---

[12] R. J. Lifton. *The Nazi Doctors: Medical Killing and the Psychology of Genocide*. New York: Basic Books, 1986.

[13] E. Staub. *The Roots of Evil: The Origins of Genocide and Other Group Violence*. New York: Cambridge University Press, 1992.

helplessness. Ultimately, this form of suppression is unsuccessful because powerlessness persists in the group's unconsciousness. Inevitably, group violence is a likely outcome.

Weston's far-reaching study of Yugoslavia as it was breaking up provides a disturbing illustration of psychological splitting and regression within large (Serbian and Croatian) groups and their leaders' abilities to manipulate and provoke conflict between ethnic groups: "In Yugoslavia we found a strong tendency toward splitting. Images were split into good/bad and into we/them categories. Almost everyone idealized their own ethnic group and demonized others."[14] The black-and-white thinking was further encouraged by nationalistic leaders who actively played on group antipathy, using propaganda aimed at creating fear, rage, and insecurity about people's safety. Slobodan Milosevic was successful at stirring up the hostilities of Serbs in Kosovo and promoting ethnic cleansing in just this manner. By evoking the collective memory of the 1539 Battle of Kosovo and insisting to his fellow Serbs that they will never be forced to leave Kosovo, Milosevic solidified the large group against its neighboring enemy, the Ethnic Albanians in Kosovo.

Terrorism as a Group Activity: Large-Group Identity

Ethnic, religious, cultural, and nationalistic groups are characterized by homogeneous subcultures in which psychological and physical boundaries between and among individual members seem to disintegrate and vanish from consciousness. The terrorist group identity and its concomitant belief system transcend the individual identities of members themselves. The group and its leadership come to replace the ideals, fantasies, and ambitions of individual members. Thus, psychological processes of deindividuation abdicate power to the group and its leadership through emotional bonds that require intense loyalties and social cohesion.

In his article, "The Origins of Ethnic Strife," Firestone writes,

> Identification with a particular ethnic or religious group is at once a powerful defense against death anxiety and a system of thought and belief that can set the stage for hatred and bloodshed. Conformity to the belief system of the group, that is, to its collective symbols of immortality, protects one against the horror of feeling the objective loss of self. In merging his or her identity with that of a group, each person feels that although he or she may not survive as an individual entity, he or she will live on as part of something larger which will continue to exist after he or she is gone.[15]

Joining the group and identifying with its leadership and ideology is a defense against death anxiety—the ultimate experience of individual vulnerability that leads to a merger (deindividuation) with the leadership and its associated large-group identity. Firestone's application of the "defense against death anxiety" is synonymous with the notion of group vulnerability (discussed earlier) and the perceived threat of outsider groups. For example, Volkan warns

> When anxiety about identity occurs, members of a large group may consider killing a threatening neighbor rather than endure the anxiety caused by losing their psychological borders: In such a climate, chosen traumas and chosen glories, mourning difficulties, and feelings of entitlement to revenge, are reactivated.[16,17,18]

---

[14] M. C. Weston. When Words Lose Their Meaning: From Societal Crisis to Ethnic Cleansing. *Mind and Human Interaction* 8, no. 1: 20–32, 1997.

[15] R. W. Firestone. The Origins of Ethnic Strife. *Mind and Human Interaction* 7, no. 4: 167–191, 1996.

[16] V. Volkan. *Blood Lines: From Ethnic Pride to Ethnic Terrorism*. New York: Farrar, Straus and Giroux, 1997.

[17] V. Volkan. Psychoanalysis and Diplomacy: Part 1. Individual and Large Group Identity. *Journal of Applied Psychoanalysis* 1, no. 1: 29–55, 1999.

[18] V. Volkan. *Killing in the Name of Identity: A Study of Bloody Conflicts*. Charlottesville, VA: Pitchstone Publishing, 2006.

These psychological processes underlie ethnic, racial, and religious acts of terrorism. A group's core identity is derived from the "pride" of attachment between members or followers and their leader(s). Members merge with like-minded blood brothers, all of whom come to idealize their charismatic leader and his governing ideology. Yet, as is the case with individual pride, group pride is often a mask for group self-hatred and low self-concept.

Large Groups and Totalistic Belief Systems

These psychological processes of merger, deindividuation, and attachment then contribute to the leader's ideological influence over the actions of members. Individual morality and conscience are replaced by a group ideology and worldview. Members forfeit their individual liberties for affiliation and identification with an omnipotent, godlike leader or guru who gives them hope for a better world.

Typically, group members come to adopt a totalistic and conspiratorial belief system that embodies the struggles of a cosmic war of good against evil. Once the merging of individual and group leadership is complete, the psychology of splitting and paranoia—"us against them"—takes over. A persecutory group identity shapes and cements the members together through a common subjective experience and shared perception of evil and threatening outsiders. Primitive thinking and fanatic belief systems then promote group members' unwitting resignation to simplistic solutions to otherwise complex societal problems. Enemies and scapegoats are identified, solidifying the group and targeting the aim of its aggression.

As Staub notes,

> History shows that people will sacrifice themselves to promote ideologies. Followers of ideologies identify some people as a hindrance and commit horrifying acts in the name of creating a better world and fulfilling higher ideals. This scapegoating occurs partly because the new social or spiritual order is defined in contrast to an existing order and partly because the ideal way of life is difficult to bring about or the new social system does not fulfill its promise.[19]

Disappointment stirs resentment and anger: "Examples include the great blood bath after the French Revolution, the Inquisition and other religious persecutions, as well as genocides and mass killings."[20] Whether it refers to religious affiliation, nationality, or ethnicity, large-group identity is defined as the subjective experience of hundreds of thousands or even millions of people who are linked by a persistent sense of sameness while also sharing numerous characteristics with others in foreign groups.[20]

Our understanding of the concept of large-group identity begins with the work of Freud and, in particular, his view of group psychology and institutions. In Freud's *Group Psychology and the Analysis of the Ego*, he suggests that individual psychology and group psychology are not mutually exclusive.[21] In particular, he argues in this and in later works that our understanding of the intrapersonal world is derived from our knowledge of the psychodynamics of self and other from infancy through adolescence and adulthood—the internalization of interpersonal (self and other) experience over time. Thus, one can come to learn that the emergence of one's sense of self, and thereby one's sense of his or her core identity, evolves from the mental internalization of self and other relations in dyads, groups, and institutions. In other words, our internalized subjective experiences, particularly those early on in life and through adolescence, then help to shape our mental

[19] E. Staub. *The Roots of Evil: The Origins of Genocide and Other Group Violence*. New York: Cambridge University Press, 1992.

[20] V. Volkan. *Blood Lines: From Ethnic Pride to Ethnic Terrorism*. New York: Farrar, Straus and Giroux, 1997.

[21] S. Freud. *Group Psychology and the Analysis of the Ego*. New York: Norton & Company, 1921.

images of our self, others, and the world. Leadership and authority are key components in our developing identity as they are central to our understanding of the nature of individual attachments and affiliations with large groups (religious, ethnic, and other primary associations) and nation-states.

Furthermore, as Naimark writes in *Fires of Hatred: Ethnic Cleansing in Twentieth Century Europe*,

> Although the modern state and integral nationalism have been critical to ethnic cleansing in this century, political elites nevertheless bear the major responsibility for its manifestations. In competing for political power, they have exploited the appeal of nationalism to large groups of resentful citizens in the dominant ethnic population. Using the power of the state, the media, and their political parties, national leaders have manipulated distrust of the "other" and purposely revived and distorted ethnic tensions, sometimes long-buried, sometimes closer to the surface.[22]

Naimark stresses the assumption of personal responsibility ultimately coming to rest on the shoulders of political elites and leaders.[22] Yet leadership does not exist without followership. It is a dyadic relationship, a merger of like-mindedness and shared responsibility. Naimark, however, is correct in pointing out the manipulative and influential power of leaders in large groups, which is critical and ought to be viewed as an appropriate starting point if one is moved to understand more deeply the phenomenon of group violence and hold accountable those most responsible. Consider the earlier example of Milosevic and his provocation of the Serbs against ethnic Albanians.

In Freud's original essay, he explains the dynamics of group psychology via the individual's emotional attachment to the group. He argues that the individual surrenders his or her autonomy and independence to the group leadership by unconsciously replacing his or her own ego ideal with that of the leadership. In other words, group affiliation that may be characterized as hypnotic and suggestive takes place by a process in which the individual relinquishes to the leadership his or her own conscience, values, liberties, and integrity. In joining the group, the self is forced into a psychologically regressive flight from individuality and autonomy to a more infantile state of deindividuation, merger, and social cohesion, which explains why one observes primitive thinking, such as splitting and compartmentalization, as well as shared fantasies and delusions among vulnerable large groups.

The group image of collective utopia is then represented for the membership by their loyalty and admiration of the group leader. So, although Naimark[22] is correct in highlighting the responsibilities of political elites in fostering ethnic cleansing and other forms of violence, his analysis marginalizes the role of followers in endorsing and empowering their leaders. As previously noted in this chapter, it is a dyadic phenomenon and thereby ought to be examined and understood as such.

Concluding Thoughts

When large groups, whether ethnic, racial, religious, nationalistic, or cultural, feel vulnerable, that is, when they feel the potential loss of their attachment and emotional investment in the group's belief system and leadership, they fear the annihilation of the group-self or (what has been called) the large-group identity. Psychological regression is a common yet primitive defense mechanism used by groups under these stressful circumstances, whether the fear is legitimate or not, real or fantasized. Psychological regression and the associated cognitive and emotional splitting are typical responses to the experience of such profound anxiety (what Firestone calls death anxiety). Under these conditions of psychological regression, members

[22] N. M. Naimark. *Fires of Hatred: Ethnic Cleansing in Twentieth Century Europe*. Cambridge, MA: Harvard University Press, 2001.

assume a collective, psychological flight behind their leaders and toward more primitive and infantile feelings. Charismatic spiritual leaders and gurus reflecting and articulating expansive visions and absolute ideologies offer the illusion of a safe haven for the seemingly fearful, disenfranchised, and powerless members of society who are searching for simple, black-and-white solutions to complex social and political problems.

Group solidarity emerges from a foundation of ethnic, religious, cultural, and nationalistic similarity and like-mindedness. There is safety in the comfort of the large-group identity and its godlike leader. The combination of homogeneity and group cohesion fosters a loss of individuality and separateness (self and other boundaries) among members. This loss of independence and critical thinking then reinforces polarized, compartmentalized thinking, which produces psychological splitting and regression among group members. It is this black-and-white, absolutist thinking rooted in infantile anxieties that fosters dehumanization of and violence against the other. In the presence of social disorganization and economic and political problems, charismatic leaders can manipulate and provoke group violence by exploiting the "us and them" mentality of the large (ethnic, religious, cultural, or nationalistic) group. By identifying the enemy and then leading the group in attack against a popular scapegoat, terrorist leaders diminish followers' anxieties while proffering them a target for their long-held resentment and hostility.

The extent to which political, religious, and ideological factors contribute to the appeal of engaging in terrorism depends in part on the leadership of the organization. It also depends on the ideologies and motivations of the individuals and/or group members that employ terrorism. What's more, to the extent that leadership, group members, and individuals are motivated to engage in terrorism, the appeal of terrorism is likely to be enhanced.

3

International and Domestic Terrorism[1]

Terrorist incidents have been going on in the United States for many years. However, the incidence and severity increased during the 1990s. For 17 years, the Unabomber baffled law enforcement officials and spread terror throughout the United States. Some of the bombs were sent through the mail in packages, and others were planted at target facilities. Eight of the bombings occurred on the west coast, five in the Chicago area, two each on the east coast and Salt Lake City areas, and one in Nashville, Tennessee. Primary bombing targets were universities, corporate and government facilities, and their personnel. Devices constructed by the Unabomber were carefully crafted pipe bombs.

The threat of terrorism impacts all communities large and small, both in the United States and throughout the rest of the world. Events of the past have shown that no place is immune from the potential of a terrorist attack. Incidents have occurred in cities of all sizes, as well as in rural America. The FBI classifies terrorism as international or domestic based essentially on geography and not the ultimate goal of the behavior. Each will be explored individually below.

International Terrorism

International terrorism involves individuals and groups that cross one or more borders to conduct operations. For example, Pakistani-backed Islamic terrorists cross the border between Pakistan and India's Kashmir. Basically, individuals and groups labeled as international terrorists operate in multiple countries around the world.

International terrorism has also been defined by US government agencies but only as it applies to the United States. Particularly, the FBI defines international terrorism as

> violent acts or acts dangerous to human life that are a violation of the criminal laws of the United States or any state, or that would be a criminal violation if committed within the jurisdiction of the United States or any state. These acts appear to be intended to intimidate or coerce a civilian

[1] Information for this chapter was drawn from the following titles: (1) J. Pastor, *Terrorism and Public Safety Policing: Implications for the Obama Presidency*. CRC Press, 2009. (2) R. Burke, *Counter-Terrorism for Emergency Responders*, Second Edition, CRC Press, 2006. (3) M. W. Nance, *Terrorist Recognition Handbook: A Practitioner's Manual for Predicting and Identifying Terrorist Activities*, Second Edition, CRC Press, 2008. (4) D. P. Schulz, *The Counterterrorism Handbook: Tactics, Procedures, and Techniques*, Fourth Edition, CRC Press, 2011. (5) K. J. Dudonis, F. Bolz, and D. P. Schulz, *The Counterterrorism Handbook: Tactics, Procedures, and Techniques*, Third Edition, CRC Press, 2005. (6) D. Perlmutter, *Investigating Religious Terrorism and Ritualistic Crimes*, CRC Press, 2003. (7) P. P. Purpura, *Security: An Introduction*, CRC Press, 2010.

population, influence the policy of a government by intimidation or coercion, or affect the conduct of a government by assassination or kidnapping.[2]

In essence, international terrorist acts occur outside the United States or transcend national boundaries in terms of the means by which they are accomplished, the persons they appear intended to coerce or intimidate, or the locale in which their perpetrators operate or seek asylum.[3] International terrorism is the most recognized and most publicized form of terrorism. This publicity is partially due to exposure. However, it may also be partly due to the foreign nature of an international terrorist that promotes more fear and lack of comprehension on the part of the target population. Because the customs and mores of the foreign nationals can be unfamiliar to the indigenous population, the lack of comprehension of these behavior patterns makes the international terrorist more viscerally frightening.

The basic propellant for international terrorism may not be understood using our present sphere of knowledge, experience, and comprehension. Each justification is tempered by culture, which puts goals and desires into a specific context that may be foreign to us. The goals and expectations can be influenced, or even created, by religious beliefs and must exist within or compete against the political framework of the religion.

On February 26, 1993, at 12:18 p.m., international terrorism struck the United States. The World Trade Center in New York City was bombed by Islamic fundamentalists. The World Trade Center boasts two high-rise towers. Each tower is 110 stories tall with several other buildings completing the complex. When fully occupied, there are more than 150,000 people in the buildings. Noontime is the busiest period of day at the complex and would be the ideal time to launch a terrorist attack to produce a large number of deaths and injuries. At the time, it was considered the worst terrorist attack conducted on American soil. The apparent motive was to weaken US support of Israel. This bombing was intended to send a message to all Americans that terrorism could happen at anytime and anywhere in the United States.

Components of the World Trade Center bomb included ammonium nitrate and fuel oil, which forms a blasting agent. Explosive effects from the 1200-pound bomb caused a crater 180 feet deep, 100 feet long, and 200 feet wide in the underground parking garage. The crater was six levels deep. A rented truck was used to transport the bomb into the parking garage. It was rumored that the truck also contained a sodium cyanide device that malfunctioned, which would have released a cloud of deadly cyanide into the building. This rumor had no foundation, and there was no cyanide involved in the explosion. As bad as the outcome was, it was far short of the terrorist goal of reducing the twin towers to a pile of rubble containing the mass grave of thousands. However, at no time was there any danger that the towers would collapse.

Following the bombing at the World Trade Center, the Clinton administration called upon Congress to strengthen US counter-terrorism policies. On February 7, 1995, Ramzi Yousef, the suspected mastermind of the World Trade Center bombing, was arrested in Pakistan. During the trial of the bombing suspects, testimony revealed that 12 locations in the United States had been targeted for sarin nerve agent attacks. The bombing of the World Trade Center was thought to be a part of a larger terror campaign being carried out by several groups of Islamic fundamentalists from several countries. The same group(s) had also been planning to bomb the UN Building, the FBI's New York office, the New York State Legislators' Building, and the Lincoln Tunnel.

Since the World Trade Center bombing, several additional plots have been discovered and stopped. In August 1997, a letter was found written by two men who were plotting to bomb a Brooklyn subway station. The letter was found in a Brooklyn apartment, demanding that six

---

[2] Federal Bureau of Investigation, 2006. Terrorism 2002–2005. p. v. Available at http://www.fbi.gov/stats-services/publications/terrorism-2002-2005/terror02_05.pdf.

[3] 18 USC § 2331: Definitions. Section 802 PATRIOT Act. Available at http://frwebgate.access.gpo.gov/cgi-bin/getdoc.cgi?dbname=107_cong_public_laws&docid=f:publ056.107.pdf, accessed April 26, 2011. Also see Findlaw. http://codes.lp.findlaw.com/uscode/18/I/113B/2331.

jailed Islamic or Arab militants be released. They included Ramzi Yousef, on trial for the World Trade Center bombing, and Omar Abdel Rahman, jailed for plotting to bomb New York City landmarks. The letter threatened the bombing of a Brooklyn subway station and subsequent attacks at other locations. On October 15, 1995, a bomb damaged an unmanned weather station used by air traffic controllers at LaGuardia Airport. Damage was sustained by a wind shear alert system, designed to notify air traffic controllers about dangerous, abrupt changes in wind speed and direction that can affect planes during takeoffs and landings. Following this, the attacks on 9/11 occurred. The al-Qaeda organization struck the United States with a horrific and well-coordinated terrorist attack. Four commercial passenger airliners were simultaneously hijacked by specially trained teams with the specific purpose of crashing them into targets in New York City and Washington, DC. Three of the four airline hijackings were successful: Two planes were crashed into the WTC's Twin Towers in New York City, and a third was crashed into the Pentagon in Arlington, Virginia, a suburb of Washington, DC. The fourth crashed into an open field in Pennsylvania after passengers disrupted the terrorist activity and thwarted the hijackers' plans. Although 125 people were killed at the Pentagon in the attack, it has almost become a footnote in the events of 9/11, with the media coverage stressing the attack on the WTC complex in New York City that claimed nearly 3000 lives.

There are several subcategories of international terrorism. These subcategories are examined in the next section.

Subcategories of International Terrorism

According to the FBI typology, international terrorism has three subcategories based on the structural organizations of the various groups. The categories are loosely affiliated extremists, formal terrorist organizations, and state sponsors of terrorism. The first category of international terrorism, loosely affiliated extremists, are designated as Sunni Islamic extremists, including Osama bin Laden and individuals affiliated with his al-Qaeda organization, and individuals of varying nationalities, ethnic groups, tribes, races, and terrorist groups who support extremist Sunni goals. The common elements among the diverse individuals is that they are motivated by political or religious beliefs and committed to the radical international jihad movement whose ideology includes promoting violence against the "enemies of Islam" in order to overthrow all governments not ruled by conservative Islamic law. These individuals also seek the removal of the US military from the Persian Gulf.

In the Middle East, the rise of Islamic fundamentalism in the modern era can be traced to the Muslim Brotherhood, founded in 1928 by Hassen al-Banna, a schoolteacher who preached for Sharia law. A militant wing known as the secret apparateur was formed, and in 1948, some of the Brotherhood members assassinated Egypt's prime minister. A short time later, alleged government agents killed Hassen al-Banna. In the early 1950s, the Brotherhood was accused in some 750 cases of arson, mostly in Cairo. The targets were mainly nightclubs, theaters, hotels, and restaurants frequented by the British and other Westerners, including tourists, in an effort to end the secular lifestyle. In 1954, after an attempt on the life of Gamal Nassar, a crackdown on the Brotherhood was carried out. After Nassar's ousting, Anwar Sadat became president and eased the restrictions on the Brotherhood, but he also fell from favor when he signed a peace accord with Israel. He was assassinated on October 6, 1981, by members of the violent Tanzim al-Jihad. The Brotherhood has spawned or inspired a number of ideological terrorist groups, such as al-Qaeda, Hamas, and Jamaat-al-Islamiyya, to mention a few. In addition, the second in command to Osama bin Laden, Ayman al-Zawahiri, was a former member of the Egyptian Brotherhood. During the 1960s, 1970s, and 1980s, radical Islamic terror groups increased in number and strength throughout the Middle East and also spread into Europe.

Consider one group that falls under this category; namely, al-Qaeda (the Base). Al-Qaeda reportedly has operations in Afghanistan, Algeria, Egypt, Morocco, Turkey, Jordan, Tajikistan, Uzbekistan, Syria, Xinjiang in China, Pakistan, Bangladesh, Malaysia, Myanmar, Indonesia,

Mindanao in the Philippines, Lebanon, Iraq, Saudi Arabia, Kuwait, Bahrain, Yemen, Libya, Tunisia, Bosnia, Kosovo, Chechnya, Dagestan, Kashmir, Sudan, Somalia, Kenya, Tanzania, Azerbaijan, Eritrea, Uganda, Ethiopia, and the West Bank and Gaza in the Palestinian areas of Israel. The goal of al-Qaeda is to establish a worldwide Islamic regime by routing out non-Islamic governments and expelling Westerners and non-Muslims from Muslim countries. This terrorist group formed in the 1980s when rebels in Afghanistan drew international support and funding from countries including the United States that did not support the USSR's occupation of Afghanistan. An operational strength of this group is that it is believed to have hundreds to thousands of members; extremist groups, such as the Egyptian Islamic Jihad and parts of al-Gama'at al-Islamiyya, the Islamic Movement of Uzbekistan, and the Harakat ul-Mujahidin, also fall under its umbrella.

Foreshadowing the American tragedy on September 11, a congressional statement dated May 10, 2001, noted that loosely affiliated extremists were considered the most urgent threat to the United States because their goals consist of carrying out large-scale, high-profile, high-casualty, terrorist attacks against US interests and citizens. It is not surprising that subsequent investigations led to changing the designation of loosely affiliated extremists to the Radical International Jihad Movement—signifying that they are no longer loosely affiliated but are exceptionally well organized. In 1998, Osama bin Laden announced the formation of the International Front for Fighting Jews and Crusades, an alliance bent on killing Americans and destroying US interests around the world. Member groups include al-Qaeda, the Egyptian Islamic Jihad, the Pakistani Society of Ulemas, the Ansar Movement, the Bangladesh Jihad, and the Islamic Army for the Liberation of the Holy Sites.

The US Department of State has reported, on numerous occasions, that al-Qaeda and its associated networks remain the greatest threat to the United States and its allies. Al-Qaeda has regrouped in Pakistan, near the border with Afghanistan. The group is adaptive to counterterrorism, creative, and seeks weapons of mass destruction. Al-Qaeda continues to target Western Europe and the United States through affiliates in the Middle East, Africa, and Europe. The Taliban, who were forced out of Afghanistan by the United States following the 9/11 attacks, today remains a threat inside Afghanistan and Pakistan. They try to maintain safe havens inside Pakistan; some link themselves to al-Qaeda, and both groups are involved in terrorism and clashes with government forces in both Afghanistan and Pakistan. The United States, the North Atlantic Treaty Organization (NATO), and other allied forces have a presence in Afghanistan.

The second category of international terrorism is formal terrorist organizations designated as extremist groups. Examples are the Palestinian Hamas and the Lebanese Hezbollah. They are characterized as autonomous, generally transnational organizations that have their own infrastructures, personnel, financial arrangements and training facilities. They have a presence in the United States with members who are engaged in fund-raising, recruiting, and intelligence gathering. They also maintain operations and support networks in the United States.

Two formal terrorist organizations are explored further: Hamas and Hezbollah. The Islamic Resistance Movement (or Hamas) was formed in 1987 and reportedly has operations in Syria, Palestinian Occupied Territories, Israel, and Lebanon. A relatively moderate faction of Hamas seeks to create a Palestinian Islamic state and accepts some kind of agreement with Israel; the goal of a second faction is to create a Palestinian Islamic state and destroy Israel. The military goal of Hamas is to terrorize Israelis through the use of random violence. Hamas operates small rebel cells that are anonymous to one another; suicide bombings are not always controlled by the top leadership of Hamas.

Hezbollah (Party of God) formed in 1983, reportedly has operations in the Middle East, Europe, Latin America, and the United States. The goal of the group is to create a revolutionary Shi'a Islamic state similar to Iran in Lebanon and eradicate non-Islamic influences and interests. Hezbollah has a military faction known as the Islamic Resistance—a small, highly effective guerrilla organization trained and directed by Iranian revolutionary guards. This unit attacks in small, highly mobile units and shrouds its operatives in secrecy, even from Hezbollah leaders. Prior to the September 11 events, Hezbollah were responsible for the deaths of more Americans than any other terrorist group.

The third category of international terrorism is state sponsors of terrorism, which consists of countries that view terrorism as a tool of foreign policy. As of May 30, 2013, the US Department of State list four countries as state sponsors of terrorism: Cuba, Iran, Sudan, and Syria. Iran represented the greatest threat to the United States because it financially and logistically supports anti-Western acts of terrorism by others. In fact, the US Department of State sees Iran as the most significant state sponsor of terrorism with Hezbollah as a key player in Iranian plans. Syria is also a supporter of Hezbollah.

Domestic Terrorism

Domestic terrorism has been defined by US government agencies but only as it applies to the United States. Specifically, according to the FBI,

> Domestic terrorism is the unlawful use, or threatened use, of force or violence by a group or individual based and operating entirely within the United States or Puerto Rico without foreign direction committed against persons or property to intimidate or coerce a government, the civilian population, or any segment thereof in furtherance of political or social objectives.[4]

Nevertheless, traditionally, domestic terrorists are viewed as individuals and groups that operate within a nation's borders. Frequently, these domestic terrorists are members of fringe groups promoting a cause. The dedication to this cause is fierce, and the feeling is that, again, the end justifies the means. Any atrocity, in their minds, pales in comparison to the consequences and injustices of the institution they are fighting. This level of dedication is almost mandated for the terrorists to be able to target their own country and people. There are several subcategories of domestic terrorism, which will be explored in the next section.

Subcategories of Domestic Terrorism

Classifications of terrorism are subject to overlap. A group's characteristics may span multiple categories, and a group may be difficult to place in any one category. In addition, terrorist groups constantly split and form new groups; older groups may become inactive permanently or "sleep" before becoming active again, and the viewpoints of terrorists change. Domestic terrorism has several subcategories based on the ideologies of various groups. For example, nationalist-separatist terrorism involves the use of violence by a religious or ethnic minority that is or believes it is persecuted by the majority.[5] One of the more well-known terrorist groups in this category is the Euskadi ta Askatasuna (ETA), a Basque separatist group that operates throughout Spain and is still active today. Special attention will be paid to left-wing, anarchist, right-wing, and special-interest terrorist groups.

Left-Wing Terrorists

The first category of domestic terrorism is left wing, and it includes terrorists who generally profess a revolutionary socialist doctrine and view themselves as protectors of the people against the dehumanizing effects of capitalism and imperialism. Their method of bringing about change

---

[4] Federal Bureau of Investigation, 2006. Terrorism 2002–2005. p. v. Available at http://www.fbi.gov/stats-services/publications/terrorism-2002-2005/terror02_05.pdf.

[5] M.-H. Maras. *Counterterrorism*. Massachusetts: Jones and Bartlett, 2013, 12.

is through revolution rather than the political process. Left-wing groups were especially popular during the 1960s and 1970s. These groups often adhered to Marxism (i.e., the political ideology of Karl Marx that is the foundation of communism). These groups, the most notable of which included the Baader-Mienhof Gang (later the Red Army Faction) in Germany and the Red Brigades in Italy, which kidnapped and later killed Aldo Moro, a former prime minister of Italy, would operate well into the 1980s.

Left-wing terrorist groups operating in the United States were against the Vietnam War and were proponents of civil rights. Although not all left-wing groups espouse violence or terrorism, during this era, those groups that became involved in violence were the Students for a Democratic Society (SDS), the Weather Underground Organization, the May 19 Communist Organization, and the Black Panthers.

The Weathermen, another offshoot of SDS formed in 1969, took its name from a Bob Dylan song. The group declared its intention to overthrow the US government. As women began to take more prominent roles in its activities, it changed its name to the less sexist Weather Underground Organization. Between 1969 and the mid-1970s, members engaged in public demonstrations causing violence and riots and were especially active during the Democratic presidential nominating convention in Chicago in 1968. They continued to place bombs at various locations, often targeting banks. Although they prided themselves on sending warnings about the devices, many resulted in casualties. Among the group's major bombings were those at a police memorial in Chicago, a federal judge's home, New York City's police headquarters in Lower Manhattan, and the Pentagon building near Washington, DC, which involved Bill Ayers. While members of the Weather Underground were preparing IEDs in a townhouse in New York City's Greenwich Village neighborhood in March 1970, the building exploded and was leveled. Group members had been preparing nail bombs for placement at the Fort Dix Army base in New Jersey.

The Armed Forces of National Liberation also known as Fuerzas Armadas de Liberacion Nacional Puertorriqueña (FALN) and Los Macheteros sought independence for Puerto Rico from the United States. FALN carried out bombings on the US mainland, primarily in and around New York. Los Macheteros is suspected of three bombings in Puerto Rico. Overall, shootouts with police and bombings characterized the violence conducted by left-wing terrorists.

In December 1974, one of their first devices, placed in a tenement in New York's Harlem neighborhood, injured a police officer who was responding to investigate a possible dead person. Their next bombing, in January 1975, was at the historic Fraunces Tavern restaurant in Lower Manhattan, where President George Washington had bid farewell to his troops after the Revolutionary War. The restaurant was a popular Wall Street lunchtime destination, and the explosion killed four people and injured more than 50 others. Later that same year, in April, members of FALN planted and exploded four IEDs at four locations in Midtown Manhattan, injuring about a half-dozen persons. In August 1977, they placed devices in additional Midtown locations, this time causing one death and several more injuries. They invariably left communiqués in telephone booths. One of their key bomb makers, William Morales, was arrested in his Elmhurst, New York, home after accidentally exploding a device he was working on. As firemen and police responded, he stuffed papers and files down the toilet even after having nine fingers severed. With only one finger, he would later escape from the hospital prison ward and make his way to Mexico. Who helped him was never completely ascertained. He claimed he did it alone.

On New Year's Eve 1982, two members of the NYPD Bomb Squad were severely injured and maimed while trying to render safe a FALN device that exploded prematurely. This group would be responsible for almost 110 bombings in New York and more in Chicago, Philadelphia, and San Francisco over a period of almost 10 years. A number of individuals were arrested for various bombings, attempted bombings, bank robberies, and other felonies. The FALN was one of the first terrorist organizations to use the double-bang tactic. This involved placing a second bomb in close proximity to the first, so that when responding officers and investigators arrived, while they were shaking hands and greeting each other, the second device would go off. After this, future first responders built defenses against this tactic into their response procedures. In

1999, to the astonishment of the entire law enforcement community as well as a large part of the general population and an overwhelming majority of the US Congress, President Bill Clinton pardoned 16 members of FALN. His justification was that none of those pardoned had been convicted of actually harming anyone. They had been convicted of conspiracy to commit robbery, bomb making, and sedition. Though perhaps they were not the persons actually placing the bombs, they helped accomplish the deed. The government wanted those pardoned to denounce any further violence; not all did.

Anarchists

The anarchists, a term more popular in the 1800s and 1900s, opposed both Marxism and capitalism and favored revolution, but they had no plan for a replacement of the government. In fact, purist and idealistic anarchists do not believe that there should be any government. They feel that each person should function free of restraint. However, most people who claim to be anarchists are more opposed to big government and the capitalist system than they are to the basic concept of government itself. To accomplish this goal, some believe that the working class must unite to bring down capitalism. After this occurs, the workers will control the means of production. Workers will establish rules that will enable them to live in harmony with one another. Anarchist philosophy had a significant impact on terrorist campaigns and groups. An early anarchist, Karl Heinzen, published a book titled *Der Mord* (translated from German as "Murder"), which justified terrorism on a grand scale.

Anarchists were blamed for numerous notorious actions, including the assassination of President William McKinley in 1901; killing eight police officers in a bombing, which resulted in the Haymarket Riots in Chicago on May 4, 1886; and for the September 16, 1920, bombing on Wall Street in New York City. This attack killed 33 people, wounded 400 others, and caused approximately $2 million in damages.[6] Contemporary anarchists are similarly interested in bringing down the capitalist system and government in general. During the 1990s, some anarchists engaged in violent protest demonstrations, usually staged by labor unions and other causes.

Right-Wing Terrorists

Right-wing terrorists stress nationalism above individual rights. Some of these terrorists seek a strong central government, and others are strongly antigovernment. Foreigners and minorities are targets of right-wing terrorists. For example, neo-Nazi groups seek to establish a strong central government that would control the means of production, either directly or through corporate monopolies controlled by selected individuals. In this worldview, the country would be very nationalistic and militarily strong. Patriotism would be stressed. The white race, Aryan nationality, and a quasi-Christian creed would occupy a favored position. Other groups would face discrimination and would have their rights restricted. While these tenets illustrate typical neo-Nazi thinking, there are other political philosophies (i.e., Sovereign Citizens, Freemen, Posse Comitatus) that are different from the neo-Nazi cause yet are still characterized as right-wing philosophies. For this reason, it is difficult to categorize or classify right-wing extremist groups. No matter how they are categorized, there will be an overlap. There are many commonalities. The vast majority of these groups are antigovernment in philosophy. Almost all espouse an element of hate toward some other group of people.

---

[6] State and Local Anti-terrorist Training (SLATT) Manual, Domestic Terrorist Groups, pp. 4–5. Available at http://info.publicintelligence.net/SLATT-TerrorismTraining/domesticterrorism.pdf.

The Ku Klux Klan (KKK), neo-Nazi Aryan Nation, and skinheads are examples of racial supremacist groups. The KKK engaged in acts of terrorism against African Americans that included the use of incendiary devices, arson, bombings, and murder. These types of terrorists are characterized by their adherence to the principles of racial supremacy and their embrace of anti-government and anti-regulatory beliefs. Formal right-wing hate groups that represent continuing domestic terrorist threats in the United States on a national level include the World Church of the Creator (WCOTC) and the Aryan Nations. Racism-based hatred remains an integral component of these groups' core orientations.

The most infamous attack by a right-wing terrorist on US soil was the 1995 Oklahoma City bombing. The Oklahoma City bombing occurred on April 19, 1995, when Timothy McVeigh drove a rented Ryder truck containing 5000 pounds of ammonium nitrate fertilizer, nitromethane, and a diesel fuel mixture to the front of the nine-story Alfred P. Murrah Federal Building. He parked near the building's day-care center after lighting multiple fuses, locked the vehicle, and walked to his getaway vehicle. The bombing killed 168 people and injured 853. Nineteen children were killed, including 15 from the day-care center. The blast destroyed about one-third of the building and damaged more than 200 nearby buildings. This was the deadliest terrorist attack in the United States prior to the 9/11 attacks.

Less than two hours after the explosion, McVeigh was stopped by an Oklahoma state trooper for driving a vehicle without a license plate and was then arrested for having a concealed weapon. Later in the day, he was linked to the bombing via the vehicle identification on an axle from the destroyed Ryder truck he had rented. In 1997, McVeigh was found guilty of murder and conspiracy and sentenced to death. He was executed by lethal injection on June 11, 2001, at the US penitentiary in Terre Haute, Indiana. Terry Nichols, a co-conspirator, was tried, found guilty, and sentenced to life without parole.

Investigators revealed that McVeigh and Nichols were members of a right-wing militia movement and bombed the federal building in retaliation for the Ruby Ridge and Waco events. In the Ruby Ridge incident in 1992, Randy Weaver, a white supremacist, was under siege at his Idaho home for trying to sell illegal firearms. During the siege, a US Marshal, Weaver's pregnant wife, and Weaver's son were killed. Weaver finally surrendered amid much publicity over the incident, which became a symbol of right-wing struggles. In the Waco incident in 1993, the Bureau of Alcohol, Tobacco, and Firearms (ATF) made tragic mistakes in trying to arrest David Koresh, a religious leader, at his compound in Waco, Texas, for illegal firearms. The first assault on the compound resulted in four ATF agents being killed, 20 injured, and an unknown number of Branch Davidian casualties in the compound. The FBI then took control of the operation, cutting off electricity and water to the compound, and shining bright lights and playing loud music at night. Some members of the religious sect came out and surrendered while others continued to wait for a message from God. After a standoff of 51 days, tear gas was fired into the compound. This was followed by the sound of explosions and the sight of intense smoke as the buildings became engulfed in flame. Seventy-five people (mostly women and children) died, and nine survived. A subsequent investigation indicated that the inhabitants of the compound set the fires.[7]

Many right-wing extremist groups have created their own religions. Most US domestic terrorist religions are more commonly known as white supremacist religions. Although they appear to have a number of significant differences, they can all be classified as Nativist Millennial Movements. Nativist Millennial Movements consist of individuals who feel oppressed by foreign colonizing governments, believing that the government removes natives from their land and eradicates their traditional way of life and their religion and takes away their means of survival. They long to return to their past, which they view as an idealized golden age, and believe that divine intervention will eliminate their oppressors. The movement is a response to colonization either by an outside culture or a ruling bureaucratic class. The colonized people

[7] C. Combs. *Terrorism in the Twenty-First Century*, Third Edition. Upper Saddle River, NJ: Prentice Hall, 2003, 178–179.

are economically oppressed, pressured by government law enforcement agents and tax collectors, and are systematically removed from their land. Historically, these movements typically referred to third-world people who were reacting to colonization by Europeans who threatened their way of life with technology and developed economies. The contemporary Euro-American nativist movement in the United States is a movement of white Americans who possess education and advanced technology but believe the Aryan white race is being subjected to genocide and systematically deprived of their land by an illegitimate government controlled by foreign and Satanic beings. The contemporary Euro-American nativist movement in the United States includes the Freemen, Identity Christians (believers in Christian Identity), neo-Nazis, Odinists, the KKK, and many other white supremacists.

Special-Interest Terrorists

The third category of domestic terrorism consists of special-interest extremists. They differ from right-wing and left-wing terrorists in that they seek to resolve specific issues rather than overthrowing the entire political system. They conduct acts of politically motivated violence to bring public attention to their specific causes. These groups occupy the extreme fringes of animal rights, pro-life, environmental, anti-nuclear, and other political and social movements. The groups most noted for acts of vandalism and terrorist activities are the Animal Liberation Front (ALF) and the Earth Liberation Front (ELF). They have caused millions of dollars in damages to businesses they consider hostile to the environment or to animal rights. Many pro-life extremists identify with right-wing extremists' religious ideologies.

Animal Rights

The ALF is concerned with animal rights, not eating animals, vegetarianism, and stopping research involving animals. The 1990s brought a wave of terrorist attacks to many parts of the world—and home to the United States. Many people in this country love animals, so the animal rights movement should not be a shock to anyone. However, there is also a dangerous side of the campaign for animal rights. In September 1992, ALF supporters set fire to a research facility at Michigan State University. A researcher's office was set ablaze, and a laboratory where mink were kept was vandalized. Damage to the offices and lab was estimated at $50,000 to $100,000. An additional $20,000 to $25,000 worth of damage occurred to the research facility. Years of data were lost. Attacks were also carried out against Utah State University on October 24, 1992, where an arson fire caused $110,000 in damage; at the University of Edmonton, Canada, 29 cats were stolen on June 1, 1992, with more than $50,000 in damage caused to the facility; the mink research center was attacked at Washington State University August 13, 1991, when 18 animals were set free and the facility was extensively damaged. Other similar incidents occurred at the University of Buffalo, University of Pennsylvania, Texas Tech University, University of Arizona, University of California/Davis, and Oregon State University. The FBI classifies these attacks as acts of terrorism.

Information taken from the Animal Rights Resource website provides some background material concerning the Animal Rights Movement: "The ALF carries out direct action against animal abuse in the form of rescuing animals and causing financial loss to animal exploiters, usually through the damage and destruction of property." Actions of the ALF are against the law: "Activists work anonymously, in small groups or individually, and do not have any centralized organization or coordination." The FBI has listed the ALF as a domestic terrorist group. Justice Department documents indicate more than 300 incidents of break-ins, vandalism, arson, and theft involving medical research facilities and university labs by animal extremists in the United States. Any facility that conducts animal research or business in animal furs or other animal body parts may become a target of this domestic terrorist group.

The ALF has claimed responsibility for a number of post-9/11 protests that failed to garner national headlines at a time when international terrorism was uppermost in the minds of law enforcement executives, the press, and the public. Included in these are a firebombing at a federal corral for wild horses near Susanville, California, that caused about $80,000 in damage; a fire at a primate research center in New Mexico; and two break-ins in Iowa, one at a fur farm that resulted in the release of more than 1000 minks and another that freed pigeons that were being raised for use in research. These were not the first break-ins or animal releases in Iowa although the earlier events had been attributed to ALF until a Canadian-based faction of the group claimed credit for the 2001 actions.

Ecoterrorists

Ecoterrorists seek to preserve nature from human destruction. The FBI considers ecoterrorists as the number one domestic threat because they continue their attacks in the United States. The ELF focuses on stopping environmental damage caused by humans. The ELF describes itself as an environmental group "that realizes the true cause of murder and destruction of life," and that it must work against "the capitalist state and its symbols of propaganda" through economic sabotage. In recruiting members, the group notes that if someone believes in the ELF ideology, follows its guidelines, and "conducts actions," he or she will become part of ELF. The guidelines are as follows:

- To cause as much economic damage as possible to a given entity that is profiting off the destruction of the natural environment and life for selfish greed and profit
- To educate the public on the atrocities committed against the environment and life
- To take all necessary precautions against harming life

Ecoterrorists, animal rights terrorists, and similar groups traditionally favor property destruction tactics, such as bomb attacks, arson, vandalism, and criminal trespass, to terrorize their intended victims. Among the groups claiming credit or suspected of being involved in terrorist acts, in addition to the ELF, are the Cropatistas, the Strawberry Liberation Front, the Anarchist Golfing Association, and Reclaim the Seeds. Although the names may sound amusing, the groups' activities are not and are termed "serious violations of federal law" by FBI agents assigned to the cases.

Antiabortionist Terrorists

Antiabortionists are generally Christian oriented with a small percentage advocating violence against abortion facilities and medical personnel. These groups generally point to five different approaches for their complaints: scriptural, legal, moral, philosophical, and medical. Antiabortion terrorists frequently are involved in fire-bombings of abortion clinics around the country. Although they are often sole issue activists, some have also been associated with violence against bars that cater to homosexual clients and churches that welcome homosexuals into worship services or that do not take what is perceived to be a strong enough stand against abortion. Not only do they differ in their political orientation from the ecoterrorism, animal rights, and antiglobalist groups, but they also differ in their organizational structure. They are usually parts of small, very close-knit groups, and cracking these cases often depends on informants although the FBI's Joint Terrorism Task Force has been heavily involved in investigating clinic bombing cases for many years.

Despite their different political and organizational orientation, the antiabortionists have also made considerable use of the Internet to publicize their cause and, in some cases, to recruit supporters and raise money. They have used a variety of websites to publicize the names of doctors who perform abortions, particularly since 2001 when the US Court of Appeals for the Ninth Circuit, one of the most liberal in the nation, overturned a $109 million verdict against a group of antiabortionists, ruling that the website maintained by the group that featured wanted posters of doctors who performed abortions was protected by the First Amendment. The appeal overturned a Portland, Oregon, jury verdict that had ordered the group to pay damages to Planned Parenthood and four doctors who had used the federal racketeering (RICO) law to claim that the site incited violence. The court ruled, in a decision that had obvious implications for cases involving web advocacy, that if the group did not threaten to commit violent acts, but "merely encouraged unrelated terrorists," its words were protected by the First Amendment.

During the 1996 Olympics, Atlanta, Georgia, became the next site of domestic terrorism in the United States on July 27, 1996, at 1:25 a.m. In spite of heavy security and enormous preparations for the possibility of a terrorist attack, a pipe bomb exploded in Olympic Park, killing two and injuring 111 people, including 10 emergency responders. It was the worst attack at the Olympics since the Munich games in 1972 when 11 Israeli athletes were killed by Palestinian guerrillas. Atlanta police were warned of the device from a pay phone near the scene of the blast at 12:58:34 a.m. The caller, believed to be a "white male with an indistinguishable accent" and American, stated that "a bomb was in Centennial Park, you have 30 minutes" (the bomb actually exploded 10 minutes earlier than the time given by the caller). A partial evacuation of the park occurred but only because police already on duty in the park happened upon the unattended knapsack that held the bomb. The device was an unsophisticated pipe bomb placed in a satchel near the concert stage in Olympic Park. Nails and screws were loaded into the bomb to create shrapnel to harm people. Police indicated they saw three pipes but did not know if they were three separate bombs or were all hooked together. Experts do not think international terrorists were involved because of the primitive type of explosive device used in the attack. Prior to the games, three members of a Georgia militia group were arrested in April 1996 for plotting to attack the Olympics. They allegedly belong to a militia group calling itself the 112th Regiment, Militia-at-Large for the Republic of Georgia. The members arrested were charged with conspiracy to make pipe bombs; they were planning to stockpile explosives, ammunition, weapons, and other military equipment for a terror campaign.

On January 12, 1997, in the Atlanta, Georgia suburb of Sandy Springs, two bombs went off at the Northside Family Planning Services. The first bomb did not cause any injuries. However, the second bomb apparently was planted and timed to kill or injure emergency responders. Thirteen emergency responders, including three federal agents, were injured, although not seriously, by the second blast. A little over a month later, another pair of bombs went off at an Atlanta nightclub called the Otherside Lounge that caters to gay clientele. Five people were injured, one seriously by the first blast. Police found a third bomb outside by the curb that was again set for emergency responders. The bomb exploded while a robot tried to disarm it. However, precautions were taken and no one was injured by the blast.

The day after the second attack, letters were sent claiming responsibility for both of the bombing incidents. A group calling itself "The Army of God" indicated it had declared and would wage a total war against agents of the federal government. The author(s) of the letter indicated they were violent opponents of abortion, homosexuality, and the federal government. Forensic evidence from all of the Atlanta bombings seems to suggest that the Olympic Park, abortion clinic, and gay nightclub bombings are all connected. On January 30, 1998, a bomb exploded at an abortion clinic in Birmingham, Alabama. The blast killed an off-duty police officer who was moonlighting as a security guard at the facility and critically injured a clinic counselor.

From January to May 1997, additional acts of violence, including the use of incendiary devices and bombs, have occurred against abortion clinics in Tulsa, Oklahoma; Falls Church, Virginia; North Hollywood, California; Bozeman, Montana; Yakima, Washington; and Portland, Oregon. During May of 1998, attacks occurred involving butyric acid at eight abortion clinics in Florida. This was the first report of the use of butyric acid against abortion clinics in more than four years. From 1992 through May of 1998, there had been 99 reports of "noxious" chemical attacks on abortion clinics. Butyric acid is a colorless organic acid with a penetrating obnoxious odor. It is a strong irritant to skin and tissue and can cause severe burns. The most significant problem with butyric acid is removing the odor. With little exception, anything the acid comes into contact with will have to be replaced. As a result, the attacks have caused more than $800,000 in damage since 1992.

Federal investigators have determined that the bombings in Olympic Park, the Sandy Springs abortion clinic, the Otherside Lounge, and the abortion clinic in Birmingham are all connected and may have been carried out by the same person(s). Tests performed by ATF and FBI laboratories in Washington, DC, have discovered some of the bomb components from the clinic and nightclub in Atlanta were identical. Shrapnel parts found at all three bombing sites came from the same foundry. During February 1998, Eric Rudolph, a 32-year-old resident of Murphy, North Carolina, was charged with the bombing of the New Woman All Women Health Clinic in Birmingham, Alabama. On October 14, 1998, Rudolph was also charged with and subsequently convicted for the bombings in Olympic Park and the abortion clinic and nightclub in Atlanta.

Domestic and International Lone-Wolf and Homegrown Terrorism

Leaderless Groups and Lone Wolves

Many, if not most, terrorist acts are perpetrated by groups organized—tightly or loosely—with a structure that may be paramilitary. They are focused on terrorist action, or they may include nonviolent political, social, or religious segments as well as extremist and activist arms. However, there are also groups that are leaderless (at least outwardly) but still supportive of direct, radical action. Terrorist acts committed in the name of such groups as the ELF and ALF may appear to be executed by lone wolf perpetrators, but in reality, there are whole networks of supporting enablers for these operatives, including publicists, counselors, tacticians, and legal advisors who communicate via websites, publications, blogs, and other media to encourage and advise. Even structured groups, such as Yemen-based al-Qaeda in the Arabian Peninsula, have so-called lone wolf adherents who commit small-scale or low-level terrorist acts in the United States.

ALF Lone Wolf

The existence of Animal Enterprise Terrorism Act (AETA) of 2006 in protecting animal enterprises has not deterred radicals from committing acts of terrorism, such as those in which Walter Bond was charged. Bond, who refers to himself as a lone wolf and has the word "vegan" tattooed across his throat, was arrested in July 2010 for arson at a Glendale, Colorado, business called the Sheepskin Factory, a retail establishment that carried a variety of products, including hats, mittens, seat covers, rugs, boots, and slippers. The merchandise was also sold through an e-commerce website. According to the affidavit with the charges against the 34-year-old Bond, he had, at one time, lived near the Sheepskin Factory and had been angered that the business profited from the deaths of animals. He also called the building housing the business a "box of matches" and indicated it was a prime candidate for a fire. By the time Bond was arrested, almost four months after the crime, the Sheepskin Factory had reopened for business with new inventory in another location. Bond vowed to "torch" the new store "in a couple of years." After the Sheepskin Factory fire, which caused $500,000 in damages, but prior to Bond's arrest, someone using the tag "ALF Lone Wolf," who may or may not have been Bond, made an Internet post stating, "[t]he arson at the Sheepskin Factory in Denver was done in defense and retaliation for all the innocent animals that have died cruelly at the hands of human oppressors. Be warned that making a living from the use and abuse of animals will not be tolerated. Also be warned that leather is every bit as evil as fur. As demonstrated in my recent arson against the Leather Factory in Salt Lake City. Go vegan!" The fire at a Tandy Leather Factory store in Salt Lake City and at the Tiburon Restaurant in Sandy, Utah—which serves foie gras—have been attributed to Bond, but investigators say the actual perpetrator may be another animal rights activist who is using Bond's arrest to publicize other ALF-oriented activities.

Islamic Lone Wolves

The issues surrounding the difficulty in anticipating lone-wolf terrorist acts and in trying to discern a pattern in them are exemplified by a shooting that occurred on June 1, 2009, in front of an Army/Navy recruiting center located in a strip mall in west Little Rock, Arkansas. Abdulhakim Mujahid Muhammad, a 23-year-old African American who had been known as Carlos Leon Bledsoe before converting to Islam, shot two young soldiers as they took a smoke break outside the recruiting station to which they had been temporarily assigned. The suspect, originally from Memphis but living and working in Little Rock, made a number of incriminating statements to local police. According to the officer's report filed with Mujahid Muhammad's arrest report, he told police that after putting three weapons in his Ford Sport Trac, he drove around and saw the Army military recruiting station with two soldiers standing out front smoking and that he "pulled onto the parking lot in front of the recruiting station, stopped his vehicle, and began shooting at the soldiers." He further stated that he fired several rounds at the soldiers with the intent of killing them before fleeing.[8]

The degree to which the local police were left to handle the case on their own is not unusual in these "lone wolf" terrorist actions. Both the arrest report and the 12-page request for a search warrant were filed by local police officers after stopping Mujahid Muhammad's vehicle based on eyewitness identifications. Despite these similarities to any local vehicle stop, in this instance, the defendant was charged with a total of 16 counts of terrorist acts in addition to one count of capital murder. As information about the suspect became known, it became obvious that the case was more than a random shooting. Little Rock Chief Stuart Thomas reported that Mujahid Muhammad had admitted that he was specifically targeting soldiers because he was angry at the Army because of attacks against Muslims overseas.

Despite the fact that the suspect was determined not to be part of a larger group planning attacks, there were also reports that he had traveled to Yemen. Subsequent investigation revealed that he had gone to Yemen to teach English, had married a Yemeni woman, and had been arrested in Yemen for carrying a fraudulent Somali passport. He had been interviewed by the FBI while in a Yemeni prison and was deported by Yemen at the urging of the American Embassy. But despite the FBI having opened a preliminary investigation on him, no further action was taken when he was returned to the United States on January 29, 2009, barely six months before the shooting. This illustrates one of the problems in keeping track of lone wolves. Although it may not release exact figures, the FBI undoubtedly receives thousands of bits of information on people like Mujahid Muhammad. Whether obtained from authorities in other countries, from its own agents, from other government agencies, or through tips that outsiders provide for any number of reasons, the number of leads makes it impossible to do more than cursory follow-up on all but a few. As with all police investigations, a case file is opened, the matter receives attention, and unless the inquiry turns up additional information that indicates an actual violation, the case is closed.

Generally, in the course of normal policing, the case is unlikely to be referred to again unless something similar is reported about the same individual or if a group of similar cases are opened. In the latter instance, there is no guarantee the cases will be linked until after something occurs. This is similar to what happened after 9/11, when deeper post-event analysis turned up bits of information about Middle Eastern men who applied to a number of flight schools around the nation, but there was nothing to point to this information as particularly relevant. The other danger of overlooking lone wolves is that, by definition, they work alone. This means it is difficult to catch them ahead of time; there are no groups, there is no buildup, there are no messages to intercept. With a cell, someone may make a mistake, someone may want to back out, someone may upset the plans or even discuss a plan, but with a lone wolf, the person may strike at any time with little or no advance planning.

[8] Arkansas Arrest/Disposition Report, defendant Abdulhakim Mujahid Muhammad, filed June 2, 2009, available online from Investigative Project on Terrorism, http://www.investigativeproject.org/case/330.

Like regular crime, some lone wolf activities could be terrorism of opportunity, meaning that although the person intended to commit a terrorist act, the actual event was somewhat unplanned and occurred at that time and in the location because the opportunity presented itself. For instance, if the two soldiers had not been outside, would Mujahid Muhammad have entered the career center and started shooting? Although his original statement to the Little Rock police tended to reinforce the random nature of the actual act, if not of his motivation, his later statements indicate a different story. In January 2010, in a letter to the local judge presiding over the case, Mujahid Muhammad changed his plea to guilty, claiming affiliation with al-Qaeda in the Arabian Peninsula (AQAP), although this has not been confirmed. The suspect's father, Melvin Bledsoe, doubts it, though, believing rather that his son was trying to fulfill a sense of martyrdom. Most terrorist experts seem to agree.[9]

Early Homegrown Terrorists

Although recent terrorist activity has focused on radical activity fostered by international concerns, the history of terrorism is replete with actions that were either purely domestic in nature or focused on international events quite different from those today. Among these were the following:

- *First VBIED in the United States.* Probably the first vehicle-borne improvised explosive device (VBIED) was a horse and wagon loaded with 100 pounds of dynamite that detonated at midday on September 16, 1920, in New York City's Wall Street area, killing 38 people and injuring more than 400. Despite vast resources expended by local and federal law enforcement and by private security firms, the crime has never been solved.
- *World's Fair 1939–1940.* During the fair in Flushing Meadows Park, New York, a suspicious package was removed from the British Pavilion by two members of the NYPD Bomb Squad. While they were attempting "render safe procedures," the device exploded, killing the two detectives. Like the Wall Street–area bombing, this case has never been solved although, in this case, investigators believed the package had been placed by Nazi sympathizers.
- *The Mad Bomber.* Between 1940 and 1956 a disgruntled former employee of Consolidated Edison, the power company in New York City, George Metesky, placed 33 IEDs, 22 of which detonated. Most were placed in movie theaters, railroad stations, throughout the subway, and in other locations that attracted large crowds. Although many people were injured and there was considerable property damage, his activities did not result in any fatalities. Metesky used the nom de plume "FP," but the news media dubbed him the "Mad Bomber." Upon capture, Metesky was judged legally insane and institutionalized. He was released after 13 years on the basis of judicial error. He never engaged in any further violence and died in Connecticut, 20 years later, at the age of 90.

Non-Islamic Homegrown Contemporary Terrorists

Antigovernment militias have existed for decades, but a more recently formed group has attracted considerable attention. Formed in 2008, the Hutaree Militia, whose name the group says means Christian Soldiers, is based in Michigan with outreach to Ohio and Indiana. It is believed that this group has connections with other militia groups, but it is not a clandestine

[9] J. Dao. A Muslim Son, a Murder Trial and Many Questions, *The New York Times*, February 17, 2010.

organization. The militia maintains a website and members have appeared on radio talk shows. While most other militia movements are paramilitary organizations, usually survivalist, antigovernment and antitaxes and Second Amendment adherents, the Hutaree group states a more Christian aim and a belief that the apocalypse is near. In one indictment against the group, members are accused of plotting to entrap and kill police officers by placing a false 911 call and attacking responding officers. They also hoped to attack ceremonial funerals generally attended by a large number of law enforcement personnel. This is not unlike a tactic that was used in Ireland by the Provisional Irish Republican Army.

Contemporary Homegrown Islamic Terrorists

Since 9/11, the FBI and other government agencies have arrested many American-born or naturalized citizens on terrorism charges. The reasons for their arrests ranged from committing violent acts, to offering support to violence, to helping finance a terrorist operation, to recruiting new terrorist operatives. Here are a few examples: Two Brooklyn, New York, men, Wesam el-Hanofi and Sabirhan el-Hasanoff, were arrested in Virginia after returning from Yemen, where el-Hasanoff took an oath to al-Qaeda. While in Yemen, he purchased software to secure communication and seven Casio watches that matched a model that had previously been used extensively in creating timing elements of IEDs. In addition, he received $50,000 from another conspirator to further terrorist actions.

An example of a domestic terrorist cell planning an attack is as follows. In 2008, a former inmate of New Folsom Prison in California, Levar Washington, 30 years old, was sentenced to 22 years in federal prison for his role in a domestic terrorist cell planning to attack US military and Jewish facilities in the Los Angeles area. Washington was recruited into the cell while in prison by Kevin James, who formed the terrorist group and required members to swear an oath of loyalty and obedience to James and the cell. Upon release from prison, cell members committed about a dozen armed robberies to raise money for the attacks. When police linked cell members to a robbery, a search of their apartment turned up a James-authored statement to be given to the media following a planned deadly attack. It read, in part, "This incident is the first in a series of incidents to come in a plight to defend and propagate traditional Islam in its purity."

"Jihad Jane," Colleen R. LaRose, a blue-eyed blonde woman born in Michigan around 1964, had never been in any serious legal trouble. By the age of 24, after two failed marriages, she had been living for the past five years in a suburb of Philadelphia with a man whose father she cared for while her companion worked. She spent a good deal of time online and posted a YouTube video saying that she desperately wanted to in some way help Muslims although she was not specific on how or why. She somehow became involved with a group of violent co-conspirators from around the world. On the day of the funeral of her companion's father, she disappeared with her computer hard drive (probably having been advised to do so) and flew to Europe. She was arrested in Ireland with two Libyans, a Palestinian, a Croatian, and two Algerians, one of whom she had married. Because she was a blue-eyed blonde, she and the members of her group believed that she would not attract attention moving to Sweden to assassinate a Swedish cartoonist, Lars Vilks, who Muslims say blasphemed Mohammed. In 2011, she pleaded guilty to providing material support to terrorists, conspiracy to kill in a foreign country, making false statements, and attempted identity theft.

George Tech student Syed Haris Ahmed, born in Pakistan in 1984, came to the United States with his family when he was 12 years old and became a naturalized citizen at 19. He and other Muslim youths who met in Canada talked themselves into becoming jihadists and were ready to take action. On his own, Ahmed visited Washington, DC, and videotaped a number of landmarks, a fuel depot in the area, and a Masonic Temple in Virginia. He then bought a one-way ticket to Pakistan and attempted to interest the Pakistan terrorist group Lashkar-e-Taiba in the tapes he had prepared. They spurned his offer due to their suspicions about the arrival of an unannounced Westerner. He returned to Atlanta where, because the authorities were aware of his actions, he was arrested and subsequently pleaded guilty to conspiracy to provide material support for terrorism in the United States and abroad.

Anwar al-Awlaki (now deceased) was born in New Mexico in 1971 to foreign parents. His father was a low-level Yemeni governmental employee. Anwar spent his later childhood back in Yemen, returning to the United States in 1991 for his education. Evidence indicates that three of the 9/11 attackers interacted with al-Awlaki and received spiritual advice from him prior to the attacks. When al-Awlaki returned to the United States, he attended Colorado State University and received a BA in engineering and subsequently earned an MA in education at San Diego State University. He served as an Imam at a mosque in San Diego. Some who knew him at the time of the 9/11 attack say that his lectures identified him as a moderate; however, this description has been disputed. Court records show that he was arrested twice in San Diego for soliciting prostitutes. He returned to Yemen and spent various stints in jails, where he voraciously read the works of radical Muslims. His writings and lectures, in English, have been directed at young American and British Muslims, with whom he had his greatest influence.

One adherent of al-Awlaki's teachings was Faisal Shahzad, also a naturalized citizen, who became known as the Times Square car bomber. He told authorities he was moved to action by al-Awlaki's writings that called for holy war against Westerners. He considered himself a follower of al-Awlaki and had contacted the Internet-savvy Imam via computer. Using his US passport, Shahzad returned to Pakistan in an attempt to connect with an unnamed militant group for training. Although he has claimed that he received training for a number of weeks by the group, terrorist experts believe that he was probably viewed with suspicion and did not receive high-level instruction. As evidence, they point to the inept device he constructed. In May 2010, Shahzad constructed a VBIED in a Nissan Pathfinder and parked it on West 45th Street in the Times Square area. He set the fuse and left the area, but a T-shirt vendor saw smoke and alerted police. Had the device been properly prepared, it could have caused great damage and significant loss of life. Shahzad was captured two days later while trying to flee the country.

Al-Qaeda's public relations man, Adam Pearlman, aka Adam Yahiye Gadahn, aka Azzam the American, was born in Oregon in 1978. His grandfather was Jewish and his grandmother Christian. He was raised Christian and at 17, while living in California with his grandparents and attending college, he converted to Islam. At 20, he moved to Pakistan where he married an Afghan refugee. Until he lost contact with his family in 2001, he had told them that he was a journalist. He would, in fact, become the public relations expert for al-Qaeda and a senior advisor to Osama bin Laden, including preparing cultural transcripts, producing propaganda videos, and translating for al-Qaeda.

He has prepared or appeared on various recruiting videos criticizing the United States and has assisted in a number of attacks and the bombing of embassies. One of his messages was an invitation to Americans "to be led out of darkness into the light" of al-Qaeda. He has been involved in or appeared in every video or communication released by al-Qaeda "commemorating the 9/11 attack to the World Trade Center." These actions led to his being indicted by the United States for "treason, for providing material support to al Qaeda," and he has been placed on the FBI's Most Wanted Terrorist List.

Concluding Thoughts

Historically and presently, countries worldwide experience terrorism. Terrorism has been classified based on geography. More specifically, terrorists and terrorist groups have been classified according to their area of operations. Domestic terrorists operate within their target country's borders. By contrast, international terrorists cross borders and often target and operate within several countries. Numerous domestic and international terrorists pursuing different ideologies exist both in the United States and abroad. Both domestic and international terrorists have demonstrated their ability to strike almost at will. Lone wolves and homegrown terrorist incidents have been revealed across the globe. What is particularly troubling about these types of terrorists is the fact that these individuals are often indistinguishable from the rest of the population and, therefore, very difficult to recognize or uncover.

Part II

Terrorist Tactics, Terrorist Capabilities

4

Terrorist Organizations and Cells[1]

Terrorist cells are secret, small teams of terrorists who operate as a group either on orders of a commander or independently. The cell is the fundamental unit of a terrorist group. Cell operations and their members are the least understood part of terrorism. Their operations are always secret and never seen until they attack.

Cells are often referred to by other names in a terrorist organization's communications and statements. Depending on the group and its national origin, cells may be referred to as fronts, commandos, groups, or wings. The Irish Republican Army called cells active service units; in Sri Lanka, the Tamil Tigers call their cells cadres. Many terrorist groups will name their cells after slain members; an example is a cell of Germany's Red Army Faction that was known as the Gudrun Essenlin Commando.

Types of Terrorist Cells

To better understand the makeup of terrorist cells, military chain-of-command terms are used. Terrorist groups do not refer to themselves with the following terms but use terms that better suit their ideology and culture.

- A command and control cell (C2) is comprised of external or internal supervisors who make final decisions and supervise the execution of an attack. They may be leaders of or participants in any of the following cells.
- Tactical operations cell (TAC-OPS). This is the person or team that actually carries out the act of terrorism. Also known as combat cells, attack cells, action teams, or operational cells.
- An intelligence cell (INTELL) collects data, makes recommendations, selects targets, and provides information to hit the target.
- Logistics cell (LOG). This includes people who are organized to provide supplies or support to the other cells. These may include bomb makers, black marketeers, doctors, lawyers, bankers, couriers, and others needed in an emergency. Also referred to as the auxiliary cell, support cell, or assistance cell.

[1] Information for this chapter was drawn from the following titles: (1) M. W. Nance, *Terrorist Recognition Handbook: A Practitioner's Manual for Predicting and Identifying Terrorist Activities*, Second Edition, CRC Press, 2008. (2) K. J. Dudonis, F. Bolz, and D. P. Schulz, *The Counterterrorism Handbook: Tactics, Procedures, and Techniques*, Third Edition, CRC Press, 2005.

- A combined cell (Combined) is a team of terrorists so small it must perform all the functions of the four cells named above. The al-Qaeda organization often uses combined cells to maximize its manpower.
- A sleeper cell is any one of the above types of cells that infiltrates a geographic region and lies dormant until activated for a mission. Sleeper cells are distinguished by their ability to blend into their surroundings until given orders to carry out their mission. Once activated, of course, the cell is no longer a sleeper.

Keep in mind that cells may operate independently or in coordination with each other, depending upon their mission.

Operative Membership Pools

Terrorist groups must draw operatives from a body of manpower known as a pool. Pools of manpower come in two forms: open and closed.

Closed pools of operatives are professional or dedicated terrorists who are consistently used by the leadership. These members are active cadres and supporters chosen for skills and reliability. They are generally a known number of personnel and may be the heart of the terrorist group. Smaller groups have used this system successfully and were only degraded through arrest or death of the operatives. The German terrorist group Red Army Faction lost its last two closed-pool operatives in 1999 with the arrest of Andrea Klump and the death of Horst-Ludwig Meyer in a SWAT raid. The group is now considered defunct.

Open pools of operatives rely on active cadre and field leadership to recruit lower-level operatives and train them to support their missions. These core personnel do not have to risk themselves completely and can form new cells as necessary. Al-Qaeda uses this system.

Terrorist Cell Size

The number of cells, the number of operatives per cell, and the group's overall structure depend upon several factors:

- *Group skills*: Better groups use small cells of three to five people. Unskilled groups use larger numbers of people. Al-Qaeda, a professional group, prefers to use large cells of four to 20 members, but they are independent enough to create their own cells. Blood-connected groups, such as criminally bent families, also tend to use larger cells. The larger the group, the greater the chance of compromise.
- *Mission risk*: If the mission is high risk, smaller numbers of operatives may be more effective. The more permissive the environment—that is, the easier it is for operatives to move around and carry out their tasks—the more people may be involved without jeopardizing an operation.
- *Manpower*: Some groups make deliberate decisions to limit the cell size for reasons mentioned above; others simply do not have enough manpower and are forced to work with the few people they have.
- *Money*: Limited resources may also limit the number of operatives carrying out a mission. Well-funded groups, such as al-Qaeda, the IRA, and Hezbollah, may be able to finance dozens of terrorists simultaneously.

How Cells and Leadership Communicate

Cells communicate with leadership and/or with each other via two methods: direct and indirect. Direct communications offer surety that the message is received, and mistakes are minimized. They are also less secure, however, and can be compromised through arrest or infiltration by agents. The methods of direct communications are the following:

- *Face-to-face meetings with known people.* A dangerous but often necessary method of communications. Newer groups that are just beginning to establish communications or groups whose loyalties can be assured by members use face-to-face meetings as a way of definitively confirming a person's identity and the authenticity of the communications. If a police or government infiltrator is discovered, the group can hold, interrogate, and even eliminate the person. Groups without blood ties or extremely strong ideological ties are more susceptible to infiltration, defection, and arrest of members, which could compromise the entire organization.
- *Face-to-face meetings using anonymous names.* This method of communications involves face-to face meetings between strangers, identified to each other only by code names or noms de guerre. Some groups, including al-Qaeda and the now defunct Abu Nidal Organization (ANO), use this system in training schools and during operations. Their members are identified only by code names, such as Abu Jihad or Abu Saif, not their real names.

Indirect communications offer maximum security and protection from interception, but also increased opportunity for errors. Messages can be lost, misinterpreted, or broken if a member or system is destroyed or lost. The indirect method requires an elaborate "lost communications" procedure and follow-up security checks.

- *Cutout communications.* Use of cutouts is an age-old indirect communication and security technique that allows the leadership to deliver orders to an operative, securely. A cutout can be any break in the direct line of communications, such as a courier or trusted agent who assists communications between two people who may not know each other. New cell members receive orders from an unknown commander appointed above them. These orders are delivered to the operatives via various indirect methods. Often, messages are in code and may be concealed by embedding in books, newspapers, and other written documents. This system generally goes undetected, but terrorist operatives must follow orders from people whose legitimacy they cannot confirm. The main strength of a cutout system is the inability of operatives, if they are arrested, to identify senior group members. This minimizes the damage caused to the organization by the compromise of an individual or cell.
- *Cutout through electronic systems.* The same indirect communications principle described above is used, but electronic media serve as the channels of communications, such as secure Internet chat rooms, three-way telephone conversations, or the use of forwarded e-mail messages that are encrypted and relayed by hand on disk.
- *Mail drop.* Here the postal system or electronic mail delivery is used to send and receive communications. Regular post or delivery services can be used to deliver written mail, floppy disks, memory chips, or SIM cards, all of which may or may not be encrypted in order to send or receive orders. Authentication may be done by code words or passwords that are sent via separate secret communications.

- *Dead drop.* Information is left at a prearranged location known only to the group members. Terrorists using dead drops reflect a measure of training by an intelligence-trained agent. Agencies suspecting usage of dead drops should contact the appropriate FBI office to ensure that trained counterintelligence officers conduct counter-surveillance.

Terrorist Command and Control Cells

Some groups may use a supervisory team of professional terrorists that operates and commands subordinate cells. Other groups go so far as to dispatch field leadership officers to check up on the status of the operation and provide the other cell leaders with mission support. Both are called command and control (C2) cells. The C2 cell generally contains two to three terrorists in the following roles:

- The operative in charge (OIC) serves as the overall mission commander as well as the tactical operations cell leader. May be near the target during the attack or observe from a distance.
- The assistant operative in charge (AOIC) is a deputy helping the OIC execute the mission.
- A driver/messenger supports the OIC and AOIC in movement and communications with leaders and other cells.

Terrorist Intelligence Cells

The intelligence cell is the eyes and ears of the terrorist organization. It is extremely important because its members conduct target selection; they guide the decision as to who or what will be attacked, when an attack will be carried out, and the most effective means for doing so. Typically, INTELL cell members are the most experienced members of the organization. Once surveillance has been conducted and tactical decisions made, the cell creates a briefing package for both the senior and field terrorist leadership. When the decision to strike is made, it is then passed on to the tactical operations cell. The package describes the plans and feasibility of the attack to terrorist leadership and is usually delivered via courier.

The intelligence cell rarely participates in an attack because its members would risk being identified—especially if counter-surveillance efforts picked up their repeated presence at a given location. Occasionally, they do participate; al-Qaeda used a combined cell in the bombing of the American embassy in Nairobi, Kenya, in which an intelligence cell member helped carry out the attack. His involvement later helped to identify the supporting terrorists and break up the rest of the cell.

Intelligence cells generally employ the following participants: cell leaders, a surveillance team, a photography team, a penetration team, and security/driver.

Cell Leader

- An experienced terrorist
- Highly trusted, "leads from the front"
- Actively participates in collecting information
- Responsible for the security of the cell
- Reports only to a designated superior or directly to the organization's leadership

Surveillance Team

The surveillance team observes and reports on targets being considered for attack. Skilled groups use dedicated, highly trained people for this task.

- Combined groups may use logistics cell personnel or non-terrorist supporters for surveillance
- May be a single individual
- Unlikely to use handheld radios to communicate with other members when actively conducting surveillance. More likely to use cell phones or report verbally after surveillance is completed
- Identifiable by position and behavior
- Look for the "four sames": same type of people, in the same place, at the same time of day, doing the same activity
- Look for behaviors that, at first glance, might appear normal, but may be out of context (for example, a couple picnicking near a lake next to a nuclear power plant may appear normal, but picnicking every day for a week or an absence of food makes this activity suspicious)

Photography Team

- Usually one or two people, male or female
- Identifiable by behavior: people using still or video cameras, overtly or discreetly
- Films subjects not typically photographed by tourists: embassies, building entrances and exits, security personnel, and so on

Penetration Team

- May be an intelligence cell or tactical operations cell member who has received the proper penetration information (for this reason, all penetration attempts need to be evaluated as the start of a real attack)
- Enters target area for surveillance purposes
- Usually one or two people, male or female
- No radio communications until the mission is complete (cell phone, hand signals, or other nonverbal methods may be used)
- May walk the attack pattern they intend to use (called a pre-attack walk-down)
- Will attempt to enter a facility using ruses, false IDs, or false stories
- May try to use unusual entrances or exits; may be seen pacing or undertaking close observation of a facility
- Will dress to look like facility staff, tourists, fishermen, hunters, runners, or the like

Security/Driver

- Usually one person, male or female
- Stands off to the side to watch the team's flank
- May double as an escape driver

- May use predetermined signals for the team to break off surveillance
- Identifiable by behavior: a single person sitting in a running vehicle, a vehicle that circles the area repeatedly, horn honking that brings other people back to a vehicle, a loitering person one block away from the objective

Terrorist Tactical Operations Cells

- *Cell leader*: This person is usually the overall mission commander, as well as the head of the attack arm. The tactical operations cell leader personally leads attack operations.
- *Tactical operatives*: The number of operatives depends largely upon the mission at stake. The operatives' job is to carry out the actual attack according to plan. This might involve assassinating a target, dropping (leaving behind) bombs, carrying out a suicide mission, or any other type of attack.
- *Rear/flank security*: The cell may require a final security check of the target before the attack, covering routes of approach that police or security forces may use when they arrive. This team member may be armed or just act as a lookout.
- *Insertion/extraction driver*: This may be the same driver from the logistics cell or a specially designated person with evasive driving skills. Teams that arrive by vehicle and expect to depart in the same vehicle designate an insertion/extraction driver. This driver may stand off from the operations area and act as a lookout; he or she may also be on the ready to provide more firepower or drop off weapons and supplies.

Terrorist Logistics Cells

- *Cell leader*: Supervises all cell members' duties and is responsible for acquiring the supplies necessary for an attack. May fulfill the duties of another cell member as well.
- *Supply officer*: Obtains needed weapons, equipment, and supplies through either legal or criminal methods.
- *Driver*: Provides transportation for tactical operations and intelligence cells and moves the group's supplies and personnel.
- *Bomb master*: Conducts all phases of assembling bombs with the exception of delivery. Rarely takes part in the attack unless the arming procedure is complex or the device is a "special" weapon, such as a dirty radioactive bomb or nuclear fission bomb. However, lone wolf terrorists, such as the Unabomber, used couriers for delivery.
- *Arms handler*: Expert in acquiring and preparing weapons and explosives components.
- *Courier*: Receives and delivers written communications, passes voice messages, makes and receives money transfers; may also locate supporters outside the organization when necessary for funding and additional assistance.
- *Emergency support teams*: These are not de facto members, but active supporters of the organization. They may include emergency medical support comprised of doctors, nurses, surgeons, and specialists who will provide services and treatment to injured

terrorists. Another component may be emergency legal support, such as lawyers and other legal professionals who will represent members of the group if arrested and work toward their release from jail. Perhaps the most important group would be those who provide emergency financial support or those who provide money and supplies in an emergency with no questions asked.

Terrorist Group Structures and Membership: Who Orders Terrorist Acts?

The leadership of a terrorist group is often publicly known and is its most identifiable part. Charismatic personalities such as Osama bin Laden (al-Qaeda), Renato Curcio (Red Brigades), Abdullah Ocalan (PKK), Velupillai Prabhakaran (LTTE), or the late Yasser Arafat (PLO) are well known and provide a face for the grievances of the group. The terrorist leadership orders and is responsible for terrorist acts even though some decisions may be left up to the field leadership or the individual operative.

Terrorist groups are generally composed of five subgroups that make operations possible: the senior leadership, field leadership, active operatives, active supporters, and passive supporters. The operational makeup of terrorist organizations is based on a pyramidal support structure. An analysis of terrorist groups since 1990 reveals that a new level of leadership between the active cadre and senior leadership is making more and more operational decisions to insulate the group's leaders: the field leadership. Decisions to select targets and to carry out operations are increasingly being made at the field leadership level. The modified pyramid includes the following levels of support:

- *Senior leadership*: These are the hard-core supporters who believe in the cause of the group without question. They include ideologues, theologians, and others who attempt to justify the acts of terrorism. The leadership creates strategic plans and decides whom to strike, what to strike, and where to strike; unlike with the terrorism of the 1960s and 1970s, leaders usually do not participate in tactical operations.
- *Field leadership*: These are the select terrorist operatives who control large geographic areas and command the active terrorists. The field leadership often designs terrorist attacks and gets them approved by senior leadership. The field leadership participates in operations in a supervisory role.
- *Active operatives*: These are the primary covert members of the terrorist organization who collect intelligence and supply and conduct the actual attacks.
- *Active supporters*: These are civilians who truly believe in the cause of the terrorist group and offer unquestioned support, sometimes acting as couriers, providing emergency safe houses, and acquiring materials.
- *Passive supporters*: Civilians who unknowingly support the terrorists' political or religious organization.

Terrorist Command and Control Structures

The type of organization a group uses depends on its level of sophistication and what works best geographically. The Defense Intelligence Agency classifies terrorist groups into two command and control structures: centralized authority structure and decentralized authority structure.

1. *A centralized authority structure.* This structure provides the terrorist cells and manpower with all support, intelligence, and supplies from one source either in depots or caches belonging to the organization. The benefits are unified and controlled action as well as making large quantities of resources available for missions. The difficulty of this structure is that it creates a large group that can be infiltrated. Well-known traditional communist and guerrilla terrorists, such as the German Red Army Faction and the Italian Red Brigade, used this structure.
2. *A decentralized authority structure.* This structure allows groups at the individual or cell level to provide for themselves with minimal direction or support from the group's leadership. The benefits are that they can make decisions based on detailed local intelligence, have better awareness of the security environment, and use few group resources. This structure is also more prone to fractionalizing or groups acting in rogue operations, however. International groups, such as al-Qaeda, or groups that operate in difficult security environments, such as Hamas and the Palestinian Islamic Jihad, prefer this structure.

Organizational Models

The purpose of a terrorist organization is simply to ensure that the absolute most effective and secure terrorist activities are carried out successfully. Each group may select the best model based on its area of operations, security, and resources. These models are provided to show that terrorist groups generally have simple communications and command structures. Terrorist groups are structured in one of the three general organizational models: functional, operational, and independent.

1. *Functional structure*: This is a centralized structure. The group is commanded by the senior leadership, which passes orders down directly to a command and control cell or to cells that operate strictly in their specialty area (intelligence, tactical operations, and logistics). This is one of the oldest and most secure of organizational structures because the terrorist group's unique cell functions are kept highly compartmentalized. Each cell may be completely unaware of the other cells' existence; often, cells do not communicate directly with each other. If one cell is stopped or arrested, the other cells remain in place, and the mission may even continue if a replacement cell arrives in time. Communications within this form of structure take place between the terrorist senior leadership and each cell with secure methods.
2. *Operational structure*: This is a decentralized structure. The group is commanded by its senior leadership, which passes orders down to a series of "combined cells." These combined cells run their own intelligence, supply, and attack operations with the same group of people. This is a highly risky structure for operatives because the arrest of one cell member can stop all operations. Al-Qaeda uses this structure.
3. *Independent cell structure*: This is a centralized structure that is similar to the operational structure described above, except that there is no independent senior leadership. The group operates as one body and performs all the cell functions necessary to carry out an attack. Cell members may perform several different roles.
4. *Networked structure*: With advances in personal communications and the intensity of counter-terrorism security, fewer and fewer organizations continue to operate in the systematic top-to-bottom command structure like the hierarchical systems.

> More and more internal organizations require loosely connected structures, which offer flexibility, speed of communication, and layered security. Over time, organizations desired to eliminate a single central joint command and control, which could disable the entire group if killed or arrested. With the advancements of computer and mobile phone connectivity, these groups started to communicate and form "networks" along the lines of their verbal, written, and electronic communication and relationships.

Networks can be all of those, but they can also be the notional lines of affiliation of like-minded individuals with general goals and targets. Networks allow a group to share ongoing initiative and allows for increased flexibility. Networks work through key hubs called "nodes," which do the following:

- Distribute responsibility
- Provide redundancy for lost nodes
- Avoid unnecessary C2 approval process
- Contact only critical cells
- Can use computer technology or couriers

A node is a singular point within a network that can be an individual, cell, group, or other networked organization within or connected to a group's structure. Nodes work most effectively when all nodes are ideologically similar. Dissimilar nodes can work with both ideological and non-ideological nodes, thus making networks mix criminal, cross-religious, and cross-political groups to achieve a singular goal.

Nodes are connected by lines of relationship. These are called diyads (see Figure 4.1). Diyads can be face-to-face meetings, communications, or personal relationships. Networks tend to create geometric structures that have particular characteristics.

Chain networks (Figure 4.2) pass communications, materials, information or goods from one node to the next in a near-linear fashion. These structures are favored by the following:

- Smugglers
- Money launderers
- Drug chains

A wheel network is one where all nodes can communicate with a central hub. The outer nodes can communicate with each other freely. It is a common feature of economic/financial systems.

A hub or star network (Figure 4.3) is one in which all nodes communicate with or through a central hub. The hub can simply be a passageway and does not necessarily have to make decisions.

An all-channel network (Figure 4.4) is an organizationally "flat" structure in which no hierarchical command is above it; therefore there is no "head of the snake" to decapitate. This structure is communications-intensive and command and control is distributed within the network. This network has difficulties as the nodes can be infiltrated or neutralized.

Hybrid networks are combinations of various networks. Disparate structures can be linked including the following:

- Chain network for money laundering
- Wheel network for financial
- All channel network for C2

The key to breaking these networks is to look for linkage between the networks (see Figures 4.5 and 4.6).

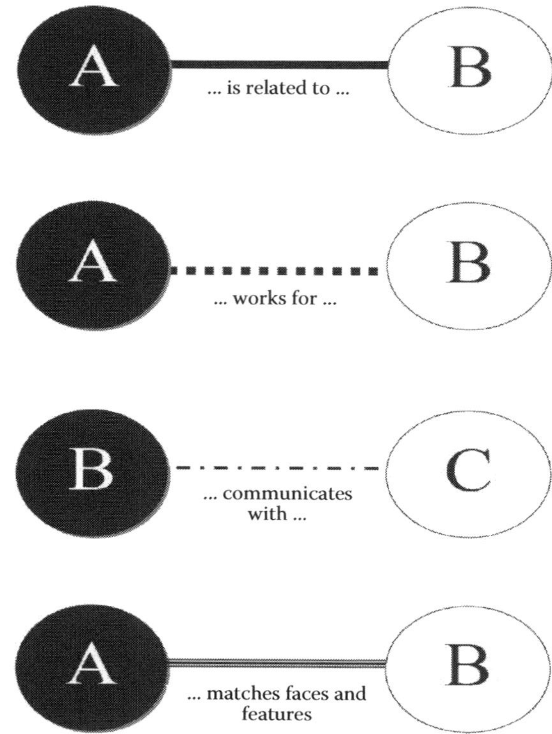

Figure 4.1 Nodal diyads. (From M. W. Nance, *Terrorist Recognition Handbook: A Practitioner's Manual for Predicting and Identifying Terrorist Activities*, Second Edition, CRC Press, 2008. With permission.)

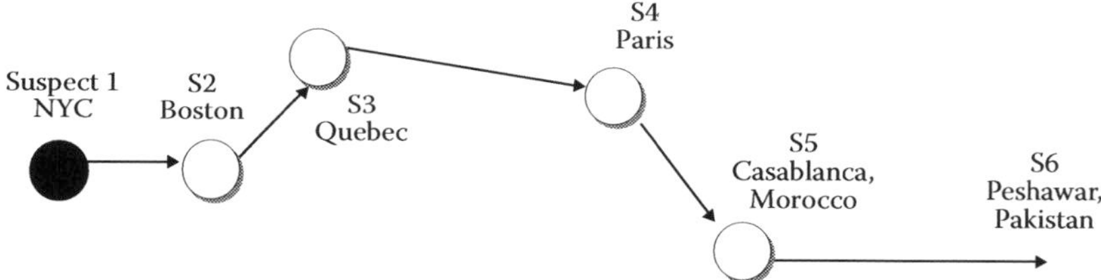

Figure 4.2 Chain network. (From M. W. Nance, *Terrorist Recognition Handbook: A Practitioner's Manual for Predicting and Identifying Terrorist Activities*, Second Edition, CRC Press, 2008. With permission.)

Religious Terrorist Organization Structure

- *Spiritual leader*: Typically, this is a charismatic person who sets the spiritual and political agenda for the group. The leader has direct communications with the group's "public" (such as a political party or social services organization) wing but maintains secret communication paths with the operational (terrorist) division
- *Council or other body of religious leaders*: A cohesive group that supports and advises the spiritual leader on the use of terrorism and its religious or political suitability
- *Laypeople and supporters*: Active supporters who support the decisions and teachings of the spiritual leader even if they involve terrorist acts

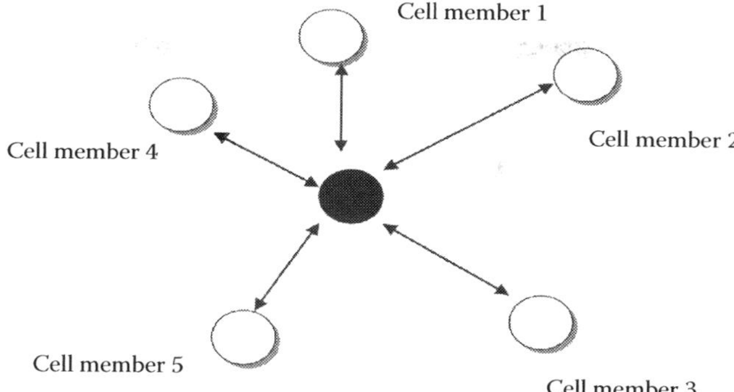

Figure 4.3 Hub or star network. (From M. W. Nance, *Terrorist Recognition Handbook: A Practitioner's Manual for Predicting and Identifying Terrorist Activities*, Second Edition, CRC Press, 2008. With permission.)

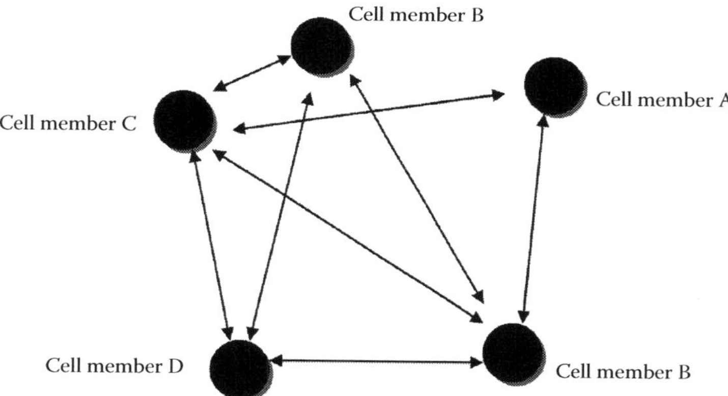

Figure 4.4 All channel network. (From M. W. Nance, *Terrorist Recognition Handbook: A Practitioner's Manual for Predicting and Identifying Terrorist Activities*, Second Edition, CRC Press, 2008. With permission.)

- *Political wing*: Active supporters who provide political power, influence, and money
- *Covert terrorist wing*: Militants who use violence to advance the spiritual goals of the spiritual leader (see Figure 4.7).

Political Terrorist Organization Structure

- Political leader: This is generally a charismatic figure who sets the overall political goals of the group.
- Political deputy/operations officer executes and/or distributes orders from the leader.
- Operational liaison officer passes on the secret orders of the leadership to the operatives who will carry out terrorist acts (see Figure 4.8).

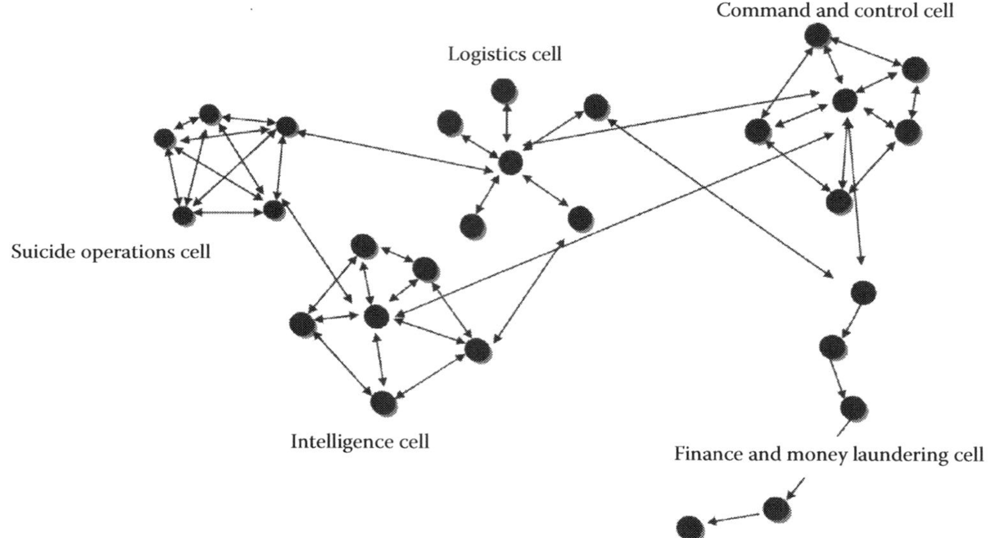

Figure 4.5 Hybrid network, low density. (From M. W. Nance, *Terrorist Recognition Handbook: A Practitioner's Manual for Predicting and Identifying Terrorist Activities*, Second Edition, CRC Press, 2008. With permission.)

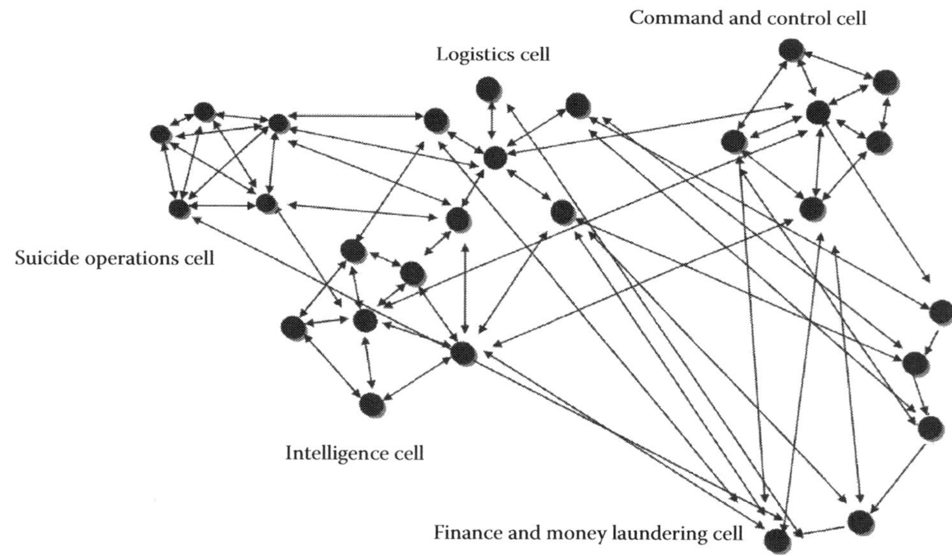

Figure 4.6 Hybrid network, high density. (From M. W. Nance, *Terrorist Recognition Handbook: A Practitioner's Manual for Predicting and Identifying Terrorist Activities*, Second Edition, CRC Press, 2008. With permission.)

Combined Cell Organization Structure

A self-contained covert unit, the combined cell can be used by terrorists of any ideological leaning. This group may be one person (a lone wolf) or a small group of people operating together (combined cell). This system is highly advocated by white supremacist and neo-Nazi groups within the United States. Technically, al-Qaeda seeks out and supports independent combined

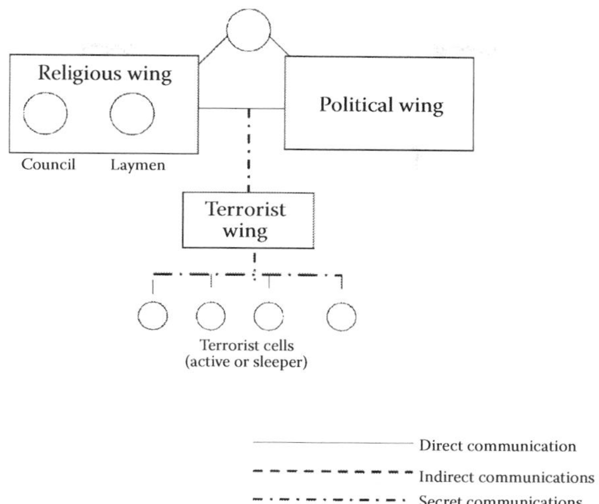

Figure 4.7 Religious terrorist organization structure. (From M. W. Nance, *Terrorist Recognition Handbook: A Practitioner's Manual for Predicting and Identifying Terrorist Activities*, Second Edition, CRC Press, 2008. With permission.)

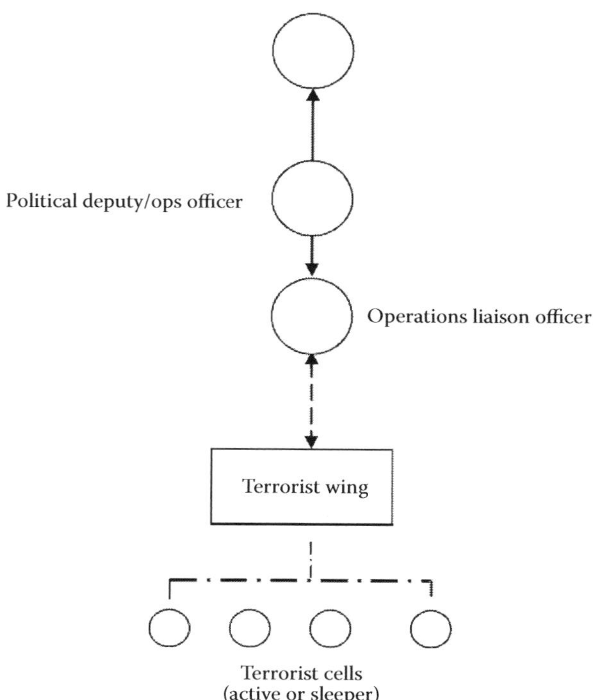

Figure 4.8 Political terrorist organization structure. (From M. W. Nance, *Terrorist Recognition Handbook: A Practitioner's Manual for Predicting and Identifying Terrorist Activities*, Second Edition, CRC Press, 2008. With permission.)

cells within countries and provides guidance and finances to their operations but has little direct control over their structure or targets. These groups are marked by members who conduct all the necessary support, intelligence, and attack operations with the same group of people.

Case Study: Ecoterrorism

They call themselves "elfs," act in autonomous groups with little or no chain of command, and recruit loyalists though a website that had been maintained by a publicist in Portland, Oregon, who claimed not to know the names of any members of the group. Making it even more difficult for the police and the private security professionals to track their activities, members of the Earth Liberation Front (ELF; hence the term elfs) have claimed credit for activities that cross the jurisdiction of a number of law enforcement agencies, including the FBI; the Bureau of Alcohol, Tobacco, Firearms, and Explosives; the Bureau of Land Management; and the US Forest Service. In addition, because of the ill-defined organizational structure, members who may or may not be acting independently have committed crimes in many parts of the country and have targeted prime companies, universities, researchers, farmers, and real estate developers, resulting in a nightmare of cross-jurisdictional problems for any investigator trying to determine where the elfs might strike next. The movement is so loosely organized that trying to get a handle on it has been described as trying to grab a fistful of water.

ELF opposes urban sprawl; deforestation; and more vaguely, any acts its members view as "harmful to the environment," which include work with genetically modified food stocks, typically referred to as "Frankenfood." The difficulty in recognizing the violent nature of some of their activities as well as the elusive nature of many of the domestic terrorist groups makes them particularly difficult to protect against. Members of the groups are often young, upper middle class, and white, and their activities are often centered on areas close to where they live. Few have had any involvement with the police other than possibly other eco-protests, so they are difficult to trace, and only rarely are their fingerprints or descriptions already on file. In some cases, the activists have been employed by or for their targets, making it even more difficult to prevent their access to a facility or their ability to learn the facility's vulnerability.

The elusive nature of the attackers makes it fairly easy for them to undertake detailed pre-raid surveillance of a facility without being detected. The shadowy nature of ELF is exemplified by its self-proclaimed former spokesperson, Craig Rosenbraugh, of Portland, Oregon, who claimed, in 2002, that he had resigned his position as spokesperson after invoking his Fifth Amendment right against self-incrimination before a US House of Representatives subcommittee. Still speaking for the group at a time when three Long Island, New York, youths pled guilty to federal arson charges, he agreed with his attorney's view that the pleas would have little effect on the group because it "operates under an ideology, not a physical membership, so it is really impossible to dissolve."

Yet James F. Jarboe, an FBI domestic terrorism expert, called the group one of the most dangerous domestic terrorist groups based on two factors: its increased activities and the amount of damage its supporters have caused. According to FBI estimates, ELF and its partner in crime, ALF, have committed more than 2000 criminal acts and caused more than $110 million in economic losses and damages since their inceptions. A Eugene, Oregon, detective attributed the group's danger to its impossibility to infiltrate. Because few of the members know one another and they hold no meetings or issue no instructions to one another, there is little or nothing to track. He contrasted it with the Mafia, where a potential undercover operative can sometimes gain access through recommendations from a made member of a particular family.

But among ecoterrorists, there is no family to infiltrate; there is only a very small group of people who get together to commit a crime and take credit for their act only through a press release or on a website. In a self-published monograph, ELF boasted that very few of its actions have resulted in arrests, claiming that the group "has been extremely successful in evading law enforcement due to its anonymous cell structure."

Concluding Thoughts

From within, virtually all groups use variants of cellular organizations at the tactical level to enhance security and to task organize for operations. Historically, terrorist organizations displayed an organized, hierarchical approach to organization and operation. This approach allows for a top-down direction normally led by an overall organization or individual. In a hierarchical approach, terrorist cells may be identified by five main categorizations all led by both an overall command cell and a smaller, more unit-specific column command. The smallest elements of terrorist organizations are the cells that serve as building blocks for the terrorist organization. One of the primary reasons for a cellular or compartmentalized structure is security. The compromise or loss of one cell should not compromise the identity, location, or actions of the other cells.

A cellular organizational structure makes it difficult for an adversary to penetrate the entire organization. Personnel within one cell are often unaware of the existence of other cells and, therefore, cannot divulge sensitive information to infiltrators. With the face of modern terrorism changing from an organized group with a discernible leader to a more ideological approach undertaken by inspired followers, so does the operational structure change. Although the hierarchical approach is still in place today in a more fragmented fashion, the groups or individuals are using more of a networked approach connected not so much in a linear way but in a less tangible and indirect manner. There may still be a command cell or an individual or group dictating actions of followers, but the line of communication is not direct. Very often, current groups are self-organized—leading to single-actor or small-group "lone wolf" operations—without any direction other than the ideology itself.

5

Terrorist Planning, Surveillance, Targeting, and Operations[1]

At its most rudimentary level, conducting a terrorist operation consists of following a generically created, yet ultimately effective, cycle. This cycle is known as the terrorist attack cycle and has been analyzed and reworked by countless counterterrorism officials since the inception of the threat. Although some discuss the possibility of it consisting of six steps and others, four, the reality is that at the cycle's core lies a very general yet germane set of actions that are required to launch and accomplish an effective attack. Thus, an essential element in counterterrorism is understanding this cycle. Doing so helps officials better prepare, respond, and possibly interdict the next terrorist attack.

Successful terrorist operations are seldom self-contained undertakings. This holds true for large international terrorist groups that leave a much longer logistics trail and for so-called "lone wolves" who act alone or within a very limited circle of witting or unwitting accomplices. Even lone wolves are not free from the burden of applying the tools of their trade. Very few individuals have the requisite technical, physical, financial, and logistical skills to mount an operation without reaching out to like-minded individuals or sympathizers for assistance. In the age in which we live, considerable assistance can, of course, be gleaned online. Nonetheless, surfing the Internet for information can take one only so far, and it carries with it its own set of perils and vulnerabilities. Furthermore, at some point, this online knowledge and technical skills must be translated into real-world applications and actions.

In looking at individual terrorist operations, sometimes officials exhibit a bit of myopia in that they tend to think that any method of attack that does not follow the pattern of recent attacks must be new. A closer look, however, reveals a set of recurring themes. And although the methods of attack are constantly being refined in an attempt to adapt to existing security countermeasures, the terrorists' basic repertoire remains pretty much fixed.

For example, the November 2008 attacks in Mumbai, India, were carried out by individuals highly trained in light infantry tactics and equipped with assault rifles, grenades, and relatively small explosive charges. Such tactics had been discarded in recent times in favor of large-scale, mass-casualty attacks, but they can be traced back to the very beginnings of the current wave of terrorism that dates at least from the second half of the 20th century. Although the Mumbai attackers took advantage of some newly available commercial

[1] Information for this chapter was drawn from the following titles: (1) M. W. Nance, *Terrorist Recognition Handbook: A Practitioner's Manual for Predicting and Identifying Terrorist Activities*, Second Edition, CRC Press, 2008. (2) R. McPartland, Terrorist tradecraft I: The attack cycle. In M. J. Fagel (ed.), *Principles of Emergency Management: Hazard Specific Issues and Mitigation Strategies*, CRC Press, 2011.

technologies—global positioning systems, voice-over Internet protocol, personal data assistants, etc.—the basic tactics they used were not all that different from those used by members of the Japanese Red Army in an attack in May 1972 on Tel Aviv's Lod Airport. In this attack, the perpetrators hid their assault rifles with removable stocks in violin cases and, upon entering the airport, removed the weapons from the cases, assembled them, and started firing indiscriminately, ultimately killing 26 people. This same scenario was reprised more than 13 years later, when on December 27, 1985, the Abu Nidal group, using Libyan-supplied assault rifles and grenades, launched virtually simultaneous attacks on the El Al and TWA ticket counters in Rome's Leonardo da Vinci–Fiumicino Airport and on passengers waiting to board a flight to Tel Aviv at Vienna's Schwechat Airport. It was even reported that the Abu Nidal attackers were doped on amphetamines, mirroring similar reports about the Mumbai attackers. The cycle replicates itself because it works and is effective. A terrorist group will continue to do what is effective and deemed accomplishable.

Aside from understanding the cycle and all its phases, counterterrorism officials must also be cognizant of the motivation and goals of the terrorist or extremist. Although ideologies differ between various terrorist groups, their motivation and goals need to be examined at an elementary level. Knowing what the attack planners set out to accomplish helps in determining their next target location, target group, and potential method of attack. Before one can begin looking at specific plot mechanics, it is important to recognize why a terrorist group, or possibly a single extremist, is motivated to undertake such a planned yet despicable act. It is also critical to understand basic cell structure and operational parameters of a terrorist group as well as the terrorist attack cycle itself.

The Terrorist Attack Cycle

The way in which a single terrorist or terrorist group plans for and executes an attack is known as the "terrorist attack cycle." The cycle is a predetermined group of steps undertaken before, during, and possibly after the event that, if followed properly, can lead to a successful operation. The necessity to understand and recognize the terrorist attack cycle is no longer limited to members of the intelligence community (IC). Today, members from other fields, law enforcement, and emergency responders, among others, need to know the way in which an attack is planned and executed in order to better mitigate, prepare for, and respond to a terrorist attack.

Contrary to popular belief, the execution of a terrorist attack is not random. Rather, there is a process that can be generically applied to all terrorist attacks, regardless of their scope. Attacks are often meticulously planned with inception to delivery times ranging from six months to years. The planning is often segmented, and each phase is often carried out by separate individuals allowing for maximum operational security. Overall, operational planners of the attack look to exploit their adversary's weaknesses while avoiding all their strengths, often leading to the selection of "soft targets" or those areas, locations, or people, carrying a weak security profile.

The cycle consists of five stages, each with its own unique set of requirements, and is normally carried out by specific member(s) of the overall terrorist cell. Not all phases are necessary for every mission. All is dependent on the overall goal of the attackers. For example, not all events require an escape plan. A case in point is attacks that involve suicide bombings. Depending on the size of the group and the complexity of the operation, the cycle itself is scalable and will often appropriately match the planner's level of experience, expertise, and resources. The five general phases are normally allotted time constraints and often come with organizational limitations (Figure 5.1). Understanding this cycle and nuances within it is critical in any discipline to know and understand in order to better prepare for and mitigate against this threat.

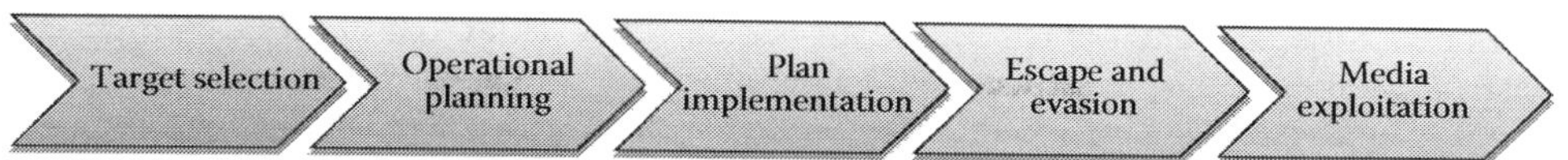

Figure 5.1 Five phases of the terrorist attack cycle. (From M. J. Fagel (ed.), *Principles of Emergency Management: Hazard Specific Issues and Mitigation Strategies*, CRC Press, 2011; R. McPartland, *Terrorist Tradecraft I: The Attack Cycle*. With permission.)

Phase I: Target Selection

Considering that most targets of terrorism tend to be utilities of public use (e.g., hotels, office buildings, shopping areas), the targeting aspect of the cycle is usually not easily predicted. Terrorists tend to overlay their own ideology with specific goals in order to choose the target that best suits their message. They often look to targets of symbolic value or those that can garner the most media attention and then combine it with a consideration for specific target groups in order to increase the impact of the attack and possibly avoid collateral damage.

They tend to avoid "hard targets" or those locations, people, or areas with a higher, more reinforced level of security. The softer targets consisting of civilian populations and civilian infrastructure will often result in a more successful mission and a higher number of casualties and deaths. This intended result, coupled with the impact both psychologically and financially on the targeted population, makes the choice of choosing a softer target much more enticing.

During the *Target Selection Phase*, operatives' research as much about the potential target as possible. The depth and detail of the collection depends on the terrorists' resources and the overall scope of the operation. Oftentimes, there might be multiple collection processes placed in motion to look at multiple potential targets at once in order to prioritize and have various options to consider.

Historically, target research was conducted on-site by operatives using average collection methods, such as videotaping, taking photographs, and simply writing down notes about a particular area. Today, however, the methods used to collect information are different and more remote. The reason for this is twofold. First, with the invention and overall depth of the Internet, operatives need not physically see a location in order to collect the majority of all information needed. Through remote portals, such as live street and traffic cameras, and typographical sites, such as Google Earth, selection members are allowed to collect necessary information remotely and from the safety of their own living rooms. The second reason is the increased law enforcement awareness and the greater likelihood of discovery. Using the Internet and more remote methods of information collection is not only the easier method but is also a necessity.

Law enforcement agencies are more aware of the information collection methods of terrorists. Many are trained to look for signs of preoperational surveillance and security probing. Preoperational surveillance involves the collection of information through various means conducted over a certain period of time before commencement of the operation whereas security probing is when operatives test current security methods or procedures through legal means, such as turning doorknobs of possibly unlocked doors or asking sensitive questions of assigned security personnel.

Target selection is the beginning of the planning cycle and is the first in a series of steps in the pre-incident phase of the actual attack. Understanding the methods makes interdiction of terrorism possible. The next phase is terrorists' operational planning and preparation.

Phase II: Operational Planning and Preparation

After the selection of the target is completed, the operation and method of the attack becomes the next issue. Terrorist attacks often require meticulous planning and preparation. Historically, this is done by a separate cell's member(s), but as of late, given that many of the potential attacks domestically have come from radicalized, homegrown extremists, the function of planning may originate from those that conducted the original surveillance and selection.

During the selection process, through the use of on-site or remote surveillance, operatives have not only found a suitable target but also the possible "Achilles heel" of the said target. Pinpointing possible weak areas in security or even the physical façade itself allows the planners to then formulate an attack plan and decide upon an effective method. The planning process involves multiple steps including the following:

- Conducting additional surveillance on the target location
- Selection of an attack method and possible weapon to use
- Careful consideration of funding issues and personnel needed
- Gathering of materials and weapons and possibly building the device
- Selection and formation of an attack team
- Rehearsals or dry runs of the attack to finalize the decided-upon method

Terrorist Preparations: Tactics, Safe Houses, and Supplies

Tactic Selection

There are several different types of attacks that terrorists can engage in, such as explosive bombings, arson, assassinations, light infantry weapons attack, armed raids, abduction, barricades, human guided weapon attack, aviation attack, maritime attack, vehicle commandeering and theft, industrial and infrastructure attack, and physical intimidation and maiming.

Explosive Bombing Attack

The explosive bombing is the most widely used type of terrorist tactic. Explosive bombings are used in most terrorist attacks. The reason is that characteristics of bombs are favorable to creating the highest impact. Explosive bombings are recognized as being universally available and cheap; featuring multiple, easy delivery methods; being highly concealable; and offering outstanding destruction-to-weight ratio. There are three types of explosive bombings that terrorists can engage in: manual bombings, standoff bombings, and vehicle bombings. The first type, manual bombings, are those bombs that are placed by hand, and they include the following:

- *Drop bombing*: A bomb left or dropped off at a location
- *Toss*: A bomb tossed at a target
- *Drive-by*: A bomb tossed from a moving vehicle
- *Courier delivered*: A bomb given to a second person who knows the device is a bomb and delivers it to the target
- *Surrogate delivered*: A bomb given to a person who does not know it is a bomb and unknowingly carries it to the target
- *Remotely detonated*: A bomb detonated by electronic control from a distance away
- *Victim activated*: A bomb that explodes when the victim starts a vehicle or trips a detonation device
- *Planted or landmine*: A bomb placed on a roadside or under a roadway that explodes when a victim steps on it or rolls over it

The second type, a standoff bombing, involves bombs that are launched from a distance. These include the following:

- *Shoulder launched*: A bomb is shot from a rocket launcher that must be mounted on the shoulder of a terrorist.
- *System launched*: A bomb is fired from a system, such as a mortar, vehicle-mounted rocket launcher, or other improvised device, that shoots it a great distance.

The third type is vehicle bombings. These bombs are attached to or target a vehicle or are the weapon itself. Some forms of vehicle bombings include the following:

- *Planted device or landmine*: A bomb is deliberately placed on or under a vehicle.
- *Booby-trapped on site*: A vehicle has a bomb attached to the chassis while it is at the victim's residence or office.
- *Booby-trapped off site*: A vehicle is turned into a bomb after the car is taken away by the terrorist, modified, and returned without the victim knowing it.
- *Remotely detonated*: A bomb is detonated from a distance, usually electronically.
- *Victim activated*: A car bomb explodes when the victim starts the vehicle, moves it, or sits in it.

Arson

Arson is the simplest form of terrorism. It can be done by the most junior member of an organization. Arson can occur by setting fire to a building, gas station, ammunition dump, oil, fertilizer or grain storage facility, petroleum refinery, or a ship transporting flammable liquids. All of these tactics can be effective weapons of mass destruction. If carried out correctly, it could be very difficult to trace the act to a terrorist group. Arson can be committed as follows:

- *Arson by hand*: This is the initiation of a fire by hand with a lighter, matches, and/or accelerants, such as gasoline and other fuels.
- *Device-initiated arson*: A mechanical explosive device is filled with an accelerant that creates and spreads a fire. Many are designed by professional arsonists. Samples of arson devices have been posted on the Internet by the Earth Liberation Front to encourage the use of arson in its cause by active supporters.
- *Device-activated fire attack*: Purpose-built devices, such as Molotov cocktails, white phosphorus incendiary grenades, magnesium destruction devices, and more.
- *Vehicle-carried fire attack*: Flame grenades, incendiary mortar launchers, or flame-throwers mounted on a vehicle chassis.

Assassination

Assassination is the tactic used to selectively eliminate a specific enemy of a terrorist group. Assassination may use techniques associated with other terrorist tactics (such as an explosives bombing or light infantry weapons attack) because the target is usually one or a small group of important people. The selectivity of the target makes assassination its own special tactic.

- *Blade assassination*: This technique was the primary terrorist assassination technique for centuries until the firearm came along. Sharp objects, such as knives, daggers, swords, and other piercing equipment, are used.
- *Poison assassination*: Poisoning is an ancient technique of introducing a toxin into a victim until it cannot be counteracted. In 1978, Bulgarian intelligence killed Georgi Markov, a Bulgarian defector, with an umbrella tipped with the toxin Ricin,

an extract of the castor bean. Al-Qaeda was known to experiment with toxins in Afghanistan and may have succeeded in turning them into weapons of mass destruction as opposed to personal assassination weapons.

- *Blunt-force assassination*: Another time-tested technique is beating the victim to death with the hands or a blunt object.
- *Hanging or garrote assassination*: A silent killing technique, strangulation by rope has been used in every period of history as a terrorist weapon. In modern terrorism, it is usually reserved for the execution of a victim already in captivity, execution of traitors, and on-the-spot assassinations. Kidnapped US Marine Lieutenant Colonel William Higgins was shown to have been hanged by the Hezbollah terrorist group although evidence reveals he may have died from torture.
- *Firearm assassination*: Usually a small-caliber pistol is used in a firearms assassination: The killer steps behind or in front of the victim and kills with one clean shot to the head or multiple shots to the body. In 1987, four American service members were assassinated by the Filipino New People's Army "Sparrow" assassination squads in this exact manner.
- *Sniper assassination*: The use of high-caliber, bolt-action or magazine-fed, purpose-built sniper rifles or accuratized military or hunting rifles to kill a victim.
- *Explosives assassination*: The use of commercial, homemade, or improvised explosives to kill a victim with bombs delivered by booby trap, landmines, rockets, a suicide bomber, or another direct method that hits the target, usually while stopped.
- *Drive-by vehicle assassination*: The spraying of a large quantity of bullets from an automatic rifle, submachine gun, or pistol when driving by the target in a vehicle.
- *Light infantry weapons assassination*: A surprise attack from a hidden place that combines a team of people using the full firepower of bombs, rifles, machine guns, and/or rockets to kill a victim and neutralize bodyguards.
- *Explosives ambush assassination*: A surprise bomb attack on the route the victim takes, exploding a device left on or near the road.

Light Infantry Weapons Attack

Light infantry weapons assault (LIWA) takes place when a small terrorist unit or cell assaults a target with light military weapons and explosives, such as assault rifles, hand grenades, and shoulder-launched rockets. These attacks reach for success by laying down a large volume of concentrated firepower. The effectiveness of a LIWA is the training that the terrorist cell has prior to the assault. Many terrorist groups create professional and well-trained infantry soldiers highly capable of conducting a LIWA. Some terrorist groups, such as Hezbollah in Lebanon, have superb ground combat capability comparable to our Special Operations Forces. LIWAs with small arms and mortars by terrorist groups and paramilitaries drove the well-trained Israeli army out of Lebanon with numerous and increasingly effective assaults. All land warfare weapons and attacks can be used against airbases, ships, piers, and facilities.

The typical LIWA attack may take one of two forms: an assault or an ambush. A LIWA is a concentrated, highly dynamic infantry-style attack on a target or victim. The assaulters in the terrorist cell will generally focus on either seizing and holding their target or just destroying and killing its occupants. In December 2001, a Pakistani-backed terrorist team stormed the Indian Parliament with a LIWA team and killed more than 35 people. By contrast, a LIWA ambush is a weapons ambush that can be done with assault rifles, anti-tank rockets, surface-to-air missiles, or explosives. The target can be anything or anyone. It will be unexpected, intense, fast, and extremely violent in execution. It is generally designed to kill the victims or neutralize security forces. The difference between the LIWA ambush and a weapons assassination (LIWA/combined arms) is that the LIWA is a full-scale attack in which heavy volumes of fire are applied, as in a war, versus a precise single shot—although the result may be the same.

Armed Raid

Raids are military-style operations conducted generally to destroy a facility, seize weapons, or rob banks. They are often popular tactics for new groups and wannabe guerrillas who need to demonstrate a limited operations capability or experienced groups that want to seize high-value targets for short periods. In a highly videotaped shootout in North Hollywood on February 28, 1997, two masked gunmen with several fully automatic assault rifles tried to rob a bank. The event led to large-volume gunplay between the police and the robbers with the civilian population caught in between. Though not an act of terrorism, this typifies the armed terrorist raids prevalent in Latin America and Asia.

- *Weapons seizure raid*: Amateur terrorists conduct armed raids on government armories, police stations, police outposts, or commercial gun shops to acquire guns, explosives, and ammunition.
- *Money seizure raid (bank robbery, etc.)*: Gunmen conduct robberies to acquire the funds necessary to pay active cadres and fund future terrorist attacks.
- *Destruction of garrison/personnel raid*: This raid is designed to completely destroy the buildings, equipment, and people at a government facility. In 2002, the government of Nepal suffered more than 500 soldiers, police, and civilians killed in garrison raids by communist terrorists.
- *Decoy/feint raid*: The decoy/feint is conducted to draw police and law enforcement away from the actual intended target. Each attack a terrorist carries out should be evaluated as a potential decoy/feint. Police should stand by for a secondary attack.

Abduction (Kidnapping, Hostage Taking)

Victims of abduction are often kidnapped by terrorists for cash ransoms to fund other terrorist activity or held hostage to gain political leverage over governments or to make a victim give them access to a secure facility. Kidnappers use many different techniques. Most victims are held by a special guard cell for as long as the negotiations continue. They are usually kept in poor conditions over a time span that may last from a few hours to several years. There are several different types of abductions:

- *Ruse abduction*: The use of police, military, or another false pretense to get the victim to comply with the abductor until it is clear that it is an abduction.
- *On-foot or on-street abduction*: Abduction occurs on the street, usually on foot, in a spot where the victim has been led or that is part of a victim's set routine, which the terrorist has discovered by surveillance.
- *Home-invasion or surreptitious-entry abduction*: Terrorists sometimes deliberately storm a residence and take hostages away. This is a home invasion. A surreptitious entry is when a terrorist stealthily enters a residence and quietly abducts the victim before anyone realizes the victim is gone.
- *Vehicle-stop abduction*: When victims are on the road, it is absolutely necessary for terrorists to stop the vehicle to conduct the abduction. The stop can be done via ruse, such as a false police roadblock or creating an accident. The Red Army Faction pushed an empty baby carriage into the path of an abduction victim to force his convoy to stop suddenly.
- *Site abduction*: Terrorists conducting attacks on corporate work sites, remote infrastructure, and critical facilities may require a large force. In December 2000, the

FARC of Colombia conducted a site raid in neighboring Ecuador seizing 10 Western oil workers and a corporate helicopter.

- *Mass abduction*: An unusual tactic is the abduction of dozens, hundreds, or sometimes thousands of hostages without a barricade situation. In 1995 and 2002, the Chechen Muslim rebels who later became the al-Qaeda–supported Islamic Army of the Caucasus conducted three mass abductions with thousands of hostages in Russia. They twice used them as human shields until they could escape. The ELN and FARC of Colombia have also conducted mass abductions of lesser numbers, but they kept most of these victims as hostages until the ransoms were paid.

Barricade or Hostage Barricade

Terrorists on a raid may seize, then barricade themselves in a facility to gain attention. They generally take hostages and may execute some of them to press their demands. This type of situation requires professional hostage negotiators and immediate containment by a competent security force. This is a common and dramatic tactic to confront a government with the fact that terrorists have seized a facility and taken hostages. At this point, the terrorists usually make grandiose statements before the news media. Hostage barricades can last for months. In the 1970s, most hostage barricades ended in favor of the terrorists. When the 1996 hostage barricade at the Japanese embassy in Lima, Peru, occurred, most nations learned to end these barricades with deadly offensive action. There are also terrorist barricades that do not have hostages. Here, terrorists seize a facility to demonstrate they have the power to do it but take no hostages. They may raise political banners, make demands, and engage in a suicide battle with police or law enforcement if they feel the demonstration has no further use.

Human-Guided (Suicide/Martyr) Weapon Attack

This is the most feared and rapidly expanding form of terrorism worldwide. There are two forms of human-guided (HG) weapon attack: the suicide attack and the martyrdom attack. The phrase "suicide attack" can refer to both types. The recent use of the phrase "homicide attack" is inaccurate because it reflects the result rather than the tactics. Any fatal terrorist attack can be a homicide attack. A suicide attack is a nonreligious, politically motivated terrorist attack whose operatives understand that there is little to no possibility of escape; the terrorists are prepared to die or will kill themselves at the end of the attack, or a terrorist's body is the explosive device's guidance system. This may include making plans to commit suicide before capture or fighting until killed.

The martyrdom attack is a technique that is used by religious extremist terrorists who believe that they will attain a special place in their next life or "heaven" if they die while killing their enemies. This attack is guided and delivered by a human being who has absolutely no intention of returning from the mission alive. In fact, returning alive may be a disgrace. In September 1999, a 39-year-old man, tacitly associated with the Egyptian Muslim Brotherhood, attacked President Mubarak with a knife, knowing full well that US Secret Service–trained bodyguards would gun him down. He did it with little planning, saw an opportunity to commit martyrdom, and died in the attempt. Some HG suicide/martyrdom tactics include the following:

- *HG suicide/martyrdom explosives–manual delivery*: The delivery of an explosive device carried in a bag or wrapped around the body of a bomber. The bomber will blow up with the device.
- *HG suicide/martyrdom bomb–vehicle delivery, land* (aka suicide car bomb or truck bomb): This is an attack using a car or truck driven into or near the victim by a terrorist operative who explodes the bomb, killing the driver and destroying the target. Between 1983 and 2002, numerous suicide car bombs were launched against American embassies in the Middle East and Africa, killing more than 400 people.

- *Vehicle delivery, maritime*: The LTTE and al-Qaeda use small high-speed boats as floating human-guided bombs that explode once they reach their target. The October 2000 attack on the American destroyer USS Cole (DDG-67) in Yemen was a classic example of maritime martyrdom bombing. The Sri Lankan LTTE may be the world master of maritime suicide attacks: It has destroyed dozens of Sri Lankan navy ships with high-speed explosive boats driven by the "Sea Tigers."
- *Vehicle delivery, skyjacking/aircraft as weapons system*: This tactic involves the use of an aircraft as a human-guided explosive device or improvised cruise missile. In 1973, Israeli Air Force fighters shot down a Libyan Airlines 727, Flight LN 114, over Sinai, believing it was a terrorist-hijacked aircraft preparing to crash into Tel Aviv. It was, in fact, lost in a sandstorm and suffering a navigational error. All 113 passengers aboard were killed. In December 1994, Algerian Islamic extremists hijacked an Air France flight from Algiers to Marseille. Intelligence gained on the ground revealed that the aircraft was refueling to fly to Paris with the aim of blowing up the plane over Paris or crashing it into the Eiffel Tower. While the plane was being refueled, French GIGN commandos then stormed the aircraft and killed the hijackers. The September 11, 2001, skyjackings in America were the first successful use of this tactic in terrorism.
- *Light infantry weapons suicide/martyrdom attack*: This is a terrorist attack in which the attackers use military firearms and hand grenades against a knowingly hardened position in which death is almost guaranteed. In June 2002, Palestinian Islamic Jihad operatives started a wave of successful two- and three-person martyrdom attacks on Israeli settlements in the face of overwhelming firepower. The attackers are invariably killed after they have killed as many victims as possible. On July 4, 2002, an Egyptian gunman conducted an armed attack on an El Al ticket counter at the Los Angeles International Airport. He fired from two weapons and then used a knife, trying to kill as many Israelis as possible until gunned down by El Al security officers.

Aviation Attacks

Aviation attacks are planned missions attacking passengers, aircraft, airports, or air facilities of the victim society. The most common type of aviation attacks are skyjackings and in-flight bombings. The skyjacking of an aircraft creates a mobile hostage barricade. The skyjackers seize the aircraft for ransom of the passengers or as a human-guided weapon system. This type of operation can take place in flight or on the ground. Extortion and violent intimidation are used in an effort to have the skyjackers' demands met. Often victims are paraded and executed before the news cameras. During the 1970s, some aircraft were symbolically blown up for television at the end of the operation. If the aircraft is disabled or forced to remain on the ground, the operation becomes identical to a hostage barricade.

In-flight bombings have also occurred. These attacks have been numerous and have killed thousands since the first in-flight bombing in 1949. The 1985 Air India 747 bombing destroyed the aircraft over the Atlantic Ocean, killing 329 passengers. The bomb was placed in checked baggage by a passenger who never boarded the flight. This was proven when another bag checked by the same Sikh terrorist exploded at Narita Airport in Japan. It was destined for another Air India 747. The 1989 bombings of Pan Am Flight 103 over Lockerbie, Scotland, and UTA Flight 772 over the Tenere Desert in Chad were carried out by three Libyan intelligence agents who never boarded the aircraft and an agent who got off at an intermediate stop. All of these bombings occurred when the passenger who checked the bags never boarded the flight—a key clue. The 1993 World Trade Center bomber Ramzi Yusef was convicted of plotting to simultaneously blow up 12 airlines over the Pacific Ocean using bombs placed under seats. A different technique was used by the so-called al-Qaeda–associated "Shoe Bomber" Richard Reid, who attempted to light a fuse linked to explosives hidden in his shoe. An explosion of this sort over the main fuel tank would have blown up the aircraft over the Atlantic.

On-ground bombings of airplanes have occurred as well. In Rome on December 17, 1973, Palestinian terrorists rushed through the airport gate security area, shooting. They then stormed the passenger area firing machine guns, and paused only to throw an incendiary bomb onto a loaded American Airlines 707. The explosion and fire killed all of the 29 people aboard and destroyed the aircraft. The terrorists continued the attack by skyjacking a Lufthansa airliner and later escaped. In other incidents, bombs that were to have exploded in the air have blown up instead on the ground. In 1986, such a bomb exploded in Sri Lanka while an airliner was taxiing, killing 16 passengers and wounding 41.

Additionally, small-arms, ground-to-air attacks have occurred. Armed gunmen with machine guns and rifles have attacked aircraft while taxiing on the ground for takeoff with the intent to damage or blow up the aircraft's full fuel tanks. One such incident occurred in Zurich, Switzerland, in 1969 when gunmen behind the perimeter fence fired AK-47 rifles on El Al Flight 432. The attack was stopped when an Israeli air marshal jumped off the plane and opened fire on the terrorists. Moreover, terrorists have engaged in rocket or missile ground-to-air attacks (MANPAD/SAM). A rare attack is the use of an unguided rocket, such as an American M-72 light anti-armor weapon (LAAW) or Russian-built RPG-7 rocket launcher, to blow up an airliner on the ground. In April 1985, a terrorist fired a Russian RPG-7 rocket at a taxiing Jordanian airliner. The rocket struck the aircraft but failed to explode. A successful attack could have been catastrophic had the rocket hit the fuel tanks.

Furthermore, terrorists have engaged in MAN portable air defense (MANPAD) missile (aka surface-to-air missile or SAM) attacks. In this attack, terrorists employ a sophisticated missile designed to shoot down aircraft and helicopters by damaging the engines and starting a fire. More than 30 incidents of the use of MANPAD missiles have been documented since 1970, killing well over 400 passengers. Many of the attacks were in sub-Saharan Africa (Angola). In 1973, five terrorists were arrested in Rome with two missiles as they prepared to shoot down an Israeli airliner. In 2002, an al-Qaeda–owned SA-7 missile missed a US Air Force E-3 Sentry aircraft taking off from an airbase in Saudi Arabia. On November 28, 2003, al-Qaeda terrorists fired two SA-7 missiles at an Israeli airliner taking off from the Mombasa, Kenya, International Airport. Both missiles missed.

Maritime Attacks

Maritime terrorism first evokes the image of piracy at sea. This is a common crime, but the seas have been increasingly a location for terrorism. There are many examples of terrorists seizing vessels and using them later as suicide platforms. They have abducted crews from oil platforms and dive boats with tourists as well as hijacking arms shipments to be used in later operations.

Terrorists also run shipping companies to legally generate funds. Vessels can be pirated (carjacked) to act as floating weapons of mass destruction that can ram vessels or be used to create explosive devices. Flammable fuel carriers, such as oil tankers, natural gas carriers, or even grain transporting ships, are subject to seizure and detonation without authorities knowing until the last moment.

A common tactic of maritime terrorists is to engage in an amphibious assault. Terrorists use small craft to come ashore and make direct armed assaults on targets. Terrorist commando groups have conducted amphibious assaults using small rubber boats, such as the Zodiac, to land ashore and infiltrate or attack a nation's shores. In the 1970s and 1980s, Israeli forces stopped Palestinian amphibious commando raids along the Israeli coast. Zodiac rubber raiding craft were launched from merchant vessels (mother ships) in the eastern Mediterranean Sea and were to motor ashore. In a March 1978 raid, 11 Palestinian terrorists landed on a Haifa beach, killed an American citizen, and hijacked a passenger bus. The subsequent rescue attempt by the army killed 25 passengers and nine terrorists. Seventy other civilians were wounded.

Terrorists have also been known to engage in a light infantry weapons assault from shore. This is a simple attack that could be effective against poorly guarded gates and perimeters near ships or ports. In July 1988, terrorists from the Abu Nidal Organization conducted a LIWA attack by storming the pier at the port of Piraeus after a car bomb, designed to breach the security perimeter, prematurely detonated. Two of the assault teams were killed in this explosion. The remainder of the cell seized the passenger ship City of Poros. The terrorists sprayed the passengers with machine-gun and rocket fire, killing nine and wounding 98. A further maritime attack by terrorists involved their using the vessel as a weapon. As mentioned earlier, this tactic was used in the 2000 USS Cole bombing.

Vehicle Commandeering (Hijacking) and Theft

Truck or car hijackings can provide terrorists a surveillance platform, an infiltration vehicle, an explosives weapons platform, a weapon of mass destruction (with chemicals or fuels), a sniper hide, a mortar carrier, an anti-aircraft gun mount, a resupply vehicle, an escape transport, or a lucrative source of financing.

- *Highjacking for weapons system*: A vehicle is stolen or hijacked to be converted into a bomb or other weapons platform.
- *Escape platform hijacking*: A vehicle is stolen specifically to transport the terrorist group to and from the attack site.
- *Transportation hijacking*: The vehicle is stolen to move people, equipment, or hostages to and from safe locations.

Industrial and Infrastructure Attack

Industrial and infrastructure attack includes conventional weapons, plausible accidents, or improvised devices used to destroy chemical plants, petroleum refineries, electrical grids, road systems, rails, or bridges or to block transportation. Domestic terrorists use this strategy often to bring pressure onto a government through the discomfort of the people. The terrorist group may decide to knock out large segments of services that a government provides to the public to demonstrate to the people that they cannot gain comfort or be protected in the most basic acts, such as driving safely on the highway, or be provided with consistent power and water supplies, fuel or oil revenues, or uninterrupted communications.

Groups could also attack infrastructure to cause a release or activation of a weapon of mass destruction. For example, four members of the True Knights of the Ku Klux Klan were convicted of planning an armored car robbery in Wise County, Texas, but intended to explode diversionary bombs at a natural gas processing/storage facility to cover the robbery. They believed the facility contained lethal gases that could create a disaster.

Physical Intimidation or Maiming

Terrorists often use maiming to express a point related to loyalty within the organization or to punish uncooperative civilians. Victims may be beaten or maimed instead of assassinated by terrorist supporters as a symbolic gesture. These types of attacks may yield intelligence about operatives in the country, because they may come into contact with the police and hospital systems. Officers may learn good information from maimed terrorists or supporters about other members of the terrorist group.

Safe Houses

The safe house is one of the key nodes of terrorist operations. A detected and seized safe house may compromise cells, plans, and materials to be used in an attack. A safe house may be detected by informants, by suspicious neighbors, or through activities of surveillance teams. Virtually every terrorist group has a series of safe houses used as bomb factories, supply centers, or weapons armories. The location of a safe house gives an indication as to the kind of mission with which it is connected.

A safe house is a secure location where a terrorist can prepare for or recover from operations. A safe house may also be used as a command and control center, a planning room, and a briefing room as well. If a safe house is a planning center, it may include the following:

- Intelligence cell planning board
- Surveillance board with photos of targets
- Watch assignment board
- Map wall
- Mock-up tabletop or sand models
- Videotape for propaganda and rehearsal

In 2000, for example, the New Zealand authorities arrested five Afghan refugees for planning a terrorist attack on Sydney, Australia's Lucas Heights nuclear power plant. Their safe house in Auckland, New Zealand, was a full command center with a conference room, marked-up map boards, planning materials, and a photo board of entries and exits at the nuclear plant. In another case, a joint Pakistan Inter-Services Intelligence (ISI)/Central Intelligence Agency (CIA) raid in February 2003 netted Khalid Sheik Mohammed, a senior al-Qaeda leader. His safe house included computers, plans, and address books of al-Qaeda associates.

A major use of the terrorist safe house is as a weapons armory. Armory raids could yield exact plans of attack and deprive the tactical operations cell's equipment for the mission. The type of attack can generally be determined through the weapons and equipment found in the safe house. For example, the German government carried out a series of counterterror raids in 1988 called Operation Autumn Leaves, discovering a terrorist supply center in Frankfurt full of Yugoslavian AK-47 rifles, grenades, 14 blocks of dynamite, six sticks of TNT, and 12 pounds of Semtex plastic explosives. This raid also unearthed intelligence that led to further raids on other safe houses and a car in which a Toshiba model 453 radio was found that turned out to be an altimeter-equipped bomb identical to the one that blew up Pan Am Flight 103 over Scotland.

Furthermore, secure terrorist safe houses may burrow into the ground and create a large weapons storage bunker. In May 1993, a terrorist weapons bunker exploded in a suburb of Managua, Nicaragua. It turned out to be a way station for many different terrorist groups supported by the Sandinista Liberation Front. Tons of explosives and hundreds of assault rifles, machine guns, RPG-7 rockets, and launchers were found. It also included hundreds of real-name and false passports. Surprisingly, two of the valid identification documents were of Canadian citizens Christine Lamont and David Spencer, who were captured in Brazil in 1989 for the terrorist abduction of the supermarket billionaire Albilio Diniz.

Detection of Terrorist Supply Chains: Terrorist Supply Is an Indicator of Future Activity

No matter what operation terrorists select, they will always need supplies. The detection of the supply chain can lead directly to cells and planned missions. Small amateur terrorist groups and individuals can buy commercial chemicals to make homemade explosives or buy commercial weapons, such as hunting rifles, pistols, or shotguns, and make firebombs, propane tank mortars, and improvised chemical gases from pool supplies.

Residences and lodges can be used as temporary laboratories, storage facilities, and safe houses. As terrorists and/or terrorist groups grow in sophistication, they require more extensive logistics support, financing, and administration. Some groups, such as the Irish Republican Army (IRA), al-Fatah, or the Kurdistan Workers Party, have an entire supply bureaucracy supporting them. No matter the size of operation, tracking suspicious legal and illegal supplies and supply sources can lead you directly to terrorist cells.

Terrorist organizations that have made a decision to strike a target or start the process of finding targets must supply the operatives tasked with the mission with finances and supplies. Irrespective of the level of operation or the number of people involved, terrorists will have various needs. For example, for safe houses, these needs are rent, food, electricity, cable television (possibly for intelligence collection), and storage. To activate and sustain this type of support, terrorists need an identity and banking services. Intelligence and law enforcement agencies may be able to detect this type of support by finding discrepancies between who pays the rent or utilities and who actually lives in the safe house.

Terrorist Methods of Acquiring Supplies

Terrorists can legally and illegally acquire supplies. On the one hand, terrorists may use themselves or supporters to acquire materials and supplies legally on the open market. On the other hand, terrorists may steal the equipment they need themselves or purchase it on the black market. Specifically, terrorists may use low-level criminal methods, such as robbery or theft, as a way to acquire equipment, systems, and weapons or their components. They may also use highly involved and developed criminal pathways, pipelines, and institutions to covertly acquire material. This includes international gun smuggling, illicit commercial transactions, and false bank transfers.

Terrorist logistics at a local level are generally legal, but underworld criminals are extensively used, too. It is this contact with the underworld and the strange pattern it creates of legal and criminal activity that make terrorist logistics cells detectable. To detect such terrorist logistical cell activity, authorities canvass criminal and public informants. These authorities seek out informants and check for tips and reports that will yield terrorist attack pre-incident indicators, such as unusual illegal weapons purchases without any paperwork (or bribes given to forge paperwork), and/or by unusual pathways: unusual purchase of legal products. There could be multiple purchases of these explosives precursors and unusual payments: The suspect purchases guns, supplies, or components with large quantities of cash, electronic fund transfers from new checking accounts, money orders, multiple Western Union transfers (instead of one single transfer), fake credit cards, and real credit cards that do not match the buyer.

Depending on the quality of the initial target-selection process, the planning phase can be done more secretly and oftentimes more remotely. The amount of work needed is entirely dependent on how well the target information was collected and processed. If the information is vague, incorrect, or incomplete, the planning team or lone wolf has no choice but to revisit the scene and begin the collection process again. Planning and preparation can take months to years to complete. The length of time depends on the size of the operation and the skill of the planners. Something on the magnitude of the September 11, 2001, attacks or the coordinated, armed assaults in Mumbai, India, in 2008 were elaborate, requiring various skill sets of the attack team members as well as an abundance of resources. Other smaller planned attacks may involve fewer people, less sophisticated skill sets, and minimal resources, allowing for a faster turnaround time from selection to planning completion.

Phase III: Plan Implementation

After carefully selecting the target and deciding upon the best method of attack, the third and most imminent part of the cycle is the *Implementation Phase* or the actual deployment of attack members and the attack itself. The last chance for interdiction by any member of the law enforcement community is during the implementation phase. During this phase, attack team members or lone wolves are mobilized from their respective safe houses and deployed to the attack area.

Transportation is a critical need of a terrorist group, offering speed to get to the target, insertion and extraction, or a firing platform. Terrorists, like criminals, prefer to use untraceable vehicles for their missions. Some may opt to rent vehicles. Vehicles are not limited to cars or trucks. Many groups are adept at using aircraft, boats, and movement on foot to carry out or support their operations. Some types of vehicles that have been used by terrorists are as follows:

1. *Getaway cars*: These vehicles are selected for the following factors, depending on the missions:
    a) *Size*: A small car may be desired for urban areas or car bombs. Large SUVs may be needed for off-road work.
    b) *Horsepower*: Terrorists will pick cars with the maximum available horsepower and may modify the engine to gain more than the car is rated.
    c) *Seating capacity*: A vehicle with substantial seating capacity may be needed for armed raids or missions that require more than four terrorists. In Latin America and Africa, terrorists use pickups as improvised personnel carriers during raids.
    d) *Intended purpose*: The mission will dictate the type of vehicle needed. An SUV may be needed as a large bomb. The PIRA uses vans as mobile sniper platforms for its large Barrett .50-caliber sniper rifles or as mortar carriers for its scuba tank mortar shells.
    e) *Availability*: How easily could a specific vehicle be stolen or hijacked? Can the vehicle be rented without being traced? These are the questions each group asks and plans for.
    f) *Armor*: Do terrorist leaders need to equip themselves to survive an ambush? For instance, the mission may entail having to go through a hailstorm of fire. In that case, terrorists may buy or steal a purpose-built bank armored car. Many Colombian and Mexican narco traffickers and their terrorist groups use armored vehicles similar to those used by government officials (e.g., Land Rovers and Mercedes).
2. *Motorcycles*: Terrorists may use motorcycles to conduct reconnaissance or as highly flexible assassination platforms. The FARC of Colombia and the Greek group November 17 have used two-person motorcycle attack teams to assassinate victims. Colombians prefer high-speed drive-by attacks with a small submachine gun, such as an Uzi. The Greek November 17 group used two riders with a .45-caliber pistol. The key to a motorcycle assassination profile may be that both riders wear full-face helmets.
3. *Recreational vehicles* (RVs): Special attention should be paid to these vehicles. The RV is a self-contained operations platform. Many police agencies use them for command centers, laboratories, and negotiation centers. Terrorists could also use RVs for a number of purposes, including the following:
    a) Mobile safe house
    b) Mobile attack coordination and command center
    c) Mobile armory and chemical-biological laboratory
    d) Mobile hostage jail
4. *Vans, buses, and trucks*: Special attention should be paid to these vehicles. The larger the vehicle the terrorist has, the greater the range of uses it could be put to. Panel vans, roll-back trucks, converted passenger buses, and commercial tractor-trailer trucks are perfect platforms for the following:
    a) Large-scale explosive devices
    b) Chemical weapons
    c) Long-range mobile sniper platforms
    d) Mortar carriers
    e) Personnel carriers

5. *Aviation and Flight Support*: Some terrorist groups, such as the Palestine Liberation Organization (PLO), the Revolutionary Armed Forces of Colombia (FARC), and al-Qaeda, have access to excellent air support, including small airplanes, executive jets, charter airplanes, and helicopters.

   a) *Private/personal aircraft*: Al-Qaeda had a T-39 Saberliner passenger jet to transport weapons and leadership from Pakistan to Sudan and Kenya. Furthermore, Osama bin Laden is alleged to have used executive jets supplied by private citizens of Saudi Arabia or the United Arab Emirates.

   b) *Specialized aircraft*: Crop dusters and helicopters are believed to have been sought by members of al-Qaeda for chemical or biological warfare dispersal systems. North Korean intelligence agencies use specialized small aircraft, such as the An-2 Colt and Hughes MD-500 "Little Bird" helicopters, to smuggle agents in and out of South Korea or for commandos to seize airfields.

   c) *Friendly airlines*: Terrorists often fly on airlines that are friendly to the philosophies of their leadership or accept their cash. Afghanistan's Ariana (before the Taliban was defeated), Iran Air, Libyan Arab Airlines, Syrian Airlines, and financially strapped sub-Saharan African airlines that are open to bribes can fly operatives to countries where it may be possible to transfer to a regular airline without suspicion being aroused.

   d) *Mercenary/corporate flight logistics*: Many contract airlines may actually be mercenary flight services. In the past, Russian, Yugoslavian, and Ukrainian flight companies were infamously known for flying anyone almost anywhere for a price.

6. *Maritime Transportation*: In many parts of the world, terrorists use the ocean as an excellent mode of infiltration and supply. Support vessels include the following:

   a) *Motor vessels*: Commercial merchant vessels have been used by terrorist groups worldwide to transport weapons and operatives and for suicide attacks. Members of the Tamil Tigers routinely lure patrol boats alongside only to blow up both ships. Some merchant vessels act as mother ships to carry smuggled supplies to small boats on enemy shores. This is actually quite an effective way of moving heavy materials and manpower.

   b) *Small craft/skiffs/Zodiac raiding craft*: Inflatable rubber boats or high-speed boats can be used to shuttle supplies and people to and from planned missions. The PLO, FARC, and Abu Sayyaf Group use small boats for resupply and for piracy or abduction.

   c) *Commercial maritime logistics*: Many legal transportation methods exist, including the lease or purchase of containers, sea-land cargo boxes, and even taking legal jobs on ships.

Interdiction by law enforcement and interaction by any member at this point is possible in the *Implementation Phase* but is solely dependent on the level of secrecy the group has attained as well as the amount of planning and safety methods put in place during the planning process.

Modern terrorists are, more than ever, using computers, high-technology communications equipment, and various levels of communications security. With the sophistication of today's technology, a secure communications pathway can be set up virtually anywhere, even on a mobile handheld wireless device, such as a BlackBerry. Terrorists employ computers to create target databases using information technology. Highway abductions increasingly involve terrorists who go online to check the database and determine the most lucrative abduction they could stage. The FARC group of Colombia actually has a victim database that includes earnings information on all millionaires in the country, so if they are encountered at an illegal roadblock, they can be immediately abducted. Other groups use computers to store target data, photos, and reports. The computer is also a perfect communications device. Many groups, such as the al-Qaeda–backed Islamic Army of Aden-Abiyan, use computers as a primary communications system via e-mail and chat rooms. Al-Qaeda also has a policy of using floppy disks to deliver reports by hand for follow-on transmission from insecure locations, such as Internet cafés and friends' homes.

Terrorists need secure communications systems. Terrorists assume that their manual electronic communications are often intercepted. For them, the communications pathway only needs to be open as long as the operation is not detected before the mission is completed. They need a buffer of time in which secret encoded communications should be undetected and thus need codes strong enough to hold off being broken until the last possible moment. The techniques that terrorists have used to communicate secretly include the following:

1) *Written codes and ciphers*: Older groups that have been trained in tradecraft by the Soviet Union or a foreign intelligence agency may still use written or document-based code and cipher systems.
2) *Internet encryption*: Commercial programs that encode e-mail messages offer a highly sophisticated way to ensure the security of their communications using software programs, such as Pretty Good Privacy (PGP), or weaving messages inside digital photos using steganography.

Telephones may be a moderately secure way for terrorists to communicate. Digital encryption and other voice-masking security modules that attach to communications equipment can be purchased in the open market. Though not secure against agencies with the right tools, they can render some intercepts incomprehensible for the short term. The nationwide boom in telephone and proprietary cellular systems, such as T-Mobile, Verizon, and Sprint, makes random efforts to collect information difficult. US law enforcement wiretaps involve many legal hurdles although that changed with the 2001 USA Patriot Act. Throwaway global phone cards are found everywhere. Timothy McVeigh—the man who bombed the Oklahoma City federal building, killing 168 people—communicated with his fellow conspirator Terry McNichols via public phone. After his arrest, the FBI conducted an impressive tracking study of each call placed publicly through McVeigh's phone card, which was purchased under a false name. Satellite telephones give terrorists direct access to quick communications links with people on the other side of the world. Terrorists can easily purchase into systems such as INMARSAT, GlobalStar, and Iridium using Thrane & Thrane or Nera phone terminals, Motorola, Kyocera, or subscribe to the new Thuraya satellite mobile phone system (dedicated to the Middle East and Africa) for instant global communications. In addition, terrorists may use secure radio systems, similar to police radios, to coordinate their attacks and movements. The terrorists involved in the takeover and hostage barricade at the Japanese embassy residence in Lima, Peru, openly wore handheld VHF/UHF radios. Commercial radios made by Yaesu, Motorola, and Marconi have been seen in terrorist hands.

Phase IV: Escape and Evasion

Even though members of the first responder community may have missed the initial three phases and are now handling the aftermath of the attack, there is still a good chance that capture is possible depending on the ability of the attack members to escape. The fourth phase of the terrorist attack cycle involves possible escape from the scene and then overall capture. Not all plans will include an escape plan, and those that do not become much easier to accomplish and prepare for. Oftentimes the escape plan is more complicated and unpredictable than the attack itself.

Counterterrorism officials need to be aware of the critical nature of this phase while still conducting lifesaving or investigative methods immediately after the incident. A possible victim could be a terrorist and that piece of debris, a critical piece of evidence. Those in the surrounding areas must also be aware that although they may not be responding to the actual incident, those that they may come in contact with who are acting suspiciously could be those involved in the incident. Given the suicidal nature of many recent attacks, the attack team members may not escape or be aware of any escape plan. The planners, however, or those involved in the other aspects of the preparation may.

Phase V: Media Exploitation

The fifth and final phase of the attack cycle comprises media exploitation immediately after the attack. Understanding that most groups want to take recognition for the incident to further gain support for their cause and notoriety of members, attackers will attempt to use either the mainstream media or other nonconventional means (Internet, web postings, etc.) to send this message. Some groups may use their own branch of media collection and dissemination whereas others will rely on national broadcast centers to propagate the terrorists' message and cover the attacks. Terrorism generally thrives on media attention. The purpose of terrorist operations is to transmit fear and publicize a cause. No matter how destructive an attack, and no matter whether anyone claims it, the event will succeed in generating publicity—and terror.

Concluding Thoughts

Given the changing face of modern terrorism and the increasing switch from operational groups to lone individuals, these five phases, at their core, are the framework for any terrorist attack. The five phases of a terrorist cycle include target selection, operational planning and preparation, plan implementation, escape and evasion, and media exploitation. While all phases were discussed, the primary emphasis in this chapter was on terrorists' target selection and terrorist planning, preparation, and implementation of their plan. Special emphasis was placed on terrorist tactics, safe houses, supplies, mobility, and communications. Some incidents may be more elaborate than others involving longer durations between each cycle whereas others may not. The fact remains that counterterrorism officials must be in tune with the nuances of each in order to prepare for and possibly interdict the next attack.

6

WMD and CBRN[1]

Introduction

By the end of the past century, the threat of mass casualty terrorism had begun to edge its way onto the agendas of defense and law-enforcement agencies. The arrival of the millennium and the worldwide celebrations that would accompany it had taken on sinister connotations for many officials. There was a concern that cults, disgruntled individuals, or terrorist organizations might view the dawn of a new century as a signal to take violent action to help prompt the coming of some long-awaited utopia. The air was filled with apprehension as many officials believed that the multitudes gathered at various New Year's celebrations might prove to be tempting targets for individuals or organizations bent on violence. The fact that enormous crowds of revelers could be wiped out by a weapon of mass destruction (WMD), a chemical, biological, radiological, or nuclear (CBRN) device whose use is intended to inflict widespread casualties and/or physical destruction, was not lost upon officials. When the millennium passed quietly, a collective sigh of relief could be heard in police and defense ministries around the world.

---

[1] Information for this chapter was drawn from the following titles: (1) J. J. F. Forest and S. Salama, Jihadist tactics and targeting. In G. Ackerman and J. Tamsett (eds.), *Jihadists and Weapons of Mass Destruction*, CRC Press, 2009. (2) M. Binder and M. Moodie, Jihadists and chemical weapons. In G. Ackerman and J. Tamsett (eds.), *Jihadists and Weapons of Mass Destruction*, CRC Press, 2009. (3) C. Loeb, Jihadists and biological and toxin weapons. In G. Ackerman and J. Tamsett (eds.), *Jihadists and Weapons of Mass Destruction*, CRC Press, 2009. (4) C. D. Ferguson, Radiological weapons and jihadist terrorism. In G. Ackerman and J. Tamsett (eds.), *Jihadists and Weapons of Mass Destruction*, CRC Press, 2009. (5) C. P. Blair, Jihadists and nuclear weapons. In G. Ackerman and J. Tamsett (eds.), *Jihadists and Weapons of Mass Destruction*, CRC Press, 2009. (6) S. M. Presley, G. P. Austin, P. N. Smith, and R. J. Kendall, Threats and vulnerabilities associated with biological and chemical terrorism. In R. J. Kendall, S. M. Presley, G. P. Austin, and P. N. Smith (eds.), *Advances in Biological and Chemical Terrorism Countermeasures*, CRC Press, 2008. (7) J. R. Masci and E. Bass, *Bioterrorism: A Guide for Hospital Preparedness*, CRC Press, 2004. (8) S. K. Loyalka, Nuclear terrorism: Nuclear weapons. In T. K. Ghosh, M. A. Prelas, D. S. Viswanath, and S. K. Loyalka (eds.), *Science and Technology of Terrorism and Counterterrorism*, Second Edition, CRC Press, 2009. (9) S. K. Loyalka and M. Prelas, Nuclear terrorism: Threats and countermeasures. In T. K. Ghosh, M. A. Prelas, D. S. Viswanath, and S. K. Loyalka (eds.), *Science and Technology of Terrorism and Counterterrorism*, Second Edition, CRC Press, 2009. (10) J. A. Larsen and J. J. Wirtz, WMD terrorism: New threats, revised responses. In M. A. Opheim, N. Bowen, and P. R. Viotti (eds.), *Terrorism and Homeland Security: Thinking Strategically About Policy*, CRC Press, 2008. (11) K. J. Dudonis, F. Bolz, and D. P. Schulz, *The Counterterrorism Handbook: Tactics, Procedures, and Techniques*, Third Edition, CRC Press, 2001. (12) D. P. Schulz, *The Counterterrorism Handbook: Tactics, Procedures, and Techniques*, Fourth Edition, CRC Press, 2011.

Evidence exists, however, that terrorists did intend to launch attacks to coincide with the millennium. In December 1999, police in Jordan rounded up an al-Qaeda terrorist cell that was about to strike. Seventy-one drums of "acids" were uncovered in their weapons cache. Closer to home, Ahmed Ressam, who has been linked to al-Qaeda, was arrested on December 19, 1999, while entering Port Angeles, Washington, from Canada. Alert border patrol agents discovered high explosives hidden in the trunk of his car. Months later, intelligence analysts determined that Ressam had intended to bomb Los Angeles International Airport on New Year's Day in 2000.[2] The fact that these al-Qaeda operatives were thwarted and that they were primarily armed with high explosives sharpened the debate about the likelihood of mass casualty terrorism, especially involving weapons of mass destruction.

Some argued that terrorists would shy away from attacks that produced massive death, injury, and destruction. Agreeing with Brian Jenkins' famous observation that terrorists wanted people watching, not dead, they pointed out that it would be difficult to harness an attack that produced thousands of casualties to achieve some political objective.[3] Such a heinous act would unite potential supporters, opponents, and fence sitters against the terrorists, dooming not only their organization, but also their political goals. They also noted that even though terrorists had come to possess WMDs, such weapons required demanding technical skills and operational savvy if they were to be used to produce large amounts of death and destruction.

September 11 and Terrorists' Designs

The September 11, 2001, al-Qaeda suicide attacks on the United States ended the debate about the likelihood of mass casualty terrorism. The 2004 Madrid train bombings, the Bali tourist bombings in 2002 and 2005, the 2003 bombing of the Marriott Hotel in Jakarta, the 2005 London Underground and Amman hotel bombings, and the George W. Bush administration's revelations about foiled terrorist plots continue to highlight al-Qaeda's interest in launching terrorist attacks intended to produce as many casualties as possible.[4] The nexus of WMD and terrorism poses one of the gravest threats to the national security of the United States and its global partners. A successful major WMD terrorist attack could result in mass casualties and produce far-reaching economic and political consequences.

Skeptics agreed that mass casualty terrorism involving CBRN weapons was possible, but they asserted that the threat was greatly exaggerated. By contrast, others focused on the consequences of a terrorist attack involving weapons of mass destruction and how such an attack might change the course of history. They agreed that terrorists generally did not resort to mass casualty terrorism, that it was difficult to use such an event to achieve political objectives, and that significant technical and operational hurdles made it difficult to obtain and employ CBRN weapons. But they also noted that just because an activity had not yet occurred, this was not a compelling reason to believe that it would not occur in the future.

CBRN and Terrorists' Capabilities

In the aftermath of the September 11, 2001, attacks against the World Trade Center and the Pentagon, analysts have devoted considerable effort to assessing al-Qaeda's ability to use CBRN weapons. On the one hand, the international response to Islamic terrorism has hampered al-Qaeda's ability to launch attacks, and networks and cells have been disrupted. On the other hand, dispassionate assessments of the likelihood that al-Qaeda might launch a terrorist attack

---

[2] National Commission on Terrorist Attacks upon the United States. *The 9/11 Commission Report*. New York: W.W. Norton & Co., 2004, 174–179.

[3] B. Jenkins. *The Potential for Nuclear Terrorism, RAND Report P-5876*. Santa Monica, CA: RAND, 1977, 8.

[4] Three plots were directed against targets inside the United States. One involved Jose Padilla's interest in launching an attack with a radiological device; the others involved the use of hijacked airliners to attack west and east coast targets. See Peter Baker and Susan B. Glasser, "Bush Says 10 Plots by Al Qaeda Were Foiled," *Washington Post*, October 7, 2005, p. A1.

using WMD are not reassuring. Lewis Dunn, for instance, notes that al-Qaeda operatives have attempted to acquire chemical and possibly nuclear weapons and that plots have been uncovered involving ricin, cyanide, and radiological weapons.[5] Nevertheless, Dunn also concludes that al-Qaeda has come to rely on explosives as its primary terrorist weapon and the use of chemical, biological, or nuclear weapons would entail significant technological and operational challenges that would require innovation, a course of action that is extraordinarily risky from the terrorists' perspective. Audrey Kurth Cronin has reached a similar conclusion that terrorists probably prefer conventional weapons but that WMD use cannot be ruled out because "terrorism seeks to shock."[6] Nonetheless, it is the assessment of most analysts and the US government that WMD might become increasingly available to terrorists. As a result, the threats emanating from both state and non-state actors could increase.

If they somehow managed to acquire them, would terrorists, such as al-Qaeda operatives, use CBRN weapons in a terrorist attack? Or does the threat of terrorism involving WMD represent a barrier that will not be crossed in the future? To address these questions, this chapter explores nuclear, radiological, biological, and chemical weapons (each of which is examined individually below) and the different types of terrorism that can be perpetrated using these weapons. It then examines the possibility of their use by domestic and international terrorists.

Nuclear Weapons

Nuclear weapons are the ultimate means of destruction, and humanity can ill afford acquisition of such weapons by terrorists. Nuclear material, however, is difficult, but not impossible, to obtain. Not only can raw nuclear-grade materials be obtained, but complete nuclear warheads are said to be available for purchase at the underground market for the right price. Since the breakup of the Soviet Union in the 1990s, intelligence reports indicate that a number of nuclear warheads are unaccounted for and may have fallen into the hands of underworld criminals and black marketers. Complicating the matter is that many of the now independent former socialist republics laid claim to assets of the Soviet Union, including weapons factories and the military equipment located within their borders. This included nuclear material for power usage as well as weapons and materials used in their manufacture. As newly created and independent countries, many were desperately short of hard currency, and such nuclear material would be viewed as a valuable commodity by a major terrorist organization or rogue nation.

Nuclear Material Acquisition and Weapon Production

Nuclear weapons may emerge on the black market, for instance, if they are stolen from the large remaining stocks of Russian nonstrategic nuclear weapons or from the growing numbers of warheads in the Pakistani and Indian arsenals. Informal, entrepreneurial networks have already emerged in the realm of nuclear technology, materials, and know-how. In 2004, revelations that the Pakistani scientist A. Q. Khan probably provided information about gas-centrifuges used to produce weapons-grade uranium and nuclear bomb designs to North Korea, Iraq, Iran, Libya, and Syria shocked the nonproliferation community.[7,8] Iran, a designated state sponsor of terrorism, is actively pursuing an indigenous nuclear weapons program. Many observers worry that

[5] L. A. Dunn. *Can al Qaeda Be Deterred from Using Nuclear Weapons?* Center for the Study of Weapons of Mass Destruction, Occasional Paper #3. Washington, DC: National Defense University, July 2005.

[6] A. K. Cronin. Terrorist Motivations for Chemical and Biological Weapons Use: Placing the Threat in Context. *Defense & Security Analysis*, 20, no. 4: 317, December 2004.

[7] C. Clary, A. Q. Khan and the Limits of the Non-proliferation Regime. *Disarmament Forum*, no. 4: 33–42, 2004.

[8] D. Albright and C. Hinderstein. Unraveling the A. Q. Khan and Future Proliferation Networks. *The Washington Quarterly*, 28, no. 2: 111–128, 2005.

the Iranian nuclear industry might become a clandestine source of fissile material for terrorists. Indeed, the threat of fission weapon construction, acquisition, and use by terrorists has become more credible with the spread of nuclear technology and international instabilities and dynamics.

Nonetheless, nuclear weapons are extremely difficult to produce because their manufacture requires a large industrial infrastructure. The actual design of a workable explosive requires sophisticated analysis and synthesis. Building a nuclear weapon might be within the realm of possibility, however, if a group was able to get its hands on fissile material, such as highly enriched uranium (HEU) or plutonium. The physics and engineering of nuclear weapons are well understood; the challenge lies in creating or obtaining the fissile material. By contrast, a radiological dispersal device (RDD) would be much easier to build. An RDD is a conventional bomb wrapped in radioactive material; when detonated, radioactive material is spread by the blast. Unlike the HEU or plutonium needed to make a nuclear weapon, low-level radioactive materials can be used in an RDD; these materials are plentiful in modern societies because they have a myriad of industrial and medical uses in everyday life. Most observers are not too concerned that terrorist networks will actually build a nuclear weapon. Instead, they worry that terrorists might find a way to procure a weapon through theft or purchase.

The Prospect of Nuclear Attack

Nuclear terrorism could comprise attacks against nuclear installations and the dispersal of radioactive materials through the use of conventional explosives and other means, as well as the use of nuclear weapons. Targets of nuclear terrorism would be large cities and infrastructure, private and public. Nuclear installations (manufacturing and storage facilities, nuclear power plants, and research reactors) and shipments (raw material, fresh fuel, and used fuel) are all plausible targets for acquisition of nuclear material or attacks that could lead to the release of radioactivity from these installations or activities. Nuclear power plants are often located in remote areas and research reactors contain relatively small amounts of radioactive material. Neither are likely to undergo a nuclear explosion except in special circumstances, but chemical explosions/fires or plane crashes at these sites can cause great difficulties and eventual release of radioactivity and harm.

Motivations for nuclear terrorism exist, both in large terrorist groups and in some countries. There is likely to be a greater move toward nuclear threats as terrorists exhaust other means and tactics and as they become more experienced, sophisticated, and knowledgeable. Nuclear threats are plausible as together with motivations, materials, and expertise for making crude weapons may be acquired, means for delivery may be available, attacks on nuclear installations or their sabotage may be feasible, and nuclear weapons may be stolen or purchased.

Intelligence sources have revealed that terrorist organizations, particularly al-Qaeda, have shown an interest in nuclear power plants. Indeed, since at least 1993, Islamic terrorists have made serious attempts to acquire fissile materials and nuclear weapons. Several individuals linked to jihadist groups have been arrested or detained for plotting or attempting to acquire nuclear weapons or materials, yet, to date, there have been no confirmed incidents of a jihadist-linked individual or a jihadist group successfully obtaining fissile materials suitable for a nuclear weapon or an intact nuclear warhead.[9]

Most active among jihadist groups seeking to acquire nuclear weapons and weapons-grade nuclear materials has been al-Qaeda; according to the US government, their determined efforts to acquire nuclear materials began "at least as early as 1992."[10] In fact, there are reports

[9] See, for example, Commission on the Intelligence Capabilities of the United States Regarding Weapons of Mass Destruction, Report to the President (Washington, DC: WMD Commission, 2005), 272. Available at http://www.wmd.gov/report/wmd_report.pdf.

[10] United States of America v. Usama bin Ladin, Indictment 98Cr., United States District Court Southern District of New York, 19. Available at http://cns.miis.edu/pubs/reports/pdfs/binLadin/indict.pdf. See also Testimony of Mamdouh Mahmud Salim, as quoted in P. Bergen. *The Usama bin Ladin I Know*. New York: Free Press, 2006, 339.

that al-Qaeda continues to maintain a strong desire to employ nuclear weapons against the United States and its allies.[11] Al-Qaeda has made several efforts to secure intact nuclear devices and fissile materials and has reportedly been prepared to pay many millions of dollars to do so.[12] To date, jihadists and other terrorists have been unsuccessful in all publicly known attempts to acquire intact nuclear weapons. Despite this unsuccessful history, however, there are no indications that serious interests by jihadists in acquiring a nuclear capability will abate in the near future. Whether or not they will succeed is one of the modern era's most daunting questions.

Four broad factors will have a direct effect on any probable outcome:

1. The quantity of global fissile materials and the security associated with these stocks.
2. Global stockpiles of intact nuclear weapons and their security have an obvious bearing on the odds of terrorists successfully obtaining a nuclear capability.
3. The spread of nuclear know-how and weapons to other states could dramatically alter any calculus used to determine the odds of terrorists being successful in their nuclear endeavors.
4. The number and sophistication of terrorist groups will likely have an enormous bearing on future developments. If their numbers remain the same or grow, it is very likely that their odds of eventual success will increase.

Radiological Weapons

Terrorists, in general, might choose to use a radiological weapon for one or more purposes: causing harm to human health through exposure to ionizing radiation, provoking psychological effects through stimulation of people's fears of radiation as well as disrupting people's lives and livelihoods, and causing significant economic damage through radioactive contamination of valuable property. Although radiological weapons can take many forms, the common ingredient required for success is radioactive material. This material emits ionizing radiation, which can knock electrons off atoms, thus creating ions. These ions, if present in large enough amounts in human tissue, can cause damage potentially leading to harmful health effects, such as radiation sickness or cancer.

A radiological weapon must not be confused with a nuclear weapon, and the effects of the two weapons differ greatly. For example, a radiological weapon cannot produce a nuclear chain reaction and will not, consequently, result in a massive explosion. The one characteristic common to nuclear and radiological weapons is that both employ radioactive material. A nuclear explosion through fission would produce massive amounts of radioactive material whereas a radiological weapon cannot produce additional radioactive material beyond the amount that was originally contained in the weapon.

Radiological weapons can take a variety of forms, from very crude explosive devices to sophisticated dispersal mechanisms. Unfortunately, the news media have latched on to the term "dirty bomb" to describe all types of radiological weapons, which conveys a very limited sense of the variety of these weapons. The popular image of a dirty bomb usually consists of conventional explosives, say dynamite, strapped to some type of radioactive material. When the explosives are ignited,

---

[11] See, for example, F. Davies, "Pakistani Urged al-Qa'ida to Obtain Nuclear Weapons, Authorities Say," Knight Ridder Washington Bureau, February 11, 2005; "US Charges Pakistani With Urging al Qa'ida to Acquire Weapons," Press Trust of India, February 14, 2005; "Qaeda Wants to Smuggle N-material to US," *The Nation*, November 17, 2004; "Bordering on Nukes," *Time Magazine*, November 22, 2004.

[12] See, for example, "Al-Qa'ida's WMD Activities," James Martin Center for Nonproliferation Studies.

the resulting blast disperses the radioactive material. The fact is that this dispersal mechanism may do a very poor job at effectively spreading out radioactive material in ways that can do serious harm to health or result in significant radioactive contamination that is hard to clean up.

To optimize the production of aerosolized material, terrorists would have to be skilled in conventional explosives and know how to choose the correct types and amounts of explosives depending on the chemical composition and amount of radioactive material present. They would also need to have knowledge of the chemistry and physical form of the radioactive source. In particular, they would need to know whether the source is a solid, liquid, or powder, and whether it is a metal or chemically bound to other elements. In sum, to move beyond a simple dirty bomb, a terrorist group would have to assemble experts with the correct skill sets and knowledge of the radioactive material they have accessed or are attempting to access. If a terrorist group bent on using a radiological weapon had these skills, a larger palette of radiological weapons would be available to them.

For most scenarios involving radiological weapons, very few, if any, people near the scene of an attack would succumb to serious and immediate health effects. To experience these effects, people would have to receive relatively high exposures of ionizing radiation. Because radiological weapons are typically designed to disperse radioactive material over wide areas, the dispersed material would pose a far less potent health threat compared to concentrated amounts of radioactivity near a person. However, if people ingested or inhaled significant amounts of radioactive material, they might well develop serious health effects. Also, people exposed to even tiny amounts of excess radiation have a very small, but nonzero, increase in the probability of developing cancer. Nevertheless, because it could take several years to decades for cancer to develop, many people might live in fear of developing cancer after exposure to even small amounts of radiation in the aftermath of a radiological attack. Therefore, the psychological and social consequences of a radiological attack could linger for many years after the incident and dwarf the physical health effects.

The radioactive material in a radiological weapon can come from many sources. Nuclear power plants, research reactor facilities, hospitals, blood banks, universities, food irradiation centers, oil well sites, and shipbuilding and construction sites are many of the major places where radioactive materials are used and stored. Some of these places are more vulnerable than others to terrorists obtaining radioactive material. Of the places listed above, nuclear power plants would probably have the most rigorous security and would have radioactive materials that are too radioactive to handle without thick shielding and too heavy to carry without special equipment. At nuclear power plants, spent nuclear fuel is highly radioactive and could give a lethal radiation dose in a few minutes without adequate shielding. Moreover, a spent nuclear fuel assembly at a power plant typically weighs many tons.

Spent fuel from research reactors, on the other hand, may not contain nearly as much radioactivity as spent fuel from nuclear power plants because many research reactors operate at power levels much lower than nuclear power plants. Also, a spent fuel assembly at a research reactor can weigh much less than a spent fuel assembly at a power plant and thus might be more susceptible to transport by thieves. Of course, a terrorist group would have to surmount the barrier of finding out where the spent fuel is located within a facility. Reconnaissance and insider assistance could help provide this information. At any location where radioactive materials are used, terrorists would have to determine how to gain access, identify where radioactive materials are situated, and figure out how to remove the materials. If removal proves too much of a problem, the terrorists could try to blow up the material in place. Such a scenario may or may not achieve the terrorists' intended objectives unless the location itself is considered to be of high enough tactical value to elicit the desired response from the terrorists' intended audience.

Certain locations where radioactive materials are used or stored appear more accessible than others relative especially to high-security nuclear power plants. For instance, hospitals and universities are designed to be open to the public. Thus, terrorist reconnaissance of these locations may not attract authorities' attention. But without specific information about where radioactive materials are located, the terrorists may not identify these locations without additional assistance from insiders or from external sources of information, such as websites about the facilities. Thinking through potentially promising pathways for terrorists to try to acquire radioactive materials, security experts have identified—in addition to insider assistance and theft from facilities—alternative acquisition routes, including deliberate transfer by a government, unauthorized transfer by a government official or a facility custodian, looting during coups or other times of political turmoil, licensing fraud, organized crime, exploiting weaknesses in transportation links, sellers of illicitly trafficked radioactive material, and finding orphan radioactive sources (which have been lost, stolen, or fallen outside of regulatory control).[13]

Much attention has been focused on the possibility of a nuclear bomb being sought after by terrorists. Neither nuclear nor explosively dispersed radiological devices (called dirty bombs) have been used in a major terrorist attack to date, but dozens of attempts to acquire radioactive material have been documented worldwide since the 1970s. While security experts have shown intense interest in radiological terrorism, there have been relatively few examples of terrorists in general showing unambiguous interest in radiological weapons. The first reported incident of jihadists acquiring radioactive material and demonstrating this fact was in November 1995, when then-Chechen leader Shamil Basayev called a Russian television crew to tell them that there was a partially buried container of cesium-137 in Moscow's Ismailovsky Park. But the container was not blown up. Thus, Basayev may have only wanted to show that his group could carry out a radiological attack without actually following through, achieving a psychological effect on the Russian population without risking massive retribution from Russian authorities.

The known cases of al-Qaeda's interest in radiological terrorism to date, however, indicate a relatively unsophisticated understanding of how to effectively use radioactive materials. For example, in January 2003, British investigators reported that al-Qaeda may have acquired radioactive materials and then constructed a dirty bomb near Herat, Afghanistan. However, an unnamed American official told the Associated Press that the report was unsubstantiated.[14] Additionally, in September 2006, the leader of al-Qaeda in Iraq, Abu Hamza al-Muhajir, better known as Abu Ayyub al-Masri or "Ayyub's Father the Egyptian," called for nuclear scientists and explosive experts to assist his organization in making biological and "dirty" radioactive weapons.[15] What's more, since 2006, additional evidence has pointed to increasing interest and perhaps sophistication in the use of radioactive materials by jihadists. In March 2006, the Global Issues Report discussed instructions about making radiological weapons posted on the militant Islamic online forum AlGhorabaa.net.[16] Despite evidence indicating jihadists' interest in radiological terrorism, they confront significant barriers, including governments' and industry's increasing efforts at hardening targets, securing radioactive sources, and replacing certain types of sources with nonradioactive alternative technologies and deploying radiation detectors to increase the likelihood of interdiction.

Biological Weapons

Biological weapons are produced from pathogenic microorganisms or toxic substances of biological origin, formulated in such a way that they are capable of disabling and/or killing people,

[13] For a fuller treatment of this pathway analysis, see C. D. Ferguson and W. C. Potter with A. Sands, L. Spector, and F. L. Wehling, *The Four Faces of Nuclear Terrorism*. New York: Routledge, 2005, 271–278.

[14] Associated Press. BBC Says al Qaeda Produced a 'Dirty Bomb' in Afghanistan. *New York Times*, January 31, 2003.

[15] Associated Press. Zarqawi Successor Exhorts Scientists: Tape Urges Experts to Join Fight in Iraq. *Washington Post*, September 29, 2006, A15.

[16] Center for International Issues Research. Dirty Bomb Instructions Posted on Hostile Web Forum. *Global Issues Report*, March 2, 2006.

crops, and livestock, and combined with an apparatus/method used to deliver the biological harm to the target population. Biological agents are the microorganisms and toxins that cause disease and could be used for manufacturing biological weapons. The biological agents that have been associated with weapons development can be divided into five key groups:

1. Bacteria
2. Viruses
3. Rickettsia
4. Fungi
5. Toxins (bacteria, viruses, and toxins are the most well-known types of biological weapons agents)

Biological terrorism, or bioterrorism, can be defined as the calculated use of microorganisms or toxins produced by living organisms that may have been enhanced or modified to more effectively and efficiently cause disease in, debilitate, or kill other living organisms in an attempt to intimidate or coerce a government, the civilian population, or any segment thereof in furtherance of political, religious, or social objectives. The difficulty in detecting biological terrorist attacks is that symptoms of illness do not appear immediately as would occur in a chemical, nuclear, or conventional weapon attack. Because most biological weapons consist of living organisms, symptoms will occur only after an incubation period that may last days to weeks.[17,18] Many times, the initial symptoms could appear as a common cold or influenza and might be mistaken for a normal outbreak of infectious disease. Until large numbers of individuals report illness, the attack could go undetected. This is especially likely to be the case during annual cold and flu season. If the agent used can translate as a communicable disease, the infection could spread rapidly across a large population before health preventative measures are effectively put in place. Rapid growth in international travel further complicates the issue, allowing sick persons incubating disease to move around the globe, spreading the infection across multiple transit pathways and borders.

Dissemination Challenges

Biological and toxin weapons can be disseminated into target populations through a variety of different methods, depending on their form. The most effective means of disseminating an agent is in the form of a wet or dry aerosol—a cloud of solid particles suspended in the air. Wet aerosol mixtures are easier to produce but more difficult to deploy in a manner that will result in high levels of casualties, and they are unlikely to be subject to re-aerosolization. Dry aerosol mixtures, on the other hand, are more difficult to produce than wet aerosol mixtures. Dry aerosols are also more likely to be subject to the phenomenon of re-aerosolization after deposition, thus enabling them to potentially continue to infect target populations. Smallpox, for example, can survive up to 24 hours after release. In fact, the smallpox virus can be released and spread among millions of people before it is detected because its incubation period is approximately two weeks. A US government exercise that simulated a terrorist release of smallpox showed that more than three million people could die within 30 to 60 days of the appearance of the first incidence. The usage of a human deployed biological weapons system—a suicide operative deliberately infected with a disease, such as smallpox—is the most viable terrorist weapon and far more attainable than a nuclear weapon.

---

[17] Australia Group. Australia Group Common Control Lists. Available at http://www.australiagroup.net/en/controllists.html.

[18] USAMRIID. *USAMRIID's Medical Management of Biological Casualties Handbook*, Sixth Edition. Available at http://www.usamriid.army.mil/education/instruct.htm, April 2005.

Factors that can determine the effectiveness of a biological or toxin attack include the choice of agent, type of formulation, and the manufacturing process employed. Terrorists also have to contend with incremental degradation over time due to transporting materials from the point of acquisition or production to the point of use, not to mention ensuring a suitably virulent strain has been properly and effectively weaponized. Technical means of delivery include the use of cluster bombs, artillery shells, rockets, and sophisticated sprayers, but the use of such large-scale delivery systems is usually associated with military development of biological weapons. Nontechnical and cheaper modes of dissemination include using animal vectors (e.g., fleas and mosquitoes), improvised crop dusters designed for agricultural spraying purposes, backpack sprayers, and even purse-sized atomizers. While it may be easier from a technical perspective to contaminate food or water sources, this method is generally less effective than open-air aerosol dissemination because of the dilution of the agent in the food or water, quality control processes, and limited distribution of the agent. There has been much speculation and fear over the prospect of food supplies being contaminated with biological agents; however, achieving large-scale casualties with this method remains technically difficult and depends on the type of agent used and the method in which it is formulated and delivered.

Another delivery method (mentioned earlier) could include self-infection with a contagious agent, such as smallpox or plague. There are uncertainties with this method, of course, with serious and even fatal risks to the deliverer as well as the risk of indiscriminately infecting and even killing group members, leaders, followers, family, and friends.[19] The success of the delivery of a biological agent in the open air is dependent on meteorological and terrain conditions, such as wind velocity, temperature, precipitation, and humidity, thereby making success difficult to predict.

Nevertheless, biological weapons are much more accessible, cheaper, and easier to produce than nuclear weapons, yet potentially could have comparable destructive power. Unlike other tools, biological weapons could be used covertly. This could increase their destructive effect, but also make it harder to catch or even identify the perpetrators, another factor that might encourage their use. Many biological agents, including some that can be effectively weaponized, are relatively inexpensive and available, with sources in biological supply companies, hospital and commercial laboratories, and in nature.[20] Indeed, some biological weapons are relatively easy to produce by skilled laboratory personnel with a minimum of necessary materials or advanced equipment. This is not a hypothetical threat: Coalition forces in Afghanistan uncovered trace amounts of ricin and anthrax at several locations. Evidence captured along with Khalid Shaikh Mohammed in March 2003 also suggests that al-Qaeda was planning an ambitious effort to manufacture anthrax.[21] However, preparing and delivering biological agents in a manner sufficient to cause large numbers of casualties would require a far higher degree of knowledge and skill as well as financial and technical resources.[20,22]

Recent advances in genetic engineering, biotechnology, vaccine production, and other life sciences research, however, are rapidly diffusing the knowledge, equipment, and materials needed to produce both crude and sophisticated biological weapons. Increased access to the Internet has expanded the availability of the knowledge and specialized equipment needed to produce biological weapons, such as seed stocks and culture collections, well beyond traditional scientific and technical communities. Research once limited to national-level weapons programs

---

[19] A. Dolnik. Die and Let Die: Exploring Links between Suicide Terrorism and Terrorist Use of Chemical, Biological, Radiological, and Nuclear Weapons. *Studies in Conflict and Terrorism* 26, no. 1: 17–35, January–February 2003.

[20] US Congress, Office of Technology Assessment. Proliferation of Weapons of Mass Destruction: Assessing the Risks, OTA-ISC-559, US Government Printing Office, 1993.

[21] A. K. Cronin. Terrorist Motivations for Chemical and Biological Weapons Use: Placing the Threat in Context. *Defense & Security Analysis*, 20, no. 4: 315–316, December 2004.

[22] J. B. Tucker. Introduction. In J. B. Tucker (ed.), Toxic *Terror: Assessing Terrorist Use of Chemical and Biological Weapons*. MIT Press, Cambridge, MA, 2000.

can now be conducted in civilian settings. As just one measure of how widely disseminated the relevant knowledge is, more than 42,000 people around the world are members of the American Society for Microbiology, most with graduate degrees in microbiology.[23] Along with rising levels of scientific education have come greater freedom of travel, wider dissemination of information through the Internet, and advancing use of bioengineering techniques—all developments that can deliver great benefits but that also can enable bioterrorists to strike.

Aum Shinrikyo and Bioterrorism

There have been several attempted incidents of bioterrorism. The Japanese terror cult Aum Shinrikyo experimented with anthrax, botulinum toxin, cholera, and Q fever and even attempted to obtain Ebola during trips to Africa. This cult was unknown to the general public, especially outside Japan. The leader of the group was a half-blind former acupuncturist named Shoko Ashara who turned to religion and mysticism. He was born in 1955 as Shoko Matsumoto. At one point, he owned a folk medicine shop before traveling to Tibet to study Buddhism and Hinduism. In 1984, he founded the Aum Shinsen Club, recruiting 15 original followers. Within a few years, the organization had grown to 1300 members. There was international growth as well, particularly in the Soviet Union and, following its collapse, Russia and the other newly independent republics. The ranks swelled with tens of thousands of new members. The organization later changed its name to Aum Shinrikyo, or the "Supreme Truth," in which Ashara was considered to be a god by his followers. At its peak, the movement counted almost 40,000 members in six countries. Ashara's aim of his organization eventually became the overthrow of the Japanese government.

This group's biological attacks began in April 1990, when the sect made several attempts to spread botulinum toxin from a vehicle driving around government buildings in central Tokyo and at the US Navy base in Yokohama. On a number of occasions between 1990 and 1995, the cult attempted to release biological agents on selected targets in Japan but were unsuccessful in causing casualties, mostly as a result of utilizing nonvirulent strains and unsophisticated delivery apparatuses.[24] Specifically, Aum Shinrikyo tried to aerosolize anthrax spores from the roof of an eight-story building that the cult owned in Tokyo. Experts have said that the anthrax strain was not virulent enough to have the intended effect although pet deaths and odd smells and stains were reported at the time.[25] Moreover, in March 1995, preparations were made to release botulinum toxin in the Tokyo subway using attaché cases equipped with vents and blowers to be triggered by the vibrations of the subway. The attack fell through, reportedly because the appointed cult member chose not to fill the cases.[25] No casualties were reported from any of Aum Shinrikyo's bioterrorist attempts. The biowarfare effort was led by a graduate-level microbiologist. The cult had two laboratories and was building a more advanced lab when it was raided after the sarin attack.[26]

Aum Shinrikyo, a well-funded and well-educated terrorist group, working over a period of years with two of the deadliest biological agents, apparently was unable to harm a single person. The experience of Aum Shinrikyo shows that despite the nightmare scenarios that can be devised, deadly dissemination of biological agents may not be easy. The cult had scientific resources; officials estimated Aum Shinrikyo had 10,000 members in Japan and 30,000 in Russia, many of them well educated with scientific or technical training. About 1400 of the Japanese adherents and 5500 of the Russians were hardcore followers, living

---

[23] About ASM, American Society for Microbiology. Available at www.asm.org/general.asp?bid=14777.

[24] K. B. Olson. Aum Shinrikyo: Once and Future Threat? *Emerging Infectious Diseases, Centers for Disease Control and Prevention*, Special Issue. Available at http://www.cdc.gov/ncidod/EID/vol5no4/olson.htm.

[25] K. B. Olson. Aum Shinrikyo: Once and Future Threat? *Emerging Infectious Diseases*, 5: 513, 1999.

[26] A. E. Smithson and L.-E. Levy. Ataxia: The Chemical and Biological Terrorism Threat and the US Response, Report No. 35, The Henry L. Stimson Center, Washington, DC, 2000, chap. 3.

in Aum facilities. The cult had financial resources as well. Its net worth was estimated at $1 billion or more with money raised through a chain of restaurants, a computer company, expensive training courses, tithing, and other means.[27] A less reassuring moral can also be drawn from the fact that a well-funded and well-educated group had no scruples about repeatedly attempting such a project—trying to indiscriminately unleash mass destruction through disease.

In small amounts, some biological agents are relatively easy to culture and to deliver as shown by several small-scale events:

- In 1984, members of a religious cult called the Rajneeshees added Salmonella typhimurium to restaurant salad bars in Oregon, sickening 751 people. The cult operated a health clinic and state-licensed laboratory; members cultured the salmonella from "bactrol discs" purchased from a medical supply house, ostensibly for laboratory quality assurance testing.[28]
- In 1990, nine people in an Edinburgh apartment block became ill with giardiasis, apparently after an infected person intentionally contaminated water tanks on the roof.[29]
- In 1996, a hospital laboratory technician in Dallas used Shigella dysenteriae type 2 taken from a hospital lab to contaminate pastries she placed in a break room, sickening a dozen coworkers.[30]

Even small-scale use of biological weapons with low-tech means can cause large scale social, psychological, and economic consequences. A case in point is the 2001 anthrax attacks.

2001 US Anthrax Attacks

On September 28, 2001, a 38-year-old assistant to NBC TV newscaster Tom Brokaw noticed a lesion on her cheek and sought medical assistance at a local hospital. Within two weeks, the woman's sores were diagnosed as a cutaneous, or skin-based, form of anthrax. In short order, news surfaced about other anthrax-laced letters sent to the headquarters of major television networks, the *New York Post* newspaper, New York Governor George Pataki's office, and that of Senator Tom Daschle, Democratic Party leader in the US Senate. The Morgan postal service center in New York City was shut down for several days, and the Brentwood postal facility in Washington, DC, was shut down for a lengthy period of time. One of the first places where anthrax-laced mail was confirmed was the headquarters of American Media, Inc., in Boca Raton, Florida. In addition, a number of other mail-handling facilities were contaminated to varying degrees by tainted letters or packages through them.

The 2001 anthrax incidents showed that this long-feared pathogen could be prepared as a weapon and distributed by low-tech means—in this case, as letters sent through the US mail. It showed that responding to even limited use of a deadly biological agent could have heavy economic and emotional costs. Indeed, the 2001 anthrax attack on the US Senate proved more frightening than destructive. The media coverage surrounding the contamination of the Senate office buildings and the unfortunate deaths of several victims created a perfect storm of rumor and panic. In the end, it involved only 11 cases with five deaths. But the events of 2001 heightened

[27] D. E. Kaplan. Aum Shinrikyo (1995). In J. B. Tucker (ed.), *Toxic Terror: Assessing Terrorist Use of Chemical and Biological Weapons*. MIT Press, Cambridge, MA, 2000.

[28] W. S. Carus. The Rajneeshees (1984). In J. B. Tucker (ed.), *Toxic Terror: Assessing Terrorist Use of Chemical and Biological Weapons*. MIT Press, Cambridge, MA, 2000.

[29] C. N. Ramsay and J. Marsh. Giardiasis due to Deliberate Contamination of Water Supply. *Lancet*, 336, no. 8719: 880–881, 1990.

[30] S. A. Kolavic, A. Kimura, S. L. Simons, L. Slutsker, S. Barth, and C. E. Hayley. An Outbreak of *Shigella dysenteriae* Type 2 among Laboratory Workers due to Intentional Food Contamination. *JAMA*, 278, no. 5: 396–398, 1997.

concern about bioterrorism in several ways. The September 11 terrorist attacks on the World Trade Center and the Pentagon showed that terrorists could carry out a technically sophisticated, well-coordinated, long-range plan on US soil. It showed they could devise a novel and unexpected technique. And perhaps most ominous, it seemed to confirm that they were eager to cause mass civilian casualties, without limit, rather than targeting their attacks more narrowly.

In the 2001 anthrax attacks against the United States, the perpetrator chose to deliver the powdered anthrax spores through the US postal system. One of the main reasons why more casualties did not occur is because the delivery method was extremely unsophisticated. This attack, and the one perpetrated by Aum Skinrikyo, demonstrate that even with a "working" biological weapon, if the delivery method is unsophisticated or the terrorist group does not take into account important meteorological, terrain, and other factors, the outcome of the attack may be much less severe.

For jihadists or any other terrorist group to successfully obtain and use a biological or toxin weapon, the group would likely have to display three key characteristics: (1) sufficient motivation, (2) an efficient organizational structure, and (3) the requisite technical capability.[31] Open-source evidence indicates that jihadist terrorists have been actively seeking out the resources, equipment, and technical know-how to obtain a biological weapon. These are numerous incidents that illustrate that jihadists have progressed beyond mere rhetoric when it comes to bioterrorism.

The most illustrative of the threat of jihadist BW terrorism is a 2008 report on the status of al-Qaeda's WMD program. On February 3, 2008, it was reported that al-Qaeda member Abu Khabab al-Masri, formerly believed to have been deceased from a 2006 US airstrike in Pakistan, was, in fact, alive and in charge of resurrecting al-Qaeda's WMD program.[32] While experts suppose that the research is currently focused on the development of cyanide, chlorine, and other poisons unlikely to cause mass casualties, the potential for simultaneous biological weapons development cannot be ignored.[32] Intelligence reports indicate that Masri has begun to set up rudimentary labs in the mountains of Pakistan and has recruited some scientists for the cause.[33] Prior to the invasion of Afghanistan in 2002, al-Masri, who is a trained chemical engineer, wrote and distributed training manuals with information on the development of both chemical and biological weapons.

Why would a terrorist group choose a biological weapon over other types of weapons, especially those known for their reliability and easy accessibility, like conventional explosives? Their ability to cause widespread death and disease, their indiscriminate nature, the shortage or complete lack of vaccines and therapeutics to treat many of the diseases caused by biological agents, their capability to invoke images of suffering and horror, and their similarity to apocalyptic biblical diseases and plagues, make them appealing to jihadists and other terrorist groups. Biological weapons are thus appealing to jihadists for many of the same reasons as nuclear and radiological weapons because they provide the opportunity to inflict serious physical, psychological, and economic harm on targets.

Chemical Weapons

Chemical weapon terrorism (or chemical terrorism) refers to the use of toxic chemicals to disrupt normal functions and to sicken or kill victims within the zone of release. More specifically, chemical terrorism or the use of chemical threat agents or weapon agents for terrorism, can be

[31] Nuclear Threat Initiative. Characteristics of CBW Terrorists. Available at http://www.nti.org/h_learnmore/bwtutorial/chapter01_05.html.

[32] J. Meyer. Al-Qa'ida Said to Focus on WMDs. *Los Angeles Times*. Available at http://www.latimes.com/news/nationworld/world/la-fg-khabab3feb03,1,1300705.story, February 3, 2008.

[33] IntelAnalysis. Al-Qa'ida Said to Focus on WMDs. Available at http://intelanalysis.org/2008/02/04/al-qaeda-said-to-focus-on-wmds/, February 4, 2008.

defined as the calculated use of hazardous toxic compounds or substances that may have been enhanced or modified to more effectively and efficiently debilitate or kill humans in an attempt to intimidate or coerce a government, a civilian population, or any segment thereof in furtherance of political, religious, or social objectives.

Chemical weapons fall into several categories, depending on the manner in which they cause physical effects: blister, blood, choking, and nerve agents. Blister agents, or vesicants, are oily liquids that inflict chemical burns on the skin or any other part of the body with which they come into contact, including the lungs if they are inhaled. Blister agents, such as mustard gas, were used extensively in the last two years of World War I. Mustard agents can cause damage to the eyes and respiratory system by direct contact and inhalation. Blister agents were also used to some effect in the war between Iraq and Iran in the 1980s.

Blood agents refer to chemical agents that use cyanide as an important ingredient and achieve their effects by traveling through the bloodstream to sites where the agent can interfere with oxygen utilization at the cellular level. Hydrogen cyanide, which is also a widely used industrial chemical, and cyanogen chloride are the most important agents in this group. Blood agents (cyanide compounds) have an undeserved reputation as an effective chemical warfare agent. Because they are so volatile, it is difficult to maintain effective concentrations for extended periods of time. However, at high concentrations, cyanide does kill very quickly.

Choking agents attack the airways and cause swelling and edema in the lung tissues. These were perhaps the most widely used agents during World War I and include such chemicals as chlorine and phosgene, both of which are in widespread commercial use today. In June 1990, the Liberation Tigers of Tamil Eelam (LTTE) became the first insurgent, guerrilla, or terrorist organization to stage a chemical weapons attack when it used chlorine gas in its assault on a Sri Lankan Armed Forces camp at East Kiran. As Bruce Hoffman notes, this attack was relatively crude: Several large drums of the chemical were transported from a nearby paper mill and positioned around the camp's perimeter, and when the wind currents were judged right, the attackers released the gas, which wafted into the camp.[34] More than 60 military personnel were injured, and the LTTE captured the facility. However, though this was part of the first round in a renewed military offensive, the LTTE did not use a similar weapon in subsequent attacks, in part due to revulsion among their core supporters and constituencies.[35]

Nerve agents are perhaps the most widely feared category of chemical weapon because of the speed and severity of their impact. Discovered as a byproduct of 1930s research into organophosphorous insecticides, these agents inhibit the function of vital enzymes in the human body that inactivate acetylcholine, which mediates the transmission of certain types of nerve impulses. This results in the characteristic uncontrolled muscle movements associated with exposures to nerve agents. Nerve agents include tabun (GA), sarin (GB), soman (GD), and other G-series agents, as well as V-agents (VE, VM, and VX) discovered by British scientists in the late 1940s. The Iraqis are believed to have used nerve agents in their war with Iran, and the Aum Shinrikyo cult used sarin in its attacks in Matsumoto (1994) and Tokyo (1995). Indeed, having failed at bioterrorism, Aum turned to chemical weapons with greater effect. In the 1990s, the cult members began using sarin and VX nerve gas, targeting specific enemies in seven attacks within a year. In the worst of these, seven people died and more than 100 were injured when cult members sprayed vaporized sarin for 10 minutes in June 1994 in a parking lot in the city of Matsumoto. Even after the 1995 Tokyo subway attack (where the group punched holes in plastic

[34] B. Hoffman. CBRN Terrorism Post-9/11. In R. Howard and J. J. F. Forest (eds.), *Weapons of Mass Destruction and Terrorism*. New York: McGraw-Hill, 2007.

[35] J. V. Parachini. Comparing Motives and Outcomes of Mass Casualty Terrorism Involving Conventional and Unconventional Weapons. *Studies in Conflict and Terrorism*, 24, no. 5: 389–406, September 2001.

bags with sarin to release it in the subway), the cult still sought to cause mass casualties, making two unsuccessful attempts to release hydrogen cyanide gas in the Tokyo subways. Following the 1995 Tokyo subway attack, Japanese authorities discovered that the cult had also explored other nerve agents, including soman, tabun, and VX (in addition to its unsuccessful efforts to use the biological weapons anthrax and botulinum toxin).

Chemical agents vary in composition and how they affect the body with most chemical agents coming in liquid form. The exceptions are riot-control agents that are solids, usually in the form of a fine powder. Chemical agents can produce a variety of effects, depending upon their volatility and persistence to evaporation. Some of these effects can occur within seconds, while others arise hours and even days later. The components that constitute the chemical agent are a major factor in how quickly it will evaporate. There are also other factors to consider, including temperature, wind velocity, and the surface upon which the agent comes to rest.

Like all hazardous materials, chemical agents can exist as solids, liquids, or gases, depending on the existing temperatures and pressures. When chemical agents are weaponized, they are in the liquid state within the weapon. When the container (weapon shell) explodes, the agent is expelled as a liquid or aerosol, which is a group of small solid particles or liquid droplets suspended in gas. For instance, mustard and nerve agents are not gases at normal temperatures and pressures. Therefore, to be an effective terrorist agent, they must be heated to produce vapor, and the vapor has to be disseminated in order for people to breathe it.

Acquisition, Manufacture, and Use

Once a group has selected the agent that it would like to use, it must take appropriate measures to acquire the chemical and produce a weapon for subsequent use. Terrorists have two basic approaches available to them to obtain chemical weapons, each of which has unique attractions and drawbacks. The first approach is to acquire chemical weapons by theft, "gift" (such as from a state sponsor), or purchase. The second is to produce the chemical agent, and its delivery mechanism using precursors and other materials that are themselves purchased, stolen, or otherwise obtained. A choice of whether to select one or both of these two basic approaches must be made irrespective of whether the group plans to employ military chemical weapon agents or the aforementioned toxic industrial chemicals.

The acquisition and use of toxic industrial chemicals may represent the most effective method for terrorist groups to obtain a chemical weapon capability. Many highly toxic chemicals, including anhydrous ammonia, chlorine, hydrogen fluoride, phosgene, and others, are produced, stored, and transported in very large quantities in support of normal day-to-day industrial activities. Security for these chemicals is frequently minimal or nonexistent, and it is reasonable to suppose that a determined terrorist group would be able to gain access to significant quantities without too much difficulty.

A more likely alternative for those seeking access to military chemical weapon agents is to produce them indigenously along with the necessary delivery systems. This contingency has received extensive attention from many analysts who often differ on the ease of producing chemical weapon agents. Some contend that the production of military agents, especially nerve agents, is an extremely difficult enterprise. Others adopt the position that the production of relatively small quantities of the agent, on the order of a few tens of kilograms, can be achieved without too much difficulty by moderately skilled personnel using widely available equipment. Still others contend that it is not so much the production of the agent that is the major barrier, but the mating of agent and delivery device in such a way that ensures that the agent will be disseminated effectively and act in the way it is intended.

The basic requirements for manufacturing chemical weapons from scratch include precursor chemicals and an assortment of dual-use chemical equipment, potentially including corrosion-resistant piping and reaction vessels. All else being equal, the more basic the initial precursor chemicals the terrorists obtain, the more reaction steps will be required to produce the desired chemical agent and the longer and more complex the production process becomes. Certain processes for more complex chemical agents (such as certain of the G-series nerve agents) are extremely dangerous and require specialized equipment that can withstand corrosion, high temperatures, and high pressures.[36,37] Nonetheless, several alternative synthesis methods exist for producing most chemical weapon agents, and it is likely that terrorists would try wherever possible to avoid those that use high-temperature and high-pressure reactions in order to obviate the need for special equipment and reduce the possibility of injury or discovery resulting from an accidental release.[38,39]

Vesicants are simpler to produce than nerve agents, both in terms of the chemical precursors required and the processes and materials needed for manufacture, but it is unlikely, although not impossible, that these will be selected. These agents are generally slow in their effects, may require large quantities to have a widespread affect, and lack lethality, reducing their attractiveness to terrorists, who have frequently indicated their interest in generating mass casualties. The main attraction of vesicants would be the ease with which they can contaminate a large area and the potential they have to produce significant economic disruptions while efforts are undertaken to decontaminate all potentially exposed facilities and persons. In contrast, nerve agents are lethal even in very small doses and have a rapid effect, and even trace quantities can produce distressing physical symptoms, such as dimming and blurring of vision. On the other hand, these attractive qualities are counterbalanced by the difficulties associated with nerve-agent production, which requires a series of complex reactions between precursors and intermediates that are difficult to obtain and are frequently corrosive or toxic. The services of a suitable chemical engineer would be a necessary requirement for success.[40]

Finally, the group producing the agents would need to take special precautions to avoid prematurely exposing themselves to the agents. Depending on the level of risk the group is willing to accept, these precautions could range from basic spill and inhalation protections, such as impervious gloves and gas masks to obtaining nerve agent antidotes, such as atropine. Although the latter step might increase the possibility of detection, it could be useful for ensuring that those involved in the production of the chemical weapon agent survive long enough to complete their task. Acquiring the required equipment may or may not be difficult, depending on the location of the jihadist manufacturing effort. In heavily industrialized societies, such as Europe, obtaining the necessary equipment for small-scale batch production of chemical weapon agents should not be an insurmountable obstacle. The dual-use nature of many precursor chemicals and equipment puts the synthesis of limited quantities of chemical weapon agents within the reach of almost all terrorist organizations with the requisite expertise. Obtaining exotic precursor chemicals may be difficult, but those that cannot be purchased may be available through

---

[36] As an example, Tucker notes that the aluminum phosphorus complex (APC) process for the production of sarin creates an explosive hazard and produces large volumes of toxic byproducts. The more traditional DMHP process requires the use of highly toxic and corrosive hydrogen fluoride gas. This is also the case with the production of VX. Production of the key precursor transester (QL) requires working with chemicals that react violently to water and catch fire if exposed to moist air. The final reaction stage also involves an extremely energetic reaction. J. B. Tucker, *War of Nerves: Chemical Warfare from World War I to al-Qaeda*. New York: Pantheon, 2006, 111, 134, 159.

[37] J. B. Tucker. *War of Nerves: Chemical Warfare from World War I to al-Qaeda*. New York: Pantheon, 2006, 111, 134, 159.

[38] N. Gurr and B. Cole. *The New Face of Terrorism: Threats from Weapons of Mass Destruction*. London: I. B. Tauris, 2002, 51.

[39] R. A. Falkenrath, R. D. Newman, and B. A. Thayer. *America's Achilles' Heel: Nuclear, Biological, and Chemical Terrorism and Covert Attack*. Cambridge, MA: MIT Press, 1998, 107.

[40] The important consideration to note here is that the person need not be a specialist who has already worked with CW agents. The important thing is that they have some familiarity with small-batch production of chemicals.

targeted thefts, depending on the level of chemical activity in the local economy. Once again, such attempting to steal chemical weapon agent precursors and related technology would increase the risk that the group might be detected. An alternative would be to produce precursors from their more basic chemical ingredients.[41]

Aum Shinrikyo and Chemical Terrorism

Since Aum Shinrikyo's 1995 sarin gas attack on the Tokyo subway, the question of whether terrorists could develop more effective chemical weapons has been the subject of intense debate. The Aum experience, however, is one of only a limited number of historical cases of terrorist attempts to exploit chemistry for malicious purposes. A key question is whether the case of Aum Shinrikyo is, in fact, representative of the difficult challenges that non-state actors face in trying to harness the life sciences and related technology or whether Aum was a unique situation, a one-of-a-kind combination of profound bad luck and organizational dysfunction that will not be repeated.[42]

In any case, Aum Shinrikyo provides an instructive example, highlighting aspects of terrorist group capabilities for the production of military-grade chemical weapons. Aum was a large, well-resourced group based in a highly developed industrial society. The group actively recruited educated individuals who possessed a multitude of useful technical skills in the fields of biology and chemistry. Drawing on the skills of its members, the group was able to successfully produce small quantities of nerve agents, including sarin, soman, tabun, and VX. Over a period of six months, beginning in November 1993, the group produced some 30 kilograms of sarin, which was subsequently used in attacks against both individuals and large groups of people. The group also constructed a large facility that was intended to produce as much as two tons of sarin per day as part of a plan to amass a stockpile of 70 tons of agent. Although this large production facility was not able to produce any sarin before the group's activities were ended by Japanese authorities, Aum's ability to design, construct, and begin to operate the facility was unprecedented. However, it is not clear whether another terrorist group would be able to duplicate Aum's success by constructing and operating a similar facility.

A much more significant element of the Aum case is the group's ability to make several tens of kilograms of sarin using laboratory methods over approximately six months. In doing so, the group highlighted the point that the production of so-called classic chemical weapon agents does not require the latest cutting-edge science and technology although access to skilled personnel remains critical. In fact, they exploited science that is more than 70 years old and quite well understood by a large number of people worldwide. The agent was produced at a facility located in a Tokyo suburb that, while impressive for a non-state actor, involved relatively crude production techniques and technologies. In addition to producing useful quantities of the agent, Aum was also able to develop and deploy a somewhat effective vehicle-mounted delivery system, which was used in the 1994 Matsumoto attack. Nevertheless, not all of Aum's attempts to produce workable delivery systems were as successful or as sophisticated as that used in the Matsumoto attack. Most famously, the Tokyo subway attack was conducted using plastic bags filled with liquid sarin that were punctured by umbrella tips and left to evaporate. This crude delivery technique, combined with the relatively poor quality of the sarin in terms of its purity, were major factors in limiting the number of casualties in that attack to only 12 victims.

The Aum case is particularly interesting for what it says about the ability of a well-funded organization with access to skilled personnel to produce and deliver military-style chemical weapon agents. In contrast to Aum's successes, the efforts of al-Qaeda, and jihadist groups in general to

---

[41] Office of Technology Assessment. Technologies Underlying Weapons of Mass Destruction, 1993, 30–31.

[42] J. A. Russell and C. Clary. Globalization and WMD Proliferation Networks: Challenges to US Security. Report of a Conference Sponsored by the Naval Postgraduate School. June 29–July 1, 2005, 9.

demonstrate a similar production capability have been much less impressive. Al-Qaeda has been suspected of seeking to produce chemical weapons ever since the group came to the attention of US authorities. However, to date, neither al-Qaeda nor the wider jihadist movement has demonstrated the ability to produce even small quantities of military agents. The most significant effort to date was that undertaken in Afghanistan in the late 1990s and early 2000s. Investigations following the US invasion of that country highlighted al-Qaeda's interest in these weapons, noting the existence of laboratories and documentation related to chemical weapon agent production. The bulk of these efforts were focused on the manufacturing of cyanide derivatives and industrial chemicals. There was little or no evidence to suggest that the group had demonstrated an ability to manufacture nerve agents.

Ultimately, although terrorist groups have some familiarity with the use of chemicals and chemical processes, these skills have been limited to that basic subset required to manufacture high explosives. In general terms, the efforts of terrorist groups to produce their own chemical weapons have thus far proven ineffective. A fundamental problem appears to be an inadequate understanding of the chemical processes involved and the difficulties in securing personnel with the appropriate skills. At the same time, terrorists' (overall) past lack of success in developing and producing chemical weapon agents should not be allowed to foster complacency when considering future prospects.

How the chemical terrorism challenge will evolve is a function of significant, ongoing, and often rapid change—first and foremost in the underlying science and technology but also in the security landscape, social organization, strategic priorities, the form and function of conflict, and elsewhere. These changes are converging to create an environment marked by greater complexity and uncertainty, which, in turn, will heighten unpredictability. Managing risks in this environment will constitute the greatest challenge to policymakers in both counterterrorism and the chemical weapon arena in the future. But it will be an unfamiliar challenge. It will be less and less about what the terrorists have and more and more about what they know and how they may try to misuse that knowledge. In the past, their knowledge base and technical know-how have been limited; in light of current trends, that could change.

Concluding Thoughts

Terrorism has evolved over time, reflecting the ideologies, organizational preferences, and technological sophistication of those who attempt to kill the innocent to achieve their political objectives. Future attacks could thus involve WMD with levels of casualties and destruction heretofore never seen within the United States and abroad. Chemical, biological, nuclear, and radiological weapons would provide terrorists with different capabilities and pose different operational challenges.

Based on their characteristics, physical properties, and effects, chemical weapons differ significantly from their nuclear and biological counterparts. Simple chemical weapons are relatively easy to procure, for example, but relatively large quantities of an agent, dispersed in the right quantity over the targeted area, are needed to produce mass casualties. The effects of chemical weapons are normally seen over a smaller area, and they have been traditionally viewed as more effective at the tactical or operational level rather than at the strategic level. In contrast to biological weapons, which are generally slow acting, the effects of exposure to chemical weapons can become apparent within minutes or, at most, hours of initial contact. The strategic value of chemical weapons derives primarily from their psychological impact. Forcing a frightened population, or even military units, to don gas masks or protective gear can produce both physical and psychological effects of significant magnitude.

Although terrorists have demonstrated interest in the full range of CBRN weapons, chemicals are the most likely weapons to be used in the near term. By contrast, nuclear weapons pose fewer challenges in terms of use, but they are extremely difficult to manufacture or procure on the black market. While nuclear weapons have the potential to be many orders of magnitude more devastating than chemical weapons, they are also significantly less likely to be used in the medium term or even long term. In short, a terrorist attack involving nuclear weapons constitutes the quintessential low-probability, high-consequence scenario. Biological weapons are a somewhat less high consequence vis-à-vis nuclear weapons while the probability of their use is slightly higher. Chemical weapons, on the other hand, are unique insofar as they combine significant potential consequences with a generally accepted high probability of use. The basic technologies underlying chemical weapons are essentially ubiquitous in the modern world, and many analysts have concluded that the required materials and processes are well within the capabilities of determined terrorist groups. This contrasts with nuclear weapons, for which the necessary materials are very hard to obtain, and biological weapons, for which the technologies and methods have proven very difficult to master.

Terrorists also have an operational code and history that leads them to prefer certain types of weapons over others. Aum Shinrikyo experimented with biological agents, but chemical weapons were incorporated as part of its belief structure. Al-Qaeda has attempted to launch attacks using lethal chemical or noncontagious biological agents, but it has not yet used a radiological dispersal device or contagious biological agent, weapons it could probably acquire. As this chapter shows, terrorists are dabbling with WMD although no group has yet employed them with maximum effect.

One of the greatest challenges facing security professionals today is determining if and when jihadists could use biological and toxin weapons. It cannot be assumed that because a jihadist terrorist organization has stated that they desire to use WMD and have made rudimentary attempts to acquire biological weapons that they will succeed in doing so or even proceed to choose a biological weapon as their favored method of attack. Serious questions, including whether or not their ideology (the perception and application of which may vary across jihadist cells) permits the indiscriminate use of the weapon (assuming it is a communicable agent), along with organizational factors, access to financial resources, and technical capabilities must be weighed carefully. Still, the apparent resurrection of al-Qaeda's WMD program; the number of uncovered plots to develop or obtain radiological, biological, and chemical weapons by other jihadist terror groups; and the increasingly global availability of life sciences materials and technical know-how illustrate that the threat of jihadist WMD terrorism cannot be ignored.

From the perspective of tactical deployment, CBRN materials pose many risks to operatives throughout the planning and preparation stages of an attack. A lack of familiarity and comfort with toxins, pathogens, or radiological materials could expose would-be perpetrators to greater operational risks than they may be willing to accept (assuming that they are aware of such risks and do not take precautions to mitigate or protect against them). In any case, many of the elements and materials necessary for these weapons are expensive and regulated through various domestic licensing systems and export control regimes, making it difficult to acquire them without attracting the attention of local authorities. Further, these central elements are notoriously difficult to weaponize and deploy effectively, and the highly specialized knowledge required for a successful WMD attack is rare among terrorists. Overall, there are a lot more things that can go wrong with CBRN weapons than with conventional explosives. With all these considerations, the return on investment in CBRN is seen as lower than that associated with conventional, homemade explosives, such as those used in Bali, Madrid, London, and so many other terrorist attacks in recent years.

By and large, despite globalization and numerous technological advances over the past decade, it is noteworthy that more (and more successful) attacks using weapons of mass destruction have not been seen. Indeed, based on predictions of the past decade, governments should be awash in terrorist attacks using improvised chemical, biological, radiological, or nuclear weapons by now. But they are not and for several good reasons, including the limited availability of CBRN materials, the relatively rare ideological justification for their use, the limited tactical and strategic benefits they offer, and the many operational disadvantages that are associated with a WMD attack. Understanding the advantages and disadvantages of CBRN weapons is necessary in order to appreciate the difficulties that terrorists face in rationalizing their acquisition and use.

7

Terrorist Funding[1]

Terrorist organizations need money and resources not only to carry out an operation but, perhaps most importantly, to recruit, maintain safe havens, train, travel, take care of day-to-day expenses, and, in some groups, provide for the families of dead martyrs. The assets required to fund such extensive, global operations synonymous with modern terrorist groups come from a variety of licit and illicit sources, such as individuals, organizations, and the criminal enterprise. One widely used estimate is that economic activity–related terrorist group activity accounts for a staggering $1.5 trillion, or 5% of annual global output.[2] Furthermore, the cost of doing business may be rising for terrorists, especially al-Qaeda. Similar to a business expanding into franchises, splinter groups need resources to sustain themselves, driving the cost of doing business higher. Also, as terrorist plots increase in complexity or delve into the WMD realm, the cost of equipment, expertise, and keeping operations off law enforcement's radar will rise. These emergent needs will likely lead groups to previously untapped sources for money, manpower, and other support.

An old soldier's axiom provides excellent context to the importance of pursuing terrorist and criminal financing: "Amateurs study tactics; professionals study logistics." The money trail is perhaps the key to preventing future operations, more so than any other aspect of terrorism investigative work. A transaction can typically be broken down into a series of smaller steps, allowing investigators to further penetrate an operation. The identification of individual, illicit transactions, the behavior of the actors accomplishing licit transactions, and other information gathered from video surveillance, cell phone records, and computer Internet Protocol (IP) addresses can certainly unravel plots and destroy organizations. Therefore, understanding the methodologies employed and keeping an eye on developing techniques are critical to successful investigatory penetration. This chapter examines the sources of funding for terrorism and the ways in which terrorists move and store their licit and illicit funds.

Classifying Terrorist Sources of Support

Terrorists use diverse methods to procure the capital necessary to finance their organizations and activities. Historically, governments have funded terrorism. Specifically, law enforcement, internal security, intelligence, or other official agencies have been used by governments to conduct terrorist acts against foreign nations, the nation's own people, or foreign dissidents.

[1] Information for this chapter was drawn from the following titles: (1) M. Kraft and E. Marks, *US Government Counterterrorism: A Guide to Who Does What*, CRC Press, 2010. (2) J. L. Hesterman, *The Terrorist-Criminal Nexus: An Alliance of International Drug Cartels, Organized Crime, and Terror Groups*, CRC Press, 2013.

[2] A. Cowell. Terrorism's Cost in a Global Economy. *New York Times*, November 9, 2003.

State-directed terrorism has also occurred. This type of terrorism is ordered and controlled by a nation that uses a terrorist group as a tool in carrying out government policy. The term "state sponsored" is often used in place of the more accurate "state directed." Examples include Harakat ul-Ansar (Pakistan) and the Mujahideen al Khalq (Iraq). Additionally, state-sponsored terrorism has occurred: terrorist groups that operate independently but receive financial, material, intelligence, or operational support from one or more foreign nations. These groups enjoy the approval and support of nations but are not told what or where to strike. Because governments only marginally control them, they are harder to deter. Examples include the Irish Republican Army (IRA), Hamas, and the Palestinian Islamic Jihad (PIJ). State support involves the intentional and direct financial support of terrorist organizations and activities by an established and recognized state government. For example, Colonel Muammar al-Qadaffi, dictator of Libya, is known to support extremist and terrorist organizations. He has used the government's wealth from the oil industry in Libya to support the IRA, the Palestine Liberation Organization (PLO), the Popular Front for the Liberation of Palestine (PFLP), the Democratic Front for the Liberation of Palestine (DFLP), and the Popular Front for the Liberation of Palestine-General Command (PFLP-GC) to the tune of approximately $100 million dollars a year. A more common form of terrorism does not involve governments. These are terrorist groups that are completely independent of support of a foreign government. These terrorist groups are potentially the most dangerous because they are not subject to political pressures. Al-Qaeda is an independent terrorist group. These terrorists receive their funds from a variety of sources.

Earning, Moving, Storing

When the FBI transported Ramzi Yousef by helicopter over Manhattan following his capture in 1995 for the bombing of the World Trade Center's Twin Towers, an FBI agent pulled up Yousef's blindfold and pointed out the lights of the World Trade Center were still glowing. As the FBI agent stated, "They [are] still standing." Yousef is reported to have responded, "They would [not] be if I had enough money and explosives." This chapter examines the sources of funding for terrorism. To frame the discussion of terrorist and financing activities, it is important to first differentiate between traditional methods employed by groups and their members to earn, move, store, and/or launder their assets. This model is especially helpful when applied to transnational and virtual finance issues.

Earning

Legal investments can fund terrorist organizations and operations. In the early 1970s, the Palestine Liberation Organization (PLO) started buying partnerships in airlines as well as purchasing duty-free shops in airports with financial backing from Libya and other Arab countries. Osama bin Laden, for example, was using a network of retail shops selling honey, owned by him and other members of the al-Qaeda organization, to generate funds for terror missions. These stores were located throughout the Middle East, Pakistan, and especially Yemen. They provide a legitimate source of income for bin Laden's terrorist network.

Cultural or Ethnic Support Organizations

One such source is cultural or ethnic support organizations. Legitimate organizations that support cultural or ethnic causes or goals of their people may, in some cases, provide financial support to other groups pursuing the same goals that are involved in terrorist activities. The IRA was supported financially by the Irish Northern Aid Organization (NORAID), based in the United States. NORAID has branches all over the country and is a main collections source of supporters' contributions. Until 1991, the US government allowed funds to be collected by Arab groups to fund the Office of Jihad Services or Maktab al-Khadimat (MAK) in order to recruit fighters against Russia, but many eventually joined al-Qaeda.

Charities

Charitable organizations have also funded terrorism. The use of charities to raise funds for terrorist groups is a persistent concern in the counterterrorism community. Modern charities are global in nature, and many are the equivalent of large-scale corporations. The use of charities to raise funds is desirable primarily because of the ability to quickly comingle illicit funds with licit funds, making a direct link between the financier and terrorist act virtually impossible. Further, for contributors wishing to finance a terrorist group, their identities are protected due to lack of a paper trail and the charity's ability to hide within and be protected by a large, overarching religious organization. For example, per the US Treasury, despite the best efforts of the UN, the United States, and others, Hamas still raises tens of millions of dollars per year using charitable fund-raising as a cover. Unfortunately, the Internet and virtual "nonbanks" have unintentionally kept illicit charities in business.

Nongovernmental organizations can be established to funnel legitimate donations from supporters to fund terrorist organizations and activities without the explicit knowledge of the donors. The Afghan Support Committee (ASC) is a nongovernmental organization established by Osama bin Laden. The ASC claims that donations to the organization are given to widows and orphans and then uses the donated money to fund al-Qaeda operations.

Zakat

Zakat-al-Mal is another fund-raising mechanism receiving far less attention than charities but possibly with greater significance. In a little-known report prepared for the UN by terrorist-financing expert Jean-Charles Brisard, Zakat is singled out as the most important source of terrorism funding, and most of the funds are moved through the legal banking system.[3] The literal meaning of the word "Zakat" is cleansing and growth. Zakat is charitable giving, part of every devout Muslim's obligations; it typically peaks during the season of Ramadan, and is paid on or before Eid. An individual who possesses wealth equal to or above a set minimum amount (called Nasab) is obliged to give Zakat. The Qur'an specifies eight purposes for which the money from Zakat can be used[3]:

1. The poor
2. The needy
3. Those employed to administer the collection, distribution, and administration of Zakat as compensation
4. Individuals who have been recently reconciled to the "Truth" (Mu'allafat-al-Qulub), including new Muslims or those who are willing to support the Muslim state but need to be compensated
5. Freeing of those in bondage or slavery
6. Those in debt
7. In the cause of Allah: Those who are going out or working in the cause of Allah (including the task of conveying the message of Islam) or in a battle declared by an Islamic state for just cause
8. The wayfarer: a traveler who is in need of help during his travel

Certainly, the interpretation of these Zakat destinations could be varied with donors believing their intentions are pure but with money funding illegal or terrorist activities. According to Brisard's estimate, Saudis contribute approximately 10 billion US dollars per year in Zakat

[3] J.-C. Brisard. Terrorism Financing: Roots and trends of Saudi terrorism financing. Report prepared for the President of the Security Council, United Nations, Dec. 19, 2002. Available at http://www.investigativeproject.org/documents/testimony/22.pdf.

donations, which then usually take the form of bank transfers to approximately 240 charities. He estimates that between $300 and $500 million gathered through Zakat were given to al-Qaeda in the years leading up to 9/11.[4] The lack of bookkeeping for Zakat makes it difficult to identify contributors or beneficiaries. Also, countries are extremely sensitive about the monitoring of religious giving. In response to intense scrutiny of the Zakat system following the attacks and international pressure, Saudi authorities removed Zakat "collection boxes" from outside of their mosques and businesses, but the amount of money collected in those boxes represented only $60,000 a year.[5] Although plenty of funds collected through Zakat reach the intended recipients, much of it goes to questionable sources and activities. In Pakistan, for example, scholars note that Zakat recipients have included "orphans" with living parents, "impoverished women" decorated in gold jewelry, and "old people" who had long since died.[6] The anonymity and mixing of funds collected through Zakat makes this method extremely vulnerable to terrorist fund-raising activities.

Illicit Activities

Terrorist operations are funded by criminal activities, some of which include kidnapping for ransom, drug trafficking, narco-trafficking protection, illegal taxation, and illegal banking activities. Kidnapping for ransom involves terrorists collecting money for the assured safe release of hostages. The FARC of Colombia is believed to have made more than $200 million in ransom from the release of abducted Colombian citizens. In addition, terrorists engage in illegal production and transportation of drugs for profit, which are channeled into terrorist operations. Terrorists have also engaged in narco-trafficking protection, which is the collection of money, usually a set percentage of profits, for the assured security and protection of cultivators and smugglers of drugs. FARC provides security and protection for the coca farmers in Colombia for a fee of 10% of the profits. In 1986, this alone provided the FARC with almost $3.38 million each month. Moreover, terrorists have engaged in illegal taxation, which is the collection of a percentage of citizens' incomes in areas under the control of a terrorist organization. Furthermore, terrorists have engaged in illegal banking activities, such as the direct involvement and assistance, by a financial institution, in the financial operations of a known terrorist organization. In particular, in 1985, the CIA and British Intelligence (MI6) linked the Bank of Credit and Commerce International (BCCI) to the funding of terrorism. Osama bin Laden had accounts with BCCI when it was shut down in 1991.

Moreover, terrorist funding has been obtained via protection rackets, which involve the collection of fees for security and protection services provided by a legitimate company with known ties to a terrorist organization. In Northern Ireland, both the Irish Republican Army and Ulster Defense Regiment (UDR) have created a number of apparently legitimate private security companies throughout the areas they control. These "security companies" offer legitimate services to all businesses in their area for a regular legitimate fee. They will exhibit the brutal nature of terrorism only when a potential client refuses the services offered. Legal businesses may be used by terrorists. These are legally operated and owned firms whose income is used to fund terrorist organizations and activities. Basically, payments are knowingly made to a terrorist organization for protection, secrecy, or false service of some kind.

---

[4] J.-C. Brisard. Terrorism Financing: Roots and trends of Saudi terrorism financing. Report prepared for the President of the Security Council, United Nations, Dec. 19, 2002. Available at http://www.investigativeproject.org/documents/testimony/22.pdf.

[5] Center for Strategic and International Studies (CSIS). Transnational Threats Initiative, 1, no. 10, 1–4, July 2003. Available at http://csis.org/files/media/csis/pubs/ttu_0307.pdf.

[6] US House Committee on Financial Services. Anti-Money Laundering: Blocking Terrorist Financing and Its Impact on Lawful Charities, May 10, 2010.

Commodities Smuggling and Organized Retail Crime

The exploitation of high-use products within the United States is an increasingly popular fund-raising tool for criminal and terrorist groups. In commodity-smuggling schemes, high-demand products, such as cigarettes, are purchased in one state and sold in another with a higher tax rate. To generate income for Hezbollah, cigarettes were smuggled from North Carolina into Michigan for resale at a higher price without Michigan's higher cigarette taxes being paid. The profits were sent to Lebanon and financed attacks on Israel. This not only reaps a profit for the criminal group, it causes loss for the victimized state, as would-be buyers leave the traditional marketplace to make black-market purchases.

In organized retail crime (ORC), products are not purchased but stolen and then resold by a criminal enterprise to reap the profit. Products are shoplifted, acquired through cargo theft, or purchased with stolen credit cards. Individuals known as "boosters" then convert the product on the street for profit. ORC organizations are very sophisticated and compartmentalized and operate similarly to criminal entities involved in drug trafficking or human smuggling. Stolen products range from perfume to the latest ORC hot product, Tide laundry detergent.

Operation Milk Money was a federal investigation of an ORC ring involved in the theft and interstate transportation of stolen baby formula. The primary targets were Honduran nationals who stole and resold thousands of cans of powdered baby formula on a monthly basis with an estimated annual loss to the retail industry in excess of $1 million dollars. Financial transactions were accomplished to conceal the nature, source, ownership, and control of the illicit proceeds. One target structured approximately $208,744 in cash by making deposits in amounts less than $10,000 in an attempt to avoid FINCEN's (Financial Crime Enforcement Network) reporting requirements. Operation Milk Money resulted in 21 arrests.[7]

The US Immigration and Customs Enforcement (ICE) is the lead agency battling ORC through its Homeland Security Investigation (HSI) arm. In July 2009, HSI initiated an ORC pilot program and the follow-up SEARCH initiative (Seizing Earnings and Assets from Retail Crime Heists) to help combat the transnational organized crime networks involved in this illicit activity. The interstate and international shipment of stolen goods and corresponding movement of illicit proceeds from their sale make charges related to Title 18 United States Code 1956, laundering of monetary instruments, possible. SEARCH pulls together the efforts of federal, state, and local law enforcement, prosecutors, and the financial and retail community to provide a multifaceted approach to deterrence and prosecution.

Profits generated from commodity smuggling and ORC are laundered through the US financial sector. Therefore any vulnerability in banking or money services business (MSB) systems, whether technological, human, or other, will be exploited by actors to move or store their illicit proceeds. FINCEN is heavily involved in disseminating information regarding red flags and typologies to MSBs and financial institutions. All types of money-laundering techniques and exploitation of e-commerce have been detected as related to commodities smuggling and ORC. Since 2009, ICE has initiated more than 120 criminal investigations with 63 arrests and more than $6 million in property seized.[8]

Intellectual Property Crime (IPC)

IPC is occurring throughout the world and generates an unbelievable amount of profit. In fact, counterfeit-goods trade is estimated at $450 billion annually, representing 5% to 7% of global trade value. In the United States alone, losses to counterfeiting are staggering, estimated by the

---

[7] J. Hopper. Formula for Theft Success: Steal Food for a Baby. *ABC World News*, April 13, 2011. Available at http://abcnews.go.com/US/baby-formula-targeted-organized-retail-theft-rings/story?id=13293485#. UfnUWa6ur31.

[8] J. Larocca. ICE Announces Expansion of ORC Pilot Program. February 14, 2011. Available at http://blog.nrf.com/2011/ 02/14/ice-announces-expansion-of-orc-pilot-program/.

FBI at $200 to $250 billion annually.[9] Intellectual property refers to the legal rights corresponding to intellectual activity in the industrial, scientific, and artistic fields. These legal rights, most commonly in the form of patents, trademarks, and copyrights, protect not only the moral and economic entitlement of the creators but also the creativity and dissemination of their work.

Counterfeiting is the creation of false currency with the intention of recirculation. It is believed the Iranian-backed Lebanese terrorist group Hezbollah produced and distributed hundreds of millions of high-quality US hundred-dollar bills and used them for black-market purchases. The quality of these forgeries prompted an entire change of US paper currency. Based on this understanding, IPC refers to counterfeited and pirated goods, manufactured and sold for profit without the consent of the patent or trademark holder. IPC is a black-market activity operating parallel to the formal economy and includes the manufacturing, transporting, storing, and sale of counterfeit or pirated goods. Examples of pirated goods are CDs, DVDs, cigarettes, clothes, shoes, designer purses, and computer software. Any hot commodity is ripe for exploitation; for example, when Rosetta Stone rose in popularity, it became a favorite for counterfeiters who then sold their products on Craig's list or eBay and laundered money through PayPal. No product line is safe from counterfeiters, and even inexpensive items, such as NFL pennants or condoms, have been replicated.

IPC is a lucrative criminal activity with low initial investment and high financial returns, possibly even higher than drug trafficking. For instance, an Xbox game costing 40¢ to duplicate can be sold on the black market for $20, realizing unbelievable profit. The link between organized crime groups and counterfeit goods is well established. IPC is a global criminal activity on the rise and quickly becoming a lucrative method of funding for a number of terrorist groups.

Why might IPC become an increasingly important source of illicit financing for terrorist groups? One reason is that local law enforcement finds it difficult to treat IPC as a high-priority crime, typically due to their lack of manpower resources or technical investigative knowledge. In a large heist, federal law enforcement naturally must engage. However, when it comes to duplicating Rosetta Stone DVDs in a small operation and selling them at flea markets or on eBay, the investigation and prosecution costs may seem greater than the value of stopping the operation. If IPC is pursued in smaller cases, the result is often seizure of goods or halting of production but no further investigation of the money trail, which is often complex and robust with untraceable cash-based transactions.

Trafficking in counterfeit goods is a relatively easy criminal activity. A terrorist could make profit solely from the sale of counterfeit or pirated goods and does not need to be involved in the actual production or fabrication. Thus there are relatively low entry costs, and the illicit profit margins are high. The profit/risk ratio is attractive not only to criminals, but also to loosely networked terrorist groups who do not have the capacity to generate funds through sophisticated criminal activity. Demand for "knockoff" products is widespread due to public perception that purchasing these goods is not a criminal offense and a general lack of understanding regarding underlying criminal activity. Think of the numerous vendor stands found in big cities, hawking "designer" purses, scarves, and sunglasses bearing the same logos and identifiable as fakes only by the trained eye. Counterfeit goods are now part of mainstream America, which has an insatiable desire for luxury goods with most lacking the resources to purchase them. This low-risk/high-return activity and others like it bear watching as we close down other sources of terrorist funding.

Identity Theft

The sophisticated white-collar crimes of identity theft and credit card fraud are no longer just a consumer issue. When federal investigators unraveled the 9/11 money trail, it suddenly became clear that identity theft was an issue related to global terrorism and national security. The hijackers used phony identification, Social Security numbers, and birth dates to establish bank accounts and

[9] FBI. Intellectual Property Crime Rights Coordination Center. Available at http://www.iprcenter.gov/.

create their lives in the United States. Landlords, flight schools, banks, and other institutions were victims and unwitting contributors to the terrorist operation. Seven of the hijackers obtained identification cards through the Virginia Department of Motor Vehicles (DMV) even though none lived in the state. They took advantage of rules allowing individuals to meet residency requirements with a simple notarized letter, a system fraught with fraud and long abused by immigrants, immigration lawyers, and local notaries. Despite previous warnings from the FBI and DMV investigators, the department maintained the rudimentary identification system.[10]

Identity fraud and related crimes in the financial sector are often the source of terrorist fundraising. According to identity theft expert Judith Collins of Michigan State University's Identity Theft Crime and Research Lab, "All acts of terrorism enacted against the United States have been facilitated with the use of a fake or stolen identity."[11] Terrorists need to blend in when working the logistical aspects of the operation, such as obtaining clothing and components of weapons and, most importantly, fulfilling transportation needs, such as rental vehicles and airline tickets. Most Americans do not use cash for these purchases, and the terrorists would bring unwanted attention if they were to do so, hence the need for credit cards. Passports are also extensively used by terrorists moving between countries of interest and the target; the use of stolen identities and fake passports has been documented in many terrorism cases in the past 10 years.

More attractive because of its transparency and ability to access a subject's credit for a longer period is an emergent criminal act called "skimming." Skimming was first detected as a criminal tactic when master counterfeiter and terrorist supporter Youssef Hmimssa was arrested just days after 9/11 when he was caught providing fake visas and other identification documents to a suspected terrorist cell in Detroit. His apartment yielded documents, including a day planner that the government says contained sketches of a US air base in Turkey, and a videotape of potential future terrorist targets in Los Angeles, New York, and other locations. He confessed his crimes and has gone public to explain how easy identity theft and fraud is to perpetrate.

In 2003, Hmimssa was called to testify to the Senate Finance Committee to enlighten lawmakers, and his testimony was both riveting and troubling. In support of his efforts, Hmimssa recruited a fellow Moroccan, both a taxi driver and a waiter at a north suburban restaurant, to steal customers' credit card numbers. He provided his codefendant with a pocketsize device resembling a pager. With a single swipe, the skimming device copied encoded information on the card's magnetic strip. The driver/waiter would swipe customer credit cards through the device and then give the skimmer to Hmimssa, who downloaded the information using a laptop computer. In all, the pair skimmed about 250 credit card account numbers and bilked customers out of more than $100,000. In the past few years, criminals have become savvier and have started putting skimmers on gas pumps and ATM machines. With wireless technology, the card data is immediately transferred. Identity theft and related crimes have been detected in many terrorist cells in the past five years.

Ahmed Ressam, a member of the Armed Islamic Group (with ties to bin Laden), was caught in December 1999 at the US–Canadian border with 100 pounds of explosives stashed in the wheel bed of the trunk of his rental car. He had assumed the name Benni Norris, which he used to obtain a passport, false birth certificate, and student ID as well as to open bank accounts. He told authorities he relied on welfare and petty crime, including credit card fraud and trafficking in identity documents, for support. He was linked to a theft ring suspected of stealing more than 5000 items, including computers, cellular phones, passports, and credit cards, with the goal of financing Muslim extremist groups.[12] In his so-called millennium plot, Ressam planned to set off a large explosive device at the Los Angeles International Airport. Others involved with the operation told FBI agents they supported themselves through credit card fraud and used

---

[10] R. O'Harrow. Identity Crisis: Meet Michael Berry. *Washington Post*, August 10, 2003.

[11] F. Perri. The Fraud–Terror Link: Terrorists are Committing Fraud to Fund Their Activities. *Fraud Magazine* 12, no. 4, 28–52, July–August 2010. Available at http://www.fraud-magazine.com/article.aspx?id=4294967888.

[12] R. O'Harrow. Identity Crisis, *Washington Post Magazine*, August 10, 2003.

proceeds from the scam and others to finance their mission. They used countless stolen and fraudulent identities, including 13 stolen from the membership computer of a Bally's fitness club in Boston. They also had plans to buy a gas station and use the business as an avenue to secretly obtain credit card numbers, placing a camera in a location where it would be possible to watch people punching in their PIN numbers.

Al-Qaeda uses credit card scams and identity theft extensively. The 9/11 hijackers had a scheme in Spain to raise money for the attacks, and according to authorities, "[t]he pattern was very clear within the North African contingent of al-Qaeda members operating in Europe. Every time you arrest one of them he has 20 different identities and 20 different credit cards."[13] Other suspected terrorist cells operating in the United States, Canada, and Europe have employed a variety of scams to steal millions of dollars from credit card companies.

The link between terrorists and sophisticated white-collar crimes, such as identity theft and related fraud, is irrefutable. Technological advances have only made this crime easier to commit, and it remains a lucrative means of raising funds for terrorist groups.

Other Fund-Raising Methods

Fraud is a scheme that involves the deceptive collection of some kind of benefit, such as money. Manufacturers' coupons generate eight billion dollars annually—inserts from recyclers, newspaper distributors, and small newsstands are purchased in bulk to collect the unused coupons. The coupons are then clipped, sorted, and shipped for reimbursement. Funds are then smuggled out of the United States and used to fund terrorist activities.

One type of fraud is government subsidy fraud, which involves the fraudulent collection of government-funded cash subsidies for the purposes of procuring money for the funding of terrorist organizations and activities. In Ireland, for example, Thomas "Slab" Murphy generated more than three million dollars each year for the IRA by using various forms of subsidy fraud. Murphy collected subsidies by exporting goods, mostly pigs, cattle, and grain, from southern Ireland into Northern Ireland. A subsidy was offered to exporters to counteract the discrepancy in taxes. The goods were then smuggled back across the border into southern Ireland, where they could once again be exported north. Using a "straw buyer" in the process, it was continued over and over again with the same goods. The money was channeled into terrorist activities.

US officials believe that "a substantial portion" of the estimated millions of dollars raised by Middle Eastern terrorist groups comes from the $20 to $30 million annually brought in by the illicit scam industry in America.[14] These scams, as related to Nigerian transnational crime, include advance-fee schemes conducted through e-mail such as "you've won the lottery," inheritance notifications, or correspondence appearing to be from a family member who is traveling and needs emergency funds. This criminal activity typically originates in Nigeria and is known as "419 fraud," referring to Section 419 of the Nigerian penal code addressing such crimes. Proceeds from 419 fraud have now been linked to the lethal al-Qaeda affiliate terrorist group Boko Haram.[15] In some instances, alert front-line personnel at wire service companies or banks are able to intervene to stop a fraudulent 419 transaction completion. However, criminals are changing tactics to avoid detection, giving explicit instructions to customers on how to structure payments.

Mortgage Fraud: Emergent Earning Method

As governments closed formal funding streams, terrorists and criminal enterprises simply find other avenues of exploitation. For instance, mortgage loan fraud is the fastest-growing

---

[13] R. O'Harrow. Identity Crisis, *Washington Post Magazine*, August 10, 2003.

[14] US Senate Committee on Homeland Security and Governmental Affairs. Hezbollah: Financing Terror through Criminal Enterprise, 2005.

[15] Ultrascan. Ultrascan HUMiNT: Boko Haram. Available at http://www.ultra-scan.nl/Ultrascan_Humint_Boko_Haram_gSi_from_inside_-alert. pdf.

white-collar crime in the United States, climbing dramatically from 4500 cases in 2001 to almost 30,000 cases in 2011. The housing boom fed fraudulent activities with billions of dollars changing hands and expedited loan processes requiring minimal paperwork. The FINCEN Suspicious Activity Report (SAR) summaries contain a plethora of information regarding money laundering and terrorist financing activities. By asking financial and other reporting institutions to indicate not only the primary reporting identifier (in this case, mortgage fraud) but secondary activities as well, data emerges regarding other embedded criminal activities.

Since the mortgage market has slowed, criminals are now engaging in "rescue fraud": loan modification, debt elimination/consolidation, and foreclosure rescue scams preying upon innocent homeowners who are desperate to save their homes. As foreign entities and continuing criminal enterprises engaged in home loan–related fraud, it is easy to see that the country's economic crisis was also a national security crisis, something many fail to recognize.

Moving: A Paper Chase in a Paperless World: Informal Value Transfer Systems

Money is typically moved through nontransparent systems in which terrorists and criminals can hide transactions and the movement of funds across borders. Legitimate systems are sometimes used although the means of movement will be illicit in nature. Informal value transfer systems (IVTSs), such as hawala, are still being exploited, despite renewed regulation and scrutiny. Financial transactions through licit systems may be also layered, adding additional protection to the movement. The sophistication and international aspect of such laundering activities have long been underestimated; one expert believes that terrorist organizations have shown the same skills as any Wall Street investor in channeling assets into legal structures and businesses in pursuit of their broader goals.[16]

FINCEN defines an IVTS as any system, mechanism, or network of people receiving money for the purpose of making the funds or an equivalent value payable to a third party in another geographic location, whether or not in the same form.[17] Transactions generally take place outside the conventional banking system, leaving only handwritten records, if anything, in their wake. Expatriates and immigrants often use IVTSs as a trusted and ancient process to send funds to friends and family in their home countries.

Companies conducting business in countries without a formal financial system also use IVTSs. Due to their versatility, anonymity, and location outside of the regulated US banking system, IVTSs are extremely vulnerable for exploitation, and terrorists and criminals routinely use the method to launder proceeds from illicit activities. After a 2010 FINCEN advisory regarding the continued illegal or suspicious use of IVTSs to move money, specifically detailing how criminals were working around current laws, financial institution SAR filings increased by 559% over the next year. The massive filings indicated that despite attempts to "regulate" IVTSs, the illicit transfer activity business is booming. Before the FINCEN IVTS advisory, SAR filers primarily described suspicious activity as occurring between the United States and Latin American countries. However, after the advisory, filers reported not only exchanges with Latin America, but also many suspicious Middle Eastern transactions, most involving the United Arab Emirates (UAE), Yemen, and Iran.

FINCEN continues to address the problem of licensed MSBs in the United States doing business with unlicensed entities abroad. For countries lacking a formal banking system and wishing to do business in traditional, unlicensed manners, IVTS remains vulnerable to money laundering and criminal/terrorist financing activity. For some foreigners living in our country, IVTS is the only way to send money home.

---

[16] Ultrascan. Ultrascan HUMiNT: Boko Haram. Available at http://www.ultra-scan.nl/Ultrascan_Humint_Boko_Haram_gSi_from_inside_-alert. pdf.

[17] FINCEN. Informal Value Transfer Systems. Advisory 33 (2003). Traditional Terrorist and Criminal Financing Methods, 2003.

Hawala

Much has been written about the use of an IVTS system called "hawala" by terrorists to move money. Attention was focused on the hawala method when it was discovered that the al Barakaat informal banking system was used multiple times to move funds for al-Qaeda. The group used hawala to help finance the American embassy bombings in Kenya and Tanzania in 1998 and again in 2001 to move massive funds out of Afghanistan in advance of US military operations.

Most assume that improved hawala filing requirements and increased scrutiny of cross-border financial transactions closed the door on IVTSs; however, the increase of SAR filings and data released by FINCEN is worrisome. US Treasury officials admit that hawala transfer is still posing challenges for those trying to shut down methods of illicit transfer. The language in the USA PATRIOT Act regarding hawalas is found in Subtitle C, which makes it a crime to run an unlicensed money-transmitting business, punishable by five years in prison. However, thousands of hawalas operate in the United States in mom-and-pop types of operations, and it is estimated that more than $30 billion leaves our country annually through this money transfer method.[18] The sheer number of hawala operations in the country makes this law almost unenforceable unless nefarious activity is detected through some other activity. Informal banking systems are ancient and known by many names reflecting cultural origins. "Hawala" and "hundi" are terms commonly referred to when describing Indian, Pakistani, and Middle Eastern IVTSs.

Hawala is a system in which money does not physically cross international borders. The transfer is quick (can send money internationally in the time it takes to place a phone call), easy, and based on trust. The money is not physically moved across any borders; for instance, the sender gives the cash to an agent in the United States, who calls an agent at the forward location and has the sum immediately delivered to the recipient. Receipts are typically not given on either end of the transaction, and no log is kept regarding the identities of the sender and receiver. The amount of money transferred is the only concern, thus a paper trail is nonexistent. The agents work out the monetary issues between themselves to balance their books, usually by transferring goods, paying off other debts, etc. The system is unregulated and undocumented and provides the obscurity desirable to terrorists.

Governments have taken action to regulate this informal, nontraditional transfer system. In the "Abu Dhabi declaration" on hawala, some Arab states agreed to implement a reporting system. In the UAE, business applications are now required, and hawaladars are certified. However, as we attempt to inject standards internationally, the cultural significance of this ancient system cannot be overlooked. Islamic banking traditions appeal to Islamic people; they are familiar and trustworthy. For instance, remitters know their money is not being invested in pork, used for gambling, or used in other ways contrary to their faith, concerns that keep them from using the US banking system. Also, many of the areas where relatives of expatriates live are inaccessible by other means, such as Western Union. Additionally, money transmittal companies charge steep fees whereas hawalas run concurrent with another business, typically offering transactions at no cost to the customer. The bottom line is that the hawala system of informal monetary transfer cross-border persists, especially in countries with OFAC sanctions.

Storage

Groups may store assets in commodities that maintain or increase in value over time, such as diamonds or gold. Precious metals and stones are regarded as currency in many parts of the world and are relatively easy to smuggle, untraceable, and able to escape detection by canine or x-ray. Bulk cash can also be considered a method of storage.

---

[18] C. d'Estree and L. A. Busby. US Response to the Events of September 11, 2001: The USA PATRIOT act, Title iii. Law in the War on International Terrorism, 2001.

Storing, Moving, and Earning: Precious Metals and Diamonds

According to the GAO, the commodities terrorists tend to exploit are of high value, easy to conceal, and hold their value over time.[19] The 2003 Money Laundering Strategy further warns that "while maintaining our vigilance over traditional means of value transfer, we must also focus on alternative means—trading in commodities such as gold, gems and precious stones and metals."[20] The precious-stone and -metal market is certainly an area susceptible for exploitation. For example, gold's shape can be altered into any form through smelting, a desirable attribute to smugglers. Six al-Qaeda operatives arrested in Berlin for plotting attacks in 2003 were financing their operation with gold smuggled from Dubai in an elaborate two-year scheme that included melting, adding extra materials, then reshaping it into benign-looking objects and selling at a profit at $7.5 million.

Gold smuggling in India is prevalent with couriers doing everything from hiding the metal in their bodies to disguising it as food. The terrorist group that attacked Mumbai in 2003 and 2008, al-Qaeda affiliate Lashkar-e-Taiba, was financed partially by a notorious gold smuggler, Dawood Ibrahim, the "Don of Mumbai." Gold smuggling remains prevalent in certain areas of the world; however, diamonds probably serve as the best example of a traded, global commodity that could be exploited by terrorists to earn, move, and store their assets. Douglas Farrah, a former *Washington Post* correspondent and author of the book *Blood from Stones*, broke a story garnering worldwide attention in December 2002 regarding purported links between al-Qaeda and the diamond market. This connection was widely reported in the press and caused upheaval and concern among those in the diamond industry. Federal law enforcement agencies have extensively investigated his claims but will neither officially confirm nor deny that his sources exist, his information is reliable, or there is an al-Qaeda connection to the diamond industry.

However, it is an established fact that al-Qaeda was involved in diamond-mining and diamond-trading organizations in the 1990s, and although these operations did not come to fruition, it certainly speaks to their interest in and prior knowledge of the industry.[21] Hezbollah has long been known to be in the diamond-smuggling business between Lebanon and the west coast of Africa, especially in cash-strapped Sierra Leone. Diamonds are especially easy to smuggle because of their low weight. According to the Congressional Research Service in 2002, one pound of uncut diamonds is worth approximately $225,000.[21] If the diamonds are cut and polished, there are 2200 carats in a pound, meaning the street worth could be in the tens of millions of dollars. This is compared to a pound of cash ($45,000) and a pound of gold at 2012 prices ($25,000). Diamonds are untraceable, making them more attractive than serial-numbered bills. Stones are odorless and thus can be smuggled past working dogs and equipment designed to identify smuggled drugs and money; they can also be swallowed or hidden in other objects, such as stuffed animals and clothing. Diamonds are often unmarked and untraceable and can easily be used in lieu of cash in business transactions. Diamond mines are located in remote, poor, and often lawless areas of Africa. The area of possible al-Qaeda activity, according to Farrah, were the diamond markets of Sierra Leone and Liberia. Mr. Farrah's investigation into al-Qaeda financing reported that they started pursuing the diamond market after assets were frozen by the United States following the embassy bombings in 1998.[22]

If factual, this supports the theory that as we close traditional funding sources, al-Qaeda may move into nontraditional areas to earn, move, and store assets. Looking at the antithesis always helps when developing countermeasures in the finance realm. Therefore, we should

[19] GAO. Federal Agencies Face Continuing Challenges in Addressing Terrorist Financing and Money Laundering. March 4, 2004.

[20] US Departments of the Treasury and Justice. National Money Laundering Strategy. 2003.

[21] GAO. Terrorist Financing: US Agencies Should Systematically Assess Terrorists' Use of Alternative Financing Mechanisms. November 2003.

[22] D. Farah. Report Says Africans Harbored al Qaeda; Terror Assets Hidden in Gem-Buying Spree. *Washington Post*, December 29, 2002.

explore the factors that might preclude criminal and terrorist groups from delving into the diamond world. For example, significant expertise in gemology is an absolute necessity; diamonds exported from Africa are uncut and to the untrained eye simply appear to be dirty glass. Also, diamonds are not as easily laundered as cash or even gold; they have a targeted market and resources are expended in purchasing, movement, and selling activities. Even though paper trails are mostly nonexistent in black-market trade, multiple transactions create witnesses, something very undesirable to terrorist organizations. Finally, there may be significant cultural issues to overcome for the terrorists involved. For instance, the Antwerp diamond market is dominated by those of the Jewish faith, thus business activities associated with unloading the diamonds for cash might be a very significant hurdle for a traditional Muslim terrorist group. Strengthening all of these areas in the industry could keep bad actors from penetrating. At the very least, diamonds are traded on the black market and used by African warlords to fund some of their violent activity, giving advent to the terms "blood diamonds" or "conflict diamonds."

In 2002, 45 nations (including the United States) met in Switzerland to discuss illicit diamond sales and use of profit to pay for weapons in African wars. The State Department appointed an official as a special negotiator for issues regarding these "conflict diamonds," and the group developed new regulations for governments of diamond-producing nations, now known as the Kimberley Process Certification Scheme. Participating governments must not only license diamond miners but also develop "tamper-proof" ways to ship and move rough diamonds across borders. On the buying end, cutting centers (such as those in Antwerp) must ascertain and certify the origin of the rough diamonds.[23] These cutters are the terrorist's last "wicket" because cut-and-polished diamonds are practically untraceable. Unfortunately, certain aspects of the Kimberley Process are voluntary and unenforceable with some African nation-states refusing to participate. These aspects make the diamond market ripe for exploitation for criminals and terrorists.

Financial Terrorism: Money Laundering

Money laundering can lead to financial terrorism or, at least, financing terrorism, and many well-known financial institutions have had officers involved in moving money in and out of offshore banks. Some manipulations and movement of money are done for the purposes of avoiding taxes or legal restrictions and regulations, but often, and this is what makes the movement of funds money laundering, the machinations are performed to legitimize ill-gotten funds of illegal businesses, criminals, and terrorists.

Money laundering happens after funds are secured by criminals and terrorists through licit or illicit activity; they typically seek to "launder" the proceeds. Money laundering is the practice of engaging in financial transactions in order to conceal the identities, sources, and destinations of the money in question. Traditional money laundering makes "dirty" money "clean" after the crime has been committed. Think of traditional criminal money laundering as simply putting a dirty one-dollar bill into a vending machine, hitting the "change return" button, and receiving four clean quarters. Now think on a larger scale. For example, casinos are extremely vulnerable to money laundering; the patrons exchange the dirty money for chips and then cash out. Or they hold the chips and cash out when ready. Alternatively, laundering can be as complex as washing money through an international corporation or a chain of businesses.

The crime has been committed, and the resulting money must be dealt with. However, terrorist-related money laundering is a far different activity. The crime (terrorist operation) has not yet occurred. The money is clean, such as donations from charities or through Zakat,

[23] The Kimberley Process. Available at http://www.kimberleyprocess.com.

and will be put to use to fuel the terror operation in some manner. Therefore, the laundering operations are slightly different in scope and activity although no less complex and hard to detect.

Fronts, Shells, and Offshores

Fronts, shells, and offshores are corporate methods used by organized crime and terrorists to launder money. Front operations are legitimate businesses whose books are used to wash the money. Often, another operation is going on out the back door, such as drug trafficking or prostitution, and the dirty money is pushed back through the front, the legitimate business.

Consider the case of European and Caribbean-based al-Qaeda supporters, Youssef Nada and Ahmed Idris Nasreddi, who ran the Bank al Taqwa, a designated financier of the 9/11 operation. They also operated multiple businesses, including Nasco, which makes cereal and baked goods and sponsors soccer tournaments in Nigeria. All of these activities were complicated fronts and fund-raisers for their money-laundering business, and the intertwining of licit and illicit funds made the case extremely difficult for terrorist financing officials to prove. Bin Laden himself knew the value of fronts and made extensive use of a "honey house" and bakery businesses in Yemen to store and move his clean money prior to 9/11.[24]

An example of how a US company could possibly be used in this manner is the Boston software firm PTECH, Inc. In late 2003, employees alerted the FBI that a key investor was Yasin al-Qadi, who was on the US Treasury Department's list of Specially Designated Global Terrorists. Mr. al-Qadi is a Saudi businessman suspected of diverting millions of dollars to al-Qaeda and Hamas while at the helm of the State Department terrorist-designated charity Blessed Relief foundation. Al-Qadi's investment in PTECH was a way to conceal money that could later be used for terrorist operations.[25]

As our country continues to experience economic turmoil, businesses, universities, and other enterprises seeking investors must be ever vigilant that they do not become a conduit for money laundering or worse. A "shell" is a slightly more complicated business venture; simply put, it is a company that does not exist. The minimalist forms of a shell would be a hotel room with a phone and answering service, an empty office space with a fax machine, or even a post office box at a local mail services store. Criminals will pay cash for the rented space, set up a toll free phone number, run ads in newspapers and online, and then collect money through mailed checks or credit card numbers for a nonexistent service or product. They quickly close the business, staying a step ahead of authorities. In the most complicated form, a shell could also be an "offshore" venture or investment racket; in the global environment, with communications technology, this is certainly an easy way to raise funds without risk of detection.

Bulk Cash Smuggling

A less sophisticated way of moving cash is through smuggling. According to the Treasury Department, bulk cash smuggling refers to moving currency, traveler's checks, or similar instruments across borders by means of a courier rather than through a formal financial system. Although it is risky because the mission will fail if it is detected, bulk cash smuggling is still attractive to terrorists; it is easy to move large quantities of money at once, there is no paper trail or third parties involved (other than the courier), and the group maintains total control over movement. Also, in the Arab culture, it is not uncommon for individuals to carry a large

[24] US Senate Subcommittee on Terrorism, Technology and Homeland Security. Terrorism: Growing Wahhabi Influence in the United States, June 26, 2003.

[25] J. Seper. US Agents Raid Software Firm, Seeking al Qaeda Money Link. *Washington Times*, December 7, 2002, 2.

amount of currency on their person, so bulk cash may not draw attention. Bulk cash smuggling is the preferred method for drug dealers to move money across borders.[26]

When bulk cash is smuggled in support of the narco trade or terrorist financing, the amounts moved are staggering. For instance, in December 2003, at least six men believed to have links to al-Qaeda and carrying what some intelligence reports estimated was $23.5 million were apprehended in Syria as they attempted to leave the country.[27] Treasury officials believe al-Qaeda may be relying more on couriers because of the crackdown on the traditional banking sector.[28] While US authorities have also spotted couriers with bulk cash leaving Saudi Arabia and Kuwait, they have not been able to stop them because US officials have no jurisdiction.

E-Gambling and E-Gaming: Emergent Money-Laundering Concerns

The e-gambling and e-gaming industries have exploded in the past five years and are a hotbed of illegal activity. From child predators preying through interactive Xbox games to drug sales and using the benign virtual gaming platform as an anonymous, untraceable communication tool, what started as a fun and exciting industry is now heavily scrutinized for illegal activity. These platforms are also ripe for money-laundering activity as once value is assigned to something, whether real or virtual, it becomes usable to launderers and vulnerable for exploitation.

E-gambling casinos have always been an attractive way to launder money because cash can be exchanged for chips, which are then held, transferred to another actor, or simply cashed out at a later time. E-gambling provides a new venue for money laundering, adding anonymity and the ability to transfer funds across borders outside the traditional banking system. The US government was initially unsure how to proceed with e-gambling and was very cautious in terms of companies within our borders. Companies in Europe capitalized on the void and the insatiable appetite of potential customers, and Europe is now the world's biggest online gambling market, accounting for an estimated $12 billion of that sector's almost $30 billion in revenue for 2010. Overseas, governments have not shied away from e-gambling despite inherent risks, largely due to the enormous profitability. The government of Denmark, for instance, takes 20% of the gross earnings from companies hosted in their country. Countries like Gibraltar, Malta, and Montenegro also seized the opportunity to establish online gambling venues and have ongoing disputes with the United States as our country attempts to halt proliferation of online betting.

Many US citizens patronize e-gambling companies on foreign soil; in fact, Antigua is thought to hold 25% of the US e-gambling market. Prior to the rise of the Internet, money-laundering activities in the gambling and gaming world came with a trail of paper, surveillance video, and witnesses, making it somewhat easy for law enforcement to investigate. However, many laws do not pertain to e-gambling enterprises and apply only to on-the-ground casino operations. Compounding the problem is the simultaneous boom in nonbanks and the prepaid-card industry. These factors are contributing to a worrisome "perfect storm" scenario.

Since it has more experience with the sector, the best vulnerability assessments regarding e-gaming and e-gambling are coming out of the European Union. According to the Levi Report,[29] the most comprehensive review of e-gambling to date, the following are areas of risk regarding e-gambling:

---

[26] ICE. Operation Cornerstone. Available at http://www.ice.gov/cornerstone/.

[27] D. Farah. Syria Seizes Six Arab Couriers, $23 Million. *Washington Post*, December 20, 2003.

[28] J. Aversa. Nations to Discuss Ways to Cut Off Terrorists' Financing. *Associated Press*, February 4, 2004.

[29] M. Levi. *Money Laundering Risks and E-gaming: A European Overview and Assessment*. Wales, UK: Cardiff University, 2009.

1. Online gaming firms can credit winnings or unused funds back to an account other than the one on which the original bet was made.
2. Virtual fronts and shells can be established, providing a way to anonymously run gaming transactions and move money.
3. It is now possible to play "peer-to-peer" games, in which value transfers can occur between human players. An example of exploitation is if two players are complicit in money-laundering activity or want to transfer funds off the radar; one will deliberately lose the game, and the other will send him or her funds. "Dirty" money can be easily moved this way.
4. Payment can be made in (and out) of the game via anonymous use of nonbanks or prepaid cards.

E-gaming Bitcoins are an experimental digital cash commodity, typically earned, stored, and moved through e-games or auction sites or by providing services online. Accounts can be set up anonymously, and Bitcoins are a peer-to-peer commodity, meaning money can be moved between player accounts without third-party involvement. They are also acceptable for payment at many stores and even some restaurants and hotels. Bitcoins can also be cashed out through anonymous prepaid cards or through nonbanks, such as PayPal. Hackers have been able to steal Bitcoins from player accounts and the gaming hosting companies themselves.

Online gambling companies do collect a significant amount of data on the IP addresses, gaming, and gaming finance patterns of their customers, which are used to construct profiles against which to assess the risks posed by particular customers. Gaming sites are not as fastidious about recognizing and reporting customer trends and patterns. Also, because there are no regulations regarding registration, third-party Bitcoin dealers have emerged on the Internet, further obscuring transactions and increasing the money-laundering risk. Other actors have designed computer programs creating Bitcoins; they anonymously cash out and simply disappear.

Unfortunately, lacking guidance or regulation, e-gambling companies vary on customer spending limits or ceilings. Typical of traditional casinos, the company will engage only if the betting ceiling somehow threatens the livelihood of the business. Naturally, gambling sites with the highest spending and betting ceilings are more at risk for money laundering and other nefarious activity. A stronger legal construction could provide a better framework for e-gambling and e-gaming companies to lessen the vulnerability and money-laundering risk.

Combating Terrorist Financing

Curbing and possibly cutting off funding for terrorists is a major part of the international effort to take the offensive against terrorists—undermining their ability to organize and stage large attacks, to recruit supporters, and to fund the families of operatives. This proactive approach supplements other aspects of counterterrorism that are either more specific in nature—such as trying to prevent specific attacks before they take place or tracking down and apprehending terrorists who do conduct attacks—or are more physical and defense (antiterrorism) oriented, such as airport scanners and barriers around buildings.

The efforts to counter terrorism financing predate 9/11 but have been stepped up in a major way since then. The US government has sought to stem the flow of financial resources to terror groups for decades through various designation and sanction programs. The initial efforts focused on state sponsors of terrorism. The Export Administration Act of 1979 (Section 6j) authorized the secretary of state to designate a government that provides funding or other forms of support to terrorists or terrorist organizations as a state sponsor of terrorism.[30]

[30] 50 USC App. 2401 et seq.

Designation of a state as a sponsor of terrorism triggers a variety of sanctions, including cutoffs of US foreign assistance, a ban on defense exports and sales, control over exports for dual-use items, and miscellaneous financial and other restrictions. To discourage investment and trade, this designation also denies companies or individuals from claiming foreign tax credits for income earned in the designated terrorist states.[31]

In 1994, as a result of intelligence reports indicating that terrorist groups were increasingly using front companies and "charities" to obtain funding—and in the wake of a series of terrorist attacks in the Middle East—the Clinton administration drafted legislation to make it illegal to provide funding or other forms of material support for specific acts of terrorism or for foreign terrorist organizations (FTOs). Enacted as the Antiterrorism and Effective Death Penalty Act of 1996, this legislation specifically criminalized not only financial contributions, but also the provision of financial services to groups designated as FTOs by the Secretary of State.[32] In January 1995, as the legislation was introduced in Congress to begin its long journey through the process of committee hearings, briefings, and floor debate, the Clinton administration issued Executive Order (E.O.) 12947 to immediately freeze the assets of 12 terrorist groups (10 Palestinian and two Jewish) that threatened the use of violence to thwart the Middle East peace process. This was pursuant to the authorities of the International Emergency Economic Powers Act.[33]

Since then, the list of designated entities has expanded tremendously. After the bombings of the US embassies in Nairobi, Kenya, and Dar-Es-Salaam, Tanzania, in August 1998, steps were taken to strengthen international efforts to counter terrorism. The United Nations approved an international treaty—the International Convention for the Suppression of Terrorism Financing—that obligated all member nations to take steps to curb terrorism fundraising efforts. The convention makes it an offense to provide funding for terrorist attacks, whether or not the attacks have actually taken place. Parties to the convention are required to either prosecute or extradite the offenders.

To help other nations strengthen their capabilities to counter financing, the State Department's Office of the Coordinator for Counterterrorism, which provides policy guidance to the Antiterrorist Training Assistance Program (ATA) in the Bureau of Diplomatic Security, directed the ATA to develop a course to train foreign officials in countering the financial underpinnings of terrorist financing. The course was created in cooperation with the Departments of Justice and Treasury, drawing on anti-money laundering and financial crime expertise and programs already deployed in the war on drugs. Only two countries actually received the courses by the time of 9/11, but this program laid the groundwork for the more comprehensive Counterterrorism Financing (CTF) capacity building programs that were launched in the wake of those attacks.

The 9/11 attacks on the twin towers of the World Trade Center in New York City, the Pentagon in Washington, and Flight 93 in the fields near Shanksville, Pennsylvania, prompted the top government leadership to give more priority to countering terrorism financing. The government also strengthened intelligence, law enforcement, and other tools by providing more resources and also making organizational changes in key agencies, such as the Treasury. The 9/11 Commission report said, "[a]fter the September 11 attacks, the highest-level US government officials publicly declared that the fight against al-Qaeda financing was as critical as the fight against al-Qaeda

[31] State Department, State Sponsors of Terrorism. Available at http://www.state.gov/s/ct/c14151.htm. Also see testimony of Juan Carlos Zarate, assistant secretary of Treasury for terrorist financing and financial crimes, to the House of Representatives Financial Services Subcommittees on Domestic and International Monetary Policy, Trade and Technology and Oversight and Investigations, September 30, 2004. Available at http://www.investigativeproject.org/documents/testimony/297.pdf.

[32] Antiterrorism and Effective Death Penalty Act of 1996: A Summary. Congressional Research Service Issue Brief, June 3, 1996. Available at http://www.fas.org/irp/crs/96-499.htm.

[33] 50 USC 1701 et seq. (IEEPA), the National Emergencies Act (50 USC 1601 et seq.), and section 5 of the United Nations Participation Act of 1945, as amended (22 USC 287c)(UNPA), and section 301 of Title 3, United States Code.

itself. It has been presented as one of the keys to success in the fight against terrorism: if we choke off the terrorists' money, we limit their ability to conduct mass casualty attacks."[34]

Developing ways to quickly and securely raise, launder, transfer, store, and access funds is a top priority for all terrorist groups, from al-Qaeda and its various globally oriented affiliates to regionally focused groups like Hamas and Hezbollah.[35] The funding is important not only for buying guns and explosives. This is an important, but often a minor, part of a terrorist operation. Money is needed for transportation, safe houses, and sometime bribing local officials. And for groups that operate charitable fronts, the funding helps support health clinics and other facilities that, in turn, help the terrorist groups recruit supporters. Terrorist groups, such as al-Qaeda and Hamas, also spend considerable resources to support the families of their operatives. One of the Bush administration's first initiatives after September 11, 2001, was aimed directly at terrorism financing. On September 23, 2001, President Bush issued Executive Order 13224[36] to designate and block the assets of organizations and individuals linked to terrorism.[37]

The new executive order broadened the Treasury, Justice, and State Departments' mandates to designate individuals and entities (not only foreign terrorist organizations) as material supporters of terrorism. Since 2001, designations of terrorist financiers by the Treasury, State, and Justice Departments have been used to disrupt terrorist networks by blocking their assets and deterring would-be terrorist supporters from providing financial resources to terrorist groups, pursuant to E.O. 13224. To detect, disrupt, and deter the funding of terror networks, contemporary US CTF strategy is based in four areas[38]:

- Law enforcement and intelligence operations
- Public designations and asset freezes
- Setting international standards to counter terrorist financing
- Foreign capacity building programs

To implement the strategy, the US government basically built upon and expanded existing anti-money laundering (AML) and financial crime programs. Among the government's tools used to monitor financial activities are the following:

1. Foreign Terrorist Asset Tracking Center, which works to identify foreign terrorist groups, assesses their funding sources and fundraising methods, and provides information to law enforcement agencies as to how the funds are moved about.
2. Operation Green Quest is a Customs Service–led multiagency initiative involving investigators from the Internal Revenue Service, the Treasury's Office of Financial Assets Control, and the FBI, who target sources of funding for terrorist groups. The Terrorist Financing Task Force was formed to identify, disrupt, and dismantle the financial operations of charities and nongovernmental organizations associated with Osama bin Laden and al-Qaeda.

---

[34] J. Roth, D. Greenburg, and S. Wille. National Commission on Terrorist Attacks upon the United States: Monograph on Terrorist Financing, 2004, p. 1.

[35] M. Levitt and M. Jacobson. The US Campaign to Squeeze Terrorists' Financing. *Journal of International Affairs, University of Colombia* 62, no. 1, 2008. Available at http://jia.sipa.columbia.edu/files/jia/67-85_levitt_jacobson.pdf.

[36] Executive Order 13224, issued September 23, 2001. Available at http://www.state.gov/s/ct/rls/other/des/122570.htm.

[37] Treasury Department. What You Need to Know about Sanctions. Available at http://www.treasury.gov/resource-center/sanctions/Programs/Documents/terror.pdf.

[38] US Government Accountability Office. Terrorist Financing: Better Strategic Planning Needed to Coordinate US Efforts to Deliver Counter-Terrorism Financing Training and Technical Assistance Abroad, 2005, 2–3. Available at http://www.gao.gov/new.items/d0619.pdf.

In transitional money laundering, "bad" money, such as that obtained from criminal activities, goes through various transactions to conceal its source. With terrorism, funds are often obtained from "good" sources, such as legitimate charities or unwitting donors of similar ethnic backgrounds, and used to buy weapons, pay for safe houses, bribes, travel, etc. However, the processes of moving—and trying to track—the money are basically similar, and thus the counterterrorism financing efforts initially drew heavily on the expertise of the anti-money laundering experts in the Departments of State and Treasury, the Drug Enforcement Administration (DEA), and other agencies.

In the areas of law enforcement and intelligence operations, the Federal Bureau of Investigation (FBI), the Treasury Department, and the intelligence community enhanced their activities and cooperation with foreign counterparts to identify, disrupt, and dismantle terrorist financing networks. The problem of curbing money flows has become more complex as terrorist groups use hawalas[39]—informal transaction systems that bypass the regular banking system, involving couriers or money laundering schemes, such as buying cigarettes cheap in a southern state and selling them to a state with high taxes or buying used cars in the United States and shipping them overseas where they get a higher price. For example, in February 2011, the Drug Enforcement Administration and the Treasury Department publicly cited the Lebanese Canadian Bank for a money-laundering operation on behalf of Hezbollah's activities in shipping cars and other goods overseas for sale at a profit.[40]

Another major problem has been donations by wealthy individuals, especially in Saudi Arabia and other Gulf countries, to front groups for al-Qaeda and other terrorist groups. In an effort to counter this, the US government has engaged in diplomatic efforts to encourage other nations to crack down on such money flows and has sent teams of experts to help train officials in individual countries. Although some countries have publicly taken steps to discourage such contributions, some US officials privately express doubts that these countries have been vigorous in investigating potential abuses.[41]

Concluding Thoughts

Nefarious groups earn money through a variety of activities. Donations from wealthy supporters and the personal wealth of group members are two of the "cleanest" sources. Osama bin Laden is thought to have used a great portion of his own personal fortune to directly fund al-Qaeda's terrorist activities. Without bin Laden's personal wealth and infusion of cash into the group, al-Qaeda may not have succeeded or be the vast enterprise it remains today. By nature, these funding streams are not business activities and are thus untraceable, impermeable ways to generate funds. International charities and the use of "tithing" by religious believers is the next desirable activity, mixing illicit and licit funds to complicate the money trail. When necessary, the organization may move on to other activities, such as involvement in commodity smuggling, intellectual property crime, organized retail theft, identity theft, "419" scams, and mortgage fraud. Many international terrorist groups are also involved in the drug trade; for example, the

---

[39] INTERPOL. Hawalas. Available at http://www.interpol.int/public/financialcrime/moneylaundering/hawala/default.asp.

[40] DEA. Drug Investigations Lead to Treasury 311 Patriot Act Designation against Lebanese Bank Tied to Hizballah. February 10, 2011. Available at http://www.justice.gov/dea/pubs/pressrel/pr021011.html.

[41] Interviews with authors. Also see T. L. Friedman. Bad Bargains, *New York Times*, May 10, 2011. Available at http://www.nytimes.com/2011/05/11/opinion/11friedman.html?_r=1&hp. He quotes a Saudi writer, Mai Yamani, daughter of a former oil minister, who said that Saudi Arabia has spent about $75 billion during the 1980s to propagate Wahabism throughout the Arab world and continues this after 9/11. See M. Yamani. Extremist ideology can only revive bin Laden's ghost. *Beirut Daily Star*, May 5, 2011. Available at http://www.dailystar.com.lb/Opinion/Commentary/2011/May-05/Extremist-ideology-can-only-revivebin-Ladens-ghost.ashx#axzz1M4FfLHLe.

Abu Sayyaf group exploits marijuana plantations in the Philippines; the Taliban leverages the poppy crop; and Hezbollah, FARC, and al Qaeda are all involved in the Latin American drug trade.

Despite governments' best efforts, terrorist and criminal groups continue to exploit tried-and-true methods of earning, moving, and storing funds, such as charities; Zakat; and the counterfeiting, smuggling, and theft of commercial goods. As the case studies illustrated, groups will adapt for success and pursue avenues with the least resistance and greatest vulnerability. Fueled by globalization and the proliferation of the uncontrolled Internet, it seems that going outside of the formal network to earn, move, store, and launder money may be easier than ever.

Financing is the lifeblood of a terrorist enterprise. Traditional criminal money laundering makes "dirty" money "clean" after the crime was committed; terrorists launder "clean" money by moving and storing it for the purposes of financing training and future operations. The use of NPMs makes both illicit activities possible, and the generation of additional funds during the laundering process is a bonus and made easier due to technology. Both groups also stand to benefit from the liaison between telecommunications, nonbanks, and Internet commerce. Money is no longer specifically handled by banks and credit unions but also by gas stations, drug stores, and retailers. The roles and participants in the process are not easily defined nor are their specific or legal responsibilities. The lack of physical evidence in mobile transactions, compounded by the ease of moving and storing money through various NPMs, should be of great concern to policy makers and the law enforcement community.

Part III

Terrorism Preparedness, Terrorism Response

8

Homeland Security[1]

A new period in American history started on September 11, 2001, when the United States was attacked from within its own borders. That event, referred to as 9/11, thrust homeland security to the top of the national agenda. In the American system of government, homeland security is now firmly a primary domestic public policy area, just like education, healthcare, the environment, national defense, and others.[2] The subject of homeland security is quite broad. Although just about every citizen knows homeland security has to do with protecting the nation from harm, many do not truly understand what homeland security is. Thus, an important and necessary starting place is to understand what is meant by homeland security.

This chapter provides an overview of the emerging discipline of homeland security and focuses on its establishment and components. It also presents definitions of homeland security and homeland defense. Finally, this chapter explores the strategy for homeland security in relation to terrorist threats, looking in particular at preparedness for and responses to terrorism.

The Establishment of Homeland Security

The Cold War era in United States history lasted for 45 years. The dismantling of the Berlin Wall in 1989, the reunification of Germany in 1990, and the dissolution of the Soviet Union in 1991 marked the end of the Cold War. The United States spent the majority of the 1990s examining threats to America, trying to define the new world order, and projecting America's role in it. Throughout the decade, numerous studies, panels, task forces, and commissions warned of forthcoming dangers for the nation and the need for greater homeland defense as part of national security.

The US Commission on National Security/21st Century, known also as the Hart–Rudman Commission, was particularly prescient in its initial report published in September 1999. The

---

[1] Information for this chapter was drawn from the following titles: (1) D. L. June, Gemini: Terrorism and Homeland Security. In D. L. June (ed.), *Terrorism and Homeland Security: Perspectives, Thoughts, and Opinions*, CRC Press, 2010. (2) D. Jones. Homeland Security: Emerging Discipline, Challenges, and Research. In J. Pinkowski (ed.), *Homeland Security Handbook*, CRC Press, 2008. (3) C. P. Nemeth. *Homeland Security: An Introduction to Principles and Practice*, Second Edition, CRC Press, 2012. (4) M. R. Ronczkowski, *Terrorism and Organized Hate Crime: Intelligence Gathering, Analysis, and Investigations*, CRC Press, 2003. (5) P. R. Viotti. In M. A. Opheim, N. Bowen, and P. R. Viotti (eds.), *Toward a Comprehensive Strategy for Terrorism and Homeland Security: Thinking Strategically About Policy*, CRC Press, 2008. (6) T. A. Johnson. *War on Terrorism: A Collision of Values, Strategies and Societies*, CRC Press, 2008.

[2] T. R. Dye. *Understanding Public Policy*, Eleventh Edition. Upper Saddle River, New Jersey: Pearson Prentice Hall, 2005.

first conclusion of the report stated that America will become increasingly vulnerable to hostile attack on our homeland, and our military superiority will not entirely protect us.[3] National security policy makers knew that a high potential existed for attacks against American citizens on US continental territory. According to the Department of Defense (DOD), the US homeland is "[t]he physical region that includes the continental United States, Alaska, Hawaii, United States territories and possessions, and surrounding territorial waters and airspace."[4] For the first time since the surprise attack on Pearl Harbor in 1941, the United States suffered a serious, direct attack on its homeland on September 11, 2001, when terrorists flew commercial airliners into New York City's World Trade Center towers, the Pentagon, and a field in Shanksville, Pennsylvania.

This was not the first time the United States experienced terrorism.[5] Nonetheless, terrorism evolved during the decade of the 1990s into "a core threat to international security."[6] Some of the most devastating assaults against the United States were the terrorist bombings of Khobar Towers in Saudi Arabia in 1996, the American embassies in Kenya and Tanzania in 1998, and the *USS Cole* in Yemen in 2000. Then, on September 11, America absorbed the culmination of terrorist attacks, which "eclipsed anything previously seen in terrorism" and were "unparalleled in their severity and lethal ambitions."[7]

The national response to the 9/11 attacks resulted in the most sweeping changes to federal government organization since the National Security Act of 1947. The Act and amendments to it created the National Security Council, formed the Central Intelligence Agency (CIA), and combined the military services into a newly named Department of Defense. The national security policymaking structure and processes generated from the law served the nation well during the Cold War. However, new legislation and executive branch actions after 9/11 brought significant changes for the first time in more than half a century.

In 2001, President George W. Bush issued Executive Order 13228, which established the Office of Homeland Security and the Homeland Security Council within the Executive Office of the President. That same year, Congress passed the USA Patriot Act of 2001, officially the Uniting and Strengthening of America by Providing Appropriate Tools Required to Intercept and Obstruct Terrorism Act, which created new crimes, new penalties, and new powers for searches, seizures, surveillance, and detention of terrorist suspects. A year later, Congress passed the Homeland Security Act of 2002, which created the cabinet-level Department of Homeland Security (DHS). In the largest federal government reorganization since the beginning of the Cold War, the DHS was activated on March 1, 2003, with nearly 180,000 personnel from 22 federal organizations. The mission of the department is to prevent terrorist attacks within the United States, reduce America's vulnerability to terrorism, minimize the damage, and ease recovery from attacks once they do occur.

While safety and security issues are permanent national concerns, the examination of how to predict and prevent threats to the national homeland took on added importance after 9/11. The previous patchwork of aligned and even competing government agencies was obvious. Even the 9/11 Commission critiqued the lack of information sharing and turf games between competing

---

[3] Hart–Rudman Commission. New World Coming: American Security in the 21st Century, Major Themes and Implications. Phase I Report on the Emerging Global Security Environment for the First Quarter of the 21st Century, September 15. Washington, DC: US Commission on National Security/21st Century, 1999, p. 4.

[4] Department of Defense. Homeland Security. Joint Publication 3–26. August 2. Washington, DC: Department of Defense, 2005, p. GL-8.

[5] See Chapter 3 of this volume.

[6] A. K. Cronin and J. M. Ludes (eds.). *Attacking Terrorism: Elements of a Grand Strategy*. Washington, DC: Georgetown University Press, 2004, p. 1.

[7] A. K. Cronin and J. M. Ludes (eds.). *Attacking Terrorism: Elements of a Grand Strategy*. Washington, DC: Georgetown University Press, 2004, pp. 303–304.

agencies. The agencies cooperated, some of the time. But even such cooperation as there was is not the same thing as joint action. When agencies cooperate, one defines the problem and seeks help with it. When they act jointly, the problem and options for action are defined differently from the start. Individuals from different backgrounds come together in analyzing a case and planning how to manage it.

The drive toward a new agency was rooted in a host of compelling rationales. Unity of purpose and mission was surely at the forefront. The "one" agency mindset represented a significant change of ethos for the intelligence community. No longer would the Central Intelligence Agency (CIA), Federal Bureau of Investigation (FBI), National Security Agency (NSA), and North American Aerospace Defense Command (NORAD) see themselves as individual players in the fight against terrorism, but instead they are part of the collective and simultaneously unified effort to detect and prevent harm to the homeland. DHS refers to these shifts in operational mentality as an "evolution of the paradigm"[8]—a movement away from the decentralized to a totally centralized approach in the management of threat. DHS would be the centerpiece of these efforts. The Homeland Security Act of 2002[9] seeks to minimize the threat of another 9/11 and poses its mission in broad terms. Part of the act lays out the mission of DHS.[10] The primary mission of the department is to do the following:[11]

- Prevent terrorist attacks within the United States
- Reduce the vulnerability of the United States to terrorism
- Minimize the damage, and assist in the recovery, from terrorist attacks that do occur within the United States
- Carry out all functions of entities transferred to the department, including by acting as a focal point regarding natural and man-made crises and emergency planning
- Ensure that the functions of the agencies and subdivisions within the department that are not related directly to securing the homeland are not diminished or neglected except by a specific explicit act of Congress
- Ensure that the overall economic security of the United States is not diminished by efforts, activities, and programs aimed at securing the homeland
- Monitor connections between illegal drug trafficking and terrorism, coordinate efforts to sever such connections, and otherwise contribute to efforts to interdict illegal drug trafficking

The act further compartmentalizes the agency into four main areas of responsibility, namely border and transportation; emergency preparedness and response; chemical, biological, radiological, and nuclear countermeasures; and information analysis and infrastructure protection. The organizational chart of DHS in 2008,[12] shown in Figure 8.1, portrays those with crucial responsibility for DHS. The significance of these categories cannot be overemphasized. In border and transportation, DHS assumed control over security services relating to our borders, territorial waters, and transportation systems. Immigration and Naturalization, Customs, the Coast Guard, and animal protection issues are now DHS functions.

---

[8] Homeland Security Council. National Strategy for Homeland Security (October 2007), 3. Available at http://www.whitehouse.gov/infocus/homeland/nshs/2007/sectionII.html or http://www.whitehouse.gov/infocus/homeland/nshs/NSHS.pdf.

[9] Homeland Security Act of 2002, US Code 6 (2002), § 101.

[10] Homeland Security Act of 2002, US Code 6 (2002), § 101.

[11] Homeland Security Act of 2002, US Code 6 (2002), § 101 (b).

[12] US Department of Homeland Security Organization Chart. Available at http://www.dhs.gov/xlibrary/assets/dhs-orgchart.pdf, 2012.

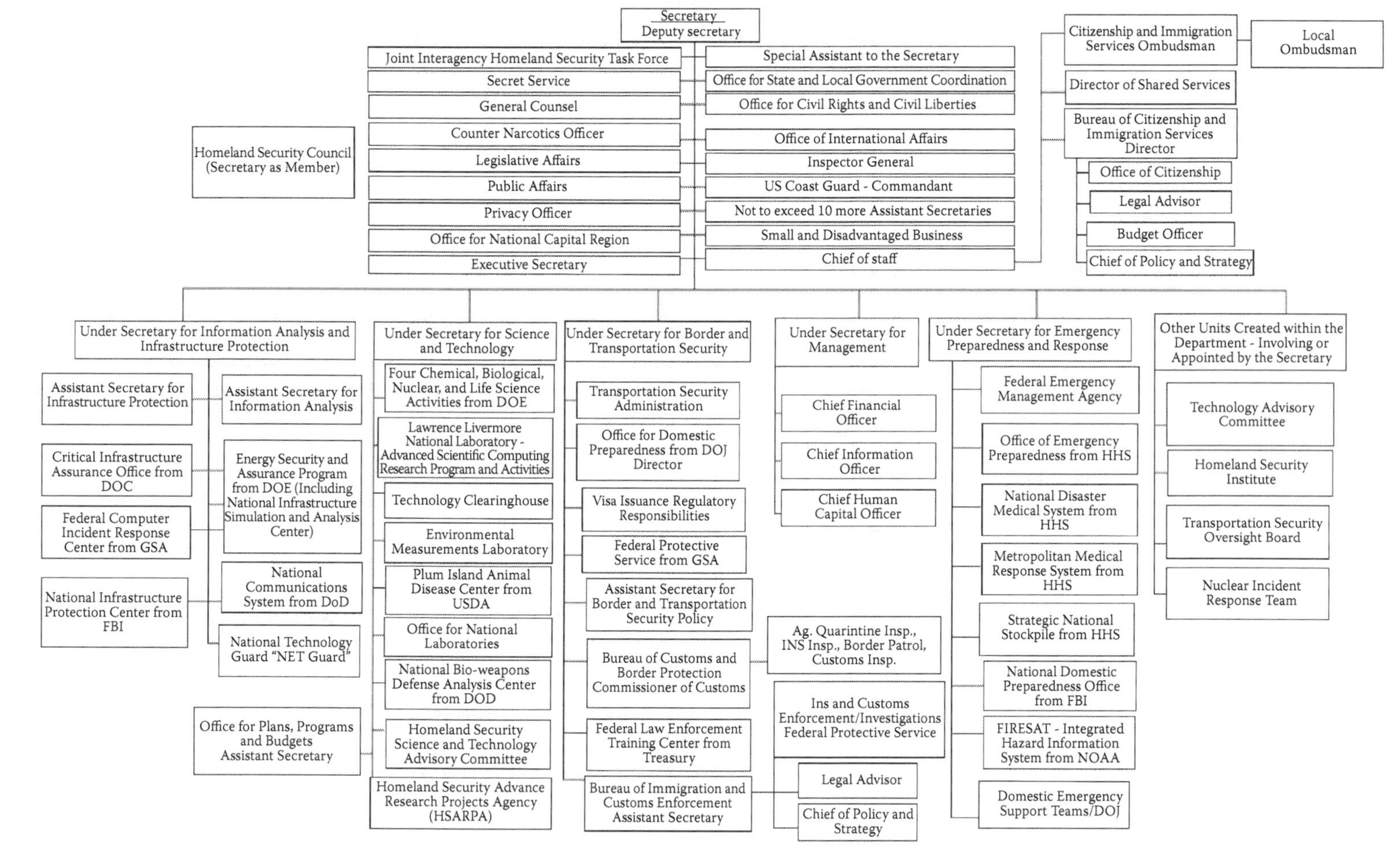

Figure 8.1 DHS organizational chart in 2008. (From C. Nemeth, *Homeland Security: An Introduction to Principles and Practice*, Second Edition, CRC Press, 2013. With permission.)

In emergency preparedness and response there was a complete merger of the Federal Emergency Management Agency (FEMA) operations into DHS. FEMA became an organization dedicated not only to natural disaster, but also to man-made events. Federal interagency emergency programs were subsumed into DHS as well as critical response units relating to nuclear and pharmaceutical events. In matters involving prevention of chemical, radiological, and nuclear terror, DHS plays a central, coordinating role. Efforts here would be one of centralization and coordination of diverse department activities across the spectrum of government agencies. Guidelines regarding weapons of mass destruction were rapidly promulgated. In the area of intelligence and threat analysis, DHS acts as a central repository for information pertaining to threats to the homeland. Data from traditional intelligence organizations, such as the CIA, FBI, NSA, Immigration and Naturalization Service (INS), and Drug Enforcement Administration (DEA), are catalogued and disseminated as needed. DHS now works closely with the FBI's Office of Intelligence. As for infrastructure, DHS is responsible for the evaluation and protection of the country's primary infrastructure, including food and water systems, health and emergency services, telecommunications, energy, chemical and defense industries, and common carrier transportation. Issues of infrastructure continue to be pressed by both the executive and legislative branch.

Finally, the DHS of 2003 extended its program reach to state, local, and private sector justice agencies. One of the hallmarks of DHS is the cultivation of governmental—both interagency and intra-agency—cooperation. DHS saw the essential need for mutual trust and respect between competing agencies so that the mission of DHS might be implemented. DHS erected an "intergovernmental affairs office" to coordinate the numerous initiatives emanating from the agency. Accordingly, the task of DHS is to foster the unified culture of prevention and information sharing so needed in the fight against terrorism. DHS is many things to many entities and, in the final analysis, a clearinghouse as well as an operational center for policy on homeland safety and security. The current structure of DHS is charted in Figure 8.2.

Another significant action was the formation of United States Northern Command, known as "USNORTHCOM." With the responsibility for protecting the homeland, US Northern Command was established on October 1, 2002, and reached full operational capability on September 11, 2003. Another key law was the passage of the Intelligence Reform and Terrorism Prevention Act of 2004, which created the position of Director of National Intelligence and reformed the US intelligence enterprise to be more unified. Together, the magnitude of the actions after 9/11 clearly establishes homeland security as a permanent fixture in American government and society at least for the foreseeable future.

Additionally, after the attacks on America, the Federal Government published numerous strategies and supporting plans to protect the nation from terrorism threats. The White House, DHS, DOD, and other agencies issued or updated key strategy documents and plans beginning in 2002. Since then, at least 21 major strategies and plans related to homeland security are guiding the national effort. Federal, state, and local governments continue to produce additional strategies and implementation plans.

Definitions of Homeland Security and Homeland Defense

Just like defining terrorism, terrorist activity, or a terrorist, homeland security has many meanings to different people. There is also a distinction between the roles of the DHS in homeland security and the DOD in homeland defense.[13] To protect and defend the United States and preserve the freedoms guaranteed by the Constitution, the nation must secure its homeland from

[13] T. Goss. Who's in Charge? New Challenges in Homeland Defense and Homeland Security. *Homeland Security Affairs II*, no. 1: Article 2, 2006.

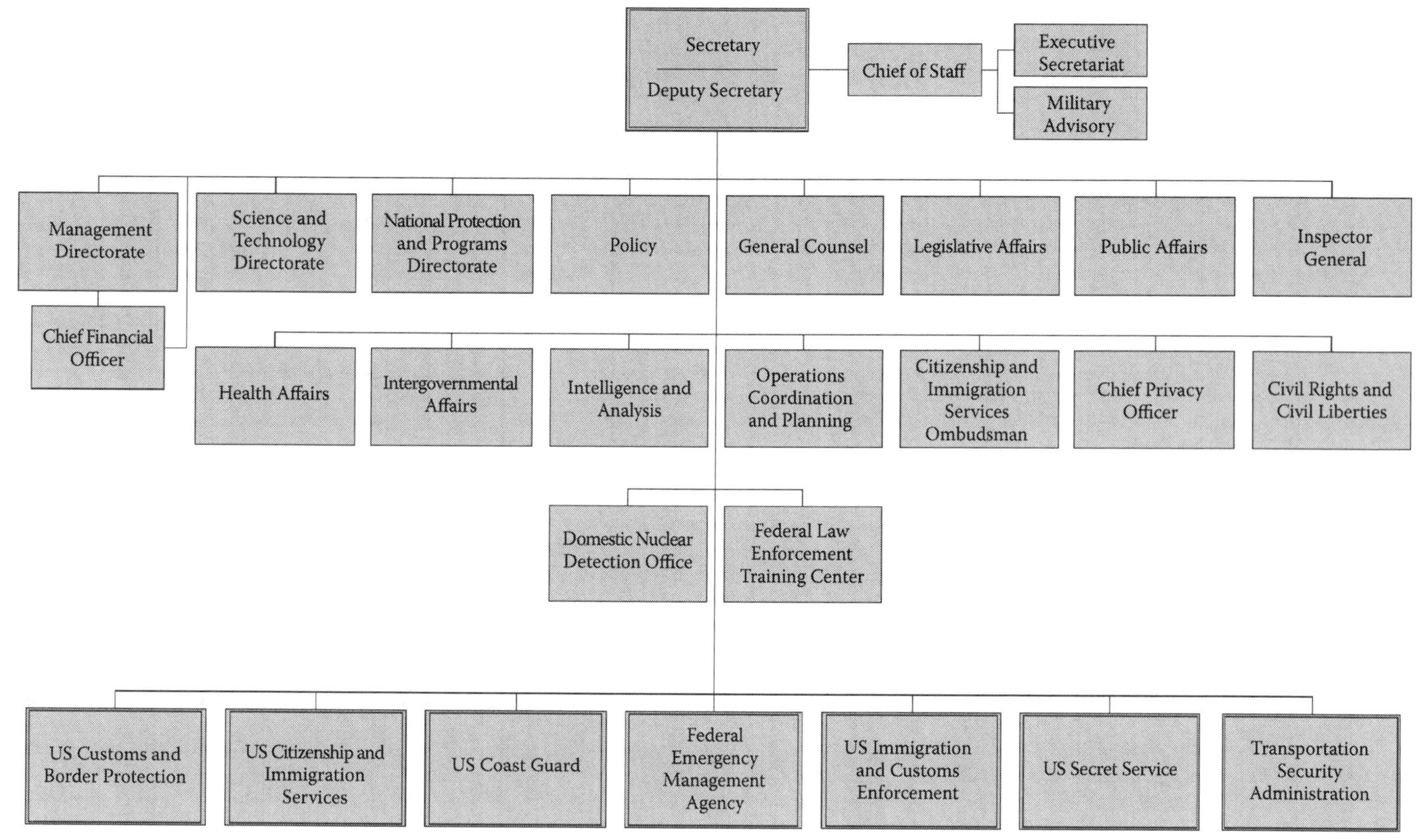

Figure 8.2 DHS organizational chart as of April 1, 2013. (From C. Nemeth, *Homeland Security: An Introduction to Principles and Practice*, Second Edition, CRC Press, 2013. With permission.)

threats and violence, including terrorism. Homeland security is the first priority of the nation, and it requires a national effort. According to the National Strategy for Homeland Security, homeland security is "a concerted national effort to prevent terrorist attacks within the United States, reduce America's vulnerability to terrorism, and minimize the damage and recover from attacks that do occur."[14] The DHS is the lead federal agency for the homeland security mission. The department organizes and leads the homeland security efforts of all levels of government—federal, state, local, and tribal—as well as private and nonprofit sector organizations. Additionally, the department's responsibilities extend beyond terrorism to preventing, preparing for, responding to, and recovering from a wide range of major domestic incidents, natural disasters, and other emergencies.

The DOD has a key role in homeland security. However, its role does not include preventing terrorists from entering the United States and apprehending and arresting terrorists within the nation's borders. These responsibilities belong to the DHS and the Department of Justice (DOJ), respectively. The DOD supports homeland security through homeland defense and defense support of civil authorities (also referred to as civil support), which are two distinct but interrelated mission areas. These missions are the responsibility of US Northern Command. According to the DOD, homeland defense is "[t]he protection of United States sovereignty, territory, domestic population, and critical infrastructure against external threats and aggression or other threats as directed by the President."[15] The DOD is responsible for homeland defense, which includes protection against "external threats" that may be planned and executed internally. For homeland defense missions, the DOD is the lead or primary agency. Defense support of civil authorities or civil support is "DOD support, including Federal military forces, the Department's career civilian and contractor personnel, and DOD agency and component assets, for domestic emergencies and for designated law enforcement and other activities."[16] The DOD provides defense support of civil authorities when directed by the President or Secretary of Defense in response to state governor requests for assistance for domestic incidents to include terrorist threats or attacks, major disasters, designated law enforcement, civil disturbances, and other emergencies.

Throughout the nation's history, US law and policy have limited the military's role in domestic affairs. The Posse Comitatus Act of 1878 generally prohibits the US military from direct participation in civilian law enforcement activities. However, Congress has enacted exceptions to the Posse Comitatus Act that allow the armed forces, in certain situations, to assist civilian law enforcement agencies in enforcing the laws of the United States. Some examples are counterdrug activities, assistance with crimes involving nuclear materials, emergency situations involving chemical or biological weapons of mass destruction, and use of the Insurrection Act to suppress insurrections. The use of military personnel in law enforcement roles is conducted within strict compliance with the constitution and laws and only under the direction of the President and Secretary of Defense.

Response to Terrorism: Homeland Security

Governmental response to terrorist acts has had one very major consequence: The resulting actions have lost Americans many of the freedoms they famously enjoyed, for instance, weapons searches and screenings for entrance to all governmental and public buildings, the freedom

[14] White House. National Strategy for Homeland Security. July. Washington, DC: The White House, 2002, p. 2.

[15] Department of Defense. Homeland Security. Joint Publication 3–26. August 2. Washington, DC: Department of Defense, GL-9, 2005.

[16] Department of Defense. Strategy for Homeland Defense and Civil Support. June. Washington, DC: Department of Defense, 2005, pp. 5–6.

from privacy due to acts like the Patriot Act (enacted immediately after the Pentagon and World Trade Center bombings), the ability to take certain items aboard a plane, and warrantless interception of communications. As each terrorist act is played out, the primary response has been to increase security measures, which, in the long run, has created an erosion of personal freedoms and choices. Thus, perhaps, the terrorists are actually winning the war on terrorism. In the world, terrorist activity continues on a near daily basis. The war on terrorism continues, but no longer by that name. As long as people in the world are willing to kill themselves in order to murder and maim others, terrorism will remain as a prominent security threat.

Preparedness and Response in Terrorist Acts

A common-sense approach to modern living is preparedness. One could conservatively estimate that only one in 10 people (most likely the percentage is much lower) are trained in CPR (cardiopulmonary resuscitation), the ABCs (airway, bleeding, and circulation) of medicine, and even fewer are aware of procedures to follow and what to expect in a large natural disaster, such as an earthquake, fire, or flood. Beyond personal concerns, response, and action, what of the larger-scale emergencies, such as evacuation of a major city and the treatment of casualties, or perhaps food, clothing, shelter, and medical attention for those injured or displaced? Most public buildings have evacuation plans and guidelines, including drawings depicting routes and directions for quick and easy evacuation, posted somewhere near elevators and other obvious locations. But who takes the time (even while waiting for an elevator) to read and understand them? As a guest in a hotel, how many people actually read the emergency evacuation instructions or even bother to note the location of fire alarms and extinguishers? Surprisingly, or not surprisingly, the quick answer would be few. The public mindset is a collective "it will not happen here" or "it will not happen to me." But obviously, emergencies, natural and man-made, do occur "here" and to "me." For these reasons, there is significant governmental concern about preparation for emergencies related to terrorism and the ability to respond in a timely and appropriate manner. However, it must also be recognized that plans and procedures must trickle down to local and individual levels.

Training

Recognizing the Problem

A "playbook" or course lesson plan should begin with an analysis or definition of the problem. Framing the problem in terms of "trends" leads the trainee to look at the whole scope of the matter from historical perspectives to present day, and to look at and anticipate the future of terrorism with the evolution of accompanying violence attendant on an act of terrorism.

Reflexes and Rehearsals

Once the background and framing of the problem is complete and solution examples are explored and ratified, testing of the models must be undertaken to determine the degree of workability and whether government and individuals can react as intended. Since the bombings of 9/11, municipalities have rehearsed planned scenarios to gauge readiness and capabilities of resources, such as first responders, medical facilities, and evacuation procedures.

Preparation and rehearsals by official agencies is a giant step, similar to the civil defense programs during the Cold War era of the 1950s, but there is a glaring difference. The civil defense preparedness programs stored food, water, blankets, medical supplies, among other items, in strategic locations while schools and businesses practiced building evacuations, "drop and cover" exercises, and received information about responding to emergencies.

Preparedness Exercises

Prepare, Prepare, Prepare

How does a government or municipality prepare for a "what if" scenario? It begins with imagining and preparing reasonable and probable scenarios and formulating a relevant plan to deal with the problem. How is a large city that has only two or three main traffic arteries, is crisscrossed with bridges or railroad tracks, and/or has a large body of water (an ocean) on one or two sides evacuated? What if one of those traffic arteries or the bridge is demolished by explosives beginning the terrorist emergency? How about a suicide bombing in a large and heavily populated shopping center, nightclub, or amusement park where there are several fatalities and injuries? Can the governmental response handle all the elements of such a heinous action? Are there sufficient medical facilities available for response to care for the injured, dying, and dead? Can the police set up a "crime scene" for investigation and search for evidence while keeping out the onlookers, the curious, and the souvenir hunters? Is there a policy and procedure for handling the local and national news media that will be flocking to the scene? Are there public information facilities and personnel capable of handling the news media rush for information? How about the public, who will be rushing to the scene to look for loved ones or perhaps jamming the telephone circuits attempting to contact someone who may have fallen victim? How will crowd and traffic control be directed?

Practice, Practice, Practice

After constructing the scenario and defining its parameters (not overlooking all possible contingencies), the plan must be rehearsed with a self-examination critique as an after-action report detailing what was right and how to improve what went wrong. The plans should be reviewed and updated at least quarterly and rehearsed at least annually. Of course the funding for rehearsals will be limited, but a well-rehearsed plan and response will save perhaps thousands of lives.

Individual Preparation, Planning, and Practice

Individual preparation begins with making a survey of a home, checking for sufficient fire alarms and fire extinguishers, planning escape routes in the event of fire, including relocation and family meeting sites, preparing an evacuation bag, and storing medical equipment and food and water for a minimum of three days for each person living in the home, among other things. Planning for an emergency is finding a solution to a problem before it becomes a problem. Once the emergency checklist is complete, the next phase is planning.

The plan should be simple (complemented with all the necessary resources) and easy to implement in the event of an unexpected evacuation or response. The people occupying a house or building should know exactly where all emergency equipment and supplies are stored for quick access. Critical telephone and contact numbers—police, fire, medical, and relevant persons to contact—should be available and within reach.[17] Some items usually overlooked on checklists for preparation and planning for an emergency are an availability and access to cash, vehicle fuel, and solar or cranked power radio. Practice means refining reflexes and eliminating any unforeseen difficulties while completing a task with minimal room for error. A family must rehearse its response and preparations through alarm drills and practicing specific scenarios of home evacuation.

[17] It is a good idea to have such a list laminated to protect it from weather, tearing, etc. It might also be minimized in size to fit into a wallet or pocket.

Government Response to Emergency Situations

Planning

It has often been repeated that a terrorist attack happens with surprise and violence. Prime examples are the bombings of the World Trade Center in 1993, the Murrah Federal Building in 1995, and of course, the World Trade Center and Pentagon bombings in 2001.[18] All of these events required instant and efficient governmental response as did the hurricane striking the Louisiana Delta area in 2005 (Hurricane Katrina). From the smallest hamlet to the largest mega-urban complex in America, city supervisors and planners at all levels of government, including local, county, state, and federal, must consider every type of emergency imaginable.

Drawing upon the experiences of New York, Oklahoma City, Washington, D.C., and the victims of Hurricane Katrina, planners can anticipate problems related to mass evacuation, massive injuries, fires, flooding, looting, and numerous logistical problems, such as supplying food, water, and shelter. They also anticipate the obstacles that arise during search and rescue procedures, as well the ways in which to maintain a stable government. During the planning phase, rapid response teams consisting of military (and National Guard), police, fire, medical, Red Cross, Salvation Army, and other support units should be included, readied, and prepared for any type of life-saving emergency, including terrorist attacks.

Preparation

A page of history from the Civil Defense (CD) preparedness days of the 1950s and 1960s Cold War era should be revised and updated through local, state, and federal government crisis management planning. The CD program consisted of identifying relocation buildings and sites and arranging deposits of food, clothing, water, blankets, and other emergency supplies necessary for survival. The cached equipment was inspected, updated, and rotated on a routine basis.

To engage a similar program will require major funding, allocation of resources, and determination of safe relocation sites, such as were provided by the civil defense program. The government (local to federal) should have regular programs of informing and educating the public in the planned practices and procedures of the political entity (city, county, state, federal) for reacting to emergency. This can be done through public meetings and news media outlets like the local newspaper and television. The old civil defense programs also featured dedicated radio frequencies for issuing instructions during an emergency crisis. The frequencies were tested regularly so the public would be aware of which frequency on which to focus their attention. This program should also be revised and include television and mobile telephones (through flash and text messaging) as immediate instruction resources.

The first order of business in preparing for a response to a terrorist attack is in prevention. Counterterrorism units of the government (city, county, state, and federal levels) must develop data and information that can be analyzed to provide strategic and tactical intelligence to detect, deter, and disrupt a planned terrorist activity. This intelligence should be shared among all levels of government—a lesson well learned from the 2001 bombings and the 9/11 Commission Report. Another important aspect of the 9/11 Commission Report stated, "[t]here was a significant lack of imagination" (on the parts of the intelligence community and enforcement agencies; the terrorists certainly exercised their imagination in conceiving and carrying out the attacks).

In the planning and preparation phases (especially when dealing with the terrorists), imaginative approaches—both to what the terrorist may do and to ways of countering it—must be explored, considering the likelihood of an event occurring, and the means and ways of preventing or reacting to it. An old cliché has become a standard guide for a terrorist-generated emergency, especially with the assistance of advanced technology: "If it can be imagined and paid for by the terrorist, it can be done." Therefore, a corollary or consequential cliché would be: "If a defense force

[18] See Chapter 3 of this volume.

can imagine and pay for an anticipated action, it can be prevented or minimized." Consequently, emergency planners have to consider all possible types of emergencies (perhaps the demolition of a major dam and resulting flooding), and sufficient funding must be provided or appropriated to respond to whatever the estimated cost of the emergency and restoration to normalcy.

Response

The better planned and prepared individuals and governments will be able to respond in a timely manner, quickly, and efficiently to any imagined and anticipated real emergency, whether it is by natural occurrence (fire, flood, or storm) or man-made by a group of ideological terrorists (a semi-military militia) or an individual. The entire emergency response community, from an individual to the most highly trained organization and political body, must have an agenda, placing response to an emergency situation at the top of their priority lists.

Emergency response is a responsibility of the governmental jurisdiction in which the emergency occurs. However, it is also important for the individual on each team to be able to react appropriately in a crisis situation. The appropriateness can only come through planning and practice or rehearsal. An educated public is the best defense against man-made emergencies, and a prepared public practiced in the ways of response can minimize overall physical and psychological damage.

Concluding Thoughts

The term "homeland security" encompasses much of the emergency, military, and law enforcement sector once dedicated to a variety of relevant responsibilities to the defense of a nation. While safety and security issues are permanent national concerns, the examination of how to predict and prevent threats to the national homeland took on added importance after 9/11. The homeland security strategy is in the broadest understanding a response to threats of all kinds; although the focus in the United States since 9/11 primarily has been on the real-and-present dangers of terrorist attacks.

There is a need for all elements of a nation—from federal, state, and local governments to the private sector to local communities and individual citizens—to help create and share responsibilities in a culture of preparedness. This culture of preparedness, which applies to all catastrophes and all hazards, natural or man-made, rests on four principles: a shared acknowledgement of the certainty of future catastrophes and that creating a prepared nation will be a continuing challenge; the importance of initiative and accountability at all levels of society; the role of citizen and community preparedness; and finally, the roles of each level of government and the private sector in creating a prepared nation. Built upon a foundation of partnerships, common goals, and shared responsibility, the creation of a culture of preparedness is among the most profound and enduring transformations in the broader effort to protect and defend a homeland.

In developing a strategy for homeland security in relation to terrorist threats, domestic remedies are sought in providing better intelligence and early warning of attacks, maintaining detection in transit and at airports and other transportation nodes or terminals, and developing and exercising plans for damage limitation and consequence management. The strategy of homeland security should focus on how to prevent or thwart a terrorist attack and, if an attack occurs, how to manage the consequences and limit or mitigate damages to lives and property. An effective strategy for homeland security, then, incorporates approaches to reducing the threat of terrorism by taking actions both domestically and externally. The next chapters examine the measures that are implemented to do just that.

9

Mitigating Terrorism[1]

The Department of Defense defines antiterrorism as the "defensive measures taken to reduce vulnerability to terrorist acts."[2] Antiterrorism also includes defensive and preventive measures taken to reduce vulnerability to terrorist attack. Such defensive and preventive measures may include installing physical security systems, providing and analyzing foreign and domestic intelligence, distributing information about threats, and training for response to potential future incidents. Limited response to a potential attack, such as an augmentation of security forces, is also an antiterrorism measure. Making the community and the public aware of potential terrorist threats is another key antiterrorism tool.

Antiterrorism measures are primarily passive and seek to discourage terrorist cells or organizations from attacking a target by decreasing their chances of success. Examples of government organizations or entities that employ antiterrorism measures include embassies, diplomatic staff, government offices, military units, etc. Because of their defensive nature, antiterrorism measures are a better fit for corporations and private individuals. This chapter examines various antiterrorism measures employed by private organizations and companies that are designed to mitigate the threat of terrorism; namely, terrorist defense planning, the use of private security guards, and target hardening. Preceding this, the fundamentals of antiterrorism planning are explored.

Antiterrorism: The Fundamentals

There are five fundamentals to antiterrorism planning:

1. *Threat vulnerability assessment.* This is a realistic assessment based on the actual threat to an organization or installation and the organization's ability to defend against that threat.
2. *Security measures.* This is a mixture of procedural and physical barriers designed to reduce the vulnerability of the organization or installation to an attack identified in the

[1] Information for this chapter was drawn from the following titles: (1) R. Johnson, *Antiterrorism and Threat Response: Planning and Implementation*, CRC Press, 2013. (2) R. Dzikansky, M. Kleiman, and G. Slater, *Terrorist Suicide Bombings: Attack Interdiction, Mitigation, and Response*, CRC Press, 2011. (3) M. W. Nance, *Terrorist Recognition Handbook: A Practitioner's Manual for Predicting and Identifying Terrorist Activities*, Second Edition, CRC Press, 2008. (4) D. P. Schulz, *The Counterterrorism Handbook: Tactics, Procedures, and Techniques*, Fourth Edition, CRC Press, 2011.

[2] Department of Defense Directive no. 2000. August 18, 2003, certified current as of December 13, 2007, enclosure 2, p. 21. Available at http://www.dtic.mil/whs/directives/corres/pdf/200012p.pdf.

threat assessment phase—in other words, fences, alarms, locks, guards, access control, etc. These measures will increase or decrease with the prevailing terrorism threat.

3. *Observation plan.* Personnel should be trained to recognize the threat when they see it. Most terrorist attacks are preceded by an extensive period of surveillance, and this surveillance can be detected by trained observers. This information is used to modify security measures and alert counterterrorism forces.
4. *Random antiterrorism measures.* A terrorist or terrorist organization conducting surveillance against an organization or installation will try to develop a picture of the facility's security plans and procedures. It will seek to learn about the layout and routine of this establishment. In antiterrorism planning, routine is considered a weakness. Random antiterrorism measures deter an attack by sowing doubt in the minds of the attackers. By constantly changing details of the target's defensive posture, terrorists will not be able to form a clear picture of the target's defenses and therefore cannot ensure a high probability of success. This, in itself, is often enough reason for a terrorist group to move on to another, less prepared target.
5. *Response planning.* What will an organization do if surveillance is detected? What will an organization do if it is attacked? Response planning is crisis-response planning. If an organization's personnel are well trained and rehearsed, the effects of a terrorist attack can often be swiftly contained. This model is flexible, comprehensive, and robust, and adapts quickly to corporate or individual needs. Most corporate security departments conduct threat assessments, vulnerability mitigation, and response planning. Some do observation planning. Almost none do random antiterrorism measures. What they lack is the overall unifying theory—the understanding of how each component contributes to the others.

To combat terrorism, security officials should expend effort in observation planning and deterrence measures, which is at the heart of antiterrorism planning. This practice is known as terror defense planning.

Terror Defense Planning

In today's world of high-stakes terrorism, there are few individuals or organizations in either the private sector or law enforcement that will question the need for planning in order to meet the threat of terrorism. The events of 9/11, the London transit bombings, and the Mumbai attacks, and even such unsuccessful attempts as the Christmas Day "underwear" bomber in 2009 and the Times Square car bomber less than six months later, have demonstrated that the tactics of terrorists know no bounds and out-of-the-box planning is now the rule rather than the exception. In fact, there is no other area in which there is a greater need for cooperation among federal, state, and local law enforcement and the private sector than terrorism defense.

In the pre-9/11 days, when questions arose, they were generally about costs and potential benefits resulting from these expenditures. In the aftermath of 9/11, questions of cost have been put aside, but as terrorist attacks diminish or the perceived threat subsides, budget issues are again being raised—in times of financial downturn when money is tight. History shows, unfortunately, that security operations are frequently the first to feel the budget axe. It must be remembered, however, that the moral obligation to protect people's lives cannot be evaluated in dollars.

For law enforcement's consideration, there is a legal obligation to protect lives. It is the foundation of the police mandate. On the part of the private sector, the obligation can be derived from what the courts have called "foreseeability" in vicarious liability suits. Thus, in the private sector, an incident, such as hostage taking, could be considered a foreseeable occurrence under the vicarious liability statutes and case law, particularly if the company is doing business with a country or group that has been or is known to be a focal point of terrorist activity. In effect, such a company can be foreseen to be a potential target of violent action and therefore must operate under a legal obligation to protect its employees and property and perhaps even its customers. Although terrorists are the most identifiable source of such violent action, disgruntled employees are also potential perpetrators of violence as are common criminals. Courts have held companies liable for failure to react appropriately when such incidents occur.

The preincident plan is a guide to dealing with terrorist threats on a pragmatic level. Whether developed by a law enforcement agency, by private security personnel, or ideally, through a joint effort between the two, a preincident defense plan is a living—rather than an archival—document. It must be reviewed periodically and updated or altered as necessary. Terrorist defense planning can be divided into three component areas:

1. Preincident
2. Incident
3. Postincident

Preincident planning involves all the planning, anticipation, "what if" modeling, and intelligence gathering that can be done in advance. With today's "outside the box" thinking a must, cooperation between police and the private sector is especially crucial because information and intelligence can be shared and the most efficient use of resources can be made.

Incident planning involves the development of a course of action in the event of terrorist activity or if suspected or potential terrorist action occurs or is even threatened. Again, communication between the private-sector company or organization that may be a target and the public safety community is essential. Lastly, postincident, or consequence, planning is concerned with handling events in the aftermath of a bomb threat, explosion, hostage taking, kidnapping, or other attack and deals with emergencies, physical damage, any possible collateral damage, and the need to get operations back to normal as quickly and safely as possible. During this period, continued cooperation between the private and public sectors is still essential. It should be noted in today's tense environment that many companies maintain disaster recovery plans that will enable minimal operations to be relocated to a satellite location within a short period even before addressing the long-term effects of an attack.

Structuring a Preincident Plan

Preincident planning involves preparing for an occurrence that everyone hopes will never come to pass. The planning process is complex, involving information gathering (intelligence), risk analysis, organization, training, determining logistical needs, and purchasing necessary supplies and equipment required to handle an extraordinary event. What is the purpose of planning? First, it establishes the amount or level of potential risk to which a community, corporation, government entity, property, building, or other facility or an individual executive or group of individuals, may be exposed vis-à-vis terrorist operatives.

Once the risk is assessed, policies must be in place to implement and adhere to procedures. It should be remembered that such a plan is a living document and must be updated and revised as circumstances change. Such circumstances include, but are not limited to, remodeling or other changes to physical facilities; changes in personnel, particularly those named in the document even by position or title; and changes in external political, economic, and international events.

The incident segment of a defense plan is, in reality, an operations manual for handling the initial phases of a terrorist attack of any nature. It should explain what actions are to be taken, when they should be taken, who should take them, and how these actions should be carried out. Even in the chaos of the World Trade Center disaster, the presence of a basic recovery plan allowed core businesses to maintain at least some level of business services. The collapse of the Twin Towers, accompanied by an extraordinary loss of life among the senior ranks of the emergency service personnel, especially within the New York Fire Department, revealed serious flaws in the planning process. A number of postincident reports severely criticized the placement of the command in such close proximity to the scene of potential and, as it turned out, literal disaster.

Postincident activity should include everything required to assist representatives of authorized agencies who may investigate the incident as well as to restore the location to a point at which normal operations may resume. Postincident planning also involves metrics for assessing the long-term effects of the incident and provides a method for evaluating the strengths and weaknesses of the defense response so everyone can be better prepared should there be another incident. In this "lessons learned" phase, it is important to include all levels of participants, so all points of view can be taken into consideration. In the case of the World Trade Center attack, the devastation was so great that some small companies never recovered and even larger firms that lost hundreds of employees suffered the consequences for years afterward.

Information Gathering

Although this might seem contradictory, information gathering with regard to terrorist operations is at once the easiest and most difficult of tasks. It is easy because much of this information already exists—in files, letters, official documents, records of municipal and other government agencies, libraries, computer and Internet databases, and similar sources. The difficult part of information gathering is that there is no certainty as to what kind of information will be most helpful. Likewise, there are no guidelines for how much information is enough. One thing is certain: New information will be flowing constantly, altering previous assumptions and conclusions as well as opening whole new areas of concern. In today's world, there are many options—from televisions to the Internet to mobile communication devices—in order to follow global events. The advent of and advancements in reporting from all locations around the world give real-time information to law enforcement and security professionals.

There are a host of resources at the disposal of the security professional, including specialized repositories on everything from terrorist activity to security hardware. The Internet has made such information easily available to the security profession although the same information is also accessible to terrorist operatives. Some of the sources are subscription oriented, but a great many are free, including GlobalSecurity.org, which offers comprehensive information on military and terrorism subjects, including ongoing and past military and counterterrorist operations. There also are a variety of other websites that provide information on biological and chemical agents and various weapons of mass destruction.

In addition to the privately administered websites, the government has a number of sites that provide terrorism information, including one at the Centers for Disease Control and Prevention, which also provides information on diseases and biological agents. Other federal agencies, including the Federal Emergency Management Agency (FEMA), the Department of Homeland Security (DHS), and the Department of State as well as many states and educational institutions maintain websites that provide security practitioners with useful information on counterterrorism-related issues. This method of gaining information, coupled with a strong liaison with law enforcement on the local and federal levels, should provide any security practitioner with a handle on what to do.

A word of caution: Information overload can easily occur, so the appropriate level of data gathering, in both amount and periodical updates, should be ascertained early in the process. For the most part, private security does not require the amount and depth of information that the law enforcement community requires. On the other hand, corporate security officials may require more geographically focused data, particularly when foreign operations are involved, than would a local police department. As the 9/11 and later investigations revealed, however, terrorist cells can be located almost anywhere in the country or in the world. In any event, there is a tendency to gather so much information that it can be difficult to process and properly evaluate—almost to the point of rendering it worthless. There is also the problem of organizing and retrieving information when it is needed in a timely fashion. Whatever the sources and however the data are collected, there are three general categories of information: targets, target profiles, and terrorists.

Targets

Information on who and what can be a target is subdivided into two categories. The first type of target involves primarily physical facilities, not only those located in the United States, but also American-related facilities anywhere around the world. The second type of target is personnel, individuals who may make useful kidnapping or hostage victims to terrorists. Once targets are identified, information should be assembled that covers the type or types of facilities and individuals and what it would take to reestablish operations after an emergency situation.

Whether target identification information is being gathered on behalf of a municipality, a quasi-public corporation, or a private company, the data are simply an enumeration of assets, including human resources, buildings and real estate, inventory, other physical assets, and intangibles, such as goodwill, name recognition, and publicity value. In other words, a target is anything or anybody that could be burned, bombed, stolen, damaged, contaminated, taken over, occupied, kidnapped, or held hostage. All of these potential targets should be listed (or inventoried) and major characteristics identified. Individuals have personnel files with home addresses, medical histories, dependents' names, and names of next of kin. Buildings have blueprints; floor plans; and drawings of electrical and heating, ventilation, and air conditioning (HVAC) systems; as well as fire alarm and other security systems. Vehicles have operating and repair manuals. Real estate has descriptions and dimensions in the deed and title files. All of this information must be gathered, so it can be assessed, filed, updated, copied, stored, or handled by whatever policy is decided upon during the risk analysis phase. Target identification should include rankings of vulnerability and information on what it would take to get the entity up and running again after an emergency situation. Needless to say, all information on targets should be given the highest security priority and should be backed up with copies off premises but in a relatively easy-to-access location.

Target Profiles

This refers to subjective information dealing with an individual's perceptions of all the identified potential targets. Much of target profiling is based upon not only analyzing the current trends of bomb attacks, but also reviewing attacks that occurred several years prior. If a municipality is involved in compiling a possible list of targets, obviously the city or town hall is included, but so should all schools because of their high profile for media interest. The same goes for law enforcement facilities, which have prime symbolic value, particularly for right-wing terrorists. If corporate targets are included, considerations include evaluation of the company's image within the local community, the country, and perhaps even the world. Who are the company's suppliers, customers, investors, and perhaps primarily, what is the company's product or service?

Individuals in the company should be evaluated for their symbolic or strategic importance as a target. Corporations may have to think of ancillary targets that may have an impact on their ability to operate and how well they provide security for their operations. For instance, an electric utility may provide excellent security for corporate headquarters and the main generating plants but leave the substations, service trucks, payment stations, and transmission lines with minimal protection. Even if the decision is made not to protect the miles of transmission lines, a cost analysis should be made by all parties concerned in order to justify that decision.

Almost anything can be attacked, and many of the targets selected by terrorists can be classified as "soft," that is, any target that may be frequented by the public and receive no special security protection. In attacking these types of targets, the terrorists seek not to disrupt a key installation, but to kill as many people as possible. This will give the perception that a terrorist group is operating "under the radar" and can strike with impunity.

In devising a target profile, it is imperative to include the quality of responding emergency services: the local police, fire, medical, and other emergency agencies. Questions should cover whether the response teams are volunteers or professionals and if there are specialists, such as bomb technicians or hostage negotiators, included in the first responder teams. If not, how long will it take to have them on the scene? What is the response time for emergency situations? What are the cooperative arrangements, if any, with agencies that provide support or supplemental backup? Are local hospital facilities adequate to handle mass casualties, and if not, how fast can that type of medical assistance be available? How long does it take local power and gas companies to respond to emergencies? These subjective and qualitative questions will help in evaluating the risk potential for possible terrorist targets.

Target Analysis

One of the more difficult challenges facing defense planners is accurately assessing the likelihood of any particular person, piece of property, or service becoming the target of a terrorist attack. Overestimating the threat potential means wasting dollars, personnel time, and effort. On the other hand, underestimating the threat could result in physical injury or death as well as millions of dollars in damages, ransoms, or liability judgments. The failure of the intelligence agencies to detect the 9/11 attack drew much attention—most of it viewed with perfect 20/20 hindsight—but whatever led up to the attack, the assault itself was so far outside of contemporary thinking that it is no surprise that everyone was caught by surprise.

Target or threat analysis includes not only the likelihood of becoming a target, but also whether or not offered defenses are sufficient to discourage potential attacks or protect individuals and organizations in liability suits. Many terrorist attacks today, especially in the international arena, are directed at US government facilities, but US private-sector organizations sustain the largest number of attacks even if they are not of the same magnitude as those against official government facilities.

Based upon data from the Terrorist Threat Integration Center, now known as the National Counterterrorism Center (NCTC), which was established in January 2003 and includes elements from the Central Intelligence Agency (CIA), the Federal Bureau of Investigation (FBI), and DHS, the US State Department said there were 82 anti-US terrorist attacks in 2003, up slightly from 77 attacks in 2002. Terrorist incidents worldwide and the number of deaths attributed to terrorist activity declined from their high points in 2006 and 2007 to approximately 11,000 incidents in 83 countries during 2009. These affected more than 58,000 victims, including 15,000 fatalities, according to the NCTC.

The Near East and South Asia were the locations of nearly two thirds of the 234 high-casualty attacks, defined as causing 10 or more deaths. Attacks in Afghanistan were almost double the number in 2008, and terrorist attacks increased in Pakistan for the third year in a row. Though terrorist attacks in Iraq continue to decline, during the five years from 2005 to 2009, Iraq has seen more terrorist activity and deaths resulting from terrorism than any other country. This does not include attacks against US military units in Afghanistan and Iraq because these are directed toward combatants and thus, by definition, are not terrorist attacks. The NCTC reports that "Islamic extremists conducted several attacks in the United States, including two that resulted in fatalities."[3] The NCTC further stated that "[t]hese attacks represent the most significant activity by such extremists in the United States since 2001." In East Asia and the Pacific, terrorist attacks declined 16% between 2008 and 2009 due mostly to decreased activity in the Philippines. Terrorist attacks increased 19% in Africa with nearly 700 of the reported 850 incidents occur-

[3] National Counterterrorism Center. 2009 Report on Terrorism, Washington, D.C.

ring in either Somalia or the Democratic Republic of the Congo. Fatalities resulting from these attacks rose to 250.[4]

In conducting an analysis, all forms of terrorism should be considered—domestic and international terrorists whether right-wing, left-wing, religious, or unknown orientation. Any business entity outlined below should consider these concepts and determine where they fit into the equation:

1. Any business or organization that has an operation or facility in a politically sensitive country.
2. A company heavily involved in the military-industrial complex. This could include any company or subcontractor with a defense contract and anyone supplying goods or services, or both, to the defense sector of the economy.
3. Financial institutions, especially those involved in financing (or co-sponsoring with the government) programs that are antithetical to the aims of various terrorist organizations and their causes, for example, a bank holding government-backed loans to countries where terrorist organizations are active.
4. Businesses that are working with advanced technologies, particularly if they are weapons-oriented, defense systems–oriented, or both.
5. Companies involved in the processing or use of petrochemicals or other environmentally sensitive products. This is especially applicable in South America, where oil pipelines and refinery operations are located in remote regions.
6. Utilities, particularly those whose service disruption would have a dramatic impact on the public.
7. Companies with manufacturing operations in the Third World or developing countries, especially where low wage rates could leave the companies open to charges of exploitation.
8. Companies with operations in politically sensitive countries: traditionally Israel, Sri Lanka, Spain (particularly the Basque areas), and current hot spots, such as the former socialist republics of Central Asia and anywhere in the Middle East, including the Arabian Peninsula, the Philippines, Pakistan, Malaysia, the Venezuela-Colombia region, Kenya, and Zimbabwe. Terrorist activity is fluid and subject to ebbs and flows and thus can crop up almost anywhere or recur after years of relative calm.
9. Companies that, by virtue of ever-changing political winds, may find themselves on the wrong side of emotional political issues. These include, but are not limited to, forest production companies (particularly true of rainforest products), makers of abortion or birth control products, researchers who use live animals in their testing processes, researchers or agribusinesses involved in genetically modified foodstuffs, consumer product manufacturers, food processors, real estate developers, and manufacturers or users of nuclear power products.
10. Corporations that, because of their size, history, marketplace, dominance, or status as cultural icons, have become symbolic of the United States, capitalism, or both, such as Coca-Cola, McDonalds Corp., Microsoft, IBM, and virtually any international commercial bank.

Law enforcement officials with companies or organizations located in their jurisdictions that may be potential terrorist targets should ask questions such as the following:

[4] National Counterterrorism Center. 2009 Report on Terrorism, Washington, D.C.

1. Has the company or organization ever been the target of a terrorist attack?
2. Has the company's or organization's name ever been mentioned in a derogatory manner in any radical oratory, literature, website, online chat room, or other communication medium? This includes whether the company has been the target of demonstrations locally or at facilities outside the local jurisdiction.
3. Is the entity in any way affiliated with a company or organization that would have answered in the affirmative to either of the first two questions?
4. Does the company supply raw materials, packaging, or any other goods or services to such companies or organizations?
5. Does the company or organization receive materials from or ship goods to or through "sensitive" countries or territories?

The challenge in target analysis is to look at an operation through a microscope, noting suppliers, customers, distribution networks, end users, financial supporters, and even public statements and personal politics of leading officials. If an organization is defensive enough, it will be able to surmise, even in the unlikeliest scenarios, who might want to mount an attack. While many terrorist and radical groups are well known, there are many others whose presence is virtually unknown and whose grievances are unaired. Thus, the chief component in determining who may pose a terrorist threat to a company, or organization, or locality, is identifying anyone who may be able to conjure grievances, however far-fetched or historically remote they may seem.

Organization

The organization of a preincident or defense plan for a large exposed company is not an easy task to accomplish. It requires the assignment of authority and responsibility for everybody, from the highest level of management down to the rank and file, who must know whose orders to follow. The prime components of organizing are establishing levels of responsibility and structuring a chain of command for the team. Individuals assigned to decision-making positions in any defense plan structure should be chosen for their ability to act under pressure. Bureaucrats, drones, slow but steady functionaries, or impulsive hunch players should be passed over in favor of those who possess the ability to keep their wits about them in difficult circumstances. The difficulty in this selection is that private industry allows little opportunity for observing individuals in stressful situations that will allow for evaluation. Finding such individuals is, of course, the best-case scenario, and reality may precipitate deviations from the ideal. To overcome this problem, many companies and other organizations are turning to individuals with antiterrorism field experience to assist them during the planning process—sometimes as part of a full-time security team.

Any organization, whether a law enforcement agency, private company, or public institution, such as a school or hospital, has established lines of authority and a chain of command for normal day-to-day operations. These individuals may be adequate for the daily operations of a business, but in an emergency situation precipitated by a terrorist attack may require special operating rules. A terrorist defense plan could well call for a variation in the routine and a crisis team taking over control from the usual hierarchy. Such a change could include transferring the seat of power from the chief administrator's office to a command center that is better protected or has more space or better and more secure communications. This would operate until the arrival of first responders and follow-up public safety officials, who will then assume command of the situation.

The structure of the chain of command—with lines of communication as short and direct as possible—can take many forms, depending upon the nature of the target and type of emergency.

More important than how the chain of command is structured is the fact that such a chain has been planned, exists, is in place, and everyone is aware of it. The changeover to crisis management can be made rapidly and orderly as long as everyone knows who is in charge and who has what authority and what responsibilities. Only then can the challenge of dealing with, and resolving, the emergency conditions proceed with any reasonable expectations of success.

Defining levels of responsibility is an important component in the chain of command. Each person in a decision-making or leadership role should be aware of, and well schooled in, his or her responsibilities and extent of authority. The limits of that authority must also be well understood. Training for those individuals should include drills and quizzes as to who must make what decisions, as well as "what if" modeling in hypothetical situations.

In addition to individuals being fully aware of their roles, responsibilities should be spelled out in writing in the defense plan, so that the operation can proceed accordingly even if key personnel have been replaced over time. The organization of a well-defined and thoroughly schooled crisis team is required until public safety units arrive. In some cases, especially in rural areas or smaller communities, this may take longer than in more urban locations. Some elements of crisis teams may be in place, such as a first aid squad or fire brigade, especially in large manufacturing operations. Other teams that should be formed, if they are not already in place, are an evacuation team, which, as we will see later, is not the same group as the wardens who conduct drills; a bomb search team; and a consequence management unit to aid in such things as medical emergencies, evaluating the condition of the area where the incident occurred, and assisting authorities with their investigations. There should also be a risk assessment team that meets to assist in creating and maintaining the defense plan as well as evaluating threats and situations as they arise.

In organizing a crisis team and its subunits, every attempt should be made to eliminate overlap of duties among members. In the event of an actual emergency, it is likely that each individual would be occupied with specified tasks and unable to handle multiple assignments. The amount of personnel available may be a limiting factor, but eliminating overlap as much as possible should be part of the initial planning considerations.

In evaluating potential team members, maintenance staff and building engineers are especially helpful because of their knowledge of the facilities; layouts; and heating, air conditioning, and ventilation systems. There is a distinction to be made between maintenance people and janitorial or cleanup crews. Janitorial staff is often composed of part-time or contract employees with minimal skills and responsibilities and thus may not be the best choices for important responsibilities during an emergency.

The composition of an "action team," defined as the staff responsible for evacuation and search, among them, should include supervisory and management personnel. People in position of authority are more likely to be listened to in times of emergency. As a practical matter, more wardens will probably be needed for an evacuation team than, say, a search team because every staircase and exit must be covered during an evacuation. Evacuation personnel will report to the same location for each and every drill or in the event of an actual emergency. This means that those employees who are on the premises every day, all day, are preferred for such assignments.

Training

During training on a terrorist preincident plan, responsibilities must be communicated to all participants at all levels of involvement because these people are members of a coordinated unit in which teamwork is required. The foundation for coordinated teamwork is through understanding of individual assignments. Training of some of the specialized teams used in crises can be accomplished without the necessity of outside assistance; however, local and state police agencies as well as specialized security professionals can better provide assistance in conducting the training.

Training sessions should include a complete explanation of the defense plan, the theory involved, and the detailed application in order to provide operational flavor to all those involved. The classroom sessions should be followed by tests and drills of each aspect or phase of the plan, which should then be critiqued so alterations can be made accordingly. Finally, a full-scale crisis simulation should be conducted. Once the simulation has been conducted and evaluated, regular testing of plan components should be scheduled at least as regularly as fire drills. A full-scale mock crisis drill should be conducted annually, at the minimum, unless local conditions dictate greater frequency.

Perhaps the biggest deficiency in terrorist defense planning and crisis management comes in the area of replacing and training personnel. When a plan is adopted initially, there usually is sufficient enthusiasm and commitment to ensure well-trained teams. As individuals are promoted, transferred, or replaced within the organization, large gaps can develop in the defense plan's organization or personnel. Familiarizing newcomers with their responsibilities in the plan and regular simulations of crises and disasters—even just selected phases of the whole plan—is simply good management. Such drills not only school newcomers, but also reacquaint experienced personnel with their roles and duties. The whole effort presents opportunities for reviewing the plan and altering or updating where required. The planning and training is a difficult sell to management, especially in times of cost-control initiatives. However, management would be remiss, perhaps even in a legal sense, to completely ignore the situation, dismissing such a possibility on the premise of its unlikeliness to occur.

Reducing Casualties: Private Security Guards and Hardening Buildings

Ideally, the best way to combat terrorism, in general, and suicide bombings, in particular, is to interdict the suicide bomber before he or she carries out an attack. That prevents people from being killed or maimed and the wider community from becoming traumatized. The more difficult, but not impossible, way of stopping a prospective suicide bomber is to identify and capture him or her as he or she tries to carry out an attack. The frequent inability to foil suicide bombings leads many to think that there really is not much one can do in dealing with a suicide bombing. This is simply not true. If the wall of security—the behavioral profiling, the hiring of trained security guards, and the like—does not prevent a suicide bombing, there are steps that can be taken in advance to reduce casualties. Israelis have taken many of these steps in their efforts to eliminate and reduce the withering effects of these bombings. The tactics used by them are explored below.

Private Security

Throughout the 1980s and 1990s, Israel's most blunt instrument was a private security program that proved reasonably useful as a last-minute defense against suicide bombers. With their military background and a feeling that they were protecting their families, however indirectly, Israeli private guards were prepared to "take the bullet," which, in their cases, meant keeping a suicide bomber from getting inside the premises even if the bomber blew himself up next to the guard. At this stage, American private security guards do not have the same mindset that Israeli guards do: willing to put their lives on the line to protect civilians. If terrorists begin a suicide bombing campaign in the United States, one assumes that American guards would "take the bullet," if required, as their Israeli counterparts have sometimes been forced to do.

Success for the security guard means preventing the suicide bomber from entering the premises, and, indeed, alert security guards have stopped suicide bombers before they could get inside. If the suicide bomber gets inside the premises, he will almost always kill and wound more people than if he had blown himself up outside. Ideally, the guard will identify and stop the bomber from blowing himself up. But realistically, success for the guard means reducing or preventing as many deaths and wounded as possible.

Despite their limitations, security guards represent a last line of defense. The creation of a professional private security program proved of immeasurable help in Israel's fight against suicide bombings. After the Palestinians began employing suicide bombing as a weapon of choice against the Israelis, Israel had to employ any tactic it could to fight the bombers. The favored Middle Eastern terror tactic in the 1970s and 1980s was airplane hijackings in which the Palestinian goal was to free the passengers in exchange for the release of Palestinian prisoners in Israeli jails.

The defense against hijackings was greater vigilance against potential hijackers. Inasmuch as Palestinian terror was confined to the skies, there was no need for a private security guard to be posted at every central bus station, department store, office building, and the like. Even when Palestinians launched suicide bombings in Israel, security professionals assumed that bombers would be highly selective, targeting only such high-profile figures as the prime minister, cabinet members, and the army chief of staff or other symbols of power, such as the electric grid and gas and port facilities.

The prime minister's office and home in Jerusalem along with the Knesset were turned into military fortresses, but few other buildings were given such high-level security. Though Israel's security outlook required the outlay of millions of Israeli shekels to protect these high-profile targets, Israeli security officials look back upon that expense as largely a waste because the terrorists wound up not attacking symbols of power. When Palestinian terrorist organizations unleashed their suicide bombers against Israeli targets, they aimed at places where Israelis gathered in large numbers.

These locations had great advantage for the suicide bombers. Each coffeehouse or restaurant had far less security than that provided to a prime minister. For Israelis to guard each and every place where people gathered seemed frustratingly useless. If a suicide bomber found too much security at one coffeehouse, he could easily find another with weaker security down the block. However, once suicide bombings against public places began in earnest in the mid-1990s, placing security guards at their entrances seemed increasingly necessary. In addition, the Israel Police, which had the chief responsibility in the fight against domestic terror, flooded the streets.

The police minister at that time, Roni Milo, even ordered all police cars to keep their flashing lights on their car roofs on at all times—not just when heading for an emergency—to give Israelis the impression of an omnipresent and large police presence in the streets, thus calming their nerves. In fact, the tactic may have backfired by causing the public to believe that the police cars were on their way to another suicide bombing, which is not exactly what the police minister had in mind.

In Israel, security guards were trained to study the behavioral patterns of potential suicide bombings, but even the most professional guard could, at best, prevent the suicide bomber from blowing up inside the premises. Guards did identify would-be suicide bombers as they tried to enter a restaurant or bus terminal; on a few occasions, realizing that he or she had been spotted, the bomber prematurely detonated his or her bomb, killing the guard, who died a hero having saved numerous lives inside the premises.

Requiring Israeli youth to serve as security guards after serving in the army would have added a harsh burden to those young people. The Israel government ordered its young men and women to join the army at age 18 and serve three years for men, two years for women. After serving in the military, Israel's youth wanted to travel or attend a university, not guard public places. Besides, the Israeli government was unable to take on the financial burden of hiring and training a professional group of security guards. Accordingly, the government enacted laws that passed the financial burden on to the private sector.

As a result, the government relied on private security companies to supply the needed personnel. The Israel Police took responsibility for creating the training doctrine for the private guards, overseeing its implementation, and the hiring of trainers who ran courses and performed background checks on potential security guards. Israel benefited greatly from the fact that most private security guards had recently graduated from the military and were willing to work at affordable rates.

All schools were required to have secure physical barriers with an armed guard stationed at all entrances. Trained security guards were posted at shopping mall entrances, restaurants (of a certain size), hotels, and most other public venues, such as event spaces where weddings, bar mitzvahs, and Passover seders, were held. Security guards appeared outside many public facilities from supermarkets to movie theaters, checking bags of visitors. It was the norm for Israelis to wait in line for mandatory (as opposed to random) security checks of their bags for explosives. Guards used metal detectors, but they did not ask men to take off their belts or request men and women to remove their shoes, instead relying almost entirely on spotting someone suspicious. X-ray machines were used mainly at government offices, airports, and central bus and train stations.

In the same way that American-based security guards have been trained in how to stop a shoplifter from leaving a store, Israeli guards, in meaningful contrast, have learned how to keep a potential suicide bomber from entering the premises or from blowing himself up in a crowd outside a public place. Israeli security officers have a shorthand way of describing the contrast: In America, the security guard faces "in." In Israel, the security guard faces "out."

On a number of occasions, Israeli security guards, whether relying upon a visual read or metal detectors, have been successful in identifying suicide bombers as they approached a target. Though the bomber sometimes detonated his explosives outside the target, many lives were saved by the guards' careful screening technique. However, a guard's lax behavior at the Maxim Restaurant in Haifa on October 4, 2003, showed that weak security could be devastatingly lethal.

Should intelligence agencies supply private security guards with information about potential suicide bombers? For years, these agencies debated the question among themselves. American intelligence does not provide classified information to private security guards concerning terrorists about to carry out an act of violence. But in Israel, the police routinely pass on what Americans would consider classified intelligence to senior executives at private firms. Those executives then pass the intelligence on to their security guards. Routinely armed with normally classified intelligence about potential suicide bombers, well trained to detect suspicious behavior, and highly motivated, these private security guards often proved their on-the-spot value. Here are some examples:

- *April 24, 2003, train station, Kfar Saba.* A suicide bombing occurred at the entrance to the brand-new Kfar Saba train station northeast of Tel Aviv. At 7:20 a.m. the bomber arrived, hoping to get into the station, where numerous Israelis were waiting on platforms for arriving trains. Sensing that the man was suspicious, a security guard refused to let him into the station, demanding to see his identity papers. The bomber changed his plan and set off the bomb there and then, killing the security guard and wounding nine others.
- *April 30, 2003, Mike's Place, Tel Aviv.* A suicide bombing had taken place at 12:45 a.m. when a terrorist approached Mike's Place and blew himself up at the entrance to the bar, killing three people and wounding another 60, including a security guard named Avi Tabib, who had properly identified the bomber as suspicious and had kept him from entering the restaurant, where many more people had congregated.

  The guard faced terrible odds. Even had he put the bomber through a metal-detection scanner, the detasheet (detonation sheet) explosive that the bomber was carrying would have gone undetected. After the guard grabbed the bomber, the man realized that he could not get into the restaurant; he set off his explosives near the entrance, killing "only" three people and injuring the guard.
- *July 11, 2004, Caffit restaurant, Jerusalem.* Malak Nasser A-Din, a 41-year-old Hamas terrorist, stood outside the popular café, Caffit, on Emek Refaim Street, planning to kill the security guard and then rush into the café and detonate his bomb. Instead, spotting the guard, the would-be bomber suddenly walked away and was subsequently arrested.

Apart from private security guards, Israel has enjoyed the advantage of an enlisted civilian public that has stayed on full alert even during so-called quiet periods. In addition to private security guards, Israeli bus drivers, unarmed and devoting full attention to driving carefully, have sometimes played a significant role in identifying suicide bombers and taking action against them to reduce casualties in a bombing.

Hardening Public and Private Places

Placing security guards outside entrances to public places provides "last-minute" security. To reduce casualties, security guards have to act at the last minute or even the last few seconds before a suicide bombing. But Israelis learned that acting before a suicide bombing can reduce casualties as well.

One way to take action long before a suicide bomber sets off on a mission is to harden (or fortify) a public place; the object of hardening the place is to reduce casualties should a suicide bomber blow himself up, whether in a car or standing outside the venue near or inside a crowd. The security officer is always trying to find an answer to a perceived threat as opposed to threats that are unrealistic. If word reaches security officers that a terrorist has a nuclear weapon, the officer does not need to harden a target. Certain threats, like the threat of a nuclear weapon, simply have no reasonable answer. The security officer's job is to take responsibility and provide professional answers to reasonable threats based on available resources.

The far more realistic threat, as the Israelis discovered, is from suicide bombers. Before the mid-1990s, Israel paid scant attention to the hardening issue as the wave of bombings only began in 1993. After that, a wave of suicide bombings against Israel drove its security officials to think about fortifying, or hardening, public and private places against that specific threat. Between 2000 and 2002, when a second wave of suicide bombings was hitting Israel, this time on a weekly basis, the government learned the hard way that it had to step up its hardening efforts against suicide bombings quickly.

How Should One Harden a Facility?

Each target should be hardened according to the specific threats faced and the available resources. Israeli security officers always describe a security program as an individual process peculiar to each site, or "tailoring a security suit." There are specific steps that should be taken to "harden" facilities:

1. Perform background checks on all employees.
2. Search people coming into a public building.
3. Install a good camera system that photographs both inside and outside a building to determine if someone is engaging in surveillance near the building.
4. View monitors regularly; then send recordings and information about anyone suspicious to law enforcement.
5. Whenever and if possible, building managers should put in place physical barriers, such as planters or cement blocks that can block an explosive-laden vehicle from getting close to its intended target. The barriers will almost certainly minimize casualties and building damage.
6. Attention should be given to all exterior building windows and the possible secondary blast effects. Solutions run the gamut from different types of glass to add-on film to interior fragment reducers, such as blast curtains. Exterior building windows should be covered with blast-resistant film to mitigate shattering from the blast effect of explosives.

7. If the building, especially a sensitive one, has a garage, cars entering should be checked, including car trunks, to make sure that they are not carrying explosives. The height of roofs in a parking garage should be lowered to prevent large vehicles (which could potentially carry enough explosives to take down a building) from entering.

Fortification of schools is a top priority in Israel, and there are valuable lessons to learn from the Israeli experience. Here is what the Israelis learned: Guards need to be placed outside all school entrances. Security and building maintenance officials need to learn how to check a school building's heating, ventilation, and air conditioning systems because terrorists might try to place explosives or chemical or biological agents inside them. Access to these systems must be limited and controlled. All exterior doors and operable windows should have alarms and motion sensors. A gate or fence should be installed along the perimeter of a school. Schoolchildren should be taught "terror awareness" at an early age; youngsters should be instructed not to pick up anything from the ground and to report anything suspicious to teachers. What they find just might be an explosive. In Israel, such instruction begins in pre-kindergarten. Israelis know that it is never too early. Teachers, principals, and security guards are responsible for security functions in Israeli schools. Those are the only school personnel who should carry the obligation of ensuring the safety of schoolchildren.

The Lesson of Istanbul

While on assignment in Israel, Mordecai Dzikansky visited Istanbul soon after suicide-bombing attacks rocked the city. The first of the two Istanbul incidents occurred on November 15, 2003, at 9:26 a.m., when a suicide bomber struck at Neve Shalom, the city's largest synagogue. Five minutes later, a second suicide bomber attacked the Bet Israel synagogue. Dzikansky found indisputable evidence that hardening a target prior to a suicide bombing reduces casualties significantly. That lesson offered New York City—and the rest of America as well—a way to reduce casualties in such a bombing.

Upon arriving in Istanbul, Dzikansky wanted to know whether either target had been hardened, and if so, which had fared better. As it turned out, Neve Shalom, which had 11 dead and 125 wounded, had been fortified; Bet Israel, with 12 dead and almost twice as many wounded (220) had not been. Seventeen years earlier, on September 6, 1986, Arab gunmen had entered Neve Shalom and killed 22 worshippers. The Palestinian terrorist and founder of al-Fatah, Yasser Arafat, had been blamed. Inasmuch as suicide bombers were employing a tactic of striking twice at the same place, fortifying Neve Shalom made much sense. Because of the 1986 attack, all sorts of security improvements had been put in place: bullet-proof entrances, security checks of congregants, six large pillars outside the building to act as barriers against direct hits, and video cameras installed to monitor people and the street. Bet Israel had not made any of these improvements.

The pillars at Neve Shalom worked, keeping the truck from getting closer to the synagogue, preventing deaths, and limiting injuries inside. The video camera recorded the truck as it came to a slow crawl and then, while still moving, exploded in front of the Neve Shalom synagogue. Heavy structural damage was sustained, but far less than at the Bet Israel bombing site. Bet Israel, in contrast to Neve Shalom, was left porous: The street at its main entrance was closed off to vehicular traffic, and security personnel were stationed at the door. But the street at its back entrance was open to traffic. Though five security officers and one police officer had been stationed at the back entrance, all six were killed when the bomber blew himself up. Nor did Bet Israel have pillars at either of its two entrances, allowing the bomber to get close to the building.

Concluding Thoughts

Measures that seek to mitigate terrorism are those that are designed to deal with the impact of a terrorist attack once it has materialized. Antiterrorism measures seek to do just that by including terror defense plans designed to enable both public and private sectors to prepare for a terrorist attack. This defense planning includes the collection of information on terrorists' profiles and tactics. The core of terror defense planning includes the creation of preincident, incident, and post-incident plans, which should be updated on a regular basis. The private sector is often overlooked in antiterrorism. However, it plays a critical role in mitigating terrorism. Lessons can be learned from other countries' use of private security personnel in their antiterrorism efforts. A case in point is Israel. In Israel, private security has been used to harden targets to great effect: often resulting in the reduction of casualties in a terrorist attack and, at times, discouraging a terrorist from engaging in an attack.

10

Deterring Terrorism[1]

The Department of Defense defines counterterrorism as the "offensive measures taken to prevent (preempt), deter (disrupt), and respond to terrorism."[2] It includes those active measures used to find and destroy terrorist organizations or cells. They are offensive in nature and the almost exclusive domain of governments, acting through their militaries, intelligence agencies, and law enforcement organizations. These measures are often taken in response to a terrorist attack after it occurs. Within the context of a US military response, counterterrorism includes the overt or clandestine use of forces to locate and neutralize terrorists and their facilities, rescue hostages, and recover intelligence on terrorists. Accordingly, counterterrorism may include a wide variety of measures, from armed military action (such as the 1998 Tomahawk cruise missile attack on the Zawar Kili terrorist training center in Afghanistan) to clandestine operations (for instance, the Drug Enforcement Administration/Federal Bureau of Investigation/Central Intelligence Agency sting that led to the arrest of Lebanese hijacker Fuwaz Yunez in 1987).

A government has no higher obligation than to protect the lives and livelihoods of its citizens. Here, governments should employ methods that will cut off terrorists from the network of individuals, institutions, and other resources they depend on for support and that facilitate their activities. The network, in turn, will be deterred, disrupted, and disabled. Conventional wisdom holds that terrorists and terrorism cannot be deterred: terrorists do not fear punishment or death, nor do they possess the territory and population of a state, and they are therefore immune from psychological coercion via threat of retaliation.

Smith and Talbot argue, however, that deterrence—specifically psychological coercion through denial as opposed to traditional deterrence by punishment—cannot only be applied to terrorism, but also can be utilized at the tactical, operational, and strategic levels for an overall coercive effect. In developing this application, the chapter presents terrorism as a dynamic process described by interrelated essential elements and communication flows. It then presents concepts of deterrence as these enter into this dynamic process and disrupt its elements and linkages, thus shaping coercive influences, removing terrorist options, and forcing decisions that alter terrorist plans and actions.

---

1 Information for this chapter was drawn from the following titles: (1) J. M. Smith and B. J. Talbot, Terrorism and Deterrence by Denial. In M. A. Opheim, N. Bowen, and P. R. Viotti (eds.), *Terrorism and Homeland Security: Thinking Strategically About Policy*, CRC Press, 2008. (2) T. A. Johnson, *War on Terrorism: A Collision of Values, Strategies and Societies*, CRC Press, 2008. (3) R. Johnson, *Antiterrorism and Threat Response: Planning and Implementation*, CRC Press, 2013.

2 Department of Defense Directive no. 2000. August 18, 2003, certified current as of December 13, 2007, enclosure 2, p. 21. Available at http://www.dtic.mil/whs/directives/corres/pdf/200012p.pdf.

At the base or tactical level, the operative coercive mechanism for deterrence of an act of terrorism is denial of opportunity, which delinks the terrorist action cadre from its intended victim or victims. At the higher operational level—deterrence of a series of related terrorist actions or a campaign of terror—the mechanism is denial of capability, which disrupts organizational recruitment and maintenance, training, access to weapons and sanctuary, communications, finance, and other resources needed to undertake hostile actions. At the highest and most important or strategic level—deterrence of terrorism itself or defeat of the strategy—the mechanism is denial of objectives or marginalization of the terrorist message from both its target population and its support base, leading to ultimate failure.

The chapter concludes with a discussion of how to implement a framework to create these effects with specific attention to both international perception and influence and domestic preparation and insulation. A wide range of efforts is required to create the synergistic deterrent effect within and across the tactical, operational, and strategic levels. Cognizant that terrorism is a form of strategic communication, implementation must be informed by the effort to use international effects and influence to shape messages to and among the regional and global terrorist "core" audience and potential supporters and domestic effects that shape both US government and population reactions to terrorist threats and actions. Only this total, deliberate, and strategic approach can achieve a deterrent effect on this otherwise intractable adversary.

Terrorism as a Dynamic Process

The term "terrorism" is today used to describe a wide range of tactics, campaigns, and strategies of criminal and political violence. This chapter is specifically addressing terrorism as deliberate violence undertaken for political objectives with the attainment of these objectives resulting from psychological effects on targets beyond the direct victims of the violence. Smith and Talbot look to second- and third-order psychological effects of political violence—an examination that goes well beyond the physical act, weapon, and victim to the larger motivation, preparation, and orchestration of terrorism and the terrorist as well as to the instrumental creation of fear or terror as the primary lever seeking to cause changes in government policy and action, particularly in driving popular demands on that government for the changes sought. At the same time, the act sends messages to create, deepen, and reinforce support for the terror and the terrorist group among its core audience, and it seeks to engender sympathy and support among wider regional and global audiences to foster its cause and secure both general and tangible support. It is both political violence and psychological communication—sometimes called "propaganda of the deed"—undertaken as asymmetrical warfare against an otherwise superior adversary.[3]

One way to conceptualize terrorism and to design effective anticipatory and response efforts toward deterrence is to depict it as a systematic process (a cause to action to effects chain, as depicted horizontally in Figure 10.1). The focal point for much of the terrorism analysis is the terrorist act—the terrorist committing a violent act employing some weapon against a selected victim. Although the terrorist, the act, the weapon, and the victim constitute an important tactical level of analysis relevant to the overall effort to combat terrorism, it is insufficient either to understand fully or to respond effectively to the threat. The process model developed here adds the operational and organizational underpinnings to the terrorist and his act, and it also includes the essential consequences and audiences terrorized or influenced by such acts.

[3] Dan Gressang's presentation "Reconsidering the Functionality of Terrorism: Implications for Security Planning" to the International Studies Association in Chicago, February 23, 2002, spurred the development of the strategic communication dimensions added to this model.

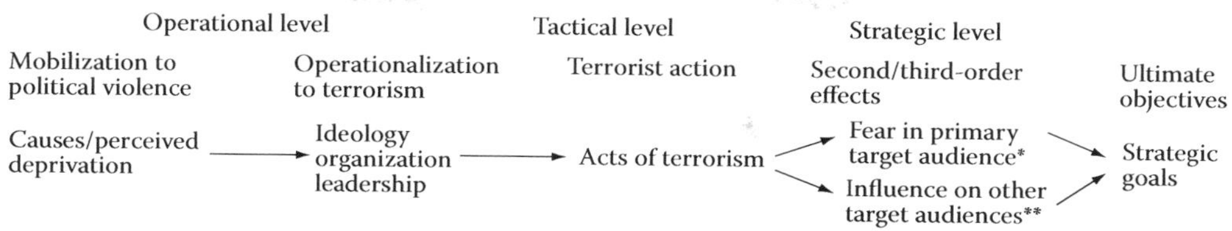

Figure 10.1 Essential process elements, dynamic linkages, and audiences. (From M. A. Opheim, N. Bowen, and P. R. Viotti (eds.). *Terrorism and Homeland Security: Thinking Strategically About Policy*, CRC Press, 2008; J. M. Smith and B. J. Talbot. *Terrorism and Deterrence by Denial*. With permission.)

The operational level of analysis—a focus on cause and organizational response—adds the foundation and structure of terror from its underlying causes and roots of discontent through the organizing infrastructure of recruitment, training, support, communications, and weapons procurement—all that goes into motivating, organizing, preparing, supporting, and sustaining a quasimilitary structure and strategy. It also includes focus on the complex psychological and organizational transformation from discontent to violence or the action link that brings all of those motives and capabilities to the act of terrorist violence.

Terrorism does not end with the act of violence; that is only the beginning. It is the fear generated in the minds of the target audiences—not the victim—that provides the lever through (and only through) which the terrorist organization can hope to attain its objectives. Terrorism is a tool used by the relatively weak to attack a strong adversary, an asymmetrical tool that bypasses adversary strengths and seeks out the soft and vulnerable underbelly of society as the focus of influence. It is this second-order psychological effect on the "target of terror" that is the key to influencing adversary decisions and policies. The terrorist act also is to reinforce and expand the group's influence on and support from its core support base, its broader regional or cultural base, and even the global audience—all "targets of influence."[4]

Terrorism and Deterrence by Denial

As briefly outlined, viewing terrorism as an interactive process above indicates points of attack for an effective strategic response. These components and the dynamics between them are defining the terrorist group; its critical characteristics; and its operational, tactical, and strategic dimensions. They also point to its relative strengths and weaknesses, indicating potential responses to counter effectively its key strengths and capitalize on its weaknesses. Terrorism can be blunted—its damage prevented, deflected, or limited by tactical response policy elements. And it can be preempted or altered, even ultimately defeated, by strategic countermeasures that target and attack its operational and strategic bases or operational centers. This process context—its essential elements developed and related within an overarching strategic perspective—is at the center of both the terrorist threat and the strategic response to that threat. It provides not only a template for a comprehensive threat assessment, but also a framework for systematic response.

[4] The terms "target of terror" and "target of influence" are from D. J. Hanle, *Terrorism: The Newest Face of Warfare*. Washington, D.C.: Pergamon-Brassey, 1989, as adapted by T. S. Thomas in *Beneath the Surface: Intelligence Preparation of the Battlespace for Counterterrorism*. Washington, D.C.: Joint Military Intelligence College, November 2004, 11.

Tactical Level: Deterrence by Denial of Opportunity

The tactical level of deterrence aims at prevention of an act or acts of terrorism. It seeks to delink terrorism from its victim. This can be accomplished by denying either the victim access to the terrorist through protection and hardening or by denying the terrorist access to the victim or weapon through efforts to block entry and obstruct movement. Potential "victims" with high value and high symbolic visibility can be protected through physical means and protective measures. Making it difficult to reach or attack specific victims can cause terrorists to look elsewhere or to change (delay or defer) their decisions to act. Making it difficult to gain entry to the country, to travel with impunity within the vicinity of the priority victim, or to access weapons of choice or their essential components can also have this preventive effect.

Another key point here is that if short-term deterrence fails and an act of terrorism does occur, then the visible effectiveness of the response can have strong and larger-scale deterrent effects toward future acts and continued terrorism. An effective implementation of crisis and consequence management—strength of response, rescue, recovery, and clear leadership within those efforts—will limit the degree of "terror" in the local and national population, blunt the fear, and shorten the period of major psychological impact.

Accurate and timely attribution of the attack to the responsible party or parties and identification of weapons components employed by these terrorists will allow decisive retribution and a clear chain of movement toward effective prosecution of both perpetrators and their weapons suppliers. Rapid recovery followed by both symbolic and substantial reconstruction and reconstitution also will blunt much of the long-term effect. This limits the "terror" outcome, and it helps with the strategic preparation of the population for a sustained campaign to combat terrorism, also limiting the likelihood of the terrorist obtaining any favorable effect through future attacks. Less than fully effective deterrence today does not signal total failure; today's attack response can contribute significantly to tomorrow's strengthened deterrent outcomes.

Operational Level: Deterrence by Denial of Capability

Actions that contribute to effective deterrence at the operational level address the organizational and operational process. In organizational terms, the United States can seek to affect the legitimacy and attractiveness of the organization's cause, its ability to recruit members and supporters, and most significantly its process of socialization and mobilization toward violent action. These are often broadly based and long-term counterterrorism efforts.

Shorter-term actions include attempts to disrupt the operational process by removing access to sanctuary and open support, putting and keeping terrorist leadership underground and on the run. Terrorist action can be disrupted by denying access to weaponry—at least its worst forms—training grounds and resources, free movement and associated travel documents, secure communications, and finance. Specifically, governments can accomplish this by denying or neutralizing what terrorists need to operate and survive:

- *Leaders.* Leaders provide the vision that followers strive to realize. They also offer the necessary direction, discipline, and motivation for accomplishing a given goal or task. Most terrorist organizations have a central figure who embodies the cause in addition to several operational leaders and managers who provide guidance on a functional, regional, or local basis. The loss of a leader can degrade a group's cohesiveness and, in some cases, may trigger its collapse. Other terrorist groups adapt by promoting experienced cadres or decentralizing their command structures, making the challenge in neutralizing terrorist leaders even more challenging.
- *Foot soldiers.* Foot soldiers include the operatives, facilitators, and trainers in a terrorist network. They are the lifeblood of a terrorist group; they make it run. Technology

and globalization have enhanced the ability of groups to recruit foot soldiers to their cause, including well-educated recruits. Governments should not only continue to capture foot soldiers, but also work to halt the influx of recruits into terrorist organizations as well. Without a continuing supply of personnel to facilitate and carry out attacks, these groups ultimately will cease to operate.

- *Weapons.* Terrorists exploit many avenues to develop and acquire weapons, including through state sponsors, theft or capture, and black market purchases.[5] They employ existing technology—explosives, small arms, missiles, and other devices—in both conventional and unconventional ways to terrorize and achieve mass effects. They also use non-weapon technologies such as the airplanes on September 11. One of the greatest and gravest concerns, however, is WMDs in the hands of terrorists.[6] Preventing their acquisition and the dire consequences of their use is a key priority of this strategy.
- *Funds.* Funds provide the fungible, easily transportable means to secure all other forms of material support necessary to the survival and operation of terrorist organizations. Terrorists raise funds through a variety of means, including soliciting contributions from supporters; operating businesses, NGOs, and charitable fronts; and engaging in criminal activity, such as fraud, extortion, and kidnapping for ransom. They transfer funds through several mechanisms, including the formal banking system, wire transfers, debit or "smart" cards, cash couriers, and hawalas, which are alternative remittance systems based on trust. Effective disruption of funding sources and interdiction of transfer mechanisms can help starve terrorist networks of the material support they require.[7]
- *Communications.* Communications allow terrorists the ability to receive, store, manipulate, and exchange information. The methods by which terrorists communicate are numerous and varied. Terrorists rely on couriers and face-to-face contacts with associates and tend to use what is accessible in their local areas as well as what they can afford. They also use today's technologies with increasing acumen and sophistication. This is especially true with the Internet, which they exploit to create and disseminate propaganda, recruit new members, raise funds and other material resources, provide instruction on weapons and tactics, and plan operations. Without a communications ability, terrorist groups cannot effectively organize operations, execute attacks, or spread their ideology.
- *Propaganda.* Propaganda is used by terrorists to justify violent action as well as inspire individuals to support or join the movement. The ability of terrorists to exploit the Internet, and 24/7 worldwide media coverage allows them to bolster their prominence as well as promote radical ideology and conspiracy theories to potential recruits in all corners of the globe. Besides a global reach, these technologies allow terrorists to propagate their message quickly, often before an effective counter to terrorist messages can be coordinated and distributed. These are force multipliers for our enemy.

In addition, denying terrorists the tools to travel internationally and across and within our borders significantly impedes their mobility and can inhibit their effectiveness. They rely on illicit networks to facilitate travel and often obtain false identification documents through theft or in-house forgery operations. Governments should develop and enhance security practices and technologies to reduce vulnerabilities in the dynamic transportation network, inhibit terrorists

[5] See Chapter 5 of this volume.

[6] See Chapter 6 of this volume for further information on WMD terrorism.

[7] See Chapter 7 of this volume for further information on terrorist financing.

from crossing US borders, and detect and prevent terrorist travel within the United States. These efforts will include improving all aspects of aviation security, promoting secure travel and identity documents, disrupting travel facilitation networks, improving border security and visa screening, and building international capacity and improving international information exchange to secure travel and combat terrorist travel.

Moreover, governments should deny terrorists the support and sanctuary of rogue states. To break the bonds between rogue states and terrorists, governments work to disrupt the flow of resources from states to terrorists while simultaneously working to end state sponsorship of terrorism. State sponsors are a critical resource for terrorists, often providing funds, weapons, training, safe passage, and sanctuary. Some of these countries have developed or have the capability to develop WMD and other destabilizing technologies that could fall into the hands of terrorists. The United States currently designates four state sponsors of terrorism: Iran, Syria, Sudan, and Cuba. The United States maintains sanctions against them and promotes their international isolation—until these countries end their support for terrorists, including the provision of sanctuary.

Iran remains the most active state sponsor of international terrorism. Through its Islamic Revolutionary Guard Corps and Ministry of Intelligence and Security, the regime in Tehran plans terrorist operations and supports groups, such as Hezballah, Hamas, and the Palestine Islamic Jihad (PIJ). Iran also remains unwilling to account for and bring to justice senior al-Qaeda members it detained in 2003. Most troubling is the potential WMD terrorism nexus that emanates from Tehran. Syria also is a significant state sponsor of terrorism and thus a priority for concern. The regime in Damascus supports and provides haven to Hezbollah, Hamas, and PIJ.

The designation of Iraq as a state sponsor was rescinded in 2004 as it transitioned to democracy, ceased its terrorist support, and became an ally in the War on Terror. Similarly, the United States in June 2006 rescinded the designation of Libya, which has renounced terrorism and since September 11 has provided excellent cooperation to the United States and other members of the international community in response to the new global threats we face. Libya can serve as a model for states that wish to rejoin the community of nations by rejecting terror.

Another counterterrorism goal is to disrupt the flow of resources from rogue states to terrorists. Furthermore, counterterrorism seeks to deny terrorists control of any nation they would use as a base and launching pad for terror. Terrorists have strived to claim a strategic country as a haven for terror. From this base, they could destabilize the Middle East and strike America and other nations with ever-increasing violence. Governments should, therefore, prevent terrorists from exploiting ungoverned or under-governed areas as safe havens—secure spaces that allow our enemies to plan, organize, train, and prepare for operations.

Ultimately, governments should seek to eliminate these havens altogether. Physical sanctuaries can stretch across an entire sovereign state, be limited to specific ungoverned or ill-governed areas in an otherwise functioning state, or cross national borders. In some cases, governments may want to exercise greater effective sovereignty over its lands and maintain control within its borders but lacks the necessary capacity. As such, the counterterrorism goal should be to strengthen the capacity of such countries to reclaim full control of their territory through effective police, border, and other security forces as well as functioning systems of justice. To further counter-terrorist exploitation of under-governed lands, governments' effective economic development should be promoted to help ensure long-term stability and prosperity. In failing states or states emerging from conflict, the risks are significant. Spoilers can take advantage of instability to create conditions terrorists can exploit.

Nations should continue to work with foreign partners and international organizations to help prevent conflict and respond to state failure by building foreign capacity for peace operations, reconstruction, and stabilization so that countries in transition can reach a sustainable path to peace, democracy, and prosperity. Where physical havens cross national boundaries, governments should continue to work with the affected countries to help establish effective cross-border control. Yet some countries will be reluctant to fulfill their sovereign responsibilities to combat terrorist-related activities within their borders. In addition to cooperation and sustained diplomacy, governments should continue to partner with the international community to persuade other states to meet their obligations to combat terrorism and deny safe haven under U.N. Security Council Resolution 1373. Yet safe havens are not just limited to geographic territories. They also can be nonphysical or virtual, existing within legal and cyber systems.

Some legal systems lack adequate procedural, substantive, and international assistance laws that enable effective investigation, prosecution, and extradition of terrorists. Such gaps offer a haven in which terrorists and their organizations can operate free from fear of prosecution. In the United States, we have developed a domestic legal system that supports effective investigation and prosecution of terrorist activities. Other countries may or may not have these capabilities. Accordingly, they need to build their legal capacity to investigate, prosecute, and assist in the prosecution of the full range of terrorist activities—from provision of material support to conspiracy to operational planning to a completed act of terrorism.

What's more, the Internet provides an inexpensive, anonymous, geographically unbounded, and largely unregulated virtual haven for terrorists. Terrorists use the Internet to develop and disseminate propaganda, recruit new members, raise and transfer funds, train members on weapons use and tactics, and plan operations. Terrorist organizations can use virtual safe havens based anywhere in the world, regardless of where their members or operatives are located. Use of the Internet, however, creates opportunities for governments to exploit. To counter terrorist use of the Internet as a virtual sanctuary, governments should discredit terrorist propaganda by promoting truthful and peaceful messages. In due course, governments should seek to deny the Internet to the terrorists as an effective safe haven for their propaganda, proselytizing, recruitment, fundraising, training, and operational planning.

With effective intelligence and international support, governments can sometimes preempt terror preparations and attack. Governments can interdict these organizational and operational processes, and they can at least limit group capabilities and attack severity. In the end, governments seek to isolate the terrorist from support bases and sources of sanctuary and to limit his or her ability even to undertake acts of terrorism.

Strategic Level: Deterrence by Denial of Objectives

Strategic deterrence of terrorism is aimed at creating the clear perception in the mind of the terrorist leadership that their goals cannot be achieved by means of a terror campaign against the United States; their strategy cannot succeed, and any action on their part can only leave them exposed to all levels of audience as ineffective, irrelevant, and unworthy of attention or support. This level of deterrent action builds from the tactical and operational levels specifically to limit the psychological vulnerability and to build the psychological strength of the target—in this case, the United States public and its government. Preparing the American target to mute the effects of terrorism is, first, a function of education prior to attack. Fear of the misunderstood magnifies the impact of terrorism, and knowing something about the true weakness and understanding the terrorists' motivations and objectives can provide an effective damper on the generation of "terror." Knowing what is going on across an attack through open and nonsensational information is essential to limiting fear. These effects, along with strong and visible tactical and operational efforts to prevent and respond to terror, will go far toward insulating the target from the full, desired terrorist reaction. Effective prevention, mitigation, and response combine to marginalize and mute the terrorist message. Because the terrorist is already an ineffective, marginal player on the global stage in all other dimensions of power and influence, such a negative impact on his strategic "message" dooms him to failure. Terrorism without "terror" cannot succeed as a political strategy, and failure ultimately will feed on itself, destroying the terrorist cause and effort.

All of these levels and components of terrorism and deterrence are graphically displayed in Figure 10.2. While that depiction only provides the framework for deterring terrorism, the

Figure 10.2 Terrorism dynamic process model with deterrence overlay: strategic response based on causal analysis of terrorist threat. (From M. A. Opheim, N. Bowen, and P. R. Viotti (eds.), *Terrorism and Homeland Security: Thinking Strategically About Policy*, CRC Press, 2008; J. M. Smith and B. J. Talbot, *Terrorism and Deterrence by Denial*. With permission.)

following discussion of implementation gets at the broad, combined, and synergistic effects on the target audiences of terrorism and of the response; the international and domestic audiences or targets of influence and targets of terror. It is ultimately here that success or failure for the United States or for the terrorist occurs.

International Implementation: The "Away Game"

The implementation of the components of a comprehensive, synergistic strategy has to be centered on the international community because the most significant threats to the United States stem from transnational terrorism. This represents the "away game" within the overall effort, focusing on affecting the terrorists before they manifest their threats in the US homeland and specifically on the "targets of influence" that provide essential support, sanctuary, and sustenance to the terrorists and terrorism. This effort, besides the operational preemption and interdiction actions mentioned above, centers on creating operational and strategic effects to deny terrorist capabilities and attainment of the objectives of terror. The success of the strategy to combat terrorism depends significantly on the image and influence of the United States in the regional and cultural world from which this threat stems.

International implementation efforts must first identify the target population that provides the terrorists with recruits as well as a support base. Second, with the target population in mind, the United States must develop an influence strategy that marginalizes the terrorist message, which means it must initially define the core message at the strategic level and then outline appropriate counters against it. This simply boils down to getting out the real truth. Finally, the United States must also offset the operational-level propaganda efforts of the terrorists that attempt to mask the rationale for US military operations in their region of concern while at the same time distorting the truth behind their own involvement in terror attacks, which attempt to draw implausible parallels to "just causes." Terrorists might even devise conspiracy theories designed to inspire doubt as to who are the real instigators of acts of terror. At the operational level, the United States can also use the media to analyze the results of terrorist attacks and point out to the targets of influence that often those attacks leave many innocents as victims—including members of the target of influence populations, which, if properly publicized, could turn significant numbers of supporters against the attacks.

Identifying and Influencing the Target Population

The growth of Islamic terrorist groups like al-Qaeda in terms of both recruitment and popularity depends on developing supporters. They are reliant on these supporters for political and economic support as well as safe havens in states where they are persecuted by the governments, such as Saudi Arabia and Egypt. An influence campaign against Islamic-inspired terrorism should focus on the most likely supporters of the global jihad inspired by al-Qaeda's actions against the United States. The strategic and operational elements of the influence campaign are explored below.

Denial Strategy: Marginalizing the Terrorist Message

A corresponding effort must focus on development of a proper influence strategy to marginalize the terrorist message, which means we must first define the message. In the case of al-Qaeda, its longer-term, overall goal apparently is to bring about a "new world order." Its terror campaign is aimed at the United States and Israel because they make up what it labels the "far-away enemy." This far-away enemy is distinct from the "near enemy"—the corrupt Arab and other Muslim state governments that prevent the implementation of Sharia (God's law) and whose existence prevents the unification of the umma (the Muslim community) under a single caliphate (understood to be a divinely inspired government). It is Western governments, particularly the United States, that protect corrupt Muslim governments from overthrow by their own populations.

Al-Qaeda also believes that the United States is interested in dominating and subjugating the region (aided by Israel) because of its oil resources and due to a religious divide—God-fearing Muslims versus Godless, materialistic Westerners. The United States is blamed for initiating what Samuel Huntington refers to as a "clash of civilizations." Thus, based upon fatwas (religious rulings) and other pronouncements issued in the past by al-Qaeda leaders, such as Osama bin Laden and Ayman al-Zawahiri,[8] the far-away enemy must be driven from Muslim lands to save Islam from destruction; the jihadists are to effect the downfall of corrupt governments, ushering in a return of the caliphate.

Countering this al-Qaeda appeal is complicated by the early error by President Bush, alluding to a "crusade" against terrorism that, consistent with Huntington's clash-of-civilizations thesis, was interpreted in the Muslim world as the latest chapter of anti-Muslim efforts—a direct, historical reminder of the European Christian campaign to recapture the Holy Land during the 11th and 12th centuries. This slip of the tongue—repeated frequently in Middle East media—set the context in many minds for an adverse interpretation of US actions in the region. It was relatively easy for bin Laden and others to liken US interventions in Afghanistan and Iraq to modern crusades aimed at destroying Islam in those regions.

An influence campaign at the strategic level should refute al-Qaeda's and other terrorists' messages directly, attempting, at the same time, to make the Arab and Muslim worlds well aware of US public and private assistance to Muslims worldwide. This counter-message should also highlight respect for religious practices of Muslims and others within the United States and underscore the freedoms and economic successes enjoyed by American Muslims. The generosity of both public and private American donors to charitable causes should be made known as a counter to the image of America as if it were a corrupt and Godless nation bent only on material gain.

[8] See Chapter 3, "Striking at the Faraway Enemy," for further discussion, in G. Kepel, *The War for Muslim Minds*. Cambridge: Harvard University Press, 2004, 70–107. Additional references on bin Laden and al-Qaeda include M. Scheuer, *Imperial Hubris*. Washington, D.C.: Potomac Books, 2004, see Chapter 5; and Y. Bodansky, *Bin Laden: The Man Who Declared War on America*. Roseville, CA: Prima Publishing, 2001.

Denial of Capability: Public Diplomacy and Disrupting Recruitment and Retention

Terrorists fighting the global jihad have distorted the rationale for US involvement in the Middle East. Jihadists paint an image of the United States bent on making war against Islam in order to control Muslim oil. But this can be countered by comparing US involvement in the first Gulf War—to liberate Kuwait from Iraqi occupation and to defend another Muslim country, Saudi Arabia. In fact, the United States neither took control of Kuwaiti oil, nor did the US forces residing in Saudi Arabia stay in place but, rather, subsequently withdrew from Saudi soil. The message needs to underscore that the US military is not in the Middle East to stay or to occupy the territory.

A related operational-level concern is al-Qaeda's attempts to justify each individual attack with its overall rationale for global jihad. Osama bin Laden went to great lengths to legitimize the September 11 suicide hijackings as a logical extension of the Palestinian suicide bombings against Israel, which began in earnest after the failure of the Camp David peace talks during the summer of 2000. By 2001, images of Israeli repression and Palestinian funerals filled Middle Eastern airwaves, which, in bin Laden's view, provided sufficient legitimacy to the Arab street for his massive suicide attack plan.

Still, a famous al-Jazeera television cleric condemned the hijackings by stating that "the anti-Israeli suicide attacks of the Palestinians could be justified as martyrdom … since they were part of a defensive jihad aimed at reclaiming Palestinian Islamic land that had been usurped by the Jews … [But, the] September 11 hijackers [were] suicides rather than martyrs, because, contrary to Muslim teachings, they had unduly taken the lives Allah had given them … the difference … was that America is not a legitimate target of defensive jihad."[9] Such condemnations against al-Qaeda's operational justification for September 11 and other attacks needs to be presented repeatedly to audiences to underscore how such terrorist actions are contrary to Islamic teachings, thus countering claims by al-Qaeda to the contrary.[10] If a potential martyr doubts that his actions will lead him to paradise, then he is less likely to carry out his attack. But more importantly, doubts among potential terrorist supporters hurt recruitment and retention necessary to sustain operations.

Still, CIA expert Michael Scheuer asserts that "US public diplomacy cannot negate the impressions formed by real-time video from Palestine, Iraq, and Afghanistan that shows Muslims battling aggressive Western forces, thus validating in their minds bin Laden's claim that the West intends to destroy Islam."[11] Scheuer believes that ultimately it is the radical Islamists who have the upper hand when it comes to control of the Arab media. Be that as it may, the Arab media are not really so monolithic. Western efforts to influence Middle East publics are an uphill contest but an important one nonetheless.

Another factor often contributing to resistance against condemning known terrorists is the widespread belief in conspiracy theories. Rumors after the September 11 attacks, for example, initially blamed the Israeli Mossad (Secret Service) or in some instances even the CIA, for the attacks in New York and Washington, and some even went so far as to claim that email was sent to all Jews working at the World Trade Center informing them to stay home on that tragic date. So why do people cling to conspiracy theories? Johnson reports that "while the idea of a Muslim hero standing up to the United States has appeal, many Muslims remain deeply disturbed by

[9] G. Kepel, *War for Muslim Minds: Islam and the West.* Cambridge, MA: Belknap Press, 2006, 102–103.

[10] Too detailed to present in depth here, Patai describes the need among Arabic speakers to repeat and exaggerate threats in order to make them understood while, at the same time, repeating the threat also removes the psychological pressure to carry it out, which may also explain why some terrorist threats never come to fruition. See R. Patai, *The Arab Mind.* New York: Charles Scribner's Sons, 1983, 49–65.

[11] Scheuer is the noted CIA expert on Osama bin Laden. See M. Scheuer, Al-Qaeda's Next Generation: Less Visible and More Lethal, *Terrorism Focus* 2, no. 18: 3, October 2005.

terrorist tactics."[12] They do not want to believe such acts could be carried out in the name of Islam, defiling the very religion the attacks were supposed to defend. Publicizing admissions of responsibility for terrorist actions as well as counterarguments to the conspiracy theories that abound in this region of the world are essential if the West is to have any opportunity at all to counter the claims of terrorist groups.

Domestic Implementation: The "Home Game"

The international or "away game" is critical to the success of the comprehensive effort to deter and defeat terrorism; however, the domestic components of the strategy or the "home game" are also critical to achieving the overall synergy that defines success. Terrorism must be attacked before, during, and after it is carried out. The domestic effort is aimed directly at preparing and mitigating impacts on the "target of terror," generating tactical and strategic effects to deny terrorists the opportunity to achieve their objectives. The domestic effort certainly revolves around the actions taken to harden victims against attack, to limit terrorist access to those victims, and to limit access to weapons of choice to carry out attacks. These actions contribute to effective prevention of terrorist attacks. The "home game" equally involves efforts to mitigate the effects of attacks that do take place. And the mitigation, response, and recovery actions during and after a terrorist attack that is not prevented all contribute to longer-term strategic deterrent effects against terrorism.

Educating and Preparing Domestic Publics

Uncertainty and a lack of understanding breed fear and magnify the already negative emotions generated by casualties and destruction of properties—both fueling and deepening the terror that flows from calculated acts of violence. On the other hand, education based on accurate information effectively delivered contributes to mental preparation and "hardening," thus reducing, to some degree, adverse effects on the mass population. Education of this kind is needed well prior to any terrorist attack if such knowledge and understanding are to serve as a solid foundation for effective crisis communication and management.

Former Speaker of the House Thomas "Tip" O'Neill's dictum on American politics (that "all politics are local") also applies to the most fundamental level of domestic terrorism; all terrorism is local. The effects, the search for useful information by the public in the face of crisis, and the fundamental propensity to experience greater or lesser degrees of fear—the depth and extent of "terror" generated by the incident—are all firmly rooted at the local level. In crises, one's perceptions are reality, and local factors most significantly shape those perceptions of the most directly impacted "target" audience. Even those far removed from the immediate scene can be profoundly influenced by the role of the news media. In essence, "journalists are first responders:"[13]

> This country [is not] ready to deal with a catastrophic terrorist attack, and government preparedness may not be the biggest problem. Indeed, one of the most critical parts of … infrastructure—the nation's news media—[does not] appear near the top of anyone's list of concerns. They should be of utmost concern to those responsible for homeland security.[2]

---

[12] J. L. Johnson. Exploiting the Weakness in the Far Enemy Ideology. *Strategic Sights* IV, no. 6: June 2, 2005.

[13] R. Atkins. The News Media Could Be Our Weakest Link. *Washington Post*, January 26, 2003, B3.

The United States and other nations need clear, well-designed educational materials to address the technical and human dimensions of the terrorist threat and need a prepared noninflammatory channel of presentation for those materials in times of crisis. A comprehensive homeland security strategy must capitalize on quality materials and experiences to target localized delivery of education and the information. It must involve establishing cooperative relations with local media outlets. This is not easy, as adversarial relations may exist between government and the media at various levels, but being able to harness the support of the media in extending information during these times of crisis is a critical variable in implementing a successful homeland security strategy. The implementation of a comprehensive strategy to create deterrent effects requires measures at both international and domestic levels of implementation. These measures do require a strategic guiding hand to ensure comprehensive, complementary implementation and synergistic deterrent effects. This coordination of the effort must remain a central area of emphasis at every level.

Concluding Thoughts

In summary, deterrence by denial was applied to the capability (the operational level), opportunity (the tactical level), and objectives sought by groups, movements, or insurgencies that are considering the use of terrorism as a tactic to advance their cause (the strategic level). This approach flows from a causal analysis of what leads to the use of terrorist tactics in the first place. Strategy implementation calls for pursuing both external or international actions—the "away game" as well as various domestic measures—the "home game." Success comes from efforts to marginalize the terrorist message and deter or preclude attainment of terrorist objectives, thus defeating strategically the group, movement, or insurgency threatening the US homeland.

As this analysis showed, first, there is no one "magic bullet" that can be used to defeat terrorism. Terrorism aimed at the United States today is a complex, asymmetrical threat. And this threat demands an equally complex, asymmetrical, adaptive, and cumulative response package. Second, each of the response actions and strategies is individually important. Each element of effective response advances the effort to blunt and defeat terrorism. Finally, even if all of the actions addressed are implemented immediately, terrorist violence likely would still continue—at least in the short term. Over the longer term, however, the net effect can indeed be a deterrent effect, leading the terrorist leadership, core support base, and regional or ideological community to select other, less violent means of addressing their political, economic, and social grievances.

11

Intelligence-Driven Counterterrorism[1]

The role of intelligence in combating terrorism is critical. In the counterterrorism fight, it comes from several directions. First, intelligence comes from a nation's intelligence agencies. Much of what they get they collect directly or obtain through intelligence-sharing agreements with other countries. Diplomacy is very important in intelligence as good relations with an ally, combined with a willingness to share your own information, can yield great results.

Intelligence also comes from law enforcement agencies. They have a great advantage when collecting information on the domestic front as they are less likely to attract as much attention as national-level agencies, and they may not have the same legislated restrictions. Finally, intelligence comes from the field. Counterintelligence forces cultivate their own sources in the areas where these relationships are likely to pay off. Security professionals working in critical infrastructure sectors are of particular interest as it is through attacking these sectors that terrorists could achieve the greatest return on their investment. The information that counterintelligence forces receive is processed. This includes collating the information for date and location, assessing its viability, and conducting analysis to see how it fits into the overall threat picture. Finished intelligence reports are written and sent to parties with an interest in the product. This chapter examines the intelligence process, looking in particular at intelligence-led policing, the intelligence cycle, and international cooperation in information sharing.

Intelligence-Led Policing

The law enforcement and intelligence communities always have had very different ways of looking at the problem posed by terrorism. Law enforcement's traditional approach to any criminal act was to conduct an investigation, establish "probable cause," make an arrest, and get a conviction. This was entirely in keeping with the procedures prescribed by our system of laws. The swift completion of this process was expected to have a deterrent effect on would-be criminals, who would know that any crimes they contemplated in the future would be dealt with similarly.

[1] Information for this chapter was drawn from the following titles: (1) J. F. Pastor, *Terrorism and Public Safety Policing: Implications for the Obama Presidency*, CRC Press, 2009. (2) A. N. Guiora, *Homeland Security: What Is It and Where Are We Going?* CRC Press, 2011. (3) B. Elias, *Airport and Aviation Security: US Policy and Strategy in the Age of Global Terrorism*, CRC Press, 2009. (4) M. W. Nance, *Terrorist Recognition Handbook: A Practitioner's Manual for Predicting and Identifying Terrorist Activities*, Second Edition, CRC Press, 2008. (5) R. McPartland, Terrorist Tradecraft I: The Attack Cycle. In M. J. Fagel (ed.), *Principles of Emergency Management: Hazard Specific Issues and Mitigation Strategies*, 2011. (6) R. Johnson, *Antiterrorism and Threat Response: Planning and Implementation*, CRC Press, 2013. (7) C. P. Nemeth, *Homeland Security: An Introduction to Principles and Practice*, Second Edition, CRC Press, 2012.

Other than that, there were clearly defined limits as to how far law enforcement could go in taking preemptive steps to disrupt a potential crime. The intelligence community, on the other hand, operated under a different set of rules, especially with regard to collecting foreign intelligence. The only "probable cause" it needed was a reasonable expectation of gathering foreign intelligence. The intelligence community, not being involved in the criminal process, was not concerned with such things as rules of evidence and chain of custody because it never expected its findings to be presented in a court of law. This does not mean that law enforcement and the intelligence community did not, or could not, work together on terrorism cases.

A useful starting point is to provide a definition. According to the National Strategy for Homeland Security, intelligence-led policing is[2]

> a management and resource allocation approach to law enforcement using data collection and intelligence analysis to set specific priorities for all manner of crimes, including those associated with terrorism. ILP is a collaborative approach based on improved intelligence operations and community-oriented policing and problem solving, which the field of law enforcement has considered beneficial for many years. Today, it is being adopted by a variety of law enforcement entities.

A driving force behind intelligence-based policing has been Homeland Security Presidential Directive No. 6. Its stated goal is to integrate and use information to protect against terrorism. Specifically, the goals are to do the following:

1. Develop, integrate, and maintain accurate information about individuals known or suspected of preparing for or in aid of any terrorist acts on US soil. Use that information for prosecution to the fullest extent of the law.
2. Support federal, state, county, tribal, and local visa screening processes.
3. Similarly, in Homeland Security Presidential Directive No. 11, the goal is to develop comprehensive terrorist-related screening procedures. Specifically, these goals are to detect, identify, track, and interdict foreign or domestic citizens that pose a threat to homeland security.
4. Safeguard legal rights, including freedoms, civil liberties, and information privacy guaranteed by federal law.

One way to bring this element of public safety policing into a structural assessment is to consider the acquisition of information. Inherent in policing and, for that matter, almost any industry is the need to obtain, process, analyze, and disseminate information. In the old days, this was rather straightforward. A crime was committed; it was observed by a citizen who yelled for help. The police came and arrested the offender based on the statement of a witness. This "information flow" was sometimes enhanced by observations of the officer or by statements made by the offender. Over time, various technological enhancements made the acquisition of information more readily obtainable. Police moved in vehicles enabling them to observe much more "data" from the street as they drove from location to location, from beat to beat, from beat to sector, and from sector to the larger community. Telegraphs, "call boxes," and then radios within the vehicle, and later handheld radios, greatly increased the acquisition of additional information. Telephones used to report crimes facilitated this information flow. Other technologies, like burglar and holdup alarms, helped transmit information from the protected facility to monitoring centers, to police dispatch centers, then to responding police vehicles. The dynamics of interfacing and collating information from public camera systems, crime mapping, predictive software, access control systems, and similar technologies are critical to the provision of public safety

[2] National Strategy for Homeland Security. Homeland Security Council, Office of the President of the United States, October 2007.

services. They are also key sources of information that can be used within the intelligence process. These and many other technologies have fostered rapid flows of information designed to prevent crime or capture the criminal.

Currently, societies are awash in data. The amount of data and information transmitted within society is overwhelming. It is data overload. Police are processing substantial amounts of information from seemingly ever-increasing sources. Indeed, one of the "innovations" was to cultivate the flow and quality of human information by emphasizing relationships within the community. In this way, foot patrols enabled police to observe details of crime indicators that may go unnoticed by rapid vehicle patrols.[3]

Walking also helped facilitate conversations with citizens and business owners designed to foster relationships so data and information flows would be enhanced. Beat meetings were also said to open up the dialog to a larger audience, enabling community concerns to be aired. In these meetings, the information flow was to go both ways: from the community to the police and from the police to the community. Other more strategic information flows were fostered with community and political leaders at regularly scheduled meetings.

Internally, police agencies developed information reports and special attention notices that are read at roll calls. More generalized—and sometimes more important—information is transmitted via bulletins, teletypes, and other electronic means. Accountability sessions are held to assess the effectiveness of tactical and strategic remedies designed to impact crime patterns and trends. These patterns and trends are facilitated by increasingly sophisticated data-analysis methods, by crime-mapping software, by "real-time" information transmitted by such technologies as cameras and alarms, and by an overall increase of technologies designed to transmit and discern information.

These technological enhancements, like those in the larger society, have resulted in "information overload." Seemingly ever-increasing sources of information, more sophisticated layers of data, and the rapid transmission of both have created operational dilemmas within police agencies. Added to this dilemma is the fact that failing to "connect the dots" from any information source can result in a tragedy like 9/11. Indeed, reading the 9/11 Commission Report, one is struck by the failure to make sense of numerous pieces of information. These range from pilot training patterns, immigration and identification data, intelligence reports, and the like that were missed or fell through the cracks. Consequently, police agencies are in the process of reorienting themselves around better use of the vast amount of data and information that are available. This desire is at the heart of ILP. In this way, the problem for American policing is not so much getting the intelligence but making sense of it and sharing it with those who can use it.

As stated earlier, prior to 9/11, significant amounts of information in the possession of law enforcement was noncriminal in nature (i.e., pilot training that did not emphasize landing skills). By itself, such information did not provide the basis of reasonable suspicion of a terrorist or criminal conspiracy. Traditionally, police have been trained to focus on criminal behavior. The threat of terrorism, however, requires police to focus their attention on data or observations that do not necessarily indicate criminal intention or conduct.

Attributes of Intelligence-Led Policing

One basic distinction between ILP and traditional police investigations is the concept of information and intelligence. Information is unprocessed (raw) data. It is gathered or collected in its original form by the agent or officer. Information can be gleaned from a number of sources, including informants, documents, surveillance, wiretaps, observations, cameras, alarms, and

[3] R. C. Wadman and W. T. Allison. *To Protect and To Serve: A History of Police in America*. Upper Saddle River, NJ: Pearson/Prentice Hall, 2004.

the like. The need to process and interface these information sources is critical. Processing this information, however, does not transform it into intelligence.

Intelligence is much more defined and refined. It is the output of analysis, generated by applying the intelligence process by a trained analyst. More pointedly, intelligence is the analysis of information that is assessed for validity and reliability through inductive and deductive logic. In short, this equation is illustrative: information/data + analysis = intelligence. These terms can be further broken down into the following distinctions. Data can mean raw print, images, or signals. It can be classified, such as technical intelligence signal intercepts, or unclassified, such as fliers distributed during a demonstration or posts on Internet message boards. Information is data that have been collated and processed in order to produce a document that is of generic interest, such as a police report. Intelligence is those products that allow a specific group or organization to make an informed decision, such as an intelligence briefing.[4]

Types of Information Obtained from Intelligence-Led Policing

There are several types of intelligence, three of which will be explored further: namely, tactical, strategic, and evidentiary. Tactical intelligence is information developed by law enforcement through case research and analysis of direct sources, such as surveillance, countersurveillance, covert operations, informants, and eavesdropping. This type of intelligence is operational and ongoing. This information is designed to generate targets and investigations by collating and assessing information. It seeks to identify key problem areas, suspects, and/or groups. It may also be developed through analysis of indicative intelligence.

Strategic intelligence is the culmination of both indicative intelligence and tactical intelligence, providing a broader perspective. It is a more thorough examination of data and events. It is used to evaluate and analyze critical issues, factors, and organizations, such as street gangs or terrorist groups. It involves a predictive component by identifying evolving or emerging trends and patterns. Because of its strategic value, this type of intelligence is often used for policy-making decisions, operational planning, and crime prevention strategies. It can also be used as a management evaluation tool or as an "internal consultant."

Finally, evidentiary intelligence is designed to foster criminal prosecutions. In this way, it is similar to traditional criminal investigations. Because the information may be used in court, procedural and constitutional collection requirements will take on a heightened sense of legitimacy. Of course, any information obtained in violation of the law will not be admitted into the trial. In addition, the sources and methods of the intelligence-gathering process may be scrutinized by the court system. Consequently, as with any other investigation, it is necessary to avoid any and all "shortcuts" throughout the intelligence process. One never knows what case will result in prosecution. The best practice, of course, is to perform each intelligence case file as if it may appear in court.

The Intelligence Cycle

The intelligence cycle has four separate but interrelated elements. Before examining them, it is important to consider that all steps of this cycle should be focused on the needs of the end user. The end users can be police administrators, criminal investigators, patrol officers, political leaders, and even the general public. The end users need to embrace the process so that they will participate. Similarly, the end users need to understand both the great potential and the limitations of intelligence operations. The elements of the intelligence cycle are planning and direction; collection, analysis, and dissemination. Each one is examined below.

---

[4] Law Enforcement Prevention and Deterrence of Terrorist Acts, Version 1.0. Department of Homeland Security, 2/9.

Phase 1: Planning and Direction

During this phase, the incident reporting processes are developed by establishing policies and procedures. The planning and direction element is the foundation that the entire process is built upon. The functions of this part of the process are to develop and prioritize goals and objectives. As mentioned earlier, goals and objectives must take into account the needs and desires of the end users. It is to provide and then manage resources to meet these goals.

Phase 2: Collection

In this phase, information is developed and submitted through predetermined channels, in which the intelligence personnel receive and process the information. Information can come from a wide variety of sources and therefore can come in through many different conduits. As mentioned earlier, the information can come from a variety of open sources, or it can derive from covert methods. Regardless of the source, the collection of information must be done in a systematic and consistent fashion.

Because the intelligence process starts with information; where information comes from is of some consideration. Information is typically subdivided into two categories: open source and covert. According to Central Intelligence Directive 2/12, the definition of "open source" is "publicly available information (i.e., any member of the public could lawfully obtain the information by request or observation) as well as other unclassified information that has limited public distribution or access." As much as 95% of all information is open source. Examples of open source information include the following:[5]

- Business directories
- Media reports (newspapers, magazines, television, other publications, radio)
- Internet searches, chat rooms, databases, and Internet websites
- Telephone directories and people finders
- Commercial information providers
- Credit bureaus
- City, county, and state agencies (public records)
- Court records (unless sealed)
- Professional exchanges (conferences, professional chat, roundtables)

Conversely, covert or "private" information sources include the following:

- Law enforcement records and reports
- Schools records and reports
- Public utilities records and reports
- Employment records and data
- Banking and financial institution records and data
- Military records and reports
- Arrest and warrant evidence, information, statements
- Interviews, public contacts, traffic stops, etc.
- Police operations

---

[5] Law Enforcement Prevention and Deterrence of Terrorist Acts, 2/10.

- Undercover operatives (confidential source or informant)
- Physical surveillance (either remotely via videotape or in person)
- Electronic surveillance

Terrorist intelligence collection is the gathering of any usable information related to a particular group or event by any method. Data can be collected through regular intelligence sources and methods. Many of these methods may be classified as well due to the critical need to protect the source and the special techniques necessary to gain that information.

Types of Intelligence Gathering

The intelligence community deals with a broad array of information regarding potential terrorist threats in various forms that can typically be categorized into one of three primary source categories: signal intelligence (SIGINT), imagery intelligence (IMINT), and human intelligence (HUMINT). Other forms of intelligence information may be categorized as measurement and signature intelligence (MASINT) or open source intelligence (OSINT). While OSINT plays an important role in the context of counterterrorism and homeland security intelligence, MASINT plays a more limited role in information gathering regarding terrorist operatives and nonstate groups. Collectively, these various delineations of intelligence based upon its source characteristics define the various intelligence-gathering disciplines.

In the context of counterterrorism intelligence gathering, SIGINT refers primarily to the interception of communications signals, such as telephone conversations, emails, text messages, and so forth, transmitted over communications channels, including telecommunications networks. Because this intelligence gathering primarily deals with communications, it may sometimes be referred to as COMINT for communications intelligence, a subset of the broader SIGINT category that also includes various forms of electronic intelligence (ELINT).

In addition to SIGINT, the intelligence community gathers IMGINT from various aerial platforms, including manned and unmanned reconnaissance aircraft and satellites. In reference to intelligence collected on terrorist groups, IMGINT may consist of aerial or satellite tracking of activity at suspected terrorist training sites or operations bases in places like Afghanistan. Although IMGINT, and more especially SIGINT, can provide valuable information regarding terrorist operatives, their movements, and possible terrorist plots, most intelligence experts believe that a richer source of information can be gained through interpersonal interaction or HUMINT gathering.

HUMINT can be gathered from various sources, such as foreign government and business contacts, using a variety of techniques although, in the context of dealing with nonstate groups, such as terrorist organizations, meaningful HUMINT may only be achievable by using clandestine group membership, group structure, group leadership, and group plans and aspirations to carry out acts of terrorism, including possible plots to carry out attacks against aviation targets. In addition to clandestine intelligence operations, information can be retrieved from the Internet as well. It is known that terrorist groups have used the Internet extensively to disseminate propaganda, recruit new members, exchange information regarding ideologies, conduct fundraising, and to make threats and issue warnings.[6] Such information may provide important clues regarding ongoing plots or terrorist attacks in the planning stages. Additionally, terrorist groups may use online chat rooms or other social networking resources to discuss ideologies with potential recruits, concoct and coordinate terrorist plots, and exchange information on how to plan and carry out attacks.

Therefore, besides providing OSINT, the Internet may provide important SIGINT traces that can potentially be followed to try to identify terrorist networks. For example, by looking on the Internet for deadly chemical or biological agents as well as chat room and social networking

[6] B. Elias. *Airport and Aviation Security: US Policy and Strategy in the Age of Global Terrorism*. Boca Raton, FL: CRC Press, p. 160, 2009.

exchanges about such topics, intelligence analysts may be able to trace terrorist networks and identify suspect individuals. However, because computer-savvy terrorists may be able to effectively cloak their locations and identities while using the Internet, sophisticated electronic tracing and forensic techniques may be needed to uncover the identities and locations of suspected terrorists who communicate and disseminate information over the Internet.

Phase 3: Analysis

This phrase results in development of intelligence assessments through the application of scientific testing. Here, the information is organized, evaluated, and stored. These functions are accomplished so that the information can be brought to the refinement stage when needed. The goals of this phase are threefold:

- Evaluate the information to determine its reliability, validity, and value.
- Sort and organize the information into categories and into a logical order.
- File the information so that it can be retrieved at a later time.

Proper filing of information is critical because the system must have adequate security to prevent unauthorized access. It also must be open enough to allow the flow of information to the end users. Certain requirements relating to the filing and safeguarding of information must be maintained. These include administrative, technical, and physical safeguards (including audit trails). These safeguards must be adopted to insure against unauthorized access and against intentional or unintentional disclosure. Further, the information shall be labeled to indicate levels of sensitivity, levels of confidence, and the identity of submitting agencies and control officials.[7]

It is often said that analysis is the heart and soul of the intelligence cycle. It is the refinement of the raw information into a usable product. The goals and objectives of the analysis component are to provide additional meaning to raw information by linking individual pieces of raw information into a cohesive intelligence assessment. In essence, the analysis should answer this key question: What does the collected information mean?

There are various techniques used to facilitate this analysis. These include time event charting, link analysis, crime analysis, criminal profiling, and behavioral evidence analysis. These analytical assessments can be quite sophisticated. As such, an explanation of these techniques is beyond the scope of this chapter.

The Basics of Analyzing Intelligence and Predicting Terrorism Events

Terrorism intelligence analysis is conducted in order to do the following:

1. Identify the existing terrorist threat conditions in a country or jurisdiction.
2. Rapidly identify terrorist attack preincident indicators (TAPI) that show changes in the existing terrorist threat conditions.
3. Accurately predict trends that may be building into an attack.
4. Direct conclusions to the relevant authorities for action.

To do this job well, authorities need to carry out the never-ending process of CACRR, which stands for collect, analyze, conclude, report, and respond (see Figure 11.1). CACRR is defined as follows:

1. Collect indicators and intelligence on terrorists from all sources.
2. Analyze the information and process indicators into a logical sequence.

[7] 28 CFR Part 23.20 (g).

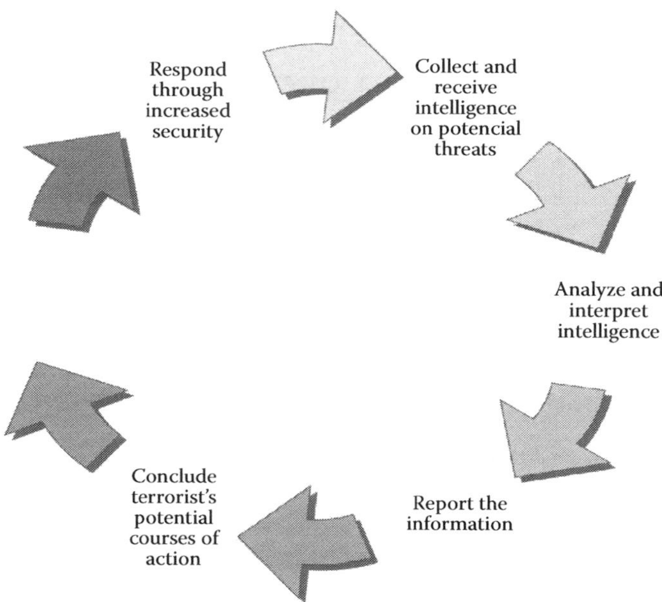

Figure 11.1 The collect, analyze, conclude, report, and respond process. (From M. W. Nance, *Terrorist Recognition Handbook: A Practitioner's Manual for Predicting and Identifying Terrorist Activities*, Second Edition, CRC Press, 2008. With permission.)

3. Conclude the terrorists' potential courses of action.
4. Report rapidly up the chain of command.
5. Respond with overwhelming force or increased security measures.

Within this process, you will make a prediction based on information and evidence about where, what, when, why, and how you believe the terrorist will strike. The terrorists' potential attack options, known as their courses of action (COA), will be forecasted in an estimate. This estimate may provide authorities with the opportunity to provide intentions and warning (I&W) of terrorist attacks in an effort to provide the 3Ds of homeland security: detect, deter, and defend. COAs listed in an I&W estimate will provide the intelligence to detect the attackers in the planning stage, deter them through increased security, and/or defend against an attack. Authorities need to be cautious and pause when indicators point to terrorist activity. They should also be mindful of asking intelligence-focused questions rather than queries from a law enforcement standpoint. Taking stock and asking the right questions will lead to better understanding and results. Estimating versus speculating: How do we know when a terrorist is going to attack? The short answer is, we do not. The long answer is, given that terrorists are human, they are predictable. This predictability—coupled with good intelligence collection and analysis—is the basis of making a trustworthy intentions and warning (I&W) projection of what the terrorists may do. The projection of the terrorists' COAs will be based on known information about terrorist strategies and tactics; the weaknesses of potential targets in an area; and the fusion of intelligence reports, observations, and evidence into logical conclusions.

The intelligence report that carries your preincident indicators, potential courses of action, and conclusions is often called an I&W estimate, which is a summary of evidence and information that often ends with a prediction on the courses of action available to terrorists. Many people believe that making estimates, especially those that have different or competing conclusions, is a waste of resources. This inherent distrust comes from past intelligence failures such as

Pearl Harbor, the Tet Offensive in Vietnam, and the 1993 and 2001 World Trade Center attacks. In fact, each of these examples had many intelligence indicators, and if read correctly, they could have tipped us off to the attacks. Proper estimates are made up of evaluated preincident indicators. One starts to connect the proverbial "dots" of the terrorist intelligence picture by completing an analysis and placing all the evidence in the estimate. Who is responsible for "connecting the dots"? The person who draws up the estimate should spell out the dot picture in the conclusion section of the estimate, but ultimately the reader is also responsible for interpreting the data presented. This means that everyone who reads the document and sees the indicators is responsible for connecting the dots and making the call.

The Basics of Predicting and Preventing Terrorism

While prediction is not a hard science, intelligence analysis is. By utilizing the steps outlined below, the chances of projecting the correct COA and preventing a terrorist act will improve.

Law enforcement officers, public decision makers, and other officials, come into contact with confidential information related to terrorist activities usually presented in one of three forms:

1. Sensitive intelligence from an external agency, such as the FBI, NSA, CIA, or subagencies in the Department of Homeland Security
2. Direct observation from a bystander, surveillance team, or other party
3. Informant intelligence from someone very near or in the group

The information may be "raw" intelligence, or it may be processed into an estimate. In most cases, it will be scrubbed of sensitive sources and methods to give you only the critical kernel of information that you need. For example, information from a sensitive source may be sanitized to simply state, "A terrorist act is planned for x date in x location by x group."

Analysis of Intelligence about Terrorism

Analysis will help in predicting the who, where, when, why, and how of terrorist activities. Analysis is the study of all information contained within a complex problem and its placement into a logical sequence that points to a possible course of action. These COAs give us adequate I&W on the threats. When tips are received, observations are made, or other information is gained; this enhances knowledge of terrorists. Someone almost always sees or hears the indicators of an attack but may not realize that this evidence is an intelligence indicator.

Terrorist Attack Preincident Intelligence Indicators (TAPIs)

Every terrorist incident has preincident indicators. TAPIs are the individual bits or data fragments of intelligence information that produce patterns and allow the investigator to understand the potential courses of action. Law enforcement refers to these as evidence, tips, and hints. Preincident indicators can collectively or in part lead to the detection of terrorist activities. Three such indicators are explored below: group-related, target-related, and incident-related indicators. Additionally, the quality of indicators are also examined.

Classes of Indicators

Group-Related Indicators

Group-related indicators are techniques, methods, equipment, or operations that give clues as to the group preparing to carry out operations. Groups may have areas of operations they specifically operate in, targets they specifically wish to strike, and weapons that they favor. Many groups declare terrorist "campaigns" or may strike on significant dates. The International Association of Counterterrorism & Security Professionals (IACSP) prints an annual calendar of dates significant to terrorist groups, which may help identify group indicators.

Structural expansion is a group indicator that requires excellent intelligence of the terrorist group's baseline operations. It requires knowledge of the usual complement and makeup of a cell or day-to-day patterns of the group at each level. Accelerated recruitment or expansion of the number of members in a cell may indicate impending operations. For example, if a suspected cell in an area is reported to contain three or four low-level logistics members, and your investigation discovers that several new members arrive with explosives and weapons training, it constitutes a localized structural expansion that may indicate preparations for an impending attack.

Target-Related Indicators

Target-related indicators are fragmentary or whole data that lead investigators to believe a specific target is under consideration for attack. Threats, manifestos, or declarations by terrorist groups are good target-related indicators because they often specifically spell out who is at risk. However, noting that a building is under repeated surveillance by a consistent person or group indicates it is a potential target. For people who may be targets, actions by a potential victim, such as routine travel or regularly scheduled visits, may increase chances of attack. The Secret Service aggressively attempts to predict "target indicated" threats because the President and senior staff must so often travel to conduct business in public and on schedule.

Incident-Related Indicators

Incident-related indicators may be events or reported incidents that may not appear directly related to terrorist activity but may be a single link in the chain for a major incident. The 9/11 skyjackers' complete disregard for learning to land an aircraft—even abandoning an aircraft on a runway at a major airport—was a clear indicator of suspicious activity. Dry runs and rehearsals either on the actual target or in a specific training base are also good incident-related indicators.

Quality of Indicators

Ambiguous Indicators

Ambiguous indicators are tips or observations that do not clearly spell out a definable threat. These could be any of the detectable activities of terrorists that are not immediately identified. Most indicators are ambiguous. For instance, a terrorist suspect is observed with a book on chemistry (may indicate planning).

Unambiguous Indicators

Unambiguous indicators are tips or observations that show clear activities of terrorism. For example, a terrorist suspect is caught at a safe house exhibiting physical symptoms of both smallpox and inhalation anthrax.

Tip-offs

Tip-offs are solid unambiguous intelligence indicators that give clear, uncontestable warning or clues to an imminent event. The airline tickets, completed bombs, and detailed plans found in a Philippines safe house were the tip-offs to Project Bojinka, the 1994 al-Qaeda plan to blow up 12 airliners simultaneously over the Pacific Ocean.

Chatter

Chatter is an intelligence community word that refers to many intelligence sources providing indicators in an increasing crescendo of indirect indications that some event is imminent. Its origin is from Cold War signals intelligence, wherein enemy communications would increase as an event grew closer. In terrorism, this is not literal. The chatter may be increasing reports, observations, and tips.

While indicators are the basis of estimates, they are of no value unless filtered through three testing agents: pertinence, source reliability, and credibility or validity of the source.

Pertinence (of Indicator)

All information must be evaluated for pertinence or relevance. Indicators are like jigsaw puzzles: Data fragments may or may not appear related until the puzzle's picture firms up. Authorities should ask themselves: Does the information received relate to the estimate you are making or perhaps another estimate? Information comes from many sources, and seemingly unrelated data may be pertinent. Seemingly obscure indicators should be kept in a database to be brought back up when you need them. For example, information that a suspected terrorist had selected a window seat on the left side of the plane during each flight from Hartford to New York might seem obscure or irrelevant unless the analyst considers that the individual might be attempting to become familiar with the landmarks, flight path, and approach to a specific target in New York.

Source Reliability

Each source of information must be evaluated for reliability. Additionally, the reporting agency should also be evaluated, using the same standard. The agency and source are always evaluated separately. Is this information and the person reporting reliable? Does it hold up to scrutiny? The phrase "consider the source" is always valid when reliability and credibility are being considered. Government-generated terrorism reports usually give both a source of the information and an evaluation rating. An A-rated source is rare unless the source has deep and broad experience with the information to the point where it is unquestionable (for example, a foreign diplomat who has been 100% reliable in the past). B-validated information is more common. For example, an undercover officer is a source for the Drug Enforcement Administration estimate you read. He reports an indicator of a possible chemical weapons factory at a house that was thought to be a crystal methamphetamine lab. The source has great experience in drug lab processing and is usually correct. Based on this information, the source may be rated as source reliability B. The source agency—in this case, the DEA—is also evaluated as B.

Credibility or Validity of the Source

Credibility refers to the probable truth of the source information. This information must be evaluated by asking the following questions:

- Is it possible for the reported event to have taken place?
- Is the source information consistent with itself?
- Is the report confirmed or corroborated by different sources or agencies?
- Does the report agree or disagree with other information?
- If the report does not agree with other information, which is most likely to be true?

The Analytical Process

There are two main stages of intelligence analysis: evaluation and integration.

Analytical Process: Evaluation

Once information has been checked for reliability, accuracy, and pertinence, it must be turned into usable intelligence. This is done through a myriad of analytical processes, tools, and techniques. The heavy intelligence analysis techniques used by US intelligence and law enforcement intelligence divisions, including matrix manipulation, visual investigative analysis charting, link analysis, time charting, and the program evaluation review technique (PERT), are too advanced for a chapter of this scope.

Many computerized intelligence analysis programs exist for these techniques and can enhance any analysis done mentally, especially when visualization is necessary. For the average reader, this chapter offers the following simplified techniques that can be used on a daily basis and in every aspect of the job. Some of the techniques include the following:

Inductive Analysis (aka Plausible Reasoning)

The US Defense Intelligence Agency defines inductive analysis as "the process of formulating hypotheses on the basis of observation or other evidence." Inductive reasoning is learning from observing patterns and drawing a conclusion about the activity. A tragic example is the passengers of the fourth hijacked flight on September 11, who quickly induced that their plane would also be used as a suicide weapon after receiving cell phone calls informing them of the fate of three other hijacked aircraft.

Deductive Analysis (aka Demonstrative Reasoning)

Deductive analysis is the process of reasoning in which a conclusion is reached from a theory. This method starts with a premise and comes to a logical confirmation of the theory through gathered evidence or observation.

Pattern and Frequency Analysis

Pattern and frequency analysis is the study of certain characteristic patterns that can be identified and predicted. If a tactic is being used again and again as a group gains experience, a pattern is established, and the group may move on to a different tactic. Repeated observations of known terrorists entering the country, living with or meeting each other, conducting surveillance on the same target, or repeatedly purchasing legally obtained items that can be used to create terrorist weapons can all be pattern indicators.

Analytical Process: Integration

Raw data fragments, collected and summarized intelligence facts, photo imagery, and open-source information are not intelligence until they are evaluated and integrated with other sources of information into a usable summary. It is also known as multisource integration, intelligence fusion, or intelligence synthesis. Integration is a process that brings all facts and indicators together to produce a hypothesis. Information from imagery, visual surveillance, and wiretaps of the suspects would be integrated into a report along with other data to create a complete picture of the intentions of the terrorists. Integrated intelligence product should reveal to the analyst if the likelihood of an attack from terrorist action is increasing or decreasing. However, integrated intelligence is only considered a "final product" when it has been evaluated against known or projected intelligence of the capabilities of the group of interest and all of the courses of action have been spelled out. A simple method of integrating all of the key factors necessary in predicting potential threat courses of action is called the Four-Ts technique. The Four Ts are terrorists, targets, time, and tactics. This field analysis technique relies on placing what is known about the four categories into a logical sequence and then drawing a conclusion about the terrorists' COAs from the data at hand. It takes an enormous amount of the guesswork out of the analytical process by allowing you to see the key data in the critical categories.

Phase 4: Dissemination

In this phase, reports are tendered or disseminated according to protocols and guidance. As critical as the merits of the analysis are, it stands to reason that intelligence that is not shared has little value. Said another way, intelligence is worthless if it is not disseminated in a timely manner to those who need it or can use it. Hence, the dissemination component is the distribution of the final product. The end product should consider the following factors:

- Identify the target audience
- Convey information clearly and in a manner understandable to the target audience
- Provide a time parameter in which the information provided is actionable
- Provide a recommendation for action
- Allow for feedback

International Cooperation, Intelligence Gathering, and Threat Assessment

International cooperation must be understood in the context of both limits and necessity; the former because homeland security measures are inherently limited, and the latter because international cooperation is essential to facilitate domestic security. Though there is a certain risk to a comparative approach—benefits unequivocally outweigh the costs. Learning from positive and negative examples implemented by countries facing similar and dissimilar threats alike enhances articulation, development, and implementation of measures intended to protect the public. To that end, international cooperation forges professional relationships and partnerships among similar government agencies and parallel national institutions; while each nation-state bears ultimate responsibility for protecting both its civilian population and national assets, developing cooperative measures between nation-states facing similar threats is mutually beneficial.

Maintaining US homeland security inherently involves international cooperation in threat assessment. The United States cannot respond to all threats against the homeland without the appropriate intelligence. What follows is an examination of the US effort to promote intelligence sharing in the context of institutional limits that are—in many ways—the true "bugaboo" of intelligence sharing.

Intelligence is highly time-sensitive; timely and relevant information directly contributes to effective operational counterterrorism. Timeliness, then, is an essential aspect of intelligence; not only is the information itself important, but when it is received is essential to determining its relevance and operability. Therefore, one of the most important concerns in the post-9/11 world has been developing mechanisms to facilitate timely analysis of enormous amounts of information to produce relevant intelligence that can be easily shared and understood by others.

The National Counterterrorism Center (NCTC) represents the main US effort to unite the many intelligence agencies and sources in a way that coordinates and enables the efforts of all the intelligence agencies. Created in 2004, the NCTC consists of a team of intelligence experts from US intelligence agencies and departments. With access to 30 different networks used by the various agencies, NCTC oversees the administration of NCTC online or NOL. This database allows users the ability to access counterterrorism information and intelligence. Additionally, the NCTC provides "alerts, advisories, warnings, and assessments on topics of interest that are widely disseminated to domestic and overseas operators and analysts."

Nevertheless, the involvement of other nations—essential to successful intelligence gathering and analysis—is largely contingent upon their efforts and willingness to utilize available resources and integrate them effectively into their own investigative and intelligence efforts. However, several factors necessarily limit the amount and type of information and intelligence the United States can and should share with other nations. First, security concerns require that sensitive information and intelligence be carefully guarded and made available only to those with a demonstrated need to know. Clearly, maximizing the availability of intelligence to international partners presents several promising benefits; other nations could integrate US intelligence products with their own in efforts to identify, disrupt, and prevent terrorist attacks and activities. Additionally, finding ways for the United States to share intelligence with other nations will naturally create opportunities to receive and integrate intelligence products from other nations. That said, it will be necessary to integrate foreign intelligence experts into a national-level intelligence effort in order to capitalize on the resources, knowledge, and understanding of the other nations. While this again raises legitimate security considerations (source protection) regarding introducing foreign actors into intelligence coordination and decision-making, any meaningful efforts at international intelligence sharing must go beyond mere sharing of sterilized information.

The first step to effective international cooperation in homeland security is to forge lasting international partnerships with different countries and multistate organizations, such as the EU. The United States must strive to continue positive trade relations with different countries as trade is vital to security. In order to promote true, effective partnerships, the United States must maintain open communication with liaisons between partner countries and organizations. Partner countries and organizations should speak through liaisons from counterpart agencies, departments, and organizations (such as the Red Cross) from each country or multistate organization, to ensure active communication about security and threat assessment and to promote effective use of international cooperation in counterterrorism.

Partner countries must work together to develop a coordinated international security plan. That plan must outline steps for coordinated travel security, border security, and for determining and acting on known and unknown threats. For example, partner countries and multistate organizations must work together to enforce security measures, such as watch lists and cargo restrictions. Partner countries must communicate possible threats to travel security and must create a set plan of action for disaster, terrorist attack, and terror threat scenarios. The plan should outline each multistate organization/country's role within the greater security plan. The plan should articulate the coordination of country-specific agencies, departments, and organizations and outline how each entity must act in the face of a terror threat.

A coordinated plan is vital to effective international cooperation in homeland security. For example, the United States could learn from the EU's cooperative efforts to strengthen its member states' borders. The United States could benefit tremendously from aiding and cooperating with both Canada and Mexico in managing their external borders. Increasing the security of our neighbors' borders could help reduce the number of third-country nationals attempting to enter the United States through our northern and southern borders. This is particularly important, as terrorists are likely to attempt to cross those borders in order to avoid the rigors of entering the United States directly from another continent.

Finally, the United States and its international partners must ensure institutionalized continuity both between nation leaders and between each nation's key agencies and department liaisons. Institutionalized continuity on an international level refers to the idea that there must be a set process for which to continue, to pass on, the articulated security plan from one nation leader to the next. Each leader, liaison, and representative must ensure that he or she understands the coordinated security plan and must continue to improve upon the technology, intelligence, and training in order not only to develop, but also to maintain a high level of international security. This requires a dialogue between partner nations asking: Does the security strategy work? It requires the creation and continuity of parameters by which to measure international effectiveness. What is the ultimate goal? What are the expectations as to security training and financial ability? Ultimately, there must be an articulated, institutionalized plan to ensure the continuity of security between nation leaders and all agency/department counterparts in order to promote effective international cooperation and ensure an effective homeland security strategy.

Concluding Thoughts

The intelligence cycle is comprised of four components: direction, collection, processing, and dissemination. The intelligence cycle is an iterative process in which collection requirements based on national security threats are developed, and intelligence is collected, analyzed, and disseminated to a broad range of consumers. Consumers sometimes provide feedback on the finished intelligence products, which can be used to refine any part of the intelligence cycle to ensure that consumers are getting the intelligence they need to make informed decisions and/or take appropriate actions. It is the patterns and connections that analysts are looking for. It is the overall fit of the information into particular facts and circumstances that the intelligence analyst seeks. Just as crucially, the idea of intelligence has become fixated on things beyond basic knowledge, and in a sense, tending toward technology and gadgets over the basic acquisition of information. Many professionals in the intelligence community remind us that intelligence is first and foremost knowledge—something gathered and then disseminated.

Intelligence estimates as a whole are not subjective. The sections in which the possible or probable courses of action are predicted may appear subjective but, in fact, are deeply rooted in the indicators collected. Estimates are solid information and indicators. It should give adequate intentions and warning on a given threat if one has collected good data and integrated them properly. Predictions of the terrorists' COAs are what may be found in the conclusion after the evidence is spelled out. It is how these indicators are analyzed and interpreted that may be somewhat subjective. Stereotypes, lack of information, and lack of attention to indicators leads to speculation and unreliable conclusions. These forms of guessing and speculation are not considered intelligence. Another problem, especially within the terrorism intelligence community, is that estimates are usually overly cautious. Most reports are extensive summaries of highly detailed indicators yet leave readers to draw their own conclusions.

In order to create an effective homeland security strategy, the United States must take measures to promote international cooperation in counterterrorism. To establish effective international cooperation in homeland security, the United States must take measures including the following: forging international partnerships, sharing intelligence related to security, creating a coordinated international security plan, and finally, implementing international institutionalized continuity.

Part IV

Regional Focus on Terrorism

12

The Terrorist Threat in Latin America[1]

While the United States considers the threat from Middle Eastern organizations and is vigilant against this threat, there are other threats against not only the American homeland, but against Americans worldwide. This threat originates from some of the neighbors of the United States to the south. The United States has seen attacks from Puerto Rican nationals, anti-Castro organizations, and other groups. This chapter looks at organizations that have been involved in terrorist activities in the Americas in the past. The State Department reports that "[t]he threat of a major terrorist attack remains low for most countries in the hemisphere. Overall, governments took modest steps to improve their counterterrorism (CT) capabilities and tighten border security, but corruption, weak government institutions, ineffective or lack of interagency cooperation, weak or nonexistent legislation, and reluctance to allocate sufficient resources limited progress."[2]

In a news story published on March 31, 2008, Admiral James Stavridis, then commander of the United States Southern Command and current commander of the US European Command and NATO's supreme allied commander of Europe, stated, "[The United States] consider[s] Latin America and the Caribbean to be potential bases for future terrorist threats to the United States and others in the Americas."[3] Part of the reason for this threat is the outlaw nature found in this hemisphere. There is extreme poverty, economic systems that rely on no official markets, and government and law enforcement corruption. This permits terrorist organizations to thrive and establish bases within Latin America.

Foreign terrorism is not new to the United States. In 1950, two members of the Puerto Rican Nationalist Party attempted to assassinate President Truman. Several years later, four Puerto Ricans entered the visitor's gallery of the House of Representatives firing numerous shots, injuring several members of Congress.[4] Another Puerto Rican organization, the Fuerzas Armadas de Liberación Nacional (FALN), has "claimed responsibility for more than 120 bombings of

---

[1] Information for this chapter was drawn from the following titles: (1) J. A. Bacigalupi, Terrorist Threats South of the Border. In D. L. June (ed.), *Terrorism and Homeland Security: Perspectives, Thoughts, and Opinions*, CRC Press, 2010. (2) A. D'Avila, Mexico Violence That Threatens Our Southern Border: Ripening Conditions for Escalated Terrorism Domestically and Internationally Immediately South of the United States. In D. L. June (ed.), *Terrorism and Homeland Security: Perspectives, Thoughts, and Opinions*, CRC Press, 2010. (3) J. L. Hesterman, *The Terrorist-Criminal Nexus: An Alliance of International Drug Cartels, Organized Crime, and Terror Groups*, CRC Press, 2013.

[2] Office of the Coordinator for Counterterrorism, US Department of State. Country Reports on Terrorism. *Western Hemisphere Overview*, April 30, 2007, Chapter 2. Available at http://www.state.gov/s/ct/rls/crt/2006/82735.htm.

[3] US Admiral Says Caribbean Possible Terrorist Threat. Available at http://www.caribbean360.com/news/caribbean/Stories/ 2008/03/31/newS0000005643.html.

[4] M. Roig-Franzia. A Terrorist in the House. *The Washington Post Magazine*, February 22, 2004, p. w12. Available at http://www.latinamericanstudies.org/puertorico/lolita-house.htm.

military and government buildings, financial institutions, and corporate headquarters in Chicago, New York, and Washington, D.C., which killed six people and injured dozens more."[5] More recently, Cubans residing in the United States have been involved in bombings and assassinations, including the firing of a bazooka at the United Nations building and the car bombing of a former member of the Chilean government.[6] This chapter explores the threat of terrorism from several countries: Argentina, Bolivia, Brazil, Chile, Colombia, Cuba, Ecuador, El Salvador, Guatemala, Mexico, Nicaragua, Panama, Paraguay, Peru, Suriname, Trinidad and Tobago, and Venezuela. Each of these countries and the threat of terrorism from and within these countries are explored individually below.

Argentina

Argentina remains a stable country. However, a recent shift toward the left suggests the possibility of increased activity. Several terrorist events in the past (prior to 2005) resulted in property damage and casualties. Since then, American businesses have received email and bomb threats and were, at times, the focus of protests and demonstrations, but actual reporting and confirmation of these types of incidents declined.

Intelligence and news reports suggest that there are Hezbollah supporters and members within the immigrant Syrian and Lebanese communities of the triborder area between Brazil and Argentina.[7] Hezbollah and Iran remained the chief suspects for the July 18, 1994, terrorist bombing of the Argentine-Israeli Mutual Association (AMIA) that killed 85 and injured over 200 people.[8] However, some news reports suggest that the perpetrators were not members of Hezbollah.

Bolivia

Bolivia is one of the poorest countries in South America. Lack of resources, corruption, and the infiltration of terrorist organizations from neighboring Peru plague Bolivia's fight against terrorist organizations. In the 1970s, Bolivia was the victim of organized terrorist attacks on its population. According to the US State Department, "The Bolivian government released Francisco 'Pacho' Cortez, a member of the National Liberation Army (ELN), who was arrested in Bolivia after the statute of limitations on his case expired. Bolivian authorities also arrested Aida Ochoa, a suspected member of the Tupac Amaru Revolutionary Movement (MRTA), in October 2005 but then released her in early 2006."[7] The arrest of Ochoa suggests that Peruvian terrorist organizations are extending their influence to Bolivia. The Bolivian district attorney prosecuting a gang leader allegedly responsible for the murders of three foreign tourists in Bolivia said the gang had received training from Sendero Luminoso (Shining Path). Aliheydar Rzayev acknowledges the involvement of organized crime with terror organizations, stating that

---

[5] G. M. Pérez. Fuerzas Armadas de Liberación Nacional (FALN). *The Electronic Encyclopedia of Chicago*. Available at http://www.encyclopedia.chicagohistory.org/pages/489.html.

[6] J. Franklin. Terrorist Network Operating Openly in the United States. *Znet Daily Commentary*, April 30, 2005, Available at http://www.zmag.org/Sustainers/content/2005- 04/30franklin_.cfm.

[7] Office of the Coordinator for Counterterrorism, US Department of State. Country Reports on Terrorism. *Western Hemisphere Overview*, April 30, 2007, Chapter 2. Available at http://www.state.gov/s/ct/rls/crt/2006/82735.htm.

[8] M. Loyola. All Along the Watchtower: The War on Terror Has Arrived in Latin America, and Is Headed Our Way. *National Review Online*, March 18, 2009. Available at http://article.nationalreview.com/?q=MjvjMDFjMty3Mzi4M2e2yje5Mze0ymy2Mz rmotQ1zty=.

in "some countries of Latin America, such as Peru, Bolivia and Columbia, activity of terrorist organizations is closely tied to the Mafia."[9]

Brazil

Brazil is the largest country in South America. "Political and labor strikes and demonstrations occur sporadically in urban areas and may cause temporary disruption to public transportation."[10] As in other countries, these demonstrations may evolve into violent confrontations between law enforcement and the perpetrators. Intelligence reports suggest that Colombian terrorist groups operate in border areas of Brazil. However, the State Department knows "of no specific threat directed against US citizens across the border in Brazil at this time."[10]

Triborder Area (Argentina, Brazil, and Paraguay)

The governments of the triborder area have long been concerned with arms and drug smuggling, document fraud, money laundering, and the manufacture and movement of contraband goods through this region. Hezbollah and Hamas appear to use the triborder region to raise funds by participating in illegal activities. In "August 2008, the US Southern Command and the [Drug Enforcement Administration], in coordination with host nations, targeted a Hezbollah drug trafficking ring in the Tri-Border region of Argentina, Brazil and Paraguay."[11]

Chile

The State Department considers the potential for terrorist activity in Chile to be low. There has been some politically motivated violence among indigenous communities in southern Chile. None has affected Americans. Potential for civil disturbance is low although demonstrations, sometimes violent, do occur.[12] A recent terrorist-related incident occurred when police arrested Miguel Tapia Huenulef for an alleged "arson attack on a private estate" and for an attack on the public defender's office in Temuco. During the arrest, the police "claim they found a stash of dangerous weapons," including "a submachine gun, ammunition clips, two grenades and bomb-making materials."[13]

Colombia

Colombia faces a continuing terrorist threat from the Fuerzas Armadas Revolucionarias de Colombia (Revolutionary Armed Forces of Colombia–FARC), the Ejercito de Liberación

---

[9] A. Rzayev. Financing of Terror: Interconnection of Criminals and Terrorists. *Global Politician*, September 11, 2007. Available at http://www.globalpolitician.com/23428-terror-sponsors

[10] US Department of State, Bureau of Consular Affairs. Brazil: Country Specific Information. Available at http://travel.state.gov/travel/cis_pa_tw/cis/cis_1072.html, March 15, 2013.

[11] M. Levitt. Hezbollah: Narco-Islamism. The Washington Institute for Near East Policy, March 22, 2009. Available at http://www.washingtoninstitute.org/templatec06.php?ciD=1257.

[12] US State Department. Chile, Country Specific Information. Available at http://travel.state.gov/travel/cis_pa_tw/cis/cis_1088.html.

[13] B. Witte. Chile: State Seizes Mapuche 'Terrorist'. *The Patagonia Times*, March 16, 2009. Available at http://www.patagoniatimes.cl/index.php/20090316769/news/human-rights-indigenous-news/chile-State-SeizeS-MaPuche-terroriSt.html.

Nacional (National Liberation Army–ELN), and remaining elements of the former Autodefensas Unidas de Colombia (United Self-Defense Forces of Colombia–AUC). Government action weakened Colombian-based terrorist groups. However, these groups continue their terrorist activities of murder, kidnapping, and terror.

Recently, the FARC has resumed active military operations against, primarily, police and government targets. The Department of State "continues to warn US citizens of the dangers of travel to Colombia. While security in Colombia has improved significantly in recent years, violence by narco-terrorist groups continues to affect some rural areas as well as large cities. The potential for violence by terrorists and other criminal elements exists in all parts of the country."[14]

The FARC's military operations consist mostly of tactical-level encounters and the use of kidnapping and extortion.

> The FARC is a terrorist group dedicated to the violent overthrow of Colombia's government. It consists of approximately 10,000 armed guerillas organized into 77 'fronts' and four urban militias. The FARC has also evolved into the world's largest supplier of cocaine. The FARC's 10th Front is responsible for attempting to obtain control, by military force, of the Arauca Department of Colombia, an area bordering Venezuela. To support its terrorist activities, the FARC's 10th Front supplies and arranges cocaine shipments from airstrips in Venezuela and the Colombian border with Venezuela.[15]

The FARC suffered several significant losses in its military leadership in the past few years, resulting in a loss of members. While some reports place the group's strength at 10,000, other estimates place the FARC's strength at only about 3000 armed combatants. They operate primarily in rural areas, but occasionally conduct operations at urban centers. During March 2009, the FARC increased attacks against government and infrastructure, causing some casualties and damage.

By contrast, the ELN, which first appeared in January 1965, claims to fight against oppression from the Colombian government. This organization appears to have minimal conventional military forces. Its main operations include kidnapping for ransom and attacks on petrochemical infrastructure for protection "taxes."

Furthermore, AUC, known as the paramilitary forces, was formed to retaliate against the leftist guerrillas. The AUC was an elite paramilitary force, heavily armed, well organized, and, of course, illegal; it was created to protect its sponsors from the threats of the guerrillas using terror. Supposedly demobilized in 2006, recent reports suggest a resumption of activities of the right-wing paramilitary forces. Included in the AUC's protection methods are homicides, mutilation, and dismembering of agricultural leaders (supposedly linked to the FARC), as well as massacres designed to send a message to opponents of the group.

Cuba

The State Department claims that the Cuban government continued to permit US fugitives to live legally in Cuba and is unlikely to satisfy US extradition requests for terrorists harbored in the country. Likewise, Cuba contends that the United States does not honor extradition requests; specifically, for Luis Posada Carriles, who was accused of being the mastermind of several assassination attempts against Castro and being involved in the mid-flight destruction

[14] US Department of State, Bureau of Consular Affairs. Travel Warning, March 25, 2009. Available at http://travel.state.gov/travel/cis_pa_tw/tw/tw_941.html.

[15] US Department of Justice. Associates of Colombian Terrorist Organization Charged with Conspiracy to Import Ton-Quantities of Cocaine. Available at http://news.prnews-wire.com/Displayreleasecontent.aspx?acct=104&Story=/www/story/03-20-2009/0004992200&eDate=.

of a Cubana de Aviacion aircraft with 70 passengers and crew on board.[16] There does not appear to be any factual basis for active participation of Cuba with terrorist organizations, and there are no guerrilla or terrorist organizations based in Cuba. However, Cuba's relationship with Iran, Venezuela, and other countries opposed to the United States suggests the possibility of links to some terrorist organizations.

Ecuador

Ecuador's greatest counterterrorism and security challenge was the presence of Colombian foreign terrorist organizations, frequently linked with narcotics trafficking organizations, along its northern border. Members of the Revolutionary Armed Forces of Colombia (FARC) and the National Liberation Army (ELN) were widely present on the Colombian side of the border and regularly entered Ecuadorian territory (generally as unarmed civilians) for rest and resupply. The Ecuadoran government discovered several training camps for these groups on the Ecuadorian side of the border.[17] During 2008, Colombia conducted an armed military incursion into Ecuadoran territory to attack a FARC military camp, resulting in the capture of several members of the terrorist group as well as a laptop computer with substantial information on terrorist links to other countries and organizations. This incursion caused a breach in the relations between Ecuador and Colombia as well as between Venezuela and Colombia.

Ecuadorian police suspected several small Ecuadorian groups of domestic subversion and involvement in terrorism. Of greatest concern was the estimated 200-member Popular Combatants Group (GCP), a faction of the Marxist-Leninist Communist Party of Ecuador. Its members are mainly students trained in the use of firearms and low-yield pamphlet bombs, which they deployed in major cities without casualties. Also of concern were the Political Military Organization (OPM) and Alfarista Liberation Army (ELA), which were reputed to have ties with and support from Colombian narcoterrorists.[17] However, with a leftist President at the helm of the country, these leftist organizations will probably wither and disappear.

El Salvador

El Salvador was the only Latin American country with troops serving alongside US forces in Iraq. While it continued supporting the US-led coalition, the election of a leftist President will present a shift in its policies. The main terrorist organization in the country, the Frente Farabundo Marti para la Liberación Nacional (Farabundo Marti National Liberation Front–FMLN), reorganized itself after a long civil war and became a formal political party. As time passed, the FMLN candidates achieved substantial success, and in the recent presidential elections, the FMLN candidate won the presidency. The main threat faced in the cities and countryside of El Salvador is organized crime. Currently, there are no known terrorist organizations based in El Salvador.

Guatemala

Severe resource constraints of technology and manpower, corruption, and an ineffective criminal justice system hindered efforts against transnational crime threats, such as drug trafficking

[16] Office of the Coordinator for Counterterrorism, US Department of State. Country Reports on Terrorism. April 30, 2007, Chapter 3. Available at http://www.state.gov/s/ct/rls/crt/2006/82736.htm.

[17] Office of the Coordinator for Counterterrorism, US Department of State. Country Reports on Terrorism. *Western Hemisphere Overview*, April 30, 2007, Chapter 2. Available at http://www.state.gov/s/ct/rls/crt/2006/82735.htm.

and alien smuggling, especially through remote areas of the country.[18] The country remains relatively free of terror activity. In 1968, a rebel faction assassinated "Gordon Mein, [the] ambassador to Guatemala."[19] During the 1980s, numerous death squads operated in Guatemala, mainly kidnapping dissidents, torturing, and then killing them. Currently, the main threat against US nationals comes from traditional criminal activity linked to the poor economic situation found in the country.

Mexico

Mexico continually works with the United States in combating drug trafficking. It has worked in the past on the war on terror by trying to prevent terrorist entry into the United States through the common border. However, in recent years, the increased operations by drug cartels have resulted in numerous deaths to visitors and law enforcement officers. The US State Department continued a travel advisory for Mexico due to the Mexican drug cartels engaging in an

> increasingly violent conflict—both among themselves and with Mexican security services—for control of narcotics trafficking routes along the US-Mexico border. Some recent Mexican army and police confrontations with drug cartels have resembled small-unit combat, with cartels employing automatic weapons and grenades. Large firefights have taken place in many towns and cities across Mexico but most recently in northern Mexico, including Tijuana, Chihuahua City, Monterrey, and Ciudad Juarez."[20]

According to the Federal Research Division of the Library of Congress, "Mexico's government officially recognizes the existence of just three insurgent groups." Mexico's military, however,

> has identified as many as 16 guerrilla bands. The best known is the Zapatista National Liberation Army (Ejército Zapatista de Liberación Nacional–EZLN), with which the government has had an uneasy truce since the insurgents staged a violent, short-lived 1994 revolt in the southern state of Chiapas. The other two are the People's Revolutionary Army (Ejército Popular Revolucionario–EPR), which operates mainly in Guerrero and Oaxaca states, and an EPR offshoot formed in 1998 called the Revolutionary Army of the Insurgent People (Ejército Revolucionario del Pueblo Insurgente–ERPI). Media reports indicate that as many as 25 insurgent groups may be active in the country. Except for the EZLN, most of the insurgent groups number no more than a few dozen to a few hundred militants. Several of the guerilla bands are recent offshoots of the Popular Revolutionary Army (EPR), a leftist insurgency based in the mountainous state of Guerrero.[21]

These organizations probably pose no threat to the United States but could pose a threat to US nationals traveling in Mexico.

Mexico is well known for its drug production and is a main supplier of marijuana and methamphetamines to the United States with sales estimates ranging from $13.6 billion to $48.4 billion yearly. There are about seven main cartels or organizations operating in Mexico. The

---

[18] Office of the Coordinator for Counterterrorism, US Department of State. Country Reports on Terrorism. *Western Hemisphere Overview*, April 30, 2007, Chapter 2. Available at http://www.state.gov/s/ct/rls/crt/2006/82735.htm.

[19] List of US Diplomats Killed Abroad. *USA Today*. Available at http://www.usatoday.com/news/world/2008-01-01-2036205597_x.htm.

[20] US Department of State, Bureau of Consular Affairs. Travel Alert, Mexico, February 20, 2009. Available at http://travel.state.gov/travel/cis_pa_tw/pa/pa_3028.html; Terrorist Threats South of the Border 297.

[21] Federal Research Division, Library of Congress. Organized Crime and Terrorist Activity in Mexico, 1999–2002. Available at http://www.loc.gov/rr/frd/pdf-files/orgcrime_Mexico.pdf, p. 34.

Gulf, Sinaloa, and Juarez cartels are the three main players. They have about 13, 17, and 21 Mexican states, respectively, that they have a presence and bases in. The Tijuana cartel and Gulf cartel have merged to form the "Federation" to gain a bigger portion or territory for profit.[22] These Mexican cartels are increasing their involvement with gangs in the United States, such as the Latin Kings and Mara Salvatrucha (MS-13) for distribution in the southwest. The cartels do not care which gangs they sell to or what rivalries may come between them. They also use corruption or intimidation of law enforcement officials to make progress in their operations. Reports suggest that as many as 1500 of 7000 of Mexico's Investigative Agency are or have been under investigation for working for the Sinaloa cartel. Competing cartels fight for influence over law enforcement and the media and use intimidation and murder. Murders have been on the increase in Nuevo Laredo, at approximately 600 since 2003. Between 1800 and 1900 Mexicans were killed in related violence in the first 36 weeks of 2007.

One of the major battlegrounds for the drug cartels has been across the border from El Paso, Texas, in Juarez. Its police chief was forced to resign after receiving a threat that one policeman per day would die if he did not resign.[23] Plaguing the battle to disrupt the cartel is the level of corruption found among Mexico's military and paramilitary forces, making it all the more difficult to control the cartels and eliminate the violence and murders. Deaths related to drug trafficking have doubled from 2275 in 2007 to 5207 in 2008, mostly attributed to La Familia. La Familia left its calling card at a nightclub after decapitating and tossing five heads on the dance floor, claiming, "[t]he family [does not] kill for money. It [does not] kill women. It [does not] kill innocent people, only those who deserve to die. Know that this is divine justice."[24] La Familia uses decapitations with messages in an intense propaganda campaign to intimidate, terrorize, and inhibit action by the local authorities. News of its activities has appeared on national news, Internet videos, and half-page advertisements in newspapers. Mexican drug cartels are sending assassins into the United States to kill Americans to the point that Phoenix, Arizona, has now become the kidnapping capital of America with 370 in 2008.[25] Already there is a list published of Americans and law enforcement who are targeted for assassination. Killings, kidnappings, firefights, and home invasions linked to drug cartels are happening more frequently in both Mexico and in the United States.

Los Zetas

The Gulf cartel employs groups, such as Los Zetas, Negros, MS-13, and Guatemalan Kaibiles (special forces). The Zetas, as reported, were formed by deserters of the Mexican military's Special Air Mobile Force Group (GAFES) in 1990. The Zetas are more highly trained militarily, are able to use sophisticated weapons and conduct more complex operations. It has been reported that these soldiers were trained in the United States (unconfirmed) and then were bribed/bought to join the cartel. The Zetas membership initially included special forces, but they have recently been recruiting military, paramilitary, and civilians due to shortages. The Zetas perform assassinations, kidnappings, weapons trafficking, drug dealing, money laundering, and money collection for the Gulf cartel. They also control trafficking routes along the eastern edge of the US–Mexico border. The Zetas have also trained smaller groups, such as La Familia, who have carried out numerous executions in Michoacan.

---

[22] C. W. Cook. Mexico's Drug Cartels. CRS Report for Congress, 2007.

[23] M. Cuevas. Nine Bodies Found in Common Grave Near Ciudad Juarez, Mexico. CNN, 2009. Available at http://www.cnn.com/2009/WORLD/americas/03/14/mexico.bodies.found/.

[24] G. W. Grayson. *La Familia: Another Deadly Mexican Syndicate*. Foreign Policy Research Institute, 2009. Available at http://www.fpri.org/enotes/200901.grayson.lafamilia.html.

[25] M. Webster. Phoenix and Tucson Police Report over 400 Kidnappings of Americans by Mexicans, 2009. Available at http://www.articlesbase.com/news-and-society-articles/phoenix-and-tucson-police-report-over-400-kidnappings-of-americans-by-mexicans-767650.html.

Los Zetas should be viewed not as a criminal enterprise but as a lethal, complex army. They have specialized training in navigating and operating in all terrains; they have river swimmers, divers, jungle experts, and training in urban warfare. Money from their drug trade and other nefarious activity enables Los Zetas to buy top-of-the-line equipment; they have tanks, surface-to-air missiles, RPGs, night vision equipment, boats, helicopters, and aircraft. They often operate in small-fire teams and use snipers and counter snipers. Their executions are savage; they often set their targets on fire, decapitate them, and saturate their bodies with bullets. The violence is escalating in their ongoing battle with the Sinaloas. In May 2012, Heriberto Lazcano gave orders for the massacre and dismemberment of 49 innocent civilians in the so-called Mother's Day massacre.

They also engage law enforcement and the military, using ambush tactics and the element of surprise to kill officers before they can react. A new tactic in the States may be to monitor law enforcement activity, looking for patterns or routines, and then ambush and kill. In southern Arizona, "spotters" are routinely used by drug cartels to locate and report back to drug and human traffickers the location of Border Patrol agents and other law enforcement so they can avoid arrest. These spotters are heavily armed, stealthy, and capable of targeting law enforcement. The killing of Border Patrol agent Brian Terry, who was shot with an AK-47 in Rio Rico, Arizona, was celebrated in the cartel world as a victory. The brazen shooting was a first and possibly opened a "new chapter" with regard to tactics and escalation of violence against law enforcement, in which they are not merely watching and monitoring but shooting.

It is estimated that only 50% of the Zetas' money is in the drug-trafficking business, and they have routinely shown the ability to expand into unexpected areas to launder and generate money. For example, in June 2012 horse racing complexes owned by brothers in New Mexico and Oklahoma were the targets of a law enforcement investigation that uncovered a multi-million-dollar money-laundering scheme by the Zetas. Another source of Zeta revenue is the Pemex Corporation oil pipelines in Mexico. The company estimates that 5000 siphons have been attached to their pipelines and three million barrels of oil were stolen in 2011 alone for a loss of $475 million to the company.[26]

Lastly, the Zetas are known for sending "messages," including a recruiting banner in an area where the average daily wages are around five US dollars. The sign calls out to any soldier or ex-soldier and says, "Why be poor? Come work for us" and "We're offering you a good salary, food and medical care for your families."[27] The Zetas have also targeted the *ni-ni*, young boys who go to neither school nor work, by offering them money and "prestige." In May 2012, the group employed a new propaganda tactic, one not previously seen in the cartel battles. Thousands of leaflets were dropped from aircraft during the early morning hours over the Sinaloa capital city as a warning to the governor of the region and Chapo Guzman, leader of the Sinaloas, to stop working together or face dire consequences (see Figure 12.1).

Nicaragua

Nicaragua has seen a former guerrilla organization, accused of numerous terrorist acts, assume the presidency of the country in free and open elections. The Frente Farabundo Marti para Liberación Nacional (Farabundo Marti Liberation Front–FMLN) participated in a guerrilla war that resulted in thousands of deaths and significant damage to property during the long civil

[26] P. Corcoran. Oil Theft Is Big Business for Mexican Gangs. *InSightCrime: Organized Crime in the Americas*, March 20, 2012. Available at http://www.insightcrime.org/insight-latest-news/item/2373-oil-theft-is-big-business-for-mexican-gangs.

[27] M. Roig-Franzia. Mexican Drug Cartels Making Audacious Pitch for Recruits. *Washington Post*, May 7, 2008.

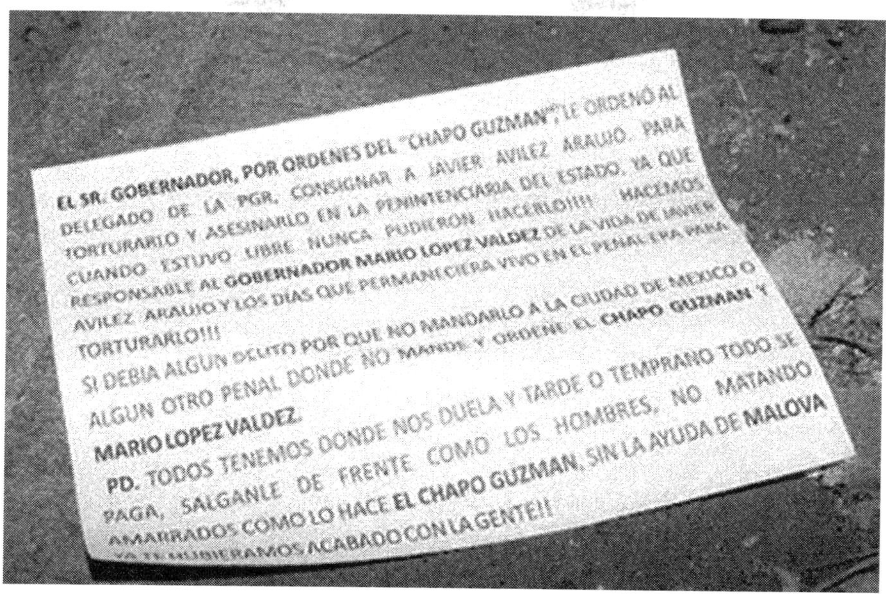

Figure 12.1 Zeta leaflet, unattributed photo taken by Mexican law enforcement. (From J. L. Hesterman, *The Terrorist-Criminal Nexus: An Alliance of International Drug Cartels, Organized Crime, and Terror Groups*, CRC Press, 2013. With permission.)

war. Since the signing of a peace agreement between the government and the FMLN, the former guerrillas used the ballot box to gain access to the government. They held mayoral positions in a many large cities, including the capital (which they lost in the 2008 election) and have done a credible job according to world observers. Many analysts consider the country may shift further left with the election of the FMLN's President. As in other developing countries, with the decline of world economic markets, there has been an increase in petty and violent crimes in major urban centers. The State Department warns that violent crime "is increasing and petty street crimes are very common. Gang activity also is increasing, though not at levels found in neighboring Central American countries. Pickpocketing and occasional armed robberies occur on crowded buses, at bus stops, and in open markets."[28]

Panama

The Panama Canal, as Panama's principal economic asset, could be a lucrative terrorist target that would influence world economies. FARC rebels from neighboring Colombia, as they do in Ecuador, use border areas to hide and conduct base camp operations. The State Department warns US citizens that "travel to Darien Province" is dangerous. It further states that while "no incidents have occurred at [resorts in the Darien Province], US citizens, other foreign nationals and Panamanian citizens have been the victims of violent crime, kidnapping and murder in this general area."[29]

[28] US Department of State, Bureau of Consular Affairs. Country Specific Information: Nicaragua. Available at http://travel.state.gov/travel/cis_pa_tw/cis/cis_985.html.

[29] US Department of State, Bureau of Consular Affairs. Country Specific Information: Panama. Available at http://travel.state.gov/travel/cis_pa_tw/cis/cis_994.html.

Paraguay

Paraguay faces a complex task in its triborder region. Because of the difficult terrain and isolation, it is difficult for the central or regional governments to provide adequate security within the area. Additionally, the presence of an immigrant community in the region contributed to the possible presence of Islamic terrorists using this area as a base of operations for terrorist activities. The State Department reports that citizens of the United States "have on occasion been the victims of assaults, kidnappings, robberies, and rapes."[30] The recent election of Fernando Lugo, a former Roman Catholic Bishop and strong advocate of liberation theology, shifted the political landscape of Paraguay to the left. While there are no national terrorist organizations, there exists fear of Islamic terrorist organizations residing and operating in the triborder area.

Peru

The main terrorist threat in Peru is Sendero Luminoso (Shining Path–SL). This organization's goal is to establish a leftist revolutionary government similar to those found in Cuba and other leftist countries. This organization was most active in the 1980s and 1990s, costing more than 69,000 lives. The group suffered its major setback when the government arrested its leader, Abimael Guzman, and sentenced him to life in prison. Additionally, the number two military leader, Hector Aponte Sinarahua "Clay," also died. During the 1990s, SL suffered many setbacks and almost disappeared. However, with the growth of narcotics trafficking and the decline of the world economy, the organization has reemerged.

Another revolutionary organization that in the past used terrorist tactics is the Movimiento Revolucionary Tupac Amaru (Tupac Amaru Revolutionary Movement–MRTA). Military operations of this organization decreased since 1996. It is possible that MRTA members, following the lead of the FMLN in Nicaragua, began entering legitimate political organizations of the left. "MRTA members decided the best way to fight the war was to attack the holdings of Peru's wealthy elite, but sought to cause the least amount of injuries possible by frequently warning of its attacks in advance. Experts say Tupac Amaru has been less violent, in general, than Shining Path."[31] An interesting finding in this organization is the presence of US citizens as part of the group. In 2000, the Peruvian judicial system found Lori Berenson guilty of conspiring to attack the Peruvian National Congress and sentenced her to 20 years in prison.[32] In addition to these threats, the FARC uses remote areas of the joint Peru-Colombian borders to establish base camps and purchase weapons.[33]

Suriname

Suriname's Minister of Justice and Police claimed, in December 2007, that criminal organizations were planning attacks in Suriname. "According to the minister, there were arrests over a

---

[30] US Department of State, Bureau of Consular Affairs. Country Specific Information: Paraguay. Available at http://travel.state.gov/travel/cis_pa_tw/cis/cis_997.html.

[31] K. Gregory. Shining Path, Tupac Amaru (Peru, Leftists). Council on Foreign Relations, September 25, 2008. Available at http://www.cfr.org/publication/9276/.

[32] "Descartan modificación de condena a Lori Berenson por estado de gestación," 24 horas libre, September 17, 2008. Available at http://www.24horaslibre.com/politica/1221644078.php.

[33] Office of the Coordinator for Counterterrorism, US Department of State. Country Reports on Terrorism. April 30, 2007, Chapter 6. Available at http://www.state.gov/s/ct/rls/crt/2006/82738.htm.

two-week period late in the year, and investigations had pointed to involvement of the FARC and unspecified African crime organizations."[34]

Trinidad and Tobago

This Caribbean island, one of the world's producers of natural gas, is the "home of one of the first attempts at violently establishing a modern Islamic extremist state in the region after the attempted Islamic coup in July 1990." The group responsible, Jama'at al Muslimeen, under the control of Imam Yasin Abu Bakr, is alive and thriving in Trinidad. Major General Gary D. Speer, former Acting Commander in Chief of the US Southern Command, in April 2002, stated: "The recent bombing outside the US Embassy in Peru preceding President Bush's visit is indicative that other domestic terrorist groups pose threats to the United States elsewhere in the hemisphere. These include, but are not limited to, the Sendero Luminoso (Shining Path) and Tupac Amaru Revolutionary Movement (MRTA) in Peru and the Jama'at al Muslimeen (JAM) in Trinidad and Tobago."[35]

Venezuela

When President Hugo Chavez was in power, Venezuela had distanced itself from the United States. During the Bush administration, the Secretary of State identified Venezuela as a state "not fully cooperating with US antiterrorism efforts. In light of Venezuela's actions, the United States imposed an arms ban." This resulted in Venezuela's contracting with Russia for the purchase of advanced aircraft and combat systems.

An individual claiming to be a member of an Islamic extremist group in Venezuela placed two pipe bombs outside the American Embassy in Caracas on October 23, 2006. Venezuelan police safely disposed of the two pipe bombs and immediately made one arrest. The investigation by Venezuelan authorities resulted in the additional arrest of the alleged ideological leader of the group. At year's end, both suspects remained in jail, and prosecutors were pressing terrorism charges against them.[36]

While some in the Bush administration claimed there was a strong link between terrorist organizations and Venezuela, the head of the Organization of American States (OAS), Jose Miguel Insulza, testified before US Congress that "[t]here is no evidence, and no member country, including this one [the United States] has provided the OAS with any such proof."[37] The recent death of Hugo Chavez could signal a change in US-Venezuela relations; however, if and to what extent this occurs remains to be seen.

---

[34] Caribbean Nations Make US Terror Report. *Caribbean World News*, May 1, 2008. Available at http://www.caribbeanworldnews.com/middle_top_news_detail.php?mid=692.

[35] C. Kelshall. Radical Islam and LNG in Trinidad and Tobago. Institute for the Analysis of Global Security, November 15, 2004. Available at http://www.iags.org/n1115045.htm.

[36] Office of the Coordinator for Counterterrorism, US Department of State. Country Reports on Terrorism. *Western Hemisphere Overview*, April 30, 2007, Chapter 2. Available at http://www.state.gov/s/ct/rls/crt/2006/82735.htm.

[37] AFP. OAS Chief to US Congress: No Venezuela–Terrorist Link. April 10, 2008. Available at http://afp.google.com/article/aleqM5ipnXwhoq34tlujMqpPj9ozvXwznw.

Concluding Thoughts

Admiral Stavridis stated that the United States "consider[s] Latin America and the Caribbean to be potential bases for future terrorist threats to the United States and others in the Americas." In this chapter, the threat of terrorism from and within these countries was examined. What is clear from this analysis is that leftist-leaning elections in South and Central America and other political alarms, such as drug trafficking, organized crime, and terrorism in these regions, highlights the need for each government to deal with the domestic causes of these problems and the need for the stabilization of cooperation between governments.

13

Terrorism in the European Union[1]

The Case of Germany

Located in the center of the European continent, Germany has one of the most extended borderlines among the EU member states. It shares land borders with no less than nine countries. These direct neighbors are Austria, Belgium, the Czech Republic, Denmark, France, Luxemburg, the Netherlands, Poland, and Switzerland. The overall length of land borders is 3757 kilometers; the two coastlines at the North and the Baltic Sea have an additional length of 2389 kilometers.[2] These basic figures illustrate the historical importance of border control as one element in the context of counterterrorism policies.

This is even true in light of the fact that the border issue has to be assessed in a very particular political context in Europe. The "new" international terrorism struck Germany and Europe at a moment when the abolishment of border controls was one of the top priorities on the political agenda. On the one hand, governments consider the disappearance of borders between the member states as one of the fundamental achievements of the coalescent development in Europe. The disappearance of formal borders transpired at a time when a critical assessment of the EU and its existing bureaucracy and the merit of control-free movement of people and goods was considered one of the most visible and perceptible advantages in EU citizens' everyday lives. However, in the aftermath of 9/11, many of the measures introduced around border security and the control-free movement of goods and people were brought into question. Virtually all governments attempted to counterbalance the loss of border-related control opportunities by implementing surrogate measures. These will be presented and critically assessed here in detail.

In addition, Germany's experience with terrorism will be referred to as well. First of all, this is due to the fact that the present statutory regulations in the penal code have their origin in the fight against the domestic terrorism of the 1970s. Second, Germany has been quite intensively touched by the activities of the 9/11 terrorist events. Not surprisingly, this recent experience has clearly fueled policy developments in this field.

---

1 Information for this chapter was drawn from the following title: M. Klichling and A. Maguer, Border Security in Germany since 9/11. In K. W. Sundberg and J. A. Winterdyk (eds.), *Border Security in the Al-Qaeda Era*, CRC Press, 2009.

2 Further information is provided by the Federal Office of Statistics at http://www.destatis.de.

Germany's Experience in Terrorism: Old versus New Risks

Like several other European countries, Germany had experience with domestic terrorism long before 9/11. The country was first struck by serious terrorist assaults as a result of a process of political radicalization among parts of the post-1968 movement that produced a serial terrorist threat throughout the 1970s and 1980s. At that time, a left-wing terrorist group emerged that was initially named the Baader-Meinhof Group after its two main founders, Andreas Baader and Ulrike Meinhof, and eventually renamed the Red Army Faction (RAF). After the main period of activities of that group during the 1970s (see Table 13.1), the most prominent members of the first generation were either tried and convicted or had committed suicide. Nevertheless, it was only after German reunification in 1990 that the group, after a longer period of inactivity, officially disbanded although not without committing a final murder in 1991.[3] Disclosure of documents from the former GDR[4] revealed that the RAF had been supported by the GDR ministry of state security and the state security police from the late 1970s on. Group members who had not been caught in the West, in particular persons of the "subsequent" or "second generation" of the RAF, were invited to settle in the GDR. Equipped with new identities from the GDR government, they lived inconspicuous lives as ordinary working class people behind the Iron Curtain, shielded from investigations and prosecution by the Federal Republic of Germany.[5] Other leftist groups were the Movement of June 2nd (J2M, circa 1975), a sub-group of the RAF that temporarily acted independently, and the Revolutionary Cells (RZ) (circa 1975); both of them, however, were less prominent and committed significantly fewer atrocities with most of their activities concentrated in Berlin (see Table 13.1).[6]

Notwithstanding the domestic character and the nationally oriented political focus of these groups, elements of transnational terrorism can already be found in these early times. These become evident with regard to the fact that the RAF and the RZ had connections to terrorist groups in the Middle East through Palestinian training camps and by being involved in joint activities, such as the OPEC attack of 1975 in Vienna, Austria, and the aircraft hijacking events of 1976 in Entebbe, Uganda, and 1977 in Mogadishu, Somalia.[7] Other "domestic" RAF assaults such as the 1975 attack on the German embassy in Stockholm, Sweden, were conducted abroad as well; therefore, they meet the definition of what nowadays is called transnational terrorism.

Another early German experience with transnational terrorism was the Palestinian assault upon the Olympic team of Israel during the 1972 summer games in Munich, when two athletes were immediately killed and another 11 kidnapped, who all later died in the course of a failed rescue mission by German police. Besides that latter Palestinian attack, which had a direct and immediate impact on visa regulations and control policies at German borders and airports, all these domestically oriented terrorist threats brought no significant changes in border controls, which at that time still had a totally different structure.

The incidents were assessed and combated as political crimes challenging national security from the inside. Consequently, legal initiatives had their focus on criminal law and criminal procedure; in both legal areas, significant amendments were implemented.[8] More or less irrelevant for the development of border control policies was also the homegrown right-wing terrorism

[3] Detlev Rohwedder, who was the director of the Treuhand agency responsible for the privatization of the industry in the former GDR, is assumed to be the last victim of the RAF. See the following for more information: J. O. Engene, *Terrorism in Western Europe: Explaining the Trends Since 1950*, Cheltenham, UK, and Northampton, MA, USA, 2004.

[4] Former (communist) East Germany had the official name German Democratic Republic (GDR).

[5] For more details on the RAF history and state reaction, see S. Aust. *Der baader-meinhof-komplex*, Hamburg, 1997.

[6] J. O. Engene. *Terrorism in Western Europe: Explaining the Trends since 1950*. Cheltenham, UK, Northampton, MA, US, 2004.

[7] T. Wittke. *Terrorismusbekämpfung als rationale politische Entscheidung*. Frankfurt am Main, 1983.

[8] H.-J. Vogel. Strafverfahrensrecht und Terrorismus—eine Bilanz. *Neuer Juristische Wochenschrift* 31: 1217–1228, 1978.

Table 13.1 List of RAF-Related Terrorist Incidents of the 1970s

Assaults/Attacks by the RAF	Date	Explanation
Arson in Frankfurt department stores	April 2, 1968	Committed by the Baader-Meinhof Gang, the antecedent of the RAF
Baader liberation	May 24, 1970	Andreas Baader liberated from prison, first "official" RAF action
Triple bank robbery in Berlin	September 29, 1970	Probably only 2 of the 3 robberies were actually committed by the RAF
Petra Schelm killed in Hamburg	July 15, 1971	RAF member Petra Schelm killed by police during a shootout in Hamburg
Norbert Schmid killed in Hamburg	October 22, 1971	Police officer Norbert Schmid killed by RAF during a shootout in Hamburg
Herbert Schoner killed in Kaiserslautern	December 22, 1971	Police officer Herbert Schoner killed during an RAF bank robbery
Bombing of US 5th Army Corps headquarters in Frankfurt	May 11, 1972	Part of the RAF's "May Offensive"
Bombing of police buildings in Augsburg and Munich	May 12, 1972	Part of the RAF's "May Offensive"
Failed assault on federal judge Buddenberg in Karlsruhe	May 15, 1972	Part of the RAF's "May Offensive"
Bomb attacks against the Springer Building in Hamburg	May 19, 1972	Part of the RAF's "May Offensive"
Bombing of US Army headquarters in Heidelberg	May 24, 1972	Part of the RAF's "May Offensive"
First hunger strike	January 17, 1974	Forty prisoners go on hunger strike to protest Ulrike Meinhof's isolated confinement; this is the first of 10 hunger strikes
Stockholm embassy attack	April 24, 1975	RAF occupies the German embassy in Stockholm, kills two staff members
Death of Holger Meins	November 9, 1975	Holger Meins dies in prison after being on hunger strike for 54 days

(*continued*)

Table 13.1 List of RAF-Related Terrorist Incidents of the 1970s (Continued)

Assaults/Attacks by the RAF	Date	Explanation
Suicide of Ulrike Meinhof	May 9, 1976	Ulrike Meinhof commits suicide by hanging in prison
Siegfried Buback murder	April 7, 1977	Federal Attorney General Buback is shot in Karlsruhe along with driver and bodyguard
Raid on an arms dealer	July 1, 1977	Two RAF members raid an arms dealer in Frankfurt
Failed attack on the Federal Attorney General's office	August 25, 1977	A missile attack on the Federal Attorney General's office in Karlsruhe fails by chance
Hanns Martin Schleyer kidnapping	September 5, 1977	President of the Employer's Union Schleyer is kidnapped in Cologne, four bodyguards killed in a subsequent shooting
Murder of a Dutch policeman	September 22, 1977	Knut Folkerts kills a Dutch police officer in Utrecht during a traffic control
Hijacking of LH airliner *Landshut*	October 13, 1977	Te *Landshut* is hijacked by a group of Palestinian terrorists to attain the release of the RAF Stammheim prisoners. Stormed on October 18 by German special police unit GSG 9 in Mogadishu
Schleyer killed in Mülhausen	October 18, 1977	Schleyer is discovered dead in a car, killed the day before by the RAF
Stammheim suicides	October 18, 1977	Baader, Ensslin, and Raspe commit suicide in the terrorist prison in Stuttgart-Stammheim
Suicide of Ingrid Schubert	November 12, 1977	Ingrid Schubert commits suicide by hanging in prison
Jürgen Ponto murder	July 30, 1977	Dresdner Bank CEO Ponto is shot in his house in Oberursel by the RAF
Attempted assault on NATO Supreme Allied Commander	June 25, 1979	A bomb attack on the NATO commander fails in Casteau, Belgium

that, besides one singular event when a bomb exploded during the 1980 Munich Oktoberfest, emerged as late as the 1990s and, for quite a while, was centered in the federal states of former Eastern Germany. Jewish sites (synagogues and community centers) and people, including Africans, Vietnamese, and other individuals of assumed foreign origin, were the main targets.

The most relevant statutes applicable for the prosecution of terrorist offenses are Articles 129 and 129a of the German Penal Code. First of all, Article 129, which traditionally had been the central organizational statutory offense in Germany, relates, in a more general manner, to the formation of criminal organizations. Section (1) provides that "whoever forms an organization, the objectives or activity of which are directed towards the commission of crimes, or whoever participates in such an organization as a member, recruits for it or supports it, shall be punished with imprisonment for not more than five years, or a fine." Additionally, Section (4) refers to serious cases by stipulating that imprisonment from six months to five years shall be imposed: "if the perpetrator is one of the ringleaders or supporters or there exists an especially serious case."

Through the Counterterrorism Act of August 1976,[9] an extra organizational offense with particular focus on terrorist groups was introduced. Article 129a at that time provided in its section (1) that

> (1) Whoever forms an organization, the objectives or activity of which are directed towards the commission of
>
> 1. Murder, manslaughter, or genocide
> 2. [Specified] crimes against personal liberty
> 3. [Specified] crimes dangerous to the public or whoever participates in such an organization as a member, supports it or recruits for it, shall be punished with imprisonment from six months to five years
>
> (2) If the perpetrator is one of the ringleaders or hintermen, then imprisonment for no less than three years shall be imposed.

In the following years, the provision was further amended, *inter alia*, by increasing the statutory penalties for the formation of the organization to imprisonment from one year to 10 years. Participation, recruitment, and support were formally upgraded to a separate section (3), providing the original sentencing range. Still, to date, Germany has no separate provision on the financing of terrorism. Based on case law interpretation established in the 1970s by the Federal Court of Appeals (the highest instance in criminal matters in Germany), these cases are regularly subsumed under the statutory alternative "support" as provided in the above-mentioned section (3) of Article 129a.[10]

The consequences taken by the legislature are completely different and much more complex with regard to the new international terrorism. Unfortunately, Germany has played a significant role as a "relaxation room" for the so-called "sleepers" of 9/11. In retrospect, it was found that Mohammad Atta and several other suicide pilots were living openly for some time in Hamburg, some of them as students. A remarkable number of other individuals were part of that "Hamburg Cell"; some of them were either tried in Germany or in the United States for conspiracy or concretely aiding and abetting the 9/11 murders (see Table 13.2). One of those people, Abdelghani Mzoudi, was finally acquitted at the last minute due to insufficient cooperation by US agencies, which were unwilling to disclose any of the relevant evidence to the German courts.[11,12]

---

[9] Antiterrorismusgesetz [Counterterrorism Act] of 18 August 1976, BGBl. I (*Federal Law Gazette*, part I), p. 2181.

[10] M. Kilchling. Rechtliche Instrumente zur Bekämpfung der Terrorismusfinanzierung im internationalen Vergleich. In G. Gehl (ed.), *Terrorismus—Kriegdes 21.* Jahrhunderts? Weimar, 2006, 87–113.

[11] L. Blaauw-Wolf. The Hamburg terror trials—American political poker and German legal procedure: An unlikely combination to fight international terrorism. *German Law Journal* 5: 791–828, 2004.

[12] C. J. M. Safferling. German Prosecution of 9/11—A Failure and Disappointment? *German Law Journal* 5: 515–524, 2004.

Table 13.2 List of 9/11-Related Proceedings and Suspicions in Germany

Name	Group	Date	Charges	Status
Mounir al Motassadeq	al-Qaeda/Hamburg Cell	11/01	Aiding to murder in 246 cases	15 years imprisonment
Abdelghani Mzoudi	al-Qaeda/Hamburg Cell	10/02	Aiding to murder in 3066 cases	Acquitted
Eight suspects	al-Qaeda/"Attawhid library"	07/02	No charge	Preliminary investigations
Mohammad Ali Hassan al-Mudschad	al-Qaeda	01/03	Conspiracy, support of al-Qaeda and Hamas	Extradited to the US, 75 years imprisonment
Mohammad Moschen Jahja Sajjid	al-Qaeda	01/03	Conspiracy, support of al-Qaeda and Hamas	Extradited to the US, 45 years imprisonment
Other Members of the Hamburg Cell				
Mohammad Atta	al-Qaeda	Pilot of fight AA 11, which hit the north tower of the WTC		
Marwan al-Shehhi	al-Qaeda	Pilot of fight UA 175, which hit the south tower of the WTC		
Said Bahaji	al-Qaeda	Wanted for the 9/11 attacks, still at large		
Ziad Jarrah	al-Qaeda	Pilot of fight UA 93, which crashed in Shanksville, Pennsylvania		
Ramzi Binalshibh	al-Qaeda	Arrested in 2002, probably held captive in Guantánamo		
Zakariya Essabar	al-Qaeda	Arrest warrant in Germany, still at large		

As a consequence of these facts, the German Penal Code was further amended in the course of the post-9/11 legislation through which the provisions on criminal and terrorist organizations (Articles 129 and 129a of the Penal Code) were further extended.[13] In addition, Article 129b was introduced, based on the fact that organizations having their main field of activity outside Germany can be tried here, too. This additional step was necessary because the related provisions had been designed and interpreted by the Federal Court of Appeals in accordance with the concrete history of the RAF terrorism of the 1970s—a fact that had the effect that only domestic groups could be tried on the basis of the traditional organizational offenses.[14] It is remarkable that prosecution related to groups from abroad is considered a matter of national interest and therefore subject of an *ex ante* authorization by the Federal Ministry of Justice. Article 129b now explicitly provides that

> (1) Art. 129 and 129a shall apply to organizations abroad. If the offence relates to an organization outside the member states of the European Union, this shall not apply unless the offence was committed by way of an activity exercised within the Federal Republic of Germany or if the offender or the victim is a German or is found within Germany. In cases that fall under the previous sentence the offence shall only be prosecuted on authorization by the Federal Ministry of Justice. Authorization may be granted for an individual case or in general for the prosecution of future offences relating to a specific organization. When deciding whether to give authorizations, the Federal Ministry of Justice shall take into account whether the aims of the organization are directed against the fundamental values of a state order which respects human dignity or against the peaceful coexistence of nations and which appear reprehensible when weighing all the circumstances of the case.

After the 2002 amendment, the statutory offense of Article 129a reads as follows:[15]

> (1) Whosoever forms an organization whose aims or activities are directed at the commission of
>   1. Murder under specific aggravating circumstances, murder or genocide or a crime against humanity or a war crime
>   2. [Specified] crimes against personal liberty, or whosoever participates in such a group as a member shall be liable to imprisonment from one to ten years
>
> (2) The same penalty shall be incurred by any person who forms an organization whose aims or activities are directed at
>   1. Causing serious physical or mental harm to another person
>   2. Committing [specified] offences endangering the general public
>   3. Committing [specified] offences against the environment under §330a (1) to (3)
>   4. Committing [specified] offences under the Weapons of War (Control) Act
>   5. Committing [specified] offences under the Weapons Act; or by any person who participates in such a group as a member, if one of the offences stipulated in no. 1 to 5 is intended to seriously intimidate the population, to unlawfully coerce a public authority or an international organization through the use of force or the threat of the use of force, or to significantly impair or destroy the fundamental political, constitutional, economic or social structures of a state or an international organization, and which, given the nature or consequences of such offences, may seriously damage a state or an international organization.

---

[13] 34th Penal Code Amendment Act of 22 August 2002, BGBl. I (*Federal Law Gazette*, part I), p. 3390.

[14] H. Meyer. *Terror und innere Sicherheit—Wandel und Kontinuität staatlicher Terrorismusbekämpfung*. Münster, 2006.

[15] Translation taken from M. Bohlander, *The German Criminal Code. A Modern English Translation*, Oxford, UK: Hart, 2008.

(3) If the aims or activities of the group are directed at threatening the commission of one of the offences listed in subsection (1) or (2) above, the penalty shall be imprisonment from six months to five years.
(4) If the offender is one of the ringleaders or hintermen the penalty shall be imprisonment of not less than three years in cases under subsections (1) and (2) above, and imprisonment from one to ten years in cases under subsection (3) above.
(5) Whosoever supports a group as described in subsections (1), (2) or (3) above shall be liable to imprisonment from six months to ten years in cases under subsections (1) and (2), and to imprisonment of not more than five years or in fine in cases under subsection (3). Whosoever recruits members or supporters for a group as described in subsection (1) or subsection (2) above shall be liable to imprisonment from six months to five years.
(6)–(9) [...].

The statutory offense now covers all crimes and complies with the "minimum maximum penalties" provided by the EU Framework Decision on Combating Terrorism.[16,17] Furthermore, totally new elements can be identified: In particular, the legal definition provided in the last sentence of section (2), and the extension of punishability to the recruitment of supporters according to section (5). In the past, only recruitment of group members was prohibited.

Meanwhile, the state of security in Germany became more precarious. Quite obviously, the country is no longer a "relaxation room." On the contrary, it has become a target, too. In recent times, several threats were prevented through the arrest of suspects (see Table 13.3). The most ominous incidents so far were certainly that of the Cologne suitcase bombers and the uncovered plans intended by the so-called Sauerland Group. In the Cologne case, the suitcase bombs were placed in two commuter trains; in the Sauerland case, it seems that the police stepped in right before the bombs were filled with the fluid explosives for immediate use.

Unlike the early groups, the "new" terrorism is considered to be a deindividualized phenomenon that constitutes a new form of terrorist threat.[18] As a result, a whole set of measures that go beyond the "classical" penal and criminal procedural focus by which the former domestic terrorism was addressed have now passed the legislature. A number of these legislative initiatives have direct relevance to the field of border control.

Rudimentary Control Regime: Germany's Border Security in the Schengen Open Border Era

Before the developments in border control policies and legislation are presented in more detail, the principles of the legal and factual framework for border controls in Germany will be briefly outlined. This is considered because, as part of the general trend toward unification in Europe, the border regimes have already been subject to a dramatic change for more than two decades. In order to establish a "common area of freedom, security and justice" as proclaimed at the Tampere summit of the European Council in 1999,[19] it is common policy of most European governments that all border controls between the member states should be abolished.

This principle and the related legal and practical consequences have been laid down in the Schengen Open Border Agreement of 1985[20] and in several subsequent intergovernmental

---

[16] Council Framework Decision of 13 June 2002 on Combating Terrorism (2002/475/JHA), O.J. No. L 164, pp. 3–7.

[17] E. Dimitriu. The E.U.'s Definition of Terrorism: The Council Framework Decision on Combating Terrorism. *German Law Journal* 5: 585–602, 2004.

[18] O. Lepsius. Liberty, Security, and Terrorism: The Legal Position in Germany. *German Law Journal* 5: 436–460, 2004.

[19] See, for example, COM/2000/0167 final.

[20] The Schengen Treaty and related texts can be obtained from the EU documentation on the Schengen Acquis, O.J. no. L 239 of 22 September 2000.

Table 13.3 List of Other Arrests and Trials Related to al-Qaeda and the New Islamic Terrorism

Event	Affiliation	Date	Arrested Suspects	Notes	Charges
Strasbourg Christmas market	al-Qaeda	12-00	Aerobui Baendali Lamine Maroni Fouhad Sabour Salim Boukhari	Sentenced to 10 to 12 years imprisonment	Planning of bombing of the Strasbourg Christmas market
Alawi assault	Ansar-el Islam	12-04	Ata R. Mazen A. H. Rafk Y.	Sentenced to 7.5 to 10 years imprisonment	Planning of assault of former Iraqi prime minister during Berlin visit
Düsseldorf al-Qaeda trial	al-Qaeda	1-05	Ibrahim Mohamed K. Yasser Abu S. Ismael Abu S.	Sentenced to 3.5 to 7 years imprisonment	Planning of terrorist attacks in Iraq
Gelsenkirchen attack		8-06	Eight suspects	No arrest warrant due to lack of evidence	Planning of the bombing of a tanker ship
Cologne Suitcase Bombers		7-06	Youssef Mohamed al-Hajdib, Fadil el S., Dschihad Hamad and two additional Lebanese	Hajdib sentenced to life imprisonment in first instance; appeal currently pending. Fadi el S. was acquitted. The other three are imprisoned in Lebanon	Attempted bombing of two regional trains in Cologne and Dortmund
Sauerland Group	Islamic Dshihad Union	7-06	Fritz Gelowicz Adem Yilmaz Daniel Schneider	Currently on trial in Düsseldorf	Planning of several terrorist attacks on targets in Germany
Arrest of an Algerian		7-02		Arrested in Stuttgart	Wanted for various charges of extremism and terrorism in France

(*continued*)

Table 13.3 List of Other Arrests and Trials Related to al-Qaeda and the New Islamic Terrorism (Continued)

Event	Affiliation	Date	Arrested Suspects	Notes	Charges
House search and arrests		10-02	Several suspects	Premises in several states were searched, several suspects arrested	Planning of terrorist attacks in Germany; membership in a terrorist association
House search and arrests		2-03	Four suspects	Premises in several states were searched, four suspects arrested	Planning of terrorist attacks in Germany; membership in a terrorist association
Arrest in Gelsenkirchen		3-03	One suspect	Acquitted due to lack of evidence	Membership in a terrorist association
House searches in various states		1-05	Eleven suspects	Eleven suspects arrested during a razzia	Membership in a terrorist association
Arrest in Munich		4-05	Two suspects	Suspicious of financing of al-Qaeda	Financing of terrorism
Arrest in Marburg		4-05	Ismail Abu S.	Suspicious of planning terrorist attacks	Planning of terrorist attacks in Germany; membership in a terrorist association
Arrest in Osnabrück		10-06	Ibrahim R.	Broadcasting audio and video messages from Osama bin Laden	Membership in a terrorist association
Arrest in Frankfurt		6-07	Burhan B.	Arrested at airport prior to journey to Jordan	Membership in a terrorist association
Arrest in Frankfurt	Islamic Jihad Union (IJU)	9-08	Hüseyin Ö. Omid S.	Associated with the Sauerland Group	Attempt to construct bombs with various chemical components
Arrest at Cologne airport	Islamic Jihad Union (IJU)	09-08	Omar D. Abdirazak B.	Arrested in KLM aircraft, suspected of traveling to a jihad training camp in Pakistan	Membership in a terrorist association

treaties, all named after Schengen, Luxemburg, where the original treaty was signed. The Treaty ultimately aims to establish total freedom of movement for everybody within and between the "Schengen countries" without any kind of border control by police or customs authorities. Although closely linked to the European Union, the Schengen Agreement is formally an independent intergovernmental system of border management that, on the one hand, includes several non-EU partners, such as Iceland, Norway, and recently Switzerland; on the other hand, some of the EU member states, such as Ireland and the United Kingdom, have decided not to join the Schengen Acquis.

This development also had consequences for the visa regime. In addition to the traditional national visa, any member state can also issue Schengen visas based on which foreigners enjoy the same freedom as citizens to move between and to stay within any of the Schengen states. In addition, as a consequence of the fact that entrance control has moved to the external borders, even a national visa allows for entry in and transit through another member state to the state of final destination that has issued the national visa.

According to the Schengen Codex,[21] member states have only restricted possibilities to temporarily suspend the non-control principle in urgent situations of security relevance. In recent years, this has, in fact, been the case. For example, following the initiative of the French government, after the London bombings of July 2005, border controls were reintroduced at the French-German border until February 2006. During that period, French border police forces were closely supported by the German Federal Police. In addition to such terrorism-related reinforcement of control, other examples with direct security relevance were in evidence as well. Germany has thus far suspended non-control twice, during the 2006 FIFA football world championship and the G8 summit of 2007[22] and Austria during the UEFA European football championship in 2008.

Since the accession of Switzerland to the Schengen Treaty, Germany has no more external land borders.[23] All borders between Germany and its neighbors have been downgraded bit by bit to control-free internal borders in the course of the Schengen process. Additional external borders that are formally relevant in our context are, first, the seaports. However, freight control is the most important issue there, much more important than passenger control. For sea cruises, lists of passengers and crew members now have to be transmitted in advance.[22]

Second, with respect to passenger control in particular, airports have, without doubt, the largest practical impact both in terms of quantity and quality. Airports today have the highest priority for border control policies, as airports are, at the same time, internal and external borders. Whereas in 2007, the German seaports counted some 12.57 million passengers,[24] German airport authorities counted some 183.58 million people arriving or departing from the 17 international airports;[25] of these, 62.53 million were Schengen passengers.[26] The quantitative differences also become obvious when looking at the numbers of illegal entries: only 136 of

[21] Regulation (EC) No. 562/2006 of 15 March 2006, O.J. no. L 105, p. 1.

[22] Federal Ministry of the Interior. Bundesministerium des Innern 2008. Schengen Erfahrungsbericht 2005–2007. http://www.bmi.bund.de, 2008.

[23] Switzerland's accession to Schengen became operational on 12 December 2008 for the land borders and on 25 March 2009 for the airport control regime.

[24] German Marine Office. Bundesmarine, Jahresbericht 2007—Kennzahlen zurmaritimen Abhängigkeit der Bundesrepublik Deutschland. http://www.dmkn-beta, 2008.

[25] Another 5.79 million passengers traveled through regional airports.

[26] German Airport Association. Arbeitsgemeinschaft Deutscher Verkehrsflughäfen (ADV). 2008. Verkehrsergebnisse der internationalen Flughäfen—2007. http://www.adv.aero/download/presse/kumulierte_Werte_07.pdfde/gfx/daten_nat.php.

such incidents were registered in all seaports in the first half of 2007 as opposed to some 1391 at airports.[27]

Initially, Schengen-related control reduction included the deconstruction of barriers not only at any land borders but at airports as well. In accordance with the Schengen Treaty, European governments also aimed at abolishing all passport controls for air passengers coming from or leaving for another Schengen member state. This principle was implemented by establishing a dual system for passenger transfers at all airports in the Schengen countries, allowing for control-free passage except for the general security check, which is a procedure more or less exclusively conducted by private agencies under the control of the civil airport authorities. However, this initial idea has undergone quite a significant transition since 9/11: For departing passengers, passport controls once again became a regular procedure even though they are conducted today mostly by civil airport or airline staff rather than by police personnel. Depending on the location, double or even triple ID checks have become common before one has reached the gangway or aircraft. The originally intended universal "Schengen liberties" can nowadays mainly be enjoyed by passengers upon arrival.

One can say that today, the prevention of potential terrorists getting access to aircraft has higher priority than the prevention of terrorists entering the country by air. The latter aim is more subject to general police activities. With regard to border control, this can, of course, work only under the premise that terrorists come from outside the Schengen area and will be identified and caught when trying to enter via an external border. At both land and air borders, all passengers arriving from outside are strictly controlled. This includes an immediate check through the electronic Schengen Information System (SIS) or a prior SIS check, which is routine prior to the issuing of a Schengen visa. Probable domestic terrorists (citizens or persons from abroad with residence in a Schengen country, such as the "sleepers" or other members of the Hamburg Cell during the planning and preparation phase of the 9/11 attacks), however, fall out of the system and, therefore, are subject to other, internal control regimes, which will be discussed in more detail below.

Developments in Border Control Legislation and Policies Related to Terrorism

In addition to the general developments based on the European Schengen Acquis, the most significant changes in border control legislation and policies in Germany have their cause indeed in post-9/11 anti-terrorism initiatives. These policies have been developed in light of, and as a consequence of, the Schengen process, which can be summarized as a radical, long-term cutback of border controls. Citizens now have the freedom to travel freely, crossing any national border between the member states free of police and customs control. Incoming travelers from outside enjoy the same freedom once controlled at the first external border of the Schengen area.

However, measures have been introduced in order to substitute for the loss of control facilities. One of those instruments was introduced with the Schengen Treaty itself, which provides the legal basis for so-called suspect-free controls. In a first step, it allows police to stop and check any individual at any time within a zone of 30 kilometers from an internal border (so called mobile border controls).[28] The federal states of Bavaria and Baden-Württemberg allowed their police forces such suspect-free controls even beyond these 30 kilometers, followed by other

[27] Federal Ministry of the Interior. Bundesministerium des Innern 2008. Schengen Erfahrungsbericht 2005–2007. www.bmi.bund.de, 2008.

[28] In order to prevent states from introducing new "relocated" inland border control regimes as a substitute for the abolished ones, neither regular nor systematic controls are allowed (Art. 24 of the Schengen Treaty of 1985 and Art. 99 of the Convention for the Implementation of the Schengen Treaty of 1990).

states. In May 1998, the federal parliament passed a bill that allowed such controls on a general basis, which, in essence, transformed the country into a great border territory.[29]

With special attention given to the coastlines, the border control area was significantly extended. Instead of the regular 30 kilometers, control activities are allowed within a 50-kilometer zone; in addition, the Federal Ministry of the Interior was given the power to extend by decree, whenever necessary, the 50 to 80 kilometer zone.[30] These extensions aim at providing sufficient room for security controls even in coastal regions with a meandering borderline characterized by tideland, bays, river mouths, etc., which obviously have caused practical problems in the past.[31]

This latter amendment was part of a total of three legislative "packages," thus far (the national "security" or "anti-terrorism packages," which have been implemented by the national legislature since 2001). Each of these packages was comprised of an array of concrete regulatory elements. The first one provided three measures that have a direct link to border control. In addition to the aforementioned extension of the control belt in seashore areas, airport security was enhanced by introducing a mandatory security check of all airport personnel. In addition to information from the internal and external secret services, even information taken from the files of the former GDR's ministry of state security can be used in monitoring and security checks, especially when new employees are hired. And finally, fingerprints were introduced as part of visa procedures. More generally, police and other security agencies were furnished with additional financial funds of €1.5 billion for staff and equipment.[32] In order to raise the necessary income, tobacco and several other taxes were raised through an explicit Financing of Counterterrorism Act.[33] An additional element of the package was the amendment of the offense statutes on terrorism conduct (see above), notwithstanding the fact that it was implemented through a separate piece of legislation.

The second step was the implementation of the Combating Terrorism Act of 2002.[34] Unlike the "first package," which had its focus mainly on repressive measures, the "second package" centered on the preventive area.[35] Consisting of approximately 100 regulations by which 17 different laws, statutes, and statutory orders were amended or introduced, it can be considered as the main piece of direct post-9/11 legislation in Germany. In particular, the powers of the federal internal secret services (Federal Intelligence Service[36] and Federal Office for the Protection of the Constitutional Order),[37] of the external secret service (Military Counterespionage Service)[38] and of the Federal Criminal Police Office (BKA) were extended.

The new competencies clearly go beyond traditional "strategic" information. They can now retrieve data from banks, postal offices, telephone companies, and airlines. All these powers aim at providing border control agencies with information to identify individuals having contact to extremist groups. Furthermore, operational data exchange regarding actions or movements of

---

[29] BT-Drucksache 13/10790 of 26 May 1998.

[30] Art. 2 of the Federal Police Act [Bundespolizeigesetz].

[31] K.-H. Blümel, M. Drewes, and K. M. Malmberg. *Bundespolizeigesetz kommentar*, Third Edition. Stuttgart, Munich, Hanover, Berlin, Weimar, Dresden: § 2 annot. 45, 2006.

[32] H. Meyer. *Terror und innere Sicherheit—Wandel und Kontinuität staatlicher Terrorismusbekämpfung*. Münster, 2006.

[33] Financing of Counterterrorism Act [Gesetz zur Finanzierung der Terrorbekämpfung] of 10 December 2001, BGBl. I (*Federal Law Gazette*, part I), p. 3436.

[34] Combating Terrorism Act [Terrorismusbekämpfungsgesetz] of 9 January 2002, BGBl. I (*Federal Law Gazette*, part I), p. 361.

[35] O. Lepsius. Liberty, Security, and Terrorism: The Legal Position in Germany. *German Law Journal* 5: 436–460, 2004.

[36] Bundesnachrichtendienst–BND.

[37] Bundesamt für Verfassungsschutz–BfV.

[38] Militärischer Abschirmdienst–MAD.

terrorist persons or networks, forged or falsified travel documents, and weapons was improved. Alien law and asylum law was amended in order to prevent counterfeiting, forgery, and fraudulent use of identity papers and travel documents and to ensure that refugee status is not abused by terrorists by not recognizing political motivation as a ground for refusing requests for extradition of alleged terrorists. Additional measures aimed at advancing identification techniques through biometric features in order to facilitate identity checks and to further improve border controls. And finally, having armed air marshals from the Federal Border Security Guard on board German vessels was introduced.

Besides all these legal regulations of the second antiterrorism package, which deal with very specific matters, there was an important organizational change that, without doubt, brought the most significant and far-reaching change to the security architecture in Germany. On July 1, 2005, the Federal Police was set up.[39] This change is so fundamental because it undermines the traditional division of power between the federal and the state level as provided by the constitution, a division partly abolished now. As a consequence of the negative experiences during the Third Reich, a centralized national police force would best be prohibited in the future. Therefore, policing became the exclusive power of the federal states. Besides the Federal Criminal Police Office, which originally was not more than a clearing and coordination agency without any direct executive power, there existed only two centralized federal agencies with, limited, police powers; these were the former Border Security Guard (*Bundesgrenzschutz*) and the former Railroad Police Guard (*Bahnpolizei*). These two agencies were transformed into the new Federal Police (*Bundespolizei*).

According to Article 2 of the Federal Police Act, the Federal Police has exclusive responsibility for border security. This includes not only border protection in its traditional sense but the prevention of any kind of endangerment of public security and public order in connection with border transit.[40] Whereas the field of activity of the former border security guard was restricted to the prevention of threats coming from outside the borders into Germany, the new Federal Police is responsible now for any kind of threat or danger irrespective of whether a concrete threat has its origin inside or outside the country. By enlarging the scope of responsibility, the German legislature aimed to ensure that, in the post-9/11 era, export of hazardous material shall be prevented as intensively as the importation of hazardous material. Hence, in qualitative terms, the new agency has full police powers, which means that a second, parallel, police structure was established. Besides border control, the Federal Police is also responsible for the security at the 17 international airports, in all national railway stations, on board German aircrafts, and in Lufthansa premises worldwide. However, border control does not necessarily have to be conducted by officers from this agency. The law provides that border control can be devolved to the customs authorities (Article 68 of the Federal Police Act) (a devolution of competency that is of high practical impact). In order to be even better prepared to counter terrorist threats, the Federal Police was the subject of a fundamental reorganization of its structures, which became effective on May 1, 2008. In addition to traditional border control, the Federal Police is involved in a variety of different supra-national cooperation structures, such as the European border agency FRONTEX, the railway police network COLPOFER, and the Baltic Sea Region Border Control BSRBCC.

The Federal Police is also involved in a further organizational innovation aimed at improving the fight against the "new" international terrorism, which was introduced in December 2004 when the Joint Terror Defense Center in Berlin (GTAZ)[41] was established. Besides the denomination as such—the Center's function is threat assessment rather than "defense" in its

---

[39] Act on the Renaming of the Border Security Guard into Federal Police [Gesetz zur Umbenennung des Bundesgrenzschutzes in Bundespolizei] of 21 June 2005, BGBl. I (*Federal Law Gazette*, part I), p. 1818.

[40] K.-H. Blümel, M. Drewes, and K. M. Malmberg. *Bundespolizeigesetz kommentar*, Third Edition. Stuttgart, Munich, Hanover, Berlin, Weimar, Dresden: § 2 annot. 45, 2006.

[41] Gemeinsames Terrorabwehrzentrum.

generic meaning—it is also remarkable that this is the first institution in Germany in which all authorities that are involved in matters related to terrorism cooperate on a daily basis. The purpose of the Center is the bundling of all information gathered by the different institutions and the strengthening of the competence of analysis.[42] Besides the practical aspects, this new institution signifies even a double breach with the fundamental, previously irrevocable, principles of the division of power. Since the foundation of the Federal Republic of Germany in 1949, there was consensus about the necessity of a strict separation of state police and security and other agencies on the federal level; even stricter was that of police from intelligence services.

Notwithstanding this historical "taboo," officers from the Federal Criminal Police Office, the Federal Intelligence Service, the Federal Office for the Protection of the Constitutional Order, the Military Counterespionage Service, the State Police Offices, the State Offices for the Protection of the Constitutional Order, the Federal Police, the Customs Police Office, the Federal Attorney General, and the Federal Agency for Migration and Refugees now regularly meet in the GTAZ. In addition to the daily briefings that aim at rapid exchange of information, the GTAZ's agenda includes operational planning, situational analyses, and long-term threat analyses as well. The setting up of this service is in line with a general development in Europe toward the institutionalization of multi-agency bodies in counter-terrorism matters.[43] At a European level, Europol usually is an additional key player at such meetings.

In order to provide a better data basis for the joint center in Berlin as well as for local police authorities, a new joint database was set up in September 2006. Its legal basis is provided by the Joint Database Act,[44] which allows for the exchange and joint use of data that traditionally had been restricted for internal use by the recording authority only. Based on the new system, scattered data on the marital status, profession, telephone and banking information, knowledge of weapon possession, and the religious affiliations of suspects can be provided by the system upon request.[45] In the political debate, the latter item was the subject of the most intensive controversies.[46] In most of Europe, public sensitivity toward this issue is high and can be compared to that of the race issue in the United States and other countries. In March 2007, the database was officially opened by the Federal Minister of the Interior.

The most recent legal activity with relevance in our particular context is the third "anti-terrorism package," called the Combating Terrorism Extension Act.[47] It amends several laws, such as the acts concerning the Federal Intelligence Service, the Federal Office for the Protection of the Constitutional Order, and the Military Counterespionage Service, the telecommunications interception laws, the air security act, the street traffic law, the law on private associations, the customs law, and the passport law. In addition to data of post and telephone companies and financial institutions, the aforementioned security authorities now also have access to information from airlines concerning names and addresses, all relevant transport details, and booking details. Unlike in the United States, information on religion and dietary

---

[42] H.-J. Kerner, C. Stierle, and I. Tiedtke. Kriminalitätsbekämpfung durch Behörden des Bundes—Ein Überblick über nationale, europäische und internationale Elemente. *Kriminalistik*: 292–304, 2006.

[43] R. Neve, L. Vervoorn, F. Leeuw, and S. Bogaerts. First Inventory of Policy on Counterterrorism. WODC Cahier 2006-3a. The Hague, 2006.

[44] Gesetz zur Errichtung gemeinsamer Dateien von Polizeibehörden und Nachrichtendiensten des Bundes und der Länder (Gemeinsame-Dateien-Gesetz) [Joint Database Act] of 22 December 2006, BGBl. I (*Federal Law Gazette*, part I), p. 3409.

[45] H. Meyer. *Terror und innere Sicherheit—Wandel und Kontinuität staatlicher Terrorismusbekämpfung*. Münster, 2006.

[46] F. Roggan. Die "neue Sicherheitsarchitektur" der Bundesrepublik Deutschland—Anti-Terror-Datei, gemeinsame Projektdaten und Terrorismusbekämpfungsgesetz. *Neue Juristische Wochenschrift*: 876–881, 2007.

[47] Terrorismusbekämpfungsergänzungsgesetz [Combating Terrorism Extension Act] of 5 January 2007, BGBl. I (*Federal Law Gazette*, part I), p. 593.

habits is not yet the subject of surveillance. In the future, biometric data will also be used for the issuance of passports; before this recent amendment, this data was only necessary for the visa procedure.

In addition to the national developments summarized before, a new international initiative with a specific focus on the transnational prosecution and prevention of terrorism within the control-free Schengen area was launched. The 2005 Prüm Convention, named after the small town in the Eifel Mountains in the federal state of Rhineland Palatinate, is an intergovernmental European treaty between Austria, the Benelux countries, France, Germany, and Spain. It deals with the strengthening of police cooperation, cross-border cooperation, and data exchange in matters of terrorism, cross-border crime, and illegal migration and will have a significant impact on the development of the security architecture in Europe. This convention is very interesting as it may develop in the same way in which the Schengen Treaty once did (that is, it may encourage other EU member states to join). Sometimes titled "Schengen III," the Prüm Convention (also called the Prüm Treaty) certainly has the potential to become a kind of replay of Schengen[48] and to become, sooner or later, part of the EU *acquis*. Indeed, in June 2007, the European Commission published a decision according to which great parts of the Prüm Convention should be integrated in to the *acquis communautaire*.[49]

Chapter 3 of the convention pertains to the prevention of terrorism and provides, for example, the transmission of personal data of persons who might commit terrorist actions to any police or justice service of any of the signatories without any previous requirement. This is a very obvious and very important change regarding the rules of information transfer between European countries.[50] More generally, the Prüm Convention grants the member states and their police forces the possibility to require and above all to retrieve any information available in any other member state. This "availability principle" can lead to a mutual openness of the data. Although this principle had been evoked within the EU Commission before,[51] it is the Prüm Convention that actually turned this principle into life and reality and made it enter into the real practice of police forces. In fact, it provides disposability of data for a much wider range of objectives (that is, many more global objectives, such as the prevention of crime and the maintenance of order during public events). This may produce problems concerning both national and EU laws for the treaty application although the Prüm Convention itself assumes the supremacy of EU rules over those of the Prüm Convention.

Concerning the internal Schengen borders, cooperation centers have been established since 1997, when the first German-French cooperation center was set up in Kehl, Germany.[52] Since then, many of these centers have developed alongside internal borders in Europe, and some attempts have been made after 9/11 for them to receive additional powers in the general fight against terrorism. However, except for the very specific case of the cooperation centers in the French-Spanish border region, none of the other actors in the field of counterterrorism was willing to share such powers. The lack of human resources and the regional anchorage of those centers, as well as the fear of central services being ignored by the network of such centers in the EU, have been very strong factors in keeping the centers away from this field of activity.

[48] G. Bonvicini. The Treaty of Prüm—A Replay of Schengen? Available at http://www.europeum.org/ess2008/doc/w1r2.pdf, 2007.

[49] EU Press Document, IP 07/803 of 12 June 2007.

[50] F. Dehousse and D. Sifflet. Les nouvelles perspectives de la cooperation Schengen. *Studia Diplomatica* vol. LIX/2: 199–212, 2006.

[51] O.J. no. C 187 of 03.07.2001.

[52] A. Maguer. Les frontières intérieures Schengen, dilemmes et stratégies de la coopération policière et douanière franco-allemande. *Freiburg im Breisgau*, 2004.

Last, but not least, some side aspects of other international counterterrorism initiatives that have some impact on border control practices should be mentioned here in brief.[53] These include, for example, the previously mentioned EU Framework Decision on Combating Terrorism, the European Arrest Warrant, and the array of rules and guidelines concerning money laundering control, which, as a more or less direct policy reaction to the 9/11 events, include the financing of terrorism, too, either as a component of or as an equivalent to money laundering in its traditional sense.[54] The most important issue of border security that will also be addressed in more detail below is the cash controls according to the FATF 40 plus 9 recommendations. This instrument was adopted by the European Union through a binding regulation[55] and implemented in Germany in Article 12a s. 2 of the Customs Act.

Impact of Border-Related Security Reforms

The impact of all the border-related security reforms as outlined above can be analyzed from different perspectives. Our focus of this section is twofold. The first one is that of the travelers in particular and the citizens in general. The second one is the sphere of police and other control forces.

Impact on Travelers and Citizens

The importance of the border as a line to be crossed by persons and goods has completely changed over time, and paper travel documents are no longer as important in the context of border crossing. Whereas they have lost weight, the importance of electronic control technologies has grown. The very control of traveling people and above all the one that is operated by the post-industrial countries—the United States and Western Europe first—is achieved long before the travelers have even reached the border they want to cross. Thanks to electronic technology, biometric data can be obtained by the control forces in a shorter time than the physical travel takes.[56] The paper document does not matter anymore once the "virtual or electronic profile" of the traveling person has satisfied the security criteria of the control forces. It is not the crossing of the border, and therefore not the border, that is of relevance in this context anymore but the movement of persons as such. This is true above all for the control policies in the United States, which have been partially disconnected with the actual crossing of their territorial borders. In Europe, and especially in Germany, under the Schengen system, the link between border crossing and control still prevails, however, with a strong focus on the border of the European Union, which has been crossed first by the traveler, especially in the case of a non-EU citizen traveling.

Article 17 of the Prüm Convention provides the presence of armed police forces to be allowed on board airplanes and in some of the airport zones but does not regulate precisely whether or how they may be able to intervene. As a matter of fact, in Germany, the actual prevention of danger in the air depends on the intervention of the Federal Air Force (*Luftwaffe*), and only on it. One major reason is that it is the only armed force to dispose of the actual means of prevention and defense in the air environment.[57] Some authors have therefore asked the question whether

---

[53] For more details, see H.-J. Albrecht, Counterterrorism policies in Germany. Research in brief/forschung aktuell No. 38. Max Planck Institute for Foreign and International Criminal Law. Available at http://www.mpicc.de/ww/de/ext/forschung/publikationen/forschungaktuell.htm, 2006.

[54] M. Kilchling. Rechtliche Instrumente zur Bekämpfung der Terrorismusfinanzierung im internationalen Vergleich. In G. Gehl (ed.), *Terrorismus—Kriegdes* 21. Jahrhunderts? Weimar, 2006, 87–113.

[55] Regulation (EC) No. 1889/2005 of 26 October 2005 on controls of cash entering or leaving the Community, O.J. no. L 309, p. 9.

[56] D. Bigo. Contrôle et mobilité des personnes. *Revue de la gendarmerie Nationale*, 2è trimestre 2008: 35–42, 2008.

[57] K. Paulke. *Die Abwehr von Terrorgefahren im Luftraum*. Hamburg, 2005.

there may be after all the possibility for the state governments to employ their own regional police forces as sky marshals, like the federal government. Either way, the presence of armed police forces during a flight and the changing rules to be observed in the air defense management in Germany can generate some feelings of insecurity among passengers. Indeed, regarding the rules to be observed toward civilian airplanes, some aspects of the air defense have changed in German law. In particular, it has to be underlined that, under the 2004 Air Security Act, armed air forces are authorized, under strong conditions, to make use of their specific weapons against a civilian airplane.

Another change regarding the scope, or target, of border control that has a significant impact on travelers relates to the cash control regime. Since 2005, people who want to travel into or out of the national territory have to declare to a Customs agent when they are carrying €10,000 or more in cash. Moreover, the Customs officers may conduct physical controls on persons, luggage, and cars in order to search for, and seize, undeclared cash. Recently, a coordinated control action—Operation Athena—was conducted in the first week of September 2008 at the German-Swiss border, including transborder trains, and at all 17 national airports. During the operation, and for its particular purpose, customs checked some 13,000 persons, searched some 22,000 pieces of luggage, and seized some €5.5 million.[58] In the course of such controls, the use of sniffer dogs specialized in detecting money is a regular instrument.[59] Thus, based on legal provisions introduced to tackle the financing of terrorism, a great number of travelers are affected by such controls that, unofficially but clearly, have tax evaders as their main target, not terrorists. It was reported that airports were temporarily blocked while Operation Athena was going on.[60]

More generally, many authors have seen serious long-term consequences of 9/11 for foreigners, especially in Germany. This might affect not only those who are traveling but also, and maybe even first of all, those who have been living for years in Germany.[61] All foreigners living in Germany, as well as their German family members, have to register themselves in the central registration system for foreigners. This administration tool has been, in many ways, criticized for being discriminatory and viewed as a universal instrument of state control upon a very precise category of the population in Germany. This tool has been said by some authors to have been used in an increasing manner after 9/11.[61] Indeed, the personal data registered in this central file can be sent to any of the federal and state services that may require pieces of information from it (social services, police, custom services, etc.). This central registration service functions just as a second control tool after the border crossing, and as such, may be even more efficient than border controls because of its universal (federal, interstate, and interservices) availability.

Legal changes have tightened the entry and living condition of foreigners in Germany. The new immigration law of 2004 often has been seen as a law on security immigration limitation. This new law allows quicker expulsions under the suspicion of extremism and provides for a wider range of grounds for expulsion. Moreover, since 2005, no appeal can be filed against an expulsion decision of the Federal Administrative Court.

It has been noted that police controls of Muslim people have increased in the past few years, and some doubts have been expressed whether they may even cause more trouble than security. The power to control anyone without any precise cause for suspicion was introduced in Germany in the 1990s, as a compensation for the disappearance of systematic physical controls at the federal borders. Ever since this method of control was implemented, it was observed that those most concerned by these controls were actually foreign-looking persons. Indeed, the

---

[58] Available at http://www.zoll.de/f0_veroeffentlichungen/f0_sonstiges/w0_2008/z28_bargeldkontrolle/index.html.

[59] Focus-Money 43/2008, 84; see http://www.focus.de/finanzen/steuern/tid-12233/bargeldkontrollen-seite-2-kritische-grenzen_aid_342866.html; see also http://www.focus.de/finanzen/steuern/zoll-schwarzgeld-schnueffler-auf-vier-pfoten_aid_334542.html.

[60] For further details, see http://www.focus.de/politik/deutschland/schmuggel-operation-athena_aid_334680.html.

[61] R. Gössner. *Menschenrechte in zeiten des terrors*. Hamburg, 2007.

disappearance of border controls have never been thematized as a possible cause of increasing terrorism but only of increasing petty crime and above all of illegal immigration.

In addition, governmental representatives have never argued that border controls are an effective tool in the fight against terrorism, and it is unlikely that it should be seen any more as such. This is even true with regard to airports, as it has to be considered that their particular impact and security relevance arise from the fact that they are direct or indirect targets for terrorists. In fact, administrative tools as well as the policies tend to complicate both immigration issues and terrorism problems[62] and dissolve both issues into the same bunch. This is particularly true for the EU member states' policies toward Africa. In this framework, the fight against terrorism has led the EU member states to policies that might negatively affect the intended securitization of EU territory. The development of conditional aid as well as the increasing costs that are imposed on African immigrants especially might generate more frustrations and the very threat that the European governments fear.[63]

Impact for Police and Control Forces

The events of 9/11 have prompted many EU countries to introduce many significant changes to their national security strategies and policies. Since the events of 9/11, governments have been considering that internal and external security did not need to be dissociated in security policies. In Germany, it has to lead to an increasing effectiveness of the use of prevention and early recognition tools against terrorist threats.[63] This change has to be accomplished by an increased exchange of data and by strategies that became possible through the linking up of all security and intelligence offices at all governmental levels. For some authors, this change has been particularly drastic, especially in regard to the Federal Office for the Protection of the Constitution, the Military Counterespionage Service, and the Federal Intelligence Service, which still were, at least partly, structured according to the Cold War way of working—that is, above all in mutual dissociation from any other security service and secrecy.[63] For the other German security services, this, in turn, may have been less virulent because the federal structure in Germany was always characterized by a very high level of networking. The most important change came with the growing weight of the federal level within the German security system. In many ways, the security services at the federal level obtained, or anchored, their supremacy over various security fields, in particular the fight against terrorism. Therefore, it can be said that it is just a consequence of the fact that the borders have lost their strategic importance as control territories within the European Union that federal bodies have been searching for new paths to retain control in the field of security and possibly to increase their role and weight in this context.

The first of these changes refers to the above-mentioned transformation of the former Border Security Guard into the Federal Police. A number of authors have considered this change as an attempt by the federal government to establish a generalist police service that stands in direct competition—not to say rivalry—with the traditional state police services.[64] It has been argued that, on the contrary, the Federal Police should not be authorized to abandon its quality as a specialized police force to become a general security force; even the new name Federal Police received critical comments.[64]

The second major trend for the German control services affects the military. There have been discussions on the competency of the military forces to prevent or combat dangers in cases

[62] R. Dover. Towards a Common EU Immigration Policy: A Securitization Too Far. *European Integration*, 30, no. 1: 113–130, 2008.

[63] C. A. von Denkowski. Herausforderung des 21. Jahrhunderts: Schutz des Staates im asymetrischen Konflikt. In P. Nitschke (ed.), *Globaler terrorismus und Europa*. Wiesbaden, 2008, 147–170.

[64] H. A. Wolff. Die Bundesländer und die Gew ährleistung der inneren Sicherheit. In J. Mertes (ed.), *Antworten auf den internationalen Terrorismus*, Frankfurt am Main, 74, 2007, 67–76.

that would overstrain the regular police means. Especially in the case of an airplane attack, it was proposed that the military be authorized to bring down an attacking airplane. However, the Constitutional Court explicitly prohibits such an option.[65] More generally, the court further ruled that the military can intervene as a police force, that is, without any use of military means. Some authors doubt if it can be practicable in case of an emergency to make a distinction between military and non-military means and technologies. At all events, under the present legal circumstances, the use of military means and technologies for purposes of domestic security would require a modification of the constitution. So far, however, this has always been another taboo in security policies; its break could bring even more destruction into Germany's long-standing security system.

The third major trend concerns the growing responsibility of the federal level in some fields, such as terrorism. The federation obtained exclusive jurisdiction over the defense against dangers arising from international terrorism under certain circumstances. The Federal Criminal Police Office is responsible if either the danger affects more than one state or the state agencies are not capable of dealing with the problem in an efficient way or an exclusive competency of another authority cannot be established. Through this change, the federal level, which traditionally held most of the legislative power pertaining to criminal law matters, has now gained additional administrative and operative capacities in this field. So far, such federal executive powers were restricted to terrorism and other matters of national security.

The general trend toward increasing responsibility at the federal level in the area of domestic security could be criticized when contrasted to the parallel trend toward a privatization of at least some parts of the internal security.[66] However, the German police and intelligence services have not been the only bodies that face changes in their structures and work procedures in the course of the fight against terrorism since 9/11. Another sector that has also been increasingly involved in the surveillance of terrorist conduct is the banking sector, which has to implement surveillance systems for money transfer.[67] In addition to the control systems based on the organized-crime-related money laundering legislation,[68] the European Union issued a further directive[69] according to which banks and financial institutions are now obliged to declare and authorize any money transfer within the Union. Indeed, the Common Market had opened the borders to money transfers without providing sufficient control instruments to security authorities, neither on the member states nor at the community level.

Germany is one of the few member states that had organized its own control system, but it was of minor strategic interest as long as no uniform and EU-wide control system was implemented. Besides, all the bank-related control measures operated by the private finance sector controls have to focus on physical cross-border transfers of money at the border territory. Here, the border line is given a new and very important function that may work only at external borders of the EU—that is, as far as Germany is now concerned, essentially at air and sea borders. This control system is rather questionable as it might affect the privacy of many people without any real and concrete purpose. There are, in particular, two aspects that characterize the complexity of such a system of financial control. First, surveillance cannot be conducted without any point of suspicion; and second, controls on such a large scale cannot avoid affecting people who are not at all concerned with the control goal as could be witnessed during the aforementioned

---

[65] Ruling of the Constitutional Court of 15 February 2006, 1 BvR 357/05.

[66] H. A. Wolff. Die Bundesländer und die Gew ährleistung der inneren Sicherheit. In J. Mertes (ed.), *Antworten auf den internationalen Terrorismus*, Frankfurt am Main, 74, 2007, 67–76.

[67] C. Ohler. Terrorismusbekämpfung mit den Instrumenten der Finanzmarktaufsicht. *Die Verwaltung* 41, no. 3: 405–434, 2008.

[68] For more details, see M. Kilchling, Rechtliche Instrumente zur Bekämpfung der Terrorismusfinanzierung im internationalen Vergleich. In G. Gehl (ed.), *Terrorismus—Kriegdes 21.* Jahrhunderts? Weimar, 2006, 87–113.

[69] Directive of 13 November 2007 on payment services in the internal market (2007/64/EG), O.J. no. L 319, p. 1.

Operation Athena. It has been considered that the security and control authorities should be able to legitimize in a very precise manner every concrete control initiative.

Notwithstanding the above-mentioned issues, the cooperation between federal and state security agencies has nonetheless increased—if not in operational practice fields, then at least in the fields of intelligence and data resources. The best example is the joint anti-terror database in which any state and federal security service shall gather and register their pieces of information about terrorism and terrorist risks. This reflects a fundamental change of the structures and the working procedures within the German services that no longer rely on the very border as a strategic territory for the fight against terrorism. One could even say that, paradoxically, German services dealing with terrorism and terrorist risks have, on the contrary, retreated from that very operational territory in order from now on to work from afar. Likewise paradoxical is the observation that this intelligence work "from afar," which is in operation with computers rather than on scene, has not alleviated in any way the burden of suspicion upon the traveling foreigners in their everyday experience but made it both heavier and more global.

As far as border procedures are concerned in the context of police cooperation, the Prüm Convention has obviously introduced a tremendous change regarding the reality of judicial and legal (penal law) borders between the Prüm member states even compared to the border agreements of the Schengen Treaty and the subsequent Schengen-related cross-border cooperation agreements. It totally disconnects the border territory from police control strategy. It also brings fluency into the police and data exchanges from one member state to another in a way and to an extent that has not been attained elsewhere before. Moreover, it gives new legitimacy to international public law vis-à-vis to the complexity of the EU internal law-making processes. As a matter of fact, the many attempts to coordinate the counterterrorism policies within the EU since the 1990s have not reached a considerable solution until now. Furthermore, even the position of EU Coordinator for the fight against terrorism, which was created after the Madrid attacks of 2004, has not been reoccupied since the departure of its first holder in 2007.

On the other hand, no satisfactory response has yet been given to the subject of data protection. This has been one of the most criticized aspects of the Prüm Convention. Many authors have focused on the weak standards of protection arising from the fact that no general data protection rules have been imposed on the different member states.[70] In particular, doubts arise regarding the capacity of police forces to respect the obligation to bind each piece of information they gather to a precise police and control goal. A second important question of data protection deals with the actuality and legal ownership of the data.[71] In fact, in addition to a strong mutual trust in the respective data protection capacities required for effective day-to-day police work, strong legal bases and control structures for this data protection appear absolutely necessary for the long-term functionality of police data exchange in a globalized world.

Concluding Thoughts

In the greater political context of border control, two totally contradicting developments can be witnessed today. On the one hand, there is the greater policy of freedom of control-free travel everywhere in Europe, which from the traditional perspective of police and security agencies is quite counterproductive. On the other hand, in response, new strategies and tools have had to be developed in order to intensify border controls that now extend beyond airports and other external borders.

In the course of the border cutbacks, Germany handed over a major part of the responsibility for border controls to those neighboring countries to which the external borders have moved.

[70] See Datenschutz nachrichten. 2006. 1:12–15.

[71] D. Bigo. Contrôle et mobilité des personnes. *Revue de la gendarmerie Nationale*, 2è trimestre 2008: 35–42, 2008.

This became particularly obvious when Poland and the Czech Republic effectively joined the Schengen community in 2007—to the effect that the turnpikes opened and the "great barrier" moved eastward. Germany has been preparing for this change in two ways. First, in anticipation of the fact that the German security forces could not rely anymore on their own border checks, significant financial and personnel resources were invested in order to train and further support Polish and Czech authorities with the setting up of the new external border regimes toward Belarus and Ukraine. In addition, new cooperation structures at the new internal borders were implemented. Efficient exchange of information between the German and the foreign police forces gained in fundamental significance as this is the only way to obtain information about incoming travelers from third countries.

Of course, this requires not only appropriate structures and human and material means, but also a very high degree of mutual trust in the reliability of the information coming from the neighboring countries that are now in charge of controlling the external border for the whole Schengen community. However, in the case of Germany and Poland, with their still painful common historical past, this was not the easiest part of the construction of the new control system of the Schengen zone. The second way in which Germany prepared for the period after 2007 was to develop a new management of traveler control for its own police forces, that is, a control system that has been disconnected from any physical border control.

The drastic bureaucratic and organizational changes, however, further affected the domestic security system as a whole. In the post-9/11 era, Germany witnessed one of the largest institutional, intra-governmental changes since the end of World War II: the transformation of the former border security guard into a "full" federal police authority. Such an accumulation of centralized police power that works independently of and in competition with the state police powers would have been impossible without the 9/11 assaults. In light of the fact that, traditionally, policing was the exclusive power of the federal states, this recent development can be assessed as nothing less than a "revolutionary" development. The huge federal police headquarters building currently under construction in Berlin stands as a visible symbol of this transformation. In addition, the Joint Terror Defense Center brought a further breach with fundamental, so far irrevocable principles of division of power. For example, not only is there a division between the federal and state police and other agencies but also a clear division of powers and jurisdiction between the different levels of police and intelligence services.

To date, only one traditional constitutional taboo in the German system of domestic security still stands, which is the fact that armed forces cannot operate inside the territory of the Federal Republic, not even in case of a natural disaster. It must remain open here as to whether, and to what degree, the development of the national security forces as it has been portrayed here could have happened without the Schengen development. However, it is clear that the price to be paid by the people for their liberty to cross borders without passport control is high. And the price is further increased for the purpose of the prevention of terrorist threats under such circumstances.

14

Border Security in the Middle East[1]

The Case of Iran

Iran, one of the world's oldest continuing civilizations, is located in the tumultuous border region between the Middle East and Asia and shares hundreds of kilometers of border with the war-torn nations of Afghanistan, Iraq, and Pakistan. Iran's territory covers half the coastline of the Persian Gulf, including the Strait of Hormuz, through which much of the world's oil supply moves.[2] It borders the Caspian Sea, the Caucasus in Central Asia, and South Asia, where a great deal of the world's heroin supply is produced, several major terrorist groups are based, and huge reserves of oil and gas are just beginning to be extracted.

Historically speaking, however, borders in the Middle East are one of the most artificial ones in the world since, apart from Egypt and Iran, these borders were merely drawn on the sand during the 19th and 20th centuries by the imperial powers of Britain and France while expressing their rivalries. Before that, the borders in this region did not have such strong political ramifications as, to a large extent, they were the expression of cultural differences between Iranians, Turks, and Arabs. It was the discovery of oil that created competition and rivalry concerning control of this resource, which has consequently turned the Middle East into one of the most volatile regions suffering from constant, multifaceted forms of crisis. Iran, one of the largest countries in the region, with immense geopolitical importance, shares borders with 15 countries. Many of these countries, until the 18th and 19th centuries, were part of Iran and were lost to the superior military might of either Russia (Azerbaijan) or Britain (the western part of Afghanistan); hence, these countries still share a strong cultural and historical identity with Iran, which adds to the complexities of its relationship with its neighbors.

In addition to the geographic position of Iran within the Middle East, the Islamic Revolution of 1979 fundamentally changed Iran's political and security affairs domestically, which, in turn, has had a noticeable impact on its regional and international influence. For more than two decades, the Islamic Republic of Iran has been radically trying to redefine its geopolitical borders within the Middle East on the basis of the religious unity of followers of Islam and increasingly exhibits a hostile approach to Western countries, in particular to the United States and Israel. But now it seems this ideological-revolutionary concept has been shifted to a nationalistic

---

1 Information for this chapter was drawn from the following title: H. Aghababaei and H. Rezaei, Iran–Borders of an Islamic Republic in the Middle East. In K. W. Sundberg and J. A. Winterdyk (eds.), *Border Security in the Al-Qaeda Era*, CRC Press, 2009.

2 CIA World Factbook, Iran. Available at https://www.cia.gov/library/publications/the-world-factbook/geos/ir.html, 2008.

strategy. The export of revolutionary Islam beyond the borders of Iran is no longer the dominant discourse in Iranian national, regional, and security affairs.[3]

Undeniably, Iran has emerged as a significant regional power, and its future direction will play a pivotal role in the economic and security affairs of what much of the globe reasonably considers the center of the world.[4] The combination of political repression and economic underdevelopment, the increasing presence of American and NATO forces all around its borders, militant tribal and sectarian conflicts, deep ethnic links on all sides of its borders, terrorist insurgency, and a steady advocacy for Islamist networks have made Iran a formidable threat to the stability of the Middle East, one of the main oil and gas supplying regions of the world. Since September 11, 2001 (hereafter referred to as 9/11), Iran's borders have become permeated by Taliban and al-Qaeda cells that are dug into tribal areas between Iran, Pakistan, and Afghanistan. The instability around its borders affords suitable opportunity for international criminal organizations involved in narcotics trafficking to use Iran for their criminal activities within the region, specifically moving heroin out of Afghanistan, through Iran, and into Europe.[5]

This chapter will primarily highlight border security in Iran, viewing specific issues of border security and ongoing regional concerns from an Iranian perspective. The aim is to provide a framework for understanding border security as perceived by an Islamic state that is generally outside conventional Western study.

Iranian Political Geography and Common Borders

Since the fall of 1980, when Iraqi military forces invaded Iran (the Iran-Iraq War), the Persian Gulf has been the center of political transformation along with important international economic developments, particularly with respect to the world supply of oil. This region has been continually witnessing reciprocal consequences of international crises, which have led to an abundance of violent conflicts.[6] Eight years of widespread and destructive war between Iran and Iraq, the Iraqi invasion of Kuwait, and most recently, the intervention of American and primarily Western military forces in Iraq and Afghanistan demonstrate how this region has experienced significant conflict over the years. Most of these conflicts, such as the Iraqi invasion of Iran in 1980 and the invasion of Kuwait in 1990, were a result of boundary and territorial claims to re-map existing national boundaries.[6]

Iran, being a powerful player within the region, has claim to approximately 2400 kilometers of shoreline and 5400 kilometers of land border.[7] This sizable territory provides Iran the ability to play a significant role within this sensitive geostrategic theater. An example of how Iran's geography and territorial holdings impact regional and global stability and security would be the waterway of the Hormuz Strait, situated within the Persian Gulf and within Iranian territorial waters. It is through the Strait of Hormuz that much of the world's oil supply transits. Should Iran ever close this waterway, it is conceivable to imagine that the international markets would experience a sharp downturn as a result in the reduction in global oil supplies.

---

3 R. Takeyh. *Hidden Iran: Paradox and Power in the Islamic Republic*. New York: Times Books, 2006.

4 M. K. Albright. Remarks before the American–Iranian Council, March 17, 2000, Washington, D.C., as released by the Office of the Spokesman, US Department of State. Retrieved from http://usinfo.org/wf-archive/2000/000317/epf502.htm, 2000.

5 S. Ekovich. Iran and New Threats in the Persian Gulf and Middle East. *Orbis* 48(1): 71–87, 2004.

6 International Crisis Group. Iran: Where Next on the Nuclear Standoff? Middle East Briefing No. 15 Amman/Brussels, November 24, 2004.

7 H. Panahi. *Persian Gulf Geopolitics with Emphasis on the Strategic Points of Bosehr and Khormosa. Humanities and Social Research Center*. Tehran: Jahde Danegahi Publications, 2003.

Having Pakistan and Afghanistan as its neighbors, Iran's eastern borders have special status in the post-9/11 era. According to a United Nations Office on Drugs and Crime (UNODC) survey, Afghanistan is currently the world's leading producer of illegal narcotics with more than 93% of the world production of opium (heroin) emerging from the region.[8] Most of the Afghan–Iran border in the southwest and the Pakistan–Afghan border in the south are virtually uncontrolled by government forces. As a result, it is suspected that there are hundreds of unofficial border-crossing points between Afghanistan, Iran, and Pakistan, which smugglers and traffickers alike are believed to frequent.[8] In addition, because of severe and ongoing economic, social, and political turmoil within bordering Afghanistan, human trafficking and illegal immigration through Iran's borders have increasingly been seen as a national security threat by the Iranian leadership.

Kurdish populations in the west and northwest (the borders with Iraq and Turkey) have had their own problems for a considerable period of time.[9] Traditionally, because of the close relationships between Iraqi Kurds and the Iranian government, the entrance of opponent Kurds to Iranian borders has consistently caused special security concerns for Turkey. Similarly, opponent Kurd settlement in Iraq and Turkey has proven a significant concern for Iran's border authorities. During the eight-year war between Iran and Iraq (1980–1988) and in the subsequent unstable post-war period, opponent militant groups, such as the Kurdish armed parties together with the Mujahadin-e Khalq Organization (MKO), have threatened the security of Iran from inside Iraq. As a result of these armed militia groups being allowed to exist within Iraq, the borders between Iran and Iraq have remained a virtual war zone ever since the early 1980s, continuing today.

During the intervention of Allied forces in Iraq, Iranian officials admitted that al-Qaeda members and other terrorist groups crossed through Iran's borders to Iraq. The United States has accused Iran of assisting these terrorists financially or equipping them with weapons. On the opposite side, Iranian officials have consistently charged Western countries for failing to control the movement of militants and arms from Iraq into Iran. A specific account of these grievances is the attacks on the Iranian border cities of Ahvaz and Dezful by militants living within Iraq, where hundreds of innocent Iranian civilians have been killed or wounded. These mutual accusations have made the Iraq War into a strategic struggle between Iran and the United States.[10] Therefore, such issues related to the Iran–Iraq border are of high importance for the security and stability of the whole Middle East.

Strategic Classification of International Borders

There are three types of borders worldwide:

1. *Secure borders between brother, friend, or allied nations or states.* Not only nations or states that share a common border, but that also have no fear of their neighbor taking arms against them and can expect amicable economic and social exchange. These borders, which traditionally begin to decline over time,[11] are themselves classified into two groups:
    a. *Secure borders of the historically allied.* Such as the United States–Canada, France–Belgium, and Australia–New Zealand borders. None of Iran's borders are in this situation.

---

[8] UNODC. 2007. Afghanistan Opium Survey 2007. Available at http://www.unodc.org/pdf/research/AFG07_ExSum_web.pdf.

[9] I. Besikci. *International Colony Kurdistan.* New York: Taderon Press, 2004.

[10] S. Hersh. Shifting Targets. *New Yorker,* October 2007. Available at http://www.newyorker.com/reporting/2007/10/08/071008fa_fact_hersh, 2007.

[11] Y. Karimipour and H. Kamran. A New Glance at the Strategic Classification of Borders (with Stress on the Borders of Iran). *Faculty of Literatures and Humanities* 160, no. 48: 555–568, 2001. Available at http://journals.ut.ac.ir/user/.

   b. *Secure borders of the strategically allied.* Such as the borders of Western European countries and the China–North Korea, Russia–Mongolia, and Thailand–Malaysia borders. Iran's borders are not classified in this category, either.

2. *Strategically threatened borders.* These kinds of borders are functionally the opposite of secure borders. The neighbors never feel comfortable with one another. Examples of strategically threatened borders include the India–Pakistan border, the Greek–Turkey border, and Israel's borders with Lebanon, Syria, and Egypt. Iran's last frontiers with the Soviet Union and Tsarist Russia, as well as with the Ottoman Empire, are included in this category.

3. *Topical-threat border.* Although neighboring states within these types of borders typically are not inclined to attack the other, there does exist an atmosphere of insecurity due to illegal trafficking of humans, smuggling of weapons, transiting of narcotics caravans, or conducting of anti-governmental insurgencies. Examples of these types of borders include the Iran–Pakistan border, Iran–Afghanistan border, Iran–Turkey border, and the Iran–Iraq border. All of Iran's borders typically fit this category.[12]

Global examples of this category could arguably also include the US–Mexico border and many of the Western–Eastern European borders. Over the decades, the movement of smuggled and trafficked people and contraband has become commonplace both along the US–Mexico border and the Western–Eastern European borders. However, in the aftermath of 9/11, the United States and the Western European nations have all increased a militarized presence along their boundaries with increased patrols and new technologies meant to inhibit the illegal crossing of illegal migrants and contraband goods.[12]

Security-Threatening Factors in Iran Borders

Drug Trafficking

Within Iran, there are over a million people believed to be addicted to opium (i.e., heroin). This fact, officially admitted by Iran, has been blamed on drug trafficking from the Pakistan-Afghanistan borderlands into Iran. Iran is the main consumer of Afghan opium. Historically, Afghanistan's drug industry was a component of the United States' Cold War policy within the region. In order for the United States to fight its Cold War against the Soviet Union during the invasion of Afghanistan in 1979, US intelligence and military forces supported the Afghans and other Muslim jihadists in their resistance to Soviet occupation. This support thereby furthered the West's interests within the region without it taking overt military action. The drug production and trade in this region was easily ignored for the sake of the war against communism. Since this period, the tribal areas between Iran, Afghanistan, and Pakistan have become the world's top opium producers, currently supplying more than 70% of the world's heroin.[13] Apart from the root causes of this narcotic production within the countries neighboring Iran, there is no doubt that the production of drugs and the trafficking through Iran's borders or distribution inside Iran have caused irreparable security, political, economic, and human damage to Iran itself.

---

[12] Y. Karimipour and H. Kamran. A New Glance at the Strategic Classification of Borders (with Stress on the Borders of Iran). *Faculty of Literatures and Humanities* 160, no. 48: 555–568, 2001. Available at http://journals.ut.ac.ir/user/.

[13] UNODC. 2007. Afghanistan Opium Survey 2007. Available at http://www.unodc.org/pdf/research/AFG07_ExSum_web.pdf.

In recent years, the largest province in Iran, Khorasan, which neighbors Afghanistan, has been steadily confronting violent conflicts with armed smugglers in the form of murder, kidnapping, and robbery. This conflict has dramatically impacted the security and welfare of the Iranian people (especially children and women) within some bordering districts, where violence is a common occurrence. The range of this conflict has not been limited to the eastern provinces of Iran either, but has also penetrated the central and western regions, threatening Iran's national security. Between 1999 and 2001, insecurity and violence also expanded to the center of Khorasan province, Mashhad's mountains, and other cities, such as Chenaran, Quchan, Esfarayen, Sabzevar, and Neyshapour. Some armed gangs of smugglers have entered Golestan province, disseminating violence and crime. During the years 1996–2001, more than 3500 people were taken hostage by these groups, with almost 210 people being killed. Best estimates indicate that 7625 members of these armed groups have passed across the borders with Afghanistan.[14]

In recent years, the Judiciary of the Islamic Republic has been excessively using the death penalty in the form of public hangings of those arrested in relation to transborder smuggling and trafficking. In governmental language they are called *Ashrar*, an Arabic term used for those who use violence in public and who fight with the authorities of the Islamic governments. The common perception of Iran's judicial authorities is that when dealing with members of these armed groups it is warranted to suspend the human rights of these criminals in the interest of the state. Trials and convictions for those accused of participating with these armed groups are summary and quick.

Goods Smuggling

More than 85% of Iran's revenue is generated through the oil sector, and hence the economy is largely marked as inefficient. In order to reduce the harmful consequences of state monopolies and in the name of supporting internal economic development, the Islamic Republic of Iran has sharply restricted imports, mainly by placing high duties on foreign goods. Under these economic conditions and considering the emergence of a consumer society within Iran, the smuggling of foreign goods has become common. For instance, in 2005 Iran's Chief of Police estimated that more than $6 billion worth of goods, such as computers, electronics, tea, and cigarettes, were smuggled into the country from other Persian Gulf countries—mainly Dubai.[15]

Because of the existence of extensive subsidizations in most sectors of Iran's economy, petroleum products, pharmaceuticals, breads, and many other goods (items that are imported into Iran with governmental subsidization) are being smuggled to neighboring countries by Iranians wanting to afford a consumer lifestyle. Considering that the gasoline prices in Iran are less than 35 cents per liter, smugglers are able to make a significant profit by illegally exporting petroleum out of Iran. This offers one example of how internal subsidization has sparked the smuggling of goods out of Iran.

Although the fight against smuggling has been a main security concern for the Iranian government, it is still a daily occupation for those inhabiting Iran's border regions. According to statistics offered by Custom Organization of the Islamic Republic (COIR), automobiles, machinery, alcoholic beverages, textiles, chemical materials, and spare parts constituted the majority of smuggled goods into Iran between 2005 and 2006.[16] Also, the most smuggled goods from Iran during this period were gasoline, oil products, petrol, gold bullion, and food products.[15] Statistics also show that in 2006, the number of people suspected to be involved in smuggling

[14] Q. H. Ebrahimbay Salami. The Perspective of Persistent Development in East of Iran. *Geographic Research Quarterly* 77: 46–66, 1998.

[15] Al-Arabiya News Channel. Available at http://www.alarabiya.net/articles/2008/05/12/49719, 2008.

[16] Letter No. 22/83/253/344073 dated 1386/12/28 by the Islamic Republic's COIR.

was 45,139 with around 12,736 having been arrested and convicted.[17] According to this same letter, in the first 11 months of 2007, there was a 10% decrease in the number of cases involving smuggling yet a 23% increase of people convicted of smuggling (12,736 to 15,738 convictions). In the Hormozghan province, the main center for goods smuggling because of its proximity to central international commercial points, such as Dubai, during 1991 to 1994 more than 70,000 people were captured by border police for the transportation of smuggled goods.[18] Furthermore, during the years of 1985 to 1994, there were a total of 39,784 judicial cases involving smuggling within the province.[19]

Terrorism

Oppositional Groups

Although the Iranian Revolution of 1979 was inherently a popular nonviolent event, Iranian society has witnessed a wave of violence between the Islamic government and different political opposition groups from 1980 to 1988. Mostly these conflicts took place at the bordering provinces, sometimes extending beyond Iran's borders. During the first years of the revolution, revolutionary border forces battled with Marxist-Stalinists of Kurdish and non-Kurdish groups in the border cities in Torkaman Sahra and Kurdistan. Later, since 1981, the MKO (Mojahedin-e Khalq Organization) also resorted to armed struggle against the ruling clergy, which led to a bloody confrontation resulting in a large number of deaths and casualties and much property damage during this period. After the brutal reaction by the regime and drastic actions, including murder, executions, and imprisonment of its members by the Iranian government, the main members and advocates of the MKO initially fled to Europe but later took refuge inside Iraq.

Since 1982, most of the terrorist actions within Iran have been planned from within Iraq by exiled members of the MKO. This armed oppositional organization until the end of the war was involved in cross-border attacks against the Iranian armed forces. Still, its major military action took place in the summer of 1988 at the end of the war, when with the support of Iraq's armed forces, especially the air force, it launched a major attack and tried to take over some major Iranian cities in the west in an attempt to bring down the Iranian government. This operation, which was called "the Eternal Light," took place when Iran had accepted a cease-fire with Iraq based on the UN Security Council's Resolution 598, which was meant to end the eight years of devastating war with Iraq.

The MKO's forces, known as the National Resistance Army, succeeded in breaking down borders and penetrating deep into the Kermanshah province of western Iran. However, their speedy advance came to a halt when Iranian armed forces quickly smashed the ill-conceived and poorly executed attack, handing the MKO a severe defeat. There exists overwhelming evidence that the former Iraqi regime supported the MKO militarily, financially, and politically and that the organization until very recently continued to perpetuate acts of terrorism both inside and outside of the Islamic Republic of Iran. In the 2007 Country Reports of the UN Counter-Terrorism Committee, it is stated that "in the last 3 decades, the MKO terrorist organization has perpetrated more than 612 terrorist operations in Iran or against the Iranian interests outside the country, including through hijacking, abduction, bombing and indiscriminate terrorist attacks against civilians."[20]

On the other side of Iran's border with Turkey there is another separatist opposition, which, through military means, aims at unifying the Kurdish regions in Turkey, Iraq, and Iran into a

[17] Al-Arabiya News Channel. Available at http://www.alarabiya.net/articles/2008/05/12/49719, 2008.

[18] Hormozghan provincial, letter no. 10, 7-1374.

[19] Y. Karimipour and H. R. Mohammadi. The Obstruction of Smuggling Good, from Truth to Dream. *Geographic Research Quarterly* 73: 210–224, 2005. Available at http://www.Archive of SID.ir.

[20] UNODC. Agreement to Strengthen Border Cooperation between Afghanistan, Iran and Pakistan Reached in Tehran. Available at http://www.unodc.org/unodc/en/press/ releases/2008-05-08.html, 2008.

country. This group, known as the Party for a Free Life in Kurdistan (PJAK), is active within the northwestern part of Iran, where it attempts to offset Iran's internal security through acts of terrorism. Presently, the PJAK is the most noted armed group within the western borders of Iran, especially in the provinces of Ilaam, Kermanshah, Kurdistan, and West Azerbaijan. The PJAK is comprised of the Labor party of Turkey's Kurdistan, or PKK, and openly supports and promotes the ideals of Abdullah Ujalan, their Stalinist leader in prison in Turkey.

The PJAK has emerged as a result of the exile of opposition Kurdish groups from Iran, groups such as Komoleh and the Democratic Party of Kurdistan. The political base of these parties resides mostly in Europe rather than in Kurdistan. This physical distance causes a lapse, one might say, between theory and practice, which, as a result, has helped the creation of armed radical groups within Iranian Kurdistan. That, also, has created difficulty for the leaders of autonomous regions of Iraqi Kurdistan as both Talebani (the current president of Iraq) and Barzani (the head of Iraqi Kurdistan) and their supporters had the systematic support of the Iranian government.

Although the PJAK does not have as strong a political background or popular support as other main Iranian Kurdish groups, these, to a large extent, have postponed their armed struggle, and hence it is this group that causes security tension in the western borders of Iran. Through a security agreement between Turkey and Iran, both countries share a common security approach with regard to this group. This strong mutual security cooperation made the PJAK vulnerable. In August 2007, Turkey's Foreign Minister defended Iran's external operation against the PJAK in northern Iraq by stating that Iran had the right to defend its borders. In response, the Iranian Foreign Minister approved Turkey's attack against the PPK on November 3, 2007, during a meeting in Istanbul.

Obviously, there is a strategic convergence and a consensus around border security matters among the governments of Iran, Turkey, and Syria, specifically concerning the repression of the opposition Kurdish groups, especially the PKK and PJAK. The Kurdish opposition groups have therefore encountered extensive pressure and are increasingly under military and political pressure to abandon their armed and terrorist methods. Ironically, unlike the existing hostility between the Iranian government and armed Iranian Kurds, friendly relations with Iraqi Kurdistan are on the rise.

Iraqi Kurdish officials have an autonomous regional government that allows them to build political and economic links with other nations, such as Iran. A large part of the Iraqi Kurdistan economy depends on imports from Iran. With these current strong economical ties, if Iran were ever to close its border with Iraq, the Kurdistan economy would surely be negatively impacted. Iranian products, such as appliances and electronics, flood Kurdish cities, and petrol smuggled in from Iran helps Iraqi Kurds overcome high oil prices. The security affairs of Iraqi Kurdistan are so interconnected with Iranian security concerns that Iraqi Kurdistan is not in a position to support armed Iranian Kurds in their conflict with the central government. If Iraqi Kurds decided to support Kurds in Iran, they would be forced to seek political and economic support from other neighbors, such as Turkey and Syria, which is, given the current situation, highly unlikely. Still, such an economic and political shift could lead to clashes among Kurdish political parties so that those controlling areas bordering Turkey and Syria could gain an upper hand over the parties based near Iran. Therefore, Iraqi Kurds are tolerant of the opposition groups located in northern Iraq as long as they do not engage in military actions against Iran. Regarding the PJAK, the Iraqi Kurd officials are cooperating with Iran to control this group, which is based high in the mountains. However, Iran, while deeply worried about its own Kurdish population seeking autonomy, from time to time, accuses Iraq's Kurdish regional government of failing to crack down on Iranian Kurd opposition groups in northern Iraq.

Religious-Tribal Extremists

A mixture of harsh policies against religious minorities in the eastern border regions under an Ahmadinejad presidency, the rise of religious radicalism among the Sunnis in these regions, illiteracy, tribal extremism, and the drug smuggling industry has resulted in an increasing threat to security for Iran along its border with neighboring Pakistan. In the southeast of Iran, radical Sunni militants, very similar to al-Qaeda, claim the central Shia government has constantly discriminated against their populations. The activities of Sunni militants, together with organized criminal groups who smuggle opium out of Afghanistan, have created a very insecure situation for the region. Between 2007 and 2008 there has been a reported increase in kidnappings aimed both at civilians and Iranian officials, terrorist acts, road blockages, and human trafficking. This area in southeastern Iran is one of the poorest and the most violent provinces of Iran. The area is one of the main routes for smuggling drugs from Afghanistan to Europe and the scene of frequent gun battles between drug smugglers and Iranian security forces. A number of Iranian soldiers have been ambushed or kidnapped over the past few years.[21]

A militant bandit-radical group called Jundallah—or Army of Allah—is the most active terrorist group in this area. Since 2006, the activities of this group have intensified within the bordering cities, including various terrorist acts in Zahidan, the center of Sistan-Baluchestan Province, in particular on the border roads of this province. While they cross borders to commit terrorist acts inside Iran, the families of this group live in border areas of Pakistan and Afghanistan. Iran claims this group is affiliated with al-Qaeda; Jundallah, however, claims they are the victims of the Iranian government's oppression and discrimination, as well as political and economic neglect. The Jundallah states that they are fighting for the social and religious rights of Sunni Baluchis in Iran.

In 2006, during a very organized insurgency, in an attack at a checkpoint in this bordering area with Pakistan, this group blocked the highway between Zahidan and Zabol (Shia city of Sistan) and killed more than 20 people, including government workers and officials.[22] This extremist group was notified by its intelligence service that government automobiles were moving from Zabol to Zahidan; dressed in the uniforms of the Iranian Police Force, members of this group stopped them, asked their religion, and killed most of them just because of their Shia faith. The group filmed the scenes of killing as well as the taking of some of the passengers as hostages, whom they transported to the border of Iran and Pakistan. In another incident, this group detonated a roadside bomb in the Zahidan region, which killed the majority of military passengers aboard a transport bus. This kind of attack, hitting an elite force in daylight in an open street, and its size and nature, was shocking for Iranian security forces[21] and provided the Iranian government with further reason to enforce its harsh policies in this border region.

Measures for Security of Borders

Regional and International Cooperation

Regional and international cooperation by Iran can play a significant role in the international struggle against terrorism. From time to time, there are positive signs that the Iranian political system is willing to show its interest in fighting terrorism and organized crimes at a regional level. An example of this is Iran's recent ratification of security cooperation agreements with Italy and Saudi Arabia.[23] These agreements generally include provisions for cooperation in combating crime, terrorism, and money laundering; the surveillance of borders and territorial waters; and the designation of working committees to implement these provisions. Iran has also signed agreements on security cooperation with Kuwait, Bahrain, Yemen, Azerbaijan, Belarus, and Bosnia.[24] The 2007 Country Report of the UN Counter-Terrorism Committee mentions in detail that Iran has entered into conventions and agreements with its neighboring countries as well as others to promote its commitment in fighting terrorism and securing its borders.

---

[21] BBC News. Iran Blast Points to Ethnic Tensions. Available at http://news.bbc.co.uk/2/hi/ middle_east/6363181.stm, 2007.

[22] BBC News. Twenty-Two Killed at Iran Border. Available at http://news.bbc.co.uk/2/hi/middle_east/4816442.stm, 2006.

[23] UNODC. 2007. Afghanistan Opium Survey 2007. Available at http://www.unodc.org/pdf/research/AFG07_ExSum_web.pdf.

[24] UNODC. Crime and Justice Situation in Iran. Available at http://www.unodc.org/pdf/iran/drug_crime_situation/rule_of_law/CrimeandJusticeLaws.pdf, 2007.

The following represents an overview of Iran's attempts to engage and address various security issues.

Cooperation plan in the framework of the Economic Cooperation Organization (ECO). The ECO meeting, held on November 1, 2006, in Tehran, has been considered to be a turning point in enhancing regional cooperation on anticrime and counterterrorism measures.

Cooperation plan in the frame of Iraq's neighboring countries. Regarding security and counterterrorism issues, Iran is cooperating with Saudi Arabia, Syria, Egypt, Bahrain, Iraq, Turkey, and Jordan within a special international framework for the meetings of the Interior Ministers of Iraq's neighboring countries plus Egypt and Bahrain. The first session of these meetings was held in Tehran on November 30 and December 1, 2004. The Islamic Republic of Iran is also a party to the protocol on cooperation for fighting terrorism and organized crime as well as enhancing border security that was signed among Iraq and its neighbors, plus Bahrain and Egypt, in the second meeting of the Interior Ministers of Iraq's neighboring countries in Jeddah on September 19, 2006.

Cooperation plan for reinforcement and support of post-Taliban Afghanistan government. Terrorism and drug trafficking efforts are mutually reinforcing each other between the borders of Iran and Afghanistan. Based on ideological hostilities between Sunni radicals and the Shia faith, Iran has been officially supporting the new government of Afghanistan to counter the terrorism threat. In the context of cooperation with the government of Afghanistan on the fight against drug trafficking, Iran has commenced the training of the Afghan Anti-Drug Police Force members, which has further enhanced border cooperation between the two countries and promoted intelligence and operational cooperation with Afghanistan. In this direction, Iran has constructed numerous border stations, which have been handed over to the Afghan border police.[25]

Further, to enhance regional capacities for cooperation, a quadrilateral intelligence committee composed of the representatives of Iran, Afghanistan, Pakistan, and the United Kingdom, with Germany serving as observer, has been set up and has thus far convened several meetings. Within the framework of the UN Border Project, a trilateral cooperation between the Islamic Republic of Iran, Pakistan, and Afghanistan is expanding and strengthening. On May 8, 2008, the trilateral meeting between ministers from the Islamic Republics of Afghanistan, Iran, and Pakistan was held in Tehran. The result was an agreement on measures to strengthen border cooperation between the three countries in order to stem the flow of drugs from Afghanistan. Three countries agreed to improve cross-border telecommunication exchange on counter-narcotics. Further, they agreed to intensify the interdiction of precursor chemicals under Operation TARCET. UNODC will provide training and equipment for this purpose. Iran will also commit to establishing a permanent Secretariat for the Triangular Initiative and a regional center for intelligence exchange through UNODC's assistance.[26]

Iran is also an active participant within the Paris Pact. The Paris Pact has enhanced regional cooperation and could contribute to further restricting the activities of drug traffickers and terrorist groups in the region. Although limited in nature, the Paris Pact is a first step toward ongoing cooperation and contact between Iran and the UNODC in the fight against drug trafficking out of Afghanistan.

Security agreement between Caspian Sea countries. According to Section 22 of the letter of agreement signed in Tehran in 2007 during the meeting of authorities of the seashore

[25] Fars News. Iran to Train Afghan Police. Available at http://www.farsNews.com/, February 28, 2006.

[26] UNODC. Agreement to Strengthen Border Cooperation between Afghanistan, Iran and Pakistan Reached in Tehran. Available at http://www.unodc.org/unodc/en/press/ releases/2008-05-08.html, 2008.

countries of the Caspian Sea (Iran, Russia, Kazakhstan, Azerbaijan, and Turkmenistan), all five countries consider international terrorism, separatism, oppressive interventions, extremist and also illegal exchange of narcotics, weapons, and other forms of transnational organized crime as threats to security of the world community and international political stability. Under this agreement, all sides are committed to unconditionally convict terrorist actions as criminal offenses apart from motives, forms, and manifestations anywhere and by anyone, especially those actions that threaten the peace and security of the area. All sides also admit that terrorism should not be connected to any religion, nationality, ancestry, or racial groups.

Under Section 23 of the agreement, all parties confirm their support for extensive mutual or multilateral cooperation in the fight against terrorism, illegal trade of narcotics, weapons, and transnational organized crimes with the use of key and coordinating roles of the United Nations.

Security cooperation pact with Saudi Arabia. As a result of two competing faiths within Islam (Sunni and Shia Islam), Iran and Saudi Arabia are engaged in a rivalry as both try to expand their influence over other Muslim nations. Any joint approach to security and peace between these two leading Middle Eastern countries might strongly affect other bordering countries. In particular, in order to change the current unstable situation in Iraq and Afghanistan, the world community is in urgent need of cooperation by these two countries.

Since June 2001, there has been an unusual and relatively functioning security agreement between Iran and Saudi Arabia. According to Article 2 of this agreement, both countries are committed to preventing and combating organized crime and terrorism. They agreed to coordinate their antiterrorism and organized crime activities through the following fields of cooperation: to exchange information about people and groups related to organized crime and terrorism; to exchange experiences about time, place, situation, style, and method of organized crimes and terrorism and necessary legal measures for the prevention of such acts; to exchange experts and specialists for expanding common mutual cooperation about scientific research in the field of criminology and crime detection; to hold common police education with the agreements of committed sides; to organize and exchange joint working groups about the scientific research in criminology and crime detection; and some other areas.

According to Article 3 of the agreement both sides are committed to coordinate their activities in order to make the best use of their resources. For that reason, they will regularly discuss their cooperation in the following fields:

1. Fighting against human trafficking and smuggling goods at borders
2. Cooperating in the field of rescue operations at sea
3. Preventing any hostile political activities by opponents of each of two countries in another country

Security agreement with Turkey. To coordinate their efforts against subversive activities along the borders and exchange of information about terrorism, Iran and Turkey established the High Security Commission in 1988. The High Security Commission has thus far held eight sessions and many others at sub-commission working level. As a result, the Iran–Turkish border has been closed to the activities of PKK elements and illegal movements. In the last security meeting between authorities of the two countries, there were talks about a security contract to hold regular security meetings between them. Turkey's Interior Minister announced that, in this new type of agreement, both sides have emphasized the necessity of deepening and continuing the mutual security cooperation. In another part of this announcement, it was indicated that because of the increase in terrorist activities in the area that have caused losses to both country, Iran and Turkey are committed to solving this mutual problem through exchange of information and security cooperation.

Security cooperation agreement with Italy. Considering the radical ideological content of the Islamic Republic, this agreement can be considered exceptional. According to Article 1 of the Agreement, the parties are committed to cooperating with each other in order to guarantee security and fight transnational organized crimes in any form with the purpose of prevention, conducting research, and fighting against organized crimes, terrorism, narcotics smuggling and illegal border passages, and related criminal activities.[27] In this relationship the Italian Deputy National Anti-mafia Prosecutor visited the Islamic Republic of Iran in February 2006.[28]

Executive Measures

Iranian society has been plagued by drug traffickers and terrorists along its border areas with Afghanistan and Pakistan. Hence, combating the terrorist groups and organized narcotics traffickers has been a top priority for the Iranian security sector. Facing these ever-growing social and security problems, Iran has been adopting different levels of preventive measures during the past two decades with regard to securing its borders. Some of these measures are as follows:

Preventive Measures

In the aftermath of 9/11, the UN Security Council made a number of obligations for UN members to enhance the control of borders so as to prevent the transborder movement of terrorists. Iran, in cooperation with the international community, has obviously tightened its borders with Afghanistan in order to help the repression of al-Qaeda cells that were trying to cross through Iran. Iran blockaded many common cross points along its shared border with Afghanistan. Iran has also constituted a council with the title of Council for Organization of Legal Passages of Entrance and Exit in order to coordinate its action with the residents living near borders. This council, which was approved by the office of the supreme council, is to arrange necessary executive policies and form coordination in common executive methods. Supervision over legal passages of exit and entrance issues of the country with regard to total coordination of border issues are among the main responsibilities of this council.[29]

Logistical and Intelligence Support for Armed Forces on Eastern Borders

Over the past eight years, the Armed Forces of Iran have continually reinforced its border guards along the 900-kilometer border with Afghanistan, including three additional brigades along with logistics and support units that are ordered to identify and arrest individuals suspected of terrorist and drug-trafficking activities. In addition, the Iranian border guards, including the police, armed forces, and security personnel at all points of entry to the Islamic Republic of Iran (airports and land and sea points of entry) were reinforced and briefed about their responsibility. The list of individuals and groups associated with al-Qaeda, circulated as Security Council document SC/7166 of 8 October 2001, was distributed to the border guards to help them control the points of entry to the country and the rest of the borders.

Expansion of COIR Tools on Border Points

The Customs Organization has been developing rapidly. COIR now screens most passengers at Iranian entry and exit checkpoints, utilizing advanced inspection scanners and equipments (X-ray, Gateway, handheld detectors, and inspection camera systems). It should be noted that COIR carries out its duties in close cooperation with the Iranian Police Department. Regarding passenger control measures on international flights, the Islamic Republic of Iran, as a member of the Chicago Pact, is committed to ensuring aviation safety and security in accordance with

---

[27] Official Gazette, 17196/2003.

[28] UNODC. Agreement to Strengthen Border Cooperation between Afghanistan, Iran and Pakistan Reached in Tehran. Available at http://www.unodc.org/unodc/en/press/releases/2008-05-08.html, 2008.

[29] Official Gazette, No. 10103.

international standards and practices. Furthermore, new equipment have been set up in Iranian airports (eight international and 80 domestic airports) in order to meet this obligation.

The National Anti-Terrorism Committee

There is a National Anti-Terrorism Committee in Iran that is responsible for ensuring the necessary coordination and information sharing among the relevant agencies involved in the fight against terrorism. The Ministry of Intelligence and law enforcement agencies, including the police force, are also involved in exchange of information and intelligence related to suspected terrorist activities through INTERPOL and other relevant channels. The activities of the mentioned committee are overseen by the Supreme National Security Council. This committee has established a Working Group to study the requirements and the potentials for establishing a data bank and other mechanisms for further coordination among them in connection with gathering, compiling, and analyzing information about terrorist groups and the best possible practices in countering and preventing terrorist activities.

Excavation of Canals, Earthworks, and Border Guardhouses

The widespread and long-standing practice of poppy and cannabis cultivation within the tribal areas of Afghanistan and Pakistan have resulted in more than 80 years of illegal narcotics trafficking through the Iranian provinces of Khorasan and Sistan-Baluchistan—one of the world's largest drug-trafficking routes. In 2000, after a noticeable increase in the level of violence and drug trafficking in these provinces, the Iranian government began a massive project to "control and physically block the eastern borders" so as to curb the movement of illegal drugs and apprehend criminals using the border to traffic narcotics and people.

Since 2000, more than $20 million a year has been allocated for the redesigning and reinforcement of Iran's borders with the eastern portion being the main priority. This massive undertaking, which spans more than 925 kilometers along the Iran-Afghanistan border, from Sarakhs in Khorasan province to the farthest end of Sistan-Baluchestan, has been undertaken with great vigor. Along the eastern border of the Khorasan Province, a 500-kilometer asphalt road has been built in order for police patrols to do their work more efficiently. Further, Iran has constructed 23 dams, 390 kilometers of canals, and 695 kilometers of excavation and clearing; erected more than 125 kilometers of barbed-wire fence; and built approximately 70 guardhouses and towers and 60 operational and security bases along the eastern borders.[30]

Moreover, Iran recently introduced electronic control projects at sensitive border crossing points. After the fall of the Taliban government and improvement of relations with the Afghanistan government, some of the guardhouses and security border bases of Afghanistan were repaired with the aid of the Iranian government. Iran firmly supports the coordination and cooperation of security forces on the two sides of the border as a solution to narcotics smuggling.[31]

Training of Special Airline Security Guards

Iran has a tough airline security mandate. In Iranian airports, there are several kinds of security forces, including police forces, officers of the intelligence service, and the Islamic Revolutionary Guard Corps (Sepah Pasdaran). Because of the continuous threats to security of internal and international flights to Iran, which have existed since the Islamic Revolution of Iran, control of passengers and accompanied goods and security during flight has given over to the special and skilled forces of Islamic Revolutionary Guards. This organization has proved to be very successful in the prevention of hijacking as well as in the capture of hijackers.

---

[30] H. Zarghani. *An Introduction to International Borders*. Tehran: Daneshgah-e Oloom-e Entezami Publications, 2007.

[31] N. Moshiri. Iran Takes on Drug Smugglers. Al Jazeera (English). Available at http://english.aljazeera.net/news/middleeast/2008/06/200862620538368661.html, June 27, 2008.

Creation of Border Markets

One of the main goals of Iran's security policies aims at bringing stability to its border cities. One of the ways in which it has tried to achieve this is the creation of an economic development program for inhabitants along its borders. Presently, there are 50 such border markets distributed among all 13 border provinces of Iran.[32] This initiative is aimed at preventing smuggling activities and promotes the prosperity of border residents through lawful trade. The indirect objective of this project is to reduce the inclination of residents to join terrorist groups and give an incentive for residents to cooperate with security forces in controlling the smuggling of goods, weapons, and narcotics. In accordance with Article 7, the residents alongside these border points are given the ability to import and export goods without having to pay the normal customs fees and duties.

Covert Suppressive Operations

Following the al-Qaeda terrorist attacks of 9/11, along with the fall of the Taliban in Afghanistan, there has been a great deal of discussion within political circles and in the world press that al-Qaeda has been using Iran to transport weapons and goods. Local authorities of Iran have always denied these reports and stated that the official position of Iran is not to support the efforts of al-Qaeda.[33] In fact, some Iranian officials have stated they have suppressed al-Qaeda activities within Iran. For instance, Mr. Younesi, the former Intelligence Minister of Iran, admitted that members of al-Qaeda have entered into Iran; however, he claimed that the Iranian forces had captured these terrorists at its borders and deported them back to their country of origin. He said, "[p]resently we have encountered five waves of al-Qaeda terrorists since the fall of the Taliban regime. The first wave was the one, which, after suppression of the Taliban, was along the long border with Afghanistan, when several thousand Afghans or other nationalities entered the country illegally. We decided to confront them."[34]

According to then Intelligence Minster Younesi, Iran had adopted a multilayer strategy to fight al-Qaeda in Iran. First, Iran adopted a policy of prevention through tougher border controls. Gradually Iran noticed that some members of al-Qaeda lived inside Iran and were using Iran's territory for terrorist operations. The Iranian Intelligence Services immediately identified and arrested them. Indeed, this encounter was very vital for Iran itself. The former Minister of Intelligence even disclosed that Iranian security and intelligence authorities had identified al-Qaeda members and arrested them. Former Minister Younesi introduced the next wave by stating, "[t]his wave has been focused on the Ansar Al-Islam (Islam's Helpers) with their bases mostly in Iraq. We have identified and captured them, and most of them have been tried and imprisoned. Therefore, the prosecution of advocates of al-Qaeda was the fourth wave of this organization in the eastern borders."[35] In explaining the fifth and final wave of this organization, he stated that "the fifth wave against al-Qaeda was to deal with those groups that were organizing and forming various groups for terrorist operations and for supporting al-Qaeda. Among them we identified some religious students and Sunni Molavies (clerics). Presently, we have identified and captured, expelled, dismissed or sentenced more than a thousand people. Approximately 200 of these people are now in prison."[36] Besides this interview with the former

---

[32] Ministry of Commerce of Islamic Republic. Page of Border Markets. Available at http://www.moc.gov.ir/BorderShops.htm, 2008.

[33] ISNA (Iranian Students News Agency). 2002. Interview with authorities of border provinces Khorasan, Kurdistan, Sistan and Baluchistan and Kermanshah. News No. 8104-00232. http://www.isna.ir.

[34] ISNA (Iranian Students New Agency). 2006. Interview with Mr. Younesi, former Intelligence Minister of Iran. News. No. 8711-14490. http://www.isna.ir.

[35] ISNA (Iranian Students New Agency). 2006. Interview with Mr. Younesi, former Intelligence Minister of Iran. News. No. 8711-14490. http://www.isna.ir.

[36] ISNA (Iranian Students New Agency). 2006. Interview with Mr. Younesi, former Intelligence Minister of Iran. News. No. 8711-14490. http://www.isna.ir.

Intelligence Minister of Iran, through an official report of Iran to the UN Counter-Terrorism Committee of the Security Council in 2007, this issue has been reaffirmed. The report argues that besides members of al-Qaeda, security forces of Iran have taken measures to capture and suppress terrorist groups, such as the PJAK, Mujahedin Khalq (MKO), and other rebel groups that commit terrorist operations in order to smuggle narcotics.

Concluding Thoughts

The 1979 Iranian revolution and the emergence and dominance of radical Islam less than three years after the revolution added to the complexity of geopolitics of the Middle East as now the Islamic ideology of the ruling clergy had a very different understanding of political borders within their advocated doctrine. Hence, in effect, they refused to recognize these political borders as they tried to draw new geographical borders based on the universal government of Islam. Within this new definition of borders, Iran saw itself as the land that accepted neither the domination of the United States nor the Soviet Union (the slogan of neither East nor West) and saw as its duty to give its backing for Muslims' struggles in any country. Hence, it advocated the export of revolution—not through making the country an example, something that could be learned from, but through violent means by arming opposition groups in those countries. However, the devastating eight-year war with Iraq, political isolation, constant struggle with opposition groups and organized drug traffickers, and, in recent years, the ability of al-Qaeda forces to cross Iranian borders have forced the Iranian regime to become much less ideological and more practical. Hence, since the 1990s, we observe the change of attitude in regard to Iranian borders.

In the post-9/11 era, the Islamic Republic of Iran has a number of major concerns in relation to border security issues. This is particularly true in the eastern and western regions. A lack of effective border police in Afghanistan and Pakistan to combat the smuggling of drugs and human beings, the war in Iraq, armed oppositional activities in Kurdish provinces, and the penetration of armed terrorist groups across borders with Turkey and Iraq, together with increasing narcotics smuggling by organized criminal groups across the Iran-Afghanistan borders, have all caused Iran to regard border security as an important element of its overall national security strategy. Hence, the Iranian government has a real need and desire to secure its borders, not least of all because failure to do so weakens its authority among the public, which is vital for the security of the regime itself.

There are signs that elements within the regime, which might be called rogue elements, occasionally use these border-related threats as opportunities to support armed groups to bring them under their influence. But the willingness of the regime to cooperate with its neighbors and other countries on security issues provides a favorable situation for Western countries, especially the United States, to engage the Iranian regime constructively and make it more accountable for its actions and policies. Furthermore, while attempts to isolate the regime have opened space for radicals within Iran, real engagements about border security might provide alternative strategies and weaken terrorist activities.

Iran's strategic geopolitical location, as well as its historical and cultural influence in neighboring countries, means that it has a major impact on the security of borders in the region. Hence, making Iran a partner for peace and engaging this country in a mutually constructive dialogue over borders, security, and terrorism may be the most effective way of achieving these goals. After all, as the security of borders in the oil-producing, Muslim-majority countries of the Middle East, such as Iran, is strongly linked to international peace, so the only way of securing borders and diminishing the flow of drugs and armed groups into and out of Iran is through an international effort.

15

Terrorism in Asia[1]

The Case of the Philippines

Although the problem of terrorism has become a very serious global security threat, it has deep domestic roots in the Philippines. The threat of international terrorism is inherently local in origin. There is even a view that al-Qaeda, the most notorious network of radical Muslim terrorist organizations to date, will return to their local roots.[2] Thus, it is essential to consider the domestic milieu of the terrorist threat to fully grasp its complexities and nuances. The Philippines is not spared from the threats posed by domestic terrorism. Linkages of domestic terrorist organizations in the Philippines with international terrorist organizations confound the virulence of these threats. The Philippine government even regards the local Communist insurgency as a very serious terrorist problem. This chapter, however, focuses on terrorist threats in the Philippines emanating from radical Muslim groups. Although the problem of terrorism is not entirely a radical Muslim phenomenon, the lion's share of terrorist acts and the most devastating of them in recent years are said to have been perpetrated by radical Muslim organizations.[3]

This chapter examines the following six radical Muslim organizations that have been reported to have committed acts of terrorism: the Nur Misuari Breakaway Group (MBG) of the Moro National Liberation Front (MNLF), the Moro Islamic Liberation Front (MILF), the Abu Sayyaf Group (ASG), the Rajah Solaiman Islamic Movement (RSIM), the Abu Sofia (AS) group, and the Al-Khobar Group (AKG). This chapter also includes a brief discussion on the historical context of the radicalization of selected Muslim organizations in the Philippines.

Brief Historical Background

To have a better understanding of the so-called rise of radical Muslim terrorism in the Philippines and its contemporary realities, it is imperative to discuss the subject in its proper historical perspective. Islam arrived in Sulu in the last quarter of the 13th century. In 1450, the Sultanate of

---

1 Information for this chapter was drawn from the following source: R. C. Banlaoi, *Philippine Security in the Age of Terror: National, Regional, and Global Challenges in the Post-9/11 World*, Auerbach Publications, 2009.

2 For a complete copy of the article, access BigNews Network, at http://feeds.bignewsnetwork.com/redir.php?jid=855f4c0dfb7e7357&cat=c08dd24cec417021.

3 S. Bar. The Religious Sources of Islamic Terrorism. *Policy Review*, no. 125, June and July 2004.

Sulu was established. Scholars trace Muslim radicalism or Muslim separatism in the Philippines to the mid-16th century when Spain colonized the Philippine islands in 1565.[4]

Were it not for the Spanish colonial rule, which introduced Roman Catholicism in the archipelago, particularly in the major islands of Luzon and the Visayas, the Philippines would have been a Muslim state like its Southeast Asian neighbors.[5] All Muslim radical groups in the Philippines, regardless of political persuasion and theological inclination, believe in the Bangsamoro struggle. The term "Bangsa" comes from the Malay word, which means nation. Spanish colonizers introduced the term "Moro" when they confused the Muslim people of Mindanao with the "moors" of Northern Africa.[6]

Although the use of the term "Bangsamoro" to describe the national identity of Muslims in the Philippines is still contested; Muslim leaders regard the Bangsamoro struggle as the longest "national liberation movement" in the country, covering almost 400 years of violent resistance against Spanish, American, Japanese, and even Filipino rule.[7] The first recorded military confrontation between Spaniards and the Muslims in the Philippines began as early as 1565, which ended in the Invasion of Brunei in 1578 and 1581.[8] During this confrontation, the Spaniards were said to have ably checked "the increasing Bornean political influence and commercial activities in Luzon and the Visayas by capturing the Bornean settlement in Manila in 1571."[8]

Spanish colonial rule of the Philippines lasted from 1565 to 1898. But Spain established a strong and dominant Christian community in the entire archipelago, except for many Muslim communities, which remained unconquered against the onslaught of Spanish colonialism.[7] During the US colonial rule of the Philippines (1901–1935), the Americans inherited the Moro problem.[9] The new colonial master recognized that the Moro areas had never come under effective Spanish rule. The Americans even kept the Moros out of the Philippine-American War from 1899 to 1901 by signing the Bates Agreement in which the United States agreed to protect Moros from foreign intrusions and to respect the authorities of the Sultans and other Muslim chiefs in Mindanao.[10]

But the Americans saw the Moros from the very start as a minority to be integrated into the national life of the Philippines.[11] Although political integration took place during the American period with the establishment of a Moro Province, Muslims in the Philippines continued to be seen as a religious and cultural minority, the long-term result of which was marginality, dissatisfaction, and, ultimately, rejection of the Philippine nation-state.[11] Through jihad, Moros in the Philippines continued their resistance during the American occupation. Famous among Muslim resistance movements during the period were that of Datu Tunggul, Datu Camour, and Datu Ampuanagus in Lanao (1902–1903), Datu Ali in Cotabato (1903–1905), and Datu Panglima Hassan in Sulu (1903–1905).

To put an end to resistance, some Muslim leaders laid down their arms and resorted to peaceful means to pursue their cause during the Commonwealth Period. During the Commonwealth

[4] A. Tan. Southeast Asia as the Second Front in the War against Terrorism: Evaluating the Threat and Responses. *Terrorism and Political Violence*, 15, no. 2: 115, 2003.

[5] J. Pelan. *The Hispanization of the Philippines*. Madison: University of Wisconsin Press, 1959.

[6] P. Gowing. *Mosque and Moro: A Study of Muslims in the Philippines*. Manila: Federation of Christian Churches, 1964.

[7] S. K. Tan. History of the Mindanao Problem. In A. Rasul (ed.), *The Road to Peace and Reconciliation: Muslim Perspective on the Mindanao Conflict*. Makati City: Asian Institute of Management, 2003, 4–5.

[8] C. Majul. *Muslims in the Philippines*. Quezon City: University of the Philippines Press, 1973, 29–30, 108.

[9] For an excellent account of Muslims in the Philippines during the American colonial rule, see P. G. Gowing. *Mandate in Moroland: The American Government of Muslim Filipinos*, 1899–1920. Quezon City: New Day Publishers, 1983.

[10] W. K. Che Man. *Muslim Separatism: The Moros of Southern Philippines and the Malays of Southern Thailand*. Manila: Ateneo de Manila Press, 1990, 47.

[11] D. J. Amoroso. Inheriting the Moro Problem: Muslim Authority and Colonial Rule in British Malaya and the Philippines. In J. Go and A. L. Foster (eds.), *The American Colonial State in the Philippines: Global Perspectives*. Manila: Anvil Publishing, 2005, 142–143.

Period (1935–1946), some Moro leaders participated in the 1935 National Assembly election. But only two Muslim leaders got their seats, prompting the Muslim groups to continue their fight for independence. But it was only the outbreak of the Pacific War in 1941 "that more or less blunted the Moro independence movement," which resulted in the Japanese invasion of the Philippines.[12] During the Japanese occupation, Moros joined anti-Japanese resistance groups. It has been argued that six months before US forces led by General Douglas MacArthur landed in Leyte to retake the Philippines, "the Muslim territories in Mindanao were already free of the Japanese."[13] The end of World War II led to the total defeat of the Japanese Imperial Army and to the granting of Philippine independence.

When the United States granted the Philippines independence on July 4, 1946, the Moro communities were divided into two major groups: the integrationist or the assimilationist group and the secessionist or liberationist group. The first group accepted Philippine sovereignty while the other group believes that Mindanao belongs to a separate Islamic State that also deserves independence. Those who continue to defy the authority of the Christian-dominated Philippine government assert their separate identity as Moros and refuse to regard themselves as Filipinos, arguing as follows:

> The term Filipino can only refer to a segment of our people who bowed in submission to the might of Spain. Certainly, the Muslims do not fall under the category of Filipino. Being a historic people, the Muslims therefore cannot but reject the generalization that the word Filipino applies to them as well. Because when the word Filipino is applied to a segment of our people, the implication is that the word Filipino was derived or at least named in honor of King Felipe II ... In so far as the Muslims are concerned, the application Filipino does not have any meaning to them.[14]

But the idea of Morohood is being challenged because the term "Moro" was the appellation applied to all of the Muslim population of Southeast Asia by the Portuguese, who seized Malacca in 1511.[15] As stated earlier, Spain used the same label to describe Muslim inhabitants of the Philippine archipelago. Muslims in the Philippines have owned the term Moro to describe their collective identities.

Since the granting of Philippine independence, the government has been contending with Moro separatism. In 1951, some Muslims in the Philippines waged the Kamlong uprising, which lasted until 1955. In 1957, the Philippine government organized the Commission on National Integration (CNI) to provide scholarship to young Muslims and encourage the Moros to accept the authority of the government. The government also implemented a land reform program that encouraged Christians from the North to settle in Southern Philippines. By the 1960s, the Southern Philippines "had been virtually taken over by a Christian majority except areas like Lanao, Cotabato, Basilan and Sulu."[16]

From 76% in the 1900s, the population of Muslims in Mindanao declined to 20% in the 1990s. The massive influx of Christian Filipinos to Mindanao angered the Moros. But what started the Muslim rebellion was the Jabidah Massacre in March 1968. Otherwise known as the Corregidor Massacre, it took place on the Corregidor Island of the Philippines, involving Moro army recruits being trained for Operation Merdek, a code name for the clandestine

---

[12] S. K. Tan. *Internationalization of the Bangsamoro Struggle*, Quezon City, Philippines: University of the Philippines Center for Integrative and Development Studies, 1995, 28.

[13] R. M. Alonto. Four Centuries of Jihad Underpinning the Bangsamoro Muslims' Struggle for Freedom. Available at http://www.muslimedia.com/archives/sea99/phil-jihad, 1999.

[14] A. Glang. *Muslim Secession or Integration?* Quezon City: R. P. Garcia, 1969, 21. Also cited in C. Man, *Muslim Separatism: The Moros of Southern Philippines and the Malays of Southern Thailand*, 55–56.

[15] T. M. McKenna. *Muslim Rulers and Rebels: Everyday Politics and Armed Separatism in the Southern Philippines*. Manila: Anvil Publishing, 1998.

[16] C. Majul. *Muslims in the Philippines*. Quezon City: University of the Philippines Press, 1973, 29–30, 108.

destabilization plan of the Armed Forces of the Philippines (AFP) aiming to infiltrate Sabah as part of the strategy of the Philippine government to strengthen its territorial claim. Allegedly, their trainers summarily executed between 28 and 64 Moro recruits undergoing military training.[17] Though it has been argued that the Jabidah Massacre was a myth,[18] the incident prompted Governor Udtog Matalam of Cotabato to form the Mindanao Independence Movement (MIM) declaring the establishment of an Islamic state in Mindanao.[19] Nonetheless, Matalam yielded to the request of the Philippine government to reconsider his cause. Others continued their resistance, leading to the establishment of the MNLF and other radical Muslim groups.

The Moro National Liberation Front

There is no uniform account of the origin of the MNLF. A former MNLF spokesperson even stressed that Moro rebel leaders are still debating until today as to who really founded it.[20] Though Nur Misuari was the known founding chair of the MNLF, it is argued that the organization was conceptualized and organized by Abul Khayr Alonto and Jallaludin Santos, who were, at that time, active with the Mindanao Independence Movement (MIM) founded in 1969 as a reaction to the Jabidah Massacre. The MIM aimed for the establishment of an independent state covering many parts of Mindanao, Sulu, and Palawan. In the same year, other radical Muslim leaders formed the Union of Islamic Forces and Organization (UIFO) and Anwar El Islam to fight for Moro independence. The MIM and UIFO members reportedly underwent joint combat training in Malaysia that year.

The MNLF was officially established in 1972 as a national liberation movement of Muslims in the Philippines. Unlike other Muslim resistance groups in the Philippines, MNLF has a more secular ideology. The secular ideology of the MNLF is traced to the left-leaning ideology of Misuari, who became a member of a Marxist youth organization in the Philippines, the Kabataang Makabayan (KM), or the Nationalist Youth. Key members of KM organized the Communist Party of the Philippines (CPP), which has been waging an armed struggle against the Philippine government. The CPP also has Muslim membership.

Strictly speaking, the MNLF does not embrace Islamic fundamentalism, but it religiously adheres to the concept of Moro nationalism. It aims for the establishment of a separate Moro nation in the Southern Philippines. Although the MNLF may not be strictly labeled as Islamic fundamentalist, it is arguably a radical Muslim resistance group, advocating jihad to liberate the Moro people from the oppression of what it describes as Filipino colonialism of Imperial Manila. In other words, the MNLF is a national liberation movement of radical, mostly secular-oriented Muslims in the Philippines.

Allegedly, the MNLF received support from Muslim backers in Libya and Malaysia. Its core members of 90 Muslim rebels were reportedly trained in Pulao Pangkor, Malaysia, in 1969. The "Top 90" of the MNLF completed their military training in 1971. It was in 1972, after the declaration of martial law, when they elected Misuari as Chairman of the MNLF. Hashim Salamat, who would eventually organize the MILF, joined the second group of trainees in 1972.

---

[17] "Jabidah Massacre," Available at http://www.moroinfo.com/hist8.html. Also see M. D. Vitug and G. M. Gloria. *Under the Crescent Moon: Rebellion in Mindanao*. Quezon City: Ateneo Center for Social Policy and Public Affairs and Institute for Popular Democracy, 2000, 2–25.

[18] A. M. Azurin. The Jabidah Massacre Myth. In *Beyond the Cult of Dissidence in Southern Philippines and Wartorn Zones in the Global Village*. Quezon City: University of the Philippines Center for Integrative and Development Studies, 1996, 93–103.

[19] C. Majul. *Muslims in the Philippines*. Quezon City: University of the Philippines Press, 1973, 29–30, 108.

[20] A. S. Iribani. *GRP-MNLF Peace Talks, 1992–1996: Issues and Challenges*. Quezon City: National Defense College of the Philippines, 2000, 99.

Salamat was elected chairman on foreign affairs and in 1974 acted as Vice Chairman of the MNLF. Salamat, however, never received confirmation by the MNLF central committee. In 1978, Salamat and his more Islamic followers broke from Misuari's secular leadership. In 1979, Salamat formed the short-lived Bangsamoro Liberation Organization (BMLO). But from 1978 to 1984, Salamat still used the name MNLF to describe his breakaway movement until it formed the MILF, which will be discussed further in the next section. Meanwhile, MNLF members were divided over the issue of the appropriate form of struggle during its nascent stage: parliamentary or armed.

The Organization of Islamic Conference (OIC) recognized the MNLF as the sole and legitimate representative of the Bangsamoro people. Under the auspices of the OIC, the MNLF and the Government of the Republic of the Philippines (GRP) held a peace talk in 1976 in Tripoli, Libya, to settle the Mindanao problem. This peace talk led to the signing of the Tripoli Agreement, which provided for Moro autonomy in the Southern Philippines and for a cease-fire. But after a lull in the fighting, the truce broke down in 1977. Until 1996, the MNLF engaged in armed confrontations with the AFP. The National Memorial Institute for the Prevention of Terrorism (MIPT) has classified the MNLF as a terrorist organization.[21] Though the Philippine government has not officially labeled the MNLF as a terrorist organization, government forces claimed that the MNLF was responsible for a series of urban terror bombings in Mindanao in 1975 that continued well into the 1980s.[22]

In 1986, the GRP and the MNLF held another round of peace talks to provide a just and lasting solution to the Mindanao problem, but the talks collapsed in May 1987. The MNLF reached a final peace agreement with the GRP in 1996, which led to the establishment of the Autonomous Region of Muslim Mindanao (ARMM). Misuari was chosen governor of the region and was made chairman of the Southern Philippines Council for Peace and Development (SPCPD). It was believed that by placing Misuari in charge of both institutions, "the peace settlement would gain wide recognition among the Muslim community and demonstrate to non-Muslims that autonomy can benefit all groups."[23] Other MNLF members were integrated into the AFP. In December 2004, at least 5530 officers and enlisted personnel of the MNLF were integrated into the AFP in compliance with the 1996 Final Peace Agreement. The MNLF integrees have been assigned as regular and organic personnel of the 1st, 4th, and 6th Infantry Divisions, 53rd and 54th Engineer Brigades based in Mindanao.[24]

Nevertheless, issues of mismanagement and corruption plagued Misuari during his term as governor of ARMM and chairman of SPCPD. When he failed to seek reelection as ARMM governor, he threatened to resort to violence, which he carried out in Jolo in November 2001. Misuari organized what the AFP calls the Misuari Breakaway Group (MBG) of the MNLF, which, according to the military, has resorted to terrorism. The MBG is presently drawing up support and sympathy for Misuari and conducting massive recruitment in Sulu, Basilan, Zamboanga City, and Sarangani. As of the last quarter of 2007, the MBG has the strength of 661 Muslim fighters loyal to Misuari (Figure 15.1). They operate largely in Sulu, Basilan, Zamboanga City, and Zamboanga del Norte of the Southern Philippines.

Misuari was jailed in 2003 for an act of rebellion in Jolo town, which led to the death of 100 people. But Misuari posted bail in May 2008. According to Misuari, his group is the original MNLF. But MNLF members who respect the 1996 Peace Agreement stress that they constitute

---

[21] MIPT Terrorism Knowledge Base. Moro National Liberation Front. Available at http://www.tkb.org/Group.jsp?groupID=202.

[22] See ref. 12, p. 181.

[23] J. Bertrand. Peace and Conflict in the Southern Philippines: Why the 1996 Peace Agreement Is Fragile? *Pacific Affairs*, 73, no. 1: 42, Spring 2000.

[24] Office of the Press Secretary. DND Cites Gains in Campaign vs CPP-NPA, Abu Sayyaf, Other Criminal Elements. Available at http://www.news.ops.gov.ph/archives2005/jan03.htm, January 3, 2005.

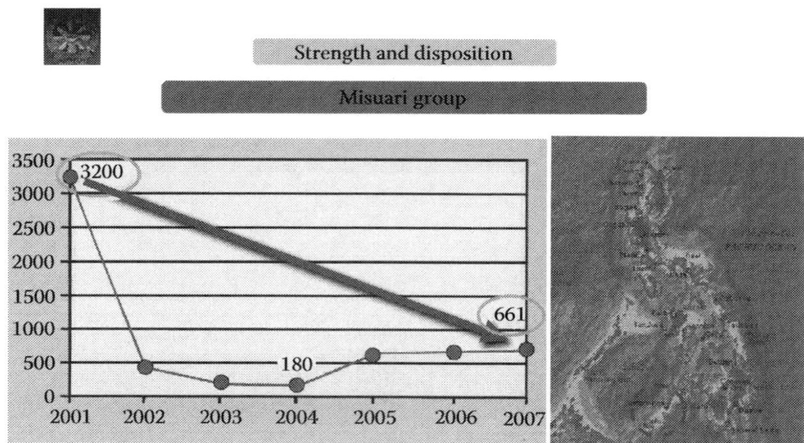

Figure 15.1 Strength of the Nur Misuari Breakaway Group. (From the Office of the Deputy Chief of Staff for Intelligence, April 2008. R. C. Banlaoi *Philippine Security in the Age of Terror National, Regional, and Global Challenges in the Post-9/11 World,* Auerbach Publications, 2009. With permission.)

the mainstream MNLF. These factions of the MNLF pose a difficult challenge for Philippine national security policy. The MBG/MNLF continues to operate in the Southern Philippines. The MBG was said to have forged alliances with the MILF and ASG to plant bombs, kidnap people, and commit murder and other acts of terrorism. According to an intelligence report, the MBG has intensified its alliance with ASG and the MILF "in the conduct of armed atrocities in pursuit of their common agenda."[25]

Ruland Ullah, a former ASG member and a state witness to the April 2000 Sipadan hostage crisis, said that ASG has hired MBG/MNLF fighters to mount terrorist attacks. MNLF members have even acted as mercenaries of the ASG for an amount of at least $1000. MNLF members allegedly provide sanctuaries for ASG members when the need arises.[26] They have also been sharing fighters to mount terrorist attacks not only in the Southern Philippines but also in Metro Manila.

On February 6, 2005, MBG forces simultaneously attacked four military posts in Sulu Province resulting in the death of 30 soldiers, the wounding of 80 others, and the evacuation of 35,000 villagers. Heavy fighting between the AFP and the MBG also broke out on February 24, 2005, as a result of the Philippine government's decision to mount heavy military operations against the MBG. The Philippine government has utilized the military service of MNLF integrees to fight not only the MBG but also the MILF.

The Moro Islamic Liberation Front

The MILF was a breakaway faction of the MNLF. As stated previously, the late Hashim Salamat, known before as the Vice Chairman of the MNLF, founded the MILF in 1978. Though Salamat traced the origin of the MILF to 1962 when he founded the Moro Liberation Front (MLF) in Cairo, it was only in 1984 when he officially used the name MILF to describe his resistance

[25] Office of the Chief of Staff for Intelligence Updates on the Activities of the ASG and the MBG. Quezon City: General Headquarters of the Armed Forces of the Philippines, 2002.

[26] J. Canlas. State Witness Bares MNLF, MILF Links with Abu Sayyaf. *The Manila Times*, March 28, 2005.

group.[27] Unlike the MNLF, which is secular in orientation, the MILF is strictly Islamic or fundamentalist, to use the Western label.

The MILF has a military arm called Bangsamoro Islamic Armed Forces (BIAF). The MILF has personnel strength of almost 11,769 as of the last quarter of 2007. They operate in almost whole areas of the Southern Philippines, particularly in Maguindanao. But according to Salamat, the MILF has registered more than 70,000 participants from BIAF and more than 100,000 trained but not armed fighters. He even claims that the MILF constitutes 70% to 80% of all fighting forces in Mindanao with a modest navy, short of warships, and some members trained as fighter pilots.[27,28]

Though there were allegations that the MILF has established strong linkages with al-Qaeda and Jemaah Islamiyah (JI), the Philippine government has not officially tagged the MILF as a terrorist organization in order not to undermine the peace talks, which, as of this writing, are in progress. Many Philippine politicians believe that tagging the MILF as a terrorist organization will cause the termination of the peace negotiations and the escalation of armed conflict in the Philippines. The MILF has renounced terrorism but persistently argued that it has a legitimate cause to wage armed struggle against the government to liberate the Moros from the bondage of Filipino colonialism.

However, intelligence sources have established a MILF link with al-Qaeda, which was traced to the Afghan war in the 1980s. Osama bin Laden reportedly instructed his brother-in-law Mohammed Jamal Khalifa to go to the Philippines in 1988 to recruit fighters. Salamat was reported to have sent 1000 Filipino Muslim fighters in Afghanistan to undergo military training. Salamat saw the training of these Muslim fighters as vital to the strengthening of the MILF. Khalifa left the Philippines in 1990, but returned to the country in 1991 to establish "a permanent al Qaeda network" to better support the MILF. Bin Laden believed that through the MILF, al-Qaeda could establish permanent presence in the Philippines to serve as its base of terrorist operations in Southeast Asia.[29]

Based on various intelligence sources, the MILF was said to have also established linkage with JI, the so-called al-Qaeda in Southeast Asia. Although MILF spokesperson Eid Kabalu said that the MILF–JI link is a recycled allegation and propaganda lodged against their organization, the International Crisis Group based in Brussels released a report describing this so-called link, stating, "[w]hile the MILF leadership continues to deny any ties, all evidence points to operational and training links. What is uncertain is whether top leaders are aware of the activity and are unwilling to admit it."[30] The MILF even earmarked a training camp for JI, called Camp Hodeiba, set up in 1994.[31] JI reportedly used Camp Hodeiba to train MILF members in urban terrorism, particularly in bomb making. But some Muslim leaders and military officials claimed that JI members were the ones actually receiving training from MILF fighters.

Aside from JI, intelligence reports also reveal that MILF has also forged a tactical alliance with the New People's Army (NPA), the armed group of the CPP. The Philippine government labels the CPP-NPA as a local Communist Terrorist Movement (CTM). Although the MILF says that it has no ties with the CTM, Salamat comments, "[w]e feel that we have almost the same

[27] H. Salamat. *Referendum: Peaceful, Civilized, Diplomatic and Democratic Means of Solving the Mindanao Conflict*. Camp Abubakre As-Siddique: Agency for Youth Affairs–MILF, 2002, 30, 34, 46, 57.

[28] H. Salamat. *The Bangsamoro People's Struggle against Oppression and Colonialism*. Camp Abubakre As-Siddique: Agency for Youth Affairs–MILF, 2001.

[29] Z. Abuza. *Militant Islam in Southeast Asia: Crucible of Terror*. Boulder, Colorado: Lynne Rienner Publishers, Inc., 2003, p. 91.

[30] International Crisis Group. Southern Philippine Backgrounder: Terrorism and the Peace Process. *ICG Asia Report*, no. 8: i, July 13, 2004.

[31] M. A. Ressa. *Seeds of Terror: An Eyewitness Account of Al-Qaeda's Newest Center of Operations in Southeast Asia*. New York: Free Press, 2003, 7.

cause."[32] Salamat even underscores, "[s]ince we have the same enemy and we face the same problem, then our religious beliefs cannot prevent us from having alliances even with the so-called godless people."[32]

In 2002, the MILF and CTM reportedly held a joint two-month "Special Explosives and Sniper Course" training at an NPA camp in Sariaya, Quezon, of Southern Luzon. The training reportedly started on November 16, 2002, and was supposed to have ended in December 2002. Due to skirmishes between the CTM and AFP forces, the training was extended up to February 2003. In March 2003, the Southern Mindanao Regional Community of the NPA reportedly dispatched around 30 armed personnel to Davao Oriental to support MILF forces fighting the government. The Far South Mindanao Region Command of the NPA also directed its front committees to support MILF forces in Sarangani. Joint elements of CPP-NPA and MILF are also operating in Misamis Oriental. According to an intelligence report, "[t]he NPA is expected to stage more joint offensives with the MILF in areas where both parties exert political and military influence."[33]

The MILF has also reportedly established links with the ASG, the most notorious radical Muslim terrorist group in the Philippines. Although the MILF continues to deny any links with the ASG, Salamat once said, "[t]he MILF shares a common goal with the Abu Sayyaf Group: to establish an independent Islamic State."[32] The MILF leadership even regards Abdurajak Janjalani as a Moro martyr.[32] Recent intelligence sources reveal that ASG and MILF members share fighters in their operations. A confession of a captured ASG member states that "sometimes the MILF would plant a roadside bomb against soldiers and the Abu Sayyaf would shoot the soldiers wounded in the blast."[34] MILF and ASG members also conduct joint training with JI operatives, particularly in the area of bomb making.

The Abu Sayyaf Group

Because of the spate of kidnap-for-ransom activities it has perpetrated, the ASG became an international sensation. But it remains the least understood radical Muslim terrorist group in the Philippines. Many scholars and journalists mistranslated ASG to mean "bearer of the sword."[35] But ASG really means in Arabic, "father of the swordsman."[36]

There is no uniform view of the ASG. The United States has listed the ASG in its list of Foreign Terrorist Organizations, while the United Nations has designated it as one of the three terrorist organizations in Southeast Asia along with al-Qaeda and the JI.[37] Some regard the ASG as

[32] H. Salamat. *Referendum: Peaceful, Civilized, Diplomatic and Democratic Means of Solving the Mindanao Conflict.* Camp Abubakre As-Siddique: Agency for Youth Affairs–MILF, 2002, 30, 34, 46, 57.

[33] Office of the Assistant Secretary for Plans and Programs. CPP-NPA-MILF Tactical Alliance. In *Moro Islamic Liberation Front Reference Folder.* Quezon City: Department of National Defense, 2004.

[34] R. Banlaoi, Leadership Dynamics in Terrorist Organizations in Southeast Asia: The Abu Sayyaf Case. Paper presented to the international symposium The Dynamics and Structures of Terrorist Threats in Southeast Asia, organized by the Institute of Defense Analyses in cooperation with the Southeast Asia Regional Center for Counterterrorism and the US Pacific Command held at Palace of Golden Horses Hotel, Kuala Lumpur, Malaysia, April 18–20, 2005. Also in J. T. Hanley, K. O. Hassig, and C. F. Ziemke (eds.), *Proceedings of the International Symposium on the Dynamics and Structures of Terrorist Threats in Southeast Asia.* Alexandria, VA: Institute for Defense Analyses, 2005.

[35] See, for example, G. H. Turbiville, Jr. Bearer of the Sword. Military Review, March/ April 2002, pp. 38–47.

[36] J. Torres Jr. *Into the Mountain: Hostages by the Abu Sayyaf.* Quezon City: Claretian Publications, 2003, 35.

[37] C. Hayer, Leadership Dynamics in Terrorist Organizations in Southeast Asia. Paper presented to the international symposium, The Dynamics and Structures of Terrorist Threats in Southeast Asia, organized by the Institute of Defense Analyses in cooperation with the Southeast Asia Regional Center for Counterterrorism and the US Pacific Command held at Palace of Golden Horses Hotel, Kuala Lumpur, Malaysia, on April 18–20, 2005.

part of the international fundamentalist movement, linked to Osama bin Laden, which aims to establish an independent Islamic state in the Philippines.[38] Others see the ASG as the agent provocateur of the Philippine military and the Central Intelligence Agency, while the Philippine government continues to condemn the ASG as a mere bandit gang that aims to amass funds through kidnap for ransom, extortion, and other criminal activities.[38]

There is also no uniform account of the origin of the ASG. It has a very nebulous beginning.[39] Existing literatures regard Abdurajak Abubakar Janjalani as the founder of ASG. Despite the nebulous origin of the ASG, the military establishment believed that in 1990, Janjalani formed the Mujahideed Commando Freedom Fighters (MCFF) to wage jihad against the Philippine government for the establishment of an independent Islamic state in the Southern Philippines. The Philippine military regarded the MCFF as the forerunner of the ASG. When the MCFF attracted some "hard core" followers in Basilan, Zulu, Tawi-Tawi, and Zamboanga, it was later called the ASG.

According to Noor Muog, one of the key leaders of the ASG now working for the Philippine government, the MCFF was a misnomer. The forerunner of the ASG was the Jamaa Tableegh, an Islamic propagation group established in Basilan in the early 1980s by Abdurajak Janjalani. This group conducted seminars, symposia, and small-group discussions to propagate Islam. It was also through this group where Abdurajak delivered some of his Islamic discourses.

The involvement of some of its followers in antigovernment rallies prompted the military to put the group under surveillance. Key followers of Jamaa Tableegh formed the nucleus of the ASG, which Abdurajak Janjalani initially called Al-Harakatul Al-Islmiyah (AHAI) or the Islamic Movement. The AHAI drew material and financial support from the extremist element in Iran, through the Hezbollah; in Pakistan, through the Jamaat-Islami and Hizbul-Mujahideen; in Afghanistan, through Hizb-Islami; in Egypt, through Al Gamaa-Al-Islamiya; in Algeria, through the Islamic Liberation Front; and in Libya, through the International Harakatul Al-Islamia. The ASG reportedly established a link with al-Qaeda in the 1990s. It was said that Janjalani befriended bin Laden while in Peshawar, Pakistan.[40]

Janjalani also became a very close friend of Ramzi Yousef, who reportedly planned, in the Philippines, the Bojinka plots, believed to be the worst terrorist plots in the country. The Bojinka plots aimed to bomb 11 US jetliners and assassinate Pope John Paul II, who visited Manila in 1995. During his travel to the Philippines via Malaysia, Yousef reportedly stayed in Basilan and trained around 20 ASG fighters. The Philippine National Police (PNP) narrates that as of September 1994, Yousef had a fully established terrorist cell in the Philippines.

The ASG was also reported to have established links with JI. Among JI personalities, Al Ghozi became the most sensational terrorist figure in the Philippines, having been identified as the major suspect in a series of bombings in the country. Known as "Mike the bomb maker," Al Ghozi was known to be Hambali's most trusted Indonesian colleague and became a student of Bashir in the 1980s. Al Ghozi used a lot of aliases while in the Philippines. Police authorities arrested him on charges of illegal possession of explosives just three hours prior to his scheduled flight to Bangkok on January 15, 2002.

In July 2003, Al Ghozi escaped from his prison cell in Manila. But through an intensified manhunt and joint military-police operations, he was killed in a shootout in Mindanao on October 12, 2003, a date coinciding with the first-year anniversary of the 2002 Bali bombing. Intelligence

---

[38] E. P. Manalo. *Philippine Response to Terrorism: The Abu Sayyaf Group*. MA thesis, Naval Post Graduate School, Monterey, California, December 2004.

[39] G. Gloria. Bearer of the Sword: The Abu Sayyaf Has Nebulous Beginnings and Incoherent Aims. *Mindanao Updates*, June 6, 2000.

[40] See Z. Abuza, Tentacles of Terror: Al Qaeda's Southeast Asian Linkages. Paper presented in the conference Transnational Violence and Seams of Lawlessness in the Asia–Pacific: Linkages to Global Terrorism, held at the Asia–Pacific Center for Security Studies, Honolulu, Hawaii, February 12–21, 2002, p. 6. Also published in *Contemporary Southeast Asia*, 24, no. 2: 427–466, December 2002.

sources reveal that the number of JI members in the Philippines collaborating with ASG was placed at 33 as of December 2004. The Philippine National Police Intelligence Group (PNP-IG) estimates a higher figure when it reports that the number of JI operatives in the Philippines may be placed at 60 as of April 2005.[41]

These JI operatives continue to exploit local Muslim secessionist rebels in the Philippines by sharing their demolition skills.[42] In connection with the 2005 Valentine's Day bombings, two Indonesians and a Malaysian allegedly belonging to the JI were arrested by intelligence operatives in Zamboanga City on February 23, 2005. But the arrest of Rohmat, alias "Zaki," on March 16, 2005, gave more substantial information about the recent JI-ASG linkages. Zaki, an Indonesian national, confessed to several crimes involving the ASG since 2000, including training members to make bombs in JI-run camps.[43] Known as the "ASG bomb trainer," Zaki admitted that he trained ASG members in bomb making, particularly the use of mobile phones as detonating devices and the use of toothpaste as bomb paraphernalia.[44] He also admitted to having coordinated the 2005 Valentine's Day bombings, which resulted in the brutal death of 10 people and the serious wounding of at least 150 others. Contrary to the public opinion and some media reports, the ASG is not a homogenous organization. The ASG is a highly factionalized group of radical Muslim terrorist groups in the Philippines. The death of Abdurajak Janjalani on December 18, 1998, aggravated the factionalization of the ASG.

The ASG strength was reduced to 383 combatants as of the last quarter of 2007, a sharp decline from its peak of more than 1000 combatants in the early 1990s. Though the ASG strength increased to around 400 in the first quarter of 2009, it is still a small organization compared with the NPA and MILF. Despite its small number, the ASG can still wreak huge terrorist havoc because of its enormous ability to solicit strong local support from Muslim relatives, friends, classmates, and neighbors of ASG fighters. Moreover, the ASG continues to have effective alliances with rogue factions of the MNLF, MILF, and some JI personalities operating in the Philippines. A police intelligence report reveals that ASG has forged alliances with MBG members or gunmen loyal to jailed MNLF leader Nur Misuari.[45]

Captured ASG members even admitted during police interrogation that they hired some MBG followers or rogue members of the MNLF to mount some piracy and terrorist attacks in Mindanao. MNLF members acted as mercenaries of the ASG for an amount of $1000 each and provided sanctuaries for ASG members during hot military pursuits. As stated earlier, ASG and MILF members have also shared fighters in some of their major operations. But some scholars still believe that the ASG and the MILF are unaligned organizations despite similar aims and comparable origins.[46] Intelligence reports, however, reveal that MILF and ASG members have been receiving joint training with JI operatives, particularly in the area of bomb making. The JI-ASG-MILF linkage, therefore, remains intact and operational.

---

[41] Interview with Police Chief Superintendent Ismael R. Rafanan, Director of the Philippine National Police Intelligence Group, held at Camp Crame, Quezon City, on April 1, 2005.

[42] A. Papa. Military: JI Members Still Training Locals. *Philippine Daily Inquirer*, January 18, 2005.

[43] Alleged Bombs Expert for Jemaah Islamiyah Regional Network Arrested in Philippine. *Channel News Asia*. Available at http://www.channelnewsasia.com/stories/southeastasia/view/138779/1/.html.

[44] Interview with General Marlu Quevedo, Chief of the Intelligence Service of the Armed Forces of the Philippines, held at Camp General Emilio Aguinaldo, Quezon City, on March 29, 2005.

[45] J. Gomez. Filipino Terror Group's Reach Grown Nationally. *Associated Press*, March 8, 2005.

[46] C. Donnely, Terrorism in the Southern Philippines: Contextualizing the Abu Sayyaf Group as an Islamist Secessionist Organization. Paper presented to the 15th Biennial Conference of the Asian Studies Association of Australia held in Canberra, June 2–July 29, 2004, p. 4.

Maritime Terrorism

Because ASG members live in the waters of Basilan, Sulu, and Tawi-Tawi, they have gained tremendous familiarity with the maritime environment. Most Muslim Filipinos living in coastal communities are known deep-sea divers. ASG members' deep knowledge of the maritime domain also gives them ample capability to conduct piracy and wage maritime terrorist attacks.

Additionally, due to its embedded seaborne abilities, ASG's first known terrorist attack was maritime in nature when on August 24, 1991, it bombed the M/V Doulous, a Christian missionary ship and a European floating library docked at the Zamboanga port. Moreover, in August 1993, the ASG abducted Mr. Ricardo Tong, a prominent shipyard owner in Zamboanga City. The abduction of Mr. Tong demonstrated that during its infancy stage, the prime target of the ASG was the maritime sector. The ASG proved its maritime terrorist capability when it waged another attack on April 23, 2000, when it kidnapped some 21 tourists, including 10 foreigners, from a Malaysian beach resort in Sipadan. On May 22, 2001, ASG guerrillas raided the luxurious Pearl Farm beach resort on Samal Island of Mindanao. This incident resulted in the killing of two resort workers and the wounding of three others. Although no hostages were taken during this attack, the Samal raid demonstrated anew the willingness of ASG to pursue maritime targets.

On May 28, 2001, the ASG waged another maritime terror when it abducted three American citizens and 17 Filipinos spending a vacation at the Dos Palmas resort in Palawan. Thus far, the Dos Palmas incident was the most notorious and the most sensationalized attack of the ASG. The incident received international coverage because several of the victims were murdered and beheaded, including an American citizen. Because American hostages were involved, the US military sent army operation forces to the Philippines to train AFP forces in counterterrorism. The US Pacific Command even extended US$2 million in assistance to the Philippines from its regional security assistance program as a result of the Dos Palmas incident. But when the lives of the two American hostages were put in danger, the US Army special operations forces changed the scope of their mission in the Philippines by facilitating the rescue of the American citizens. During a rescue operation mounted by the AFP in 2002, two victims, including an American missionary, Martin Burnham, were killed. His wife, Gracia Burnham, the well-known survivor of the kidnap incident, wrote a memoir of her captivity at the hands of the ASG.[47]

The most gruesome maritime terrorist attack of the ASG was the February 27, 2004, bombing of MV Superferry 14, a commercial vessel carrying 899 passengers. The ASG claimed responsibility for the explosion and stressed that the incident was a "just revenge" of the group for the "brutal murder" of Bangsamoro people amid the "ongoing violence" in Mindanao. The bombing of the MV Superferry 14 was carried out through the assistance of another radical Muslim terrorist group in the Philippines, the Rajah Solaiman Islamic Movement (RSIM). Some writers have traced the origin of the RSIM to the Balik Islam (Return to Islam) movement.[48]

Rajah Solaiman Islamic Movement

While founding members of the RSIM have indeed associated themselves with the Balik Islam, it is careless to associate Balik Islam with RSIM—it is like associating Islam with terrorism. Started in the 1970s, Balik Islam is a legitimate organization of at least 200,000 Christian converts to Islamic faith. Followers prefer to be called reverts based on the belief that Islam was the original religion of the Philippines. The RSIM, organized only in 2001, represents a very minuscule fraction of reverts. Though Ahmad Santos (Hilarion del Rosario Santos III) was the known RSIM commander, the group was founded with the leading role of Sheik Omar Lavilla

[47] G. Burnham and D. Merrill. *In the Presence of My Enemies*. Wheaton, IL: Tyndale House Publishers, 2003.

[48] See P. Chalk, Christian Converts and Islamic Terrorism in the Philippines. *Terrorism Monitor*, 4, no. 8, April 20, 2006. Also see International Crisis Group. Philippines Terrorism: The Role of Militant Islamic Converts. *Asia Report*, no. 110, December 19, 2005.

(Rueben Lavilla). With the arrest of Santos on October 26, 2005, Lavilla is believed to be running the daily operation of the RSIM to date. Lavilla has called RSIM members "Urban Mujahideens." In 2008, Lavilla was arrested in Bahrain and deported to the Philippines.

The RSIM was estimated to have a membership of 50 to 100 "hard core activists."[49] If we define "hard core activists" to mean individuals who have the intent and capability to wage terrorism, RSIM membership is not more than 30 members. The AFP identifies only 25 active members of the RSIM as of April 2008. These active members are reported to have been conducting recruitment drives in Luzon and in the Visayas. Though small at present, the RSIM draws its strength from its alleged continuing collaboration with likeminded terrorist groups like the ASG, JI, and al-Qaeda. The RSIM has established ties with the ASG. At the time of his arrest in October 2005, Santos served as the Chief of the ASG Media Bureau. Prior to that, ASG leader Khadafy Janjalani (now deceased) reportedly gave the RSIM the equivalent of about US $200,000 for its initial operational activities in Manila, which included the recruitment and conversion of Christians to Islam, then sent them for terrorist training.[50]

The RSIM collaborated with the ASG in the 2004 MV Superferry 14 bombing and the 2005 Valentine's Day bombings, which were reportedly planned as suicide missions.[51] The RSIM has allegedly formed its own armed wing called the Khalid Trinidad Army, a small group of terrorists named after Khalid Trinidad, an RSIM member himself. Police operatives killed Trinidad in an encounter on May 1, 2002. The RSIM was also reported to have established links with JI. Santos confessed that he collaborated with Omar Patek, one of the key suspects in the 2002 Bali bombings while hiding in Mindanao in early 2004. Patek allegedly gave the RSIM an amount of P 250,000 (US $5000) to be used in the foiled Ermita Plot. Ermita is a place in Manila frequented by foreign tourists. Santos admitted to having used this money to conduct surveillance operations in Ermita and to rent a house in Quezon City where he hid 600 kilos of explosive materials discovered by police and military authorities on March 23, 2005.

During its embryonic stage, the RSIM reportedly established links with al-Qaeda. Santos confessed that the RSIM "aided in training and giving shelter to the terrorists responsible in the September 11 terrorist attack." The PNP regarded the International Information Center, a Muslim center based in Quiapo, Manila, as a front of the RSIM. The Philippine Association of Muslimah Darul Eeman, Inc., was also reported to be a front of ASG to recruit Metro Manila–based Islam converts into its fold.[52] The following Balik Islam groups have also aroused official curiosity: Al Maarif Education Center (Baguio City), Da'rul Hijra Foundation, Inc. (Makati City), and Islamic Learning Center (Pangasinan). Police authorities said that the RSIM is the newest terrorist threat facing the Philippines today.[53]

Although the RSIM may be the smallest among the radical Muslim terrorist groups operating in the Philippines, it has trained some suicide bombers to become "martyrs of Islamic faith." Santos admitted during police interrogation to have trained potential suicide bombers from the ranks of RSIM hard-core jihadists.[54] Santos confessed that he started the training of suicide bombers as early as February 2002. Trainees were indoctrinated on the belief that "the greatest sacrifice is giving one's life for Allah and Islam." After a month of training, five RSIM members reportedly took the Shaheed (martyrdom pledge) to undergo a suicide mission scheduled in May 2002. This mission allegedly aimed to assassinate President Gloria Macapagal Arroyo (PGMA) with the use of a "truck bomb." But the raid of RSIM hideouts in Central Luzon that

---

[49] Chalk, "Christian Converts and Islamic Terrorism in the Philippines."

[50] "Summary of Report on Rajah Solaiman Movement" (April 12, 2004).

[51] Philippine National Police, "Fact Sheet on the Rajah Solaiman Movement."

[52] A paper obtained from the National Intelligence Coordinating Agency, March 1, 2005.

[53] J. Cochrane. Filipino Authorities Say the Newest Threat to the Country Is a Shadowy Terror Group Made Up of Radical Muslim Converts. *Newsweek International Edition*, May 17, 2004. Available at http://msnbc.msn.com/id/4933472/.

[54] Philippine National Police, "Executive Summary: Update on the Arrest of Hilarion Santos" (October 28, 2005).

year halted the mission. The raid resulted in the death of one and the arrest of four potential suicide bombers. The raid also indicated the strong resolve of the Philippine law enforcement authorities to clamp down on terrorists. In April 2004, the RSIM revived the mission after seven different potential suicide bombers took another Shaheed.[55] But the mission was preempted as a result of the series of counterterrorism operations conducted during May and June 2004.

RSM's alleged link with ASG has created further suspicions that Muslim converts are being used for urban terrorism. As stated earlier, the blasting of the Superferry 14 on February 27, 2004, has been described as the handiwork of an ASG-RSIM conspiracy. Redento Cain Dellosa, an RSIM member, confessed that he deliberately planted a bomb on Superferry 14. The ASG even claimed responsibility for the explosion and stressed that the incident was a "just revenge" of the group for the "brutal murder" of Bangsamoro people amid the "ongoing violence" in Mindanao. ASG Chief Khadafy Janjalani strongly warned that the "best action of ASG was yet to come." Although the Philippine government initially denied the involvement of ASG and RSIM in the incident, the Marine Board Inquiry in charge of investigating the Superferry 14 incident confirmed that the ASG indeed masterminded the explosion with the assistance of RSIM.

The RSIM, upon instruction of ASG, allegedly masterminded the three simultaneous bombings in Makati City, General Santos City, and Davao City on the eve of the Valentine's Day celebration in 2005. These bombings resulted in the death of seven people and the wounding of at least 150 others. RSIM reportedly assisted the ASG in the bombing that occurred in Makati City. The RSIM had also planned to mount another terrorist attack on the eve of the 2005 Holy Week celebration. But military intelligence operatives foiled this plan when they arrested RSIM member Tyrone Dave Santos (alias Daud Santos) in a raid conducted in an alleged RSIM building in Quezon City for carrying 10 sacks of explosive materials. These explosives were intended to be used during the Lenten season to bomb soft targets in Metro Manila in retaliation to the killing of ASG members during the aborted jailbreak in March 2005.

Abu Sofia Group

Another small but loosely labeled radical Muslim terrorist group in the Philippines was the Abu Sofia (AS) group. Military sources described the AS as a breakaway faction of the MILF engaged in banditry and kidnap-for-ransom activities. Bebis Binago, a brother of a local MILF commander, headed the said bandit group.[56] There were reports indicating that AS had established links with the ASG in terms of providing shelter to fugitive members and conducting kidnap-for-ransom activities. Though the AS did not have a veneer of ideology attached to it, its alleged links with the ASG and MILF, however, prompted police authorities to subsume it under the terrorist threat.[57]

The group was suspected for its involvement in the bombings of shopping malls in central Mindanao in 2002 and 2003. The group was also reported to having given refuge to top ASG leaders, particularly Khadafy Janjalani and Isnilon Hapilon. But the death of Binago on January 6, 2004, in a military encounter has led to the hibernation of the AS Group. Alo Binago, brother of the slain leader Bebis Binago, revived the group when he headed the kidnapping of a South Korean national in early 2006. But Alo Binago, along with two other members, was arrested on July 28, 2006, in Maguindanao province. According to the joint PNP-AFP Anti-Terror Task Force based in Sultan Kudarat, the three members of the AS Group were plotting more bombings

---

[55] Philippine National Police, "Executive Summary: Update on the Arrest of Hilarion Santos."

[56] S. Ulph. Philippine Terror War Goes On Despite Peace Talks. *Jamestown Foundation Terrorism Focus*, 2, no. 3: 3, February 3, 2005.

[57] A. Rasul-Bernardo, Ethnic Conflict, Peace and Development: A Philippine Case Study. Paper presented at the CSID 6th Annual Conference, Washington, D.C., April 22–23, 2005. Available at http://www.islam-democracy.org/documents/[df/6th_Annual_Conference-AminaRasulBernardo.pdf, p. 1.

and kidnapping activities and had been meeting with radical Muslim terrorists in Mindanao prior to their arrest.[58] Law enforcement authorities believe that some members of the AS Group are still active and continue to have links with the ASG and the MILF.[59]

Al-Khobar Group

The latest Muslim terrorist group operating mainly in the Davao del Sur, Saranggani, South Cotabato, and North Cotabato areas is the Al-Khobar Group (AKG). Though the Philippine military considers this group as a mere extortion gang, its link with Muslim personalities associated with the NPA, ASG, and MILF opens the possibility that the AKG may mutate into a radical Muslim terrorist group. According to Musali Calo, an arrested member of the AKG, the group was organized by Zabide Abdul, alias Commander Beds of the MILF.[60] The Philippine military identified the AKG as responsible for a series of bus bombings in 2008 in Mindanao, particularly in Koronadal City, Tacurong City, and Kidapawan City.

Concluding Thoughts

Muslim radicalism in the Philippines has deep historical, economic, social, and political roots. But among the radical Muslim groups in the Philippines, only the ASG and the RSIM have officially been tagged as terrorist organizations by the government. Though the MNLF-MBG and the MILF have not been officially labeled as terrorist organizations, the police and military establishments have reported their "acts of terrorism" as warranting the label. But the Philippine government is cautious in labeling the MNLF as a terrorist organization because of the 1996 peace agreement. The government also faces difficulties in labeling the MILF as a terrorist organization because of the ongoing peace talks. But all groups discussed in this chapter are called Muslim radicals, except AS, which is considered by the Philippine government as a mere bandit group. There are reports, however, of "terrorist acts" committed by these groups, prompting the police and military establishments to describe all armed groups fighting the government in Mindanao as Southern Philippine terrorist groups.[61]

The Philippine government has provided various mechanisms to actively involve local governments in the fight against terrorism. Through the cooperation of local governments, the military, and police, antiterrorist operatives were able to identify, arrest, and neutralize terrorist leaders and members operating in various local government units (LGUs) in the Philippines. The arrest and neutralization of terrorists have prevented the occurrence of some terrorist attacks that could have brought catastrophic effects on the Philippines. Due to the weakness of the Philippine intelligence system and enforcement agencies, the Philippines remains vulnerable to terrorist attacks. When terrorist attacks occur, local governments are the first victims. Preventing acts of terrorism cannot be solved through military solution alone. A more comprehensive solution that addresses the root of terrorism is imperative. Poverty and injustices are believed to serve as major roots of terrorism in the Philippines. Unless poverty is alleviated and justice is observed at the local levels, the Philippines will continue to face the vicious cycle of terrorist threats.

---

[58] Agence France Press. Three Muslim Extremists Captured in Maguindanao. *ABSCBN News*, July 29, 2006.

[59] A phone interview with military official in Cotabato City, July 30, 2006.

[60] For a news account, see M. C. Manar, "Al Khobar Leader Is MILF Commander: Arrested Bomber," *Sun Star* (February 27, 2008). Available at http://www.sunstar.com.ph/static/net/2008/02/27/al.khobar.leader.is.milf.commander.arrested.bomber.html.

[61] M. D. Vitug and G. M. Gloria. *Under the Crescent Moon: Rebellion in Mindanao*, Quezon City, Philippines: Ateneo Center for Social Policy and Public Affairs, Institute for Popular Democracy, 2000, 229.

Part V

Emerging Issues and the Future of Terrorism

16

The Arab Spring and Subsequent Effects[1]

For decades, it was a stated aim of jihadists and Islamists that the first order of business was not to destroy America or even Israel but rather to purge the Islamic world of those secular and so-called apostate regimes that refused to establish the Islamist agenda, institute Sharia (Islamic law), and promote universal jihad against Kafirs (unbelievers). The ironic result, the great unintended consequence of the "Arab Spring" as it is being termed, may be that the technology-savvy, prodemocracy, secular-oriented, spontaneously activated revolutionaries, who force abdications in some countries and ministerial changes in others, have unwittingly cleared the way for the Islamists to seize power, now that the once-implacable enemies of political Islam have been toppled.

Many in the Middle East and North Africa consider that the problems of their nations are the result of too much Islam in the public sector,[2] the practice of which (especially of the more conservative ideologies like Wahabbism) retards the advancements of modernization and technological innovation that could heal the ills of poverty and economic malaise. Conversely, the Islamists believe fervently that the same problems are caused by too little Islam and that a turn to first principles will engender a rebirth of the glorious past ages (800 CE to 1100 CE) when Islamic empires were the light of civilization, Europe being mired in the Dark Ages at that time. For the Islamists, the only true civilization is one based on a strict adherence to Sharia principles. The fact that many of these principles conflict totally with the freedoms of most Western constitutions is the primary challenge faced.

Trends and Prognostications

This chapter prospects for change (or not) in the countries affected by revolution or upheaval to date, including Tunisia, Egypt, Libya, Bahrain, Jordan, Syria, and Yemen. No one really knows the directions these various revolutions will travel. Each country afflicted may see a different outcome, and in truth, it could take years for the revolutionary dynamic to play itself out. In the end, the world will undoubtedly witness some very radical developments as the entire region

[1] Information for this chapter was drawn from the following title: A. J. Budka, The Arab Revolutions of 2011: Promise, Risk, and Uncertainty. In T. A. Johnson (ed.), *Power, National Security, and Transformational Global Events: Challenges Confronting America, China, and Iran*, CRC Press, 2012.

[2] D. Cook. *Understanding Jihad*. Berkeley, Los Angeles: University of California Press, 2005, 106–107.

is transformed. Moreover, as a part of the ripple effect, countries unaffected so far, such as Morocco, Turkey, Saudi Arabia, the United Arab Emirates, Oman, and even Iran, may experience increasing unrest or revolt over time. Therefore, this analysis begins with an examination the progenitor of the upheaval: namely, Tunisia.

Tunisia: Radical Eschew—At Least So Far

Tunisia is a small country, geographically located in the center of North Africa between Algeria and Libya. What triggered the upheaval in Tunisia? It was young Muhammed Bouazizi's self-immolation that, quite literally, caused the spark that ignited the continent-wide conflagration of upheaval, protests, and insurrections that have occurred from Morocco all the way east to Saudi Arabia and Bahrain. Mr. Bouazizi's story is now well known: He was 26 years old, long unemployed, and he decided to set up a fruit stand to make a little hard cash. Not only did the local authorities shut down his tiny enterprise for lack of the proper paperwork, they abused and humiliated him as well. His desperate response catalyzed a long-simmering national anger and resentment against Ben Ali's regime. In truth, Ben Ali's government was not only quite authoritarian in nature but also had morphed into an egregious "kleptocracy," which unabashedly flaunted its wealth, derived at the expense of the citizenry.[3] The vast majority of Tunisia's 12 million citizens made their collective will felt, and Ben Ali fled to Saudi Arabia in mid January 2011.

Elections for a new constituent assembly were set for October 2011.[4] Tunisia, which has a long history of eschewing violence and internal mayhem, despite the January 2011 "Jasmine Revolution," as it is now termed, is the one North African country for which there is belief that a secular and pluralist new government could rise as a result of Ben Ali's abdication.[5] Aiding this endeavor will be Tunisia's cohesiveness. Unlike many other Arab states, Tunisia has mostly sloughed off its tribal affiliations and adopted a national identity. Tunisians, in general, think of themselves as Tunisians first. As will be shown in this chapter, many other Arab nations do not share this national consciousness trait.

Tunisia has a well-entrenched secular culture and is considered to be one of the most socially liberal in the Muslim world. Polygamy was officially outlawed (the only Arab country to do so) soon after independence. Women are free to wear western attire and, under Ben Ali, the veil and hijab (the cloth that Muslim women wear to cover all or most of their body to indicate modesty) were forbidden in public. Interestingly, there have been recent reports of public protests in the capital of Tunis in which crowds have demanded the right for women to voluntarily wear the hijab if desired.[6] Education is compulsory for men and women until age 16, and women are found in all professions (not the case in most other Arab countries).

There is an Islamist element that has been extant in Tunisia since the early 1980s. It was vigorously repressed both under Bourguiba and Ben Ali, especially after it was discovered that the Islamists were colluding with Libya to overthrow the Tunisia state.[5] In truth, even considering the aforementioned machinations, political Islam has never been a major issue in Tunisian life, at least until this time. The main Islamist party, Al Nahda (The Awakening), participated in the 2011 October elections.

A new government is expected to be a modern democracy with separation of powers, a tenet most Islamist parties reject. But it is thought that the Tunisian brand of Islamism, at least in the

---

[3] S. Coll. Casbah Coalition. *New Yorker*, April 4, 2011, 34.

[4] T. Amara. Tunisia Election Delayed Until October 23. *Reuters*, June 8, 2011. Available at http://www.reuters.com/article/2011/06/08/us-tunisia-election-idUSTRE7571R020110608.

[5] W. Phares. Tunisia's Jasmine Revolution vs. the Forces of Counter-democracy. *American Thinker*, January 21, 2011. Available at http://www.americanthinker.com/2011/01/tunisias_jasmine_revolution_vs._html.

[6] J. Goldberg. Danger Falling Tyrants. *The Atlantic*, June 2011, 49.

beginning, will adhere to this requirement, and freedom of religion will continue to be guaranteed (even though Tunisia is about 98% Sunni Muslim in composition, anyway, with a small 1%–2% Christian, mostly Roman Catholic, presence). Tunisians are well educated in general, and even with all the previous decades of corruption, there is a sizable middle class that can provide leadership and stability. Indeed, out of all of the nations examined in this chapter, Tunisia experienced an easier government transition.[7]

Given its secular traditions, its sizeable middle class and overall well-educated public, Tunisia was equipped to overcome the challenges of the government transition. In the 2011 elections, the Islamists did much better than expected. In fact, the Al Nahda party, which had been banned under the Ben Ali regime, was elected. Specifically, "the Ennahda, or the Islamist Renaissance Party, won 41% plurality in the 2011 election."[8] In 2011, it was forecasted that if the Islamists do much better than expected, Tunisia may serve as a bellwether of sorts in that, being the least radicalized Arab nation, a strong showing by the Islamists could foretell greater election sweeps in other Arab countries. Tunisia is scheduled to vote on a new constitution and hold permanent elections for Parliament by June 23, 2013.[8] The impact of these new elections remains to be seen.

Egypt

Hosni Mubarak's long tenure provided some needed political stability for Egypt but little else. Its economy only grew at a snail's pace and could not (and still cannot) provide the needed employment or educational opportunities required to sustain a burgeoning population. Over the decades, corruption became pervasive at all levels of the huge governmental bureaucracy and internal security repression was intensified. Elections were manipulated, and the press censored and controlled. Like Ben Ali and his regime in Tunisia, President Mubarak, his family, and his closest ministers grafted billions of dollars and flaunted their wealth and acquisitions. In a nation where the average family had to live on less than $100 a month, the seeds of resentment and revolution were sown. So, suffering under a similar "kleptocracy" as the Tunisians, experiencing the same oppression and lack of opportunity, Egyptians, following the Tunisian example, spontaneously took to the streets by the hundreds of thousands and, using the same technological tools of Facebook, Twitter, and cell phones, to organize themselves, and despite suffering hundreds of deaths, overwhelmed the security forces and forced Mubarak to abdicate on February 11, 2011. As in Tunisia, this popular revolt was neither organized nor initiated by Islamists or religious extremists. It was clear from their attire that many of the young and middle-aged revolutionaries were secular-oriented, educated, and technologically astute professionals.[9]

Since Sadat's assassination in 1981, Egypt had been living under martial law, which had subjected citizens to arbitrary detention for prolonged periods without any requirement for due process. Worse, torture and brutality were rampant and routine for those incarcerated. Coupled with corruption, high unemployment, and lack of opportunity, this paved the way for the masses to revolt. Following Mubarak's abdication, Egypt's government was administered by a council of senior military officers, who held the first of these electoral parliamentary rounds in December 2011.

As in Tunisia, there was a frantic effort on the part of the population to organize political parties and begin the campaign for election. This was no small task, especially in light of the

---

[7] M. L. Roach. Morning Bell: Taking Terrorism and the Arab Spring Seriously. *The Heritage Foundation*, February 14, 2013. Available at http://blog.heritage.org/2013/02/14/morning-bell-taking-terrorism-and-the-arab-spring-seriously/.

[8] R. Wright. In 2013, Rise of the Right in Elections Across the Mideast. Woodrow Wilson International Center for Scholars, January 3, 2013. Available at http://www.wilsoncenter.org/islamists/article/2013-rise-the-right-elections-across-the-mideast.

[9] A. Darwish. Egypt: Is the Party Over? The Middle East. March 2011, p. 14.

fact that after decades of essentially one party rule, there is an obvious dearth of political experience. But the population is eager and motivated and certainly has the collective energy and will to conduct this great undertaking. The expertise already exhibited by the Egyptians in organizing the revolution will certainly aid this endeavor. However, as the new parties attempted to establish their platforms and begin the campaign, there is one bloc that already possesses the organization, the discipline, and the support of at least 30% or 40% of the population: the Muslim Brotherhood. Since its formation in 1928, and in spite of its repression by Nasser and his successors from 1954 until today, the Brotherhood has persevered and is still a major influence on Egyptian society.

The "Ikwan al-Muslimun" (The Muslim Brotherhood)

By the 1970s, a majority of the Brotherhood's leadership realized that violence was counterproductive and only resulted in increased governmental repression. A minority disagreed, split from the organization, and carried out the assassination of Sadat and other acts of terrorism during the 1980s and 1990s. Known as the "Gaamat Islamiyya," the Islamic Group, they never garnered popular support and were finally subdued by the government. Thus, the Brotherhood publicly renounced violence and stated it would work within the political system, but they never dropped their slogan and motto: "Islam is the Answer."

Quietly integrating themselves into all levels of the society and gathering substantial support, the Brotherhood has engendered immense good will among the poor, the unemployed, and the illiterate who compose the majority of Egyptian society. Its medical clinics, schools, civic projects, and charitable activities (as previously mentioned) put a constructive and peaceful face on their activity. But their ultimate goal, never foresworn since 1928, is the establishment of an Islamic, Sharia state in Egypt. The Brotherhood has learned patience over the past 80 years, and they have publicly stated, defusing any worry as to their motives, that although they will energetically participate in the elections in November 2011, they will not submit a candidate for president and will not seek to gain more than about 50% of the seats in the legislature.[10] This was a savvy and sound strategy, which promoted much good will, public approval, and even international acclaim.

The government that was elected and constituted in November 2011 faced herculean tasks. The citizenry, now that Mubarak was gone, expected a quick end to corruption and an immediate turnaround of the economy. If the efforts of the first coalition fail, the Brotherhood will not be blamed, and they can then emerge as the solution, touting their slogan "Islam is the Answer." But even as a new government takes hold, the Brotherhood will neither cease their charitable and civic efforts nor their role as the shadow government in many locales. The successes of these initiatives already have and will continue to stand in stark contrast to the former, and most likely the new, government's inability to provide for its citizens. Additionally, given an Egyptian illiteracy rate of an astounding 40%, the Brotherhood, through its private tuition-free schools, has generated huge support among this stratum of society, which will translate into votes now and in the future.[11]

Now that the government's repression of Islamists has been largely lifted and the Brotherhood has the green light to fully participate in the political process, even they (the Brotherhood) may have a difficult time restraining the energy and enthusiasm of the more militant factions. Several troubling events indicate that the Sharia supporters will not be silenced. Certain more radical

[10] C. Gillard and G. Wells. Could the Muslim Brotherhood Win Egypt's Presidency. *The Atlantic*, May 16, 2011. Available at http://www.theatlantic.com/international/archive/2011/05could-the-muslim-brotherhood-win-egypts-presidency/238914/.

[11] C. Ruddy. Egypt's Muslim Brotherhood Rising to Power. *Newsmax*, April 3, 2011. Available at http://www.newsmax.com/Ruddy/egypt-muslim-brotherhood-election/2011/04/03/id/391592.

elements are demanding an immediate abrogation of the peace treaty with Israel.[12] These same elements also demand that Egypt halt its export of natural gas to Israel and remilitarize the Sinai, which is presently a neutral zone, as dictated by the 1979 treaty. Moreover, there was an incident involving Egypt's most famous international personality, Muhammed el Baradei, who has long served as the head of the International Atomic Energy Agency (IAEA) and was admired for his opposition to the Mubarak government. A candidate for the new presidency, he was considered a secularist. Yet even he was maltreated and actually pelted with stones by Islamists and forced to withdraw from a political rally in Cairo on March 19, 2011, as he attempted to address the crowd. Calling him a tool of America, the Islamists demanded he leave Egypt.[13]

A second issue concerns the constitutional amendments approved by popular ballot on March 1. Despite Islamist assertions to the contrary, the abiding concern is that the November 2011 elections could consist of a "one person, one vote, one-time" scenario, which elects a majority of Islamists to the legislature, who, in turn, vote to dissolve the new secular state and establish a Sharia government.[14] In this regard, it has been reported that ad hoc Sharia courts have already popped up in various places in Egypt. Reportedly, these courts have tried those accused of violating Islamic law, rendered verdicts, and then carried out punishments. In one village in south Egypt, a Christian man, who had rented an apartment to a single woman, taboo under Sharia law, was found guilty and had his ear cut off as punishment and warning to the others.[15] Further evidence that a secularist loss of control of the momentum from the January 2011 revolution may be in the offing is the report that not only were Sadat's assassins released from jail, to a huge and very public celebration, but also the new military council, at the urging of the Brotherhood, allowed the repatriation of more than 3000 Muslim Brotherhood activists who had fled to Iran, Afghanistan, Bosnia, and Somalia. These activists sought exile to avoid prison. Many are from the more radical wing of the Brotherhood's membership and are militant pietists who will be expected to agitate and demand more Sharia and less secular ideology in Egypt as well as push for an end to Egypt's cooperation with the United States and Israel.

The Counterweight to the Brotherhood: The Egyptian Military

The other organized, disciplined power center in Egypt is the military, especially the Army. Despite Mubarak's fall, the military remains in firm control of the government and bureaucracy, and in truth, has done so since 1952. Nasser, Sadat, and Mubarak were all military officers, and their power base resided in the military services. It is safe to assume that the military establishment will not want to relinquish its control. Additionally, Egypt receives almost two billion dollars a year in military aid from the United States, and this will continue as long as Egypt abides by the 1979 peace treaty with Israel. Even more important for the economic health of the country are the foreign subsidies for its grain imports. The military will be resistant to major changes in Egyptian foreign policy that might endanger these military and agricultural grants. So they represent a very real counterweight to the Brotherhood or at least its more radical elements.[16]

It was forecasted that the composition of the new Egyptian government would be mostly secular and pluralistic but contain a significant Islamic presence, at least initially. But within a few years, given Egypt's extremely difficult and complex economic and social problems, it is

---

[12] A. De Borchgrave. Coming Geopolitical Upheaval. *The Washington Times*, April 11, 2011. Available at http://www.washingtontimes.com/news/2011/apr/11/the-coming-geopolitcal-upheaval.

[13] Hundreds of Islamists Stone Egypt's El Baradei. The *Vancouver Sun*, March 19, 2011. Available at http://www.vancouversun.com/technology/Hundreds+Islamists+stone+Egypt+ElBaradei/4471305/story.html.

[14] New Egypt but Same Old Sharia. *Investors.com*, March 22, 2011. Available at http://www.investors.com/NewsandAnalysis/Article/566799/201103221824/New-Egypt-but-Same-old-Sharia.aspx.

[15] S. Bouzid. Tunisia: It Could Be Normal. *The Economist*, April 2, 2011, 21.

[16] E. Margolis. Egypt's Revolution Has Just Begun. *LewRockwell.com*, April 19, 2011. Available at http://www.lewrockwell.com/margolis/margolis237.html.

believed that the population will become disillusioned with democracy and secularism and, given the constant agitation by the Brotherhood to enact more Islamic-oriented legislation, agree that "Islam is the Solution." Already Islamists are campaigning for more conservative dress by women, even Christian women.[17] In April 2011, other Islamists demanded the ouster of a Christian governor of one of the southern provinces. In Islamist ideology, Christians should not rule over Muslims. This does not bode well for the future of the secular democracy most Egyptians now expect.[18] Additionally, there was a troubling event recently witnessed in Egypt. There was the huge and enthusiastic reception on February 18, 2011, in Cairo's Tahrir Square, ground zero of the insurrection, applauding Sheikh Yusuf al Qaradawi as he delivered an Islamist harangue and voiced contumely against Israel and America. Qaradawi is a professional Sunni theologian who is very influential in the Arab world. He has infamously approved the death sentence for apostasy (abandoning the Muslim faith for another), issued a fatwa (religious edict) allowing suicide attacks against civilians in Israel, and has even bragged that Islam will conquer Europe.[19] His popular acceptance and support does not auger well for democracy, especially when one notes that a popular secular politician was denied the right to address the crowd at the very same rally. In the end, it is up to the Muslim Brotherhood and the military services to decide, along with the Egyptian people. What happened in the elections? The Muslim Brotherhood was the clear winner of the country's first democratic elections.

The new Egyptian President Mohammed Morsi, since taking office, has afforded himself sweeping powers over the judiciary and other branches of government and embarked on a foreign policy that aims to improve relations with Iran and China but distance Egypt from the United States. Since 2011, "Egypt has witnessed protests, driven by movements for human dignity, economic security, and social justice, renewing an intense debate over the best way to respond to the demands of the broader majority of Egyptians."[20]

The next elections were scheduled for April 2013; however, the Cairo Administrative Court suspended them in March 2013, pending the Supreme Constitutional Court's review of the electoral law promulgated by President Mohammed Morsi. The outcome of the elections will dictate if Egypt will stay on the same course it is currently on concerning foreign and domestic policy.

Libya: Tripping over the Tribes

Unlike in Tunisia and Egypt, many Libyans consider their tribal affiliations more important than their national identity. Basically, they think of themselves as a "Gadaffa" or a "Warfalla" first and as a "Libyan" second. Muammar Gaddafi, from the very beginning of his reign, and apparently wisely it seems, ensured that his tribe, the Gadaffa, one of the smaller tribes composing Libya's population, was allied with the larger Warfalla and Margharha tribes of the western regions of Tripolitania and Fezzan. These larger tribes were then the recipients of his economic and oil wealth largesse. It appears that these tribes, at first, supported him at the outbreak of the insurrection or at least remained neutral.[21] By shifting the locus of national power and economic

[17] D. Miller. Muslim Brotherhood Advocates Egyptian Modesty Police. *Jerusalem Post*, April 05, 2011. Available at http://www.jpost.com/MiddleEast/Article.aspx?id=215050.

[18] Y. Saleh. Christian Governor Must Go, South Egypt Protesters Say. *Reuters Africa*, April 21, 2011. Available at http://af.reuters.com/article/egyptNews/idAFLDE73K1NS20110421.

[19] R. Spencer. Egypt's Islamist Supremacist Is Man of the Hour. *Human Events*, February 23, 2011. Available at http://www.humanevents.com/article.php?print=yes&id=41938.

[20] M. Monshipouri. After the Arab Spring: Transitions and Crisis of Governability. University of California-Berkeley, February 12, 2013. Available at http://blogs.berkeley.edu/2013/02/12/after-the-arab-spring-transitions-and-crisis-of-governability/.

[21] Libya: The Colonel Is Not Yet Beaten. *The Economist*, April 2, 2011, 43.

opportunity to his own native Tripolitania and away from the Cyrenaica area, Gaddafi created longstanding resentments among the eastern tribes that bubbled to the surface during the present upheaval. It is no coincidence that the genesis of the revolt occurred in Benghazi, the main city of the Cyrenaica region. At first, it appeared that the rebels would achieve an easy victory and that the disaffected masses of a third Arab country in as many months would oust its longtime oppressor. But though initially caught unprepared and pushed off balance by the rebel offensive, Gaddafi's military forces gradually regrouped, counterattacked, and not only halted the rebels' momentum, but, in fact, pushed them back into Cyrenaica.

Although enthusiastic and full of energy, the ragtag rebels, undisciplined and lacking cohesion (not to mention adequate weapons and munitions), at first proved no match for Gaddafi's small, somewhat marginally trained but adequately equipped, tribal militias and armed forces. As noted by one reporter of *The New Yorker* magazine, dispatching from Libya, "[f]or many of them (the rebels) the fighting consists largely of performance, dancing and singing and firing into the air ... until they are sent scurrying by Gaddafi's shells."[22] The rebels were initially poorly led, virtually untrained, and woefully out-gunned. Only NATO's intervention, with air sorties attacking and destroying some units of Gaddafi's armor and mechanized forces, halted the rapid ebb of rebel fortunes and prevented a complete rout and slaughter of fighters and civilians alike. Thanks to thousands of NATO air strikes, the tide turned once again, and it was Gaddafi and his supporters who faced annihilation.

Long the international gadfly and provocateur (Libya supported international terrorism from the 1970s through the 1990s and invaded and occupied its southern neighbor Chad, the Middle East), Gaddafi was wise enough to radically change his (and Libya's) behavior when he sensed that America might have had enough of his antics and that he would, in turn, suffer the same fate as Saddam Hussein. In 2003, just after the Iraqi government was taken down by US military forces, he publically announced that Libya would abandon its pursuit of weapons of mass destruction, cease all terrorist activities against the West and the United States, and in a surprising gesture, even compensated the families of the 243 victims of the Pan American Flight 103 that exploded over Lockerbie, Scotland, in December, 1988 (in which Libya was implicated) to the tune of more than a billion dollars. Moreover, knowing that his regime represented the prime example of an apostate Muslim ruler, as identified by the jihadists of al-Qaeda, Gaddafi moved to suppress the Islamist urges of his citizens as well. Libya outlawed all Islamist activity and actively pursued any citizen professing an Islamist creed.

Interestingly, it is known that most of the thousands of Libyans who traveled to Iraq and Afghanistan to fight the American and Coalition Forces emanated from Cyrenaica in the east of Libya. The Canadian paper, the *National Post*, cited a Canadian intelligence report in 2009 that identified eastern Libya as the "epicenter of Islamist extremism" in that nation and that the mosques there had long been urging its followers to travel to Iraq to conduct jihad against the Americans.[23] There is no doubt that Islamist elements are participating in the fight against Gaddafi although, at this point, no one is sure of their exact numbers or combat effectiveness.

Moreover, according to Morgan Lorraine Roach of the Heritage Foundation, "since the fall of Muammar [Gaddafi] in September 2011, Libya's transitional government has been unable to implement rule of law throughout much of the country."[24] A case in point is what happened in Benghazi, Libya, on September 11, 2012. On this day, Christopher Stevens, the US Ambassador to Libya, among others, was killed in Benghazi, Libya, during an attack on the US consulate. Some reports indicated that this attack was not spontaneous, arguing that it was a planned

---

[22] J. L. Anderson. Who Are the Rebels? *The New Yorker*, April 4, 2011, 21.

[23] S. Bell. Libyan Rebels Islamist Ties Cause for Concern. *National Post*, March 29, 2011. Available at http://www.nationalpost.com/Libyan+rebels+Islamist+ties+cause+concern+report/4524753/story.html.

[24] M. L. Roach. Morning Bell: Taking Terrorism and the Arab Spring Seriously. *The Heritage Foundation*, February 14, 2013. Available at http://blog.heritage.org/2013/02/14/morning-bell-taking-terrorism-and-the-arab-spring-seriously/.

attack by al-Qaeda. Specifically, Ayman al-Zawahiri, the head of al-Qaeda, had released a video statement urging Libyans to avenge the death of Abu Yahya al-Libi, who had been killed in a drone strike. Others have reported that this attack was provoked by the release of a video on YouTube (*The Innocence of Muslims*), which depicted the Prophet Mohammed in a derogatory manner and was criticized as being anti-Muslim. "While the Libyan government moved quickly to denounce the attack and has offered its cooperation in finding the terrorists, little has been achieved in bringing the perpetrators to justice."[25]

Libya has a long secular tradition that many Libyans will be loath to abandon. But the jihadists have a unique opportunity to establish an Islamist state in a country previously violently hostile to jihadist aims. The temptation may prove too great, and what may be witnessed is continued fighting between the jihadists and the more secularly inclined Libyans or between the tribes of east and west. At this point, it is doubtful that the jihadists will prevail in this struggle, especially in western Libya, which is dominated by the larger and most powerful tribes. Strong Sharia governments tend to reduce tribal authority, and it is not in the interest of tribal elders, even though many are very pious and conservative Muslims, to erode their own positions. Because one still does not know very much about the make up of the rebels, the future is clouded.

Bahrain: Small Island—Big Prize

The island nation of Bahrain is actually a small archipelago in the west central Persian Gulf (or Arabian Gulf, depending on which shore you are standing on) composed of about 30 islands, many uninhabited. The largest is Bahrain Island, just 30 miles long and 10 miles wide. Bahrain, in Arabic, literally means "two seas," and before the discovery of oil, trade fishing and pearl diving were its main industries. Bahrain is no longer a significant producer of petroleum, but an oil field shared with the Saudis still provides three fourths of the national budget. Bahrain has a well-diversified economy, and banking and finance are also major industries.[26]

The Bahraini unrest is quite different from that witnessed in North Africa. The Bahraini insurrection is fundamentally sectarian in character. But the Saudis, by invading Bahrain, have left the door open for Iran to also take military action to protect their co-religionists as well. An Associated Press dispatch of April 23, 2011, accentuates the sectarian nature of this struggle. AP reported that Bahraini authorities have destroyed 16 Shiite mosques as "punishment" for the weeks of antigovernment protests.[27] It is indicative of the lack of respect that Sunnis hold for the Shia and is at the root of the problem and unrest in Bahrain. In the Sunni cosmology, the Shiites are to be ruled with an iron fist and barely tolerated. Among the ultra-orthodox Wahabbis, Deobandis, and Taliban, they can be massacred as well. The Sunnis will not hesitate to use violence to prevent the Shiites from toppling the Khalifa family. The Khalifas are adherents to Sunni Islam, although a majority (70%) of the island's population practices the Shia version. The 70% that is Shia is also racially Persian, not Arab, although Arabic is the language spoken by most. The divide between ruler and ruled runs deep and represents the fundamental issue fueling the present unrest. But the larger issue that forms the backdrop and overshadows the popular demonstrations and outright revolt we are witnessing in Bahrain today is the very real regional power struggle between Saudi Arabia and Iran. In many ways, little Bahrain is a

[25] M. L. Roach. Morning Bell: Taking Terrorism and the Arab Spring Seriously. *The Heritage Foundation*, February 14, 2013. Available at http://blog.heritage.org/2013/02/14/morning-bell-taking-terrorism-and-the-arab-spring-seriously/.

[26] L. Smith. Bahrain Falls Mainly on the Shia. *Weekly Standard*, 16, no. 28: April 4, 2011.

[27] Shiite Mosques Demolished in Bahrain Crackdown. *ABC News*, April 23, 2011. Available at http://abcnews.go.com/International/wireStory?id=13443184.

pawn in a lengthy grudge match for control and domination of the Gulf and its oil wealth and, ultimately, who will control the future of Islam itself.

The Sunnis' only consideration will be how much violence they can get away with before the Iranians threaten to intervene. So the Bahrain assessment is a relatively easy call. The Sunnis must hold onto Bahrain at all costs both for strategic political reasons (Iran on their doorstep) and for fundamental theological dictates because it would be a major sin to allow heretics to seize power. It was forecasted that they would succeed, and the Bahrain revolt will be put down. On the other hand, if the Shiites had succeeded in overthrowing the Khalifas, it would mark an important turning point and Iran's long sought domination of the Gulf would have begun. What happened in Bahrain? The Khalifas were not overthrown, and the status quo was retained. Specifically, with the help of the Saudi regime, Bahrain suppressed the uprising.

Jordan: The Once and Future Palestinian Homeland

Jordan, like Lebanon, Syria, Iraq, and Israel, was created in the aftermath of World War I and the subsequent collapse of the Ottoman Empire and the Islamic Caliphate, which had ruled these areas for hundreds of years. In late December 2010, preceding the "Arab Spring" protests, which began in January 2011, the Jordanian capital of Amman witnessed several large riots between Jordanians of Bedouin descent (who have been staunch supporters of the monarchy) and those Jordanians of Palestinian heritage. These occurred after soccer games and resulted in much criticism of King Abdallah II's wife, Queen Rifai (who is a Palestinian) by Bedouin tribal leaders, who have the opinion that the Queen is establishing a Palestinian locus of power in Jordan that could compete with the entrenched Bedouin centers.[28]

Like so many other nations, Jordan has seen its share of protests since January 2011 although they have been much milder and much less violent than in neighboring Syria, for example. As noted in an Al Jazeera report in January 2011, thousands marched to protest unemployment and inflation while demanding that the country's Prime Minister, Samir Rifai, step down.[29] Rifai and his entire government were replaced on February 1, 2011, by King Abdallah II, who also promised economic reforms. But scattered protests have continued with calls for greater participation in the government by ordinary citizens. With such a large Palestinian population, King Abdallah II risks his throne and power if he accedes to demands for an authentic constitutional monarchy.

Although there have been a few calls by some small Palestinian groups to topple the monarchy, it is the renewed vigor of the Jordanian Muslim Brotherhood that has some most concerned.[30] The Brotherhood chapter in Jordan is known as the Islamic Action Front (IAF).[30] Like many of the Palestinians who are Jordanian citizens, the IAF is also demanding changes to the election laws. As in Egypt, the fear in Jordan is that the IAF could garner significant support in the legislature and possibly a majority. The IAF maintains the same motto as their Egyptian counterparts, "Islam is the Solution," and, once in power, would demand that more Sharia laws be enacted, that the secular laws already in place be rescinded, and that ties to Israel and the United States diminish. But being a Hashemite, that is, a direct descendant of the Prophet Muhammad confers great prestige and credibility on King Abdallah II and his family. So it is likely that in spite of a growing opposition, Abdallah II can deflect calls to amend the election

[28] J. Dorsey. Rare Attack on Jordanian Queen Heightens Soccer Tensions. *Bleacher Report*, February 7, 2011. Available at http://bleacherreport.com/articles/600176-rare-attack-on-jordanian-queen-heightens-soccer-tensions.

[29] Thousands Protest in Jordan. *Al Jazeera*, January 28, 2011. Available at http://english.aljazeera.net/news/middle east/2011/01/2011128125157509196.html.

[30] J. Schanzer. The Muslim Brotherhood in Jordan. *Wall Street Journal*, February 22, 2011. Available at http://online.wsj.com/article/SB10001424052748704409004576146221164497158.html.

process and keep the IAF and more radical elements of the Jordanian Palestinian opposition at bay, at least for the foreseeable future. The mass of the Jordanian citizenry has not been susceptible to radical proposals and Abdallah II will certainly use the Bedouin/Palestinian rift to his advantage. The Hashemite monarchy still maintains the loyalty of the military and most likely a majority of the population. But King Abdallah II must find a way to reform the economy and increase economic opportunity for all Jordan's citizens or the dissatisfaction with his rule could grow.

Jordan is a progressive state in Arab terms and has an excellent educational system whose graduates find work as doctors, business managers, and professionals abroad, especially Saudi Arabia and the Gulf Emirates. This provides a safety valve of sorts, but in the long run, domestic opportunity must meet rising expectations, especially among the growing Palestinian population. So it is safe to postulate that the Hashemite Kingdom of Jordan survives the "Arab Spring" insurrections at least in the short term—three to five years. But King Abdallah II will be greatly challenged and will need to navigate the rocks and shoals of growing Islamist influence in the country and increasing political and economic expectations on the part of the Palestinian majority. The old Bedouin guard will stand with the King for now as will the military, but the future is clouded.

Syria: Waiting for the Aliwaites[31] (to Leave)

Politically, Syria represents the polar opposite of the situation found in Bahrain, where a Sunni minority is determined to maintain its rule at all costs and prevent the "heretical" Shia majority from seizing power. In Syria, the heretical (and apostate) minority is in power and has been for decades. Following World War II, Syria received its independence from the French and immediately fell into a period of political turbulence and upheaval as Syrian governments rose and fell between 1946 and 1971. In that year, Haffez Assad, the commander of the Air Force, in the last of a long series of coup d'etats that seemed to replace Syrian governments every few months, took over leadership of the nation and brought a modicum of political stability to the government.[32] Assad solidified his hold on power through brutality, mass arrests, and murder. As leader of the Syrian Ba'ath ("Resurrection" in Arabic) party, Assad was an adherent of its ideology of secular Arab nationalism and had, as his primary goal, the union of all Arabs into one great nation that would extend from Morocco to Iraq.[33] But Assad had to overcome a decided disadvantage in Syria before he could begin promoting what he viewed as the greater good of the secular, Arab nationalist ideology.

In a nation dominated by Sunni Muslims, the Sunnis represent a 70% majority (with the capital city of Damascus having the legacy of being the seat of the first great Muslim dynasty of the Sunni Umayyads, 661–750 CE), Assad's confessional lineage was a serious handicap. For centuries, the Alawis had been maligned and persecuted as heretics by Sunni and Shia alike and considered a fringe element of Islam that deserved neither respect nor consideration. The sect had fled to the mountains of western Syria adjacent to Lebanon and did their best to remain unnoticed and not antagonize the Sunni majority. All this changed when Syria became a French mandate after World War I and then procured its independence from France after World War II. Under the French, the Alawi (and the Syrian Orthodox Christians) were protected minorities that were granted more or less equal rights with the Sunnis. After World War II, most Syrians

[31] The Aliwaites have been considered, for hundreds of years, as a heresy of Shia Islam while the Shiites themselves are considered a heresy of Sunni Islam.

[32] D.-P. Jones. *The Closed Circle: An Interpretation of the Arabs.* Chicago: Harper and Row, 2002, 330, 334, 335.

[33] Egyptian leader, Gamal Nasser, espoused the secular, Arab nationalist ideology as his ultimate goal for uniting the Arab world as well. But he died in 1970, and Assad assumed the Arab nationalist mantle.

embraced the secular Arab nationalist ideology then in vogue, and the Alawi gravitated toward the military, which the Syrian Sunnis were slow to embrace. Only 12% of the population, the Alawis began to prosper[34] in the secular Ba'athist republic. By the time of Assad's coup in 1971, the Alawis controlled the military, and Assad used this power center to cement his despotism.

Hama Rules

But Sunni Islamists, especially the ever-present Muslim Brotherhood, could never abide this secular government and its Alawi ruler. As mentioned previously, the overriding unwritten theological principle is that the Shia cannot be in charge. For the very conservative Sunnis of the Muslim Brotherhood or the Saudi Arabian Wahabbis, permitting these heretical and apostate rulers to lead a country is a major sin, which must be expunged by jihad if necessary.

For these reasons, beginning in 1976, the Muslim Brotherhood of Syria initiated a concerted campaign to oust Assad and his Alawi-dominated government. Prominent Alawi ministers were assassinated and in June 1979, 83 Alawi military cadets were machine-gunned to death by a Sunni Syrian Army officer, a major outrage. Numerous car bombings occurred during that time in Damascus and other cities that killed hundreds, if not thousands, of civilians.

To combat the growing violence, Assad "… made it a crime punishable by death to be a member of the Muslim Brotherhood, or even associated with it."[34] But even this draconian legislation did not deter the Sunni's campaign. By 1982, Assad had had enough. The city of Hama in western Syria, representing a major Muslim Brotherhood stronghold, was surrounded by the Syrian tank divisions and, over a period of weeks, basically leveled. It is estimated that 20,000 to 40,000 died,[35] but the Muslim Brotherhood and its challenge to the regime had been eliminated. It was a bloody and brutal tactic but most effective, and it bought the Syrian government decades of relative internal tranquility.

Hafez Assad died in 2000 and was succeeded by his son Bashar. The "throne" had originally been intended for the elder son, Basil, but he died in a car crash in 1994. Bashar is an ophthalmologist by education and training, spent years living in London, and assumed leadership of Syria somewhat reluctantly. Bashar was originally viewed as a reformer by western pundits. One reporter put it this way: "There was a naïve assumption that Bashar had the makings of a modern leader because he was in part western-educated, spoke relatively good English, and married a professional woman who worked as an investment banker in London."[36] Bashar was unable to enact any serious changes (if he ever intended to do so in the first place), for fear that the majority Sunnis will succeed to power in any democratic national election. His focus has been the maintenance of the status quo since his accession to power, and it seemed to be working, at least until the winter of 2011.

The Syrian "Arab Spring" protests began in the city of Deraa, a Sunni-dominated city in southwest Syria on the Jordanian border, on March 18, 2011. By March 25, in an effort to quell the dissent, Bashar accepted the resignation of his entire government and promised unspecified reforms.[37] But none of these measures have halted the protests, which noticeably increased during the summer, and Bashar has now adopted a tactic out of his father's playbook and implemented his own version of Hama rules, that is, a military crackdown, which has resulted in more than 1200 deaths so far.[38] Already there have been reports of executions of Syrian soldiers who

---

[34] D.-P. Jones. *The Closed Circle: An Interpretation of the Arabs*. Chicago: Harper and Row, 2002, 330, 334, 335.

[35] E. Karsh. *Islamic Imperialism: A History*. New Haven: Yale University Press, 2007, 218.

[36] P. Beaumont. Syria Shockwaves Sweep across Middle East. *The Observer: Guardian.co.uk*, May 1, 2011. Available at http://www.guardian.co.uk/world/2011/apr/30/syria-shockwaves-sweep-middle-east.

[37] Syrian Government Resigns After Protests Sweep Country. *The European Union Times*, March 29, 2011. Available at http://www.eutimes.net/2011/03/syrian-government-resigns-after-protests-sweep-country/.

[38] N. Hassan. Syrian Death Toll Rises amid Violent Government Crackdown on Protests. *Guardian.co.uk*, June 5, 2011. Available at http://www.guardian.co.uk/world/2011/jun/05/syria-death-toll-government-violence/print.

refused to shoot into the crowds of protesting civilians.[39] Thus far, according to an estimate of the United Nations, "60,000 people have been killed in ongoing fighting," and it is reported that "government forces have committed crimes against humanity and war crimes, while some opposition forces have also carried out serious abuses, including torture and summary executions."[40]

Nevertheless, Syria has powerful friends, notably the Iranians and the Lebanese Shia Hezbollah militia (an Iranian Revolutionary Guard creation and acolyte). Bashar could request Iranian military assistance to maintain his rule (if he has not done so already). And the Saudis, by sending in troops to aid the minority Sunni government of Bahrain, have provided the Iranians a ready-made precedent and pretext to aid the minority Shia/Alawi government of Syria. Damascus is only a few hours by plane away from Iran. Whether Iran responds to any Syrian request for help remains to be seen, but the use of Hezbollah or Iranian troops to help keep Bashar and the Alawis in power is a distinct possibility. The Revolutionary Guards already have several bases in Syria that are used for training and arming Shia militias.[41] There have been reports that the Iranian commanders, who brutally put down the Iranian protests over the falsified elections in June 2009, have visited Damascus recently to assess the situation and consider options.[41] Lastly, and most ominously, it is reported that Iran's leader, Ayatollah Khomeni, has issued a fatwa that declares the Syrian protesters to be "God's enemies" and that Iran and Hezbollah should help the Assad regime crush the rebellion.[41]

In addition to the aforementioned Iranian Revolutionary Guard bases, Syria recently announced that it would allow Iran to build a naval facility at the Mediterranean port of Latakia.[42] The prospect of Iranian warships plying the Mediterranean waters in close proximity to Israel, a nation Iran has stated it will destroy, does not bode well for the future peace of the region. It is clear that Iran has its own strategic reasons for keeping the Alawis in power. But there is another option the Assad government could initiate if it appears that Alawis will lose control—strategic withdrawal. The Alawis and the other Syrian minorities who would suffer under Sunni/Muslim Brotherhood rule (the Christians, the Druze, and the Kurds) are concentrated in western Syria in and around the port city of Latakia. Assad and the Alawis could abandon most of Syria and, with Iranian Revolutionary Guard and Hezbollah assistance, establish a Shia-dominated area in the west of the country. Therefore, Syria could partition into two segments, at least temporarily. In our opinion, the regime that for decades has repressed its Sunni majority while making the claim that it stood for Arab nationalism, Arab unity, and secular freedoms is now seen for what it is and has been, usurpers practicing a version of Islam deemed heretical and ruling a fractionated nation by brutality and the jackboot.

After 40 years of brutal repression, the Assads and the Alawis know that they cannot simply walk away or surrender power to the Sunnis and, ultimately, the Muslim Brotherhood. The revenge and retribution on the Alawi community, not to mention the other minorities who supported and were protected by the secular Baathist state, would be horrific. This is political reality in this part of the world. So the Syria insurrection will continue on its sanguinary path and the body count will be high. The outcome is difficult to predict. To date,

> After a two-year civil war, Syria's Bashar al-Assad has yet to cave. The Syrian opposition movement has levied significant blows to the regime, yet support from Iran and Russia has helped to keep Assad in power. Despite more than 60,000 deaths and hundreds of thousands of people displaced,

---

[39] K. Marsh. Syrian Soldiers Shot for Refusing to Fire on Protesters. *Guardian.co.uk*, April 12, 2011. Available at http://www.guardian.co.uk/world/2011/apr/12/syrian-soldiers-shot-protest.

[40] Human Rights Watch. *World Report 2013: Challenges for Rights After Arab Spring*. February 1, 2013. Available at http://www.hrw.org/news/2013/01/31/world-report-2013-challenges-rights-after-arab-spring.

[41] R. Kahili. Iran's Leader Orders Murder of Protesters in Syria. *Big Peace*, May 8, 2011. Available at http://bigpeace.com/rkahlili/2011/05/09/irans-leader-orders-murder-of-protesters-in-syria.

[42] N. Snyder. If Assad Falls, Who Wins in Syria? *American Thinker*, April 1, 2011. Available at http://www.americanthinker.com/2011/04/if_assad_falls_who_wins_in_syr_1.html.

> the international community has done little to speed the regime's collapse ... In the midst of the carnage, terrorist groups such as the Al-Nusra Front, an al-Qaeda affiliate, have infiltrated the country and exploited the instability. The United States is currently assisting Turkey, a NATO ally, in protecting its border against potential ballistic missile attacks, yet there is no strategy for resolving the crisis.[43]

The Assad government could hang on for a few more years but, in the end, will most likely be toppled or at least driven from power in Damascus. The Sunnis will not be tyrannized in perpetuity. Some level of Iranian military assistance to the Alawi Syrian government is expected, probably covert but which, in light of the turbulence and new realities of the Arab Spring revolutions, could be massive and overt. In the end, to prevent retribution and massacres, it is believed that, with Iranian and Lebanese Hezbollah help, the Assad regime will repair to the traditional Alawi area around Latakia and establish an alternate Syrian state. Syria plays a leading role in Iran's plans for regional domination, and the Ayatollahs can ill afford to let this country slide into the Sunni and Muslim Brotherhood's hands.

Yemen: Remote, Obscure, and Al-Qaeda's Best Chance to Start Over

The Republic of Yemen occupies the southwest corner of the Arabian Peninsula and is considered an exotic obscurity even by that minute segment of the American population that may actually be aware of its existence. Poverty-stricken, lawless, fractious, and somewhat remote, even by air travel, Yemen does not command the tourist trade of Egypt or Morocco or the business allure of Saudi Arabia (its northern neighbor) or the United Arab Emirates. Nonetheless, by virtue of its location, astride the eastern shore of the sea-lane chokepoint at the southern end of the Red Sea, known as the Bab al Mandeb Strait,[44] through which an estimated 3.3 million barrels of oil flow daily, Yemen cannot be ignored by Washington policy makers and defense planners. Noting that the easily blockaded Suez Canal cuts through Egypt at the northern end of the Red Sea, the Bab al Mandeb represents another geographic vulnerability (along with the Strait of Hormuz in the Persian Gulf and the Straits of Molucca in Indonesia) to the free flow of shipping, especially oil. Thus, maintaining good diplomatic relations with whatever government rules Yemen is a necessity.

The present besieged ruler is Ali Abdullah Saleh, who acceded to power in 1978 and has reigned over Yemen's turbulent modern history ever since. Although a secular Arab nationalist by ideology, Saleh was born into a Shia family. He only obtained an elementary education, joined the Army in 1958, attained the rank of corporal and became a second lieutenant in 1963. He excelled at the political intrigues that were a part of Yemeni military life, gained promotions, and then was appointed as a military governor in 1977. After the assassination of President Al-Ghashmi in June 1978,[45] Saleh was named to the four-man provisional presidency council and actually elected president on July 17, 1978. His first official act on August 10, 1978, no longer needing intrigue and subtlety to advance his career prospect, was to execute the 30 officers who

---

[43] M. L. Roach. Morning Bell: Taking Terrorism and the Arab Spring Seriously. *The Heritage Foundation*, February 14, 2013. Available at http://blog.heritage.org/2013/02/14/morning-bell-taking-terrorism-and-the-arab-spring-seriously/.

[44] "Gate of Tears" in Arabic, which takes its name, given in ancient times, from the frequent shipwrecks caused by the dangerous currents emanating from the Red Sea emptying into the Indian Ocean. See Britannica.com, "Bab-el-Mandeb-Strait." Available at http://www.britannica.com/EBchecked/topic/361641/Bab-el-Mandeb-Strait.

[45] S. Henderson, Fighting Al-Qaeda: The Role of Yemen's President Saleh, *The Cutting Edge*, January 18, 2010. Available at http://www.thecuttingedgenews.com/index.php?article=11914&pageid=&pagename=. It is important to note that President Ghashmi was killed when an envoy from the adjoining nation of South Yemen, carrying a diplomatic briefcase containing a "secret" communication from the South Yemeni president, exploded upon opening, killing the envoy, Ghashmi, and wounding several others.

had opposed his election (proving once again that it is good to be king or at least a president with autocratic powers).[46]

The central government has always had but little control outside the capital or major cities. Recently, it had to all but abandon two Northern provinces to Shia rebels while concurrently battling a growing secession movement in the south. With more than 24 million people, the average age is an astoundingly young 18.1 years, and fully 75% of the population was born after Saleh was elected to the Presidency in 1978.[47] With a literacy rate of just 50%, an unemployment rate of at least 35%, and almost half of the population forced to live on just two dollars a day, it is not difficult to fathom the depth of the resentment and anger demonstrated these past few months by the huge youthful population against Saleh, his government, and the incredible lack of opportunity the Yemen economy offers. A *Los Angeles Times* article noted that only 5% of college graduates are able to find work.[48] Making matters worse, the tribal heritage, coupled with mountainous and rugged terrain isolates much of the population from each other. Just like in Libya, Yemenis identify with their tribal affiliation first and only secondarily with their Yemeni citizenship, most especially among the poor and illiterate.

The Yemeni uprisings began on January 15, 2011, and demonstrations have continued on an almost daily basis and have often swelled to hundreds of thousands, with Sanaa, the capital, seeing the most turbulence. To date, the often-violent government response has inflicted hundreds of deaths on the demonstrators as soldiers and snipers have fired point blank into the crowds. But this has not softened the demonstrators' resolve, and they refuse to be dispersed. Given the very young average age of the population, the Yemeni insurrection can be characterized as a true youth movement spearheaded by students, professionals, teachers, men and women.[47,49]

Many foreign observers of the Yemeni uprising are really not certain just what it is the demonstrators want to achieve or establish except the obvious demand for Saleh to step down. As one commentator noted "… while the opposition is significant in size, they do not share a common vision for Yemen …"[47] The opposition appears to be a loose coalition of secularists of the old Nasserite mold, tribal elements looking for more autonomy, socialists, and Islamists.[47] This mix will have a difficult time agreeing on the form of government once Saleh departs. Add to this the effective Shia rebel takeover of the two provinces in the North, the renewed secessionist movement to reestablish an independent South Yemen, and a burgeoning Al-Qaeda presence, one can see that Yemen after Saleh could easily devolve into fragmentation, anarchy, and civil strife.

The danger for the United States in the Yemeni turmoil is al-Qaeda of the Arabian Peninsula (AQAP), the most active and dangerous (especially now that Osama bin Laden is dead) of the several Al-Qaeda franchises that have emerged around the world. The prospect of increasing anarchy in Yemen, coupled with the difficult terrain and quasi-independent tribal fiefdoms, yield the proper environment for a secretive organization like AQAP to reconstitute its jihadist credentials and renew its activity against the United States.

Yemen's prospects are bleak. It is already a failing state by any measure, and the ouster of the autocrat Saleh, while worthy and estimable, will not be the adjuvant the country needs to pull itself out of its inevitable descent into chaos and fragmentation. The loose coalition demanding President Saleh's ouster agrees on little else. The Shia rebels in the north and secessionists in

---

[46] Ali Abdullah Saleh. *Britannica.com*. Available at http://www.britannica.com/EBchecked/topic/519196/Ali-Abd-Allah-Salih.

[47] R. Simcox. Yemen Beyond Saleh: Problems and Prospects for the US and Its Allies. *The Henry Jackson Society*, 2011, 3, 5. Available at http://www.henryjacksonsociety.org/stories.asp?id=2153.

[48] J. Fleishman. In Yemen, Tribal Tradition Trumps Education. *Los Angeles Times*, December 24, 2009. Available at http://articles.latimes.com/2009/dec/24/world/la-fg-yemen-school24-2009dec24.

[49] In an ironic remark, the secular-oriented President Saleh has stated the intermingling of men and women protestors during the demonstrations violates Islamic law and must cease.

the south will not relent from their goals to break away from Sanaa, and AQAP will increase its activity and create even more havoc for Yemen, Saudi Arabia (AQAP's primary target), and the United States. The Saleh government regularly shared intelligence concerning AQAP with the United States and allowed armed, unmanned drone over flights of Yemen that frequently resulted in strikes on AQAP targets. The concern is that any new government will not be as energetically anti-Islamist as is Saleh's regime today and that this source of intelligence will disappear.

On June 3, 2011, President Saleh was seriously injured in a rocket attack on the Presidential Palace in Sanaa and flown to Riyadh, the capital of Saudi Arabia, for treatment and convalescence. He reportedly suffered burns over 40% of his body. Although he has since returned to Yemen, given his age, and the possible seriousness of his injuries, he may not be able to reassume power. If he chooses to abdicate, a power vacuum will be created, the insurrectionists emboldened and all-out civil war possible. But any new government that emerges after Saleh will represent a fragile coalition that will most likely have less control of the countryside than does the Saleh government today.[50]

Given the country's abject poverty and dire economic straits, the youthful population that despairs of any opportunity for self-fulfillment, the 50% illiteracy rate, and the bureaucratic corruption and government torpor, one fears that AQAP's jihadist message will strike a resonant chord with many of the disaffected youth. Moreover, the attraction of jihad allows the frustrated youth to participate in a cosmic endeavor, deemed much greater than oneself, which brings with it not only some temporal benefit but the possibility of martyrdom and rich heavenly rewards. Throughout Islam's history, some percentage of its adherents has always been attracted to this creed.

In the end, in February 2012, President Saleh, stepped down from power. A new, weaker government was constituted. Particularly, "Saleh was succeeded by Abed Rabu Mansour Hadi, who served as his vice president. Hadi, who represents continuity much more than genuine change, now faces enormous challenges in stabilizing Yemen, one of the poorest and most turbulent Arab countries."[51] The fragility of this new government engenders further rebellion and fragmentation along tribal, sectarian, and regional fault-lines. This, in turn, boosts the fortunes and recruitment ability of AQAP, providing the sanctuary the group needs to reconstitute and plan new strikes at the United States and apostate regimes like Saudi Arabia. Indeed, the AQAP remains a threat to international security and even though "Yemen's government has cooperated in the Obama administration's frequent use of drone strikes, it has failed to curb AQAP's activity."[51]

Concluding Thoughts

In a larger sense, it does not matter which faction emerges victorious in the Middle East and North Africa over the next few years. Whoever it is, Islamist, secular democrat, free market advocate, socialist, or some hybrid of the these, the dire economic and social straits of all Arab societies must be solved, or there will certainly be another round of revolution a generation or two in the future. As one cogent observer of the Middle East noted some years ago, Islam fundamentally missed the Industrial Revolution and has been playing catch up ever since.[52]

---

[50] For most of modern Yemen's history, the central government authority stopped a few miles outside the capital of Sanaa and the other major cities. Tribal authority took over from there.

[51] M. L. Roach. Morning Bell: Taking Terrorism and the Arab Spring Seriously. *The Heritage Foundation*, February 14, 2013. Available at http://blog.heritage.org/2013/02/14/morning-bell-taking-terrorism-and-the-arab-spring-seriously/.

[52] F. Ajami. The Sorrows of Egypt. *Foreign Affairs* 74, no. 5: 82, September/October 1995.

The sad state of the Middle East and North African economies is dramatically highlighted when one realizes that the gross domestic product (GDP) of Italy (60 million people) is higher than all Arab states combined (including Saudi Arabia and Kuwait) with a total population of 350 million.[53] This is an astounding statistic. Much of the problem is the pervasive corruption at all levels of society. While the Mubaraks and the Ben Alis and their governmental elites diverted billions, the corruption cycle extends down to the most junior bureaucrat who, wanting to supplement his meager salary, will demand a small bribe to perform his function.[54] This endemic, petty corruption acts as a regressive tax and stymies initiative, creativity, and innovation. Only 77 international patents were filed in Egypt between 1980 and 1999, the most of any Arab country, while South Korea alone filed more than 16,000.[53] Couple this with a huge youth population bulge in which as many as half the people of a given Arab country are under 30 years of age, double-digit unemployment rates, and massive illiteracy, and one has the recipe for continued frustration, rage, and upheaval if drastic reforms are not implemented soon. For example, Egypt alone must generate 700,000 jobs a year just to provide employment for its annual high school graduates.[53]

The illiteracy problem in some Arab countries is of the utmost concern. A 2006 United Nations Educational, Scientific and Cultural Organization (UNESCO) report notes that a few countries, like Bahrain, Jordan, Kuwait, Syria, Lebanon, and Libya, have literacy rates of 80% or more while Egypt, Yemen, Morocco, and Mauritania barely make a 50% adult literacy grade.[55] In this highly technical world, lacking such basic skills as the ability to read and write can only doom a person and a society to a marginal, subsistence existence. What corporation or company would be attracted to Yemen or Egypt if half of the employees cannot read or write? Moreover, what company or individual would want to fight the bureaucratic corruption at every level to obtain the necessary permits to begin operation? At this point, the Arab world lacks a manufacturing base and, except for a few countries, like Egypt or Tunisia, really has no agricultural base as well. Everything of a technical nature and most foodstuffs must be imported. Locally produced capital goods are almost nonexistent.[56] As such, the victors of some of the upcoming elections, whoever they will be, and the newly elected of other countries, need to commit to jump-start the Arab economies. In the past, the new national leadership would inaugurate plans and designs, promise prosperity and plenty, and then resort to brutality and repression when they failed to deliver. Every tyrant now disgraced or removed in 2010 and 2011 started this way.

The events unfolding in the Middle East and North Africa since December 2010 represent a seminal period in modern history. Make no mistake, the old order, established in Egypt, Tunisia, Yemen, Syria, Libya, and Palestine in the 1950s and 1960s is passing. It has already occurred in Iraq and Lebanon and, at some point, the monarchs and leaders of Jordan, Algeria, Morocco, and Saudi Arabia will experience it as well. The last act of the secular Arab nationalist ideology is playing out, never to return. The curtain comes down on the counterfeit republics led by strong men and tyrants. There is hope, especially after witnessing the spontaneous uprisings of what appeared to be the educated and technologically savvy segment of the masses demanding more freedom and economic opportunity, that these nations will adopt a model of representative

---

[53] B. Zand. What the Arab World's Past Can Tell Us about Its Future. Spiegel Online, March 3, 2011. Available at http://www.spiegel.com.de/international/world/0,1518,druck-749537,00.html.

[54] Try obtaining a driver's license in a timely fashion without paying the required baksheesh. You will wait a very long time. See Al-Bab, Corruption in the Arab Countries, 2011. Available at http://www.al-bab.com/arab/background/corruption.htm.

[55] H. Hammoud. Illiteracy in the Arab World. *UNESCO*, 2006. Available at http://unesdoc.unesco.org/images/0014/001462/146282e.pdf.

[56] Maha. The Major Economic and Social Problems in the Arab World. *Arabwords.com*, 2011. Available at http://www.arabwords.com/990751_the-major-economic-and-social-problems-in-the-arab-world.

democracy and settle their problems with the ballot and spirited debate. Nevertheless, there is doubt that the momentum for a western-style democratic government to replace the passing old order of the Middle East can be sustained. This faction of the revolution might be ultimately eclipsed by the most organized and most disciplined, and if need be, the most ruthless segment of these national populations who, seeking to inculcate their version of Islam, will try to establish Sharia (government by theologians and Islamic law) in any nation they can.

17

Suicide Bombings[1]

The Ultimate Tool of Terrorism

Heinous and unprecedented acts of terrorism occurred during the last decades of the 20th century. These attacks ranged from hijackings of airplanes, boats, buses, and other means of transportation to the kidnapping of civilians for political blackmail or ransom. Atrocities also ranged from the blowing up of restaurants, malls, buildings, resorts, airports, airplanes in mid-air, trains, and buses to gun attacks on individuals or groups of people.

Notwithstanding their different goals, motivations, diffusion, scope of action, means, and targets of action, all these terrorist groups seek either to sow fear upon their enemies and humiliate and intimidate them into surrendering to their demands or to undertake a long-term military struggle in order to weaken the enemy by guerrilla warfare and constant bleeding. They also try to either capture the attention of the world media in order to air their grievances and attain their redress or simply to obtain, by terrorist means, objectives that they could not achieve in the arena of the battlefield. This chapter reviews the production of suicide bombing and its economy. More specifically, it explores why this tactic is fast becoming the most common tool for spreading terror; that is, how suicide bombings maximize the resulting terror and how suicide bombings are fast becoming the ultimate terrorist weapon.

The Production of Suicide Bombing

Becoming a suicide bomber is a social process; it involves socialization, and it is subject to rules and exhibits patterns. The opportunity to engage in it is likewise socially determined. Research has shown that suicide bombing requires three major elements: motivated individuals, access to organizations whose objective is to produce suicide bombings, and a community that extols perpetrators as heroes and embraces their acts as a noble form of resistance.[2]

---

[1] Information for this chapter was drawn from the following titles: (1) A. K. Mohammed, The Concept of Martyrdom. In D. L. June (ed.), *Terrorism and Homeland Security: Perspectives, Thoughts, and Opinions*, CRC Press, 2010. (2) A. K. Mohammed, Suicide Bombing as an Ultimate Terrorist Tool. In D. L. June (ed.), *Terrorism and Homeland Security: Perspectives, Thoughts, and Opinions*, CRC Press, 2010. (3) R. Dzikansky, M. Kleiman, and G. Slater, *Terrorist Suicide Bombings: Attack Interdiction, Mitigation, and Response*, CRC Press, 2011. (4) M. W. Nance, *Terrorist Recognition Handbook: A Practitioner's Manual for Predicting and Identifying Terrorist Activities*, Second Edition, CRC Press, 2008.

[2] A. M. Oliver and P. F. Steinberg. *The Road to Martyrs' Square: A Journey into the World of the Suicide Bomber*. New York: Oxford University Press, 2005.

Studies addressing motivation to commit suicide have focused on the psychology of perpetrators, inquiring whether suicide bombers exhibit measures of psychopathology or are abnormal.[3] Most observers agree that suicide bombers are rational individuals, whose resort to suicide is based on reason or a result of specific cost-benefit analysis.[4] Motivations to engage in suicide bombing include national or religious ideologies and collective/altruistic and individual/fatalistic reasons although motivation is not always accompanied by the ability to perpetrate violence on individual or organizational levels.[5]

Some observers have identified three major types of suicide bombers: those who act out of religious convictions; those who have the need to retaliate or avenge the death of a family member or loved one by the enemy; and those who are exploited by an organization, being led to agree to perpetrate an attack for minor economic rewards or promises for the afterlife.[6] Research has addressed the role of religious convictions or culturally based motivation to propel suicide bombing.[7] Frustrations from political conditions have also been listed as motives, referring to suicide as oppositional terrorism,[8] a measure employed to exact revenge, retaliate for group humiliation, or restore national honor.[9] The role of social groups—family, peer, ethnic, religious, or national—in shaping perpetrators' social identities and in internalizing collective memory of injustice, defeat, or dishonor has been noted.[7]

Some have argued that suicide bombing is not an act of desperation but of struggle,[10] as content analysis of the farewell messages recruits videotape prior to the mission suggests.[4] Suicide bombing has been explained as a means to achieve self-empowerment, redemption, and honor for individuals who experience powerlessness, downfall, and humiliation.[11] Others have called attention to the suicide as a guaranteed access to worldly pleasures forbidden in this life, and a hope for an attractive afterlife.[12]

Exposure to and contact with facilitating organizations is critical in becoming suicide bombers.[13] The organizations that produce suicide bombings provide a complete framework: wherewithal, finances, equipment, contacts, and support personnel throughout the journey. These resources comprise the infrastructure without which successful missions cannot be executed. Familiarity with prospective targets, area residents' routines, and security personnel schedules are also important as are access to and information about desirable targets, including the

---

[3] For example, see ref. 10.

[4] M. Hafez. Manufacturing Human Bombs: Strategy, Culture, and Conflict in the Making of Palestinian Suicide Terrorism. Paper presented at the National Institute of Justice Conference, Washington, D.C., 2004.

[5] B. Ganor. The First Iraqi Suicide Bombing: A Hint of Things to Come? ICT, 2003. Available at http://www.ict.org.il/articles/articledet.cfm?articleid=477.

[6] S. Kimhi and S. Even. Who are the Palestinian Suicide Bombers? *Terrorism and Political Violence*, 16, no. 4: 815–840, 2004.

[7] A. M. Oliver and P. F. Steinberg. *The Road to Martyrs' Square: A Journey into the World of the Suicide Bomber*. New York: Oxford University Press, 2005.

[8] M. Crenshaw. Suicide Terrorism in Comparative Perspective. In *Countering Suicide Terrorism*. Herzilya, Israel: The International Policy Institute for Counter-Terrorism, 2002, 19–21.

[9] J. Rosenberger. Discerning the Behavior of the Suicide Bomber: The Role of Vengeance. *The Journal of Religion and Health*, 42, no. 1: 13–20, 2003.

[10] A. Merari. The Readiness to Kill and Die: Suicidal Terrorism in the Middle East. In W. Reich (ed.), *Origins of Terrorism: Psychologies, Ideologies, Theologies, States of Mind*. Cambridge: Cambridge University Press, 1990, 121–125.

[11] R. Hassan. Suicide Bombing Driven More by Politics than Religious Zeal. Yale GlobalOnline, 2003. Available at http://yaleglobal.yale.edu/content/terrorists-and-their-tools-part-i.

[12] A. Berko. *The Path to the Garden of Eden: The World of Male and Female Suicide Bombers and Their Dispatchers*. Tel Aviv: Yedioth Ahronoth Press (in Hebrew), 2004.

[13] M. Bloom. *Dying to Kill: The Allure of Suicide Terror*. New York: Columbia University Press, 2005.

propitious time to execute a mission. Selecting candidates who can blend in the surrounding environment, have language skills to communicate with local people, exhibit confidence, wear appropriate clothes and other amenities that provide them a Western look so as not to attract suspicion is also the organization's responsibility. Without the support network, organization, and infrastructure, an individual cannot become a suicide bomber.

The symbolic value of suicide in the service of religion or nation and the honor bestowed on the suicide bomber and his or her family are also critical in the production of suicide bombing. Both secular and religiously based terrorist organizations have invoked religion when launching suicide bombings. Perpetrators who were dispatched through both types of organizations referred to one's religiously based obligation to be involved in the struggle and listed the Garden of Eden as a reward for the suicide mission.

Following the 9/11 terrorist attacks, it seems that any place is not safe. In malls, buses, cafes, convenience stores, beaches, and commercial areas, people are exposed to pictures of shattered establishments and scattered bodies. Every place today is a potential target for suicide bombing. According to Hoffman, "[f]irst you feel nervous about riding the bus. Then you wonder about going to a mall. Then you think twice about sitting for long at your favorite café. Then nowhere seems safe. Terrorist groups have a strategy—to shrink to nothing the areas in which people move freely—and suicide bombers, inexpensive and reliably lethal, are their latest weapons."[14] A suicide bombing is a bomb attack on people or property, delivered by a person who knows the explosion will cause his or her own death. It redefines basic cultural relationships and merges private, psychological motivations with public, ideologically charged actions. According to Davis, terrorists, including suicide bombers, share several characteristics: "oversimplification of issues," "frustration about an inability to change society," "a sense of self-righteousness," "a utopian belief in the world," "a feeling of social isolation," "a need to assert his [or her] own existence," and "a cold-blooded willingness to kill."[15] In addition, Bandura observes that "Islamic extremists mount their jihad, construed as self-defense against tyrannical, decadent infidels who seek to enslave the Muslim world,"[16] a view that allows them to "redefin[e] the morality of killing, so that it can be done free from self-censuring restraints."[16]

Although the concept predates the label, the term "suicide bombing" was only popularized in the 1980s in the middle of the Lebanese civil war (1975–1990). Inspired by Iran's Islamic revolution and supported by Syria, Hezbollah, claiming legitimacy in their nationalist struggle, led a suicide attack against the US Embassy in Beirut in April 1983, killing more than 60 individuals. A few months later, Hezbollah terrorists crashed an explosives-laden pickup truck into a Beirut facility housing US Marines, killing 241 US military personnel (220 Marines, 16 Navy personnel, and three Army soldiers) and 58 French airborne troops. This led to the eventual withdrawal of all US and French troops from Beirut. While suicide bombings have been used by some secular terrorist movements in the past, such as the Tamil Tigers in Sri Lanka and the Kurdistan Workers' Party (PKK) in Turkey, generally it is religiously inspired terrorist movements that have employed this as a tactic.[17]

In the Middle East, the contemporary phase of suicide bombing is rooted from the Hezbollah movement since 1982 among the Shiite population in southern Lebanon during the Lebanese civil war. A decade later, it came to the Palestinians, a group of whom formed the al-Aqsa Martyrs Brigades in late 2000 and adopted suicide bombing as a tactic in contrast to the mass casualty attacks by Hamas and Hezbollah. Suicide bombing in Israel has been a regular security problem

---

[14] B. Hoffman. The Logic of Suicide Terrorism. *The Atlantic Monthly*, 1, 40–47, June 2003.

[15] P. B. Davis. The Terrorist Mentality. In T. J. Badey (ed.), *Violence and Terrorism*, Sixth Edition. New York: McGraw-Hill, 2003, 37.

[16] A. Bandura. The Role of Selective Moral Disengagement in Terrorism and Counterterrorism. In F. M. Moghaddam and A. J. Marsella (eds.), *Understanding Terrorism: Psychological Roots, Consequences, and Interventions*. Washington, D.C.: American Psychological Association, 2004, 121, 124–125.

[17] P. B. Rich and T. R. Mockaitis (eds.). *Grand Strategy in the War Against Terrorism*. London: Frank Cass, 2003, 9.

ever since. Almost two thirds of all such incidents in Israel have occurred since September 2000. Indeed, suicide bombers are responsible for almost half of the approximately 750 deaths in terrorist attacks since then.[18]

Suicide bombing was a tactic that al-Qaeda took one dramatic stage further with the 9/11 attacks, ensuring a major dramatic impact on global public opinion. It takes martyrdom to a new level from the suicide bombing on the West Bank or in South Lebanon because the collective suicide of the 19 plane hijackers on 9/11 was purely in the cause of a global Islamic jihad rather than the more immediate political demands of local ethnic or nationalist movements. However, it is likely that the basic impulses behind the suicide terrorism of al-Qaeda remain the same as they were in other movements—it is largely an individual decision, and there is little or no evidence to suggest that the influence of a charismatic religious or political leader is sufficient by itself to drive a person to commit terrorist suicide.[19]

Suicide bombers pack together nuts and bolts, screws and ball bearings, any metal shards or odd bits of broken machinery with a homemade explosive and then strap them to their bodies. They then go to any place where people gather and detonate the bomb. Suicide bombing has the advantage of being relatively cheap as a tactic because the cost of each bomb is around $150.[20] At the same time, it is an effective response given the relative lack of success in smuggling in large-scale weapons onto the West Bank and also confirms the apparent Islamic commitment of the movement's adherence to martyrdom.[21] Moreover, terrorists do not need sophisticated and expensive technologies to make bombs; they can make bombs in their headquarters or in their houses.

The symbolic value of suicide in the service of religion or nation, and the honor bestowed on the suicide bomber and his family, is also critical in the production of suicide bombing.[22] Both secular and religiously based terrorist organizations have invoked religion when launching suicide bombing.[23] Perpetrators who were dispatched through both types of organizations referred to one's religiously based obligation to be involved in the struggle and listed the Garden of Eden as a reward for the suicide mission.[24]

Suicide Bombing in Cost-Benefit Terms

Although radical in nature, insurgents see advantages and strengths in the tactic of suicide bombings. From a cost-benefit analysis, suicide bombings seem to be a perfect tactic for the manpower-deprived insurgents. Suicide bombings sacrifice a small number of insurgents to cause damage to a much larger number of targets. As an instrument of broadcasting a political message, no other kind of attack better demonstrates an insurgent's dedication to a political agenda, and no other kind of attack has sparked as much fear. The greatest strength of suicide bombings is the fact that they are extremely hard to detect and stop. Carrying out this terrorist act is cheap because the cost of each bomb is around $150 and draws considerable international media attention to the conflict.[18]

---

[18] P. B. Rich and T. R. Mockaitis (eds.). *Grand Strategy in the War Against Terrorism*. London: Frank Cass, 2003, 9.

[19] A. Merari. The Readiness to Kill and Die: Suicidal Terrorism in the Middle East. In W. Reich (ed.), *Origins of Terrorism: Psychologies, Ideologies, Theologies, States of Mind*. Cambridge: Cambridge University Press, 1990, 121–125.

[20] B. Hoffman. The Logic of Suicide Terrorism. *The Atlantic Monthly*, 1, 40–47, June 2003.

[21] Y. Shaher. The al-Aqsa Martyrs Brigades. International Policy Institute for Counter Terrorism, March 24, 2004.

[22] J. Post, E. Sprinzak, and L. Denny. The Terrorists in Their Own Words: Interviews with 35 Incarcerated Middle Eastern Terrorists. *Terrorism and Political Violence*, 15: 171–184, 2003.

[23] M. Hafez. Manufacturing Human Bombs: Strategy, Culture, and Conflict in the Making of Palestinian Suicide Terrorism. Paper presented at the National Institute of Justice Conference, Washington, D.C., 2004.

[24] A. Berko. *The Path to the Garden of Eden: The World of Male and Female Suicide Bombers and Their Dispatchers*. Tel Aviv: Yedioth Ahronoth Press (in Hebrew), 2004.

A tactical advantage of suicide attacks over conventional terrorist tactics is the guarantee that the suicide bombing will be carried out at the most appropriate time and place with regard to the terrorists' objectives. This ensures the maximum number of casualties, which most likely would not be achieved via other means, such as the use of a remote-controlled charge or timer bomb. Basically, as "thinking bombs," suicide bombers make sure that the attacks are carried out in the most appropriate circumstance. In other words, suicide bombings strike at the right place and at the right time. This maximizes the number of casualties. Suicide bombings also draw considerable international media attention to the conflict because the act indicates a display of great determination and inclination for self-sacrifice on the part of the suicide bomber.[25]

The advantages of suicide bombing for terrorist organizations do not stop there. High-profile and much publicized suicide bombings can trigger additional, imitative suicides.[26] This suggests that mass media play an important role in terrorism. In a traditional terrorist insurgency, the exposure of an individual terrorist could be devastating for the terrorist organization. In suicide bombing, however, rather than being captured, bombers blow themselves up. This saves the organization from being exposed to authorities. This is also economical in the sense that there is not a need for an escape plan and that cost for treatment of injuries is virtually nonexistent because bombers in this tactic kill themselves in the process.

Another advantage of suicide bombing for terrorist groups is that there is a steady supply of suicide bombers. In addition to the monetary incentives for the family of the suicide bombers, they believe that bombing is not a suicide, but rather a form of martyrdom; these terrorists are looking forward to the rewards that will await them if they sacrifice their lives.[27] Suicide bombers view themselves as martyrs fighting a jihad against their heretic, apostate opponents.[28] Terrorist organizations are never out of a supply of suicide bombers because there are many individuals who strive for martyrdom as well as economic incentives.

Monetary rewards for terrorist organizations can be large. Suicide bombers sometimes draw sympathy from sources distant from the location of the attacks, especially donors who are willing to enable others to die as martyrs in the service of a cause. For example, following a supermarket bombing by an 18-year-old Palestinian girl, a Saudi telethon reportedly raised more than $100 million for the Palestinians.[29] Also, support from the Diaspora is common. According to one estimate, the Tamil Tigers have been funded by 800,000 Tamils living abroad in Australia, Canada, and elsewhere, who have sent back as much as $150 million annually. Payments and other benefits are given to the individual families of the dead Palestinian attackers.

In order to understand the threat of suicide bombers, it is helpful to examine the insurgent attacks on January 4, 2006; January 5, 2006; and January 9, 2006. On January 4, a suicide bomber snuck into a funeral packed with Iraqi mourners in Miqdadiya and detonated a bomb strapped to his torso. In the commotion that followed, a car bomber drove into the midst of the crowd and exploded, killing even more.[30] About 32 people died,[31] and 36 were wounded.[30]

---

[25] B. Ganor. The First Iraqi Suicide Bombing: A Hint of Things to Come? ICT, 2003. Available at http://www.ict.org.il/articles/articledet.cfm?articleid=477.

[26] A. Mazur. Bomb Threats and the Mass Media: Evidence for a Theory of Suggestion. *American Sociological Review*, 47, no. 3: 407–411, June 1982.

[27] E. Shuman. What Makes Suicide Bombers Tick? 2001. Available at http://www.israelinsider.com/channels/security/articles/sec_0049.htm.

[28] D. C. Rapoport. Sacred Terror: A Contemporary Example from Islam. In W. Reich (ed.), *Origins of Terrorism: Psychologies, Ideologies, Theologies, States of Mind*. Cambridge: Cambridge University Press, 1990, 103–30.

[29] B. Hoffman. The Logic of Suicide Terrorism. *The Atlantic Monthly*, 1, 40–47, June 2003.

[30] R. A. Oppel, Jr. and J. O'Neil. Attacks in Iraq Kill 120 as Post-Election Violence Escalates. *New York Times*, January 5, 2006. Available at http://www.nytimes.com/2006/01/05/international/middleeast/05cnd-iraq.html?page wanted=all.

[31] J. Straziuso. Suicide Bomber Kills 32 at Iraq Funeral. *Associated Press*, January 4, 2006. Available at http://www.apnewsarchive.com/2006/Suicide-Bomber-Kills-32-at-Iraq-Funeral/id-3fd62faf957414b9c89af9703 f9328fd.

Apparently, the funeral was for the nephew of a local political leader. Elsewhere on the same day, insurgents set off a stationary car bomb in Khadhamiya as an Iraqi police patrol passed by, killing five and wounding 15. Before the day was done, another car bomb exploded in Dora, killing a policeman and two civilians and wounding 11 more. Note that the latter two attacks occurred near the capital, which was tightly monitored by coalition forces.[30]

Suicide bombings are efficiently fatal: They result in many casualties and cause extensive damage. The number of suicide bombings increased exponentially in 2005 with an estimated 3000 deaths attributed to 360 suicide bombings last year and more than 472 suicide attacks in the five years from 2000 to 2004.[32] While the 9/11 terrorist attacks remain the deadliest of their kind, there are indications of an increase in the number of suicide bombings. That year, among the most lethal were the 54 persons killed in the July 2005 subway bombing in London and nearly 60 fatalities blamed on Iraqi suicide bombers targeting hotels in Amman, Jordan, four months later.[32]

Suicide bombing is an effective response given the relative lack of success in smuggling in large-scale weapons to the West Bank, and it also confirms the apparent Islamic commitment of the movement's adherence to martyrdom.[33] It does not come as a surprise, then, that suicide bombing has become increasingly popular. From 1980 to 2001, suicide attacks worldwide reportedly represented only 3% of all terrorist attacks but accounted for 48% of the total deaths due to terrorism.[34] In the Palestinian-Israeli conflict, suicide attacks carried out between 2000 and 2002 caused about 44% of all Israeli casualties, despite only representing 1% of the total number of attacks during the period.[35] Similarly, it is extremely difficult to counter suicide attacks once the terrorist is on his or her way to the target. Even if the terrorists are apprehended, the explosive device can still be detonated.

Another benefit of suicide bombing to terrorist organizations is that it requires a small number of people to kill hundreds of people. Once again, highlighting suicide bombings' brutal efficiency, 241 American military personnel were killed by a single suicide bomber in October 1983 in Lebanon; a single driver plowed his truck into a makeshift army camp in Sri Lanka in 1987, killing 40 soldiers. Additionally, on September 11, 2001 almost 3000 died at the hands of just 19 hijackers.[36]

Moreover, martyrdom operations are cheap with the bomb ingredients widely available as they also fill a civilian use. One Palestinian official's prescription for a successful mission includes "a willing young man (or woman) ... nails, gunpowder, a light switch and a short cable, mercury (readily obtainable from thermometers), acetone ... The most expensive item is transportation to an Israeli town. The total cost is about $150."[37] Acetone peroxide is a widely available explosive and the simplest in preparation. Its components can be easily bought in any household store without provoking suspicion—hydrogen peroxide is used for bleaching hair, and acetone is used for nail polish, as a solvent, or as an electrolyte. Acetone peroxide has one definite advantage over other types of explosives: It cannot be discovered by dogs. Specially trained dogs can discover explosives, such as ammonal, plastic explosives, and hexogen but not acetone peroxide.[38]

In addition to entailing closely related economic and strategic benefits for the terrorist organization, suicide bombing minimizes the costs that it incurs in its armed struggle against its enemies. On the contrary, the economic costs that a country sustains as a result of suicide terrorism have been

---

[32] D. R. Sands. Suicide Bombing Popular Terrorist Tactic. *The Washington Times*, paragraphs 3 and 4, 2006. Available at http://www.washtimes.com/world/20060507-102037-9660r.htm.

[33] Y. Shaher. The al-Aqsa Martyrs Brigades. International Policy Institute for Counter Terrorism, March 24, 2004.

[34] R. A. Pape. The Strategic Logic of Suicide Terrorism. *American Political Science Review*, 97: 347, 2003.

[35] A. Moghadam. Palestinian Suicide Terrorism in the Second Intifada: Motivations and Organizational Aspects. *Studies in Conflict & Terrorism*, 26: 65, 2003.

[36] J. Madsen. Suicide Terrorism: Rationalizing the Irrational. *Strategic Insights*, 3, no. 8: 2, 3, 2004. Mechanics of a living bomb. n.d. Available at http://www.waronline.org/en/terror/suicide.htm.

[37] S. Atran. The Moral Logic and Growth of Suicide Terrorism. *The Washington Quarterly*, 29, no. 2: 69, 1537, 2003.

[38] See The Mechanics of a Living Bomb, available at http://www.waronline.org/en/terror/suicide.htm, and The Making of a Terrorist, available at http://www.time.com/time/worl/article/0,8599,1883334,00.

proportionally much greater. Yet another reason why suicide bombing is fast becoming the ultimate terrorist weapon is that there is no need for an escape plan. From an operational perspective, suicide bombing is appealing as the terrorist organization does not have to plan an escape route, which is considered one of the most difficult and complicated parts of the terrorist plan. There is a great risk of the terrorist group being exposed if members of the organization are apprehended.

However, suicide bombings disenable authorities to get any information about the organization. For example, after the Madrid atrocity, when police raided an apartment to arrest others in connection with the terrorist attacks, the four inside the apartment blew themselves up rather than being captured and having to assist police in their inquiries. Likewise, Tamil Tiger rebels have traditionally carried one cyanide pill, which they can swallow in the event of imminent capture. A secretary-general of the Palestinian Islamic Jihad described suicide bombings' utility as follows: "Our enemy possesses the most sophisticated weapons in the world and its army is trained to a very high standard ... We have nothing with which to repel the killing and thuggery against us except the weapon of martyrdom. It is easy and costs us only our lives ... human bombs cannot be defeated, not even by nuclear bombs."[39] In general, suicide bombing remains a weapon of the weak in relation to a much stronger and superior enemy.

Finally, terrorist organizations are able to capitalize on the widespread media coverage that suicide bombings attract. The fate of the martyr is part of the story, and the large number of victims, again, ensures public attention. Because the gruesome effect of the violence is intended to be impressed upon an audience, the shocking nature of the attack is part of the calculation.[40] The media coverage conveys an image of extreme discipline, dedication, and skill on behalf of the terrorists in carrying out such an audacious and incomprehensible act.[41] This conversely instills a feeling of fear and helplessness among the target population in the face of a supposed invisible and unstoppable enemy.

Suicide Bombing as an Act of Martyrdom

As suggested in the previous section of this chapter, suicide bombing is becoming an ultimate terrorism tool because of the many men and women, young and old, who are willing to give up their lives for the sake of their beliefs. Children have been used in attacks as well. An al-Qaeda suicide bomber entered a hospital in Baghdad carrying a live child to gain access past the guard. The bomber was searched with no devices found but then exploded. The explosives were said to have been in the child's clothing. In terrorism studies, scholars have been examining why Islamic radical suicide bombers give up their lives freely in pursuit of achieving their ultimate goal. In tackling this problem, one must contextualize the actions of suicide bombers within the jihad concept of *shahada* (martyrdom). What drives suicide bombers to sacrifice their own lives for a cause?

Traditional explanations suggest that economic problems result in terrorism. The Palestinians' turn to suicide bombing results from the desperate situation of the populace, particularly among young people growing up angry and hopeless, some of them naively idealistic and some of them manipulated for political ends by the group's military strategists. There is a great deal of truth in these claims. In addition, many argue that globalization leads to economic insecurity and that this insecurity breeds fundamentalism, fear, and ultimately terrorism and violence. Some scholars also argue that terrorists are relatively uneducated and marginal in their societies. For example, Stern points out that terrorists are drawn from a large pool of volunteers who tend to be from the poorest segments of societies.[42] She quotes a jihadist (holy warrior): "Most of

---

[39] E. Sprinzak. Rational Fanatics. *Foreign Policy*, 120: 66, 2000.

[40] J. Madsen. Suicide Terrorism: Rationalizing the Irrational. *Strategic Insights*, 3, no. 8: 2, 3, 2004. Mechanics of a living bomb. n.d. Available at http://www.waronline.org/en/terror/suicide.htm.

[41] M. Taarnby. Profiling Islamic Suicide Terrorists, 76–82, 8, 2003. Available at http://www.jm.dk/image.asp?page=image&objno=71157.

[42] J. Stern. *Terror in the Name of God: Why Religious Militants Kill*. New York: Harper Collins, 2003.

the peoples who join these groups are from the poorest classes. Eighty-five percent come from below the poverty line; 12 percent are from the middle classes, and around three percent from the rich."[43] Furthermore, Saleh considers that the emergence of Palestinian suicide bombers is a direct consequence of the weakening of social and economic conditions.[44] Following this logic, an increase in income per capita and in the employment rate would reduce the incentive for suicide bombers to perform violent acts. According to Azam, "[e]conomic factors are a major compelling reason why young men seek opportunities in the bombing sector."[45] Low levels of education, poverty, and meager living conditions create despair, which results in anger, hatred, frustration, and, ultimately, terrorism.

However, some scholars have stressed the inadequacy of the social and economic variables in accounting for suicide bombings. Krueger and Maleckova conclude that "suicide bombers clearly are not motivated by the prospect of their own individual economic gain, although it is possible that the promise of larger payments to their families may increase the willingness of some to participate in these lethal missions."[46] Krueger and Maleckova suspect that suicide bombers' major motivation "instead results from their passionate support for the ideas and the aims of their movement."[46]

Berrebi, who explored the details of 285 Hamas and Islamic Jihad suicide terrorists, concurs with earlier findings that terrorists "are completely different than the classic characteristics of a suicidal individual"[47] and finds that suicide bombers "tend to be younger, of higher economic status, and higher educational attainment than their counterparts in the population."[48] Likewise, Berman notes that those selected for suicide bombing missions tend to be those most committed and the most capable of handling the complexities and difficulties that might arise.[49] The myth that suicide bombers are driven to their actions by the frustration stemming from poverty and ignorance is countered by the actuality that today's Palestinian bombers tend to be well educated and relatively economically stable.[50] While cash payments from abroad to families of suicide bombers continue, now all levels of the economic and educational spectrum are represented.[43] Despite well-publicized photos of families holding checks for as much as $25,000, the bomber's family may receive little direct financial incentive.[51] Therefore, the factors of economic hardship and poverty that frequently invite Western scholars to interpret suicide bombing in their light fail to account for the intensity and agenda of political Islam.

The Islamic literature points to the presence of concepts related to political struggle in Islam, which have been used over centuries in countless conflicts. While suicide bombings are not exclusive to either religious groups or religious culture,[52] such acts are becoming more religiously motivated. Atran notes that at least 70% of suicide attacks that occurred between 2000

[43] J. Stern. *Terror in the Name of God: Why Religious Militants Kill.* New York: Harper Collins, 2003.

[44] B. A. Saleh. Economic Conditions and Resistance to Occupation in the West Bank and Gaza strip: There Is a Causal Connection. 2004. Available at http://www.mafhoum.com/press7/197E14.htm.

[45] J. P. Azam. Suicide-Bombings as Intergenerational Investment. 2003, 1. Available at http://idei.fr/doc/wp/2003/suicide_bombing.pdf.

[46] A. B. Krueger and J. Maleckova. Does Poverty Cause Terrorism? The Economics and the Education of Suicide Bombers. *The New Republic*, 24: 29, 2002.

[47] C. Berrebi. Evidence About the Link between Education, Poverty and Terrorism Among Palestinians. 2003, 1. Available at http://www.cprs-alestine.org/polls/94/poll.

[48] See ref. 47, p. 4.

[49] E. Berman. Hamas, Taliban and the Jewish Underground: An Economist View of Radical Religious Militias. National Bureau of Economic Research, Working Paper w10004, September 2003. Available at http://www.nber.org/papers/w100004.

[50] S. Atran. The Moral Logic and Growth of Suicide Terrorism. *The Washington Quarterly*, 29, no. 2: 69, 1537, 2003.

[51] C. Reuter. *My Life Is a Weapon: Modern History of Suicide Bombing.* Princeton: Princeton University Press, 2004.

[52] R. A. Pape. The Strategic Logic of Suicide Terrorism. *American Political Science Review*, 97: 347, 2003.

and 2003 were religiously motivated.[53] It can be said that religion is thus the primary motivation for why extremists launch suicide bombings. Following the July 2001 suicide bombing attack in Netanya, unnamed sources from Hamas admitted that suicide bombers undergo a process of indoctrination that lasts for months. In the view of Islamic radical suicide bombers, killing oneself is no longer an act of self-destruction (*intihar*), but rather divinely commanded martyrdom (*istishad*) in defense of the faith.[54] In other words, suicide bombing is not a suicide but rather a form of martyrdom; it does not violate religious prohibitions against killing oneself.[55]

According to a BBC report, suicide bombers are recruited from mosques, schools, and religious institutions. They are likely to have shown particular dedication to the principles of Islam. They are taught the rewards that will await them if they sacrifice their lives.[56] Suicide bombers are not suffering from clinical depression or emotional difficulties; they perceive themselves as fulfilling a holy mission that will make them martyrs. Religious suicide bombers believe their goals and activities are sanctioned by divine authority.

Martyrdom, the voluntary acceptance of death as a demonstration of religious truth, is a concept central to Islam. Suicide bombers view themselves as martyrs fighting a jihad against their heretic, apostate opponents.[57] Transforming oneself into a living bomb is perceived as the equivalent of using a gun against one's enemies. The struggle is much the same, the only difference being one of chronology: The bomber dies while killing several enemies rather than after doing so.[58]

Small philological observations can sometimes introduce individuals to larger historical problems. No one familiar with Christian martyrdom will be surprised to learn that the Arabic words that Muslims use for "martyr" and "witness" are identical. The terminology is unmistakably Christian. By the fourth century, the Greek martyrs (witnesses) had acquired a technical sense and had come to denote one whose suffering and death bore witness to the truth of Jesus' passion and resurrection. Witnessing, suffering, death, and heavenly reward have since been intimately connected in Christian life and thought. Given the parallel terminology, one might expect to find a similar understanding of martyrdom in Islam.

At the level of reward, Muslim martyrs are not far from their Christian counterparts. Both are promised remission of sin and immediate life in paradise; the souls of both reside at the highest level of paradise near the throne of God; both are given the privilege of interceding with God on behalf of their coreligionists. Overall, the benefits accorded to Muslim martyrs closely resemble those in Christianity.[59] Whatever the similarities, there is one major difference in conception between Muslim and Christian martyrdom: for Muslims, one earns the title of martyr without any apparent act of witnessing. The martyr's sacrifice does not generally attest to anything specific, nor does it symbolize much beyond the obvious sense of death in the service of God's plan.

Virtually all major world traditions involve conceptual tension over the issue of self-caused death. In what is known as the Judeo-Christian tradition, suicide comes to be rejected as sinful, but it is often conceptually difficult to distinguish from voluntary martyrdom—death accepted and, in many cases, sought or embraced to attest to one's faith. Martyrdom in Islam forms an intrinsic component of the concept of jihad; hence, it does not lend itself to Western definitions

[53] S. Atran. The Moral Logic and Growth of Suicide Terrorism. *The Washington Quarterly*, 29, no. 2: 69, 1537, 2003.

[54] J. Stern. *Terror in the Name of God: Why Religious Militants Kill*. New York: Harper Collins, 2003.

[55] C. Reuter. *My Life Is a Weapon: Modern History of Suicide Bombing*. Princeton: Princeton University Press, 2004.

[56] E. Shuman. What Makes Suicide Bombers Tick? 2001. Available at http://www.israelinsider.com/channels/security/articles/sec_0049.htm.

[57] D. C. Rapoport. Sacred Terror: A Contemporary Example from Islam. In W. Reich (ed.), *Origins of Terrorism: Psychologies, Ideologies, Theologies, States of Mind*. Cambridge: Cambridge University Press, 1990, 103–30.

[58] M. Kramer. The Moral Logic of Hizballah. In W. Reich (ed.), *Origins of Terrorism: Psychologies, Ideologies, Theologies, States of Mind*. Cambridge: Cambridge University Press, 1990, 131–157.

[59] A. J. Wensinck. *The Oriental Doctrine of the Martyrs*. Amsterdam. Mededeelingen der Koninklijke Akademie van. Wetenschappen, Afdeeling Letterkunde 53: 6, 1921.

of suicide. According to Islamic teachings, *intihar* (suicide) designates despair and violent withdrawal from society whereas *shahada* (martyrdom) represents the ultimate form of giving for the well being of the community. Suicide is essentially a characteristic of individualist societies, mainly resulting from lack of integration of the individual into society. In collectivist Arab societies, there are very low suicide rates for males and virtually none for females.

The inappropriateness of Western concepts of suicide necessitates a new venue for understanding the motives of suicide bombers. The notion of altruistic suicide inspired by "religious sacrifice or unthinking political allegiance"[60] may shed light on kamikaze missions, but not on Palestinian human bombs. Whereas the kamikazes died for the sake of imperial Japan without expectation of personal reward, Arab suicide bombers feel they comply with the highest form of Islamic worship for which they have specific spiritual expectations. The dynamics of the terrorist group shape individual behavior, giving many members a strong sense of belonging, of importance, and of personal significance.

Suicide bombers often articulate a sense of personal, sacred mission. When Hezbollah introduced suicide bombing as a tactic, it soon became clear that the religious fervor of the bombers could help the organization compensate for its small numbers and inadequate military capabilities. Resentment and self-righteousness are often considered to be the underlying motivators for engaging in terrorism. Perceiving themselves as victims, the terrorists hone a hypersensitive awareness of slights and humiliations inflicted upon themselves or their particular group, and picture themselves as part of an elite heroically struggling to right the injustices of an unfair world. Typical suicide bombers are persuaded to join the movement because of both pragmatic and ideological reasons: the allure of martyrdom and the very tangible economic and social benefits his or her family will receive after his or her actions. It is, of course, difficult to ascertain what terrorists are really thinking or what really motivates them, especially considering the tendency of terrorist organizations to maintain high levels of secrecy and the contextual situation of long-standing sociocultural conflicts.

Similarly, it is easy to misinterpret the happy expressions often seen on the faces of suicide bombers. A smile may mean contemplation of eternal paradise, or it may represent satisfaction that the individual has helped the organization advance its goals one step forward.[61] Perhaps inevitably, one cannot know with certainty the extent of the suicide bombers' ideological fervor, nor can one pinpoint his or her emotional and cognitive responses to engaging in terror. Scholars and analysts are only left with observations of behavior in public, that is, the actual suicide bombing or attempt and the post-detonation interpretations of family and friends. All of this information is synthesized and extrapolated to reconstruct the influences leading up to the suicide bombing.

Martyrdom operations have gained popularity as the ultimate terrorist instrument because terrorist groups are able to benefit from the death of a member, conferring a sense of legitimacy on it.[62] Terrorist organizations glorify suicide bombing, infusing a culture of martyrdom that may include posters, songs, and flyers; this inspires others to join the organization. Indeed, even before the suicide bomber has struck, the individual is, in many ways, a living martyr.

Gender and Suicide Bombings

In most pre-modern societies, the men would fight while the women would stay home. Men, when necessary, would attack or defend. Considered the weaker of the two sexes, women would

[60] E. Durkheim. *Suicide*, trans. J. A. Spaulding and G. Simpson. New York: The Free Press, 1951, 15.

[61] M. Kramer. The Moral Logic of Hizballah. In W. Reich (ed.), *Origins of Terrorism: Psychologies, Ideologies, Theologies, States of Mind*. Cambridge: Cambridge University Press, 1990, 131–157.

[62] J. Madsen. Suicide Terrorism: Rationalizing the Irrational. *Strategic Insights*, 3, no. 8: 2, 3, 2004. Mechanics of a living bomb. n.d. Available at http://www.waronline.org/en/terror/suicide.htm.

raise children and run the home. It was as unimaginable that men would cook meals and keep the home clean as it was that women would hunt for food and defend the family in battle. Male religious leaders argued that women could not engage in battle. The leaders hoped in that way to keep women pure. If men and women trained and fought together, they were likely to touch one another, an impure act that had to be avoided. A man might have to touch a woman while preparing her for battle. Or failed Palestinian female suicide bombers could wind up in Israeli jails, where they were likely to come in contact with men, making it impossible to maintain the women's high standards of modesty; hence, the traditional ban on women acting as warriors.

And yet female combatants appear from time to time in Western history. Among the martyred female saints in the Catholic Church is Joan of Arc. Women terrorists were part of the Red Brigades in Italy, the Red Army Faction in Germany, and the Weathermen in the United States. Even within the Israeli-Arab conflict, Palestinian women were not unique to the battle: The Israel Defense Forces (IDF) has long had females in its ranks and recently as female fighter pilots. But none of these women engaged in suicide bombings.

Changing the Rules of the Game

Suicide bombing changed the traditional rules of war; female suicide bombers changed those rules even more. No longer is there a distinction between combatants (traditionally male) and noncombatants (traditionally women and children). No longer is there a distinction between terrorists (traditionally male) and innocent civilians (traditionally, men, women, and children). The revised rules that women were being employed as suicide bombers meant that bombers were even harder to identify. Any male or female might become a potential terrorist.

Accordingly, in the modern era, terrorist organizations decided that women could be used to carry out acts of terror, especially suicide bombings. One practical reason was that women tended to be more successful than their male counterparts. Because they did not arouse suspicion as a male suicide bomber might, they could meld into crowds and blow themselves up with relative ease. Female suicide bombers had another advantage over their male counterparts: They were more likely to attract widespread media coverage. With terrorist organizations competing for media attention, a female suicide bomber offered a terror group sponsoring her opportunity to increase its media profile. While all suicide bombers proved shocking, the traditional view that women gave life and did not destroy it made female suicide bombers a media draw.

On January 27, 2002, Yasser Arafat called on Palestinian women to join in the struggle against Israeli occupation. On the day that he issued the statement, a 28-year-old woman named Wafa Idris became the first female Palestinian suicide bomber. A divorced paramedic, she lived in the Am'ari Refugee Camp in the West Bank town of Ramallah. Arriving outside a shoe store on Jerusalem's Jaffa Road, she detonated a 22-pound bomb that killed her and an 81-year-old Israeli man and wounded more than 100 others. Rather than strap the bomb to her body, she carried it in a backpack. Until the attack, Palestinian women had helped plant bombs but had not blown themselves up. For that reason, the first reaction was that she could not have intended to conduct a suicide bombing: The explosion must have been accidental. But upon investigation, it was decided that she was indeed a suicide bomber. She had been angry at Israeli violence, but was not active in any of the Palestinian political, religious, or militant groups. Her motivation seemed more personal than political. Forced into marriage at a young age, she was unable to bear children and thus was considered worthless in her society. Her husband had left her for another woman with whom he had children. Worried that she might scar her family's reputation, Wafa Idris chose suicide bombing as she believed that by using this tactic she would to achieve some degree of honor.

Several terrorist groups have (or had) used females as suicide bombers, including (but not limited to) Hamas, al-Qaeda in Iraq, the Tamil Tigers, the al-Aqsa Martyrs Brigade, and the Turkish Kurdistan Workers Party (PKK). Indeed, female suicide bombers have been seen in Sri Lanka, Turkey, Iraq, Russia, Palestinian Occupied Territories, Lebanon, Afghanistan, and

Chechnya to name a few. In Iraq, female members of al-Qaeda's "Sisters" Martyr Brigades were found to have conducted suicide attacks dressed as men and mingled in line near police stations.

In Chechnya, these bombers have been called "Black Widow" suicide bombers as they are the wives of Chechnyan men who disappeared or were killed by Russian forces. They are trained and infiltrate into Russia to carry out attacks there. These Black Widows have carried out numerous attacks, such as, in 2010, they engaged in a coordinated suicide attack on the Moscow subway system; in 2004, they participated in the Beslan elementary school massacre; and in 2002, they conducted a suicide hostage barricade at a Dubrovka theatrical center.

In the last two attacks, the Black Widows engaged in mass hostage suicide attacks on the Chechen Riyadus-Salikhin Martyr's Battalion. Specifically, on September 1, 2004, the nationalist Islamic extremists of the Chechen Riyadus-Salikhin Martyr's Battalion conducted a unique form of SPBIED attack at an elementary school in the village of Beslan in North Ossetia, Russia. They first took 1400 children, parents, and teachers hostage and barricaded themselves in the school. The terrorists rigged the building with explosives tied to a deadman detonator that one terrorist had to be standing on at all times. After three days, the Russian forces attempted to storm the building, which resulted in a massacre that killed 396 people including 189 children. More than 700 were wounded. The Chechen terrorists all wore explosive belts or had detonators that would have exploded all the rigged IEDs. When attacked, they detonated their devices. This appeared to be a more refined version of the 2002 Moscow theater siege at the Dubrovka Theater where all of the 41 Chechen terrorists were prepared to destroy the building no matter what the outcome of negotiations. Here is a statement about the intentions of the terrorists that day given to Moscow television:

> Every nation has the right to their fate. Russia has taken away this right from the Chechens and today we want to reclaim these rights, which Allah has given us, in the same way he has given it to other nations. Allah has given us the right of freedom and the right to choose our destiny. And the Russian occupiers have flooded our land with our children's blood. And we have longed for a just solution. People are unaware of the innocent who are dying in Chechnya: the sheikhs, the women, the children and the weak ones. And therefore, we have chosen this approach. This approach is for the freedom of the Chechen people and there is no difference in where we die, and therefore we have decided to die here, in Moscow. And we will take with us the lives of hundreds of sinners. If we die, others will come and follow us—our brothers and sisters who are willing to sacrifice their lives, in Allah's way, to liberate their nation.

Husband-and-wife suicide bomber teams have also been used in terrorist attacks. This tactic was pioneered by al-Qaeda in Iraq (AQI) when they deployed and jointly martyred four pairs of husbands and wives driving their own suicide vehicle-borne improvised explosive device (SVBIED). An unusual example was the recruitment and death of Muriel Degauque, a former Belgian-born Christian who converted to Islam. She died in a SVBIED attack on Iraqi police in Qara Taba near Baqoubah. Her Belgian-Moroccan husband died in another SVBIED attack on US soldiers minutes later. Another ruse technique used by AQI was the deployment of families to penetrate security and detonate. One instance has been found where wives and children were being used to put on a friendly face at checkpoints so the search of the SVBIED would not be thorough. One bomber family crossed a checkpoint and then exploded at a police post.

What Motivates a Female Suicide Bomber?

At first, scholars believed that what motivated women to become suicide bombers were factors related to their gender: They resented being religiously subordinated to men; they were frustrated with their sexual inequality; they remained unmarried into a late age, not succeeding in having children; and/or they engaged in premarital sex or extramarital sex. Over time, however, other scholars determined that the same religious motivations that drove men to suicide bombing prompted a woman bomber as well.

Potential male suicide bombers are promised, for carrying out their suicide missions, a reward of 72 virgins waiting for them in heaven. But what are women suicide bombers offered? Very little is said on the subject. But a ninth-century scholar named Al-Tabarani noted that women would be reunited with their husbands upon arriving in heaven; those who had several husbands could choose the best one to be their eternal spouses. Other commentators decided that a woman who never married could marry any man in heaven.[63] Back in the ninth century, of course, no one was talking of women suicide bombers.

In the modern era, some women wanted to fight side by side with men. They sought ways to take part in the battles that men had traditionally fought on their own. But obstacles existed. Women who were part of ultraconservative patriarchic societies found it impossible to receive adequate personal training to take part in military battles involving only men. In such societies, it was taboo for a man to teach a woman military skills. The fundamentalist Islamic terror organizations, including Hamas, at first shunned female suicide bombers, but in time, Hamas came around and used women for suicide missions.

Suicide bombing was the one path open to women who wanted to take pride in fighting the enemy. Terrorist leaders had no trouble substituting female suicide bombers for males as the men were then freed for other, more complicated military tasks. Many female suicide bombers have some unfortunate personal event looming in their future, which they want to avoid: an arranged marriage, a father who refuses to let his daughter marry a boyfriend, and/or the need to restore the family's honor. All of these events give the sponsors leverage to entice women.

Concluding Thoughts

To summarize, the previous section has shown why suicide bombings will become the ultimate instrument in achieving terrorist organizations' ultimate goal. This is because suicide bombings can be carried out at very low cost. Bombs are inexpensive, can be made in the comfort of the home, and some cannot be detected. In addition, suicide bombings do not require escape routes. As bombers kill themselves, there is no fear of surrendering information. Moreover, terrorist groups capitalize on the promise of martyrdom. Suicide bombing also enhances the likelihood of mass casualties and extensive damage on the economy of the target. Lastly, it affects the public and media due to the overwhelming sense of helplessness.

This research further explored both socioeconomic and religious factors in explaining why suicide bombings or martyrdom operations will become the greatest terrorist tool. Suicide bombing is largely economic in nature; every human act is economic. In this vein, suicide bombers—male or female—make their own choices, which involve costs and benefits. Indeed, their acts and the increasing popularity of suicide bombing among terrorist organizations can be examined using an economic perspective. Iannaccone sees a supply and demand for suicide bombings.[64] Organizations that conduct such acts of terror can be regarded as firms. So the economic theory of firms and supply and demand is applicable to suicide bombings. The supply of persons willing to sacrifice themselves for a cause is more than enough. It only requires a small number of suicide bombers to inflict terror, and there is a supply, mostly young people, men and women, who are willing to give up their lives for a cause.

On the other hand, the demand for suicide terrorism comes from the firms or terrorist organizations whose leaders feel hatred and anger toward the enemy target. The fact that violence is counterproductive does not matter because those who demand suicide bombings feel satisfaction when their enemies are harmed, even if they also are harmed in the process. Undeniably,

[63] M. Tsai. Honey, I'm Dead! *Slate Magazine*, March 29, 2010. Available at http://www.slate.com/id/2249122/.

[64] L. R. Iannaccone. The Market for Martyrs. 2003. Paper presented at the 2004 Meetings of the American Economic Association, San Diego, p. 10. Available at http://www.mercatus.org/repository/docLib/MC_GPI_WP35_040807.pdf.

there is a market for martyrs and firms that organize terrorist suicide bombings. Iannaccone concludes that, in order to reduce suicide bombing, demand, rather than supply, must be reduced.[65] The following are problems that may be encountered if deterrence focuses on reducing the supply:[66] (1) Terrorist firms can function effectively even if the supply of suicide bombers is very small; (2) standard criminal penalties have little or no impact on the expected costs and benefits confronting a rational suicide bomber; (3) there are many different sources of supply and methods of recruitment, and thus if enemies block one source or method, terrorist firms can readily substitute others; and finally, (4) reducing the rate of suicide bomber success may not yield comparable reductions in the net expected benefits associated with suicide missions and may actually increase the net benefits.[67]

In the end, suicide bombing will continue to be the ultimate terrorist tool. The situation of supply-side deterrence can be likened to illegal drugs. Much of the campaigns against illegal drugs are a futile attempt to limit supply, but that just drives the cost up while doing little to reduce the quantity because the quantity demanded is rather unresponsive to changes in price.[68] Likewise, targeting suicide bombers only shoots up the price while not doing much to reduce such activity; simply stopping or killing suicide bombers will not stop terrorism because those who die will be replaced by others. In order to reduce the demand for suicide bombing, the market conditions must be altered. According to Iannaccone, "Changing market conditions provides the only true solution to the problem of suicide bombing and militant religious radicalism. Other approaches (such as targeting firms, leaders, and recruits) raise operating costs and induce substitution but leave in place the underlying demand, and hence the underlying profit opportunities, associated with this line of business."[65]

[65] L. R. Iannaccone. The Market for Martyrs. 2003. Paper presented at the 2004 Meetings of the American Economic Association, San Diego, p. 18. Available at http://www.mercatus.org/repository/docLib/MC_GPI_WP35_040807.pdf.

[66] L. R. Iannaccone. The Market for Martyrs. 2003. Paper presented at the 2004 Meetings of the American Economic Association, San Diego, pp. 13–14. Available at http://www.mercatus.org/repository/docLib/MC_GPI_WP35_040807.pdf.

[67] L. R. Iannaccone. The Market for Martyrs. 2003. Paper presented at the 2004 Meetings of the American Economic Association, San Diego. Available at http://www.mercatus.org/repository/docLib/MC_GPI_WP35_040807.pdf.

[68] F. E. Foldvary. The Economics of Suicide Bombing, paragraph 6, 2004. Available at http://www.progress.org/2004/fold353.htm.

18

The Crime-Terror Nexus[1]

Domestic terrorism from right-wing, left-wing, and single-issue groups remains a great concern for our law enforcement agencies. The growing propensity of these organizations and their members to "act out" and to step up and engage law enforcement is alarming. The radicalization of Americans continues with several successful attacks and more than 50 thwarted in our country since 9/11. The threat of the lone wolf, already embedded in society and acting alone with unyielding determination, is extremely worrisome. Factor in an unprecedented increase in hate groups and gangs in the United States, and the domestic terrorism picture is quite grim with resource-constrained law enforcement agencies struggling to juggle myriad challenges. Drug-trafficking organizations are flourishing south (and north) of our border with Mexico. Now operating in the United States, cartels are using gangs to move product and are attempting to corrupt border patrol officers to open lanes for moving people, drugs, and, potentially, worse into our nation.

The discussion of the rise of postmodern terrorist groups is deeply rooted in the soft sciences; a fusion of psychology, sociology, and organizational development and behavioral theory allows insight into many of the vexing "whys" about the terrorism phenomenon. Viewing the life cycle of terrorist groups yields a new solution set for engagement and an intuitive understanding as to why and when they liaise with actors espousing dissimilar ideologies. The "Big Three" international terrorist groups that most threaten the homeland, al-Qaeda, Hezbollah, and FARC, are morphing in structure and changing strategy and tactics. Understanding their new goals and methodology is important for policy makers, strategic planners, and operators alike.

Over the past two decades, drug-trafficking groups around the world have grown into multinational criminal corporations. Worth billions of dollars, they use terrorist methods to influence governments and protect their assets. For example, criminal organizations and drug traffickers in Colombia and Chechnya have pioneered the mass subcontracting of amateur terrorists to conduct abductions and other acts of terrorism that can earn a given group millions of dollars in ransoms and protection rackets and fund other terrorist acts. Irrefutably, the crime-terror nexus exists. The US executive branch is so troubled about the partnering of terrorists and criminals that they issued a strongly worded document in July 2011, titled the *Strategy to Combat Transnational Organized Crime: Addressing Converging Threats to National Security.* The White House, acknowledging the nexus, stated, "[t]errorists and insurgents increasingly are turning to criminal networks to generate funding and acquire logistical support."[2]

[1] Information for this chapter was drawn from the following title: J. L. Hesterman, *The Terrorist-Criminal Nexus: An Alliance of International Drug Cartels, Organized Crime, and Terror Groups*, CRC Press, 2013.

[2] The White House. Strategy to Combat Transnational Organized Crime: Addressing Converging Threats to National Security. Available at http://www.whitehouse.gov/sites/default/files/Strategy_to_Combat_Transnational_Organized_Crime_July_2011.pdf.

The synergy between groups, sharing resources and tactics, will further their collective agenda to gain power and erode security; induce fractures, internal strife, or apathy in society; and wait patiently for the opportunity to move in and take control. Commonalities shared by these dark networks make their liaison increasingly likely. Leadership is decentralized; therefore decimation, or killing the first string, will not mean the end of the organization. Modern groups are transnational and loosely organized with cells operating like business franchises with their own funding and training. Whether driven by vast sums of money, loyalty, power, or religion, the ideology is powerful glue holding the organization together. They are flexible, can change tactics and morph to avoid attention, and will expertly leverage technology for recruiting, morale boosting, and secure communication. Although these organizations have "curb appeal" to the disaffected, poor, and those seeking affiliation, members are increasingly educated, middle-class, well adjusted, and possibly just angry at "the system."

Actually, groups with dissimilar ideologies are working together to further their goals. They are also copying successful tactics, learning from each other's mistakes, and, at the very least, operating in the same physical or virtual "space." To fully grasp the complex issue of the nexus, one must first investigate root causes and the environment contributing to its rise and persistence. Transnational criminal groups now have sophisticated business models that parallel legitimate corporations. Feeding on globalization and advances in communications and logistics technology, modern transnational crime is more expansive, far deadlier, and extremely difficult to eradicate. Adding further context to the issue is an overview of the international agencies involved, methods used, and lessons learned in the fight against transnational crime, all of which should be simultaneously applied to the global war on terror. This chapter investigates the sharing and copying of tactics between groups, their surprising commonalities, and how they will and do work together to further their goals. The modern terrorist threat is asymmetric, and as such, countering it requires an asymmetric approach.

Drug-Trafficking Organizations and Terrorist Groups Interface

In the world of terrorism and crime, a "failed" operation is nonexistent. As the press covers every detail of weapon failures and the investigatory process leading to discovery and mitigation, the enemy watches and learns, perfecting their technique for the next event. Postmodern, mature groups will naturally gravitate toward a working relationship with others to leverage skills and resources. Nefarious groups not only copy successful recruiting, morale boosting, and fund-raising methodologies, but also duplicate tactics working for other organizations and study failed operations to learn how to perfect their own. Groups will work together to share tactics and techniques, especially those with "niche" capabilities who gladly sell or trade expertise. Ideology is no concern when the shared enemy is "the state," which seeks to limit influence, power, and money. A case in point is Hezbollah. Hezbollah has a strong presence in Latin America and has been detected at the Mexican border. Although they are likely in the region merely to profit from lucrative drug trafficking, authorities are now seeing their "footprint" in various cartel activities.

Nexus Geographic Area

In addition to the drug-trafficking organizations, terrorist factions and citizens from countries sponsoring terror are exploiting the chaos at the border. An investigative report prepared by the House Committee on Homeland Security, titled *Line in the Sand: Confronting the Threat at the Southwest Border* paints a worrisome picture regarding its porosity.[3] For example, in 2011,

[3] US House Committee on Homeland Security, Subcommittee on Investigations. A Line in the Sand: Confronting the Threat at the Southwest Border, 2006.

463,000 illegal aliens (IAS) were apprehended at the border; however, officials believe that just 10% to 30% of IAS crossing into the United States are detained, meaning at least four million may have successfully crossed. Illegal aliens, other than Mexicans, are also actively attempting to enter the United States through Mexico. US Customs and Border Protection (CBP) reports that in 2010 they apprehended 59,017 non-Mexican illegal aliens at the border. The law dictates that illegal aliens be detained by Immigrations and Customs Enforcement (ICE) and given a hearing. However, the courts cannot handle the workload due to the sheer number of cases; therefore, these individuals are returned to their country of origin with a future court date if they wish to return and plead their case for citizenship. Most do not and simply disappear.

Of the non-Mexican illegal aliens caught trying to illegally enter the United States, most are from Central and South American countries. The data is worrisome due to the presence of FARC, Hamas, Hezbollah, and al-Qaeda in those regions. However, of even greater concern are the thousands of IAS attempting to cross the border from "countries of concern" or state sponsors of terror, special-interest aliens (SIAs). Each fiscal year, CBP is directed by law to compile an OTM list, including SIAs. The data is not releasable to the public but may be obtained through a freedom of information act (FOIA) request to the Border Patrol (see Table 18.1). Certainly, many SIAs are smuggled by drug trafficking organizations, and the opportunity for terrorists and drug trafficking organizations to interface in this realm is extremely high.

Terrorists and others with nefarious intentions have already crossed into the United States at the Mexican border. ICE investigations revealed that many SIAs were moved from the Middle East to staging areas in Central and South America before being smuggled illegally into the United States. Hezbollah has been present and active in South and Central America for at least 20 years and now has a presence in Mexico. ICE officials have testified that members of Hezbollah have already entered the United States across the southwest border,[4] and in 2011, a former undercover law enforcement officer spoke out regarding his discovery of Hezbollah safe houses in Tijuana and Durango.[5] In September 2012, Rafic Mohammad Labbon Allaboun was arrested in Mexico and returned to the United States for violating probation. Allaboun was born in Beirut and came to the United States in 1986, becoming a dual citizen. He was arrested for credit card fraud and spent two years in jail; authorities suspected the fraud was linked to Hezbollah's money-laundering activities but could not prove the charge in court. Allaboun violated the terms of his probation and traveled to Yucatán, Mexico, where he was arrested by law enforcement; Allaboun was carrying a fake passport identifying him as a citizen of Belize at the time of arrest. Authorities suspect him of involvement with a branch of Hezbollah active in Central America and the Yucatán. Finally, Hamas is also believed to be operating in Tijuana and is likely liaising with Hezbollah or sympathizers/fund-raisers.

Al-Qaeda may be also present in the border region. An example is Ahmed Muhammad Dhakane, who was born in Somalia and moved to Brazil in 2007 to set up a large human-smuggling operation. Dhakane was arrested at the border in 2011 and applied for political asylum in the United States. However, during the application process, he failed to mention his connections to al-Barakat and Al-Ittihad Al-Islami (AIAI), both specially designated global terrorists (SDGTs) by the State Department. In fact, AIAI was, at one time, Somalia's largest militant Islamic group and officially aligned itself with al-Qaeda in the late 1990s. Dhakane confessed in court that he had smuggled seven terrorist group members into the United States across the Mexican border along with numerous men from Somalia, Nigeria, and Middle Eastern countries at the behest of the groups.[6] He is serving a 10-year sentence for his activities. In 2010, al Shabaab, also aligned

---

[4] US House Committee on Homeland Security, Subcommittee on Investigations. A Line in the Sand: Confronting the Threat at the Southwest Border, 2006.

[5] Terrorist Group Setting Up Operations Near Border. *ABC 10 News*, May 4, 2011, Available at http://www.10news.com/news/27780427/ detail.html.

[6] Investigative Project on Terrorism. USA v. Ahmed Muhammed Dhakane. Available at http://www.investigativeproject.org/case/370.

Table 18.1 SIA Data Obtained by Judicial Watch and Atlanta TV Station WSBTV through FOIA Request

Country of Interest	SIAs Apprehended in FY2007–2010
China	4157
Russia	197
Pakistan	149
Somalia	79
Iraq	59
Iran	56
Yemen	33
Afghanistan	21
Syria	12
North Korea	5

Source: Judicial Watch, Judicial Watch Obtains New Border Patrol Apprehension Statistics for Illegal Alien Smugglers and "Special Interest Aliens," 2011. J. L. Hesterman, *The Terrorist-Criminal Nexus: An Alliance of International Drug Cartels, Organized Crime, and Terror Groups*, CRC Press, 2013.

with al-Qaeda, recruited a US citizen living in Kenya, Anthony Joseph Tracy, to assist with smuggling 271 Somali nationals across the border and into the United States. Several were captured; however, most remain at large. Apart from the presence of terrorist groups in these regions, other areas of commonality between drug trafficking organizations, drug cartels, and terrorist groups include their use of similar tactics, especially, tunnels and bombs.

Tunnels

The tunnels built by the cartels to clandestinely cross from Mexico into the United States have grown increasingly sophisticated. Authorities have discovered more than 150 tunnels since 1990, most crude and incomplete but a few operational with tracks to move carts loaded with drugs across the border. In July 2012, Drug Enforcement Administration (DEA) and ICE agents discovered a 240-yard, $1.5 million tunnel under a strip mall in San Luis, Arizona, expertly constructed with six-foot ceilings and wood walls and equipped with ventilation, lighting, hydraulic systems, and other high-tech components, not the standard dirt tunnel through the sewer. DEA agents believed it was the work of experienced engineers.[7] A former US law enforcement agent with extensive experience working undercover in Mexico believes the expertise and construction features seen in the latest cartel tunneling efforts point to Hezbollah's involvement.[8]

Hezbollah has constructed a network of tunnels in Lebanon used to secure themselves from Israeli air strikes. The tunnels have medical facilities, dormitories, lighting, and heating and cooling systems. Recent reports from Beirut indicate that with the help of Iran, Hezbollah has tunneled

[7] E. Spagat and J. Billeaud. Drug Tunnels Discovered between US–Mexico Border Contained Railcar System, Tons of Pot. July 13, 2012. Available at http://www.huffingtonpost.com/2012/07/14/drug-tunnels_n_1673317.html.

[8] Terrorist Group Setting Up Operations Near Border. *ABC 10 News*, May 4, 2011, Available at http://www.10news.com/news/27780427/detail.html.

mountains in the Beqaa region and into Syria.[9] Tunnels in the Middle East are nothing new; consider the vast network discovered by coalition forces in Iraq during Operation Iraqi Freedom, including high-tech underground corridors from Saddam Hussein's palace to the airport. Also, Hamas has constructed a network of 400 main and 1000 feeder tunnels between the Gaza Strip and Egypt, many of which can accommodate vehicles. The tunnels are used to smuggle medicine, construction material, fuel, and other goods embargoed due to the ongoing Israeli-Palestinian conflict.[10]

Bombs

A new weapon in the cartel's battle for control debuted in July 2010 with the successful detonation of a vehicle-borne improvised explosive device (VBIED) in the border city of Ciudad Juárez. The Juárez Cartel deliberately targeted first responders by placing a bound, wounded man in a police uniform at the scene, luring law enforcement and medical personnel to the area. A nearby vehicle, inconspicuously laden with 22 pounds of Tovex, exploded moments later killing three people and wounding 20. Tovex is a water gel explosive widely used as a substitute for dynamite for industrial and mining purposes. Theft of Tovex in Mexico is a common occurrence. In February 2009, masked gunmen stole 900 cartridges of the substance from a US firm in Durango, Mexico.[11] In July and August 2012, a wave of car bombings in northeast Mexico targeting a city hall and the homes of security officials were detonated by the Los Zetas and gulf cartels as part of their campaign to influence local elections. VBIEDs are widely used by insurgents in Iraq and Afghanistan and terrorist groups, such as Hezbollah and al-Qaeda. However, the cartels' use of these new tactics was a game changer in Mexico's battle and prompted calls for increased vigilance on the US side of the border as the violence pushes north.

The number of Hezbollah operatives operating in Mexico has increased in recent years. In 2009, former Syrian military officer Jamal Yousef was arrested in New York City on narco-terror charges for his involvement in a weapons-for-cocaine scheme between Hezbollah and FARC, using Mexico as a safe haven. According to the indictment, a weapons cache of 100 M-16 assault rifles, 100 AR-15 rifles, 2500 hand grenades, C4 explosives, and antitank munitions was stolen from Iraq by Yousef's cousin, a member of Hezbollah, and moved to the home of family members in Mexico, also affiliated with the terrorist group. Yousef planned to deliver the weapons to FARC in Colombia in return for 2000 pounds of cocaine, but the DEA intervened; he pled guilty and faces 15 years in prison.[12] Although Yousef appears to have been a lone operator, Jameel Nasr was an international Hezbollah operative, taking direction from Lebanon to establish a Hezbollah network in Mexico and throughout South America. Nasr traveled regularly between Lebanon, Venezuela, and Tijuana and was arrested in 2010 by Mexican authorities upon his return from one of the trips. Mexican authorities said Nasr had been "entrusted with forming a base in South America and the United States to carry out operations against Israeli and Western targets."[13]

In late 2011, prosecutors in Virginia charged a Lebanese man, Ayman Joumaa, with smuggling at least "tens of thousands of kilos" of Colombian cocaine into the United States with 85,000 kilos sold to the Los Zetas Cartel. Joumaa and his associates laundered more than $250 million in proceeds through Spain, West Africa, Lebanon, Venezuela, and Colombia.[14] According to

---

[9] S. M. Yaghi. Israel Is Preparing for War Tunnels and Hezbollah Elements in the Southern Syrian Border. July 2, 2012. Available at http://www.aljoumhouria.com/news/index/15409.

[10] K. Zaboun. Gaza Tunnel Trade: Matter of Life and Death for Hamas. August 31, 2012. Available at http://www.asharq-e.com/news.asp?section=1&id=30885.

[11] A. A. Caldwell. Car Bomb in Mexico Drug War Changes the Ground Rules. *Guardian*, July 17, 2010. Available at http://www.guardian.co.uk/world/feedarticle/9178042.

[12] US District Court, Southern District of New York. Sealed Indictment: Jamal Yousef. Available at http://www.fas.org/programs/ssp/asmp/externalresources/2009/Yousef,Jamaletal.S3indictment.pdf.

[13] Investigative Project on Terrorism. Mexican Arrest Indicates Hizballah Seeking Foothold. July 7, 2010.

[14] US District Court for the Eastern District of Virginia. Sealed Indictment: Ayman Joumaa. Available at http://www.investigativeproject.org/documents/case_docs/1856.pdf.

the US Treasury Department, Hezbollah derived financial support from the criminal activities of Joumaa's network through the sanctioned Lebanese Canadian National Bank of Beirut.[15] In 2011, a former undercover law enforcement officer discussed Hezbollah interface with drug trafficking organizations, saying the group receives cartel cash and protection in exchange for giving their expertise from "money laundering to firearms training and explosives training." He also discussed his discovery of Hezbollah safe houses in Tijuana and Durango.[16]

Finally, the case of the Iranian plot to kill Saudi Arabia's ambassador to Washington, D.C., revealed how the cartels may be used to carry out attacks for rogue regimes or nation-states. In October 2011, authorities arrested Mansour J. Arbabsiar, an Iranian-American car salesman in Texas, in connection with the plot. According to his indictment, Arbabsiar's cousin in Iraq, somehow affiliated with Iran's Revolutionary Guard Corps (IRGC) Quds force, reached out to him to set up the assassination using a Mexican cartel. The plot entailed the bombing of a Washington, D.C., restaurant while the ambassador was having lunch. Arbabsiar traveled back and forth to Mexico to meet with representatives of Los Zetas Cartel to arrange the hit and provided a $100,000 down payment from Iran as a sign of good faith, a small portion of the $1.5 million that would be paid for the entire operation. Confidential informants alerted US law enforcement, who then monitored all the bank transactions, telephone calls from Iran, and Arbabsiar's conversations with people he thought were cartel members.[17]

IRA Inc.

Unfortunately, with countries hyperfocusing on al-Qaeda and its splinter groups, some terrorist factions of the Irish Republican Army (IRA) have regrouped, recruited, and grown in strength under the radar. Two splinter factions of the IRA are still active: the State Department–designated Real IRA (RIRA) and the less powerful Continuity IRA (CIRA). The IRA has long been recognized for its mastery of bomb building. The group pioneered the use of mobile phones to trigger bombs, a technique successfully used in the tragic 2004 al-Qaeda train bombings in Madrid. IRA pipe bombs have been imitated by many groups, leaving a unique and traceable fingerprint pointing to cooperation and training. Following a relative period of calm in the mid-2000s, the world was reminded that the factions of the IRA are still terrorist groups with an agenda and the resources to attack. In the March 7, 2009, Massereene Barracks shooting, RIRA dissidents brazenly ambushed and killed two British soldiers and wounded four other people during the attack at an army base. The shooting set off a string of bombings throughout the next two years, damaging courthouses and police stations as well as private homes and vehicles of law enforcement officials.

A large-scale attack occurred on February 17, 2010, when police in Newry, Northern Ireland, received a coded message from IRA bombers. They were able to clear the area around the courthouse just minutes before a 250-pound car bomb exploded. The Newry event was the first large car bomb attack in Ireland since the deadly Omagh attack in 1998 and the bombing of a police station in 2000. Officials in Ireland know that due to the sophistication of the bomb and other data not released to the public that the CIRA and RIRA are now sharing tactics and have "cross-fertilized." The police were informed that the bomb was set to go off in 30 minutes; however, the actual explosion was 17 minutes after the call. Other smaller attacks took place across Northern Ireland, including live mortars left outside police stations and a car bomb killing a police officer.

The attacks are widespread and persistent, and aimed specifically at law enforcement, the government, and financial institutions. Many attacks have also been foiled in Ireland in the

[15] S. Rotella. Government Says Hezbollah Profits from US Cocaine Market Via link to Mexican Cartel. ProPublica, December 13, 2011.

[16] Terrorist Group Setting Up Operations Near Border. *ABC 10 News*, May 4, 2011, Available at http://www.10news.com/news/27780427/ detail.html.

[17] US District Court, Southern District of New York. Sealed Indictment: Jamal Yousef. Available at http://www.fas.org/programs/ssp/asmp/externalresources/2009/Yousef,Jamaletal.S3indictment.pdf.

last few years, including a second bomb in Newry, set to go off in a major shopping district. The IRA and its factions had worked (and some are currently working) with several terrorist groups, helping them perfect their bomb-making skills. For instance, the Provisional IRA and FARC have a relationship dating back to the late 1990s when they shared bomb-building techniques. The relationship was reportedly brokered by Spain's nationalist-separatist group, the ETA. In August 2001, the "Colombia 3" case exposed the relationship when three members of an IRA faction were arrested when attempting to leave the Bogotá airport, traveling on false passports and with traces of explosives on their clothing. The three were convicted but escaped and returned to Ireland, which has no extradition treaty with Colombia.

Also in 2001, the House of Representatives Committee on International Relations published the findings of its investigation into the activities of IRA factions in Colombia, detailing the connection with FARC, identifying 15 more terrorists linked to factions of the IRA who had traveled to and from the country and estimating the IRA had received at least $2 million in drug proceeds for the training. FARC has carried out several large car bomb attacks in Colombia in the past 10 years, including a 2003 attack at a nightclub with a car laden with 200 kilograms of explosives. Interestingly, the IRA-FARC relationship was facilitated by the Spanish Basque Separatist group, ETA, which has worked with FARC for several decades. The IRA and ETA have worked together since the 1970s, exchanging technology and material. For example, a remote-controlled VBEID technique used in the first Gulf War was copied by the IRA and taught to ETA. The groups have also exchanged bomb-building material, such as the transfer of Semtex and C-4 between the groups in 2002.[18]

The IRA-Palestinian relationship is well documented and extends back to the 1970s when the groups shared bomb-building techniques in Libya and Lebanon's Bekka Valley.[19] Ireland has been vocal about their support of the Palestinian cause, even sending flagged ships to participate in the "Gaza Freedom Flotillas." Following Operation Defensive Shield in which Israel engaged in a military campaign in Gaza, a British explosives expert working with the Palestinian Red Crescent discovered 200 "exact replicas" of IRA-issue pipe bombs in Jenin.[20] Separatist groups tend to affiliate with each other, understanding the political ideology and the fight against the ruling government; therefore, it seems only natural that the IRA and its factions would align with groups such as ETA and Hamas.

Since at least 2000, the IRA has had a relationship with violent factions in the Balkans, receiving arms and sharing tactics. This association came to light with the seizure of a shipment of arms, including rocket launchers, leaving the Balkans for Ireland in July 2000. The two groups continue to liaise as evidenced by an assassination plot revealed in 2010 when an RIRA leader was arrested for attempting to hire a hit man from the Balkans to murder a British military general officer. RIRA members have also been arrested in Lithuania and Slovenia while attempting to procure arms.

Hezbollah and Hamas: Partnering for Success

Hezbollah and Hamas, also known as the Islamic Resistance Movement, operate in the same "space" in terms of benefactors such as Iran and Syria and financing activities in the tri-border area of South America. Although the ideologies differ, the two groups are forming an increasingly strong partnership in the Middle East. For instance, during the December 2008 to January 2009 Gaza War, Hamas and Hezbollah maintained continuous communication in all phases of the conflict. During the battle, Hezbollah's influence on Hamas' tactics was apparent with the group relying more on rocket attacks and less on suicide operations. Iranian sources report that Hezbollah trained Hamas in military tactics used to attack Merkava tanks, the main battle tank

[18] A. Oppenheimer. How Terrorists Acquire Technology and Training: Lessons from the IRA. *The Detonator*, September/October 2009.

[19] R. Ehrenfeld. iRa + PlO = Terror. *National Review*, August 21, 2002.

[20] The Irish–Palestinian Connection. CrethiPlethi, 2010.

employed by the Israeli Defense Forces (IDF). A Hezbollah parliamentary official confirmed the tactical exchange.[21]

IEDS, Fertilizer, and Sticky Bombs

If a tactic is successful, it will be duplicated. In the past 10 years, insurgents successfully attacked coalition forces with crude devices and devastating impact. However, the use of IEDs is not contained in war zones. In 2011, there were 4744 global IED incidents, 6278 deaths, and 17,040 wounds around the world.[22] IEDs are being used by drug-trafficking organizations, separatist groups, and antigovernment activists. Understanding the threat and how it could move to the homeland courtesy of domestic actors or radicalized lone wolves is critical to mitigate the danger.

IEDs

Military operations in Afghanistan and Iraq were greatly affected by the insurgent's use of improvised explosive devices or IEDs. IEDs are homemade, low-tech devices routinely using pressure plates and radio-controlled triggers to destroy vehicles passing on roadways or to attack soldiers on foot patrols. IEDs were responsible for 1316 of the 3171 US and coalition casualties in Afghanistan since 2001 with the bulk of the deaths occurring since 2008. Many other soldiers who survived an IED blast lost one or more limbs. Recognizing this persistent and grave threat to the troops, the Pentagon established the Joint Improvised Explosive Device Defeat Organization (JIEDDO) to respond to the threat.

Insurgents will likely spread their IEDs knowledge gleaned from recent operations as did Waad Ramadan Alwan, an Iraqi citizen who moved to Kentucky in 2009 after winning a visa as a political refugee. Unbeknownst to government officials, Alwan was an Iraqi insurgent who planted IEDs on roads traveled by US troops between 2003 and 2006. Soon after his arrival in the United States, Alwan began working with another Iraqi refugee, Mohanad Shareef Hammadi, to secure weapons to send to Iraq to aid al-Qaeda in Iraq in operations against coalition forces. A confidential source who worked for the FBI repeatedly met with Alwan, who detailed his use of IEDs in Iraq to kill Americans and made elaborate IED diagrams. Using his particular "signatures," the military was able to determine that Alwan's fingerprints were on an unexploded IED in Iraq the military had kept for evidence. Both men were arrested while they secured a shipment of stinger missiles and weapons they thought were destined for Iraq.[23]

The JIEDDO leadership recently testified about the possible use of IEDs at home, stating, "[t]he domestic IED threat from both homegrown extremists and global threat networks is real and presents a significant security challenge for the United States and our international partners."[24] Data supports this assertion; according to JIEDDO, since 2007, there are 500 attempted IED detonations per month outside of Iraq and Afghanistan. As explained in one of their *Inspire* magazine issues, one of al-Qaeda's new tactics is the call to individual jihad, motivating lone wolves into action. The Summer 2010 edition encourages lower-tech attacks through homemade bombs, giving detailed instructions on how to construct a pipe bomb and devices with timers.

Fertilizer

Urea nitrate fertilizer is used in the farming industry, and although it is rarely used in bombs due to its quick decomposition rate, under the right circumstances, it can be deadly. For example, the

---

[21] B. Berti. Assessing the Role of Hezbollah in the Gaza War and Its Regional Impact. *Terrorism Monitor* 7, no. 4, March 3, 2009. Available at http://www.jamestown.org/single/?no_cache=1&tx_ttnews%5Btt_ news%5D=34575.

[22] US House Committee on Homeland Security. Securing Ammonium Nitrate: Using Lessons Learned in Afghanistan to Protect the Homeland from IEDs, July 12, 2012.

[23] US District Court, Western District of Kentucky. Criminal Complaint: Waad Ramadan Alwan. Investigative Project on Terrorism. Available at http://www.investigativeproject.org/documents/case_docs/1568.pdf.

[24] US House Committee on Homeland Security. Improvised Explosive Device Threats, July 12, 2012.

compound was successfully used in the 1993 attack on the World Trade Center with terrorists using approximately 1500 pounds to construct the weapon. Theft of urea nitrate is common in the Middle East; for instance, in February 2010 more than 5600 tons (11 million pounds) of urea nitrate were stolen and never recovered. Another compound, ammonium nitrate fertilizer, is a powerful agent when used in bombs.

Ammonium nitrate was used by Timothy McVeigh in the Oklahoma City bombing and in the 2002 nightclub bombings by Jemaah Islamiyah in Bali in which 202 people died. The agent is extensively used in ideas and was thus banned in Afghanistan as a resource for farmers; ISAF soldiers began seizing ammonium nitrate from Afghani farmers, paying them cash and destroying their supply. Many security experts are concerned about the potential use of ammonium nitrate in the United States. A hearing, titled *Securing Ammonium Nitrate: Using Lessons Learned in Afghanistan to Protect the Homeland from IEDs*, explored tighter restrictions on the selling of fertilizer and methods for tracking sales. Dan Lungren, a California Republican and chairman of the Homeland Security Subcommittee, expressed his concern for the threat, stating, "is there any question that those who are dedicated to killing Americans would not exploit vulnerabilities in the United States to use IEDs here?"[25] In response to domestic concerns and those of our allies, ICE initiated Program Global Shield, an international law enforcement effort fighting the illicit trafficking of precursor chemicals used in nitrate explosives by monitoring their cross-border movements.

Sticky Bombs

Although variations of this device have been used in warfare since World War I, the modern version was detected in Iraq in 2004 when insurgents sporadically used a magnetic strip to stealthily attach IEDs to vehicles. Known as *Obwah Lasica* in Arabic, the magnetic bomb is a simple, homemade device turning a vehicle into a moving VBIED. In Iraq, the campaign accelerated as attackers met with success and learned from their mistakes. Bombers increased the volatility of the devices, using C4 and accelerants to increase the scope of the explosions and began specifically using the weapon as an assassination tool against Iraqi officials. Between 2008 and 2009, there were at least 400 vehicle explosions involving sticky bombs, and other groups around the world began to copy the tactics.

In January 2012, an Iranian university professor working at a key nuclear facility was killed when two assassins on a motorcycle affixed a magnetic bomb to his vehicle in Tehran. The next month, the exact same operation took place in Delhi; this time, the target was an Israeli embassy vehicle in what was labeled a revenge killing. In July 2012, an Afghan women's affairs official was killed and her husband and daughter critically wounded when a magnetic bomb exploded, destroying her vehicle. The same month, a convoy of 22 NATO trucks was destroyed when one magnetic bomb exploded, causing the other vehicles to ignite. In August of 2012, Syrian rebels used the tactic to kill two judges in the Damascus. A quick look online demonstrates that the instructions for building and using a sticky bomb are readily accessible. One site encourages their use on the hulls of ships. There is no limit to the imagination of would-be attackers, and the proliferation of this weapon should be of great concern domestically.

First Response and Threat of Secondary Devices

Unfortunately, in modern terror and crime events, the instinct to run toward the fight, not away from it, could be a deadly instinct. Consider the use of secondary and tertiary devices in Iraq and Afghanistan. For example, insurgents would set off the first IED, wait until other soldiers rush in, and then set off a second device and sometimes a third. But this is not a new tactic—both international and domestic terrorists have employed it successfully for years. International terrorist and rebel groups have successfully employed the "double-bomb" tactic to target first responders. For

[25] US House Committee on Homeland Security. Securing Ammonium Nitrate: Using Lessons Learned in Afghanistan to Protect the Homeland from IEDs, July 12, 2012.

instance, secondaries targeting responders in other notable attacks include the Jemaah Islamiyah bombing in Bali in 2002, an anti-American attack by Hezbollah at the McDonald's in Lebanon in 2003, and the 2004 police station bombing in Athens by the Revolutionary Struggle group. In March 2010, in Dagestan, a Chechen suicide bomber dressed in a police uniform approached investigators and residents who had gathered at the scene of a car bomb explosion near a school and detonated his explosive vest. In April 2010, the primary al-Qaeda–related bombing in Algeria was followed by a secondary one, detonated one hour later and killing a soldier. The same month, Chechen rebels bombed a train in Dagestan and remotely detonated a secondary device to target first responders.

Domestic terrorists also use this technique. Almost every attack perpetrated by Eric Rudolph included a secondary device, specifically targeted toward emergency personnel. For example, prior to the Atlanta abortion clinic bombing in 1997, Rudolph called in the bomb threat and watched as office members evacuated and gathered in certain areas of the parking lot. He planned this into his operation months later; after he bombed the clinic, a second device went off an hour and a half after the first, injuring seven first responders. The Hutaree Christian Militia was planning to kill a law enforcement officer and then ambush the funeral procession. If this plot had gone as planned, the secondary attack would have been a surprise and may have killed and/or injured hundreds. First responders should train on this tactic, understanding that they very likely may be the target.

Louis R. Mizell, a terrorism expert and former US intelligence agent for the State Department, has compiled a database of 300 double-bomb attacks by more than 50 terrorist groups in the world over the past 10 years. His advice: "The reality of today's double-bomb tactic dictates that first responders have three primary jobs at a site: attending to the wounded, dispersing the crowd, and finding a second bomb." Mizell's recommendations to first responders—what he calls "double-bomb protocol"[26]—are

- Teams searching for a bomb should work in concentric circles outward from the wounded.
- If manpower allows, another team should concurrently identify likely high-threat second-bomb containers outside these circles, such as lone parked cars, suspicious individuals, and trash cans.
- The wounded and attending first responders should be protected by portable barriers that have been determined bomb free, such as police cars and ambulances if possible.
- Such individuals should be aware that terrorists have studied evacuation procedures and exploited them in the past.

Law enforcement is keenly aware of the threat, and at least once a year, the FBI issues a bulletin concerning the use of secondary devices and stressing caution when arriving at the scene of an attack. The NYPD and LAPD have trained for such an event, especially in light of the catastrophic loss of life to first responders on 9/11. Training for secondary devices is the key. Similar to other counterintuitive procedures, like recovering a vehicle sliding on an icy road by steering into the spin, training will override instinct and save lives. A worrisome tactic from Afghanistan is worthy of watching; extremists will patiently train alongside coalition forces for days, weeks, or even months at a time, earning their trust. At some point, they will detonate a suicide bomb vest or draw a weapon and kill their trainers. A similar occurrence was observed in the killing of CIA agents at the Khost post by an informant, who gained their trust and was able to skip security checks and walk right into their midst and detonate his device.

Use of Human Shields by Terrorist Groups on the Rise

Law enforcement personnel should prepare for the possible use of children, women, and the elderly as human shields by terrorists (international or domestic) on our soil. Human shields tactics are the deliberate placement of civilians around targets or combatants to prevent the

[26] M. A. Gips. Secondary Devices a Primary Concern. *Security Management* 47, no. 7, 2003.

enemy from firing. The use of human shields is prohibited by the Fourth Geneva Convention, Protection of Civilian Persons in Time of War, which was passed in 1949 as a result of atrocities perpetrated by the Nazis during World War II. Specifically, the article states, "The presence or movements of the civilian population or individual civilians shall not be used to render certain points or areas immune from military operations, in particular in attempts to shield military objectives from attacks or to shield, favor or impede military operations."[27] The tactic is actively used by terrorist groups worldwide who do not adhere to Geneva Conventions or worry about worldwide condemnation of their activities.

Hamas

Independent reports give detailed evidence that Hamas used hospitals, school, homes, and mosques to hide weapons and soldiers during the Gaza War, an Israeli military initiative from December 2008 through January 2009. At 25 miles long and six miles wide, with a population of 1.5 million, Gaza is the sixth most densely populated place on earth, providing a very complex battleground situation. The UN report on the war mentions the possible use of children, women, and the elderly as human shields by Hamas. However, Malam, an Israeli intelligence think tank, produced a report using declassified material, such as videotapes, maps, and operational plans, recovered on the ground by IDF troops. The information indicates that Hamas hid IEDs in and around civilian homes and hospitals, and used children and the elderly as human shields. Of the 1444 Palestinians killed in the offensive, approximately 340 were children.

LTTE

The Liberation Tigers of Tamil Eelam (LTTE) or Tamil Tigers were defeated by the Sri Lankan government in May 2009 in a final, violent offensive on a northern beach in the Vanni region. During the months leading up to the conflict, the United States used satellites to monitor the situation, releasing photos to the public to show how LTTE herded hundreds of thousands of citizens onto the beach for use as human shields in their final standoff with government forces. Many died from starvation, execution, or due to government shelling, and some escaped only to be captured and put into government internment camps. The remaining civilians, approximately 130,000, were forced to stay in one square mile of beach and be part of the battle in May. Though there has been no final accounting of civilians killed in the final offensive, the UN estimated at least 40,000.[28]

A BBC documentary entitled *Sri Lankan's Killing Fields* documents the atrocities performed by the government and the rebels in "no fire" and "safety zones" as well as hospitals, schools, villages, and convoys of refugees deliberately pulled into the conflict.[29] In 2012, a Sri Lankan general admitted to war crimes, including the extrajudicial killing of civilians. Although it seems inconceivable to us that a terrorist group, cartel, or lone wolf would use human shields, we must remember the power of ideology, especially radical religious dogma, which empowers believers with a sense of justification for their illegal and immoral activities. One must mentally prepare and train to engage in even the most horrific of scenarios, including the exploitation of innocent civilians to further goals.

Asymmetric Threats

Terrorists have always employed asymmetric tactics to achieve their goals; they often strike in unanticipated ways to maximize results. Never has asymmetric warfare been more prevalent than in the past decade, from the use of civilian airliners as missiles on 9/11 in the United States to the seaborne staged attack on 11 targets in Mumbai in 2008. From an engagement perspective, these unexpected events can catch us unprepared and morally conflicted. For instance, on September 10, 2001, military pilots never considered they might be ordered to shoot down

---

[27] International Committee of the Red Cross. International Humanitarian Law—Treaties & Documents. Available at http://www.icrc.org/ihl.

[28] United Nations. Report of the Secretary-General's Panel of Experts on Accountability in Sri Lanka, 2011.

[29] J. Snow. Sri Lanka's Killing Fields. *BBC*, United Kingdom, 2011.

a civilian airliner in our airspace, and they did not train for this possibility. However on 9/11, a new page was added to the tactics book when the enemy used airplanes and hostages as missiles. Modern terrorist groups do not follow the Geneva Convention. Schools, hospitals, churches, shelters: everything is on the table; everything and everyone is a target.

The past decade is replete with examples; for instance, the Chechens have successfully used asymmetric warfare against the Russians. The Muslim minority group rose up following the collapse of communism as a violent separatist group, dragging Russia into two wars in the 1990s and leading to the deaths of tens of thousands of fighters on both sides of the conflict. The Chechens moved to an insurgency model and became master bombers and hostage takers, using the element of surprise in target selection and timing. In the 2002 hostage taking at Moscow's Dubrovka Theater, at least 40 attackers pulled up to the front door of the theater during the second act and entered en masse. The element of surprise was also used in the Chechen's 2004 attack on the Beslan School in North Ossetia, in which they struck on the first day of school when parents were attending an assembly and rolled up to the building in police and military vehicles. In both cases, the sieges lasted for days, and unprepared responders and military officials made poor decisions and tactical mistakes contributing to the deaths of hundreds of hostages.

The Chechen "Black Widows," or shahidkas, are women who seek retribution for the deaths of their soldier husbands and volunteer for suicide bombing missions. The use of women, children, and the disabled is another proven asymmetric tactic shared among groups. In 2008, two disabled women were unwillingly used by al-Qaeda in Iraq to attack an open market in Baghdad; the devices were strapped to their wheelchairs and remotely detonated. Also in Iraq, a female suicide bomber attacked a group of women and children at a play group gathering, killing 54. Months later, in Pakistan, terrorists bombed a hospital, specifically targeting those they wounded in an earlier attack. In 2011, a man dressed as a cleric and a small boy were walking toward a government building in Karachi; alert police approached the pair and found that they were both wearing bomb vests. In 2012, a 14-year-old suicide bomber walked into a group of his friends playing outside the NATO building in Kabul, Afghanistan, and detonated his explosives, killing six.

WMD

According to the FBI, weapons of mass destruction (WMD) are defined in US law (18 USC §2332a) under Section (c)(2) as "(A) any destructive device as defined in section 921 of this title [i.e., explosive device]; (B) any weapon that is designed or intended to cause death or serious bodily injury through the release, dissemination, or impact of toxic or poisonous chemicals, or their precursors; (C) any weapon involving a biological agent, toxin, or vector …; or (D) any weapon designed to release radiation or radioactivity at a level dangerous to human life." WMD is often referred to by the collection of modalities that make up the set of weapons: chemical, biological, radiological, nuclear, and explosive (CBRNE). These are weapons that have a relatively large-scale impact on people, property, and/or infrastructure.[30]

Organized crime and terrorists have collaborated in obtaining and selling nuclear technology and stolen nuclear materials and weapons. Indeed, the use of WMD is on the table for all groups: terrorists, criminals, and even cartels. In the name of political ideology, Bhagwan Shree Rajneesh (now known as Osho) contaminated salad bars at 10 restaurants in 1984 with salmonella, sickening 751 people. The religious cult Aum Shinryko (now known as Aleph) used sarin in a coordinated attack on subways in Tokyo in 1995, killing 13 and affecting upward of 5000 others. Although the dispersion methods were not perfected, the element of surprise led to many first responders racing to the scene without protective gear, becoming casualties themselves. Large-scale bombs, such as the one detonated by Timothy McVeigh in Oklahoma City, are considered weapons of mass destruction due to their high destruction and casualty rate.

[30] FBI. Weapons of Mass Destruction. Available at http://www.fbi.gov/about-us/investigate/terrorism/wmd.

Nuclear-smuggling activities are on the rise, and with "loose nukes" or, at the very least, unsecured material in the former Soviet Republic, the concern is high that the building blocks for a radioactive device could fall into the wrong hands. Certainly, it is known that in 1998, Mamdough Mamud Salim attempted to purchase highly enriched uranium in Western Europe to use as a building block for a nuclear weapon. In 2002, a 25-page document with information about nuclear weapons design was found in an al-Qaeda safe house in Pakistan. Al-Qaeda also attempted to purchase spent nuclear fuel, perhaps hoping to use it in a dirty bomb. In the chemical and biological realm, the 10-volume *Encyclopedia of Afghanistan Resistance* found in Jalalabad contained formulas for manufacturing toxins, botulinum, and ricin and provided methods for dissemination. At Tarnak Farms, the former Afghan training camp near Kandahar, Afghanistan, al-Qaeda not only provided firearms training but also experimented with biological warfare in a special laboratory. Ahmed Ressam, the Algerian al-Qaeda member who was caught at the Canadian border before he could execute the 2000 "millennium attack" on the Los Angeles airport, testified that al-Qaeda taught him to poison people by putting toxins on doorknobs, and he engaged in experiments in which dogs were injected with a mixture containing cyanide and sulfuric acid. Finally, al-Qaeda members were seeking to fly crop dusters that analysts believe may have been used to disseminate anthrax and chemical or biological agents.[31]

Regarding biological warfare, in 2009, Algerian newspaper *Anahar al-Jadeed* reported that 40 AQIM terrorists died at a training camp in Algeria from their infection with bubonic plague.[32] Speculation abounded: Was it a dead rat causing the deaths or an experiment gone bad? One will never know. However, *Inspire* magazine has encouraged its readers to manufacture ricin, botulism, and sarin in their homes even encouraging them to get a Muslim microbiologist to assist, if needed. Domestic terrorists may also use the al-Qaeda guides as a template for constructing their own weapons. In 2008, the FBI arrested Roger Bergendorff, who had ricin, a schematic for an injection pen, weapon silencers, and the *Anarchist Cookbook* in his Las Vegas hotel room. After recovering from ricin poisoning, he was sentenced to three and a half years in prison. Bergendorff never gave an exact motive behind his activities, but clearly it is dangerous to have private citizens tinkering with toxic biological and chemical compounds. Governments need to continue to work to get materials off of the Internet and out of the hands of would-be attackers.

Perhaps the mostly accessible WMD is chlorine, an easily obtained chemical that could sicken or kill hundreds of people under the right conditions. AQI used chlorine in several VBEID attacks against coalition forces in Iraq in 2006. Although more casualties arose from the bomb blasts, the terrorists kept trying different methodologies to perfect their technique and used it 13 more times in the war. Chlorine can be a silent killer. In 2005, two trains collided in Graniteville, South Carolina, in the middle of the night, releasing 60 tons of chlorine gas. Unsuspecting residents who heard the collision drove through the cloud, stayed in their homes, or kept working their outdoor night-shift jobs. In all, nine people died and more than 250 were sickened by the gas, which causes nausea, dizziness, and vomiting. Certainly, chlorine is easily obtained; therefore, one has to educate suppliers on how and what to report in terms of suspicious buys or patterns. Do al-Qaeda or other foreign or domestic terrorist groups have WMD?[33]

The answer to this question can be found in government reports and congressional testimony. For instance, consider the December 2008 report, titled *The World at Risk*, issued by the Graham/Talent Commission, a bipartisan group that spent six months examining the WMD issue. When Senator Graham briefed Congress, he ominously stated that "[t]errorists could mount [a] nuclear or biological attack within five years." Statements from the report are also very telling: "The

[31] J. Boureston. Assessing al Qaeda's WMD Capabilities. *Strategic Insights*, Naval Postgraduate School 1, no. 7, September 2002.

[32] Black Death Kills 40 al-Qaeda Fighters in Algeria. *Al Arabiya News*, January 20, 2009, Available at http://www.alarabiya.net/articles/2009/01/20/64603.html.

[33] See Chapter 6 of this volume for more information on this.

Commission believes that unless the world community acts decisively and with great urgency, it is more likely than not that a weapon of mass destruction will be used in a terrorist attack somewhere in the world by the end of 2013. The Commission further believes that terrorists are more likely to be able to obtain and use a biological weapon than a nuclear weapon."[34]

Synthetic manufacturing is causing increased concerns as chemically synthesized DNA can replicate those found in agents occurring in nature and, more worrisome, enhance their effects. According to Vahid Majidi, the assistant director of the FBI's Weapons of Mass Destruction Directorate, the agency is working to keep this emergent technology from falling into the wrong hands.[35] Working to prevent access to materials and instructive manuals is critical. Our response agencies must also continue to train on the threat, anticipating the absolute worst; failure is not an option in the WMD realm. Perhaps instead of studying why groups would use WMD to further their goals, it is much more productive to question why they would not use the tactic. In historic examples of nefarious use of chemical and biological weapons, they were vastly ineffective in causing the anticipated mass casualties. Reasons for not selecting this type of attack include the high probability of deadly contamination during the manufacturing process as well as selecting the proper delivery technique that will avoid detection, cause the element of surprise, and inflict mass casualties. Consider the Lashkar e-Taiba attacks on Mumbai that killed 170 people and brought the world to a standstill; although the perpetrators had conducted extensive surveillance and used satellite phones and commandeered boats for the operation, it was basically low tech and highly effective.

Concluding Thoughts

When pursuing operational objectives, drug-trafficking organizations, drug cartels, and terrorists will resort to excessive violence, have a basic lack of respect for human life/dignity, and have a disregard or contempt for the law and its enforcement agents. The sharing and copying of tactics between groups is extremely worrisome, as they continue to learn and perfect techniques. Law enforcement and international authorities must continue to monitor travel patterns of suspected go-betweens and couriers, engaging aggressively if needed to stop training and resource pipelines. The proliferation of information on the Internet contributes to this realm, and an international body with a set of governing laws would go a long way to preventing publications, such as al-Qaeda's *Inspire* and the *Anarchist Cookbook*, from reaching would-be terrorists. Governments can expect that tactics used by insurgents downrange might be copied by other groups or their operatives living in other countries.

As a final point, drug-trafficking organizations, drug cartels, and terrorists make a conscious, voluntary decision to join the organization but feel tremendous pressure to stay; leaving could mean death. The so-called drug war has been in progress since 1982; yet after billions of dollars to counter their efforts and strengthen borders, the cartels are stronger than ever. Additionally, transnational criminal organizations have become permanent fixtures on the criminal scene, and consequently, the United States has shifted from an eradication strategy to merely coping. America is learning that asymmetric approaches and use of "soft" instruments of power are essential in combating these threats, interweaved with military and law enforcement engagement, if needed. Perhaps the use of containment and deterrence strategies that policy makers typically do not find appealing is necessary as the United States tries to marginalize the threat and condense the playing field.

---

[34] Commission on the Prevention of WMD Proliferation and Terrorism. World at Risk: Report of the Commission on the Prevention of WMD Proliferation and Terrorism, 2008.

[35] US Senate Committee on Homeland Security and Governmental Affairs. Ten Years after 9/11 and the Anthrax Attacks: Protecting against Biological Threats, October 18, 2011.

19

Critical Infrastructure Protection[1]

Critical infrastructures and key resources (CIKR) sustain citizens' way of life and are essential for the economy, prosperity, security, and defense of a nation. Damage to just one sector (e.g., energy)—through a natural disaster, accident, technological failure, or act of terrorism—can cause other sectors (e.g., communications, information technology, banking, and commercial businesses) to be harmed, major inconveniences for large population groups, and multibillion dollar economic losses. Because of numerous threats and hazards facing CIKR, and the dependencies and interdependencies of sectors, nations should work with its internal partners (e.g., governments at all levels and the private sector), and those overseas, to plan and implement protection and resiliency for CIKR.

Digital control systems (DCS) and supervisory control and data acquisition (SCADA) systems enable many industries to control and monitor equipment remotely even from great distances. The Internet and IT systems facilitate the control of sensitive processes that were controlled manually on site in earlier years. CIKR sectors that use such systems include food processing, water, transportation, energy, and manufacturing, among others. Serious harm can result if adversaries access these systems. In one attack, an engineer applied radio telemetry to access a waste management system to discharge raw sewage into a public waterway and onto the grounds of a hotel. The "insider" engineer worked for the firm that supplied the DCS/SCADA system to the waste management company.

In another example, a penetration test (i.e., authorized attempt to access a system or physical site to study defenses) resulted in access to a utility's DCS/SCADA system within minutes. Operators drove to a remote substation, spotted a wireless network antenna, and from their vehicle, they operated their wireless radios and connected to the network. Following 20 minutes of work, they had mapped both the network and the SCADA equipment and accessed the business IT system. CIKR sectors must protect against this type of vulnerability. Helpful security strategies include access controls, encryption, virus protection, data recovery procedures, and manual overrides.[2] The functioning of a society relies on an interconnected web of sectors and dependencies, and if one sector is disrupted, others may falter. This is referred to as the cascade effect.

This chapter covers early critical infrastructure protection in the United States, the National Infrastructure Protection Plan, assessing vulnerabilities of critical infrastructures, and the characteristics and protection strategies of 18 CIKR sectors.

---

[1] Information for this chapter was drawn from the following title: P. P. Purpura, *Security: An Introduction*, CRC Press, 2010.

[2] P. Purpura. *Terrorism and Homeland Security: An Introduction with Applications*. Burlington, MA: Elsevier Butterworth-Heinemann, 2007, 137, 370.

Protection Challenges

The *National Strategy for the Physical Protection of Critical Infrastructures and Key Assets* identified the following protection challenges:[3]

- Critical assets:
  - Agriculture and food
  - Water
  - Public health
  - Emergency services
  - Defense industrial base
  - Telecommunications
  - Energy:
    - Electricity
    - Oil and natural gas
  - Transportation:
    - Aviation
    - Passenger rail and railroads
    - Highways, trucking, and busing
    - Pipelines
    - Maritime
    - Mass transit
  - Banking and finance
  - Chemical industry and hazardous materials
  - Postal and shipping
- Key assets:
  - National monuments and icons
  - Nuclear power plants
  - Dams
  - Government facilities
  - Commercial assets

CI is primarily owned and operated by state and local governments and the private sector. The federal government owns a limited amount of CI. For example, the federal government owns and operates the nation's air-traffic control CI. About 97% of the nation's roads and highways are owned by state and local governments with local governments owning approximately 77% of the miles of roadway. About 98% of bridges and most transit systems are owned by state and local governments. Most freight railroads are owned by the private sector. The federal government owns about 650 miles of Amtrak's 22,000 miles of rail. Many ports are publicly owned and privately operated. Most commercial service airports are owned by state and local governments. In addition, about half of the nation's drinking water systems and 20% of wastewater systems are privately owned. The majority of dams in the United States

[3] White House. The National Strategy for the Physical Protection of Critical Infrastructure and Key Assets. February 2003, p. 9. Available at http://www.whitehouse.gov.

are privately owned. Furthermore, the federal government owns and operates about 5% of the nation's dams.

Critical Infrastructures and Key Resources

Agriculture and Food Sector

The protection of the nation's agricultural and food sector is a huge responsibility shared by all levels of government and the private sector. Threats and hazards to this sector are broad and include disease, pestilence, adverse weather, acts of terrorism, and attacks by hostile nations. Various acts of deliberate contamination of food with a chemical or biological agent have been documented from across the globe. Here are a few examples from the James Martin Center for Nonproliferation Studies:[4]

- In October 2006, 350 police officers became ill because of a mass poisoning at a cafeteria located outside of Baghdad. Eleven deaths were reported. The symptoms included bleeding from the ears and nose. Cyanide was suspected as the causative agent. Suspicion focused on Sunni insurgents.
- Between 2003 and 2005, in 11 regions of Italy, one or more individuals injected bleach, acetone, or ammonia into commercial drink containers. A "copycat" theory evolved because of the wide area of victimizations. Thirty-three casualties resulted in significant economic losses for the bottled-water industry in Italy.
- In September of 1984, in The Dalles, Oregon, members of the Rajneeshee cult poisoned salad bars in 10 restaurants and one supermarket with salmonella bacteria to prevent citizens from voting in an election and to gain control of posts in the Wasco county government. About 750 people became ill. Several cult members were arrested, convicted, and imprisoned.

Although cases of foodborne illnesses are not usually intentionally caused, this problem is a serious health concern. The Centers for Disease Control (CDC) estimates that about 76 million US residents get sick, 325,000 are hospitalized, and 5000 die each year from foodborne illnesses.[5] Salmonella infection, for example, has been estimated to cause about 1.4 million foodborne illnesses each year. However, only about 40,000 laboratory-confirmed cases of salmonella are reported to the CDC annually. Foodborne illnesses are difficult to investigate and require scientific expertise. Two major challenges are detection and pinpointing the cause of tainted food. Surveillance (e.g., at hospitals) helps to link dispersed cases with common factors and symptoms.

An all-hazards approach to protecting the US agriculture and food sector is an enormous undertaking. This sector is capable of feeding and clothing people beyond the needs of the United States. The agriculture and food sector is almost all under private ownership and includes about 2.1 million farms, 880,500 firms, and more than 1 million facilities. It is dependent on the water sector for clean irrigation and processed water, the transportation sector for movement of what it produces, energy for farming and production, and banking and other sectors. The agriculture and food sector accounts for roughly one fifth of the nation's economic activity, and it is regulated at the federal level by the US Department of Agriculture (USDA) and the US Department of Health and Human Services' (HHS) Food and Drug Administration (FDA). These government bodies are sector-specific agencies (SSAs) for the agriculture and food sector as specified in Homeland Security Presidential Directive 7 (or HSPD-7). Among the many duties of the USDA, it is responsible for the

[4] James Martin Center for Nonproliferation Studies. Chronology of Chemical and Biological Incidents Targeting the Food Industry 1946–2006. Available at http://cns.miis.edu/cbw/foodchron.htm, 2009.

[5] Centers for Disease Control. CDC Congressional Testimony, July 31, 2008. Available at http://www.cdc.gov, 2009.

safety of meat, poultry, and egg products as well as agricultural health. The FDA is charged with regulation and safety for 80% of the food consumed in the United States, including domestic food valued at $417 billion, imported food valued at $49 billion, roughly 600,000 restaurants and institutional food service providers, and about 235,000 grocery stores. State and local government bodies also regulate this industry and receive guidance from the FDA.[6]

Laws that support the protection of the agriculture and food sector include the Homeland Security Act of 2002 that created the DHS and efforts to protect CIKR against, for example, agroterrorism. The Public Health Security and Bioterrorism Preparedness and Response Act of 2002 (the Bioterrorism Act) supports the FDA's identification of domestic and foreign food suppliers, inspections, and requirements that the food industry keep records of the "chain of possession" of food to aid in investigations. Under HSPD-9, the USDA, the US Department of Health and Human Services (HHS), and the Environmental Protection Agency (EPA) were directed to enhance plans for prevention, surveillance (e.g., maintaining data on outbreaks of diseases), and response to adverse events. The Project BioShield Act of 2004 focuses on the need to improve planning for the distribution of vaccines and other medical assistance to counter bioterrorism. The Robert T. Stafford Disaster Relief and Emergency Assistance Act of 1974 authorizes government leaders to distribute food to any area of the United States subject to a disaster.

Within the USDA is an Office of the Inspector General (OIG) that is the law enforcement arm of the USDA. OIG special agents, often in cooperation with other agencies, conduct investigations of criminal activity related to USDA–related laws, regulations, and programs; execute search warrants; make arrests; and carry firearms. They investigate fraud, bribery, smuggling, assaults on employees, and other crimes. A major objective is the health and safety of the public. Investigations may also focus on, as examples, a case of a meat packer allegedly selling tainted products, food tampering, or agroterrorism.[7]

The FDA, in cooperation with other government bodies, performs its public health and safety duties under several laws. FDA personnel inspect establishments, execute search warrants, make arrests, carry firearms, order recalls of products, seize products, conduct laboratory research of foods, and issue regulations. FDA special agents typically investigate counterfeit, unapproved, or illegally diverted drugs; product tampering; fraudulent health treatments; and fraud in new drug development.[8]

To assist with sector partnerships, in 2004, the Food and Agriculture Sector Coordinating Council (FASCC) was formed, composed of public and private sectors. The FASCC hosts forums for coordination of agriculture security and food defense strategies. Another protection effort is the Strategic Partnership Program Agroterrorism (SPPA) Initiative, a joint assessment program of the FBI, DHS, USDA, and HHS/FDA. The purpose of these assessments is to support the requirements of the NIPP/SSP and HSPD-9. SPPA assessments were conducted on a voluntary basis on products and commodities in the food chain to study vulnerabilities, security, and mitigation to produce generic strategies. Other initiatives include a sector-specific assessment tool, tabletop exercises (i.e., a simulated emergency scenario in which participants discuss issues, roles, procedures, or responsibilities), and online training.[9]

Water Sector

Water is essential for human survival. The water sector is vulnerable to attack by bioterrorism/chemical contamination and cyber threats. The interdependencies of the water infrastructure

---

[6] Part II, 1, US Department of Homeland Security. Agriculture and Food (May). Available at http://www.dhs.gov, 2007.

[7] US Department of Agriculture. About OIG Investigative Division. Available at http://www.usda.gov/oig/invest.htm, 2009.

[8] US Food and Drug Administration. FDA Law Enforcers Protect Consumers' Health. Consumer Health Information (August 4). Available at http://www.fda.gov/consumer, 2008.

[9] US Department of Homeland Security. Critical Infrastructure and Key Resources. Available at http://www.dhs.gov/files/programs/gc_1189168948944.shtm, 2009.

with other infrastructures are a serious concern of the National Infrastructure Protection Plan (NIPP). The water sector depends on electricity to operate water facilities, chemical plants to manufacture chlorine to purify water, and transportation systems to ship the chemicals. In August of 2003, for instance, the electricity blackout in the northeastern United States resulted in, among other problems, wastewater treatment plants in Cleveland, Detroit, New York, and other locations discharging millions of gallons of untreated sewage into waterways. In addition, the power failure at many drinking-water plants resulted in boil-water advisories.[10] Our nation depends on the water sector for critical services. These include firefighting and health care. At the same time, the agriculture and food sector, among other sectors, relies on the water sector for operations and production. According to the US Department of Homeland Security, the water sector is composed of both drinking water and wastewater utilities; there are about 160,000 public drinking-water systems and more than 16,000 publicly owned wastewater treatment systems in the United States.[11]

The Environmental Protection Agency (EPA) is the SSA for the water sector as specified in HSPD-7. Other laws that promote the protection of the water sector are as follows: HSPD-8 focuses on all-hazard preparedness and state grants for planning and training. HSPD-9 facilitates a national policy to defend the water, agriculture, and food systems; enhance monitoring and surveillance for early detection of disease, pest, and poisonous agents; develop a nationwide laboratory network; and enhance intelligence capabilities. HSPD-10 covers biodefense, and related to this topic is the Bioterrorism Act. The water sector is governed by numerous environmental laws that regulate drinking water and wastewater utilities. State governments often have direct jurisdiction over the water sector and foster security. However, to maintain primacy, states and tribes must adopt regulations for contaminants that are no less stringent than what the EPA requires in regulations.

As with other government departments and agencies, a variety of specialists are necessary for EPA operations, including administrators, accountants, IT personnel, and so forth. And, similar to the USDA, the FDA, and other federal government bodies, EPA special agents are fully authorized law enforcement officers. They investigate violations of environmental laws. The EPA not only works with the DHS to implement the NIPP, it also works with other government bodies (e.g., USDA, FDA, and CDC). EPA partners include the states, local drinking water and wastewater utilities, and national organizations (e.g., American Water Works Association). The EPA has established several programs to protect the water sector. For example, the Water Security Initiative pursues a contamination warning system to minimize damage to public health and economic impact from harm to a water system. It covers detection, response, testing, and training. As with other SSAs, the EPA promotes risk management, risk assessments, incident reporting, a culture of security, training, tabletop exercises, partnering, and information sharing.[12]

Health-Care and Public Health Sector

Imagine a city of, say, 100,000 people exposed to a bioterrorism attack, and everyone in the city is in need of medical assistance. Will the health care and public health sector in this city be capable of meeting the residents' medical needs? The volume of patients would exceed medical staff, beds, medicine, equipment, and supplies. Small-scale and large-scale medical surges can result from a wide variety of human-made and natural disasters. A medical surge is "the ability

[10] Congressional Research Service. Terrorism and Security Issues Facing the Water Infrastructure Sector (April 25), p. 1. Available at http://www.ndu.edu/library, 2005.

[11] US Department of Homeland Security. Critical Infrastructure and Key Resources. Available at http://www.dhs.gov/files/programs/gc_1189168948944.shtm, 2009.

[12] US Department of Homeland Security and Environmental Protection Agency. Water (May). Available at http://www.dhs.gov, 2007.

to provide adequate medical evaluation and care during events that exceed the limits of the normal medical infrastructure of an affected community." The concept of medical surge is essential to preparedness planning for major events requiring medical services.[13]

Health care is typically delivered at the local level, and public health is managed across all levels of government. The HPH sector is highly dependent on several other sectors: transportation, agriculture and food, energy, water, emergency services, and IT and communications. The SSA for the HPH sector is the US Department of Health and Human Services (HHS). The Pandemic and All-Hazards Preparedness Act of 2006 designated the secretary of HHS as the lead official for all public health and medical emergencies, including medical surges. States have the responsibility for developing emergency preparedness plans in coordination with other levels of government. In addition, the DOD and the Department of Veterans Affairs are expected to assist state and local entities in emergencies through their hospital facilities.

HSPD-21, issued in 2007, promotes the establishment of a national strategy for catastrophic health events. The Bioterrorism Act of 2002 noted that hospital emergency rooms are an important component of the nation's response to terrorism and diseases. This 2002 Act promotes surveillance systems at emergency rooms, public health departments, and the CDC to detect a medical emergency. The CDC is within HHS and serves in a leadership capacity during such an event. When serious medical emergencies occur, healthcare facilities experiencing a surge must be prepared through prior planning and training for a variety of scenarios. Otherwise, the healthcare site can become a disaster site subject to mob violence with medical workers themselves becoming victims and patients.

OSHA has provided guidelines to health care personnel on personal protective equipment and HAZMAT. Security officers also need training because unruly victims of a medical emergency can disrupt medical care when they may first need to be quarantined and decontaminated (depending on the nature of the emergency). HHS partners with the DHS to implement the NIPP. Numerous public-private sector councils meet to address a variety of issues, such as workforce sustainability during an emergency and medical surge. Various programs seek to enhance this sector's capabilities. Examples involve early detection of infectious diseases and other threats to health, vulnerability assessments, preparedness, and IT security.[14]

Besides the challenges faced by the HPH sector just cited, from a strictly security perspective, the challenges are numerous. Healthcare facilities often have limited access controls to permit patients to receive visitors who are often issued a visitor pass. Emergency rooms are subject to violence from causes such as intoxicated patients, irate patients and family waiting to be assisted, domestic situations, and gangs. Security strategies for emergency rooms include signs prohibiting weapons, access controls, metal detectors, and armed security officers. Security at nurseries is vital because of the threat of infant abduction. Applicable strategies are stringent access controls, ID cards for workers, closed-circuit TV (CCTV), and radio-frequency identification (RFID) bracelets for infants. Other areas of healthcare facilities requiring security are the pharmacy, parking lots, locker rooms, and the morgue.

The Joint Commission on Accreditation of Healthcare Organizations (JCAHO) promotes professionalism in this field, and compliance with its standards is required for government funding. Security plans and programs are required under JCAHO standards. The International Association for Healthcare Security and Safety is another group that facilitates professionalism. It offers publications, training, standards, and certifications. Guidance for professional operations at health care facilities can also be found through OSHA, NFPA, HIPPA, and other sources.

---

[13] US Department of Health & Human Services. Disasters and Emergencies. Available at http://www.hhs.gov/disasters/planners/mscc/chapter1/1.1html, 2009.

[14] US Department of Homeland Security. Critical Infrastructure and Key Resources. Available at http://www.dhs.gov/files/programs/gc_1189168948944.shtm, 2009.

Emergency Services Sector

When a resident of a community, a business, or other organization telephones 9-1-1 or another emergency number to report a serious incident, a dispatcher will ask specific questions about the emergency so that a decision can be made as to what services will be dispatched. The range of services includes police, fire, emergency medical, bomb squad, special weapons and tactics (SWAT), HAZMAT, search and rescue, and emergency management. These services comprise the Emergency Services Sector (ESS). The ESS is the primary protector of CIKR.

An essential system of response and recovery, it is decentralized and local across the United States. This sector consists of professionally trained and tested personnel who seek to save lives and mitigate property damage. Mutual-aid agreements among different jurisdictions enable multiple agencies to assist a locale that is dealing with an emergency that is straining its personnel and resources. Examples are a vehicle chase, a child abductor crossing jurisdictions, or a massive fire. The DHS, Office of Infrastructure Protection, is the SSA for the ESS. The US Department of Homeland Security states,[15]

> The ESS SSA engages stakeholders and coordinates ESS initiatives through the existing network of sector associations that extend to the 10 Federal Emergency Management Agency regions, the DHS/Office of State and Local Coordination, and the DHS/Office of Grants and Training. Additionally, the Emergency Management and Response Information Sharing and Analysis Center (EMR-ISAC) serves as a principal mode to coordinate sector plans and collect and share information with the ESS and other sectors.

The important role of local and state ESS should be clearly understood as emphasized by the US Conference of Mayors:[16] "When you dial 9-1-1, the phone [does not] ring in the White House … those calls come in to your city's police, fire, and emergency medical personnel … our domestic troops."

Defense Industry Base Sector

The Defense Industry Base (DIB) sector includes the Department of Defense, other government bodies, and the private-sector worldwide industrial complex. The mission of the DIB is to provide for the needs (e.g., weapons) of the military. Tens of thousands of companies and their subcontractors, including domestic and foreign entities, support these needs. The DIB depends on energy, communications, IT, and transportation, among other sectors. For national security, protection is an obvious necessity for the DIB and the sectors it depends on. The legal foundation that supports the DIB includes the Defense Production Act of 1950, Executive Order 12919, and the DOD Directive 5000.60. HSPD-7 identified the DIB as a critical infrastructure sector and designated the Department of Defense (DOD) as the SSA. The Critical Infrastructure Partnership Advisory Council enables private-sector owners and government officials to collaborate on issues and protection activities. A major issue and protection challenge is that the DIB exists in an open, global environment that compounds the difficulty of securing assets and classified information.[15]

The DIB SSP uses a risk-management framework, like other SSPs, and applies these steps: set security goals, identify infrastructures and assets, assess risks, prioritize, implement protective programs, and measure effectiveness through metrics and evaluation methodologies. This SSP emphasizes a "layered, defense in depth" approach to protection.[17] The DIB faces a serious insider threat, especially from foreign intelligence services seeking US technology to improve

---

[15] US Department of Homeland Security. Critical Infrastructure and Key Resources. Available at http://www.dhs.gov/files/programs/gc_1189168948944.shtm, 2009.

[16] P. Purpura. *Terrorism and Homeland Security: An Introduction with Applications*. Burlington, MA: Elsevier Butterworth–Heinemann, 2007, 137, 370.

[17] US Departments of Homeland Security and Defense. Defense Industry Base. Available at http://www.dhs.gov, 2007.

their military and economy. Besides private security at DOD contractor sites, another strategy to counter the insider threat is through the DOD National Industrial Security Program (NISP), administered by the Defense Security Service (DSS). This program focuses on information, personnel, and physical security to protect classified information held by businesses under a DOD contract. Private security at DOD contractor sites must adhere to NISP requirements. The US Government Accountability Office has been critical of the DSS in multiple reports.[18] Specific criticism points to DSS not properly using metrics to identify patterns of contractor security violations and inadequate training of staff in overseeing foreign contractors. The GAO has designated the protection of critical technologies as high risk.

Communications Sector

Imagine if you were unable to use your cellular phone or access the Internet. A serious disruption in the communications sector (CS) would be an enormous inconvenience and a shock to society's culture of technology. Many nations have become so dependent on the CS that we find it difficult to imagine life without this technology. The CS is an essential component of a nation's economy and supports the operations of businesses, governments, including public safety agencies, and other organizations. The CS is composed of an interconnected industry of wire line, satellite, and wireless transmission systems. Several sectors are linked to the CS. As examples, the energy sector provides power to operate cellular towers and other communications systems; the IT sector provides control systems and Internet infrastructure; the banking and finance sector relies on the CS for the transmission of transactions and operations of financial markets; and the ESS relies on the CS for receiving 9-1-1 calls and coordinating responses to emergencies. The SSA for the CS is the National Communications System within DHS. It is responsible for implementing the NIPP pursuant to HSPD-7 and bringing together public and private sectors in a coordinated protection strategy. This government-led protection effort is supplemented and integrated with private-sector initiatives. The private sector owns and operates most of the CS and is primarily responsible for its protection.

The CS concentrates on reducing risk by working to ensure that the US communications networks and systems are secure, resilient, and quickly restored following a disaster.[19] The CS has been subject to not only HSPD-7, the Homeland Security Act of 2002, and the *National Strategy for the Physical Protection of Critical Infrastructure and Key Assets*,[20] like other sectors, but also the *National Strategy to Secure Cyberspace*.[21] This document states that a top priority is awareness of infrastructure interdependencies and improving the physical security of cyber systems and communications. In addition, besides executive orders from the President that emphasize the need for reliable communications during an emergency, the Communications Act of 1934, amended by the Telecommunications Act of 1996, is the primary law governing the CS, which is regulated by the Federal Communications Commission (FCC).[22] The companies that operate the CS have a history of factoring in natural disasters, accidental disruptions, and cyber attacks into network architecture, business-continuity planning, and resiliency. The interconnected and interdependent nature of the CS has fostered information sharing and cooperative responses among companies because a network problem of one company often impacts networks owned

[18] US Government Accountability Office. Department of Defense: Observations on the National Industrial Security Program. Available at http://www.gao.gov/new.items/d08695t.pdf, 2008.

[19] US Department of Homeland Security. Critical Infrastructure and Key Resources. Available at http://www.dhs.gov/files/programs/gc_1189168948944.shtm, 2009.

[20] White House. The National Strategy for the Physical Protection of Critical Infrastructure and Key Assets. February 2003, p. 9. Available at http://www.whitehouse.gov.

[21] White House. The National Strategy to Secure Cyberspace (February). Available at http://www.white-house.gov, 2003.

[22] US Department of Homeland Security. Communications (May). Available at http://www.dhs.gov, 2007.

by other companies. As with other sectors, a risk-management approach is applied by the CS. Protection emphasizes response and recovery besides physical and cybersecurity.[23]

Information Technology Sector

The information technology sector (ITS) is essential to society today and functions in conjunction with the communications sector to provide the Internet. The DHS is the SSA for the ITS. Private- and public-sector councils represent interests in this sector and collaborate on protection. Because all sectors rely on the ITS, resiliency is a top priority. Several laws and authorities promote the ITS. Examples are HSPD-7, Executive Order 13231 (protection of IT for CI and emergencies), the Clinger-Cohen Act of 1996 (strengthens IT management in government operations), and the Cyber Security Enhancement Act of 2002 (improves sentencing for crimes such as computer fraud and unauthorized access to IT systems). There are numerous government and private-sector IT protection units and programs. The following are examples: FBI Cyber Crimes Division (focuses on offenders who spread malicious code and child pornography and engage in computer fraud and theft of intellectual property), US Department of Justice Computer Crimes and Intellectual Property Section, National Counterintelligence Center, and the US Secret Service Electronic Crimes Task Force. The US Computer Emergency Readiness Team (US-CERT) helps to protect the Internet by analyzing and reducing cyber threats and vulnerabilities, disseminating warnings, and coordinating incident response. National cyber exercises conducted by the DHS identify, test, and improve coordination of incident responses.[24]

Energy Sector

Virtually all sectors have dependencies on the energy sector (ES). When a blackout occurs and electricity is unavailable, the effect on people and the economy is huge. Imagine that certain employees are working on the 50th floor of an office building when a blackout prevents elevators from working and generators are unavailable. Will they be able to make it to the ground floor via the stairs? If they reach the ground floor, will they be able to make it home? Public transportation often relies on electricity. If a person drives a vehicle, inoperable traffic lights can lead to massive gridlock. Businesses suffer enormous losses during a blackout because the ES powers IT systems that record business transactions, telephones may be unusable, and so forth. Although emergency operations centers, hospitals, and other essential services typically have backup generators, a blackout can literally stop the everyday activities of a city and region.

Penetration-testing consultants have been probing CIKR defenses for many years to expose and correct vulnerabilities. Green reported that a team was able to hack into a power company's network overseeing power production and distribution.[25] Initially, SCADA systems were closed systems, but eventually, intranets and Internet access were added, and vulnerabilities increased. In this case, the team tapped into the distribution lists of SCADA user groups, where they harvested e-mail addresses of power company employees. Then, they sent them an e-mail stating that their employee benefits would be cut and they should click on a link to a website to learn more. When the employees clicked on the link, malware was downloaded, thereby providing the team with control over the SCADA system and an opportunity to create a power outage. The power company stopped the test as soon as the team gained control of the SCADA system. For improved security, the team recommended that the software be better engineered, that the

[23] US Department of Homeland Security. Communications (May). Available at http://www.dhs.gov, 2007.

[24] US Department of Homeland Security. Information Technology (May). Available at http://www.dhs.gov, 2007.

[25] T. Green. Experts Hack Power Grid in No Time. Networkworld (April 9). Available at http://www.network-world.com, 2008.

network be segmented so that a breach via the Internet cannot reach the SCADA system, and that employees complete training on the prevention of social engineering.

More than 80% of the US ES is owned by the private sector. The ES consists of three interrelated segments: electricity, petroleum, and natural gas. According to the US Departments of Homeland Security and Energy:[26] The electricity segment contains more than 5300 power plants. About 49% of electricity is produced by combusting coal (usually transported by rail), 19% from nuclear plants, and 20% by combusting natural gas. The remaining sources of electricity are from hydroelectric plants (7%), oil (2%), and renewable (e.g., solar and wind) sources. More than 211,000 miles of high-voltage transmission lines are used to transmit electricity from power plants. Voltage is stepped down at substations prior to being distributed to 140 million customers via millions of miles of lower voltage lines. The highly automated ES is controlled by SCADA systems.

The petroleum segment involves exploration, production, storage, transport, and refinement of crude oil. The crude oil is refined into petroleum products (e.g., gasoline and jet fuel). About 66% of crude oil required for the US economy is imported. In the United States, there are more than 500,000 crude-oil-producing wells, thousands of miles of pipeline, 133 operable petroleum refineries, and other components of the petroleum segments, which also rely on SCADA systems. Natural gas is also produced, piped, stored, and distributed. There are more than 448,000 gas wells, more than 550 gas processing plants, in excess of 1 million miles of pipelines, and about 400 underground storage fields.

The US Department of Energy (DOE), designated as the SSA for the ES, is charged with coordinating an ES SSP that is part of the DHS's NIPP. The DOE also coordinates information sharing with organizations in the ES. Numerous coordinating councils involving private- and public-sector groups share information, plan exercises, address issues, and discuss SSP updates. Several laws and presidential directives affect multiple segments of the ES. These include HSPD-7. Another example is the Energy Policy Act of 2005 that was enacted to require mandatory electricity reliability standards for the United States. The protection challenges for the ES are enormous. Emphasis is placed on preparedness, resiliency, and cybersecurity with a risk-management framework that considers enterprise-wide protection.[26]

Transportation Sector

Societies depend on the transportation sector (TS) for reliable, quick, and efficient service. The importance of this sector is often realized when we get stuck in traffic on a roadway for long periods of time, wait for a bus or train that is delayed, or learn that our flight has been delayed or cancelled. For consumers and business purposes, the transportation sector is the way in which goods are moved throughout the country and overseas.

Six key subsectors or modes of the TS are as follows:[27]

- Aviation includes 450 commercial airports, 19,000 additional airfields, aircraft, and air traffic control systems.
- Highways cover more than 4 million miles of roadways.
- The maritime transportation system includes roughly 95,000 miles of coastlines, 361 ports, and more than 10,000 miles of navigable waterways.
- Mass transit consists of multiple-occupancy vehicles, such as transit buses, trolleybuses, van pools, ferryboats, monorails, subway and light rail, and cable cars.

---

[26] US Departments of Homeland Security and Energy. Energy (May). Available at http://www.dhs.gov, 2007.

[27] US Department of Homeland Security. Critical Infrastructure and Key Resources. Available at http://www.dhs.gov/files/programs/gc_1189168948944.shtm, 2009.

- Pipeline systems refer to a vast network of pipelines that cover hundreds of thousands of miles throughout the nation, carrying natural gas, hazardous liquids, and various chemicals.
- Rail consists of hundreds of railroads, more than 143,000 miles of track, more than 1.3 million freight cars, and about 20,000 locomotives.

Besides HSPD-7, many other directives and laws affect the multitude of transportation subsectors. For instance, the Maritime Transportation Security Act of 2002 promotes port and ship security through the US Coast Guard (USCG) in cooperation with other government bodies and the private sector. The transportation subsectors are subject to many government regulations from a variety of agencies that specialize in a specific mode of transportation. Examples include the Federal Aviation Administration (FAA), within the US Department of Transportation (DOT), which regulates civil aviation, and the DOT's Federal Motor Carrier Safety Administration that regulates commercial trucking (e.g., driver requirements and size and weight of trucks).

The Transportation Security Administration (TSA) is the SSA for the TS. The TSA was formed following the 9/11 attacks through the Aviation and Transportation Security Act of 2001. Originally in the DOT, with an emphasis on airline security, the TSA was shifted to the Department of Homeland Security and now sees the need to protect all modes of transportation. The USCG is the SSA for the maritime subsector. TS SSAs work together using the NIPP Sector Partnership Model. There are separate government–private sector coordinating councils for each subsector (e.g., aviation, highway) of the TS.

Federal government bodies with transportation security responsibilities that are represented on these councils include the TSA, USCG, DOT, Department of Justice (DOJ), FBI, and DOD. Additionally, the TS works with state, local, and international governments and organizations. The risks and vulnerabilities of the TS are global and encompass supporting infrastructure and the people and goods moving through it. In addition, the TS has significant interdependencies with other sectors. For instance, the TS and the energy sector directly depend on each other to transport fuel to a variety of users and to support all forms of transportation. Priorities of the TS are to prevent and deter terrorism against all modes of transportation, enhance resiliency, and improve the cost-effective use of resources for security. Each transportation subsector has unique protection challenges, and specific, rather than generic, security strategies are designed to reduce risks. For example, access controls at airports are much tighter than for mass transit.

Banking and Finance Sector

Owned primarily by private interests, the banking and finance sector (BFS) is the backbone of the economy and consists of an assortment of more than 29,000 financial firms. These include banks, credit unions, insurance companies, and securities firms. The reach of BFS dependencies is global because of international financial markets. The BFS has identified four vital sector dependencies: energy, IT, communications, and transportation. A 2007 pandemic flu exercise allowed the BFS to study weaknesses in operations and dependencies that may occur in such a crisis.[28] Vulnerabilities also point to cybercrime, power blackouts (that can disrupt financial transactions), and terrorism (because this sector is a symbol of power, wealth, and capitalism). HSPD-7 designates the US Department of the Treasury as the SSA for the BFS, and in this capacity, it has formalized the collaboration of BFS regulators, associations, and industry subsectors. Committees and councils assess risks and vulnerabilities and prioritize needs that often focus on the protection of IT and communications.

[28] US Department of Homeland Security. Critical Infrastructure and Key Resources. Available at http://www.dhs.gov/files/programs/gc_1189168948944.shtm, 2009.

The Financial Services–Information Sharing and Analysis Center (FS–ISAC) is a private-sector group that shares protection information and best practices of incident response. Regulation of this industry by federal and state laws and government agencies is complex and challenging, especially in light of well-publicized scandals and fraud (e.g., Enron and the Madoff Ponzi scheme) and criticism of weak government regulatory authorities (e.g., Securities and Exchange Commission) and related law enforcement. Major laws that influence the BFS are the Sarbanes-Oxley Act of 2002 (requires accounting controls and accuracy in financial reporting); the USA Patriot Act of 2001 (contains anti-money-laundering provisions and strategies against financing terrorism); the Gramm-Leach-Bliley Act of 1999 (pertains to protecting the privacy of customer information); the Anti-Drug Abuse Act of 1988 and the Bank Secrecy Act of 1986 (both focus on anti–money laundering and financial reporting requirements); and Regulation H, code of Regulations (pertains to bank security and anti–money laundering). The BFS is involved in broad-based global protection initiatives. Examples are information and intelligence sharing, vulnerability assessment methodologies, crisis communications systems, emergency exercises, business continuity planning, and redundancy and backup for transactions.[29]

Chemical Industry Sector

Chemicals are essential to our lives, but they can be very dangerous if not safely manufactured, stored, transported, and applied. Accidents can occur, as well as terrorist or military attacks using chemicals. The worst chemical disaster, thus far, occurred in Bhopal, India, in 1984, when a Union Carbide pesticide plant released toxic gas. There was no emergency response. The death toll reached almost 4000 people, according to the Indian government. However, other estimates put the number of deaths at between 8000 and 10,000. There were mass funerals and mass cremations. Bodies were also disposed of in the Narmada River. About 170,000 people were treated at hospitals for burning in the respiratory tract and eyes, breathing problems, stomach pains, and vomiting. It is estimated that 20,000 people have died since the disaster of related complications, and another 100,000 to 200,000 have permanent injuries. Following the leak, a variety of animals were collected and buried, food became scarce, fishing was prohibited, and leaves on trees turned yellow and fell off. Theories on the cause of the disaster include poor maintenance, lax safety, accident, and sabotage by a disgruntled worker. The health, environmental, and occupational rehabilitation of the area continues.[30]

In the United States, the worst chemical and industrial accident occurred in 1947, in Texas City, Texas, when a fire detonated about 2300 tons of ammonium nitrate on board a ship in the city's port. At least 581 people were killed, including all 28 Texas City firefighters who were aboard the ship when it exploded and a nearby crowd who watched the fire from what they thought was a safe distance. More than 5000 people were injured. Almost all the ships in the harbor were sunk and nearly 1000 buildings in the area were leveled. Two airplanes flying in the area were destroyed and windows were shattered in Houston, 40 miles away.[31] Chemicals are pervasive within our society, communities, workplaces, and homes.

The chemical industry sector (CIS) is an integral component of the US economy, privately owned, earning revenues of about $637 billion per year, and employing nearly one million people. A variety of chemicals are produced, including basic chemicals, specialty chemicals, agricultural chemicals, pharmaceuticals, and consumer products. The CIS is dependent on (or

[29] US Departments of Homeland Security and Treasury. Banking and Finance (May). Available at http://www.dhs.gov, 2007.

[30] R. Varma and D. R. Varma. The Bhopal Disaster of 1984. *Bulletin of Science, Technology & Society* 25, no. 1: 37–45, 2005.

[31] P. Applebome. Texas City Journal, Where a Chemical Leak Seems an Accepted Risk. New York Times, November 3, 1987. Available at http://www.nytimes.com/1987/11/03/us/texas-city-journal-where-a-chemical-leak-seems-an-accepted-risk.html.

depended on by) the following sectors: transportation, energy, water, agriculture and food, IT, health care, and communications.[32] The DHS is the SSA for the CIS. The chemical industry formed a council composed of trade associations that work with the DHS to ensure that private-sector interests are considered in federal action. Federal government bodies that work with the CIS also formed a council to coordinate activities. These include the Environmental Protection Agency (EPA) and the Departments of Commerce, Justice, and Transportation. Numerous laws and regulations affect the CIS, and the EPA plays a dominant role in enforcing safety and anti-pollution regulations in this industry.

The Emergency Planning and Community Right-to-Know Act of 1986 followed the Bhopal disaster. This 1986 Act requires chemical plant management to be involved in planning for emergencies, such as a leak, and sharing information. The Clean Air Act Amendments further reinforce the role of the EPA to ensure that plant operators prevent and mitigate environmental hazards. For chemical plants along US waterways, the Maritime Transportation Security Act of 2002 requires assessments of risks to waterways. State and local governments are also involved in regulating the CIS.

The DHS views the risk of terrorist attack, theft, and diversion of hazardous chemicals as top-priority concerns. In 2007, the Chemical Facility Anti-Terrorism Standards (CFATS) became the first regulatory program that concentrates on security for high-risk chemical facilities. Section 550(a) of the act provides the legal authority for the DHS to require high-risk chemical facilities to complete security-vulnerability assessments and site-security plans and implement protection strategies that meet risk-based performance standards (RBPS) prepared by the DHS.[32] Congress directed the DHS to develop RBPS to facilitate flexibility at chemical facilities because each site has unique protection challenges. RBPS, rather than prescriptive standards (that are generic), are viewed as enhancing security because security strategies that differ among facilities complicate the plans of adversaries. A facility's risk is based on the consequences of an attack, the likelihood of a successful attack, and the likelihood that an attack would occur at the facility. The DHS has prepared methodologies and tools to assess risk. Certain facilities regulated by other laws and government bodies are exempt from CFATS. Once chemical facilities complete a security plan, the DHS will review it for approval. Updated plans, training, testing, and exercises are also required. An inadequate security plan can result in a fine and a shutdown of a plant.

Postal and Shipping Sector

Every sector of the economy depends on the postal and shipping sector (PSS). This sector is different from general cargo operations because it moves small items and is operated by just a few providers, such as the US Postal Service and United Parcel Service.[32] The PSS is subject to a wide variety of protection challenges. These include internal theft and customers shipping prohibited items (e.g., illegal drugs, hazardous materials, or weapons of mass destruction [WMD]).

The TSA is the SSA for this sector, and it concentrates on broad protection programs. At the same time, owners and operators in this sector maintain specific, proprietary security programs and strategies. The PSS has an informal council comprising the major providers in this business. Federal agencies that have also formed a council include the TSA, DHS Office of Infrastructure Protection, DHS Customs and Border Protection, CDC, and FDA. The private and public councils collaborate with each other on needs and issues. For entities on the receiving end of items from the PSS, several security precautions should be implemented. Examples include the preparation of policies and procedures for screening mail, training employees on precautions, isolating the mail receiving area in a building separate from major operations, and applying technology to screen mail.

---

[32] US Department of Homeland Security. Critical Infrastructure and Key Resources. Available at http://www.dhs.gov/files/programs/gc_1189168948944.shtm, 2009.

Critical Manufacturing Sector

HSPD-7 notes that the sector designations identified in 2003 could change as the threats and hazards facing our nation are continuously evaluated. In 2008, the DHS established the critical manufacturing sector (CMS) and designated the DHS Office of Infrastructure Protection as the SSA for this sector. Because an attack on certain parts of the manufacturing industry could disrupt multiple CIKR, the DHS, with guidance from HSPD-7, identified manufacturers of the following products for placement in the CMS: primary metals (e.g., iron and steel), machinery, electrical equipment, and transportation equipment (e.g., motors and aerospace products). For collaboration on protection issues, a government council comprising the DHS, the FBI, and several government departments formed as well as a council of manufacturing companies.[33]

National Monuments and Icons Sector

The National Monuments and Icons Sector (NMIS) consist of federally owned physical structures that represent US heritage, traditions, or values. Located throughout the United States, these resources serve as points of interest for visitors and educational activities. Protection is required for visitors, staff, and the structures themselves. Destruction of these symbols can affect the national psyche. There are minimal cyber and communications protection issues associated with this sector.[33]

The US Department of the Interior (DOI) is the SSA for the NMIS. The DOI relies on voluntary compliance and cooperation because its statutory or regulatory authority is limited (except for assets under the National Park Service) for sharing asset information, conducting risk assessments, or implementing protective programs. The legal authority for the preservation and protection of assets in the NMIS is derived from laws, such as the Antiquities Act of 1906, the National Park Service Act of 1916, and other federal statutes. The assets in this sector have their own dedicated police or security force and may rely on state and local police. The FBI is granted investigative authority of this sector through 28 U.S.C. 533 and the USA Patriot Act of 2001. A government coordinating council enables partners to share information and best practices. Because of the public nature of this sector, security strategies must be unobtrusive and include crime prevention through environmental design (CPTED). WMD detection systems are necessary at certain sites as well as civil aviation restrictions.[34]

Nuclear Sector

The nuclear sector (NS) represents about 20% of the nation's electric power from 104 commercial nuclear reactors licensed to operate in the United States. This sector includes nuclear power plants; nuclear reactors used for research, testing, and training; nuclear materials applied in medical, industrial, and academic settings; nuclear fuel fabrication; decommissioning reactors; and the storage, transportation, and disposal of nuclear material and waste. The interdependencies of this sector involve energy (as a supplier), transportation (to move radioactive materials), chemical (HAZMAT at fuel-cycle facilities), health care (nuclear medicine), and government facilities (that use radioactive materials for various purposes).[33]

The Atomic Energy Act of 1946 and subsequent amendments established government control and management of US atomic energy, whether owned by the government or the private sector. HSPD-7 assigned the DHS to protect the NS in cooperation with the Nuclear Regulatory Commission (NRC) and the Department of Energy (DOE). The NRC was created by Congress as an independent agency in 1974 to protect people and the environment from the use of radioactive materials. It regulates commercial nuclear power plants and other uses of nuclear materials. It has strong regulatory authority over this sector, especially with regard to licensing, safety,

---

[33] US Department of Homeland Security. Critical Infrastructure and Key Resources. Available at http://www.dhs.gov/files/programs/gc_1189168948944.shtm, 2009.

[34] US Departments of Homeland Security and Interior. National Monuments and Icons (May). Available at http://www.dhs.gov, 2007.

fire protection, security, and emergency preparedness. The DOE has a broad mission of advancing the national, economic, and energy security of the United States; ensuring environmental cleanup of the nuclear weapons complex; and enhancing national security through military application of nuclear energy. It is involved in a variety of protection issues, such as WMD, security of facilities and transportation of radioactive materials, and emergency preparedness. The DHS established government and private-sector councils for collaboration and to share approaches to protection. The government council consists of representatives from the DHS, NRC, DEO, EPA, FBI, and Department of State, among other government bodies. The private-sector council consists of representatives from the nuclear industry.[35]

Dams Sector

The dams sector (DS) includes dams, navigation locks, levees, hurricane barriers, and other related water retention and/or control structures. The dependencies and interdependencies of the DS are broad: water for agriculture, waterways for transportation, water for drinking and firefighting, and energy through hydroelectric power. This sector is used to prevent flooding, facilitate wildlife habitats, and serve recreational needs. The failure of a dam or other component of this sector from natural disaster, terrorism, or other cause can result in massive loss of life, property damage, and long-term consequences affecting other sectors. Protection is afforded through the Office of Infrastructure Protection, within the DHS, which serves as the SSA for this sector. Councils from both the private and public sectors collaborate to enhance protection. Numerous assets within this sector necessitate prioritization in planning protection. Security strategies for the DS include boat and vehicle barriers, access controls, CCTV, alarm systems, protection for SCADA, emergency planning, and security personnel.[35]

Government Facilities Sector

The government facilities sector (GFS) is very broad and includes buildings owned or leased by federal, state, territorial, local, or tribal governments. These facilities are in the United States and overseas. The federal government alone controls more than three billion square feet of space and more than 650 million acres of land as well as embassies, consulates, and military bases located all over the world. The GFS also covers assets managed by 87,000 local governments in the United States.[35] Many government facilities have limited access controls to enable the public to conduct business. At the same time, other government facilities (e.g., military bases) maintain strict security controls. In addition, the security of information and IT is a major concern of the GFS. The terrorist threat is another concern because the GFS represents symbolic value. Protective measures must also consider all hazards based on the characteristics of the geographic location of the assets. The DHS Federal Protective Service (FPS), as part of Immigration and Customs Enforcement (ICE), is the SSA for the GFS. The FPS coordinates a council of representatives from government entities who share information and ameliorate protection challenges. The FPS also works with the commercial facilities sector because of government leasing of space in commercial buildings.[35]

Commercial Facilities Sector

The commercial facilities sector (CFS) is very broad and includes the following subsectors:[35]

- Public assembly (e.g., stadiums, arenas, convention centers, zoos, and museums)
- Sports leagues (e.g., professional sports)
- Resorts (e.g., casinos)

---

[35] US Department of Homeland Security. Critical Infrastructure and Key Resources. Available at http://www.dhs.gov/files/programs/gc_1189168948944.shtm, 2009.

- Lodging (e.g., hotels and motels)
- Outdoor events (e.g., amusement parks, fairs, and parades)
- Entertainment and media (e.g., motion picture studios and broadcast media)
- Real estate (e.g., office/apartment buildings and condominiums)
- Retail (e.g., retail centers, districts, and shopping malls)

Most of the CFS is privately owned and operated with limited government regulations, especially in terms of security requirements. Government fire, safety, health, and other codes do apply to this sector. In addition, professional associations and trade groups, representing subsectors of the CFS, develop best practices, guidelines, and standards to enhance protection. Because the CFS accommodates access by the general public with no or minimal access controls, this sector is often viewed as a "soft target" for terrorists.

The DHS is the SSA for the CFS and has organized a private-sector council representing all of the subsectors. A related government council was also formed, and both councils share information with each other and work on protection challenges. Daily protection operations in each business of the CFS are handled individually by management. Local first responders serve as backup. The federal role is to provide threat indications and warnings and develop guides, self-assessment tools, and courses for various subsectors.[36]

Concluding Thoughts

Critical infrastructures and key resources are essential to support everyday activities, the economy, and homeland and national security. The protection of CIKR is not a new initiative; it began during the early days of the nation's history with the protection of roads and the delivery of mail. As commerce and industry expanded, and especially during times of war, the protection of CIKR became increasingly important. Today, the National Infrastructure Protection Plan (NIPP) is a unified, single, national plan to protect CIKR. It applies a risk-management and all-hazards protection approach while seeking to bring together all levels of government, the private sector, and international partners. The assessment of vulnerabilities of CIKR is an ongoing process of refining methodologies to improve assessments. One avenue is to blend both scientific and nonscientific methodologies because each approach has advantages and disadvantages. The CIKR sectors covered in this chapter have similarities and differences. Although vulnerabilities vary among the sectors, dependencies and interdependencies can result in a cascading effect that can cause massive disruptions to the way of life in the United States and harm to its economy and security. The protection of each sector is facilitated through a designated federal government body known as a sector-specific agency (SSA) that coordinates a public-private sector-specific plan (SSP). Laws and regulations are an important part of the planning process. In addition, collaboration is essential within each sector and among all sectors because of numerous stakeholders and public and private interests. CIKR needs to be adequately protected. This is a task for governments, the private sector, and all citizens.

[36] US Department of Homeland Security. Critical Infrastructure and Key Resources. Available at http://www.dhs.gov/files/programs/gc_1189168948944.shtm, 2009.

20

Technology, Terrorism, and Counterterrorism[1]

Late in February 2012, in Afghanistan, US soldiers stood near the pile of burning Qurans in a landfill at Bagram Air Base, unknowing of the violence the act would cause in the near future. Seen by Afghan workers, who transmitted the message outside the base, the incident was responsible for the deaths of more than 30 Afghans, five US soldiers, and many other violent responses.[2] There have been other incidents that undermined the social and political relationships between the United States and the Afghan people. These include the murder of 16 innocent people including women and children.[3] US soldiers taking pictures while posing with dead bodies of insurgents,[4] and US Marines urinating on dead Taliban fighters.[5]

However, the Quran-burning case is one directly related to the lack of understanding of Afghani culture by US forces. Knowledge of events such as these is diffused through social media while some information is actually volunteered with or without the intention of the information ever reaching larger social circles. Events like these are used as points of propaganda by leaders of terrorism to mobilize terrorists and potential terrorists, such as Ayman al-Zawahiri, who took command of al-Qaeda following the death of Osama bin Laden in 2011.[6]

The soldiers burning the Quran were responding in a way they thought was acceptable to the regional culture. The copies of the Quran burned were deemed to be desecrated, which is culturally correct as they had been written in by prisoners. The act of burning the desecrated Qurans was also culturally correct. However, the burning is supposed to follow specific ritualistic acts as is the burning of a worn American flag. When the Quran or the worn American flag is burned in a manner that is perceived to be demeaning, anger ensues by many of those who culturally or

---

[1] Information for this chapter was drawn from the following title: G. F. Hepner and R. M. Medina, *The Geography of International Terrorism: An Introduction to Spaces and Places of Violent Non-state Groups*, CRC Press, 2013.

[2] R. Falk. Quran Burning: Mistake, Crime, and Metaphor. *Al Jazeera*, Opinion Section, 2012. Available at http://www.aljazeera.com/indepth/opinion/2012/03/20123785644715832.html.

[3] T. Shah and G. Bowley. An Afghan Comes Home to a Massacre. *New York Times*, World Section, 2012. Available at http://www.nytimes.com/2012/03/13/world/asia/us-army-sergeant-suspected-in-afghanistan-shooting.html?pagewanted=all.

[4] D. Zucchino and L. King. Photos of US Soldiers Posing with Afghani Corpses Prompt Condemnation. *Los Angeles Times*, US Section, 2012. Available at http://articles.latimes.com/2012/apr/18/nation/la-na-afghan-photos-20120419.

[5] G. Bowley and M. Rosenberg. Video Inflames a Delicate Moment for US in Afghanistan. *New York Times*, January 12, 2012. Available at http://www.nytimes.com/2012/01/13/world/asia/video-said-to-show-marines-urinating-on-taliban-corpses.html?pagewanted=all&_r=0.

[6] Al-Qaeda Leader: Avenge Quran Burning in Afghanistan. *USA Today*, News Section, 2012. Available at http://www.usatoday.com/news/world/story/2012-05-09/al-qaeda-quran-burning/54856714/1.

ethnically have an emotional connection to the symbolic meaning of the material item and witness the event directly or indirectly.[7] It is possible that the resulting outbreak from this specific event could have been avoided with a better understanding of local cultures, including knowledge of symbolic rituals.

Knowledge of the Quran burning traveled on the global scale by information technologies—specifically, social media. Soon after the burning, US companies acted, based on human geography and use of geospatial technologies, to alleviate the anger in the most affected regions. An automated search, or a crawl as it is referred to in computational circles, was used to gather information on sentiments about the event, also referred to as *sentiment mining*. Locational properties of the sentiments were also gathered so that varying sentiments could be mapped based on location, ethnic/tribal group, and socioeconomic characteristics. The identification of sentiments over geographic areas can be referred to as an indication of the *human terrain/landscape*.

Using these technologies, the companies found that the most unstable regions, based on reactions to the burning, were the border regions between Pakistan and Afghanistan even though the protests of the burning began in Bahrain. Five thousand new Qurans were directed to tribal and religious leaders within the identified regions with letters of condolence reflecting the misunderstanding that led to the burning. In some cases, formal presentation ceremonies were used. The Qurans and apologies were welcomed by the local leaders, and a fatwa[8] of peace and forgiveness was issued by one of the leaders. The social media were then monitored to determine post-activity sentiment and found positive reaction to the US offerings in the same regions that were first identified as less stable.

The Importance of Sociocultural Understanding (Human Geography) from Global Scale to Local Level

The preceding case study provides an example of the importance of understanding and analyzing geographic variation of sociocultural groups and beliefs and diplomatic efforts in wartime. In general, not understanding sociocultural rules and customs and their patterns across the landscape can lead to conflict. The United States has been largely uninformed on the sociocultural characteristics in regions of conflict. This is most likely due to the perceived notion that geography is unimportant and a decrease in interest in topics that are not directly political and/or economic. The "War on Terrorism" that began in the President George. W. Bush era (2001–2009) was waged, for the most part, with insufficient knowledge of regional societies and cultures in Iraq and Afghanistan. The focus was on winning the war but not managing and winning the peace.

Present US involvements are different from the state-centric conflicts of the past. The Cold War is over and, although the threat of state-to-state conflict is not gone, today's wars are being fought asymmetrically, by non-state groups rising up against the states in a war for power. As these asymmetric wars continue to be waged, more attention must be given to understanding and influencing *the hearts and minds* of the people. The United States is learning firsthand the importance of understanding region and culture and the damage that can come from ignoring geography for extended periods of time. A 2004 report by the Department of Defense stated:

---

[7] A. Kalinski. Quran Burning Riots: How Geospatial Tools Helped Calm the Waters. *GPS World*, Geointelligence Section, May 9, 2012. Available at http://www.gpsworld.com/gis/geointelligence/qur-burning-riots-how-geospatial-tools-helped-calm-waters-12971.

[8] A fatwa is an Islamic law–based ruling given by a person in a leadership role in the Muslim religion. It is intended to be given by Islamic scholars, but recent fatwas have been given by Islamist terrorists whose legitimacy in initiating the fatwas is questioned by many.

> The information campaign—or as some would have it, "the war of ideas," or the struggle for "hearts and minds"—is important to every war effort, and with respect to the separation of non-violent Muslims and violent jihadists American efforts have not only failed ... they may also have achieved the opposite of what they intended.[9]

US efforts, in some instances, have created animosity between residents of countries in conflict and military forces, who are seen as occupiers and instilling a forced democracy through violence. One of the many lessons learned in US and coalition efforts overseas is that knowledge of sociocultural aspects of resident populations is vital in a battle for hearts and minds. To win irregular wars, knowledge of enemy and self is no longer enough.[10] The *ambient population* must also be considered as they are affected by the actions of all sides and drive or deter the conflict. Today's war against non-state terrorist organizations is more complex than state-to-state wars of the past. Vital post–9/11 conflict-based operational gaps have been outlined as:[11]

1. Understanding of the target-area culture and its impact on operational decisions was insufficient. There was insufficient or ineffective transfer of knowledge to follow on units via the relief in place/transition of authority (RIP/TOA) process.
2. There was limited joint service of interagency capability (organization, methods, and tools) to conduct research, visualize, understand, and explain the human terrain (i.e., the population in which the unit operates).
3. Brigade combat teams (BCTs), regimental combat teams (RCTs), and division level HQs engaged in counterinsurgency operations in Operation Iraqi Freedom and Operation Enduring Freedom lacked the operationally relevant human terrain knowledge base and social science staff experts necessary to optimize their military decision-making process.
4. Commanders were limited by the lack of joint, service, and interagency integrated capability (people, organization, methods, tools) to gather/consolidate, analyze, visualize, understand, database, and share sociocultural information effectively. The battalions, companies, platoons, and squads experienced firsthand the knowledge and capability gap.

These operational gaps are all focused on the lack of sociocultural knowledge. The realization of the lack of sociocultural knowledge and the benefits of gaining this information, as well as using geospatial technologies, has brought geographic perspectives and efforts to the forefront of operations.

Geospatial Intelligence: The Integration of Human Geography and Geospatial Technologies

Geospatial intelligence, also known as GEOINT, "is an intelligence discipline and tradecraft that has evolved from the integration of imagery, imagery intelligence (IMINT), and geospatial information".[12] "Imagery" refers to visualizations of reflected energy collected from air- and

[9] Defense Science Board Task Force. Report of the Defense Science Board Task Force on Strategic Communication. Office of the Under Secretary of Defense for Acquisition, Technology, and Logistics. Department of Defense. Washington, D.C., 2004.

[10] T. Hanzhang. *The Modern Chinese Interpretation: Sun Tzu's Art of War*. New York: Sterling Publishing Co., Inc., 2000.

[11] US Army. The Human Terrain System. Online, 2011. Available at http://humanterrain system.army.mil/.

[12] National Geospatial Intelligence Agency. National System for Geospatial Intelligence: Geospatial Intelligence (GEOINT) Basic Doctrine Office of Geospatial-Intelligence Management. September 2006.

space-borne platforms. The images are spatially and temporally specific and typically show land cover/land use characteristics. Because of the amount of coverage by satellite systems, images are available for any region in the world. Any information derived from analysis of the imagery is referred to as imagery intelligence. The images, through analysis, become more than just pixels representing ground cover. Geospatial information as a category covers a wide range of information. The uniting factor is that the information has geographic characteristics of location. This can be population distribution, political boundary, ethnic region data, or any other data with locational attributes.

Geospatial technologies and geographic information are used in the geospatial intelligence efforts of strategic operations focused on the components of the geography of thematic hierarchy spaces, places, people, topologies, and activities. Geospatial intelligence has become commonplace in counterterrorism operations, specifically in the integrated analysis of geospatial data from maps, geosensor systems, remote sensing, a geographic positioning system (GPS) integrated in a geographic information system (GIS) for decision support to locate, monitor, and assess terrorist groups and counterterrorism strategies and tactics. This integrated analysis of geospatial data leads to geospatial information, which leads to valuable knowledge for counterterrorist operations.

In the world of US intelligence, GEOINT is the only INT that operates from a completely spatial perspective.[13] As such, it has its foundations in geography and, for the task of counterterrorism, human geography specifically. Technological and data components of geospatial intelligence become much more valuable when informed with human geography knowledge. An image of settlements on the border between Pakistan and Afghanistan will only look like settlements to someone with no knowledge of the region. However, to a human geographer with prior knowledge of the region, the settlements become possible temporary shelters for internally displaced people forced out of their homes by cultural conflict or environmental hazards. The people within the shelters, possibly nomads, are most likely unaffected by government rule in the autonomous region of the border. The trained eye may be able to derive demographic and cultural information from the image, and adding further geospatial information provides more detail. Gaining detailed information on anywhere in the world is possible with geospatial technologies and human geography.

The remainder of this chapter will review aspects of geospatial intelligence, beginning with applied human geography efforts by the US Army, then on to the larger area of technology and conflict, and finally to more specific geographic data and geospatial technologies. In the discussion of various components of geospatial intelligence to follow, technologies, methods, and tools will be defined, and examples of their usefulness for counterterrorism will be given.

The US Army Human Terrain System

Much of the human terrain focus was initiated by the US Army in 2006 as the human terrain system (HTS). It began as a proof of concept effort for the Joint Improvised Explosive Device Defeat Organization (JIEDDO). The term *human terrain* describes the sociocultural variations of people over geographic space, a concept analogous to terrain analysis in physical geography and other earth sciences, which looks at variation in landforms over geographic space. The HTS has since deployed social scientists, mostly anthropologists, into conflict zones of Afghanistan and Iraq. Researchers of various social science backgrounds, including geography, sociology, political science, and psychology, have also been deployed. The research includes direct contact

[13] Other INTs include human intelligence (HUMINT), signals intelligence (SIGINT), and measurement and signature intelligence (MASINT). See National Geospatial Intelligence Agency. National System for Geospatial Intelligence: Geospatial Intelligence (GEOINT) Basic Doctrine Office of Geospatial-Intelligence Management. September, 2006.

with local populations in the form of interviews, surveys, and other types of interaction.[14] The main goals of the HTS are to "[r]ecruit, train, deploy, and support an embedded, operationally focused sociocultural capability; conduct operationally relevant, sociocultural research and analysis; [and] develop and maintain a sociocultural knowledge base" with the purpose to "[s]upport operational decision-making, enhance operational effectiveness, and preserve and share sociocultural institutional knowledge."[15]

The HTS has evolved with greater emphasis on the practice of applied human geography for operational support of the war fighter. The system is structured into requirements of expert capabilities of understanding sociocultural characteristics and management of information in all stages from gathering to advanced analysis. This information is integrated into maps and graphics used in the training of military and government personnel on sociocultural and information management.[16] The human terrain of a region is focused not only on conflict-based information, but also describes all aspects of sociocultural characteristics and patterns.

The HTS has been met with opposition from academic and scientific circles and has suffered its share of setbacks. One of the main arguments against the HTS from the American Anthropological Association (AAA) is that the HTS activities break the AAA code of ethics whereby active HTS teams have the potential to do harm to their subjects. Specifically, the AAA highlighted five concerns:[17]

- The nature of the HTS deters those workers in the field from identifying themselves as researchers, which prohibits the full disclosure of their research intentions.
- Responsibilities to the US military may result in researchers directly or indirectly harming their study subjects.
- Because of the nature of war and operating in war zones, the ability of subjects to give "voluntary informed consent" is compromised.
- Information provided to the US military can be used for the targeting of individuals.
- HTS operations can cause risk for the researchers and their subjects.

These statements and feelings from the anthropology community have been a particularly damaging strike to the HTS reputation as it was led by anthropologists. As a follow-up to the fifth concern, three researchers have died in the field as a result of conflict-based activities since the inception of the HTS program.

The HTS has also met harsh criticism from members of other military branches. Significant concerns voiced by Major Ben Connable[18] of the US Marine Corps are that the HTS ignores standing doctrine whereby the military is mandated to maintain cultural capabilities, that cultural capabilities are much improved and the US military has been proven to use "cultural terrain" to its benefit, and that the activities can work negatively against the relationship between the military and social scientists. While Connable voices his negative opinions of the army-based HTS, this does emphasize the need for cultural capabilities and shortcomings in cultural competency in the military. However, his stance is that cultural capability programs should

[14] C. A. King, R. Bienvenu, and H. Stone. HTS Training and Regulatory Compliance for Conducting Ethically Based Social Science Research. *Military Intelligence Professional Bulletin,* October–December: 16–20, 2011.

[15] US Army. The Human Terrain System. Online, 2011. Available at http://humanterrain system.army.mil/.

[16] M. C. Bartholf. The Requirement for Socio cultural Understanding in Full Spectrum Operations. *Military Intelligence Professional Bulletin.* October–December: 4–10, 2011.

[17] American Anthropological Association. American Anthropological Association Executive Board Statement on the Human Terrain System Project. October 31, 2007. Available at http://www.aaanet.org/about/Policies/statements/Human-Terrain-System-Statement.cfm.

[18] B. Connable. All Our Eggs in a Broken Basket: How the Human Terrain System is Undermining Sustainable Military Cultural Competence. *Military Review* March–April 2009, 57.

remain in house and that the military's cultural intelligence programs have greatly improved to the point where direct assistance from the academic community is not necessary.

Regardless of the ways in which cultural capabilities are being applied against terrorism, the realization that the US military lacks these capabilities is an important one. Focusing on local people and their culture within conflict areas is imperative to countering terrorism in the battle for the hearts and minds of the asymmetric conflicts of the 21st century. Civilian residents play a much larger role in the conflict than they would have in state-to-state based conflict. They are the ones most affected by the conflict, they are potential recruits, and they can help alleviate sectarian or other types of local conflict. Reliable and effective information can be attained from the *ambient population* and used to better understand the situation and mitigate foreseeable problems. It is important to consider the sentiment of the people and their responses to various stimuli.

Human Terrain Shift to Human Geography

As described previously, today's wars have highlighted the lack of sociocultural knowledge in the United States, within the US military and diplomatic corps, and of private contractors working for the United States. Human terrain was originally a limited qualitative practice of field researchers gathering information from and about local populations. Recently, the broader concept of human geography, theories, methods, and techniques from the long history of qualitative and quantitative human geography have become available for use in military and diplomatic efforts. Recent changes to the human geography perspective have expanded to include quantitative spatial analysis, geostatistics, and geospatial technologies: mapping, GIS, GPS, and remote sensing with satellite and aerial vehicles. This combination forms the basis for integrated geospatial intelligence.

Technology and War

Technology has always been an important factor in how wars are fought and won. Today's war is more terroristic and decentralized in nature. In the past, much of the technological advancement influencing war activities, as they are now, has been driven by firepower, but other technologies have played key roles. Transportation technologies led to the geographic decentralization of battles. For example, helicopters and airplanes allowed for troops to be deployed quickly to other countries. Aircraft and satellites have led to high-resolution surveillance of the battlefield. Use of GPS and drones allows the military accurately to attack regions in the world using a computer in the United States. Communications technologies have also changed warfare—from the days of Morse code to two-way radios to cellular phones. Each technological step in communications technology has changed mobility in warfare by allowing fighters more freedom and hence allowing more complexity on the battlefield. Terrorists are utilizing these and other technologies in all logistic activities.

Lind provides an overview of the relationship of weapons technology to warfare over time.[19] At each generational step, there has been a greater tendency toward disorder on the battlefield that is facilitated by technology, ideas, or both (Figure 20.1). Warfare has moved from linear to nonlinear forms in which decentralization on the battlefield (social and geographic) in the present day provides a benefit for those who are fighting against state powers. For this reason, this chronology serves to inform us about the evolution of terrorists' actions in conflicts.

---

[19] W. S. Lind. Understanding Fourth Generation War. *Military Review*, 84, no. 5: 12–16, 2004.

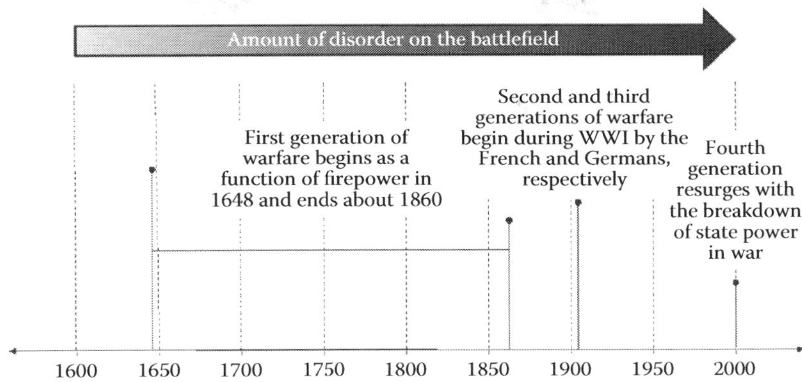

Figure 20.1 Timeline: The four generations of war. (Adapted from W. S. Lind, *Military Review*, 84, no. 5: 12–16, 2004. From G. F. Hepner and R. M. Medina, *The Geography of International Terrorism: An Introduction to Spaces and Places of Violent Non-state groups*, CRC Press, 2013. With permission.)

Through the three previous generations of war for the United States and the present fourth generation, the shaping of warfare by aspects of technology and ideas is apparent. The first generation is characterized by linearity; the second, by firepower technologies that facilitated the move away from linear battles and even forced nonlinear movement through the use of barriers; and the third, by ideas that led to maneuver warfare. The fourth generation of warfare is characterized by technologies in firepower and also by technologies for spreading ideas and capturing information, including geospatial information. It is marked by the loss of state control in war and a shift toward the people whereby more emphasis is directed toward the people, the cultures, and the information. Political boundaries are becoming less important than often nondelineated cultural boundaries, which are, at times, fuzzy. Terrorists use satellite and aerial imagery to plan actions often equal to the capabilities of nations. Information-age technologies, such as social networking and information diffusion tools Facebook and Twitter, are today seen by many as being more powerful in uprisings and fourth-generational warfare than traditional weapons.

There can be an overlap for each of these generations. For example, countries can use second- and third-generation tactics although the use of first-generation tactics can be seen as "obsolete" or "suicidal"[20] although suicide as a tactic can be an asset in war. Terrorists have found more value in the information war than with complex firepower, which is not a surprise because, traditionally, terrorists have had to use low-cost, low-tech weapons or weapons they can acquire through the enemy's losses. The difference is that today's technological advancements give almost everybody the ability to acquire and produce extreme amounts of information that, in many ways, facilitate the training, mission planning, and dissemination of propaganda.

In 1989, Lind et al. described the first three generations of war and conceptualized the fourth; though unsure, they asked, "What might it look like?"[21] They never suggested that terrorism was to be the fourth generation of war; they did state, however, that terroristic elements of warfare are (or would be, because they were writing in the late 1980s) characteristics of the theorized fourth generation, which has been used previously, though not on large (global) scales. All the

[20] W. S. Lind. Understanding Fourth Generation War. *Military Review*, 84, no. 5: 12–16, 2004.

[21] W. S. Lind, K. Nightengale, J. F. Schmitt, J. W. Sutton, and G. I. Wilson. The Changing Face of War: Into the Fourth Generation, *Marine Corps Gazette*, 73, no. 10: 22, 1989.

elements of the theorized fourth generation already exist and have been practiced throughout history. For example, Mao Tse Tung in China focused on political power before military power.[22]

The fourth-generation war can be seen as a return to the world before state dominance, in the context of war, in which the prominent strategy for warfare is guerrilla. By 2004, Lind wrote about the fourth generation as it had already begun (or resurged) and was in close resemblance to what he and other authors had theorized in 1989. His conceptualization of these four generations illustrates the link between technology, ideas, and warfare. Today, technology is facilitating the move toward nonlinearity, complexity, and decentralization of conflict strategy in the form of non-state terrorism.

Technologies of Geospatial Intelligence and Their Use in Terrorism and Counterterrorism

Geospatial intelligence was described previously as having three main components: imagery, imagery intelligence, and geospatial information. This all-encompassing geospatial technology and knowledge description leaves out important details of technologies working in the background of geospatial intelligence. The path to a useable and useful image and, finally, the extraction of information from that image is a long one. However, the ease of accessibility to advanced technologies through free online services, such as Google Earth and NASA World Wind has made complicated geospatial processes seem almost nonexistent.

Geospatial technologies are those used to collect, process, and analyze geographic data (i.e., data that have locational qualities). These technologies include GIS, GPS, and remote sensing. Geospatial technologies comprise one of the leading areas of research in the present day.[23] It is difficult to envision a world without geospatial technologies that we now use every day, that are integrated with our communications devices and modes of transportation, and that are accessible from any computer connected to the World Wide Web. They are used in terrorism and counterterrorism activities and are anticipated to continue to change the ways in which individuals live as well as the ways in which wars are waged and countered.

Geographic Data as Geospatial Information

Geographic data are data that have locational references with associated attributes. These references are typically in the form of latitude/longitude coordinates but can be linear or areal locational systems, such as miles on a roadway or presence in a specific tribal area or language area. Geographic data are widely available in many different forms and formats online. In the 21st century, the increase of computational power and storage has facilitated the increased availability of geospatial data. Coordinates are embedded into digital photographs, remotely sensed images are georectified,24 and mobile phone companies collect locational data of every customer. Online searches are now customized to factor in user locations, so a user in Los Angeles will get different results in an online search than a user in Washington, D.C., searching for the same item. For research purposes, many US agencies, such as the US Geological Survey, the National Oceanic and Atmospheric Agency, and the US Department of Agriculture, host geographic data clearinghouses online.

The acquisition of information, geospatial or otherwise, influences people to act in many situations, including conflict, terrorism, and warfare. People act on perceptions of reality and each new bit of information can change those perceptions; hence, activities of conflict will change with more information as terrorists and counter-terrorists are in search of the optimal result.

[22] T. X. Hammes. The Evolution of War: The fourth Generation. *Marine Corps Gazette* 78, no. 9: 35–44, 1994.

[23] D. Z. Sui. Geospatial Technologies and Homeland Security: An Overview. In D. Z. Sui (ed.), *Geospatial Technologies and Homeland Security: Research Frontiers and Future Challenges*. Berlin: Springer, 2008.

[24] Geo-rectification refers to the processing of image data so that they appear to be at their correct geographic location.

For example, geospatial information available online provides terrorists with the ability to better understand their operations and more accurately direct their attacks although poor and/or outdated information may also impact operations in a negative way. Either way, more information leads to a better perceived understanding of operations.

An example of the usefulness of geospatial data for terrorism research took place in 2001, when scientists identified the wall of sedimentary rock used as a backdrop for Osama bin Laden in one of al-Qaeda's early videos. Bin Laden's location was first pinpointed to two provinces in eastern Afghanistan: Paktia and Paktika. Further research on the geological aspects of the border region between Afghanistan and Pakistan using Landsat Satellite images as well as the added cultural geography knowledge of the region placed the likely location of the filming of the video in the Zhawar Kili cave region in the Khost Province.[25] Counterterrorism actions taken based on these findings are unknown but were obviously not successful. However, the potential of geospatial data and geographic knowledge from various sources for integrated analysis is clear.

Geographic Information Systems

Geographic information systems are defined as an integrated collection of hardware, software, and data with a focus on geospatial data storage, processing, analysis, and visualization. Maps are the primary means of conveying geographic information from a GIS. Maps are really models of a selected reality of the landscape. As statistics provide a value representative of numerical distribution, maps provide symbolic representations of physical and cultural features, distributions and patterns across the landscape. When maps are combined with attribute information and numerical algorithms, spatial statistics, models, and projections of spatial patterns can be generated within the GIS.

The use of GIS has proven to be a great tool in research and operations for counterterrorism on all levels and in all aspects of the emergency management cycle: mitigation, preparedness, response, and recovery. GIS is designed as a tool for visualization and analysis. Aspects of the use of GIS for terrorism/counterterrorism include, but are not limited to, cartography, identifying patterns of terrorist activity with spatial statistics, and modeling populations at risk. Much of a GIS typically sits on the back end of online applications, so not all users are highly trained technicians. Many users do not even recognize they are using a GIS as with Google Earth, Google Maps, NASA World Wind, OpenStreetMap, and others. GIS makes the sharing of spatial information possible. Terrorists are using GIS to plan attacks if they use any online navigation or locational service.

The primary value of GIS over a simple map is that the GIS uses an information systems approach. The GIS integrates many different types of geo-referenced feature data in the form of points, lines, and polygons along with raster or pixel data from remotely sensed imagery. These spatial data are combined with normally nonspatial tabular data that are provided a geographic reference or geocoded. These nonspatial data include cultural characteristics and demographic and economic data (Figure 20.2). By using GIS, patterns of the physical and human environments can be detected and better understood. This may not be possible with research that uses a single data set or multiple data sets that are not geospatially integrated.

One of the major benefits of GIS is the ability to do advanced spatial analyses, the focus of which is to find geographic patterns of people, places, or phenomena. For terrorism studies, one may be concerned with spatial patterns of terrorist attacks, recruitment, and vulnerable populations. GIS can be used in all aspects of the fundamental issues of terrorism as defined by Cutter,

---

[25] R. A. Beck. Remote Sensing and GIS as Counterterrorism Tools in the Afghanistan War: A Case Study of the Zhawar Kili Region. *Professional Geographer* 55, no. 2: 170–179, 2003.

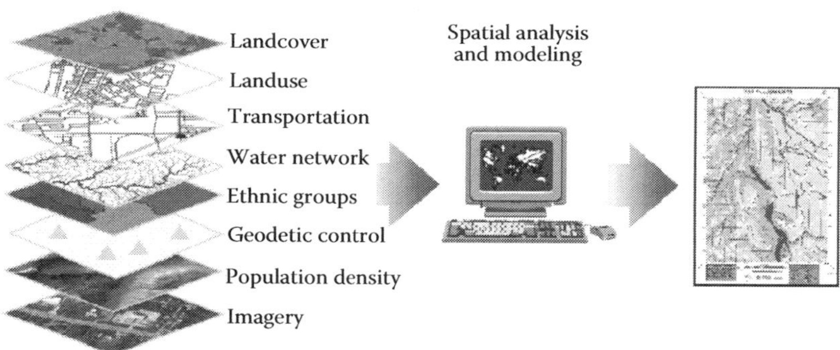

Figure 20.2 Data integration within a GIS. (From G. F. Hepner and R. M. Medina, *The Geography of International Terrorism: An Introduction to Spaces and Places of Violent Non-state groups*, CRC Press, 2013. With permission.)

Richardson, and Wilbanks:[26] reducing threats, detecting threats, reducing vulnerabilities, and improving responses. Two examples of analysis will be discussed here: a spatiotemporal analysis of terrorist/insurgent attacks in Iraq and an analysis of global terrorist social and geographic closeness (proximity) tendencies. One of the main points to consider with these analyses is that the incorporation of dynamics, whether spatiotemporal, socio-spatial, etc., is key to understanding real-world cause-and-effect relationships. Humans do not operate motionlessly, void of space and time; thus, to obtain realistic research results, researchers must conduct analyses that best reflect reality.

Analyzing the Connections between Social and Geographic Space Activities

Social and geographic space activities are interrelated. Humans tend to interact most with those who are near, and they prefer to be near to those they interact with most. GIS can assist in understanding these social and geographic space interactions. Activity locations in geographic space and connectivity in social space can be analyzed and visualized in a GIS. For example, Figure 20.3 shows a rendering of the Islamist terrorist social network to geographic space. Al-Qaeda, as an organization, sits at the center of this network while leaders Osama bin Laden and Ayman al-Zawahiri were assumed to be in the border regions of Pakistan and Afghanistan. The locations of terrorists and extent of their connections are shown.

Identifying geographic and social connection patterns is imperative in today's struggle with global terrorism. Information campaigns and social networks are much more available and influential in instances of fourth-generation warfare and netwar. Today's terrorists are global people. They travel and maintain connections all over the world. Information technologies allow organizational leaders to maintain the sufficient leadership necessary for coordinated attacks. The world is a smaller place today with decreasing costs and increasing efficiency of communications and transportation. This must be incorporated into how researchers view and analyze terrorism and the types of GIS analyses available.

In a study of geographic locations of and social connections between terrorists on a global scale, Medina and Hepner substantiated the concept of the socio-spatial network for ter-

[26] S. L. Cutter, D. B. Richardson, and T. J. Wilbanks. The Changing Landscape of Fear. In S. L. Cutter, D. B. Richardson, and T. J. Wilbanks (eds.), *The Geographical Dimensions of Terrorism*. New York: Routledge, p. 3, 2003.

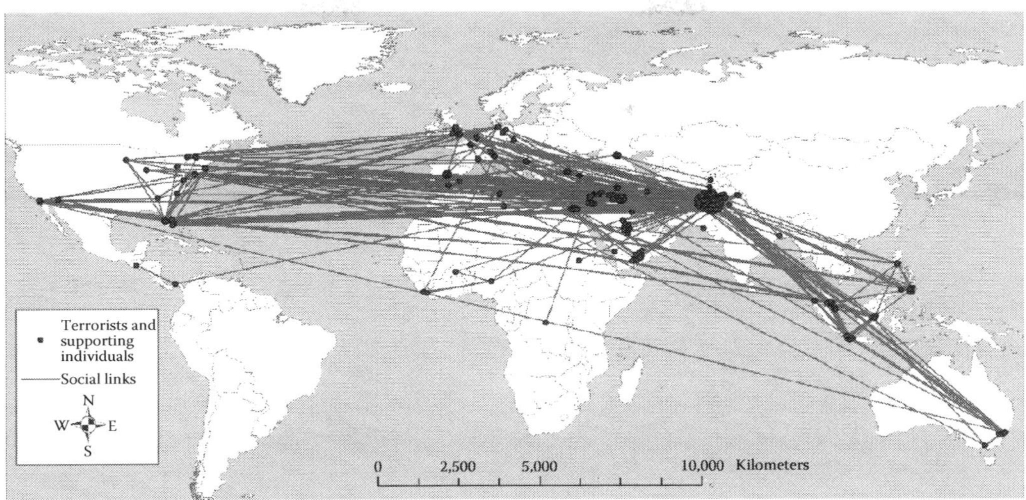

Figure 20.3 Islamist terrorist network rendered to geographic space. (From R. M. Medina and G. F. Hepner, *Transactions in GIS,* 15, no. 5: 577–597, 2011. With permission. G. F. Hepner and R. M. Medina, *The Geography of International Terrorism: An Introduction to Spaces and Places of Violent Non-state groups*, CRC Press, 2013. With permission.)

rorist network research and designed a new metric of analysis.[27] This was done by incorporating graph theoretic and social network analysis methods within a GIS. They found that operational connections between terrorists are more likely to be at relatively shorter distances and that there is a relationship between social distance and geographic distance. Adding more social connections to further degrees[28] in a terrorist social network will result in longer average geographic distance connections. Thus, terrorist social networks operate similarly to general social networks in that they prefer to interact with those that are near or prefer to be near those with whom they interact. This is not surprising when the history of the Islamist network is considered. Many connections are between longtime friends and were forged in jihadist struggles around the world. One of the most popular and partially responsible for today's Islamist network is the Russo-Afghan War in the 1970s and 1980s. Many connections in this network are family or clan based. Given these characteristics, the Islamist network can be seen as a subset of an already existing social network that does not have characteristics much different from those of the parent network.

Figure 20.4 shows the tendency for social network clustering of terrorists to be more likely within geographic clusters of terrorists. This analysis supports previously stated characteristics of geographic and social space dependencies. Member of terrorist networks need places to operate. If terrorists are clustered in a training camp or jihad arena, they are more likely to meet and form connections. If they are already connected, it is likely that at one point in time, if not now, they met at a specific place. This has implications for diaspora communities. Radical ideas are more likely to be shared with others who have similar sentiments about aspirational homelands, being alienated, and being marginalized.

The implications of this research do not lessen the importance of social connectivity through random interactions. The terrorist attacks on September 11, 2001, may have never

[27] R. M. Medina and G. F. Hepner. Advancing the Understanding of Socio-spatial Dependencies in Terrorist Networks. *Transactions in GIS* 15, no. 5: 577–597, 2011.

[28] First-degree social connections are adjacent members of one's social network. Second-degree connections are friends of friends; third-degree connections are connections with two intermediaries, and so on.

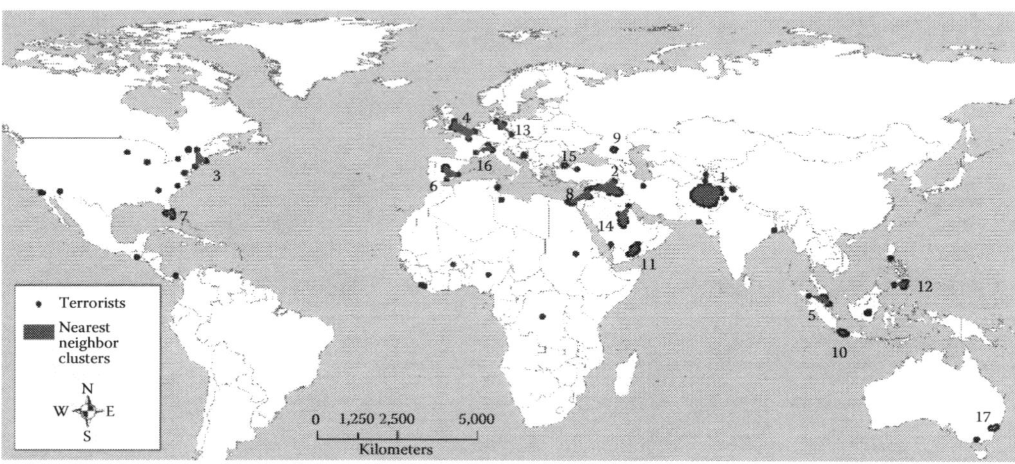

Figure 20.4 Sociospatial clusters of terrorists. (From R. M. Medina and G. F. Hepner, *Transactions in GIS*, 15, no. 5: 577–597, 2011. With permission. G. F. Hepner and R. M. Medina, *The Geography of International Terrorism: An Introduction to Spaces and Places of Violent Non-state groups*, CRC Press, 2013. With permission.)

happened if it was not for a random meeting on a train. Randomness plays a large role in Islamist network activities as it does with social networks in general. Random interactions can be connections for life, especially if those involved are of the same mindset or cultural background, which are often geographically based traits. These interactions are important and are more likely to create lasting social connections if social distances are shorter between those involved.

Furthermore, social distances are more likely to be shorter if geographic distances are shorter. It is clear to see that coincidence in space and time, whether intentional or random, is vital for terrorist network operations. These meetings strengthen relationships, especially in warlike situations, and they increase the effectiveness of interactions, such as with training camps. Some may suggest a flaw in this argument. For example, cyberterrorists seem not to need geographic space interaction. Their social networks may all be contained in virtual space. However, their operations and targets also exist in virtual space, so it is much easier to keep all interactions virtual. Terrorists operating in geographic spaces benefit much more from geographic space interactions.

One of the problems presented by this research is the lack of socio-spatial dynamics. The entities represented are static on a global scale. Some of this is the result of poor or missing data on terrorists and their activities, but more so, this is the result of insufficient GIS tools and methods. Snapshots can be considered for different time intervals but are inefficient for long time periods, and geo-visualization would benefit from an intrinsically continuous model. Some tools and methods are available for spatiotemporal analysis and visualization, but when incorporating social network connections and other factors, the possibilities from industry standard software are minimal.

While socio-spatial research is a promising area for GIS, technologies and methods are unavailable. Representing spatiotemporal dynamics and time geographies within a GIS is on the forefront of academic and industry research as is complexity science and network analysis. However, there remains a gap between the two areas. Tools and methods to analyze and visualize dynamic social networks must be designed and/or customized for present-day research. Eventually this exciting new field of complex social systems will have a collection of readily available tools and methods for important socio-spatial analysis.

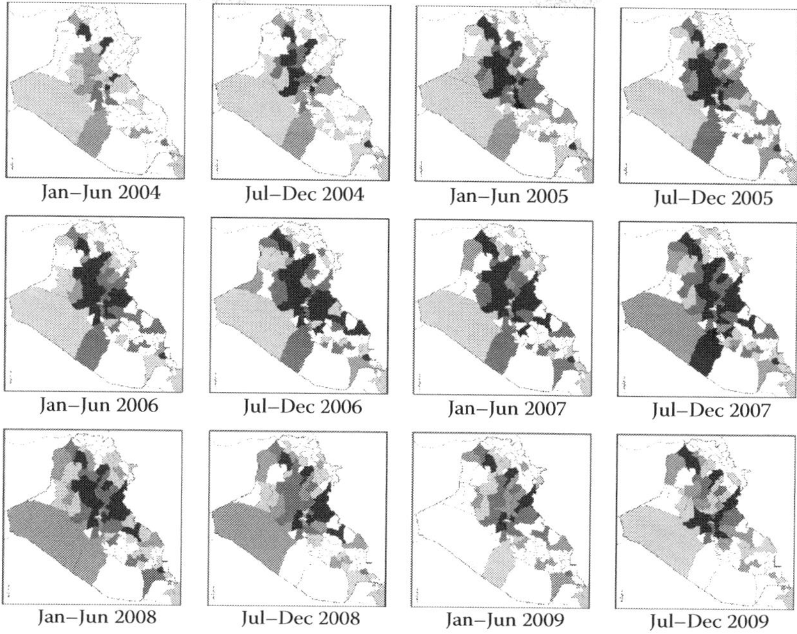

Figure 20.5 Space–time pattern of terrorist/insurgent attacks in Iraq districts, 2004–2009. (From R. M. Medina et al., *Studies in Conflict and Terrorism,* 34: 862–882, 2011. With permission. G. F. Hepner and R. M. Medina, *The Geography of International Terrorism: An Introduction to Spaces and Places of Violent Non-state groups*, CRC Press, 2013. With permission.)

GIS-Based Spatial Analysis and Visualization of Terrorist Attacks

By analyzing spatial patterns of terrorist incidents,[29] it is possible to find clusters and hot spots of events and terrorist activity. Adding in temporal aspects of terrorist behavior to identify patterns over space and time provides results that offer much more information. Identifying a cluster of attacks in a region without respect to time does not take into consideration that smaller clusters of activity may be occurring in different regions throughout a large area and that there may be spatiotemporal patterns of attacks that occur as a result of various stimuli. For example, terrorist attacks have typically been clustered in Baghdad since the US and allied troop invasion in 2003, but without consideration of time, an analyst would not be able to identify changes in behavior during trigger activities, such as elections, counterterrorist/insurgent offensives, and leader deaths that drive terrorist attacks. Spatiotemporal analyses provide a bigger picture of behavior and offer additional information. With added sociocultural information, an analyst is capable of determining, in part, why increased terrorist attacks are occurring, which can provide a better opportunity to thwart terrorism before it begins.

In a GIS-based analysis of terrorist attacks in Iraq, Medina, Siebeneck, and Hepner[30] were able to identify spatiotemporal patterns of attacks and several of the possible drivers for terrorism in Iraq. Figure 20.5 shows the spatiotemporal pattern of terrorist/insurgent attacks in Iraq

[29] Terrorist attacks in the data set used for this study are termed "incidents" by the National Counterterrorism Center, where incidents are where "sub-national or clandestine groups of individuals deliberately or recklessly attacked civilians or noncombatants" (2011).

[30] R. M. Medina, L. K. Siebeneck, and G. F. Hepner. A Geographic Information Systems (GIS) Analysis of Spatiotemporal Patterns of Terrorist Incidents in Iraq 2004–2009. *Studies in Conflict and Terrorism* 34: 862–882, 2011.

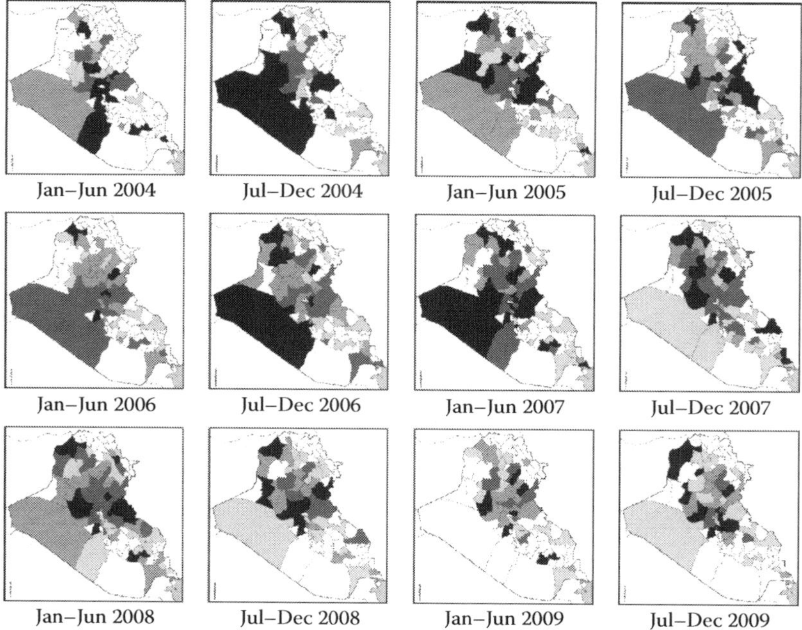

Figure 20.6 Space-time pattern of terrorist/insurgent attack intensities in Iraq districts, 2004–2009. (From R. M. Medina et al., *Studies in Conflict and Terrorism,* 34: 862–882, 2011. With permission. G. F. Hepner and R. M. Medina, *The Geography of International Terrorism: An Introduction to Spaces and Places of Violent Non-state groups*, CRC Press, 2013. With permission.)

from 2004 to 2009. The benefits of using GIS to map, analyze, and visualize the pattern of attacks over space and time are clear. One can see the growth and decline of attacks over the six-year period and the districts that need more attention or are relatively peaceful.

The previous illustration shows trends in terrorist attacks at the district scale. Attack intensity is the number of casualties divided by the number of attacks to give casualties per attack by district. Casualties in this research include deaths, injuries, and kidnappings.[31] Figure 20.6 maps the attack intensities to show the pattern differences between the incidence of an attack and the intensities of those attacks. One can see that the map of attack intensities has a much less coherent pattern.

Further sociocultural information, such as communications and transportation flows, and social network connectivity may assist in explaining the intensity patterns. The most important factor in producing damaging terrorist attacks may be spatiotemporal coincidence. The ability to be a more professional, deadly terrorist is taught and learned. It requires time and practice, and if available, benefits are gained through spatiotemporal coincidence of social network members in training camps and other centralized places.

Combining attack and intensity trends with sociocultural data can assist in explaining this violent behavior. One can identify temporal variation in reaction to sociocultural triggers. Figure 20.7 is a line graph of potential triggers for violent activity in Iraq with trends in attacks and intensities. A much more thorough investigation of spatial variation would analyze the attack trends for various districts to identify regions of greatest influence for each of the potential trigger events.

---

[31] L. K. Siebeneck, R. M. Medina, I. Yamada, and G. F. Hepner. Spatial and Temporal Analyses of Terrorist Incidents in Iraq, 2004–2006. *Studies in Conflict and Terrorism* 32, no. 7: 591–610, 2009.

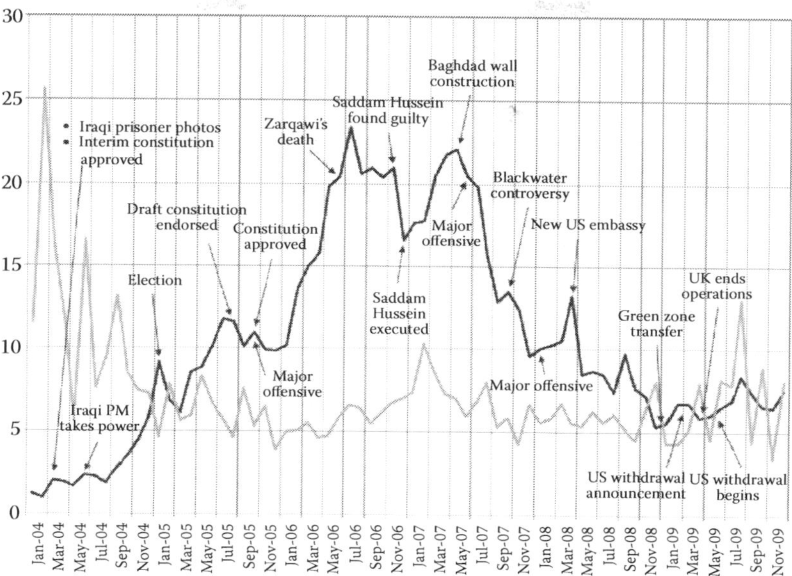

Figure 20.7 Timeline of terrorist attacks and attack intensities with added sociocultural information. (From R. M. Medina et al., *Studies in Conflict and Terrorism,* 34: 862–882, 2011. With permission. G. F. Hepner and R. M. Medina, *The Geography of International Terrorism: An Introduction to Spaces and Places of Violent Non-state groups*, CRC Press, 2013. With permission.)

For more robust conclusions, this research would benefit from analysis of more events using spatiotemporal data mining methods, in which tens of thousands of attack events could be analyzed. Additionally, one could incorporate other factors of social and physical environment—demographics, climate, and infrastructure. Sociocultural systems are very complex as are the challenges for designing models to analyze and visualize the geographic patterns of terrorism. This section serves as an introduction to the possibilities for GIS in terrorism research. Although it presents only one example, the potential of GIS for this research is much larger than can be summarized in this chapter.

Viewshed Analysis: Line of Sight

The line of sight (LoS) concept is easily described as what can be seen from various standpoints given physical and built environment obstacles. It is modeled using a viewshed analysis, which is made possible and cost-effective with today's geospatial technologies and available data. Viewshed analysis and LoS models are useful in many counterterrorism applications, including finding potential locations of sniper placement and counter sniper shelter, geo-sensor placement, and camera placement. It is also useful in determining likely locations for improvised explosive device (IED) placement. IEDs have been an ongoing problem for counterterrorist/insurgent forces in Afghanistan, Iraq, and elsewhere. The trend that makes viewshed analysis an important tool for counter-IED activities is that those who set the IED in place typically wait and hide to detonate the explosive remotely or observe/record the attack for future use in planning. This makes it more likely that IEDs will be distributed within the LoS of a vantage point where terrorists/insurgents can remain hidden.

Analyzing the viewshed for a certain area requires a vantage point and three-dimensional geographic data of the adjacent region at the extent of the desired results. The three-dimensional

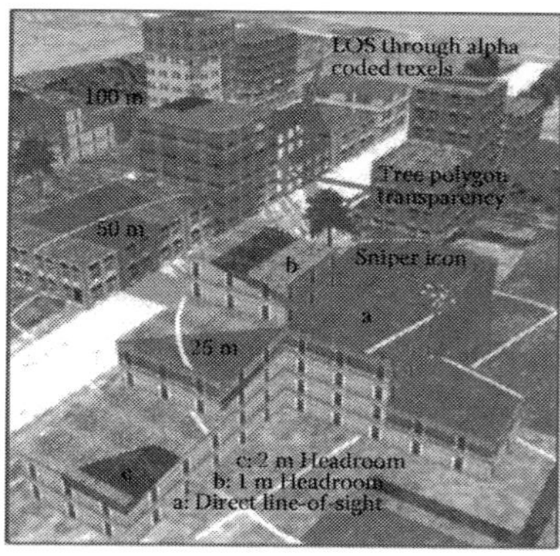

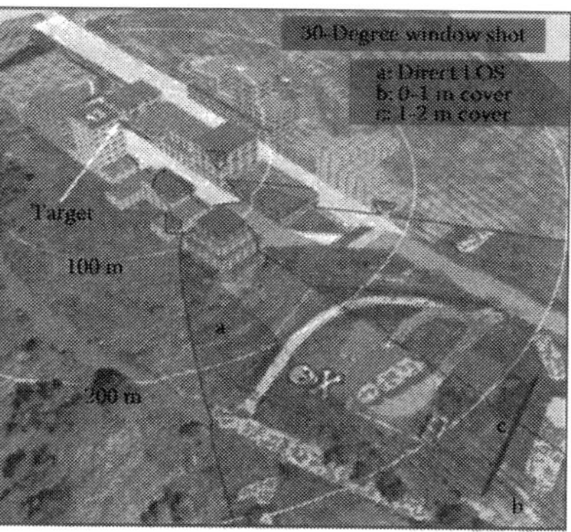

Figure 20.8 NRL–designed software for viewshed analysis in preparation for combat situations. U.S. Navy Research Laboratory. (n.d.). Navy Sniper/Counter-Sniper™: 3D Lines of Sight Mission Planning Software. (From G. F. Hepner and R. M. Medina, *The Geography of International Terrorism: An Introduction to Spaces and Places of Violent Non-state groups*, CRC Press, 2013. With permission.)

data must include physical terrain and built environment obstacles (see Figure 20.12 later in the text). Physical terrain data are available in the form of digital elevation models, and built environment data can be obtained by either manually inputting information for obstacle (buildings, walls, bridges, etc.) heights or acquiring remotely sensed data, such as light detection and ranging (Lidar) products. The data are then input into a GIS and a viewshed model is constructed using advanced algorithms. The output from a viewshed model approximates the LoS view from the selected vantage point.[32]

The Naval Research Laboratory (NRL) has developed software for use in mission planning/training and combat simulation. The potential benefits of this software in the field are clear. Safe and dangerous regions can be mapped for troops in combat situations and potential sniper/IED placement based on the best LoS can be identified in any region with geospatial data. Figure 20.8 is a screenshot from the NRL designed software, Navy Sniper/Counter-Sniper™: 3D Lines of Sight Mission Planning Software.[33]

Applications for viewshed analysis can be beneficial when used for mission planning and training. They give soldiers a visualization of regional coverage from sniper fire, which can lead to greater safety in combat situations. The greatest benefit from these types of tools, though, may be when they are utilized in the battlefield with potential for adaptive models that consider movement and number of snipers and counter snipers.

Consideration must also be given to the possible use of viewshed analysis, LoS models, and other geospatial technologies by terrorists. Undocumented reports of terrorist use of GIS and viewshed analysis for mission planning do exist. It is as beneficial for terrorists to use these tools to identify good locations for sniper placement as it is for counter sniper forces to find shelter from snipers—if not more so. In the situation in which the terrorists have more knowledge of the battlefield, this added information can make a big difference in the outcome of local conflict.

Global Positioning System

The GPS is a system of satellites launched by the Department of Defense that provide locational and navigation information with the combined use of a handheld or transportation-based

---

[32] J. E. VanHorn and N. A. Mosurinjohn. Urban 3D GIS Modeling of Terrorism Sniper Hazards. *Social Science Computer Review* 28, no. 4: 482–496, 2010.

[33] US Navy Research Laboratory. (n.d.). Navy Sniper/Counter-Sniper™: 3D Lines of Sight Mission Planning Software. Available at http://www.nrl.navy.mil/techtransfer/fs.php?fs_id=IT04.

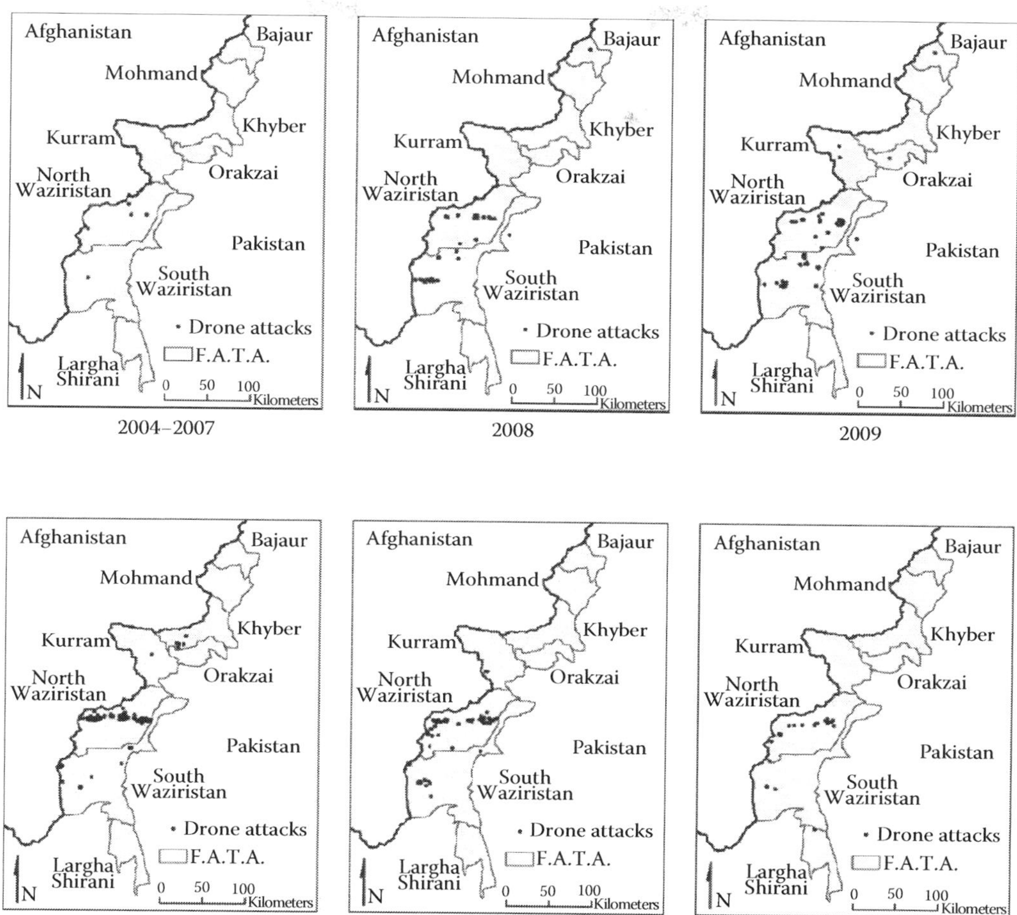

Figure 20.9 US drone attacks in Pakistan by year (2004–June 14, 2012). (Data from New America Foundation. The year of the drone: An analysis of US drone strikes in Pakistan, 2004–2012. Available from http://counterterrorism.newamerica.net/ drones, 2012. G. F. Hepner and R. M. Medina, *The Geography of International Terrorism: An Introduction to Spaces and Places of Violent Non-state groups*, CRC Press, 2013. With permission.)

receiver. GPS was originally a military venture but has since become a very successful commercial industry. GPS technologies tell one where one is, help one get where he or she wants to go, and, in the context of terrorism, helps those involved with targeting. The use of drones by the United States to target high-level Islamist terrorists remotely would not be possible without GPS technologies, which are embedded in warheads of all types.

Figure 20.9 shows the pattern of US drone targets in Pakistan from 2004 through June 14, 2012.[34] The majority of these targets have been within the FATA on the Pakistan/Afghanistan border. Many top leaders and other members of terrorist organizations, including al-Qaeda, the Taliban, and the Haqqani Network, have been killed by drone attacks, and while collateral damage exists, the accuracy of today's geospatial technologies can minimize those numbers.

[34] New America Foundation. The Year of the Drone: An Analysis of US Drone Strikes in Pakistan, 2004–2012. Available at http://counterterrorism.newamerica.net/drones, 2012.

GPS technologies will continue to be used by everybody and increasingly so as they are embedded into other location-based technologies and made more accurate. The main concern is that these technologies are easier to come by and more affordable. At some point, terrorists may use the same weapons against counterterrorist forces.

Remote Sensing

Remote sensing is defined as the "acquisition, processing, and interpreting of reflected electromagnetic radiation." It includes scanners on remote platforms, such as satellites, airplanes, unmanned aerial vehicles (UAVs), and ground-based in situ *sensors*; methods; and algorithms for the processing of spectral signal data into information.[35] Every chemical element and compound comprising our natural and human-made materials has a unique spectral identification or signature based on the manner in which specific forms of radiation are reflected by that material. These forms of radiation are actually portions of the electromagnetic spectrum, called spectral bands. Using this spectral signature approach, objects and features reflecting light in the visible portion of the spectrum can be seen with the human eye. For features and materials not having unique signatures in the visible portion, signatures in other parts of the spectrum can be discerned using spectrometers.

Remote sensing is used for many different applications including: navigation; identification of soils, vegetation, and urban areas; and detection of change in land cover/land use. For terrorism and counterterrorism activities, remote sensing is a valuable tool to acquire information from a secure location at a distance without risking lives on the ground. Remote sensing can be used for persistent surveillance, detection of change over time, identification of chemicals in the air, and a multitude of other related uses.

The most valuable application of remotely sensed imagery in terrorism and counterterrorism may simply be to visualize areas and features from a distance—to see terrain, land cover/land use types, human presence, complex urban areas, and transportation routes. Current commercially available imagery has 1 m spatial resolution, which means that objects or features on the ground that are larger than 1 m in size can be seen from a satellite 400 miles up in space. Military systems, such as the KH series of satellites, purportedly have a spatial resolution of 10 cm (4–5 in) or less. Smaller features can be delineated on aerial imagery from aircraft or UAVs, which have less areal coverage than a satellite. Remotely sensed images are used to generate realistic maps that provide more detail than is possible without air- or space-borne sensors. Also, because the platforms can be flown over the same points over time, changes in the landscape can be detected.

As sensors improve, the number of wavelengths recorded increases. Panchromatic sensors record only one value representative of the amount of reflected radiation. Multispectral sensors today record true color, infrared, and sometimes radar wavelengths of radiation. Hyperspectral sensors generally record more wavelengths than multispectral sensors, and they record them continuously (i.e., there are no gaps between the bands). The wavelengths collected by multispectral sensors are discrete. Both multispectral and hyper spectral sensors are capable of recording wavelengths that are not visible by the human eye. Other wavelengths of reflected radiation, such as infrared (near/mid/thermal IR), are detectable by sensors and assist in identifying land cover and other reflective objects that humans cannot see. Each surface has different reflectance characteristics.

Depending on the combination of bands used to produce an image, natural and human-made surfaces, such as vegetation, soils, gasses, buildings, and pavement, can be much easier to detect. Various arrangements of wavelength bands provide better visualizations for different types of ground cover. The more bands of data collected, the more detail of surface cover is provided.

All types of remotely sensed images are used for counterterrorism and security research—from panchromatic and natural color images of land use and land cover that show what is on the

---

[35] F. F. Sabins. *Remote Sensing: Principles and Interpretation*, Third Edition. New York: W. H. Freeman and Company, 1996.

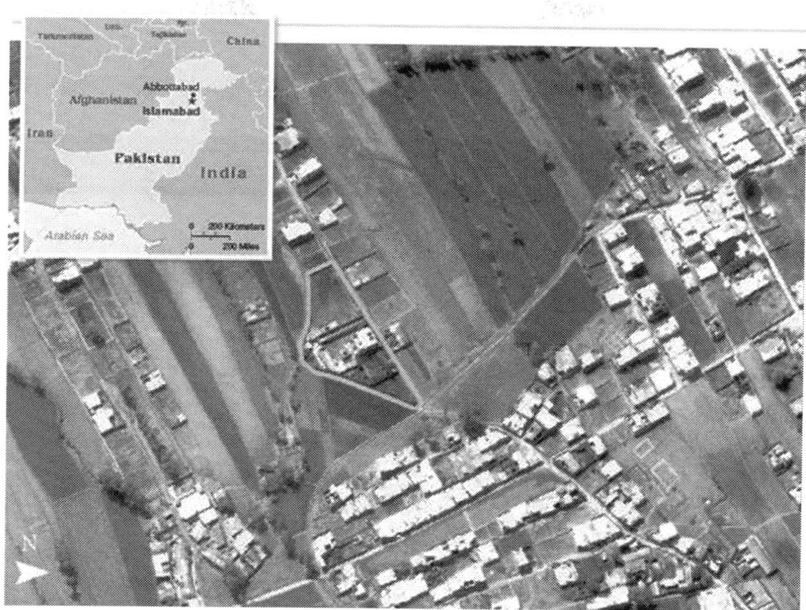

Figure 20.10 Osama bin Laden's compound, Abbottabad, Pakistan, 2011. (Courtesy of US Department of Defense. From G. F. Hepner and R. M. Medina, *The Geography of International Terrorism: An Introduction to Spaces and Places of Violent Non-state groups*, CRC Press, 2013. With permission.)

ground to terrain and elevation images that show barriers, passageways, and regions of cover to hyper spectral images that have the potential to detect agents of chemical and bioterrorism. Remotely sensed images are used in counterterrorism operations, such as the US Navy Seal raid of the bin Laden compound in Abbottabad, Pakistan, in 2011 (Figures 20.10 and 20.11) and drone targeting, also in Pakistan. If used over periods of time, sensors can be used to detect change on the ground, where triggers for conflict, such as environmental hazards, may be detected early. The ability to identify regions of hazardous climate change with knowledge of population vulnerabilities can assist in predicting future regions of conflict.

With remotely sensed images over periods of time, it is possible to detect changes in land use. Change detection has many uses, especially when combined with other geospatial information. An example of change detection is given in Figure 20.11, where Osama bin Laden's compound is shown before (2004) and after (2011) construction. Other applications of change detection for terrorism security are locating regions of internally displaced persons through temporary residence structures, locating construction of new weapons of mass destruction facilities, and identifying environmental changes that can result in regional conflicts.

Remotely sensed imagery is used for emergency management purposes: to detect hazards, vulnerable populations, escape routes, and safe zones. Following 9/11, remotely sensed images were used for many applications. Figure 20.12 shows the 9/11 ground zero site from different scales and through a Lidar sensor. Using images like these, emergency responders are able to identify damages, potential dangers, distribution of debris, and passageways and barriers. Some thermal band images were used by 9/11 responders, but onsite temperature sensors proved more useful.[36]

---

[36] C. K. Huyck and B. J. Adams. Remote Sensing in Response to September 11th. *Proceedings of the 2003 ESRI User Conference*, July 7–11. San Diego, CA, 2003.

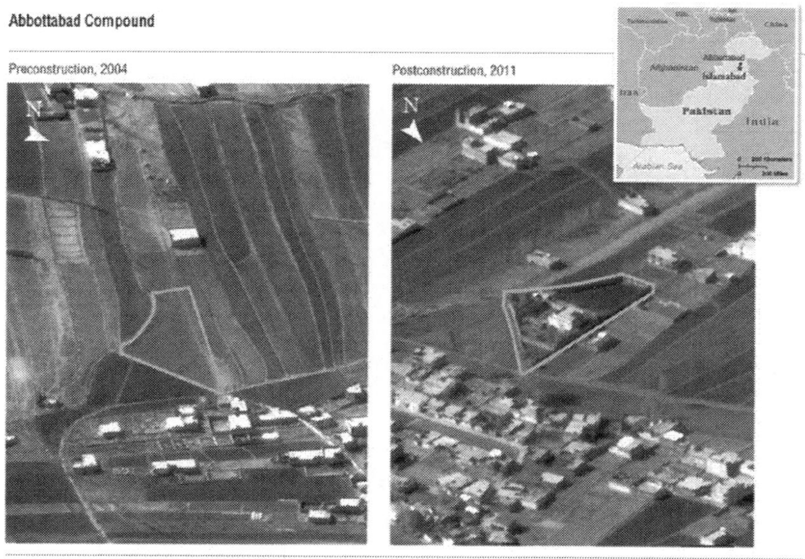

Figure 20.11 Construction of Osama bin Laden's compound. (Courtesy of US Department of Defense. From G. F. Hepner and R. M. Medina, *The Geography of International Terrorism: An Introduction to Spaces and Places of Violent Non-state groups*, CRC Press, 2013. With permission.)

Figure 20.12 Lidar images of ground zero. (From the National Oceanic and Atmospheric Administration, 2001. From G. F. Hepner and R. M. Medina, *The Geography of International Terrorism: An Introduction to Spaces and Places of Violent Non-state groups*, CRC Press, 2013. With permission.)

Figure 20.13 Zhawar Kili Al-Badr camp (west), Afghanistan. (Courtesy of US Department of Defense. From G. F. Hepner and R. M. Medina, *The Geography of International Terrorism: An Introduction to Spaces and Places of Violent Non-state groups*, CRC Press, 2013. With permission.)

One of the present-day concerns with remote sensing is the concept of *information from pixels* or *imagery-to-information*. Remotely sensed images are used to provide a visual of the ground and are available for most of the world and at many different times although at various resolutions. These images are now included in many free services provided by software companies, such as Google and Microsoft, as a background for map and direction/routing applications.

However, as useful as the remotely sensed visuals are, there is a need to extract more information from the images in defense and security efforts. Scientists and researchers are focusing more on what information they can extract from the images. This process benefits from the inclusion of other geospatial data, such as demographics, infrastructure, and economic data. For example, Figure 20.13 shows a terrorist training camp in Afghanistan taken in the 1990s. It would be beneficial for counterterrorist operations to know how many attendees the camp had, where they were from, the types of training activities being used, and the intended targets, if any. This information may be available based on the resolution, amount of detail provided, number of recorded wavelengths (also called bands) of the sensor, and knowledge of human geography.

Volunteered Geographic Information and Data Mining

The term "volunteered geographic information" (VGI) was first introduced by Goodchild in 2007. VGI is geographic information provided by users and can either be focused on a goal of producing a specific result, such as with mapping efforts to fill holes in data, or volunteered as locational information with no purpose in the mind of the volunteer, such as with geotagging[37] of digital photos. These two sources of volunteered information are termed here *intentionally* and *unintentionally* volunteered information, respectively.

[37] Geotagging refers to the added locational information, typically into digital media although the concept of geotagging could be applied to non-digital media just as effectively.

Intentionally volunteered information is a straightforward concept. It describes the process of users choosing to share geographic information with the intention that others will utilize the volunteered information for a specific application. Unintentional volunteered information refers to user information that is collected by communications tools, software applications, digital photos, or other information technologies and used without the volunteer knowing of the specific applications the information is being used for. Even though users may not have any motivation to share their geographic information, it can be collected as a contractual agreement upon initiating use of the technology or as a function of the specific technology. This type of information can be used by those collecting the information for many uses, including traffic data, individual spatial pattern data, emergency management research, and many other uses.

Most people today understand that they are sharing and, to some extent, volunteering geographic information for multiple uses. This is the result of information and communication technologies. Recent years have made some paranoid that their locational information is being harvested by cell phone companies and web applications even though large amounts of geographic information are intentionally volunteered on social networking and other communication websites and shared with the world.

Both terrorists and counter terrorists can use VGI in activities as simple as navigating to a targeted location or as complex as identifying a target based on user posts about the characteristics of specific locations. In many cases, terrorists and supporters have been open about their intentions and offer detailed geographic information in online forums and other websites. By tracking these posts over time, counterterrorist organizations can identify regions of potential conflict, threat, and, with added geographic and sociocultural data, vulnerabilities.

Information can also be mined from digital media, especially when geotagged and time coded although many times detailed spatiotemporal information is provided by the content itself. Photos and videos are now uploaded to the web at large scales and can be mined for pertinent counter terrorism and human/physical geography information. Mining of spatiotemporal data can also be used in emergency preparedness activities previous to and following terrorist attacks. Information collected on human movement patterns, which is possible through the harvesting of cell phone data, can provide knowledge of movement preferences and other environmental attributes.

The ubiquity of VGI allows for extraction of geographic information through *data mining*.[38] Data mining by counterterrorist organizations can be used to identify spatiotemporal patterns in terrorist and other radical activities and sentiments. Results of data mining do not provide an indication of why phenomena are related, but only that they are related. In this way, it is possible to detect human behavior that precedes a terrorist attack. Why that behavior precedes the attack is not initially necessary information; however, to understand the motivations and activities behind terrorist attacks completely, understanding correlations between phenomena are key.

Mobile Phones and the Ubiquity of Spatial Information and Tools

The use of mobile phones and other information technologies is ubiquitous in the information age even in areas where communications technologies were previously limited by physical or economic constraints. Mobile phones are used by many in countries that could not construct infrastructure to support landline phone services. Mobile communications infrastructure is more affordable, so in a technology sense, landline communications were "leapfrogged" by new technologies in many parts of the world.[39] For example, the number of households in Kenya with

[38] Data mining (also referred to as knowledge discovery) is the gathering of data through the use of software and algorithms. It is used to find and analyze patterns in large databases or other data sets, online and offline.

[39] R. Hahn and P. Passell. How Cell Phones Are Boosting Kenya's Economy. *US News*, Economic Intelligence Section, April 12, 2012. Available at http://www.usnews.com/opinion/.blogs/economic-intelligence/2012/04/12/how-cell-phones-are-boosting- kenyas-economy.

a phone increased from 3% in 1990 to 93% in 2011.[40] In many socially and physically vulnerable places in the world, the cell phone is the primary form of communication other than face-to-face, and if signals are not jammed or restricted, the users will have access to the Internet and other technologies.

No longer does one have to own an expensive GPS unit or be tethered to a desktop computer to access valuable locational/relative locational information. Smart phones today provide access through wireless networks to the World Wide Web and contain GPS technologies with an increasing accuracy. Even with the GPS capabilities switched off, mobile phone locations can be tracked by phone tower triangulation although with less accuracy. These phones can be considered geospatial tools. Mobile applications, termed apps, provide tools to do just about anything the user needs.

Ultimately, mobile phones increase access to communications and information and especially geospatial information. They are much more than just phones. These tools provide terrorists greater opportunities for operational efficiency and communications when carrying out an attack. Much of the geospatial technologies discussed here are accessible on a smart phone and may be built in when the phone is purchased. Real-time navigation and relative geographies are available and may assist terrorists in adapting to situations and escaping authorities. Mobile phones can be used as remote detonators and tracking tools to keep a close eye on operations and, when paired with GIS, GPS, and remote sensing, become much more powerful for operations.

Mobile phones can be used to receive and distribute social media to mobilize populations and organize movements. Social media are becoming a much more powerful tool as seen with instances in the Arab Spring in Egypt, Tunisia, and other regions. In the right setting, social media networks can be used to mobilize people for violence, send early warnings, and maintain social connectedness. In these ways, social media postings can be seen as high-tech smoke signals accessible to anyone with a smart phone.

Geosensors and Geosensor Networks

Geosensors are instruments that detect physical properties and changes in specific geographic regions. They can be used to record radiation reflectance as with remote sensing; to detect seismic activity; or to detect quantities of biological, chemical, or nuclear agents. This section is introducing sensors on the ground and not those that are air- or space-borne. When on the ground, sensors are connected in networks and in communication with each other, and the potential for complex information results is increased as is the accuracy of moving object readings. Today's networked sensors have increased capabilities for data processing, pattern detection, and decision making although this is not required.

Geosensor networks are used as counterterrorism tools for early detection of chemical, biological, radiological, or nuclear (CBRN) terrorist attacks. Combined with terrain, weather, land use/land cover, and sensor data, the release of a CBRN agent can be detected, tracked, and modeled. With early detection, the risk to vulnerable populations is greatly decreased as evacuations can begin and those incoming can be deterred. Examples of geosensor networks for counterterrorism are the joint biological remote early warning system (JBREWS) for biological agent detection and tracking by the Lawrence Livermore National Laboratory (LLNL)[41] and the wide area tracking system (WATS) for the detection and tracking of nuclear material, also by LLNL.

In battlefield situations, sensors can be placed and operated through use of UAVs as illustrated in Figure 20.14. In this figure, the sensors are dropped by UAVs in rugged terrain. The network is formed autonomously by the sensors, and information is projected skyward back to

[40] G. Demombynes and A. Thegeya. Kenya's Mobile Revolution and the Promise of Mobile Savings. Policy Research Working Paper 5988, The World Bank, Africa Region. Poverty Reduction and Economic Management Unit, 2012.

[41] Lawrence Livermore National Laboratory. Sensing for Danger: Correlated Sensor Networks Can Help Fight against Nuclear Terrorism and Other Threats, *Science and Technology Review*, July/August 2001.

Figure 20.14 Placement and operation of sensor networks by UAV. (From Lawrence Livermore National Laboratory. Sensing for danger: Correlated sensor networks can help fight against nuclear terrorism and other threats, *Science and Technology Review*, July/August 2001. G. F. Hepner and R. M. Medina, *The Geography of International Terrorism: An Introduction to Spaces and Places of Violent Non-state groups*, CRC Press, 2013. With permission.)

the UAVs. Humans can be used as sensors. Presently, volunteered information on websites, such as Twitter, is mined for geolocated information and key terms. Geolocated Google searches are used to identify global influenza patterns.[42] As more information and more detailed information are offered over time online, the potential for valuable results from mining is increased. Future technologies may see sensor networks in major cities throughout the world and mobile phones used as dynamic sensors so that sensors are anywhere people are.

Use of Geospatial Data/Information and Tools by Terrorists

While geospatial data/information and tools provide great benefits for counterterrorist activities, they also provide terrorists with useful information when organizing attacks. The same general benefits exist for both terrorist and counterterrorist sides: increased information and high-level geospatial detail. Terrorists use geospatial data for target selection and planning. Initial planning for attacks benefits from the visualization of places through geospatial data, but a more detailed account of the location and environment benefits more from "ground truthing" or visiting the potential attack site in person for a firsthand account. Terrorists have been known to visit the attack site before the actual attack for "dry runs" to get a better feel for the area and attack processes. However, in the initial target selection and mission planning stages, geospatial information can be invaluable.

The enhanced information age threat from the use of geospatial technologies for terrorism is from a combined use of GIS, GPS, and remote sensing. Google Earth alone is a powerful tool for terrorism, but when it is combined with GPS, new possibilities arise. For example, precise locations for a target based on latitude and longitude coordinates can be found using Google Earth, and a location-based detonator with an integrated GPS can be set to trigger the explosives upon

[42] For more information, see http://www.google.org/flutrends.

arrival at the target. This would ensure that suicide bombers hit their target with no hesitation by simplification of the bombing process. Bombs such as these could be placed on children, animals, modes of transportation, etc. Terrorists use cell phone GPS, laser range-finding GPS units, and Google Earth to get exact coordinates of target sites for attack. In the future, it is a possibility that terrorists may be able to buy or build missiles with GPS-based guidance systems onboard where the target coordinates need only be entered. This would give terrorists longer range and greater payload capabilities.

There have been incidents when terrorists have used geospatial data for attacks and, for coordinated attacks now, this is probably the norm. Knowledge of a potential attack location and its surrounding environment can ensure that navigations are efficient and that the target is actually reached. Location and navigation technologies are incorporated into many aspects of everyday living, so it is no surprise that they are used for attack organization.

There have been multiple cases of terrorists using freely available geospatial information. For example, Google Earth images were used to attack British military bases in Basra, Iraq, leading to one death and several injuries. The most vulnerable structures for attack within the bases, such as tents, were identified by insurgents. Google was cooperative with government concerns and removed the images from the Internet. However, the efforts were futile as the images had already been archived and printed. Versions were being distributed for attacks against the British bases. Printouts were confiscated from Iraqi insurgents.[43,44] Other examples include the al-Aqsa Martyrs Brigade incorporating Google Earth images with other maps for rocket strike target selection in Israel from Gaza[45] and Google Earth images being used extensively by Lashkar-e-Taiba for the 2008 Mumbai attacks in India.[46]

Google Earth images and imagery from other geospatial data servers are used by terrorists because they are more up to date than paper maps, provide more detail, include many attributes of the physical and human environment, have the precision necessary for different types of attacks, and are easily and freely accessible. Terrorists are benefiting from detailed topography and land use information, which includes buildings, roads, and other aspects of relative geography as well as user-volunteered photographs linked to locations where even more detail is offered, such as building identifiers and other text and heights of walls and fences for potential escape routes.

Figure 20.15 shows the Google Maps account of the Mumbai attacks generated by users with each attack site marked and information given for each attack. Digital photos of the area following the attacks are also included. One can imagine that the terrorists identified these locations previous to the attacks and used an image like this for planning and organization purposes. This image most likely looks very similar to the one the terrorists used in November 2008.

Future online geospatial applications, such as Google Earth, will only become more detailed. The next step for Google, it seems, is the incorporation of within-building navigation capabilities in their proposed Google Maps Floor Plans. This detail, already described as offering information on shopping malls and airports, could be used as a tool for terrorist attacks. One of the most interesting and probably unexpected examples of targeted attack facilitated by geospatial information is when four AH-64 Apache helicopters were destroyed by mortar attack in Iraq as a result of soldiers taking pictures of the new arrival of the fleet and posting them online. The

---

[43] K. Hearn. Terrorist Use of Google Earth Raises Security Fears. *National Geographic News*. March 12, 2007. Available at http://newsnationalgeographic.com/news/2007/03/070312-google-censor.html.

[44] T. Harding. Terrorists Use Google Maps to Hit UK Troops. *The Telegraph*, World Section. January 13, 2007. Available at http://www.telegraph.co.uk/news/worldnews/1539401/Terrorists-use-Google-maps-to-hit-UK-troops.html.

[45] C. Chassay and B. Johnson. Google Earth Used to Target Israel. *The Guardian*, World News Section. October 24, 2007. Available at http://www.guardian.co.uk/technology/.2007/oct/25/google.israel.

[46] How Google Earth Helped Mumbai Attackers. Times of India, December 19, 2008. Available at http://articles.timesofindia.indiatimes.com/2008-12-19/india/27909393_1_mumbai-.police-lashkar-terroriststerror-strike.

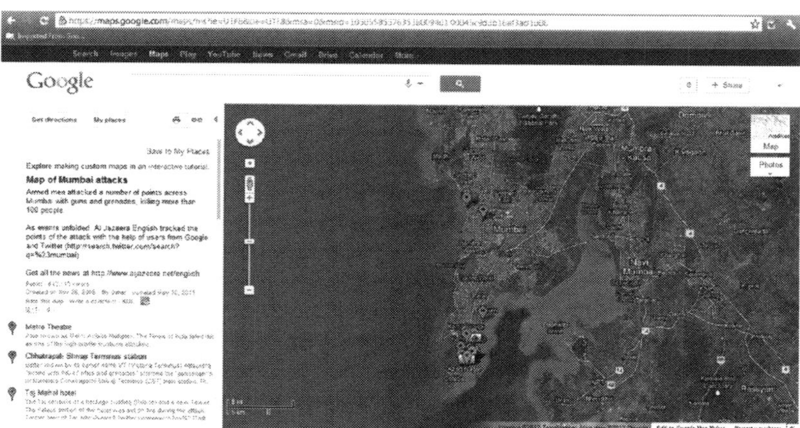

Figure 20.15 Google Maps: user-generated content for the 2008 Mumbai attacks in India. (From G. F. Hepner and R. M. Medina, *The Geography of International Terrorism: An Introduction to Spaces and Places of Violent Non-state groups*, CRC Press, 2013. With permission.)

digital photos were embedded with relatively accurate locational information (geotagged) used by insurgents to attack the precise location of the helicopters.[47]

Criteria for Publicly Available Geospatial Information

There is always a question as to what and how much geospatial data should be made public. Much available geospatial data can be used for terrorist attacks, but its usefulness may be minimal. While restricting access to some geospatial data may reduce the terrorist threat, the pros and cons must be weighed before removing these data from open sources. These same maps, images, and attribute data are useful for private sector business, civilian government, and citizens for economic development, disease monitoring, agricultural assistance, transportation, and emergency response in many nations where these data are the only support for critical decisions. In many totalitarian nations, maps are one of the most controlled types of information. In addition, how much control should government have over the flow of all types of information? As has been noted, access to information provides power to citizens and ensures transparency in democratic nations. In a study for the US government, Baker et al. developed three general guidelines to follow when deciding to restrict access to geospatial data and information.[48] The guidelines address the usefulness, uniqueness, and benefits and costs of the geospatial data in question.

The specific data set must be evaluated as to its usefulness to terrorists for mission reconnaissance, mission planning, organization, and targeting purposes. If the data are found not to be useful for violent activities, there is minimal need to remove them from the open source. Some geospatial data are very detailed and therefore can prove to be dangerous if utilized by terrorists. Aeronautical charts and many maps of critical infrastructure have been removed from the

[47] C. Rodewig. Geotagging Poses Security Risks. *US Army News Article*, March 7, 2012. Available at http://www.army.mil/article/75165/Geotagging_poses_security_risks/.

[48] J. C. Baker, B. E. Lachman, D. R. Frelinger, K. M. O'Connell, A. C. Hou, M. S. Tseng, D. Orletsky, and C. Yost. *Mapping the Risks: Assessing the Homeland Security Implications of Publicly Available Geospatial Information*. Santa Monica, CA: RAND Corporation, 2004.

Internet. Also, modifications are useful to remove critical information from maps and imagery but still provide the map and imagery to the public. Examples include removal of critical facilities from satellite imagery before its release on the Internet.

The second criterion for control of geospatial data/information involves the uniqueness of the data set. If a geospatial data set is important and unique (meaning that terrorists cannot get the same information elsewhere), it should be controlled. For example, a satellite image showing an airbase is not unique if that same airbase is shown on multiple public sources.

The final criterion considers the societal costs and benefits of restricting access to the geospatial data in question. Data sets that may be of some value for terrorist activities may be useful for public and/or private sector operations. The benefits of these data to the public enterprise may be evaluated against the actual risk of terrorist use. This does not imply that usefulness and uniqueness of data for legal use should limit the restriction of those data, but that the costs and benefits should be weighed before restriction.[49]

Concluding Thoughts

The concept of geospatial intelligence is not new although some of the geospatial technologies introduced here are. Maps have been used for every contemporary conflict, but geospatial intelligence has become more technologically advanced over the years. The transition into fourth-generation warfare does not change the need for geospatial intelligence; rather, it enhances it. Terrorist elements are more difficult to identify and find than state-based troops. They can move within, between, and around political and social boundaries that would stop their state counterparts. And the world today is changing much faster socially and physically than it has in the past.

The military understands the importance of spatial knowledge and human geography. When comparing these maps with the potential for analysis and visualization possible with today's GIS, GPS, and remote sensing technologies, it is clear that capabilities are greatly improved, but the key concepts of space, place, people, topologies, and activities remain. There is no substitute for geospatial knowledge in counterterrorism.

The present focus on geospatial intelligence and human geography is necessary for effective counterterrorism. International terrorism today is much more complex than the state-to-state conflicts of the past. Counterterrorist forces have more to do now than just win battles. They must also win over hearts and minds or at least not lose them to terrorists. This requires sociocultural understanding, which levels the field of communications between counterterrorist troops and elements of the ambient population. Sociocultural capabilities teamed with geospatial intelligence will continue to help counterterrorist forces connect with local people and save lives at home and in the field. All types of sociocultural information are important and new geospatial methods, tools, and techniques must be constructed for future counterterrorist activities.

Geospatial intelligence and technologies provide a great benefit for counterterrorism, but one should not forget that they provide terrorists with similar benefits of spatial knowledge for planning and strategy. The ease of access makes today's geospatial information and technologies a good starting point for terrorists. In the foreseeable future, there will be a trade-off between security and progress due to the distribution of geographic information.

---

[49] J. C. Baker, B. E. Lachman, D. R. Frelinger, K. M. O'Connell, A. C. Hou, M. S. Tseng, D. Orletsky, and C. Yost. *Mapping the Risks: Assessing the Homeland Security Implications of Publicly Available Geospatial Information*. Santa Monica, CA: RAND Corporation, 2004.

Appendix A: Glossary of Global Terrorist Groups

Acronym/English Name (Foreign Language Name)/Country/Area of Operations

AA: The Partisans' League (Asbat al-Ansar)/Lebanon/National
ABB: Alex Boncayao Brigade/Philippines/National
ACCU: Peasant Self-Defense Group of Cordoba and Uraba/Colombia/National
ADF: Allied Democratic Forces/Uganda/Transnational
AF: Eagle (Al Faran)/India and Pakistan/Transnational
AF: Sword of Al Fatah (Al-Fatah/Al-'Asifa)/Israel and Palestine/Transnational
AH: Iron (Al Hadid)/India and Pakistan/Transnational
AIAI: Ethiopian Islamic Union (Al-Ittihad al-Islami)/Ethiopia/National
AIAI: Somali Islamic Union (al-Ittihad al-Islami)/Somalia/National
AIS: Islamic Salvation (Front Armee Islamique du Salut)/Algeria/National
AISSF: All India Sikh Student Federation/India/National
ALIR: Army for the Liberation of Rwanda/Interahamwe DR Congo/National
AN: Aryan Nations/United States/National
ANO: Abu Nidal Organization/Israel and Palestine/Transnational
AQ: The Base or Headquarters of the World or the Islamic Front for Jihad against the Jews and Crusaders (Al-Qaeda)/Globally International
ARGK: People's Liberation Army of Kurdistan/Turkey/National
ARIF: Arakan Rohingya Islamic Front/Myanmar/National
ASG: Abu Sayyaf Group (Abu Sayyaf)/Philippines/Transnational
ASP: Anarchist Street Patrol/Greece/National
ATTF: All Tripura Tiger Force/India/National
AUC: United Self-Defense Forces/Group of Colombia/Colombia/National
AUM: Aum Supreme Truth (Aum Shinrikyo)/Japan/Transnational
AVC: Alfaro Vive, Carajo/Ecuador/National
AWB: Afrikaaner Resistance Movement (Afrikaaner Weestand Beweeging)/South Africa/National
BK: Babbar Khalsa/India/ National
BLA: Bavaria Liberation Army/Austria/National
BLT: Bodo Liberation Tigers/India/National
BOF: Brethren of the Faithful (Islamic Change Org)/Saudi Arabia/National
BSF: Bodo Security Force/India/National
CA: Conscientious Arsonists/Greece/National
CAC: Continuity Army Council/United Kingdom/National
CFF: Cambodian Freedom Fighters/Cambodia/National
CIRA: Continuity Irish Republican Army/United Kingdom/National
CNDD: National Council for the Defense of Democracy/Burundi/National
COES: Special Operations Commandoes (Comandos Operativos Especiales)/Honduras/National
DFLP: Democratic Front for the Liberation of Palestine (Jebha Demorasi lil Tahrir al Filistin)/ Israel and Palestine/International
DHKP: C/Revolutionary People's Liberation Party/Front, Dev Sol (Devrimci Halk Kurtulus Partisi/Cephesi, Devrimici Sol)/Turkey/National

DK: Army of the Pure (Dal Khalsa)/India/National
DKBA: Democratic Karen Buddhist Army/Myanmar/National
DPIK: Democratic Party of Kurdish/Iran/National
DR: Tenth Regiment (Dashmesh Regiment)/India/National
DRFLA: Democratic Revolutionary Front for the Liberation of Arabistan/Iran/Transnational
EIJ: Egyptian Islamic Jihad al-Jihad/Egypt/International
EJI: Justice Army of the Defenseless People (Ejercito Justicia de los Indefensos)/Mexico/National
ELA: Revolutionary Popular Struggle (Epanastikos laikos Agonas)/Greece/National
ELN: National Liberation Army (Ejercito de Liberacion Nacional)/Colombia/National
EPL: Popular Liberation Army (Ejercito Popular de Liberacion)/Colombia/National
EPLF: Eritrean People's Liberation Front/Eritrea/National
EPR: Popular Revolutionary Army (Ejercito Popular revolucionario)/Mexico/National
ERNK: National Liberation Front of Kurdistan (Eniya Rizgariya Netewa Kurdistan)/Turkey/National
ETA: Basque Fatherland and Liberty (Euzkadi Ta Askatasuna)/Spain/National
EZLN: Zapatista National Liberation Army (Ejercito Zapatistas de Liberacion Nacional)/Mexico/National
F-17: Force 17 Israel/Palestine/National
FAA: Fighting Ansar of Allah (Islamic Change Organization cover name)/Saudi Arabia/National
FALN: Armed Forces of National Liberation (Fuerzas Armadas de Liberacion Nacional)/United States/National
FAR: Revolutionary Armed Front (Frente Armadas Revolucionarias)/Nicaragua/National
FARC: Revolutionary Armed Forces of Colombia (Fuerzas Armadas Revolucionarias de Colombia)/Colombia/Transnational
FARF: Armed Forces of the Federal Republic (Forces Armées pour la Republique Federale)/Chad/National
FDD: Forces for the Defense of the Democracy (Forces por la Defense de la Democratie)/Burundi/National
FGF: Fighting Guerilla Formation/Greece/National
FIGL: Fighting Islamic Group in Libya/Libya/National
FLEC-FAC: Cabindan Liberation Armed Forces (FLEC-Forcas Armadas Cabindesas)/Angola/National
FLEC-R: Liberation Front for the enclave of Cabinda-Renovada Frente de Libertacao do Enclave de Cabinda-Renovada/Angola/National
FLNC: National Liberation Front of Corsica (Front de la Liberation Nationale de la Corse)/France/National
FNL: National Liberation Front (Forces Nationales de Liberation)/Burundi/National
FNT: Chadian National Front (Front Nationale du Tchad)/Chad/National
FNTR: National Front for the Renewal of Chad (Front Nationale pour le Tchad Renovee)/Chad/National
FPMR: Manuel Rodriguez Patriotic Front (Frente Patriotico Manuel Rodrigue)/Chile/National
FRETILIN: Revolutionary Front for an Independent East Timor (Frente Revolucionaria Timorense de Libertacao e Independencia)/Indonesia/National
FRF: Ricardo Franco Front (Frente Ricardo Franco)/Colombia/National
FRU: Front for the Restoration and Unity of Democracy (Front pour la Restoration d'Unite et Democratie-Dini)/Djibouti/National
GAI: GI/IG/Islamic Group (Al-Gama'a al-Islamiyya)/Egypt/International
GAM: Free Aceh Movement (Gerakin Aceh Merdeka)/Indonesia/National
GIA: Armed Islamic Group (Groupe Islamique Armee)/Algeria/International
GRAPO: First of October Anit-Fascist Resistance Group (Grupo de Resistencia Antifascista Primero de Octubre)/Spain/National
GSPC: Salafist Group for Call and Combat/Algeria/National

HAMAS: Islamic Resistance Movement (HAMAS)/Israel and Palestine/National
HIZB: Party of God (Hezbollah)/Lebanon/International
HUJI: Movement of Islamic Holy War (Harakat ul-Jihad-i Islami)/India and Pakistan/Transnational
HUJI: B/Movement of Islamic Holy War (Harakat ul-Jihad-i Islami/Bangladesh)/Bangladesh/National
HUM: Movement of Holy Warriors (Harakat ul-Mujahideen)/India and Pakistan/Transnational
IA: Islamic Amal/Lebanon/Transnational
IAA: Islamic Army of Aden/Yemen/National
IC: Islamic Call Al-Dawa al-Islamiya/Iraq/International
IFLB: Islamic Front for the Liberation of Bahrain/Bahrain/National
IJ: Islamic Jihad/Israel and Palestine/Transnational
IJH: Islamic Jihad in Hejaz/Saudi Arabia/National
IMC: Islamic Movement for Change/Libya/National
IMM: Islamic Movement of Martyrs/Libya/National
IMM: Islamic Martyrs Movement/Libya/National
IMU: Islamic Movement of Uzbekistan/Uzbekistan/National
INLA: Irish National Liberation Army/United Kingdom/National
INTERA: Interhamwe Interahamwe/Rwanda/National
IPMC-JW: Islamic Peninsula Movement for Change-Jihad Wing (Islamic Change Org cover name)/Saudi Arabia/National
IRO: Islamic Revolutionary Organization/Saudi Arabia/National
JAA: Islamic Change Organization cover name (Jamaat al-Adala al-Alamiya)/Saudi Arabia/National
JEM: Army of Mohammed Jaish-e-Mohammed/Pakistan/Transnational
JIM: Islamic Group of Malaysia (Jemaah Islamiya)/Malaysia/National
JMB: Jordanian Muslim Brotherhood/Jordan/National
JRA: Japanese Red Army (Nippon Sekigun)/Japan/International
JVP: People's Liberation Front (Janatha Vimukthi Peramuna)/Sri Lanka/National
KA: Karenni Arm/Myanmar/National
KACH: Kach (Only Thus) Group/Israel and Palestine/International
KC: Kahane Lives! (Kachane Chai)/Israel and Palestine/USA/International
KDP: Kurdistan Democratic Party/Iraq/Transnational
KLA: Kosovo Liberation Army/Yugoslavia/National
KLF: Khalistan Liberation Front/India/National
KMM: Malaysian Mujahideen of Kumpulan (Kumpulan Mujahidin Malaysia)/Malaysia/National
KNLA: Karen National Liberation Army/Myanmar/National
KOMALA: Kurdish Communist Party of Iran/Iran/National
KR: Red Khmer (Khmer Rouge)/Cambodia/National
LEO: Omar Forces (Laskar-e-Omar)/Pakistan/National
LJM: Libyan Jihad Movement/Libya/National
LLA: Laos Liberation Army/Laos/National
LMAH: Legion of the Martyr Abduallah al-Huzaifi (Islamic Change Organization cover name)/Saudi Arabia/National
LNLF: Lao National Liberation Front/Laos/National
LRA: Lords Resistance Army/Sudan/Transnational
LT: Army of the Righteous (Lashkar-e-Tayyiba)/Pakistan/Transnational
LTTE: Liberation Tigers of Tamil Eelam/Sri Lanka/National
LVF: Loyalist Volunteer Force/United Kingdom/National
MAIB: Movement for the Self-determination of the Island of Bioko (Movimiento para la Autodeterminacion de la Isla de Bioko)/Equitorial Guinea/National
MEK: MKO/National Liberation Army of Iran (Mujahideen-e-Khalq)/Iran/Transnational

MFDC: Casamance Democratic Movement Force Mouvement des Forces Democratiques de la Casamance/Senegal/National
MFUA: United Azaoud Movements and Fronts (Mouvements et Fronts Unifies de l'Azaoud)/Mali/National
MGF: Militant Guerrilla Formation/Greece/National
MIC: Movement for Islamic Change/Saudi Arabia/National
MILF: Moro Islamic Liberation Front/Philippines/National
MLB: Movement for the Liberation of Bahrain/Bahrain/National
MRTA: Tupac Amaru Revolutionary Movement (Movimiento Revolucionario Tupac Amaru)/Peru/National
NDA: National Democratic Alliance/Sudan/National
NDF: National Democratic Front/Philippines/National
NDFB: National Democratic Front of Bodoland/India/National
NF: National Front/Iran/National
NIM: National Islamic Movement (Jumbish-i-Milli)/Afghanistan/National
NIPR: Revolutionary Proletarian Initiative Nuclei/Italy/National
NLFT: National Liberation Front of Tripura/India and Pakistan/National
NPA: New People's Army/Philippines/National
NSCN: National Socialist Council of Nagaland/India/National
NTA: Anti-Imperialist Territorial Nuclei/Italy/National
OV: Orange Volunteers/United Kingdom/National

Appendix B: US/Domestic-Based Terrorist Organizations

Information comes from Jonathan R. White, *Terrorism: An Introduction*, Wadsworth Publishing, Florence, KY; MILNET website (http://www.milnet.com); ADL website (http://www.adl.org); SPLC website (http://www.splcenter.org); and the individual groups' websites.[1]

1. *American Coalition for Life Activists*. Based in Oregon; founded by Andrew Burnett, a long-time antiabortionist activist whose group endorses the justifiable homicide of abortion clinic doctors.
2. *Animal Liberation Front*. Support groups are based throughout North America; in 1993, the group reportedly planted arson or incendiary devices in four Chicago stores; based on its Web site, it does not condone violence, and membership only carries out direct action by whatever means necessary.
3. *Army of God*. Highly militant antiabortion movement that believes God has given them the duty to kill abortionists; it allegedly claimed responsibility for a number of abortion clinic bombings in Georgia and Alabama; financially affiliated with Glory to Jesus Ministries in Virginia.
4. *Aryan Nation* (aka Aryan Republican Army and Aryan National Alliance). Base of operation is located in Hayden Lake, Idaho; categorized as white supremacists, Christian Identity group; founded by Richard Butler in the mid-1970s; believe that it is its duty to populate the country with member's progeny through polygamy; allegedly seek to overthrow the American government using bank robberies as an end to their means; ideology follows Christian Identity, neo-Nazi, and paramilitary.
5. *Branch Davidians*. Thought to be an extinct operation; during their height of operation, they had bases of operation in Utah and Texas; considered by some to be a form of a cult, they are primarily firearms protestors.
6. *Christian Identity Movement*. Chapters are in approximately 18 states with an estimated 31 groups; alleged members were convicted of conspiracy to manufacture explosives; they are considered to be antiabortion and anti-banking, and they depict Jews as biologically descended from Satan.
7. *Citizens of the Republic of Idaho*. Based in St. Maries, Idaho; founded by Hari Heath; members do not believe in the bureaucracy of the US courts and government; therefore, they created their own; considered to be relatively docile.
8. *Colorado First Light Infantry*. Alleged members were charged with possessing and manufacturing illegal firearms; group publicly supports Timothy McVeigh's actions and the Oklahoma City bombing on April 19, 1995.
9. *Colorado Militia*. Based in Aurora, Colorado; professed goals are those of weapons rights.
10. *Covenant* (aka Sword and Arm of the Lord). Christian identity group started in 1971 by James Ellison on the Arkansas/Missouri state line; based in Arkansas; considered to be a violent white supremacist group with close ties to members of the Ku Klux Klan.

[1] See M. R. Ronczkowski. *Terrorism and Organized Hate Crime: Intelligence Gathering, Analysis, and Investigations*, CRC Press, 2003.

11. *Earth Liberation Front* (ELF) (aka North American ELF). Alleged members were linked to attacks against the US Forest Service, logging companies, and bioengineering corporations; group is categorized as ecological activists.

12. *Evan Mecham Eco-Terrorist International Conspiracy* (EMETIC). Formed in 1985; satirically uses the name of an Arizona governor; the group is known for spiking trees and various forms of sabotage.

13. *Freeman*. Based in Montana; group members believe the US legal system is not valid; supports an internal separatist government; alleged members were convicted for fraud and robbery; categorized as a right-wing group.

14. *Ku Klux Klan*. Categorized as a white supremacy group established during the Civil War era, December 1865; the group is primarily active in the South but allegedly has membership in approximately 28 different states with an estimated membership base of 5500 to 6000 in just over 100 different groups; subgroups go by various names including Invisible Empire, Knights of the Ku Klux Klan, United Klans of America, and the National Knights of the Ku Klux Klan.

15. *Los Macheteros*. Marxist-Leninist group formed in 1976 but emerged publicly in 1978; it wants Puerto Rico to be an independent nation; name translation means "machete wielders" or "cane cutters"; Puerto Rican revolutionary group based in Puerto Rico and operating in several northeastern states, including New York; members allegedly detonated explosives in New York and committed homicides; members are also known for their many publicly claimed robberies in the early 1980s, including one for $7.1 million in Connecticut.

16. *Michigan Militia*. Formed in April 1994 by a firearm store owner named Norman Olson and real-estate agent Ray Southwell; categorized as a large weapons rights, survivalist, and militant antigovernment organization; no major illegal activity was directly traced to this group's membership; membership was reported as high as 12,000.

17. *Militia of Montana* (MOM). Founded in February 1994 by John, David, and Randy Trochmann; categorized as a weapons rights and militant antigovernment organization; encourages members to arm themselves with guns and knives; no major illegal activity has been directly traced to this group's membership; paramilitary militia.

18. *Mountaineer Militia*. Based in West Virginia; categorized as paramilitary, antigovernment, and weapons rights organization; alleged leader was convicted in August 1997 for conspiracy to engage in the manufacture of explosives.

19. *National Alliance*. Founded by William Pierce, author of *The Turner Diaries*, in Hillsboro (Mill Point), West Virginia in 1974; categorized as a white supremacist and neo-Nazi organization; leader is Erich Gliebe.

20. *North American Militia of Southwestern Michigan*. Categorized as a paramilitary, antigovernment, and weapons rights organization.

21. *Patriot's Council*. Based in Minnesota; categorized as a violent antigovernment and tax protest organization; the group allegedly created ricin, a toxic nerve agent.

22. *Phineas Priesthood*. Inspired by the book *The Vigilantes of Christendom* by Richard Hoskins; group membership opposes homosexuality, abortions, and interracial marriages; members have allegedly committed bank robberies and abortion clinic bombings.

23. *Posse Comitatus*. Founded by Henry Beach in the early 1970s; name is Latin for power of the county; categorized as anti-Semitic and as a white supremacist organization; chapters were established in almost every state of the union and have had ties with the Arizona Patriots.

24. *Reclaim the Seeds*. Categorized as an anti-biotechnology organization; members allegedly claimed responsibility for a 2000 attack on crops at Seminis Vegetable Seeds Research Center and the Davis campus of the University of California.

25. *Republic of Texas*. Based in the Davis Mountains in West Texas; alleged leader is Richard McLaren; the organization contends that Texas was illegally annexed into the union in 1845 and that it remains an independent nation.

26. *Southern California Minuteman*. Group is allegedly against the influx of illegal aliens into the US from Mexico and has used snipers to control them.

27. *The Order* (aka The New Order). Based in Oregon, Illinois, and Michigan; founded by the late Robert Mathews; categorized as a right-wing, white supremacist, neo-Nazi, racist, and anti-Semitic group; followed by and affiliated with such groups as the Silent Brotherhood and Strike Force II.

28. *Viper Militia*. Based in Arizona; categorized as a paramilitary and antigovernment organization; allegedly had ties with Timothy McVeigh; trained to make illegal weapons and construct and detonate fertilizer bombs.

29. *World Church of the Creator*. Founded in 1973 and headquartered in Riverton, Wyoming; also based in East Peoria, Illinois; alleged leader is Matt Hale; categorized as a white supremacist group.

Appendix C: Foreign Terrorist Organizations

The foreign organization details listed here are from the Country Reports on Terrorism provided by the US Department of State.* These are not the only foreign-based terrorist organizations in existence; they are just the predominant and most active ones.

Abu Nidal Organization

aka ANO; Arab Revolutionary Brigades; Arab Revolutionary Council; Black September; Fatah Revolutionary Council; Revolutionary Organization of Socialist Muslims

Description: Designated as a Foreign Terrorist Organization on October 8, 1997, the Abu Nidal Organization (ANO) was founded by Sabri al-Banna (aka Abu Nidal) after splitting from the Palestine Liberation Organization (PLO) in 1974. In August 2002, Abu Nidal died in Baghdad. Present leadership of the organization remains unclear. ANO advocates the elimination of Israel and has sought to derail diplomatic efforts in support of the Middle East peace process.

Activities: The ANO has carried out terrorist attacks in 20 countries, killing or injuring almost 900 persons. It has not staged a major attack against Western targets since the late 1980s and was expelled from its safe haven in Libya in 1999. Major attacks included those on the Rome and Vienna airports in 1985, the Neve Shalom synagogue in Istanbul, the hijacking of Pan Am Flight 73 in Karachi in 1986, and the City of Poros day-excursion ship attack in Greece in 1988. The ANO was suspected of assassinating PLO Deputy Chief Abu Iyad and PLO Security Chief Abu Hul in Tunis in 1991 and a senior Jordanian diplomat in Beirut in 1994. In 2008, a Jordanian official reported the apprehension of an ANO member who planned to carry out attacks in Jordan. The ANO did not attempt or successfully carry out attacks in 2011.

Strength: Current strength is unknown.

Location/Area of Operation: Former and current ANO associates are presumed present in Lebanon.

External Aid: The ANO's current access to resources is unclear, but it is likely that the decline in support previously provided by Libya, Syria, and Iran has had a severe impact on its capabilities.

Abu Sayyaf Group

aka al Harakat al Islamiyya (the Islamic Movement)

Description: The Abu Sayyaf Group (ASG) was designated as a Foreign Terrorist Organization on October 8, 1997. ASG is the most violent of the terrorist groups operating in the Philippines and claims to promote an independent Islamic state in western Mindanao and the Sulu Archipelago although the goals of the group appear to have vacillated over time between criminal objectives and a more ideological intent. The group split from the much larger Moro Islamic Liberation Front (MILF) in the early 1990s under the leadership of Abdurajak Abubakar Janjalani, who was killed in a clash with Philippine police in December 1998. In 2011, Radullah Sahiron was ASG's leader.

* US Department of State. Country Reports on Terrorism. July 2012. Available at http://www.state.gov/documents/organization/195768.pdf.

Activities: The ASG engages in kidnappings for ransom, bombings, beheadings, assassinations, and extortion. In April 2000, an ASG faction kidnapped 21 people, including 10 Western tourists, from a resort in Malaysia. In May 2001, the ASG kidnapped three US citizens and 17 Filipinos from a tourist resort in Palawan, Philippines. Several of the hostages, including US citizen Guillermo Sobero, were murdered. A Philippine military hostage rescue operation in June 2002 freed US hostage Gracia Burnham, but her husband, US national Martin Burnham, and Filipina Deborah Yap were killed. US and Philippine authorities blamed the ASG for a bomb near a Philippine military base in Zamboanga in October 2002 that killed a US serviceman. In one of the most destructive acts of maritime violence, the ASG bombed SuperFerry 14 in Manila Bay in February 2004, killing at least 116 people. In 2011, ASG remained active, particularly with kidnappings for ransom, an increase in the use of improvised explosive device (IED) attacks, and armed attacks on civilian and police personnel. In 2011, ASG took close to 20 people hostage, including children, in multiple attacks, an increase over the previous year. In January, an IED killed five civilians and wounded 13 others in Makati. In March, five civilians were killed and 10 others were injured in an IED attack in Jolo. In June, a police officer was killed in Sulu; and in September, a soldier, a paramilitary member, and four civilians—including a child—were killed in an armed attack by the ASG in Basilan. Two American citizens, a mother and son, were kidnapped in July near Zamboanga. The mother was released in October while her son managed to escape custody in December. In addition, authorities believed ASG was responsible for the following attacks for which no group claimed responsibility: 1) a January 10 attack in Basilan when armed assailants fired upon a group, killing five people; 2) a September 27 attack in Basilan when 15 armed assailants fired upon a village, killing six, wounding five, and damaging the village; and a November 27 attack in Zamboanga when assailants detonated an IED inside the Atilano Pension House, killing three civilians, injuring 25 others, and damaging the hotel.

Strength: ASG is estimated to have between 200 and 400 members.

Location/Area of Operation: The ASG operates primarily in the provinces of the Sulu Archipelago, namely Basilan, Sulu, and Tawi-Tawi. The group also operates on the Zamboanga Peninsula, and members occasionally travel to Manila.

External Aid: The ASG is funded through kidnapping for ransom and extortion and may also receive funding from external sources, such as remittances from overseas Filipino workers and Middle East–based extremists. The ASG also receives funding from regional terrorist groups, such as Jemaah Islamiya, whose operatives have provided training to ASG members and helped facilitate several ASG terrorist attacks.

al-Aqsa Martyrs Brigade

aka al-Aqsa Martyrs Battalion

Description: Designated as a Foreign Terrorist Organization on March 27, 2002, the al-Aqsa Martyrs Brigade (AAMB) is composed of an unknown number of small cells of Fatah-affiliated activists that emerged at the outset of the al-Aqsa Intifada in September 2000. Al-Aqsa's goal is to drive the Israeli military and West Bank settlers from the West Bank in order to establish a Palestinian state loyal to the Fatah.

Activities: Al-Aqsa employed primarily small-arms attacks against Israeli military personnel and settlers as the intifada spread in 2000, but by 2002, they turned increasingly to suicide bombings against Israeli civilians inside Israel. In January 2002, the group claimed responsibility for the first female suicide bombing inside Israel. In 2010, AAMB launched numerous rocket attacks on communities in Israel, including the city of Sederot and areas of the Negev desert. AAMB has not pursued a policy of targeting US interests although its anti-Israeli attacks have killed dual US–Israeli citizens. In December 2011, AAMB launched rockets aimed at communities in the Negev. The attack caused no injuries or damage.

Strength: A few hundred members.

Location/Area of Operation: Most of al-Aqsa's operational activity is in Gaza, but the group also planned and conducted attacks inside Israel and the West Bank. The group also has members in Palestinian refugee camps in Lebanon.

External Aid: Iran has exploited al-Aqsa's lack of resources and formal leadership by providing funds and guidance, mostly through Hizballah facilitators.

Ansar al-Islam

aka Ansar al-Sunna; Ansar al-Sunna Army; Devotees of Islam; Followers of Islam in Kurdistan; Helpers of Islam; Jaish Ansar al-Sunna; Jund al-Islam; Kurdish Taliban; Kurdistan Supporters of Islam; Partisans of Islam; Soldiers of God; Soldiers of Islam; Supporters of Islam in Kurdistan

Description: Designated as a Foreign Terrorist Organization on March 22, 2004. Ansar al-Islam's (AI's) goals include expelling the Western interests from Iraq and establishing an independent Iraqi state based on Sharia law. AI was established in 2001 in Iraqi Kurdistan with the merger of two Kurdish extremist factions that traced their roots to the Islamic Movement of Kurdistan. On May 4, 2010, Abu Abdullah al-Shafi'i, Ansar al-Islam's leader was captured by US forces in Baghdad and remains in prison. On December 15, 2011, AI announced a new emir, Sheikh Abu Hashim Muhammad bin Abdul Rahman al Ibrahim.

Activities: AI has conducted attacks against a wide range of targets, including the Iraqi government and security forces, and US and Coalition forces. AI has conducted numerous kidnappings, executions, and assassinations of Iraqi citizens and politicians. The group has either claimed responsibility or is believed to be responsible for attacks in 2011 that killed 24 and wounded 147 people. On February 7, AI posted leaflets in Kirkuk warning of an attack on a Kurdish militia in retaliation for the arrest of Muslim women in the city. Two days later, a series of car bombs exploded in Kirkuk, destroying the militia's headquarters and injuring two nearby police patrols. The attack killed 10 and wounded 90. On October 13, 16 civilians and two police officers were killed and 43 others wounded in a double improvised explosive device attack in Baghdad. The group was also responsible for kidnappings in February and December.

Strength: Although precise numbers are unknown, AI is considered one of the largest Sunni terrorist groups in Iraq.

Location/Area of Operation: Primarily northern Iraq but maintained a presence in western and central Iraq.

External Aid: AI received assistance from a loose network of associates in Europe and the Middle East.

Army of Islam

aka Jaysh al-Islam; Jaish al-Islam

Description: Designated a Foreign Terrorist Organization on May 19, 2011, the Army of Islam (AOI) is a Gaza-based terrorist organization founded in late 2005 that has been responsible for numerous terrorist acts against the Governments of Israel and Egypt as well as American, British, and New Zealander citizens. AOI is led by Mumtaz Dughmush and operates in Gaza. It subscribes to a Salafist ideology together with the traditional model of armed Palestinian resistance. AOI has previously worked with Hamas and is attempting to develop closer al-Qa'ida contacts.

Activities: AOI's terrorist acts include a number of rocket attacks on Israel, the 2006 kidnapping of two journalists in Gaza (an American and a New Zealander), and the 2007 kidnapping of a British citizen, journalist Alan Johnston, in Gaza. AOI is also responsible for early 2009 attacks on Egyptian civilians in Cairo and Heliopolis, Egypt. AOI is alleged to have planned the January 1,

2011, Alexandria attack on a Coptic Christian church that killed 25 and wounded 100. On May 7, 2011, the group released a eulogy for Usama bin Ladin via its Al Nur Media Foundation.

Strength: Membership estimates range in the low hundreds.

Location/Area of Operation: Gaza, with attacks in Egypt and Israel.

External Aid: AOI receives the bulk of its funding from a variety of criminal activities in Gaza.

Asbat al-Ansar

aka Asbat al-Ansar; Band of Helpers; Band of Partisans; League of Partisans; League of the Followers; God's Partisans; Gathering of Supporters; Partisan's League; AAA; Esbat al-Ansar; Isbat al-Ansar; Osbat al-Ansar; Usbat al-Ansar; Usbat ul-Ansar

Description: Designated as a Foreign Terrorist Organization on March 27, 2002, Asbat al-Ansar is a Lebanon-based Sunni extremist group composed primarily of Palestinians with links to al-Qa'ida (AQ) and other Sunni extremist groups. Some of the group's stated goals include thwarting perceived anti-Islamic and pro-Western influences in the country, although the group remains largely confined to Lebanon's refugee camps.

Activities: Asbat al-Ansar first emerged in the early 1990s. In the mid-1990s, the group assassinated Lebanese religious leaders and bombed nightclubs, theaters, and liquor stores. The group has also plotted against foreign diplomatic targets. In October 2004, Mahir al-Sa'di, a member of Asbat al-Ansar, was sentenced, in absentia, to life imprisonment for his 2000 plot to assassinate then-US Ambassador to Lebanon David Satterfield. Asbat al-Ansar has no formal ties to the AQ network, but the group shares AQ's ideology and has publicly proclaimed its support for al-Qa'ida in Iraq. Members of the group have traveled to Iraq since 2005 to fight coalition forces. Asbat al-Ansar has been reluctant to involve itself in operations in Lebanon due in part to concerns over losing its safe haven in Ain al-Hilwah. AAA did not stage any successful attacks in 2011.

Strength: The group has fewer than 2000 members, mostly of Palestinian descent.

Location/Area of Operation: The group's primary base of operations is the Ain al-Hilwah Palestinian refugee camp near Sidon in southern Lebanon. The group is also in Iraq, where it has engaged in fighting US and coalition forces.

External Aid: It is likely that the group receives money through international Sunni extremist networks.

Aum Shinrikyo

aka A.I.C. Comprehensive Research Institute; A.I.C. Sogo Kenkyusho; Aleph; Aum Supreme Truth

Description: Aum Shinrikyo (Aum) was designated as a Foreign Terrorist Organization on October 8, 1997. Jailed leader Shoko Asahara established Aum in 1987, and the organization received legal status in Japan as a religious entity in 1989. The Japanese government revoked its recognition of Aum as a religious organization following Aum's deadly sarin gas attack in Tokyo in March 1995. Despite claims of renunciation of violence and Asahara's teachings, members of the group continue to adhere to the violent and apocalyptic teachings of its founder.

Activities: In March 1995, Aum members simultaneously released the chemical nerve agent sarin on several Tokyo subway trains, killing 12 people and causing up to 6000 to seek medical treatment. Subsequent investigations by the Japanese government revealed the group was responsible for other mysterious chemical incidents in Japan in 1994, including a sarin gas attack on a residential neighborhood in Matsumoto that killed seven and hospitalized approximately 500. Japanese police arrested Asahara in May 1995; in February 2004, authorities sentenced him to death for his role in the 1995 attacks. In September 2006, Asahara lost his final appeal against the death penalty and the Japanese Supreme Court upheld the decision in October 2007. In February 2010, the death sentence for senior Aum member Tomomitsu Miimi was finalized by Japan's Supreme Court. In 2011, the death sentences of Masami Tsuchiya, Tomomasa Nakagawa, and Seiichi Endo were affirmed by Japanese courts, bringing the number of Aum members on death row to 13. Since 1997, the group has recruited new members, engaged in commercial enterprises, and acquired property although it scaled back these activities significantly in 2001 in response to a public outcry. In July 2001, Russian authorities arrested a group of Russian Aum followers who had planned to detonate bombs near the Imperial Palace in Tokyo as part of an operation to free Asahara from jail and smuggle him to Russia. Although Aum has not conducted a terrorist attack since 1995, concerns remain regarding its continued adherence to the violent teachings of founder Asahara that led AUM to carry out the 1995 sarin gas attack.

Strength: According to a study by the Japanese government issued in December 2009, Aum Shinrikyo/Aleph membership in Japan is approximately 1500 with another 200 in Russia. As of November 2011, Aum continues to maintain 32 facilities in 15 Prefectures in Japan and may continue to possess a few facilities in Russia. At the time of the Tokyo subway attack, the group claimed to have as many as 40,000 members worldwide, including 9000 in Japan and 30,000 members in Russia.

Location/Area of Operation: Aum's principal membership is located in Japan; a residual branch of about 200 followers lives in Russia.

External Aid: Funding primarily comes from member contributions.

Basque Fatherland and Liberty

aka ETA, Askatasuna; Batasuna; Ekin; Euskal Herritarrok; Euzkadi Ta Askatasuna; Herri Batasuna; Jarrai-Haika-Segi; K.A.S.; XAKI

Description: Designated as a Foreign Terrorist Organization on October 8, 1997, Basque Fatherland and Liberty (ETA) was founded in 1959 with the aim of establishing an independent homeland based on Marxist principles encompassing the Spanish Basque provinces of Vizcaya, Guipuzcoa, and Alava; the autonomous region of Navarra; and the southwestern French territories of Labourd, Basse-Navarre, and Soule. Spain and the European Union have listed ETA as a terrorist organization. In 2002, the Spanish Parliament banned the political party Batasuna, ETA's political wing, charging its members with providing material support to the terrorist group. The European Court of Human Rights in June 2009 upheld the ban on Batasuna. In September 2008, Spanish courts also banned two other Basque independence parties with reported links to Batasuna. In 2010, Batasuna continued to try to participate in regional politics and splits between parts of ETA became publicly apparent in deciding a way forward.

Activities: ETA primarily has conducted bombings and assassinations. Targets typically have included Spanish government officials, businessmen, politicians, judicial figures, and security and military forces, but the group has also targeted journalists and tourist areas. The group is responsible for killing 829 civilians and members of the armed forces or police and injuring thousands since it formally began a campaign of violence in 1968. ETA has committed numerous attacks in the last four decades. Some of the group's high profile attacks include the February 2005 ETA car bombing in Madrid at a convention center where Spanish King Juan Carlos and then Mexican President Vicente Fox were scheduled to appear, wounding more than 20 people. In December 2006, ETA exploded a massive car bomb that destroyed much of the covered parking garage at Madrid's Barajas International Airport. ETA marked its 50th anniversary in 2009 with a series of high profile and deadly bombings including the July attack on a civil guard barracks that injured more than 60 people, including children. In March 2010, a Spanish judge charged ETA and Revolutionary Armed Forces of Colombia members of terrorist plots, including a plan to assassinate Colombian President Alvaro Uribe. Spanish authorities arrested more than 400 ETA members between 2007 and 2010 and have arrested an additional 52 in 2011. In 2011, in cooperation with international partners, Spanish security services arrested an additional 52 ETA member or associates. In April 2011, Spanish authorities seized 1600 kilos of bomb-making material while arresting three ETA members. In the same month, French police arrested two ETA members in Creuse, France, after they fired shots from their car and wounded a police officer while speeding through a police checkpoint. On July 7, 2011, Eneko Gogeaskoetxea, one of the alleged attempted assassins of King Juan Carlos I in 1997, was apprehended in the United Kingdom and is being held there pending extradition to Spain on several arrest warrants. The militarily weakened and politically isolated ETA, in October 2011, publicly announced a "definitive cessation" of armed activity. As the group has made and broken several past cease fires, Madrid rejected the latest announcement and continues to demand that ETA disarm and disband.

Strength: Estimates put ETA membership of those who have not been captured by authorities at fewer than 100. Spanish and French prisons together hold approximately 750 ETA members.

Location/Area of Operation: ETA operates primarily in the Basque autonomous regions of northern Spain and southwestern France but has attacked Spanish and French interests elsewhere. In previous years, ETA safe houses were identified and raided in Portugal. The group also maintains a low profile presence in Cuba and Venezuela.

External Aid: ETA is probably experiencing financial shortages given that the group announced publicly in September 2011 that it had ceased collecting "revolutionary taxes" from Basque businesses. This extortion program was a major source of ETA's income.

Communist Party of Philippines/New People's Army

aka CPP/NPA; Communist Party of the Philippines; the CPP; New People's Army; the NPA

Description: The Communist Party of the Philippines/New People's Army (CPP/NPA) was designated as a Foreign Terrorist Organization on August 9, 2002. The military wing of the Communist Party of the Philippines (CPP), the New People's Army (NPA), is a Maoist group formed in March 1969 with the aim of overthrowing the government through protracted guerrilla warfare. Jose Maria Sison, the chairman of the CPP's Central Committee and the NPA's founder, reportedly directs CPP and NPA activity from the Netherlands, where he lives in self-imposed exile. Luis Jalandoni, a fellow Central Committee member and director of the CPP's overt political wing, the National Democratic Front (NDF), also lives in the Netherlands and has become a Dutch citizen. Although primarily a rural-based guerrilla group, the NPA had an active urban infrastructure to support its terrorist activities and, at times, used city-based assassination squads.

Activities: The CPP/NPA primarily targeted Philippine security forces, government officials, local infrastructure, and businesses that refused to pay extortion, or "revolutionary taxes." The CPP/NPA charged politicians running for office in CPP/NPA–influenced areas for "campaign permits." Despite its focus on Philippine governmental targets, the CPP/NPA has a history of attacking US interests in the Philippines. In 1987, the CPP/NPA conducted direct action against US personnel and facilities, killing three American soldiers in four separate attacks in Angeles City. In 1989, the CPP/NPA issued a press statement taking credit for the ambush and murder of Colonel James Nicholas Rowe, chief of the Ground Forces Division of the Joint US Military Advisory Group. For many years, the CPP/NPA carried out killings, raids, acts of extortion, and other forms of violence. In May 2010, 40 CPP/NPA guerillas ambushed an army convoy escorting election officials in the Compostela Valley, an attack that culminated in five deaths; and 40 CPP/NPA assailants launched a synchronized landmine improvised explosive device and light arms attack against a police vehicle on August 21 that resulted in nine deaths in Cataman, Philippines. In 2011, the CPP/NPA's attacks and kidnappings continued unabated. In January, the CPP/NPA was responsible for detonating a landmine IED in Illuro Sur, Philippines, that killed five and injured two police officers. In February, two civilians were killed when 50 CPP/NPA assailants fired upon a police checkpoint in Trento, Philippines. In August, the CPP/NPA kidnapped the mayor of Lingig, Philippines, and two of his bodyguards. The group demanded a prisoner swap before releasing the hostages in October.

Strength: The Philippines government estimates there are 5000 members.

Location/Area of Operations: The CPP/NPA operates in rural Luzon, Visayas, and parts of northern and eastern Mindanao. There are also cells in Manila and other metropolitan centers.

External Aid: The CPP raises funds through extortion.

Continuity Irish Republican Army

aka Continuity Army Council; Continuity IRA; Republican Sinn Fein

Description: Designated as a Foreign Terrorist Organization on July 13, 2004, the Continuity Irish Republican Army (CIRA) is a terrorist splinter group formed in 1994 as the clandestine armed wing of the Republican Sinn Fein; it split from Sinn Fein in 1986. "Continuity" refers to the group's belief that it is carrying on the original Irish Republican Army's (IRA) goal of forcing the British out of Northern Ireland. CIRA cooperates with the larger Real IRA (RIRA).

Activities: CIRA has been active in Belfast and the border areas of Northern Ireland, where it has carried out bombings, assassinations, kidnappings, hijackings, extortion, and robberies. On occasion, it provided advance warning to the police of its attacks. Targets have included the British military, Northern Ireland security forces, and Loyalist paramilitary groups. CIRA did not join the Provisional IRA in the September 2005 decommissioning and remained capable of effective, if sporadic, terrorist attacks. On April 21, 2011, authorities defused an explosive device planted by CIRA near a statue of the Duke of Wellington in Trim, Meath, Ireland.

Strength: Membership is small, with possibly fewer than 50 hard-core activists. Police counterterrorist operations have reduced the group's strength. In June, the CIRA may have experienced further splintering when hard-liners made an apparently unsuccessful attempt to take over the leadership of the group.

Location/Area of Operation: Northern Ireland and the Irish Republic.

External Aid: CIRA supported its activities through criminal activities, including smuggling. CIRA may have acquired arms and material from the Balkans, in cooperation with the RIRA.

Gama'a al-Islamiyya

aka al-Gama'at; Egyptian al-Gama'at al-Islamiyya; GI; Islamic Gama'at; IG; Islamic Group

Description: Gama'a al-Islamiyya (IG) was designated as a Foreign Terrorist Organization on October 8, 1997. Once Egypt's largest militant group, IG was active in the late 1970s but is now a loosely organized network and formed the Building and Development political party that competed in the 2011 parliamentary elections, winning 13 seats. Egypt-based members of IG released from prison prior to the revolution have renounced terrorism although some members located overseas have worked with or joined al-Qa'ida (AQ). Hundreds of members who may not have renounced violence were released from prison in 2011. The external wing, composed of mainly exiled members in several countries, maintained that its primary goal was to replace the Egyptian government with an Islamic state. IG's spiritual leader, Sheik Umar Abd al-Rahman, is serving a life sentence in a US prison for his involvement in the 1993 World Trade Center bombing. Supporters of Sheikh Abd al-Rahman still remain a possible threat to US interests and have called for reprisal attacks in the event of his death in prison.

Activities: In the 1990s, IG conducted armed attacks against Egyptian security and other government officials and Coptic Christians. IG claimed responsibility for the June 1995 assassination attempt on Egyptian President Hosni Mubarak in Addis Ababa, Ethiopia. The group also launched attacks on tourists in Egypt, most notably the 1997 Luxor attack. In 1999, part of the group publicly renounced violence. There were no known terrorist attacks by the IG in 2011.

Strength: At its peak, IG likely commanded several thousand hardcore members and a similar number of supporters. Security crackdowns following the 1997 attack in Luxor and the 1999 cease fire along with post-September 11 security measures and defections to AQ have probably resulted in a substantial decrease in what is left of an organized group.

Location/Area of Operation: The IG maintained an external presence in Afghanistan, Yemen, Iran, the United Kingdom, Germany, and France. IG terrorist presence in Egypt was minimal due to the reconciliation efforts of former local members.

External Aid: Unknown.

Hamas

aka the Islamic Resistance Movement; Harakat al-Muqawama al-Islamiya; Izz al-Din al Qassam Battalions; Izz al-Din al Qassam Brigades; Izz al-Din al Qassam Forces; Students of Ayyash; Students of the Engineer; Yahya Ayyash Units; Izz al-Din al-Qassim Brigades; Izz al-Din al-Qassim Forces; Izz al-Din al-Qassim Battalions

Description: Designated as a Foreign Terrorist Organization on October 8, 1997, Hamas possesses military and political wings and came into being in late 1987 at the onset of the first Palestinian uprising, or Intifada, as an outgrowth of the Palestinian branch of the Muslim Brotherhood. The armed element, called the Izz al-Din al-Qassam Brigades, conducts anti-Israeli attacks, including suicide bombings against civilian targets inside Israel. Hamas also manages a broad, mostly Gaza-based network of "Dawa" or ministry activities that include charities, schools, clinics, youth camps, fund-raising, and political activities. After winning Palestinian Legislative Council elections in January 2006, Hamas gained control of significant Palestinian Authority (PA) ministries in Gaza, including the Ministry of Interior. Hamas subsequently formed an expanded militia called the Executive Force, subordinate to the Interior Ministry. This force and other Hamas cadres took control of Gaza in a violent confrontation with Fatah in June 2007, forcing Fatah forces to leave Gaza or go underground. A Shura Council based in Damascus, Syria, set overall policy, but the group began leaving Damascus in late 2011 following a disagreement with the Syrian government over its use of violence against protestors.

Activities: Prior to 2005, Hamas conducted numerous anti-Israeli attacks, including suicide bombings, rocket launches, improvised explosive device (IED) attacks, and shootings. Hamas has not directly targeted US interests although the group has conducted attacks against Israeli targets frequented by foreigners. The group curtailed terrorist attacks in February 2005 after agreeing to a temporary period of calm brokered by the PA and ceased most violence after winning control of the PA legislature and cabinet in January 2006. After Hamas staged a June 2006 attack on Israeli Defense Forces soldiers near Kerem Shalom that resulted in two deaths and the abduction of Corporal Gilad Shalit, Israel took steps that severely limited the operation of the Rafah crossing. In June 2007, after Hamas took control of Gaza from the PA and Fatah, the Gaza borders were closed and Hamas increased its use of tunnels to smuggle weapons into Gaza, using the Sinai and maritime routes. Hamas has since dedicated the majority of its activity in Gaza to solidifying its control, hardening its defenses, tightening security, and conducting limited operations against Israeli military forces. Hamas fought a 23-day war with Israel from late December 2008 to January 2009. Since Israel's declaration of a unilateral ceasefire on January 18, 2009, Hamas has largely enforced the calm, focusing on rebuilding its weapons caches, smuggling tunnels, and other military infrastructure in Gaza. Throughout 2011, Hamas carried out rocket attacks on Southern Israel. In March, an IED attack that was attributed to Hamas wounded a government employee in Jerusalem. In April, Hamas fired an anti-tank missile at a school bus, killing an Israeli teenager. Over the course of 2011, Hamas kidnapped approximately 20 Palestinian civilians and 30 political party members in Gaza. Hamas also actively worked against violent Salafi groups in Gaza during 2011, including pursuing the Army of Islam leader and elements of the Palestinian terrorist group Jaljalat, who they perceive as a threat to their control of Gaza and ceasefire with Israel.

Strength: Several thousand Gaza-based operatives with varying degrees of skills in its armed wing, the Izz al-Din al-Qassam Brigades; along with its reported 9000-person Hamas-led paramilitary group known as the "Executive Force."

Location/Area of Operation: Hamas has a presence in every major city in the Palestinian territories. The group retains a cadre of leaders and facilitators who conduct political, fundraising, and arms-smuggling activities throughout the region. Hamas also increased its presence in the Palestinian refugee camps in Lebanon, probably with the goal of eclipsing Fatah's long-time dominance of the camps.

External Aid: Hamas receives funding, weapons, and training from Iran. In addition, the group raises funds in the Persian Gulf countries and receives donations from Palestinian expatriates around the world through its charities, such as the Union of Good. Some fundraising and propaganda activity takes place in Western Europe.

Harakat-ul Jihad Islami

aka HUJI, Movement of Islamic Holy War; Harkat-ul-Jihad-al Islami; Harkat-al-Jihad-ul Islami; Harkat-ul-Jehad-al-Islami; Harakat ul Jihad-e-Islami; Harakat-ul Jihad Islami

Description: Designated as a Foreign Terrorist Organization on August 6, 2010, Harakat-ul Jihad Islami (HUJI) was founded in 1980 in Afghanistan to fight against the Soviet Union. Following the Soviet withdrawal from Afghanistan in 1989, the organization refocused its efforts on India. HUJI seeks the annexation of Indian Kashmir and expulsion of Coalition Forces from Afghanistan. It also has supplied fighters for the Taliban in Afghanistan. In addition, some factions of HUJI espouse a more global agenda and conduct attacks in Pakistan as well. HUJI is composed of militant Pakistanis and veterans of the Soviet-Afghan war. HUJI has experienced a number of internal splits and a portion of the group has aligned with al-Qa'ida (AQ) in recent years, including training its members in AQ training camps. Mohammad Ilyas Kashmiri, one of HUJI's top leaders who also served as an AQ military commander and strategist, was killed on June 3, 2011.

Activities: HUJI has been involved in a number of terrorist attacks in recent years. On March 2, 2006, a HUJI leader was the mastermind behind the suicide bombing of the US Consulate in Karachi, Pakistan, which killed four people, including US diplomat David Foy, and injured 48 others. HUJI was also responsible for terrorist attacks in India, including the May 2007 Hyderabad mosque attack, which killed 16 and injured 40, and the March 2007 Varanasi attack, which killed 25 and injured 100. HUJI claimed credit for the September 7, 2011 bombing of the New Delhi High Court, which left at least 11 dead and an estimated 76 wounded. HUJI sent an email to the press stating that the bomb was intended to force India to repeal a death sentence of a HUJI member.

Strength: HUJI has an estimated strength of several hundred members.

Location/Area of Operations: HUJI's area of operation extends throughout South Asia with its terrorist operations focused primarily in India and Afghanistan. Some factions of HUJI conduct attacks within Pakistan.

External Aid: Unknown.

Harakat ul-Jihad-I-Islami/Bangladesh

aka HUJI-B, Harakat ul Jihad e Islami Bangladesh; Harkatul Jihad al Islam; Harkatul Jihad; Harakat ul Jihad al Islami; Harkat ul Jihad al Islami; Harkat-ul-Jehad-al-Islami; Harakat ul Jihad Islami Bangladesh; Islami Dawat-e-Kafela; IDEK

Description: Designated as a Foreign Terrorist Organization on March 5, 2008, Harakat ul-Jihad-i-Islami/Bangladesh (HUJI-B) was formed in April 1992 by a group of former Bangladeshi Afghan veterans to establish Islamic rule in Bangladesh. In October 2005, Bangladeshi authorities banned the group. HUJI-B has connections to Pakistani militant groups, such as Lashkar e-Tayyiba (LeT) and the Indian Mujahedeen (IM), which advocate similar objectives. The leaders of HUJI-B signed the February 1998 fatwa sponsored by Usama bin Ladin that declared American civilians legitimate targets.

Activities: In December 2008, three HUJI-B members were convicted for the May 2004 grenade attack that wounded the British High Commissioner in Sylhet, Bangladesh. In 2011, Bangladeshi authorities formally charged multiple suspects, including HUJI-B leader Mufti Abdul Hannan, with the killing of former Finance Minister Shah AMS Kibria of Awami League (AL) in a grenade attack on January 27, 2005. Bangladeshi police also arrested many top HUJI-B leaders in 2011, including Amir Rahmatullah (aka Sheikh Farid) in April, and chief Moulana Yahiya in August. Bangladeshi police recovered arms, explosives, and bomb making materials following the arrest of HUJI-B operative Abdul Alim in May.

Strength: HUJI-B leaders claim that up to 400 of its members are Afghan war veterans, but its total membership is unknown.

Location/Area of Operation: The group operates primarily in Bangladesh and India. HUJI-B trains and has a network of madrassas in Bangladesh.

External Aid: HUJI-B funding comes from a variety of sources. Several international Islamic non-governmental organizations may have funneled money to HUJI-B and other Bangladeshi militant groups.

Harakat ul-Mujahideen (HUM)

aka HUM; Harakat ul-Ansar; HUA; Jamiat ul-Ansar; JUA; Al-Faran; Al-Hadid; Al- Hadith; Harakat ul-Mujahidin

Description: Designated as a Foreign Terrorist Organization on October 8, 1997, Harakat ul-Mujahideen (HUM) seeks the annexation of Indian Kashmir and expulsion of Coalition Forces in Afghanistan. Reportedly under pressure from the government of Pakistan, HUM's long-time leader Fazlur Rehman Khalil stepped down and was replaced by Dr. Badr Munir as the head of HUM in January 2005. Khalil has been linked to Usama bin Ladin, and his signature was found on bin Ladin's February 1998 fatwa calling for attacks on US and Western interests. HUM operated terrorist training camps in eastern Afghanistan until Coalition air strikes destroyed them in 2001. Khalil was detained by Pakistani authorities in mid-2004 and subsequently released in late December of the same year. In 2003, HUM began using the name Jamiat ul-Ansar (JUA). Pakistan banned JUA in November 2003.

Activities: HUM has conducted a number of operations against Indian troops and civilian targets in Kashmir. It is linked to the Kashmiri militant group al-Faran, which kidnapped five Western tourists in Kashmir in July 1995; the five reportedly were killed later that year. HUM was responsible for the hijacking of an Indian airliner in December 1999 that resulted in the release of Masood Azhar, an important leader in the former Harakat ul-Ansar, who was imprisoned by India in 1994 and then founded Jaish-e-Mohammed (JEM) after his release. Another former member of Harakat ul-Ansar, Ahmed Omar Sheik was also released by India as a result of the hijackings and was later convicted of the abduction and murder in 2002 of US journalist Daniel Pearl. HUM targets Indian security and civilian targets in Kashmir. In 2005, such attacks resulted in the deaths of 15 people. In November 2007, two Indian soldiers were killed in Kashmir while engaged in a firefight with a group of HUM militants. Indian police and army forces have engaged with HUM militants in the Kashmir region, killing a number of the organization's leadership in April, October, and December 2008. In February 2009, Lalchand Kishen

Advani, leader of the Indian opposition Bharatiya Janata Party, received a death threat that was attributed to HUM. HUM did not carry out any attacks during 2011.

Strength: HUM has several hundred armed supporters located in Azad Kashmir, Pakistan; India's southern Kashmir and Doda regions; and in the Kashmir valley. Supporters are mostly Pakistanis and Kashmiris, but also include Afghans and Arab veterans of the Afghan war. After 2000, a significant portion of HUM's membership defected to JEM.

Location/Area of Operation: Based in Muzaffarabad, Rawalpindi, and several other cities in Pakistan, HUM conducts insurgent and terrorist operations primarily in Kashmir and Afghanistan. HUM trains its militants in Afghanistan and Pakistan.

External Aid: HUM collects donations from wealthy and grassroots donors in Pakistan, Saudi Arabia, and other Gulf states. HUM's financial collection methods include soliciting donations in magazine ads and pamphlets.

Hezbollah

aka the Party of God; Islamic Jihad; Islamic Jihad Organization; Revolutionary Justice Organization; Organization of the Oppressed on Earth; Islamic Jihad for the Liberation of Palestine; Organization of Right Against Wrong; Ansar Allah; Followers of the Prophet Muhammed

Description: Hezbollah was designated as a Foreign Terrorist Organization on October 8, 1997. Formed in 1982, in response to the Israeli invasion of Lebanon, the Lebanese-based radical Shia group takes its ideological inspiration from the Iranian revolution and the teachings of the late Ayatollah Khomeini. The group generally follows the religious guidance of Khomeini's successor, Iranian Supreme Leader Ali Khamenei. Hezbollah is closely allied with Iran and often acts at its behest although it also acts independently. Hezbollah shares a close relationship with Syria, and like Iran, the group is helping advance Syrian objectives in the region. It has strong influence in Lebanon, especially with the Shia community. Hezbollah also plays an active role in Lebanese politics, and the group holds 13 seats in the 128-member Lebanese Parliament. Hezbollah's political strength has grown in the wake of the 2006 war with Israel and the group's 2008 takeover of West Beirut. Hezbollah provides support to several Palestinian terrorist organizations as well as a number of local Christian and Muslim militias in Lebanon. This support includes the covert provision of weapons, explosives, training, funding, and guidance, as well as overt political support.

Activities: Hezbollah's terrorist attacks have included the suicide truck bombings of the US Embassy and US Marine barracks in Beirut in 1983; the US Embassy annex in Beirut in 1984; and the 1985 hijacking of TWA flight 847, during which a US Navy diver was murdered. Elements of the group were responsible for the kidnapping, detention, and murder of Americans and other Westerners in Lebanon in the 1980s. Hezbollah was implicated in the attacks on the Israeli Embassy in Argentina in 1992 and on the Argentine-Israeli Mutual Association in Buenos Aires in 1994. In 2000, Hezbollah operatives captured three Israeli soldiers in the Sheba'a Farms area and, separately, kidnapped an Israeli non-combatant in Dubai. Although the non-combatant survived, on November 1, 2001, Israeli Army Rabbi Israel Weiss pronounced the soldiers dead. The surviving non-combatant, as well as the bodies of the IDF soldiers, were returned to Israel in a prisoner exchange with Hezbollah on January 29, 2004. Since at least 2004, Hezbollah has provided training to select Iraqi Shia militants, including on the construction and use of improvised explosive devices (IEDs) that can penetrate heavily armored vehicles. Senior Hezbollah operative, Ali Mussa Daqduq, was captured in Iraq in 2007 with detailed documents that discussed tactics to attack Iraqi and Coalition Forces; he was facilitating Hezbollah training of Iraqi Shia militants. In July 2006, Hizballah attacked an Israeli Army patrol, kidnapping two soldiers and killing three, starting a conflict with Israel that lasted into August. Senior Hezbollah officials have repeatedly vowed retaliation for the February 2008 killing in Damascus of Imad

Mughniyah, Hezbollah's military and terrorism chief, who was suspected of involvement in many attacks. Hezbollah and a Palestinian group affiliated with al-Qa'ida blamed each other for a May 2011 roadside bomb attack that wounded six Italian soldiers with the UN Interim Force in Lebanon. Two other attacks against UNIFIL peackeepers—an attack in late July that wounded six French citizens and a second attack days later that injured three other French soldiers—were believed to have been carried out by Hezbollah. Although the group did not take credit for the attacks against UNIFIL troops, Hezbollah is likely the perpetrator because of UNIFIL's efforts directed against Hezbollah throughout Lebanon. Also in 2011, four Hezbollah members were indicted by the U.N.-based Special Tribunal for Lebanon, an international tribunal investigating the 2005 assassination of Lebanese Prime Minister Rafik Hariri. The four Hezbollah members indicted by the Special Tribunal for Lebanon include Mustafa Badreddine—identified as the primary suspect in Hariri's assassination, Badreddine is believed to have replaced his cousin, the infamous Imad Mugniyeh, as Hezbollah's top military commander after Mugniyeh's 2008 death—as well as Salim Ayyash, Assad Sabra, and Hassan Anise. Hezbollah denounced the trial and vowed to retaliate, saying the four indicted Hezbollah members would not be handed over at any time.

Strength: Several thousand supporters and members.

Location/Area of Operation: Operates in the southern suburbs of Beirut, the Bekaa Valley, and southern Lebanon.

External Aid: Iran continues to provide Hezbollah with training, weapons, and explosives, as well as political, diplomatic, monetary, and organizational aid; Syria furnished training, weapons, diplomatic, and political support. Hezbollah also receives funding from private donations and profits from legal and illegal businesses. Hezbollah receives financial support from Lebanese Shia communities in Europe, Africa, South America, North America, and Asia. Hezbollah supporters are often engaged in a range of criminal activities, including smuggling contraband goods; passport falsification; credit card, immigration, and bank fraud; trafficking in narcotics; and money laundering. The Barakat Network—a criminal network operating in the tri-border area between Paraguay, Brazil, and Argentina—is an example of such criminal activity. Furthermore, two separate US government investigations implicated the Lebanese Canadian Bank as a key conduit for drug money being funneled to Hizballah.

Indian Mujahedeen

aka Indian Mujahidin; Islamic Security Force–Indian Mujahideen (ISF–IM)

Description: The Indian Mujahideen (IM) was designated as a Foreign Terrorist Organization on September 19, 2011. An India-based terrorist group with significant links to Pakistan, IM has been responsible for dozens of bomb attacks throughout India since 2005 and has caused the deaths of hundreds of innocent civilians. IM maintains close ties to other US-designated terrorist entities, including Pakistan-based Lashkar e-Tayyiba (LeT), Jaish-e-Mohammed (JEM), and Harakat ul-Jihad-i-Islami (HUJI). IM's stated goal is to carry out terrorist actions against non-Muslims in furtherance of its ultimate objective, an Islamic Caliphate across South Asia.

Activities: IM's primary method of attack is multiple coordinated bombings in crowded areas against economic and civilian targets to maximize terror and casualties. In 2008, an IM attack in Delhi killed 30 people; that same year, IM was responsible for 16 synchronized bomb blasts in crowded urban centers and a local hospital in Ahmedabad that killed 38 and injured more than 100. IM also played a facilitative role in the 2008 Mumbai attack carried out by LeT that killed 163 people, including six Americans. In 2010, IM carried out the bombing of a popular German bakery in Pune, India, frequented by tourists, killing 17 and injuring more than 60 people. In 2011, IM conducted multiple bombings killing dozens of innocent civilians and injuring hundreds more. On May 25, IM was suspected of an improvised explosive device (IED) attack in

New Delhi. On July 13, 25 civilians were killed and 137 wounded in an IED attack in Mumbai. On September 7, 15 civilians were killed and 91 others injured in a bombing in New Delhi.

Strength: Estimated to have several thousand supporters and members.

Location/Area of Operation: India.

External Aid: Suspected to obtain funding and support from other terrorist organizations, such as LeT and HUJI, and from sources in the Middle East.

Islamic Jihad Union

aka Islamic Jihad Group; Islomiy Jihod Ittihodi; al-Djihad al-Islami; Dzhamaat Modzhakhedov; Islamic Jihad Group of Uzbekistan; Jamiat al-Jihad al-Islami; Jamiyat; The Jamaat Mojahedin; The Kazakh Jama'at; The Libyan Society

Description: Designated as a Foreign Terrorist Organization on June 17, 2005, the Islamic Jihad Union (IJU) is a Sunni extremist organization that splintered from the Islamic Movement of Uzbekistan (IMU).

Activities: The IJU, based in Pakistan, primarily operates against coalition forces in Afghanistan and continues to pose a threat of attacks in Central Asia. The group claimed responsibility for attacks in March and April 2004, targeting police at several roadway checkpoints and at a popular bazaar, killing approximately 47 people, including 33 IJU members, some of whom were suicide bombers. In July 2004, the group carried out near-simultaneous suicide bombings of the Uzbek prosecutor general's office and the US and Israeli Embassies in Tashkent. In September 2007, German authorities disrupted an IJU plot by detaining three IJU operatives, including two German citizens. Foreign fighters from Germany, Turkey, and elsewhere in Europe continued to travel to the Afghan-Pakistan border area to join the IJU to fight against US and Coalition Forces.

Strength: 100–200 members.

Location/Area of Operation: IJU members are scattered throughout Central Asia, Europe, Pakistan, and Afghanistan.

External Aid: Unknown.

Islamic Movement of Uzbekistan

aka IMU

Description: Designated as a Foreign Terrorist Organization on September 25, 2000, the Islamic Movement of Uzbekistan's (IMU) goal is to overthrow the Uzbek regime and to establish an Islamic state. For most of the past decade, however, the group recruited members from other Central Asian states and Europe and has focused on fighting in Afghanistan and Pakistan. The IMU has a relationship with the Taliban and Tehrik-e Taliban Pakistan (TTP). In 2011, IMU's leadership cadre remained based in Pakistan's Taliban-controlled North Waziristan and operated primarily along the Afghanistan-Pakistan border and in northern Afghanistan. Top IMU leaders have integrated themselves into the Taliban's shadow government in the northern provinces. Operating in cooperation with each other, the Taliban and the IMU have expanded their presence throughout northern Afghanistan and have established training camps in the region.

Activities: Since the beginning of Operation Enduring Freedom, the IMU has been predominantly focused on attacks against US and coalition soldiers in Afghanistan. In late 2009, NATO forces reported an increase in IMU-affiliated foreign fighters in Afghanistan. In 2010, the IMU continued to fight in Afghanistan and the group claimed credit for the September 19 ambush that killed 25 Tajik troops in Tajikistan. On October 15, 2011, IMU claimed responsibility for a suicide assault on a US-led Provincial Reconstruction Team based in the Afghan province of

Panjshir. The attack began when a suicide bomber detonated a car packed with explosives at the front gate, killing two Afghan civilians and wounding two security guards at the base.

Strength: 200–300 members.

Location/Area of Operation: IMU militants are located in South Asia, Central Asia, and Iran.

External Aid: The IMU receives support from a large Uzbek diaspora, terrorist organizations, and donors from Europe, Central and South Asia, and the Middle East.

Jaish-e-Mohammed

aka the Army of Mohammed; Mohammed's Army; Tehrik ul-Furqaan; Khuddam-ul-Islam; Khudamul Islam; Kuddam e Islami; Jaish-i-Mohammed

Description: Designated as a Foreign Terrorist Organization on December 26, 2001, Jaish-e-Mohammed (JEM) is based in Pakistan. JEM was founded in early 2000 by Masood Azhar, a former senior leader of Harakat ul-Ansar, upon his release from prison in exchange for 155 hijacked Indian Airlines hostages in India. The group's aim is to annex Indian Kashmir and expel coalition forces in Afghanistan, and it has openly declared war against the United States. Pakistan outlawed JEM in 2002. By 2003, JEM had splintered into Khuddam-ul-Islam (KUI), headed by Azhar, and Jamaat ul-Furqan (JUF), led by Abdul Jabbar, who was released from Pakistani custody in August 2004. Pakistan banned KUI and JUF in November 2003.

Activities: JEM continues to operate openly in parts of Pakistan despite the 2002 ban on its activities. Since Masood Azhar's 1999 release from Indian custody, JEM has conducted many fatal terrorist attacks in the region. JEM claimed responsibility for several suicide car bombings in Kashmir, including an October 2001 suicide attack on the Jammu and Kashmir legislative assembly building in Srinagar that killed more than 30 people. The Indian government has publicly implicated JEM, along with Lashkar e-Tayyiba, for the December 2001 attack on the Indian Parliament that killed nine and injured 18. In 2002, Pakistani authorities arrested and convicted a JEM member for the abduction and murder of US journalist Daniel Pearl. Pakistani authorities suspect that JEM members may have been involved in the 2002 anti-Christian attacks in Islamabad, Murree, and Taxila that killed two Americans. In December 2003, Pakistan implicated JEM members in the two assassination attempts against President Musharraf. In 2006, JEM claimed responsibility for a number of attacks, including the killing of several Indian police officials in the Indian-administered Kashmir capital of Srinagar. Indian police and JEM extremists continued to engage in firefights throughout 2008 and 2009. In March 2011, Indian security forces killed chief JEM commander Sajad Afghani and his bodyguard in Sirnagar, Kashmir.

Strength: JEM has at least several hundred armed supporters—including a large cadre of former HUM members—located in Pakistan, India's southern Kashmir and Doda regions, and in the Kashmir Valley. In 2011, JEM restarted its fundraising and recruitment activities in Pakistan.

Location/Area of Operation: Pakistan, particularly southern Punjab; Afghanistan; and Kashmir.

External Aid: In anticipation of asset seizures by the Pakistani government, JEM withdrew funds from bank accounts and invested in legal businesses, such as commodity trading, real estate, and production of consumer goods. In addition, JEM collects funds through donation requests in magazines and pamphlets, sometimes using charitable causes to solicit donations.

Jemaah Islamiya

aka Jemaa Islamiyah; Jema'a Islamiyah; Jemaa Islamiyya; Jema'a Islamiyya; Jemaa Islamiyyah; Jema'a Islamiyyah; Jemaah Islamiah; Jemaah Islamiyah; Jema'ah Islamiyah; Jemaah Islamiyyah; Jema'ah Islamiyyah; JI

Description: Designated as a Foreign Terrorist Organization on October 23, 2002, Jemaah Islamiya (JI) is a Southeast Asia–based terrorist group cofounded by Abu Bakar Ba'asyir and Abdullah Sungkar that seeks the establishment of an Islamic caliphate spanning Indonesia, Malaysia, southern Thailand, Singapore, Brunei, and the southern Philippines. More than 400 JI operatives have been captured since 2002, including operations chief and al-Qa'ida (AQ) associate Hambali. In 2006, several members connected to JI's 2005 suicide attack in Bali were arrested; in 2007, JI emir Muhammad Naim (aka Zarkasih) and JI military commander Abu Dujana were arrested; and in 2008, two senior JI operatives were arrested in Malaysia and a JI–linked cell was broken up in Sumatra. In September 2009, JI splinter group leader Noordin Mohammad Top was killed in a police raid. Progress against JI continued in February 2010, when the Indonesian National Police discovered and disbanded an extremist training base in Aceh in which members of JI and other Indonesian extremist groups participated. The police raid resulted in the capture of more than 60 militants, including some JI operatives, and led authorities to former JI leader Dulmatin, one of the planners of the 2002 Bali bombing. In March 2010, Dulmatin was killed outside of Jakarta. In June 2010, wanted JI commander Abdullah Sunata was captured while planning to bomb the Danish Embassy in Jakarta. In January 2011, JI member Umar Patek was captured in Abbottabad, Pakistan, and transferred to Indonesia for trial.

Activities: In December 2001, Singaporean authorities uncovered a JI plot to attack United States, Israeli, British, and Australian diplomatic facilities in Singapore. Other significant JI attacks include the 2002 Bali bombings, which killed more than 200, including seven US citizens; the August 2003 bombing of the J. W. Marriott Hotel in Jakarta, the September 2004 bombing outside the Australian Embassy in Jakarta, and JI's October 2005 suicide bombing in Bali, which killed 26, including the three suicide bombers. A JI faction led by Noordin Mohammad Top conducted the most recent high-profile attack associated with the group July 17, 2009 at the J.W. Marriott and Ritz-Carlton hotels in Jakarta when two suicide bombers detonated explosive devices, killing seven and injuring more than 50 people, including seven Americans.

Strength: Estimates of total JI members vary from 500 to several thousand.

Location/Area of Operation: JI is based in Indonesia and is believed to have elements in Malaysia and the Philippines.

External Aid: Investigations have indicated that JI is fully capable of its own fundraising through membership donations and criminal and business activities. It has received financial, ideological, and logistical support from Middle Eastern contacts and non-governmental organizations.

Jundallah

aka People's Resistance Movement of Iran (PMRI); Jonbesh-i Moqavemat-i-Mardom-i Iran; Popular Resistance Movement of Iran; Soldiers of God; Fedayeen-e-Islam; Former Jundallah of Iran; Jundullah; Jondullah; Jundollah; Jondollah; Jondallah; Army of God (God's Army); Baloch Peoples Resistance Movement (BPRM)

Description: Jundallah was designated as a Foreign Terrorist Organization on November 4, 2010. Since its 2003 inception, Jundallah, a violent extremist organization that operates primarily in the province of Sistan va Balochistan of Iran, has engaged in numerous attacks, killing and maiming scores of Iranian civilians and government officials. Jundallah's stated goals are to secure recognition of Balochi cultural, economic, and political rights from the Government of Iran and to spread awareness of the plight of the Baloch situation through violent and nonviolent means.

Activities: In March 2006, Jundallah attacked a motorcade in eastern Iran, which included the deputy head of the Iranian Red Crescent Security Department, who was then taken hostage. The Governor of Zahedan, his deputy, and five other officials were wounded; seven others were kidnapped; and more than 20 people were killed in the attack. An October 2009 suicide bomb attack in a marketplace in the city of Pishin in the Sistan va Balochistan province, which killed more than

40 people, was reportedly the deadliest terrorist attack in Iran since the 1980s. In a statement on its website, Jundallah claimed responsibility for the December 15, 2010 suicide bomb attack inside the Iman Hussein Mosque in Chabahar, which killed an estimated 35 to 40 civilians and wounded 60 to 100. In July 2010, Jundallah attacked the Grand Mosque in Zahedan, killing approximately 30 and injuring an estimated 300 people. There were no reported attacks attributed to Jundallah in 2011.

Strength: Reports of Jundallah membership vary from 500 to 2000.

Location/Area of Operation: Throughout Sistan va Balochistan province in southeastern Iran and the greater Balochistan area of Afghanistan and Pakistan.

External Aid: Unknown.

Kahane Chai

aka American Friends of the United Yeshiva; American Friends of Yeshivat Rav Meir; Committee for the Safety of the Roads; Dikuy Bogdim; DOV; Forefront of the Idea; Friends of the Jewish Idea Yeshiva; Jewish Legion; Judea Police; Judean Congress; Kach; Kahane; Kahane Lives; Kahane Tzadak; Kahane.org; Kahanetzadak.com; Kfar Tapuah Fund; Koach; Meir's Youth; New Kach Movement; Newkach.org; No'ar Meir; Repression of Traitors; State of Judea; Sword of David; The Committee Against Racism and Discrimination (CARD); The Hatikva Jewish Identity Center; The International Kahane Movement; The Jewish Idea Yeshiva; The Judean Legion; The Judean Voice; The Qomemiyut Movement; The Rabbi Meir David Kahane Memorial Fund; The Voice of Judea; The Way of the Torah; The Yeshiva of the Jewish Idea; Yeshivat Harav Meir

Description: Kach—the precursor to Kahane Chai—was founded by radical Israeli-American Rabbi Meir Kahane with the goal of restoring Greater Israel, which is generally used to refer to Israel, the West Bank, and Gaza. Its offshoot, Kahane Chai, (translation: "Kahane Lives") was founded by Meir Kahane's son Binyamin following his father's 1990 assassination in the United States. Both organizations were designated as Foreign Terrorist Organizations on October 8, 1997. The group has attempted to gain seats in the Israeli Knesset over the past several decades but has won only one seat in 1984.

Activities: Kahane Chai has harassed and threatened Arabs, Palestinians, and Israeli government officials, and has vowed revenge for the death of Binyamin Kahane and his wife. The group is suspected of involvement in a number of low-level attacks since the start of the First Palestinian Intifada in 2000. Since 2003, Kahane Chai activists have called for the execution of former Israeli Prime Minister Ariel Sharon and have physically intimidated other Israeli and Palestinian government officials who favored the dismantlement of Israeli settlements. Although they have not explicitly claimed responsibility for a series of mosque burnings in the West Bank, individuals affiliated with Kahane Chai are widely suspected of being the perpetrators.

Strength: Kahane Chai's core membership is believed to be fewer than 100. The group's membership and support networks are overwhelmingly composed of Israeli citizens, most of whom live in West Bank settlements.

Location/Area of Operation: Israel and West Bank settlements, particularly Qiryat Arba' in Hebron.

External Aid: Receives support from sympathizers in the United States and Europe.

Kata'ib Hizballah

aka Hizballah Brigades; Hizballah Brigades in Iraq; Hizballah Brigades–Iraq; Kata'ib Hezbollah; Khata'ib Hezbollah; Khata'ib Hizballah; Khattab Hezballah; Hizballah Brigades–Iraq of the Islamic Resistance in Iraq; Islamic Resistance in Iraq; Kata'ib Hizballah Fi Al-Iraq; Katibat Abu Fathel Al A'abas; Katibat Zayd Ebin Ali; Katibut Karbalah

Description: Designated as a Foreign Terrorist Organization on July 2, 2009, Kata'ib Hizballah (KH) was formed in 2006 and is a radical Shia Islamist group with an anti-Western outlook and extremist ideology that has conducted attacks against Iraqi, United States, and Coalition targets in Iraq. KH has threatened the lives of Iraqi politicians and civilians that support the legitimate political process in Iraq. The group is notable for its extensive use of media operations and propaganda by filming and releasing videos of attacks. KH has ideological ties to Lebanese Hizballah and may have received support from that group and its sponsor, Iran.

Activities: KH has been responsible for numerous violent terrorist attacks since 2007, including improvised explosive device bombings, rocket propelled grenade attacks, and sniper operations. In 2007, KH gained notoriety with attacks on United States and coalition forces in Iraq. KH was particularly active in summer 2008, recording and distributing video footage of its attacks against United States and coalition soldiers. Using the alias "Hizballah Brigades in Iraq," KH filmed attacks on US Stryker vehicles, Abrams tanks, and Bradley armored personnel carriers. In 2009, KH continued to release videos of attacks ranging in date from 2006 to 2008 on the Internet. In June 2011, five US soldiers were killed in a rocket attack in Baghdad, Iraq, when KH assailants fired between three and five rockets at the United States military base Camp Victory, which surrounds Baghdad's International Airport.

Strength: Membership is estimated at 400 individuals.

Location/Area of Operation: KH's operations are predominately Iraq based. In 2011, KH conducted the majority of its operations in Baghdad but was active in other areas of Iraq, including Kurdish areas, such as Mosul.

External Aid: KH is almost entirely dependent on support from Iran and Lebanese Hizballah.

Kurdistan Workers' Party

aka the Kurdistan Freedom and Democracy Congress; the Freedom and Democracy Congress of Kurdistan; KADEK; Partiya Karkeran Kurdistan; the People's Defense Force; Halu Mesru Savunma Kuvveti; Kurdistan People's Congress; People's Congress of Kurdistan; Kongra-Gel

Description: Founded by Abdullah Ocalan in 1978 as a Marxist-Leninist separatist organization, the Kurdistan Workers' Party (PKK) or Kongra-Gel (KGK) was designated as a Foreign Terrorist Organization on October 8, 1997. The group, composed primarily of Turkish Kurds, launched a campaign of violence in 1984. The PKK's original goal was to establish an independent Kurdish state in southeastern Turkey, but in recent years, it has spoken more often about autonomy within a Turkish state that guarantees Kurdish cultural and linguistic rights. In the early 1990s, the PKK moved beyond rural-based insurgent activities to include urban terrorism. In the 1990s, southeastern Anatolia was the scene of significant violence; some estimates place casualties at approximately 30,000 persons. Following his capture in 1999, Ocalan announced a "peace initiative," ordering members to refrain from violence and requesting dialogue with Ankara on Kurdish issues. Ocalan's death sentence was commuted to life imprisonment; he remains the symbolic leader of the group. The group foreswore violence until June 2004, when the group's hard-line militant wing took control and renounced the self-imposed cease fire of the previous five years. Striking over the border from bases within Iraq, the PKK has engaged in terrorist attacks in eastern and western Turkey.

Activities: Primary targets have been Turkish government security forces, local Turkish officials, and villagers who oppose the organization in Turkey. In 2006, 2007, and 2008, PKK violence killed or injured hundreds of Turks. The PKK remained active in 2011, with approximately 61 credited attacks. At least 88 people were killed in the attacks and 216 wounded. Although the majority of the attacks took place in Turkey, suspected PKK members have carried out multiple attacks on the offices of a Turkish newspaper in Paris, France.

Strength: Approximately 4000 to 5000; 3000 to 3500 are located in northern Iraq.

Location/Area of Operation: The PKK operates primarily in Turkey, Iraq, and Europe.

External Aid: In the past, the PKK received safe haven and modest aid from Syria, Iraq, and Iran. Since 1999, Iran has also cooperated in a limited fashion with Turkey against the PKK. The PKK receives substantial financial support from the large Kurdish diaspora in Europe and from criminal activity there.

Lashkar e-Tayyiba

aka al Mansooreen; Al Mansoorian; Army of the Pure; Army of the Pure and Righteous; Army of the Righteous; Lashkar e-Toiba; Lashkar-i-Taiba; Paasban-e-Ahle-Hadis; Paasban-e-Kashmir; Paasban-i-Ahle-Hadith; Pasban-e-Ahle-Hadith; Pasban-e-Kashmir; Jamaat-ud-Dawa, JUD; Jama'at al-Dawa; Jamaat ud-Daawa; Jamaat ul-Dawah; Jamaat-ul-Dawa; Jama'at-i-Dawat; Jamaiat-ud-Dawa; Jama'at-ud-Da'awah; Jama'at-ud-Da'awa; Jamaati-ud-Dawa; Idara Khidmat- e-Khalq; Falah-i-Insaniat Foundation; FiF; Falah-e-Insaniat Foundation; Falah-e-Insaniyat; Falah-i-Insaniyat; Falah Insania; Welfare of Humanity; Humanitarian Welfare Foundation; Human Welfare Foundation

Description: Designated as a Foreign Terrorist Organization (FTO) on December 26, 2001, Lashkar e-Tayyiba (LeT) is one of the largest and most proficient of the traditionally Kashmir-focused militant groups. It has the ability to severely disrupt already delicate regional relations. LeT formed in the late 1980s as the militant wing of the Islamic extremist organization Markaz Dawa ul-Irshad, a Pakistan-based Islamic fundamentalist mission organization and charity founded to oppose the Soviet presence in Afghanistan. Led by Hafiz Muhammad Saeed, LeT is not connected to any political party. Shortly after LeT was designated as an FTO, Saeed changed the name to Jamaat-ud-Dawa (JUD) and began humanitarian projects to avoid restrictions. LeT disseminates its message through JUD's media outlets. Elements of LeT and Jaish-e-Muhammad (JEM) combined with other groups to mount attacks as "The Save Kashmir Movement." The Pakistani government banned LeT in January 2002 and JUD in 2008 following the Mumbai attack. LeT and Saeed continued to spread terrorist ideology as well as virulent rhetoric condemning the United States, India, Israel, and other perceived enemies.

Activities: LeT has conducted a number of operations against Indian troops and civilian targets in Jammu and Kashmir since 1993 as well as several high profile attacks inside India. Indian governmental officials hold LeT responsible for the July 2006 train attack in Mumbai and multiple attacks in 2005 and 2006. LeT conducted the November 2008 attacks in Mumbai against luxury hotels, a Jewish center, a train station, and a popular café that killed at least 183, including 22 foreigners, and injured more than 300 people. India has charged 38 people in the case, including the lone surviving alleged attacker Mohammad Ajmal Amir Kasab, who was captured at the scene. While most of those charged are at large and thought to be in Pakistan, Kasab was sentenced to death for his involvement in the Mumbai massacre. In March 2010, Pakistani-American businessman David Headley pleaded guilty in a US court to crimes relating to his role in the November 2008 LeT attacks in Mumbai as well as to crimes relating to a separate plot to bomb the Danish newspaper Jyllands-Posten. In May 2011, Headley was a witness in the trial of Tahawwur Rana, who was charged with providing material support to LeT. Rana was convicted for providing material support to LeT in June. In 2011, LeT was responsible for multiple attacks. Most of the attacks occurred in Jammu and Kashmir with the deadliest being a May 27, 2011, attack on a private residence in the city of Kupwara that killed two civilians. In a notable 2011 counterterrorism success, police in Indian-administered Kashmir shot and killed a senior LeT operative, Azhar Malik, after they surrounded a house where he was hiding in the town of Sopore.

Strength: The actual size of LeT is unknown, but it has several thousand members in Azad Kashmir and Punjab Pakistan and in the southern Jammu, Kashmir, and Doda regions. Most LeT members are Pakistanis or Afghans or veterans of the Afghan wars. The group uses assault rifles, machine guns, mortars, explosives, and rocket-propelled grenades.

Location/Area of Operation: LeT maintains a number of facilities, including training camps, schools, and medical clinics in Pakistan.

External Aid: LeT collects donations from Pakistani expatriate communities in the Middle East and Europe, particularly the United Kingdom; Islamic non-governmental organizations; and Pakistani and Kashmiri business people. LeT has global connections and a strong operational network throughout South Asia.

Lashkar i Jhangvi

aka Army of Jhangvi; Lashkar e Jhangvi; Lashkar-i-Jhangvi

Description: Designated as a Foreign Terrorist Organization on January 30, 2003, Lashkar i Jhangvi (LJ) is the militant offshoot of the Sunni Deobandi sectarian group Sipah-i-Sahaba Pakistan. LJ focuses primarily on anti-Shia attacks and other attacks in Pakistan and Afghanistan and was banned by Pakistan in August 2001 as part of an effort to rein in sectarian violence. Many of its members then sought refuge in Afghanistan with the Taliban, with whom they had existing ties. After the collapse of the Taliban as the ruling government in Afghanistan, LJ members became active in aiding other terrorists, providing safe houses, false identities, and protection in Pakistani cities, including Karachi, Peshawar, and Rawalpindi. LJ works closely with Tehrik-e-Taliban Pakistan (TTP).

Activities: LJ specializes in armed attacks and bombings and has admitted responsibility for numerous killings of Shia religious and community leaders in Pakistan. In January 1999, the group attempted to assassinate former Prime Minister Nawaz Sharif and his brother Shabaz Sharif, Chief Minister of Punjab Province. Media reports linked LJ to attacks on Christian targets in Pakistan, including a March 2002 grenade assault on the Protestant International Church in Islamabad that killed two US citizens. Pakistani authorities believe LJ was responsible for the July 2003 bombing of a Shia mosque in Quetta, Pakistan. Authorities also implicated LJ in several sectarian incidents in 2004, including the May and June bombings of two Shia mosques in Karachi, which killed more than 40 people. LJ was very active in 2011. The most notable attack occurred on December 6, in Kabul, Afghanistan, when a suicide bomber detonated an improvised explosive device in a crowd of Shia mourners, killing 48 civilians, including 12 children, and wounding 193. LJ claimed responsibility. In another attack on September 29, in Balochistan, LJ operatives ordered Shia pilgrims off a bus and shot dead 29 victims. An hour after the initial attack, gunmen killed family members travelling to retrieve the victims of the first attack. Additional 2011 attacks included a January firebombing attack that injured four police officers and six civilians, including three children; a May attack that killed eight civilians and wounded 15; another May attack that killed two police officers and wounded three; and a July 30 attack that killed 11 civilians and wounded three.

Strength: Assessed in the low hundreds.

Location/Area of Operation: LJ is active primarily in Punjab, FATA, Karachi, and Baluchistan. Some members travel between Pakistan and Afghanistan.

External Aid: Funding comes from wealthy donors in Pakistan as well as the Middle East, particularly Saudi Arabia. The group also engages in criminal activity to fund its activities, including extortion and protection money.

Liberation Tigers of Tamil Eelam

aka Ellalan Force; Tamil Tigers

Description: Founded in 1976 and designated as a Foreign Terrorist Organization on October 8, 1997, the Liberation Tigers of Tamil Eelam (LTTE) became a powerful Tamil secessionist group in Sri Lanka. Despite its military defeat at the hands of the Sri Lankan government in 2009, the LTTE's international network of sympathizers and financial support persists. LTTE remnants continued to collect contributions from the Tamil diaspora in North America, Europe, and Australia, where there were reports that some of these contributions were coerced by locally based LTTE sympathizers. The LTTE also used Tamil charitable organizations as fronts for its fundraising.

Activities: Although the LTTE has been largely inactive since its military defeat in Sri Lanka in 2009, in the past, the LTTE was responsible for an integrated battlefield insurgent strategy that targeted key installations and senior Sri Lankan political and military leaders. It conducted a sustained campaign targeting rival Tamil groups and assassinated Prime Minister Rajiv Gandhi of India in 1991 and President Ranasinghe Premadasa of Sri Lanka in 1993. Although most notorious for its cadre of suicide bombers, the Black Tigers, the organization included an amphibious force, the Sea Tigers, and a nascent air wing, the Air Tigers. Fighting between the LTTE and the Sri Lanka government escalated in 2006 and continued through 2008. In early 2009, Sri Lankan forces recaptured the LTTE's key strongholds, including their capital of Kilinochchi. In May 2009, government forces defeated the last LTTE fighting forces and killed LTTE leader Prahbakaran and other members of the LTTE leadership and military command. As a result, the Sri Lankan government declared military victory over LTTE. In 2010, some LTTE members reportedly fled Sri Lanka and have since attempted to reorganize in India. In June 2010, assailants claiming LTTE membership may have been responsible for an attack against a railway in Tamil Nadu, India. No one was injured when the targeted train was able to stop in time to prevent derailment. There have been no known attacks in Sri Lanka that could verifiably be attributed to the LTTE since the end of the war. In March 2010, German police arrested six Tamil migrants living in Germany for supposedly using blackmail and extortion to raise funds for the LTTE. LTTE's financial network of support continued to operate throughout 2011.

Strength: Exact strength is unknown.

Location/Area of Operations: Sri Lanka and India.

External Aid: The LTTE used its international contacts and the large Tamil diaspora in North America, Europe, and Asia to procure weapons, communications, funding, and other needed supplies. The group employed charities as fronts to collect and divert funds for their activities.

Libyan Islamic Fighting Group

aka LIFG

Description: The Libyan Islamic Fighting Group (LIFG) was designated as a Foreign Terrorist Organization on December 17, 2004. In the early 1990s, LIFG emerged from the group of Libyans who had fought Soviet forces in Afghanistan and pledged to overthrow Libyan leader Muammar al-Qadhafi. In the years following, some members maintained an anti-Qadhafi focus and targeted Libyan government interests. Others, such as Abu al-Faraj al-Libi, who was arrested in Pakistan in 2005, have aligned with Usama bin Ladin and are believed to be part of the al-Qa'ida (AQ) leadership structure. On November 3, 2007, AQ leader Ayman al-Zawahiri announced a formal merger between AQ and LIFG. However, on July 3, 2009, LIFG members in the United Kingdom released a statement formally disavowing any association with AQ. In September 2009, six imprisoned LIFG members issued a 417-page document that renounced violence. More than 100 LIFG members pledged to adhere to this revised doctrine and have been pardoned and released from prison in Libya since September 2009.

Activities: LIFG has been largely inactive operationally in Libya since the late 1990s when members fled predominately to Europe and the Middle East because of tightened Libyan security measures. In early 2011, in the wake of the Libyan revolution and the fall of Qadhafi, LIFG members created the LIFG successor group, the Libyan Islamic Movement for Change (LIMC) and became one of many rebel groups united under the umbrella of the opposition leadership known as the Transitional National Council. Former LIFG emir and LIMC leader Abdel Hakim Bil-Hajj was appointed the Libyan Transitional Council's Tripoli military commander during the Libyan uprisings and has denied any link between his group and AQ.

Strength: Unknown.

Location/Area of Operation: Since the late 1990s, many members have fled to southwest Asia and European countries, particularly the UK.

External Aid: Unknown.

Moroccan Islamic Combatant Group

aka Groupe Islamique Combattant Marocain; GICM

Description: Designated as a Foreign Terrorist Organization on October 11, 2005, the Moroccan Islamic Combatant Group (GICM) is a transnational terrorist group centered in the Moroccan diaspora communities of Western Europe. Its goals include establishing an Islamic state in Morocco. The group emerged in the 1990s and is composed of Moroccan recruits who trained in armed camps in Afghanistan, including some who fought in the Soviet war in Afghanistan. GICM members interact with other North African extremists, particularly in Europe.

Activities: GICM members are believed to be among those responsible for the 2004 Madrid train bombings, which killed 191 people. GICM members were also implicated in the recruitment network for Iraq, and at least one GICM member carried out a suicide attack against coalition forces in Iraq. According to open source reports, GICM individuals are believed to have participated in the 2003 Casablanca attacks. However, the group has largely been inactive since these attacks and has not claimed responsibility for or had attacks attributed to them since the Madrid train bombings.

Strength: Much of GICM's leadership in Morocco and Europe has been killed, imprisoned, or is awaiting trial. Alleged leader Mohamed al-Guerbouzi was convicted in absentia by the Moroccan government for his role in the Casablanca attacks but remains free in exile in London.

Location/Area of Operation: Morocco, Western Europe, and Afghanistan.

External Aid: In the past, GICM has been involved in narcotics trafficking in North Africa and Europe to fund its operations.

Mujahadin-E Khalq Organization

aka MEK; MKO; Mujahadin-e Khalq; Muslim Iranian Students' Society; National Council of Resistance; NCR; Organization of the People's Holy Warriors of Iran; the National Liberation Army of Iran; NLA; People's Mujahadin Organization of Iran; PMOI; National Council of Resistance of Iran; NCRI; Sazeman-e Mujahadin-e Khalq-e Iran

Description: Designated as a Foreign Terrorist Organization on October 8, 1997, the Mujahadin-e Khalq Organization (MEK) is a Marxist Islamic Organization that seeks the overthrow of the Iranian regime through its military wing, the National Liberation Army (NLA), and its political front, the National Council of Resistance of Iran (NCRI). The MEK was founded in 1963 by a group of college-educated Iranian Marxists who opposed the country's pro-western ruler, Shah Mohammad Reza Pahlavi. The group participated in the 1979 Islamic Revolution that replaced the Shah with a Shiite Islamist regime led by Ayatollah Khomeini. However, the MEK's ideology—a blend of Marxism, feminism, and Islamism—was at odds with the post-revolutionary government, and its original leadership was soon executed by the Khomeini regime. In 1981, the group was driven from its bases on the Iran-Iraq border and resettled in Paris, where it began supporting Iraq in its eight-year war against Khomeini's Iran. In 1986, after France recognized the Iranian regime, the MEK moved its headquarters to Iraq, which facilitated its terrorist activities in Iran. From 2003 through the end of 2011, roughly 3400 MEK members were encamped at Ashraf in Iraq.

Activities: The group's worldwide campaign against the Iranian government uses propaganda and terrorism to achieve its objectives. During the 1970s, the MEK staged terrorist attacks inside Iran and killed several US military personnel and civilians working on defense projects in Tehran. In 1972, the MEK set off bombs in Tehran at the US Information Service office (part of the US Embassy), the Iran-American Society, and the offices of several US companies to protest the visit of President Richard Nixon to Iran. In 1973, the MEK assassinated the deputy chief of the US Military Mission in Tehran and bombed several businesses, including Shell Oil. In 1974, the MEK set off bombs in Tehran at the offices of US companies to protest the visit of then US Secretary of State Henry Kissinger. In 1975, the MEK assassinated two US military officers who were members of the US Military Assistance Advisory Group in Tehran. In 1976, the MEK assassinated two US citizens who were employees of Rockwell International in Tehran. In 1979, the group claimed responsibility for the murder of an American Texaco executive. Although it was denied by the MEK, analysis based on eyewitness accounts and MEK documents demonstrates that MEK members participated in and supported the 1979 takeover of the US Embassy in Tehran and that the MEK later argued against the early release of the American hostages. The MEK also provided personnel to guard and defend the site of the US Embassy in Tehran, following the takeover of the Embassy. In 1981, MEK leadership attempted to overthrow the newly installed Islamic regime; Iranian security forces subsequently initiated a crackdown on the group. The MEK instigated a bombing campaign, including an attack against the head office of the Islamic Republic Party and the Prime Minister's office, which killed some 70 high-ranking Iranian officials, including Chief Justice Ayatollah Mohammad Beheshti, President Mohammad-Ali Rajaei, and Prime Minister Mohammad-Javad Bahonar. These attacks resulted in an expanded Iranian government crackdown that forced MEK leaders to flee to France. For five years, the MEK continued to wage its terrorist campaign from its Paris headquarters. Expelled by France in 1986, MEK leaders turned to Saddam Hussein's regime for its base, financial support, and training. Near the end of the 1980–1988 Iran-Iraq War, Baghdad armed the MEK with heavy military equipment and deployed thousands of MEK fighters in suicidal waves of attacks against Iranian forces. The MEK's relationship with the former Iraqi regime continued through the 1990s. In 1991, the group reportedly assisted the Iraqi Republican Guard's bloody crackdown on Iraqi Shia and Kurds who rose up against Saddam Hussein's regime. In April 1992, the MEK conducted near simultaneous attacks on Iranian embassies and consular missions in 13 countries, including against the Iranian mission to the United Nations in New York, demonstrating the group's ability to mount large-scale operations overseas. In June 1998, the MEK was implicated in a series of bombing and mortar attacks in Iran that killed at least 15 and injured several others. The MEK also assassinated the former Iranian Minister of Prisons in 1998. In April 1999, the MEK targeted key Iranian military officers and assassinated the deputy chief of the Iranian Armed Forces General Staff, Brigadier General Ali Sayyaad Shirazi. In April 2000, the MEK attempted to assassinate the commander of the Nasr Headquarters, Tehran's interagency board responsible for coordinating policies on Iraq. The pace of anti-Iranian operations increased during "Operation Great Bahman" in February 2000, when the group launched a dozen attacks against Iran. One attack included a mortar attack against a major Iranian leadership complex in Tehran that housed the offices of the Supreme Leader and the President. The attack killed one person and injured six other individuals. In March 2000, the MEK launched mortars into a residential district in Tehran, injuring four people and damaging property. In 2000 and 2001, the MEK was involved in regular mortar attacks and hit-and-run raids against Iranian military and law enforcement personnel as well as government buildings near the Iran-Iraq border. Following an initial Coalition bombardment of the MEK's facilities in Iraq at the outset of Operation Iraqi Freedom, MEK leadership negotiated a cease fire with coalition forces and surrendered their heavy arms to coalition control. From 2003 through the end of 2011, roughly 3400 MEK members were encamped at Ashraf in Iraq. In 2003, French authorities arrested 160 MEK members at operational bases they believed the MEK was using to coordinate financing and planning for terrorist attacks. Upon the arrest of MEK leader Maryam Rajavi, MEK members took to Paris' streets and engaged in self-immolation. French authorities eventually released Rajavi.

Strength: Estimates place MEK's worldwide membership at between 5000 and 10,000 members with large pockets in Paris and other major European capitals. In Iraq, roughly 3400 MEK members were gathered at Camp Ashraf, the MEK's main compound north of Baghdad at the end of 2011. As a condition of the 2003 cease fire agreement, the MEK relinquished more than 2000 tanks, armored personnel carriers, and heavy artillery.

Location/Area of Operation: The MEK's global support structure remains in place with associates and supporters scattered throughout Europe and North America. Operations have targeted Iranian government elements across the globe, including in Europe and Iran. The MEK's political arm, the National Council of Resistance of Iran (NCRI), has a global support network with active lobbying and propaganda efforts in major Western capitals. NCRI also has a well-developed media communications strategy.

External Aid: Before Operation Iraqi Freedom began in 2003, the MEK received all of its military assistance and most of its financial support from Saddam Hussein. The fall of Saddam Hussein's regime has led the MEK increasingly to rely on front organizations to solicit contributions from expatriate Iranian communities.

National Liberation Army

aka ELN; Ejercito de Liberacion Nacional

Description: The National Liberation Army (ELN) was designated as a Foreign Terrorist Organization on October 8, 1997. The ELN is a Colombian Marxist Leninist group formed in 1964 by intellectuals inspired by Fidel Castro and Che Guevara. It is primarily rural based although it also has several urban units. The ELN remains focused on attacking economic infrastructure, in particular oil and gas pipelines and electricity pylons, and extorting foreign and local companies.

Activities: The ELN engages in kidnappings, hijackings, bombings, drug trafficking, and extortion activities. The group also uses intimidation of judges, prosecutors, and witnesses and has been involved in the murder of teachers and trade unionists. Historically, the ELN has been one of the most prolific users of anti-personnel mines in Colombia. In recent years, the ELN has launched joint attacks with the Revolutionary Armed Forces of Colombia (FARC), Colombia's largest terrorist organization. Authorities believe that the ELN kidnapped at least 25 people and was involved in at least 23 attacks in 2010, some of which were carried out jointly with the FARC. The two Colombia-based terrorist groups significantly increased their attacks in 2011 as they attempted to undermine the October 30 national elections. Attacks on Colombia's oil and gas industry also significantly increased, resulting in major economic damage and numerous deaths and kidnappings. On June 25, ELN attacked a police outpost in Colon Genova, Narino, killing eight civilians, including a child, and wounding four others. On October 30—election day—the ELN attempted to kill the vice president of the House of Representatives, killing his driver but missing the vice president.

Strength: Approximately 2000 armed combatants and an unknown number of active supporters.

Location/Area of Operation: Mostly in the rural and mountainous areas of northern, northeastern, and southwestern Colombia as well as the border regions with Venezuela.

External Aid: The ELN draws its funding from the narcotics trade and from extortion of oil and gas companies. Additional funds are derived from kidnapping ransoms. There is no known external aid.

Palestine Islamic Jihad–Shaqaqi Faction

aka PIJ; Palestine Islamic Jihad; PIJ-Shaqaqi Faction; PIJ-Shallah Faction; Islamic Jihad of Palestine; Islamic Jihad in Palestine; Abu Ghunaym Squad of the Hizballah Bayt Al-Maqdis; Al-Quds Squads; Al-Quds Brigades; Saraya Al-Quds; Al-Awdah Brigades

Description: Palestine Islamic Jihad (PIJ) was designated as a Foreign Terrorist Organization on October 8, 1997. Formed by militant Palestinians in Gaza during the 1970s, PIJ is committed to both the destruction of Israel through attacks against Israeli military and civilian targets and the creation of an Islamic state in all of historic Palestine, including present-day Israel.

Activities: PIJ terrorists have conducted numerous attacks, including large-scale suicide bombings against Israeli civilian and military targets. The PIJ continued to plan and direct attacks against Israelis both inside Israel and in the Palestinian territories. Although US citizens have died in PIJ attacks, the group has not directly targeted US interests. PIJ attacks in 2008, 2009, and 2010 were primarily rocket attacks aimed at southern Israeli cities and have also included attacking Israeli targets with explosive devices. PIJ continued operations into 2011, claiming responsibility for a mortar attack in Sedero, Israel in February and a rocket attack in Ashdod, Israel, in March.

Strength: PIJ currently has fewer than 1000 members.

Location/Area of Operation: Primarily Gaza with a minimal operational presence in the West Bank and Israel. The group's senior leadership resides in Syria. Other leadership elements reside in Lebanon and official representatives are scattered throughout the Middle East.

External Aid: Receives financial assistance and training primarily from Iran.

Palestine Liberation Front–Abu Abbas Faction

aka PLF; PLF-Abu Abbas; Palestine Liberation Front

Description: The Palestinian Liberation Front–Abu Abbas Faction (PLF) was designated as a Foreign Terrorist Organization on October 8, 1997. In the late 1970s, the Palestine Liberation Front (PLF) splintered from the Popular Front for the Liberation of Palestine–General Command (PFLP-GC) and then later split into pro-PLO, pro-Syrian, and pro-Libyan factions. The pro-PLO faction was led by Muhammad Zaydan (aka Abu Abbas) and was based in Baghdad prior to Operation Iraqi Freedom.

Activities: Abbas's group was responsible for the 1985 attack on the Italian cruise ship the *Achille Lauro* and the murder of US citizen Leon Klinghoffer. The PLF was suspected of supporting terrorism against Israel by other Palestinian groups into the 1990s. In April 2004, Abu Abbas died of natural causes while in US custody in Iraq. The PLF took part in the 2006 Palestinian parliamentarian elections but did not win a seat. In 2008, as part of a prisoner exchange between Israel and Hezbollah, Samir Kantar, a PLF member, and purportedly the longest serving Arab prisoner in Israeli custody, was released from an Israeli prison. After going approximately 16 years without claiming responsibility for an attack, the PLF claimed responsibility for two attacks against Israeli targets on March 14, 2008. One attack was against an Israeli military bus in Huwarah, Israel, and the other involved a PLF "brigade" firing at an Israeli settler south of the Hebron Mountains, seriously wounding him. On March 28, 2008, shortly after the attacks, a PLF Central Committee member reaffirmed PLF's commitment to using "all possible means to restore" its previous glory and to adhering to its role in the Palestinian "struggle" and "resistance," through its military. The PLF did not successfully carry out attacks in 2011.

Strength: Estimates have placed membership between 50 and 500.

Location/Area of Operation: PLF leadership and its membership are based in Lebanon and the Palestinian territories.

External Aid: Unknown.

Popular Front for the Liberation of Palestine

aka PFLP; Halhul Gang; Halhul Squad; Palestinian Popular Resistance Forces; PPRF; Red Eagle Gang; Red Eagle Group; Red Eagles; Martyr Abu-Ali Mustafa Battalion

Description: Designated as a Foreign Terrorist Organization on October 8, 1997, the Popular Front for the Liberation of Palestine (PFLP), a Marxist-Leninist group founded by George Habash, broke away from the Arab Nationalist Movement in 1967. The group earned a reputation for spectacular international attacks in the 1960s and 1970s, including airline hijackings that killed at least 20 US citizens. A leading faction within the PLO, the PFLP has long accepted the concept of a two-state solution but has opposed specific provisions of various peace initiatives.

Activities: The PFLP stepped up its operational activity during the Second Intifada. This was highlighted by at least two suicide bombings since 2003, multiple joint operations with other Palestinian terrorist groups, and the assassination of Israeli Tourism Minister Rehavam Ze'evi in 2001 to avenge Israel's killing of the PFLP Secretary General earlier that year. The PFLP was involved in several rocket attacks, launched primarily from Gaza, against Israel in 2008 and 2009, and claimed responsibility for numerous attacks on Israeli forces in Gaza, including a December 2009 ambush of Israeli soldiers in central Gaza. The PLFP claimed numerous mortar and rocket attacks fired from Gaza into Israel in 2010 as well as a February attack on a group of Israeli citizens. In 2011, the group continued to use rockets and mortars to target communities in Israel, including rocket attacks in August and October in Eshkolot and Ashqelon, respectively, which caused no injuries or damage. In October, the PFLP claimed responsibility for a rocket attack that killed one civilian in Ashqelon.

Strength: Unknown.

Location/Area of Operation: Syria, Lebanon, Israel, the West Bank, and Gaza.

External Aid: Leadership received safe haven in Syria.

Popular Front for the Liberation of Palestine–General Command

aka PFLP-GC

Description: The Popular Front for the Liberation of Palestine–General Command (PFLP–GC) was designated as a Foreign Terrorist Organization on October 8, 1997. The PFLP–GC split from the PFLP in 1968, claiming it wanted to focus more on resistance and less on politics. Originally, the group was violently opposed to the Arafat-led PLO. Ahmad Jibril, a former captain in the Syrian Army, has led the PFLP–GC since its founding. The PFLP–GC is closely tied to both Syria and Iran.

Activities: The PFLP–GC carried out dozens of attacks in Europe and the Middle East during the 1970s and 1980s. The organization was known for cross-border terrorist attacks into Israel using unusual means, such as hot-air balloons and motorized hang gliders. The group's primary recent focus was supporting Hizballah's attacks against Israel, training members of other Palestinian terrorist groups, and smuggling weapons. The PFLP–GC maintained an armed presence in several Palestinian refugee camps and at its own military bases in Lebanon and along the Lebanon-Syria border. In recent years, the PFLP–GC was implicated by Lebanese security officials in several rocket attacks against Israel. In May 2008, the PFLP–GC claimed responsibility for a rocket attack on a shopping center in Ashqelon that wounded at least 10 people. In 2009, the group was responsible for wounding two civilians in an armed attack in Nahariyya, Northern District, Israel. In 2011, the PFLP–GC targeted Israeli communities in a March 20 rocket attack by its Jihad Jibril Brigades in the city of Eshkolot, Southern District, Israel. The attack caused no injuries or damage.

Strength: Several hundred.

Location/Area of Operation: Political leadership was headquartered in Damascus, with bases in southern Lebanon and a presence in the Palestinian refugee camps in Lebanon and Syria. The group also maintains a small presence in Gaza.

External Aid: Received safe haven and logistical and military support from Syria and financial support from Iran.

Al-Qa'ida

Variant spelling of al-Qa'ida, including al Qaeda; translation "The Base"; Qa'idat al-Jihad (The Base for Jihad); formerly Qa'idat Ansar Allah (The Base of the Supporters of God); the Islamic

Army; Islamic Salvation Foundation; the Base; The Group for the Preservation of the Holy Sites; The Islamic Army for the Liberation of the Holy Places; the World Islamic Front for Jihad Against Jews and Crusaders; the Usama Bin Ladin Network; the Usama Bin Ladin Organization; al-Jihad; the Jihad Group; Egyptian al-Jihad; Egyptian Islamic Jihad; New Jihad

Description: Designated as a Foreign Terrorist Organization on October 8, 1999, al-Qa'ida (AQ) was established by Usama bin Ladin in 1988. The group helped finance, recruit, transport, and train Sunni Islamist extremists for the Afghan resistance. AQ's strategic objectives are to remove the Western influence and presence from the Muslim world, topple "apostate" governments of Muslim countries and establish a pan-Islamic caliphate governed by its own interpretation of Sharia law that ultimately would be at the center of a new international order. These goals remain essentially unchanged since the group's public declaration of war against the United States in 1996. AQ leaders issued a statement in February 1998 under the banner of "The World Islamic Front for Jihad against the Jews and Crusaders," saying it was the duty of all Muslims to kill US citizens, civilian and military, and their allies everywhere. AQ merged with al-Jihad (Egyptian Islamic Jihad) in June 2001. Many AQ leaders were killed in 2011, including Usama bin Ladin and then second in command Atiyah Abd al-Rahman in May and August, respectively.

Activities: AQ and its supporters conducted three bombings that targeted US troops in Aden in December 1992, and claim to have shot down US helicopters and killed US servicemen in Somalia in 1993. AQ also carried out the August 1998 bombings of the US Embassies in Nairobi and Dar es Salaam, killing up to 300 individuals and injuring more than 5000. In October 2000, AQ conducted a suicide attack on the USS Cole in the port of Aden, Yemen, with an explosive-laden boat, killing 17 US Navy sailors and injuring 39. On September 11, 2001, 19 AQ members hijacked and crashed four US commercial jets—two into the World Trade Center in New York City, one into the Pentagon near Washington, D.C.; and the last into a field in Shanksville, Pennsylvania—leaving more than 3000 individuals dead or missing. In November 2002, AQ carried out a suicide bombing of a hotel in Mombasa, Kenya that killed 15 people. In 2003 and 2004, Saudi-based AQ operatives and associated extremists launched more than a dozen attacks, killing at least 90 people, including 14 Americans in Saudi Arabia. Ayman al-Zawahiri claimed responsibility on behalf of AQ for the July 7, 2005, attacks against the London public transportation system. AQ likely played a role in the unsuccessful 2006 plot to destroy several commercial aircraft flying from the United Kingdom to the United States using liquid explosives. AQ claimed responsibility for a suicide car bomb attack on the Danish embassy in 2008 that killed five people as retaliation for a Danish newspaper re-publishing cartoons depicting the Prophet Muhammad and for Denmark's involvement in Afghanistan. In January 2009, Bryant Neal Vinas, a US citizen who traveled to Pakistan, allegedly trained in explosives at AQ camps, was captured in Pakistan, and was extradited to the United States, was charged with providing material support to a terrorist organization and conspiracy to commit murder. Vinas later admitted his role in helping AQ plan an attack against the Long Island Rail Road in New York and confessed to having fired missiles at a US base in Afghanistan. In September 2009, Najibullah Zazi, an Afghan immigrant and US lawful permanent resident, was charged with conspiracy to use weapons of mass destruction, to commit murder in a foreign country, and with providing material support to a terrorist organization as part of an AQ plot to attack the New York subway system. Zazi later admitted to contacts with AQ senior leadership, suggesting they had knowledge of his plans. In February 2010, Zazi pled guilty to charges in the United States District Court for the Eastern District of New York. In a December 2011 video, new AQ leader al-Zawahiri claimed AQ was behind the August kidnapping of American aid worker Warren Weinstein in Pakistan. As conditions for his release, al-Zawahiri demanded the end of US air strikes and the release of all terrorist suspects in US custody.

Strength: AQ's organizational strength is difficult to determine precisely in the aftermath of extensive counterterrorism efforts since 9/11. The death or arrest of mid- and senior-level AQ operatives—including the group's long-time leader Usama Bin Ladin in May 2011—have disrupted communication, financial, and facilitation nodes and a number of terrorist plots.

Additionally, supporters and associates worldwide who are "inspired" by the group's ideology may be operating without direction from AQ central leadership; it is impossible to estimate their numbers. AQ serves as a focal point of "inspiration" for a worldwide network of affiliated groups—al-Qa'ida in the Arabian Peninsula, al-Qa'ida in Iraq, al-Qa'ida in the Lands of the Islamic Maghreb—and other Sunni Islamic extremist groups, including the Islamic Movement of Uzbekistan, the Islamic Jihad Union, Lashkari Jhangvi, Harakat ul-Mujahadin, and Jemaah Islamiya. TTP also has strengthened its ties to AQ.

Location/Area of Operation: AQ was based in Afghanistan until coalition forces removed the Taliban from power in late 2001. Since then, they have resided in Pakistan's Federally Administered Tribal Areas. AQ has a number of regional affiliates, including al-Qa'ida in Iraq (AQI), al-Qa'ida in the Arabian Peninsula (AQAP), al-Qa'ida in the Islamic Maghreb (AQIM), and al-Shabaab.

External Aid: AQ primarily depends on donations from like-minded supporters as well as from individuals who believe that their money is supporting a humanitarian cause. Some funds are diverted from Islamic charitable organizations.

Al-Qa'ida in the ARABIAN PENINSULA

aka al-Qa'ida in the South Arabian Peninsula; al-Qa'ida in Yemen; al-Qa'ida of Jihad Organization in the Arabian Peninsula; al-Qa'ida Organization in the Arabian Peninsula; Tanzim Qa'idat al-Jihad fi Jazirat al-Arab; AQAP; AQY

Description: Al-Qa'ida in the Arabian Peninsula (AQAP) was designated as a Foreign Terrorist Organization on January 19, 2010. In January 2009, the leader of al-Qa'ida in Yemen (AQY), Nasir al-Wahishi, publicly announced that Yemeni and Saudi al-Qa'ida (AQ) operatives were working together under the banner of AQAP. This announcement signaled the rebirth of an AQ franchise that previously carried out attacks in Saudi Arabia. AQAP's self-stated goals include establishing a caliphate in the Arabian Peninsula and the wider Middle East as well as implementing Sharia law. On September 30, 2011, AQAP cleric and head of external operations Anwar al-Aulaqi, as well as Samir Khan, the publisher of AQAP's online magazine, *Inspire*, were killed in Yemen.

Activities: AQAP has claimed responsibility for numerous terrorist acts against both internal and foreign targets since its inception in January 2009. Attempted attacks against foreign targets include a March 2009 suicide bombing against South Korean tourists in Yemen, the August 2009 attempt to assassinate Saudi Prince Muhammad bin Nayif, and the December 25, 2009, attempted attack on Northwest Airlines Flight 253 from Amsterdam to Detroit, Michigan. AQAP was responsible for an unsuccessful attempt to assassinate the British Ambassador in April 2010, and a failed attempt to target a British embassy vehicle with a rocket in October of that year. Also in October 2010, AQAP claimed responsibility for a foiled plot to send explosive-laden packages to the United States via cargo plane. The parcels were intercepted in the United Kingdom and in the United Arab Emirates. AQAP took advantage of the pro-democracy demonstrations that swept the Middle East in 2011 when similar demonstrations took place in Yemen. The demonstrations quickly turned violent in Sanaa, and as a result, the Yemeni government focused its attention away from AQAP and toward suppressing the upheaval in the capital. This allowed AQAP to carry out numerous attacks, including multiple attempts to disrupt oil pipelines, attacks on police and government personnel that killed approximately 60 people, and the October assassination of the head of the counterterrorism police force for Abyan Governorate. AQAP was also able to seize small amounts of territory in southern Yemen.

Strength: AQAP has a few thousand members.

Location/Area of Operation: Yemen

External Aid: AQAP's funding primarily comes from robberies and kidnap for ransom operations and, to a lesser degree, donations from like-minded supporters.

Al-Qa'ida in Iraq

aka al-Qa'ida Group of Jihad in Iraq; al-Qa'ida Group of Jihad in the Land of the Two Rivers; al-Qa'ida in Mesopotamia; al-Qa'id a in the Land of the Two Rivers; al-Qa'ida of Jihad in Iraq; al-Qa'ida of Jihad Organization in the Land of The Two Rivers; al-Qa'ida of the Jihad in the Land of the Two Rivers; al-Tawhid; Jam'at al-Tawhid Wa'al-Jihad; Tanzeem Qa'idat al Jihad/Bilad al Raafidaini; Tanzim Qa'idat al-Jihad fi Biladal-Rafidayn; The Monotheism and Jihad Group; The Organization Base of Jihad/Country of the Two Rivers; The Organization Base of Jihad/ Mesopotamia; The Organization of al-Jihad's Base in Iraq; The Organization of al-Jihad's Base in the Land of the Two Rivers; The Organization of al-Jihad's Base of Operations in Iraq; The Organization of al-Jihad's Base of Operations in the Land of the Two Rivers; The Organization of Jihad's Base in the Country of the Two Rivers; al-Zarqawi Network

Description: Al-Qa'ida in Iraq (AQI) was designated as a Foreign Terrorist Organization on December 17, 2004. In the 1990s, Abu Mus'ab al-Zarqawi, a Jordanian-born militant, organized a terrorist group called al-Tawhid wal-Jihad to oppose the presence of US and Western military forces in the Islamic world and the West's support for and the existence of Israel. In late 2004, he joined al-Qa'ida (AQ) and pledged allegiance to Usama bin Ladin. After this al-Tawhid wal-Jihad became known as al-Qa'ida in Iraq (AQI). Zarqawi traveled to Iraq during Operation Iraqi Freedom and led his group against US and coalition forces until his death in June 2006. In October 2006, AQI publicly renamed itself the Islamic State of Iraq and has since used that name in its public statements. In 2011, AQI was led by Ibrahim Awwad Ibrahim Ali al-Badri, aka Abu Du'a, who was designated under Executive Order 13224 on October 4.

Activities: Since its founding, AQI has conducted high profile attacks, including improvised explosive device (IED) attacks against US military personnel and Iraqi infrastructure, videotaped beheadings of Americans Nicholas Berg (May 11, 2004), Jack Armstrong (September 22, 2004), and Jack Hensley (September 21, 2004), suicide bomber attacks against both military and civilian targets, and rocket attacks. AQI perpetrates the majority of suicide and mass casualty bombings in Iraq, using foreign and Iraqi operatives. Examples of high profile AQI attacks in 2011 included a series of bombings that spanned January 18–20 that killed 139 people in Tikrit. In August, AQI vowed to carry out "100 attacks" across Iraq, starting in the middle of the Ramadan, to exact revenge for the May 2011 death of Usama bin Ladin. On November 28, AQI killed 20 police officers, government employees, civilians, and children, and wounded 28 others in a suicide vehicle–borne IED attack in At Taji, Baghdad, Iraq. On December 27, nine car bombs, six roadside bombs, and a mortar round all went off in a two-hour period, targeting residential, commercial, and government districts in Baghdad. AQI later claimed responsibility for the attacks, which killed 70 and wounded almost 200 people.

Strength: Membership is estimated at 1000–2000, making it the largest Sunni extremist group in Iraq.

Location/Area of Operation: AQI's operations are predominately Iraq based, but it has perpetrated attacks in Jordan. The group maintains a logistical network throughout the Middle East, North Africa, Iran, South Asia, and Europe and is believed to be responsible for attacks in Syria as well. In Iraq, AQI conducted the majority of its operations in Ninawa, Diyala, Salah ad Din, and Baghdad provinces in 2011.

External Aid: AQI receives most of its funding from a variety of businesses and criminal activities within Iraq.

Al-Qa'ida in the Islamic Maghreb

aka AQIM; Group for Call and Combat; GSPC; Le Groupe Salafiste Pour La Predication Et Le Combat; Salafist Group for Preaching and Combat

Description: The Salafist Group for Call and Combat (GSPC) was designated as a Foreign Terrorist Organization on March 27, 2002. After the GSPC officially merged with al-Qa'ida

(AQ) in September 2006 and became known as al-Qa'ida in the Islamic Maghreb (AQIM), the Department of State amended the GSPC designation to reflect the change on February 20, 2008. AQIM remains largely a regionally focused terrorist group. It has adopted a more anti-Western rhetoric and ideology and has aspirations of overthrowing "apostate" African regimes and creating an Islamic Caliphate. Abdelmalek Droukdel, aka Abu Mus'ab Abd al-Wadoud, is the group's leader.

Activities: Since 2007, when AQIM bombed the UN headquarters building in Algiers and an Algerian government building outside of Algiers killing 60 people, AQIM had been relatively quiet and focused on its kidnapping for ransom efforts. In 2011, however, AQIM intensified its terrorist activities. In February, AQIM targeted Mauritanian President Muhammad Abdel Aziz and detonated a vehicle-borne improvised explosive device (VBIED) in Nouakchott, injuring nine soldiers. In July, AQIM claimed responsibility for two suicide bomb attacks at the police headquarters and at a town hall in Bordj Manaiel, Algeria. The attacks killed two and injured 14 people. In August, AQIM was responsible for a double suicide attack on the Algerian Military Academy, which killed at least 18 people, and wounded 35 others. AQIM factions in the northern Sahel (northern Mali, Niger, and Mauritania) conducted kidnap for ransom operations and conducted small-scale attacks and ambushes on security forces. The targets for kidnap for ransom are usually Western citizens from governments or third parties that have established a pattern of making concessions in the form of ransom payments for the release of individuals in custody. In September 2010, AQIM claimed responsibility for the kidnapping of seven people working at a mine in Niger. AQIM released three of the hostages in February 2011, but at year's end, four French citizens remained in captivity. AQIM continued kidnapping operations throughout 2011. In January, AQIM kidnapped two French civilians in Niamey, Niger. The kidnappers later killed both hostages during a failed rescue attempt. In February, AQIM conducted its first abduction of a foreigner in Algeria since 2003 when it kidnapped an Italian tourist in Alidena. In October, AQIM kidnapped two Spanish and one Italian aid worker from a refugee camp near Tindouf, Algeria. In November, AQIM was responsible for the November 26 killing of a German man in Mali and the abduction of three men from the Netherlands, South Africa, and Sweden in Mali.

Strength: AQIM has fewer than a thousand fighters operating in Algeria with a smaller number in the Sahel. AQIM is significantly constrained by its poor finances and lack of broad general appeal in the region. It is attempting to take advantage of the volatile political situation in the Sahel to expand its membership, resources, and operations.

Location/Area of Operation: Northeastern Algeria (including but not limited to the Kabylie region) and northern Mali, Niger, and Mauritania.

External Aid: AQIM members engage in kidnapping for ransom and criminal activities to finance their operations. Algerian expatriates and AQIM supporters abroad, many residing in Western Europe, provide limited financial and logistical support.

Real IRA

aka RIRA; Real Irish Republican Army; 32 County Sovereignty Committee; 32 County Sovereignty Movement; Irish Republican Prisoners Welfare Association; Real Oglaigh Nah Eireann

Description: Designated as a Foreign Terrorist Organization on May 16, 2001, the Real IRA (RIRA) was formed in 1997 as the clandestine armed wing of the 32 County Sovereignty Movement, a "political pressure group" dedicated to removing British forces from Northern Ireland and unifying Ireland. The RIRA has historically sought to disrupt the Northern Ireland peace process and did not participate in the September 2005 weapons decommissioning. In September 1997, the 32 County Sovereignty Movement opposed Sinn Fein's adoption of the Mitchell principles of democracy and nonviolence. Despite internal rifts and calls by some jailed members, including the group's founder Michael "Mickey" McKevitt, for a cease fire and disbandment, the RIRA has pledged additional violence and continued to conduct attacks.

Activities: Many RIRA members are former Provisional Irish Republican Army members who left the organization after that group renewed its cease fire in 1997. These members brought a wealth of experience in terrorist tactics and bomb making to the RIRA. Targets have included civilians (most notoriously in the Omagh bombing in August 1998), British security forces, and police in Northern Ireland. The Independent Monitoring Commission, which was established to oversee the peace process, assessed that RIRA members were likely responsible for the majority of the shootings and assaults that occurred in Northern Ireland. In October 2011, Lithuanian authorities convicted a RIRA member for attempting to arrange a shipment of weapons to Northern Ireland in 2008. In 2011, the group was responsible for seven attacks on Northern Ireland businesses and the Police Service of Northern Ireland (PSNI) and was suspected of other incidents. In January, May, and October, the RIRA damaged office buildings, government facilities, and banks in improvised explosive device (IED) attacks, and in February authorities defused another IED before it could explode. In March, RIRA attacked PSNI officers investigating a car theft, and officials blamed RIRA for a bomb placed under a police car that killed a Catholic police officer in April. RIRA conducted two separate attacks on August 4 and August 24 that killed one civilian and wounded another, respectively.

Strength: According to the Irish government, the RIRA has approximately 100 active members. The organization may receive limited support from IRA hardliners and Republican sympathizers who are dissatisfied with the IRA's continuing cease fire and with Sinn Fein's involvement in the peace process.

Location/Area of Operation: Northern Ireland, Great Britain, and the Irish Republic.

External Aid: The RIRA is suspected of receiving funds from sympathizers in the United States and of attempting to buy weapons from US gun dealers. The RIRA was also reported to have purchased sophisticated weapons from the Balkans and to have occasionally collaborated with the Continuity Irish Republican Army.

Revolutionary Armed Forces of Colombia

aka FARC; Fuerzas Armadas Revo Lucionarias de Colombia

Description: Designated as a Foreign Terrorist Organization on October 8, 1997, the Revolutionary Armed Forces of Colombia (FARC) is Latin America's oldest, largest, most violent, and best-equipped terrorist organizations. The FARC began in the early 1960s as an outgrowth of the Liberal Party–based peasant self-defense leagues but took on Marxist ideology. Today, it only nominally fights in support of Marxist goals and is heavily involved in narcotics production and trafficking. The FARC is responsible for large numbers of kidnappings for ransom in Colombia and, in past years, has held more than 700 hostages. The FARC has been degraded by a continuing Colombian military offensive targeting key FARC units and leaders that has, by most estimates, halved the FARC's numbers and succeeded in capturing or killing a number of FARC's senior and mid-level commanders.

Activities: The FARC has carried out bombings, murder, mortar attacks, kidnapping, extortion, and hijacking as well as guerrilla and conventional military action against Colombian political, military, civilian, and economic targets. The FARC has also used landmines extensively. The group considers US citizens to be legitimate targets, and other foreign citizens are often targets of abductions carried out to obtain ransom and political leverage. The FARC has well-documented ties to the full range of narcotics trafficking activities, including taxation, cultivation, and distribution. In 2011, Colombian government investigators reported that the FARC controlled approximately 15 gold mines in the Bolivar Department and was actively involved in the extortion of heavy equipment operators at the mines. According to the investigators, the FARC could be receiving approximately $850 million annually from these activities. Over the years, the FARC has perpetrated a large number of high profile terrorist acts, including the 1999 murder of three US missionaries working in Colombia and multiple kidnappings and assassinations of Colombian government officials and civilians. In July 2008, the Colombian military made a dramatic rescue of 15 high-value FARC hostages, including three US Department of Defense contractors Marc Gonsalves, Keith Stansell, and Thomas Howe, who were held in captivity for more than five years along with former Colombian presidential candidate Ingrid Betancourt. FARC attacks increased significantly during 2011 likely due to the FARC's effort to disrupt the October national elections. Among the numerous attacks was the February 11 mortar attack in San Miguel, Putumayo, killing five civilians, including a child, and wounding two other children. Coordinated FARC attacks in late October in Narino and Arauca killed more than 30 Colombian service members. In July, a bombing of a bus, attributed to the FARC, took place in Toribio, Cauca, resulting in two deaths and 70 injuries of members of a local indigenous community. The FARC executed four Colombian military hostages on November 25. The four had been held captive for at least 12 years and were shot at close range while in chains.

Strength: Approximately 8000 to 9000 combatants with several thousand more supporters.

Location/Area of Operation: Primarily in Colombia. Activities, including extortion, kidnapping, weapons sourcing, and logistical planning, took place in neighboring countries.

External Aid: Cuba provided some medical care, safe haven, and political consultation. The FARC often uses Colombia's border areas with Venezuela, Panama, and Ecuador for incursions into Colombia and Venezuelan and Ecuadorian territory for safe haven although the degree of government acquiescence is not always clear.

Revolutionary Organization 17 November

aka Epanastatiki Organosi 17 Noemvri; 17 November

Description: Designated as a Foreign Terrorist Organization on October 8, 1997, the Revolutionary Organization 17 November (17N) is a radical leftist group established in 1975. Named for the student uprising in Greece in November 1973 that protested the ruling military junta, 17N is opposed to the Greek government, the United States, Turkey, and the North Atlantic Treaty Organization (NATO). It seeks the end of the US military presence in Greece, the removal of Turkish military forces from Cyprus, and the severing of Greece's ties to NATO and the European Union (EU).

Activities: Initial attacks consisted of assassinations of senior US officials and Greek public figures. Five US Embassy employees have been murdered since 17N began its terrorist activities in 1975. The group began using bombings in the 1980s. In 1990, 17N expanded its targets to include Turkish diplomats, EU facilities, and foreign firms investing in Greece. 17N's most recent attack was a bombing attempt in June 2002 at the port of Piraeus in Athens. After the attempted attack, Greek authorities arrested 19 17N members, including a key leader of the organization. The convictions of 13 of these members have been upheld by Greek courts.

Strength: Unknown.

Location/Area of Operation: Athens, Greece.

External Aid: Unknown.

Revolutionary People's Liberation Party/Front

aka DHKP/C; Dev Sol; Dev Sol Armed Revolutionary Units; Dev Sol Silahli Devrimci Birlikleri; Dev Sol SDB; Devrimci Halk Kurtulus Partisi-Cephesi; Devrimci Sol; Revolutionary Left

Description: Designated as a Foreign Terrorist Organization on October 8, 1997, the Revolutionary People's Liberation Party/Front (DHKP/C) was originally formed in 1978 as Devrimci Sol, or Dev Sol, a splinter faction of Dev Genc (Revolutionary Youth). It was renamed in 1994 after factional infighting. "Party" refers to the group's political activities, and "Front" is a reference to the group's militant operations. The group espouses a Marxist-Leninist ideology and vehemently opposes the United States, NATO, and Turkish establishments. Its goals are the establishment of a socialist state and the abolition of harsh high-security "F-type" prisons in Turkey. DHKP/C finances its activities chiefly through donations and extortion.

Activities: Since the late 1980s, the group has primarily targeted current and retired Turkish security and military officials. It began a new campaign against foreign interests in 1990, which included attacks against US military and diplomatic personnel and facilities. Dev Sol assassinated two US military contractors, wounded an Air Force officer, and bombed more than 20 US and NATO military, commercial, and cultural facilities. DHKP/C added suicide bombings to its repertoire in 2001 with successful attacks against Turkish police in January and September. Since the end of 2001, DHKP/C has typically used improvised explosive devices against official Turkish targets and US targets of opportunity. Operations and arrests against the group have weakened its capabilities. In late June 2004, the group was suspected of a bus bombing at Istanbul University, which killed four civilians and wounded 21. In July 2005, in Ankara, police intercepted and killed a DHKP/C suicide bomber who attempted to attack the Ministry of Justice. In June 2006, the group killed a police officer in Istanbul; four members of the group were arrested the next month for the attack. The DHKP/C was dealt a major ideological blow when Dursun Karatas, leader of the group, died in August 2008 in the Netherlands. After the loss of their leader, the DHKP/C reorganized in 2009 and was reportedly competing with the Kurdistan Workers Party for influence both in Turkey and with the Turkish diaspora in Europe. In 2011, DHKP/C continued to plan terrorist attacks, and suspected members were arrested in Greece in July. In October, a suspected DHKP/C member blew himself up with a grenade in Thessaloniki, Greece. A significant cache of weapons was found in the suspect's apartment, shared with other suspected DHKP/C members.

Strength: Probably several dozen members inside Turkey with a limited support network throughout Europe.

Location/Area of Operation: Turkey, primarily in Istanbul, Ankara, Izmir, and Adana.

External Aid: DHKP/C raises funds in Europe. The group also raises funds through extortion.

Revolutionary Struggle

aka RS; Epanastatikos Aghonas; EA

Description: Designated as a Foreign Terrorist Organization on May 18, 2009, Revolutionary Struggle (RS) is a radical leftist group with Marxist ideology that has conducted attacks against both Greek and US targets in Greece. RS emerged in 2003 following the arrests of members of the Greek leftist groups 17 November and Revolutionary People's Struggle.

Activities: RS first gained notoriety when it claimed responsibility for the September 5, 2003, bombings at the Athens Courthouse during the trials of 17 November members. From 2004 to 2006, RS claimed responsibility for a number of improvised explosive device (IED) attacks, including a March 2004 attack outside of a Citibank office in Athens. RS claimed responsibility for the January 12, 2007, rocket propelled grenade (RPG) attack on the US Embassy in Athens, which resulted in damage to the building. In 2009, RS increased the number and sophistication of its attacks on police, financial institutions, and other targets. RS successfully bombed a Citibank branch in Athens in March 2009, but failed in its vehicle-borne IED attack in February 2009 against the Citibank headquarters building in Athens. In September 2009, RS claimed responsibility for a car bomb attack on the Athens Stock Exchange, which caused widespread damage and injured a passerby. In 2010, the Greek Government made significant strides in curtailing RS's terrorist activities. On April 10, Greek police arrested six suspected RS members, including purported leadership figure Nikos Maziotis. In addition to the arrests, the Greek raid resulted in the seizure of a RPG launcher, possibly the one used against the US Embassy in

Athens in January 2007. The six, plus two other suspected RS members, face charges for arms offenses, causing explosions, and multiple counts of attempted homicide. Their trial started in December 2011, and if found guilty, the suspects face up to 25 years in prison.

Strength: Unknown but numbers presumed to be small.

Location/Area of Operation: Athens, Greece.

External Aid: Unknown.

Al-Shabaab

aka The Harakat Shabaab al-Mujahidin; al-Shabab; Shabaab; the Youth; Mujahidin al-Shabaab Movement; Mujahideen Youth Movement; Mujahidin Youth Movement

Description: Designated as a Foreign Terrorist Organization on March 18, 2008, al-Shabaab was the militant wing of the former Somali Islamic Courts Council that took over parts of southern Somalia in the second half of 2006. Since the end of 2006, al-Shabaab and disparate clan militias have led a violent insurgency using guerrilla warfare and terrorist tactics against the Transitional Federal Government (TFG) of Somalia. Several senior al-Shabaab leaders have publicly proclaimed loyalty to AQ. In some camps, AQ-affiliated foreign fighters often led the training and indoctrination of the recruits. Rank and file militia fighters from multiple clan and sub-clan factions that are aligned with al-Shabaab are predominantly interested in indigenous issues. The group's foreign fighters were generally intent on conducting attacks outside Somalia and as of late 2011 had seen their operational capacity reduced due to the military campaign against al-Shabaab. Al-Shabaab proceeded to develop ties to al-Qa'ida in the Arabian Peninsula (AQAP) during 2011.

Activities: Al-Shabaab has used intimidation and violence to undermine the TFG, forcibly recruit new fighters, and kill activists working to bring about peace through political dialogue and reconciliation. The group has claimed responsibility for several high profile bombings and shootings throughout Somalia targeting African Union Mission in Somalia (AMISOM) troops and TFG officials. It has been responsible for the assassination of numerous civil society figures, government officials, and journalists. Al-Shabaab fighters and those who have also claimed allegiance to the group have conducted violent attacks and have assassinated international aid workers and members of non-governmental organizations. In its first attack outside of Somalia, al-Shabaab was responsible for the July 11, 2010 suicide bombings in Kampala, Uganda, during the World Cup, which killed nearly 76 people, including one American citizen. Al-Shabaab's attacks continued apace in 2011 and resulted in the deaths of more than 1000 people. Among al-Shabaab's most deadly 2011 attacks were a string of armed assaults in May that killed more than 120 people, a June attack on AMISOM peacekeepers that killed 13, and an October vehicle-borne improvised explosive device attack on a government compound in Mogadishu that killed more than 70 people, including nine children. Al-Shabaab also killed the TFG Minister of Interior in June.

Location/Area of Operation: After the organization's area of control expanded in 2010, al-Shabaab lost control of significant areas of territory in 2011. By August, after a multi-front offensive against al-Shabaab, the group left Mogadishu, and the TFG and AMISOM gained control of the majority of districts in Mogadishu for the first time. Despite these losses, al-Shabaab continued to control much of southern Somalia throughout 2011.

Strength: Al-Shabaab is estimated to have several thousand members when augmented by foreign fighters and allied clan militias.

External Aid: Because al-Shabaab is a multi-clan entity, it receives significant donations from the global Somali diaspora; however, the donations are not all intended to support terrorism; the money is also meant to support family members. The loss of Mogadishu as a source of tax revenue caused al-Shabaab's revenue to diminish in 2011. However, al-Shabaab leaders and many rank-and-file fighters have successfully garnered significant amounts of money from port revenues and through criminal enterprises, especially in Kismayo.

Shining Path

aka SL; Sendero Luminoso; Ejercito Guerrillero Popular (People's Guerrilla Army); EGP; Ejercito Popular de Liberacion (People's Liberation Army); EPL; Partido Comunista del Peru (Communist Party of Peru); PCP; Partido Comunista del Peru en el Sendero Luminoso de Jose Carlos Mariategui (Communist Party of Peru on the Shining Path of Jose Carlos Mariategui); Socorro Popular del Peru (People's Aid of Peru); SPP

Description: Shining Path (SL) was designated as a Foreign Terrorist Organization on October 8, 1997. Former university professor Abimael Guzman formed SL in Peru in the late 1960s, and his teachings created the foundation of SL's militant Maoist doctrine. SL's stated goal is to destroy existing Peruvian institutions and replace them with a communist peasant revolutionary regime. It also opposes any influence by foreign governments. In the 1980s, SL was one of the most ruthless terrorist groups in the Western Hemisphere. The Peruvian government made dramatic gains against SL during the 1990s, capturing Guzman in 1992, and killing a large number of militants. In 2011, the Upper Huallaga Valley (UHV) faction of SL was largely reduced, and in December, the faction's leader publicly acknowledged defeat. Still, he did not turn himself in or disband his organization. Separately, the much larger and stronger rival SL faction in the Apurimac and Ene River Valley (VRAE) maintained its influence.

Activities: SL activities have included intimidation of US-sponsored nongovernmental organizations involved in counter-narcotics efforts, the ambushing of counter-narcotics helicopters, and attacks against Peruvian police perpetrated in conjunction with narcotics traffickers. SL killed an estimated 17 people in 2011, including 11 soldiers in a December attack on a military convoy and a military helicopter.

Strength: The two SL factions together are believed to have several hundred armed members.

Location/Area of Operation: Peru, with most activity in rural areas, specifically the Huallaga Valley, the Ene River, and the Apurimac Valley of central Peru.

External Aid: SL is primarily funded by the narcotics trade.

Tehrik-e Taliban Pakistan

aka: Pakistani Taliban; Tehreek-e-Taliban; Tehrik-e-Taliban; Tehrik-e Taliban Pakistan; Tehrik-i-Taliban Pakistan; TTP

Description: Designated as a Foreign Terrorist Organization on September 1, 2010, Tehrik-e Taliban Pakistan (TTP) is a Pakistan-based terrorist organization formed in 2007 in opposition to Pakistani military efforts in the Federally Administered Tribal Areas. Previously disparate militant tribes agreed to cooperate and eventually coalesced into TTP under the leadership of now deceased leader Baitullah Mehsud. The group officially presented itself as a discrete entity in 2007. TTP has been led by Hakimullah Mehsud since August 2009. Other senior leaders include Wali Ur Rehman, the TTP emir in South Waziristan, Pakistan. TTP's goals include overthrowing the Government of Pakistan by waging a terrorist campaign against the civilian leader of Pakistan, its military, and NATO forces in Afghanistan. TTP uses the tribal belt along the Afghan-Pakistani border to train and deploy its operatives, and the group has a symbiotic relationship with al-Qa'ida (AQ). TTP draws ideological guidance from AQ while AQ relies on TTP for safe haven in the Pashtun areas along the Afghan-Pakistani border. This arrangement gives TTP access to both AQ's global terrorist network and the operational experience of its members. Given the proximity of the two groups and the nature of their relationship, TTP is a force multiplier for AQ.

Activities: TTP has carried out and claimed responsibility for numerous terrorist acts against Pakistani and US interests, including a December 2009 suicide attack on a US military base in Khowst, Afghanistan, which killed seven US citizens and an April 2010 suicide bombing against the US Consulate in Peshawar, Pakistan, which killed six Pakistani citizens. TTP is suspected of being involved in the 2007 assassination of former Pakistani Prime Minister Benazir Bhutto.

TTP claimed to have supported the failed attempt by Faisal Shahzad to detonate an explosive device in New York City's Times Square on May 1, 2010. TTP's claim was validated by investigations that revealed that TTP directed and facilitated the plot. Throughout 2011, TTP carried out attacks against the Government of Pakistan and civilian targets, as well as against US targets in Pakistan. Attacks in 2011 included a March bombing at a gas station in Faisalabad that killed 31 people; an April double suicide bombing at a Sufi shrine in Dera Ghazi Khan that left more than 50 dead; a May bombing of an American consulate convoy in Peshawar that killed one person and injured 12; a May siege of a naval base in Karachi; the May assassination of the PNS Mehran Saudi diplomat in Karachi; and a September attack against a school bus that killed four children and the bus driver.

Strength: Several thousand.

Location: Federally Administered Tribal Areas (FATA), Pakistan.

External aid: TTP is believed to raise most of its funds through kidnapping for ransom and operations that target Afghanistan-bound military transport trucks for robbery. Such operations enable TTP to steal military equipment, which they then sell in Afghan and Pakistani markets.

United Self-Defense Forces of Colombia

aka AUC; Autodefensas Unidas de Colombia

Description: Designated as a Foreign Terrorist Organization on September 10, 2001, the United Self-Defense Forces of Colombia (AUC)—commonly referred to as the paramilitaries—was formed in April 1997. AUC was designed to serve as an umbrella group for loosely affiliated, illegal paramilitary groups retaliating against leftist guerillas. As the Colombian government increasingly confronted terrorist organizations, however, including the AUC, the group's activities decreased. After a large-scale demobilization process began in 2010, most of the AUC's centralized military structure was dismantled and all of the top paramilitary chiefs have stepped down.

Activities: The AUC has carried out political killings and kidnappings of human rights workers, journalists, teachers, and trade unionists, among others. As much as 70% of the AUC's paramilitary operational costs were financed with drug-related earnings. Some former members of the AUC never demobilized or are recidivists, and these elements have continued to engage heavily in criminal activities. The AUC did not carry out any terrorist attacks during 2011.

Strength: Unknown.

Location/Areas of Operation: Paramilitary forces were strongest in Northwest Colombia with affiliate groups in Valle del Cauca, on the west coast, and Meta Department, in Central Columbia.

External Aid: None.

Index

Page numbers followed by f and t indicate figures and tables, respectively.

Index

B

C

D

Index

E

H

I

M

N

O

P

R

S

T